Racial Domination, Racial Progress

The Sociology of Race in America

Matthew Desmond and
Mustafa Emirbayer

University of Wisconsin at Madison

Connect
Learn
Succeed™

Published by McGraw-Hill, an imprint of The McGraw-Hill Companies, Inc., 1221 Avenue of the Americas, New York, NY 10020. Copyright © 2010 by McGraw-Hill. All rights reserved. No part of this publication may be reproduced or distributed in any form or by any means, or stored in a database or retrieval system, without the prior written consent of The McGraw-Hill Companies, Inc., including, but not limited to, in any network or other electronic storage or transmission, or broadcast for distance learning.

1 2 3 4 5 6 7 8 9 0   DOC/DOC 0 9

ISBN: 978-0-07-297051-7
MHID: 0-07-297051-0

Editor-in-Chief and Vice-President: *Michael J. Ryan*
Senior Sponsoring Editor: *Gina Boedeker*
Editorial Assistant: *Daniel Gonzalez*
Marketing Manager: *Caroline McGillen*
Development Editor: *Kate Scheinman*
Senior Production Editor: *Mel Valentín*
Manuscript Editor: *Stacey Sawyer*

Design Manager: *Allister Fein*
Text/Cover Designer: *Nicole Hayward*
Visual Coordinator: *Sonia Brown*
Media Project Manager: *Thomas Brierly*
Senior Production Supervisor: *Tandra Jorgensen*
Composition: *9.5/13 Scala by Aptara®, Inc.*
Printing: *45# Pub Matte Plus, R. R. Donnelley & Sons*

Credits: The credits section for this book begins on page 649 and is considered an extension of the copyright page.

Library of Congress Cataloging-in-Publication Data

Desmond, Matthew.
  Racial domination, racial progress : the sociology of race in America / Matthew Desmond, Mustafa Emirbayer. — 1st ed.
    p. cm.
  Includes bibliographical references.
  ISBN-13: 978-0-07-297051-7 (alk. paper)
  ISBN-10: 0-07-297051-0 (alk. paper)
  1. United States—Race relations. 2. Race. I. Emirbayer, Mustafa. II. Title.
  E184.A1D36 2009
  305.800973—dc22

                                        2009030633

The Internet addresses listed in the text were accurate at the time of publication. The inclusion of a Web site does not indicate an endorsement by the authors or McGraw-Hill, and McGraw-Hill does not guarantee the accuracy of the information presented at these sites.

www.mhhe.com

For

Tessa

and

Mirangela

Table of Contents

Preface

MORE THAN A GENERATION AFTER THE CIVIL RIGHTS MOVEMENT, WE CONTINUE to lack a clear and unitary conceptual language for discussing racial domination. We continue to be tongue-tied when it comes to race and, as a result, are constrained from fully understanding our society and fellow citizens. We are even strangers to ourselves.

Old ways of thinking about race and ethnicity no longer seem to apply in a society that has moved well beyond the civil rights struggles of the 1950s and 1960s, a society that now confronts problems of racial division in some ways far more complex and ambiguous than those of straightforward segregation or bigotry (persistent as those tendencies may still be in the present day). What is needed is a new way of thinking about race for a society itself quite new. This book addresses that pressing need. It is our hope that *Racial Domination, Racial Progress* provides a more effective language with which to think and talk about—and effectively to address—the problem of racial domination in today's society. In the following pages, we plumb the depths of this problem—its origins and history, its hidden dynamics, the ways it guides our daily lives—so as to be able to dissect its meanings and significance with intelligence, confidence, and conviction.

In doing so, we break with current textbooks in several ways. We rely on innovative advances in modern social thought, advances taking place not only in sociology but also in philosophy, anthropology, political science, economics, history, and literary and art criticism—not to mention exciting developments in such literatures as whiteness studies, critical race theory, cultural studies, woman-of-color feminism, and postcolonial studies. We fuse this social thought with music, literature, poetry, and popular culture. In this book you can find the sociology of Pierre Bourdieu alongside spoken-word poetry; American pragmatist philosophy followed by country music lyrics; ideas from the likes of W. E. B. Du Bois, Toni Morrison, Alejandro Portes, Ella Baker, Edward Said, and Ruth Frankenberg (to list but a few) applied to modern society. *Racial Domination, Racial Progress* is steeped in the most up-to-date social-scientific research on race and ethnicity, as well as in examples from contemporary life, including youth culture. We have taken seriously American sociologist C. Wright Mills's famous dictum that "data is everywhere" and have called on social science to illuminate racial domination in all areas of social life.

Racial Domination, Racial Progress confronts some of today's most controversial and misunderstood issues, including immigration, affirmative action, racial segregation, interracial relationships, political representation, racialized poverty and affluence, educational inequality, incarceration, terrorism, cultural appropriation, civil society, religion, marriage and divorce, and racial identity formation. Throughout, it treats racial domination not as some "hot topic" issue to be debated in loose, unsystematic fashion but as a complex sociological phenomenon properly understood only through critical socioanalysis that arrives at conclusions after sifting carefully through the best available evidence.

Racial Domination, Racial Progress is uncompromisingly intersectional. It refuses artificially to separate the sociology of race and ethnicity from those of class and gender, while never losing sight of racial domination as its primary object of analysis. It highlights how racial domination overlaps other forms of domination based on economic standing and gender (as well as religion, nationality, and sexuality), and it does so because these bases of division are inextricably bound up with the career of racial domination.

This book's organization is nothing like that of other textbooks on race and ethnicity. Instead of proceeding, chapter by chapter, from one racial group to the next—which would only naturalize very unnatural racial divisions, emphasize our differences at the expense of our many similarities, and render the sociology of race and ethnicity nothing more than a collection of isolated snapshots of different groups—it pursues the analysis of racial domination into many of the different areas or fields of life of our society. Examining how race is a matter not of separate entities but of *systems of social relations*, it unpacks how racial domination works in the political, economic, residential, legal, educational, aesthetic, associational, and intimate fields of social life. In each of these fields, it analyses how white privilege is institutionalized and naturalized, such that it becomes invisible even to itself.

At bottom, this book is about the workings of racial domination in contemporary America (although many of its analytical concepts and sociological ideas can be applied to other national contexts). It offers you a comprehensive overview of the causal mechanisms or processes whereby racial divisions are established, reproduced, and in some cases transformed. In doing so, it necessarily engages in a serious and sustained way with history. As American novelist William Faulkner wrote, "The past is never dead. It's not even past."[1] In this book, historical processes are not relegated to a single introductory chapter; rather, historical processes inform the entire work and are explicitly addressed in each chapter.

Racial Domination, Racial Progress is not written in the uninspired and detached tone of scholastic disinterest. It does not reduce one of today's most sociologically complicated, emotionally charged, and politically frustrating topics to a collection of bold-faced terms and facts you memorize for the midterm. Rather, this book—one is tempted to call it a non-textbook textbook—seeks to connect with you, its readers, in a way that combines disciplined reasoning with a sense of engagement and passion, conveying sophisticated ideas in a clear and compelling fashion. (Accordingly, the book works just as well in lower division courses as it does in more advanced settings.) Conventional textbooks on race and ethnicity stimulate a type of reading that can only be called *contemplative*, a reading that devotes academic interest to social problems without ever being touched by them or resonating deeply with them. Such a reading ends when it ends; it goes nowhere. By contrast, we seek to stimulate *generative* readings, which simultaneously engage the world you find intimately familiar and yet also effect a sharp rupture with that world, defamiliarizing the familiar and helping you to arrive at a deeper sociological understanding of your world, offering solutions and strategies so that we all can work toward racial justice.

We seek to offer you, in short, a way of thinking about racial domination that you can apply to your everyday lives and to equip you with critical thinking skills that allow you better to address the pressing problems of racial domination with sociologically informed insight. More, we hope to cultivate in you a sociological imagination, one that rejects easy explanations and that takes into account social and historical forces that operate on an expansive scale. This is the liberating power of sociology: it allows us to objectify and criticize all the social forces that direct our lives (in ways we previously did not recognize), so that we are no longer controlled by those forces or bewildered or rendered passive in the face of them.

Racial Domination, Racial Progress, then, is not simply about one of America's most powerful driving forces—racial domination—it is also about you, the part you play in today's ever-changing world. To better understand our society is to better understand ourselves. "If this is so," you might ponder, "how, then, should I read this book?" Let us offer you two guidelines with the aim of promoting generative readings of the text.

First, as you read, think about how you can apply what you have learned to your life. When stockbrokers monitor the economy, one question dominates their minds: "How does this affect my money?" When farmers study rainfall patterns, they ask themselves but one question: "How will this affect my crops?" It should be the same way with us. As you study this book, ask yourself: "How does this information affect my life? How does it help me better to understand my innermost thoughts, relationships, family, and college experience? And, knowing what I now know, how might I throw a wrench into the gears of racial domination?" Worrying about what other people might think about this book—your classmates, friends back home, or some other readers "out there"—is no less premature and imprudent than the stockbroker worrying about other stockbrokers before checking her own stocks or a farmer fretting over another farmers' fields before caring for his own. It is commonplace for students in a course on the sociology of race and ethnicity to think the course really is for someone else. Nonwhite students tend to think such a course is intended for their white peers, while those white peers tend to think of the course as intended for students of color. A course such as this one, however, is meant for all students: immigrants and native-born citizens, white and nonwhite students, alike.

If you are a white student who thinks this course is about people of color, a study of the racialized Other, and who conceives of your own role in this class as that of a tourist in a foreign culture, think again. Much of this book is about white people, their racial privilege, and the career of whiteness. You are as much a part of the story of American race relations as your nonwhite peers; indeed, you are central to it. Likewise, if you are a nonwhite student who thinks this course is primarily meant to open the eyes of your white peers and if you think, perhaps having tasted the bitter fruit of racism, that you are here primarily to teach other students who "don't get it," think again. One does not become an expert on racial domination simply by virtue of being on the receiving end of the stick any more than an asthmatic becomes an expert on asthma simply by virtue of having it. Lucid insight into the nature of racial domination comes by way of rigorous study and analysis—the application of sociological methods of inquiry to complex problems—rather than being the inevitable result of one's position in the racial order. The point is that we all have something to learn in this class—and we all have something to teach. This book is not just about "them" but about you. It seeks to educate—and unsettle—the righteous along with the disengaged, those who have long discussed matters of racism as well as those who are just now joining the conversation.

Self-evaluation, therefore, comes first. That said—and this is the second guideline—do not be so concerned with your own life and experiences that you fail to grasp the whole. "The worst readers," German philosopher Friedrich Nietzsche once complained, "are those who proceed like plundering soldiers: they pick up a few things they can use, soil and confuse the rest, and blaspheme the whole."[2] The point is well taken. Sometimes we can fall into a pattern of reading in which we pay undue attention to what is said about our ethnic or racial group while skimming over the rest. In so doing, we can easily get hung up on a phrase here and a sentence there, thereby ignoring other important information. A close reading is admirable, but let's not fixate on details at the expense of the bigger picture. Let's read, instead, not only to facilitate self-examination but also to understand better the histories, experiences, and sufferings of ethnic or racial groups other than our own.

We are living in an age in which racial domination persists. But we also are living in an age when racial domination has come under serious and sustained attack. We are living in an age when multicultural coalitions have formed and all people, regardless of race, have taken stands against racism. And many of the most powerful and important antiracist movements have been led by young people. Considerable progress has been made, but considerable work also remains unfinished. The prerequisite for reconstructing our society is learning about it—and to understand our changing and complex world, and our place within it, we must learn about the changing and complex nature of racial domination.

Let us begin a conversation, then, a conversation through thick and thin. This conversation might make you feel uncomfortable, since topics as important and as personal as race are often difficult to discuss. You might feel a bit unsteady and awkward, clumsy even. You might feel exposed and vulnerable. Your words might trip and stumble at times, and you might say things you later regret. Take courage in the fact that many of your classmates (and perhaps even your professors) feel the same way. This is a difficult conversation for all of us: white students often are left feeling guilty or nervous, and nonwhite students often are left feeling alone or frustrated, their heartbeats returning to a normal level sometimes only hours after a class discussion. But know, too, that we have to have this conversation. We have to interrogate race, lest we allow the cancer of racism to continue to poison the promising vitality of our American society.

Supplements

Visit our Online Learning Center website at www.mhhe.com/desmondie for student and instructor resources.

For Students. Student resources include self-quizzes and Internet exercises.

For Instructors. The password-protected instructor portion of the website includes a comprehensive instructor's manual, a computerized test bank, and PowerPoint lecture slides.

Acknowledgments

Sherith Pankratz was behind this project from the beginning. This book simply would not have been possible without her enthusiasm and support. We owe her a very special and heartfelt thanks.

For logging hours of stimulating discussion and debate with us, we thank Felix Elwert, Chad Goldberg, Black Hawk Hancock, Mara Loveman, John Levi Martin, and Ruth López Turley. Crystal Moten tendered detailed feedback on Chapter 3, and Joseph "Piko" Ewoodzie gave Chapter 8 a close read. Philip Creswell and Kelsey Gernert deserve a word of thanks for their research assistance.

Peter Brinson, Matthew Dimick, Cynthia Golembeski, Anna Haskins, Rodney Horikawa, Shazia Iftkhar, Toni Johns, Sam Kho, Helen Laville, Torsheika Maddox, Kate McCoy, Zerandrian Morris, Kyle "El Guante" Myhre, Mytoan Nguyen, Matthew Nichter, David Rangel, Shane Sharp, Jennifer Patrice Sims, Adam Slez, Chris Spears, and Steven Turley all helped make this book a better one. We are grateful to Michelle Bright and Patrick Brenzel and are obliged, also, to Tod Van Gunten and his students, to members of the University of Wisconsin Multicultural Student Coalition, and to students of Sociology 922: Race Theory, for engaging this book so critically.

The following reviewers provided insightful feedback: Joyce M. Bell, University of Georgia; Caron Charlton Cates, Sam Houston State University; Douglas Hartmann, University of Minnesota; Jackie Hogan, Bradley University; Xuemei Hu, Union County College; Mary E. Kelly, University of Central Missouri; Jonathan A. Majak, University of Wisconsin—La Crosse; Wendy Leo Moore, Texas A&M University; Tomecia G. Sobers, Fayetteville Technical Community College; Kui-Hee Song, California State University—Chico; John R. Sosa, State University of New York—Cortland; Amory Starr, Colorado State University; Jennifer Stewart, Grand Valley State University; Wallace C. Strong, Yakima Valley Community College; Gloria Vaquera, University of New Mexico; Melissa F. Weiner, Quinnipiac University; LaSheila Williams, Southern Illinois University—Carbondale; Howard Winant, University of California, Santa Barbara.

Aliza Luft wrote the Instructor's Manual, and Charity Schmidt produced the PowerPoint slides. We are indebted to them for their wonderful contributions to this project.

Thomas Walker sowed the seed, and Donald Tibbs watered it—thank you, good planters. Scott Carter—a special thanks to you as well. Many thanks to Nick, Shavon, Michelle, and Maegan Desmond, for countless blessings. This book would not have been penned without financial support from the Harvey Fellowship. Tessa Lowinske Desmond's imprint graces every page, her ideas lace every word. Look, I see your tracks.

About the Authors

MATTHEW DESMOND is a Ford Foundation Fellow at the University of Wisconsin at Madison. He has received grants from The John D. and Catherine T. MacArthur Foundation, National Science Foundation, and American Philosophical Society for his research on urban poverty, race, and housing. His first book, *On the Fireline: Living and Dying with Wildland Firefighters,* was a finalist for the C. Wright Mills Award and won the Max Weber Award for Distinguished Scholarship.

MUSTAFA EMIRBAYER is a Professor of Sociology at the University of Wisconsin at Madison. Since earning his Ph.D. from Harvard University in 1989, he has edited *Émile Durkheim: Sociologist of Modernity* and has authored several prominent articles that have appeared in *American Journal of Sociology, Theory and Society* and other leading academic journals. In 2009, the American Sociological Association awarded him the Lewis A. Coser Award for Theoretical Agenda Setting.

MUSTAFA EMIRBAYER AND MATTHEW DESMOND also are the authors of *The Theory of Racial Domination,* a theoretical work that offers a new framework for understanding the structures and dynamics of race and racism. Written for race scholars, *The Theory of Racial Domination* is a companion volume to *Racial Domination, Racial Progress.*

Chapter 1

Race in the Twenty-first Century

A Cancer

As we enter a promising new millennium, we continue to be confronted with a problem as old as America itself. That problem is the problem of the color line. It is the problem of racism, of inequality and privilege, of the suffering and oppression of some groups of people at the hands of another.

Some people, however, have argued that, in these modern times, there is no problem at all. A growing number of commentators, from political leaders to radio talk-show hosts, have suggested that race no longer matters.[1] They have boasted that we have, a mere forty years after the Civil Rights Movement, "reached the promise land" that Martin Luther King Jr. so eloquently described in one of the most famous speeches of the last century: the "I have a Dream" speech, delivered on August 28, 1963. We have *arrived,* they say, at true multiculturalism. We are living in a so-called color-blind society, in which people are judged, in King's words, "not by the color of their skin but by the content of their character." Does such an optimistic idea truly reflect the state of America today?

In some respects, we have good reason to be optimistic. Thanks to the brave activists of the Civil Rights Movement, the United States no longer upholds legally enforced residential, educational, and economic segregation. Most of us will not experience grotesque acts of racial violence that many people of color experienced fifty years ago. A number of social institutions, moreover, have been thoroughly integrated, most notably the American military. The black middle class and the Hispanic middle class have grown; American Indian nations have developed effective economic development strategies based on the principle of tribal sovereignty; Asian Americans have made impressive inroads into positions of influence in politics, science, business, and the arts. There are other encouraging trends as well—in religion, sports, the mass media, voluntary associations,

1

and other significant areas in American life. In politics, one need only say the name "Barack Obama." And in the social and cultural order, Americans are beginning to appreciate the inherent value and dignity of all persons, regardless of their origins or skin color. This is especially true of the youth, who, in terms of their racial and ethnic attitudes, are probably the most open-minded and tolerant generation in U.S. history. And, today, many corporations, universities, organizations, and congregations consider racial and ethnic diversity an asset to be fostered and sought after, not a problem to be avoided. To say that nothing has gotten better certainly would be inaccurate.

But has racism been completely vanquished? Let's take a glance at race relations in the United States to find out.

- The FBI tallied 7,649 incidents of hate crime that took place in 2004 alone. (This number is underestimated, because it accounts only for those crimes *reported* to the FBI by participating law enforcement agencies.) These offenses included intimidation, destruction of property and vandalism, assault, burglary, murder, and rape. Race-based hate crimes accounted for 53% of the total number of offenses, and religion-based crimes accounted for 18%. Sixty-seven percent of the race-based hate crimes were committed against black people; and 68% of the hate crimes motivated by religious bias were anti-Semitic acts. Between 1995 and 2004, the FBI has documented 80,279 separate hate crimes, more than half of which were motivated by racial hatred.[2]

- In 2005, 37 million Americans lived in poverty. With poverty rates of 25%, Native Americans and African Americans were the poorest racial groups in the nation. Twenty-two percent of Hispanic Americans lived in poverty. Only 10% of Asian Americans and 8% of white Americans lived under similarly harsh economic conditions. In 2006, over 7 million Americas were unemployed. Four percent of whites suffered from unemployment, while that percentage jumped to 5.6% for Hispanics and more than doubled to 9.2% for blacks. Since 1940, the unemployment rate of African Americans has been nearly twice that of whites. And over half the Native Americans living on some reservations are unemployed. Despite these vast inequalities, 50% of whites recently surveyed believe that the average African American and the average white person are equally well-off.[3]

- Many of us watched as Hurricane Katrina ravaged New Orleans, exposing deep racial and class cleavages between more affluent residents, who had the means to leave the city, and the swelling ranks of the vulnerable inner-city poor, who were left behind to face the storm. Thousands of residents, most of whom were African American, were stranded in the city for days. As the body count grew larger and larger by the day, it became evident that one could not begin to comprehend what happened in New Orleans without a full-bodied understanding of social exclusion, politically enforced marginality, and ongoing processes of racism. During a televised fund-raising event, hip-hop star Kanye West vented, "George Bush doesn't care about black people!" Likewise, many Americans began asking how the richest country in the world could maroon thousands of people in such a devastated urban wasteland for days. But, in truth, we have been marooning our urban poor in substandard conditions for years.[4]

- Today, nearly 7 million people are either serving time in prison, being held in country jails, awaiting trail, or under probation or parole supervision. Almost 6 million Americans are either in prison or have been locked up at some point in their lives; that amounts to 1 in 37 Americans. Indeed, the United States has the highest incarceration rate in the world. Severe racial inequalities are at work within the criminal justice system. African Americans are eight times more likely to be incarcerated than whites. Among black men born in the late 1960s who did not earn a high school diploma, 60% had prison records by the time they reached the age of 35. Sociologists and criminologists have demonstrated that racial inequalities in the justice system are largely accounted for by examining how racial exclusion has resulted in high concentrations of poor African Americans and Latinos living in inner-city areas that offer little to no opportunity for economic advancement or survival. Researchers also have found that mass incarceration does little to lower crime rates.[5]

Given these facts—facts that barely scratch the surface of the problem—can we confidently conclude that race does not matter today? Would such logic be acceptable when considering other types of problems? Consider, for example, cancer. What if a group of citizens suddenly declared that cancer is not a problem anymore. "We solved cancer years ago," they might say. Surely upon hearing such a bold proclamation we would examine the facts, which would overwhelmingly dispute the claim. We would point to the ten million Americans with a history of cancer as well as the one million Americans expected to be victims of cancer this year. We would identify the symptoms of cancer manifest in fever, fatigue, pain, sores, bleeding, lumps, and so forth. We would consult doctors and epidemiologists who have documented case after case of abnormal cell growth and tumor development. In short, we would disavow the claim that "cancer was cured long ago" simply by pointing to the plethora of effects, signs, and symptoms of cancer obvious in everyday life.

The same logic applies to social diseases. Above we listed some symptoms of racism, evidence that race, indeed, is a fundamental part of everyday life. Race penetrates all aspects of our lives—our history, our collective memory, our schools, our jobs, our streets. It structures the inner workings of our hospitals, our prisons, our bastions of political power, and our economy. We witness its effects on our art, our entertainment, and our churches, mosques, and synagogues. Our intimate relationships—the relationships we have with family, friends, lovers, leaders, role-models, heroes, enemies, teachers, landlords, and supervisors—are influenced by relations of race. Race is even there in the basic ways we understand ourselves; it informs our inner thoughts and, indeed, our very identities as people. Life in America—and, indeed, life around the globe—is a life saturated with the reality of race.

This reality of race, like many other social realities, has grown adept at shape-shifting. Unlike cancer, which looks the same as it did one hundred years ago, the racism of our generation looks different from the racism our parents witnessed, which, of course, looked different from the racism their parents witnessed. Racism is mercurial, ever-changing. Twenty-first-century patterns of racial stigmatization, exclusion, repression—as well as promises of racial reconciliation and multicultural coalitions—do not immediately resemble those of the twentieth century. Although racial violence still occurs in America today, there are fewer victims than there were in the previous generation. And although many high schools, universities, neighborhoods, job sites, nursing homes, country clubs, restaurants, and parks remain segregated along lines of race, this racial segregation is no longer enforced by law.

Today's racism is not always obvious. It can be slippery, elusive to observation and analysis. Like a recessive tumor, twenty-first-century racism has disguised itself, calling itself by other names and cloaking itself behind seemingly "race-neutral" laws, policies, practices, and language. But it is still with us, influencing our relationships, our institutions, and our world. And it will not simply fade out of existence if we turn a blind eye toward it. A tumor will destroy a body regardless of whether its bearer recognizes it or not.

We should also keep in mind that present-day society is directed by the past. History structures the workings of today in innumerable ways, some of which are so deeply familiar to us that we fail to notice them. In the words of Émile Durkheim, a French sociologist and one of the founding fathers of the discipline, "in each one of us, in differing degrees, is contained the person we were yesterday. . . . the present is necessarily insignificant when compared with the long period of the past because of which we have emerged in the form we have today."[6] If the world we occupy is shaped by the struggles of yesterday, then we cannot divide past racism from present racism in a hard-and-fast manner.

What is more, racial inequalities, as well as racial privileges, "accumulate over generations." In other words, our standing in today's world largely is dictated by the ways in which our parents, grandparents, and great-grandparents were treated during their own lifetimes. If our parents *suffered* from systematic social exclusion and discrimination based on their race, then many aspects of our

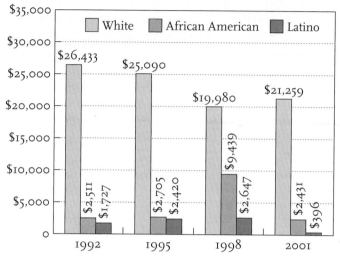

Average Family Net Worth by Race (in 2007 dollars)

SOURCE: Brian K. Bucks et al., Changes in U.S. Family Finances from 2004 to 2007: Evidence from the Survey of Consumer Finances, *Federal Reserve Bulletin*, 2009.

lives—our economic and educational opportunities, for example—will be disadvantaged. In the same way, if our parents *benefited* from the very race-based methods of social exclusion and discrimination that caused the parents of some of our peers to suffer, then we will enjoy a certain degree of privilege in today's society. The accruing afflictions or affluence of our mothers and fathers are visited upon us, sons and daughters.

To illustrate this point, let us examine different levels of wealth, a topic to which we return in a later chapter. While 61% of black families possess absolutely no net financial assets, only 25% of white households are in a similar pinch. In explaining this wide gap between white and black levels of wealth, social scientists have demonstrated that parents' net worth is the single best predictor of the net worth of young families.[7] Your level of wealth is primarily dictated by the wealth of your parents. Your parents' wealth is determined, not only by what their parents passed down to them, but also by the advantages or disadvantages they faced in the labor market. Historically, the labor market has been soaked through with legacies of racist policies and processes of exclusion. This is why the authors of *White-Washing Race* point out that "an analysis of racial inequalities in the distribution of wealth explodes any distinction between past and present racism. . . . Today's inequalities in wealth reflect the legacies of slavery, Jim Crow, and labor market discrimination."[8] We need to recognize that we are all inheritors of the history of our parents and of our society.

Racism persists as the cancer of American life. Pervasive, corrosive, dehumanizing, and deadly, modern-day racism infects the health of our society. It is our responsibility, then, as students of society, and as future citizens of our communities, to understand the realities of racism. As citizens of a world that grows more racially diverse every year, we must understand how race and racism work. And we must develop tools to analyze this social creation that is responsible for so many cleavages and inequalities in our world today. This book aims to do just that. It seeks to explain the inner logic of race and racism and to describe the nature of race relations in the present day. In addition, it hopes to provide you with a way of understanding race that is informed by historical sensitivity, critical thought, sociological analysis, and a global imagination. Put briefly, it develops a *sociology of racial domination*. To begin, let us pose a fundamental question: What is race?

A Biological Reality?

Is race a biological concept? Can modern science, using the most sophisticated techniques possible—including genetic testing—identify natural differences separating racial groups? Modern scientists have answered these questions with an unequivocal and resounding "no."

To fully understand this point, a quick biology lesson is in order. Biologists call the building blocks of life, of our bodies, the *genome*. The genome (a combination of the words *gene* and *chromosome*) of an organism is the collection of that organism's entire hereditary information, encoded in deoxyribonucleic acid, or DNA. DNA is made up of *genes*, or single units of hereditary information, and is responsible for the organism's biological development. So, how genetically different are we?

We share 99.9% of the same genes with other human beings. If you examined the DNA makeup of a Chinese golfer, an entrepreneur from the White Mountain Apache Nation, a Swedish politician, an African American surgeon, a Mexican geologist, and an Iranian sculptor, they would all be indistinguishable when it comes to racial differences. As a species, humans have dramatically low levels of genetic variation. In fact, there is more genetic variation within a single tribe of chimpanzees native to West Africa than there is within the entire human species. Regarding race, there is much more genetic variation—8.6 times more variation, to be precise—*within* traditionally defined racial groups than *between* them. Why? Evolutionary biologist Joseph Graves provides the answer: "Because there is 8.6 times more genetic variation between any given individual on the planet and another individual than there is between the populations they belong to. In other words, the variability that makes one African-American person different from another is greater than the variability between African Americans and Swedes or Tibetans or Amazonian tribes."[9]

Race does not exist on the genetic level. Scientists cannot "see race" by examining humans' DNA strands. This finding is nothing new. In *Man's Most Dangerous Myth: The Fallacy of Race*, a book published in 1942, physical anthropologist Ashley Montagu demonstrated that race is not a biologically sound concept. And long before Montagu wrote his book, Charles Darwin, the founder of modern-day biology, proclaimed that race has no biological grounding.[10]

"Obvious" Physical Differences

Nevertheless, many people still assume that racial differences are dictated by nature. One might question: "Even if genetic comparisons disclose no race-based differences among groups, don't obvious physical differences prove the natural existence of race?"

This is a fair question, but it assumes that there are such things as "obvious physical differences." People do have different skin tones, to be sure; but those tones do not fit "naturally" into the limited racial categories operating in America today. Physical traits vary enormously among people classified as racially similar. Consider the category of "white," which could include Spaniards, Russians, Italians, Afrikaners, Scots, Persians, Norwegians, Greeks, and Tajiks, not to mention thousands of people with mixed heritage. There is a vast amount of variation when it comes to "obvious physical differences"—average height, hair and eye color, and skeletal structure—between these groups.

Or consider the category "black." Aboriginal Australians, Ethiopians, Sri Lankans of India, and Trinidadians all have a dark skin tone; however, they have very different facial structures and hair types. In fact, when scientists have focused exclusively on the populations of sub-Saharan Africa, they have discovered that there is more genetic and physical variation within all the populations of sub-Saharan Africa than there is among any other populations on the globe. This means that, biologically, it is likely that a woman from the Congo would have more in common with a woman from Germany than she would with a woman from Botswana. Nevertheless, if all three women moved to the United States, the woman from the Congo and the woman from Botswana would be classified as belonging to the same race, "black," while the woman from Germany would be labeled "white."[11]

If we examine how race has been defined throughout the history of the United States—a task we will take up in detail later on—we see that "obvious physical differences" supposedly separating one race from another have been anything but "obvious." Many people who "look" white with miniscule amounts of African ancestry have been classified as black.[12] And if we think about it, the skin tone of many light-skinned blacks resembles that of Hispanics; the skin tone of many dark-skinned whites resembles that of light-skinned Native Americans; and the color of many Asian peoples' skin looks like the color of many Italians' skin.

When Korean-born artist Nikki Lee, who specializes in blending into different American subcultures, adopts the look of a young Hispanic woman in this photograph, she smudges racial lines often assumed to be obvious and fixed.

Moreover, in some parts of the world, "obvious physical differences" matter very little when it comes to partitioning people. In India, what divides people is not skin color but one's position in the caste system. A *caste system* is a social and symbolic hierarchical system of classification and separation that organizes people into rigid groups characterized by inner-group marriage, heredity, lifestyle, and occupation. Indian Hindus caught up in the caste system are grouped along a continuum ranging from those who enjoy high status and rights to those deemed "untouchable" and denied many social rights. Physical differences do not demarcate different caste groups. As the well-known American sociologist Oliver Cromwell Cox once put it, "When we refer to groups such as Chamars, Bayas, Telis, Doms, Brahmans, Kayasthas, or Jolahas [all of which are names of distinct castes], no sense of physical distinction need be aroused. We see rather only East Indians."[13]

There is nothing naturally obvious about race; moreover, this kind of thinking can lead to dangerous consequences. In biomedical research, for example, dozens of doctors falsely have assumed that a dying patient is more likely to find an organ donor among those of the same race, among those who "look" the same as the patient. This false assumption has proved deadly: it has resulted in many clinical errors and lost lives.[14]

We must resist, therefore, accepting as given the existence of obvious physical differences that demarcate the races. British social scientist Michael Banton was correct in observing that we "do not perceive racial differences . . . [but] phenotypical differences of colour, hair form, underlying bone structure and so on."[15] But we can go further still, acknowledging that the processes of racialization actually can create difference where previously no phenotypical or biological difference existed. A recent and alarming example is found within genetics. Uncritically accepting racial boundaries as legitimate demarcations of distinct populations, scientists have claimed to document different distributions of genetic sequences across racial groups. This has led some to advance claims about the genetic foundations of racial variation. However, as sociologist Troy Duster has stressed, "finding a higher frequency of some alleles [a form of a gene] in one population versus another is a guaranteed outcome of modern technology, even for two randomly chosen populations."[16]

Athletic Ability and IQ

Even though race has no genetic existence and even though obvious physical differences become quite un-obvious upon closer inspection, some people still hold fast to the idea that certain races are naturally different than others. To justify this position, they usually point to two areas where ostensible differences between racial groups appear manifest: athletic ability and IQ rankings. Let us take up each of these in turn.

Athletic Ability. "Black people are better at basketball." "Dominicans naturally excel at baseball." "Asians are excellent dancers." "White men can't jump!" Blanket statements such as these permeate popular discourse and are sometimes marshaled as evidence of biological differences between races.

Over the decades, some have claimed that African Americans are innately superior athletes. Evidence for this claim, some say, is found in the fact that African Americas seem to dominate the NBA and many Olympic games, including track and field. Sportscasters have referred to black athletes as "thoroughbreds" and "superathletes," and professional athletes themselves, black and white, have offered generalizations about athletic superiority supposedly based in racial genes.[17] Statements such as these are not supported by any scientific evidence. Claims of inherent racial ability—including myths about "fast twitch" and "slow-twitch" muscles—are disconfirmed by modern biology.[18]

In the 1920s and 30s, basketball was thought of as a "Jews' game." The top players in college and professional leagues were Jewish, and Jewish players were thought to have the biological edge, "being endowed by nature with superior balance, greater speed, and sharper eyes—not to mention, in the words of one sportswriter, a 'scheming mind' and 'flashy trickiness.'"[19] (These last two descriptive phrases come from the stereotype of Jews as "crafty.") Soon, however, Jews disappeared from the game, and many black players rose to prominence. What happened? Did nature suddenly change its mind, deciding to strip Jews of their so-called innate skills and bestow such biological gifts on blacks? Certainly not. A better explanation is a sociological one. The changing racial composition of basketball corresponded to the changing racial competition of inner cities. Traditionally, basketball has been a game for the inner-city poor: courts can be found in most urban playgrounds, and all one needs is a ball and a pair of sneakers. Jews dominated basketball in the early twentieth century because ghettos in Northern cities were teeming with Jewish immigrants. By mid-century, the nature of the inner city was undergoing a sea change, as many blacks were migrating northward from the rural South. Basketball offered these newly migrated black youth the same thing it had offered Jewish youth decades before: an accessible and inexpensive recreational activity.[20]

Turning our attention to the present day, sociologists have shown that many talented white high school athletes, many of whom come from high-income backgrounds, come to see sports as a waste of time, as "pissing in the wind," whereas numerous talented black high school athletes, many of whom come from low-income backgrounds, see sports as their one and only shot at upward mobility and social status. Accordingly, many young white athletes, no matter how talented, intentionally drop out of the "sports game" early, since they have been socialized into the conviction that pursuing an athletic career is not a wise choice to make. A sports career may seem like "small potatoes" to white youth, whereas the one-in-a-million shot at a career in the pros might seem like the "only potatoes" to black youth whose opportunities are severely limited.[21] Thus, the racial composition of professional sports rosters is more a reflection of decisions young people make—decisions guided by structures and histories of racial inequality—than it is of biological superiority. Of course, there are a handful of "exceptions to the rule," black players, such as Grant Hill or Ken Griffey, Jr., who came from prosperous backgrounds. But we should bear in mind that exceptions do not prove the rule—especially if that rule is biological.

Are blacks naturally superior athletes? The question has been answered by biology—the only evidence that counts for this kind of question—and the answer is no. The racial composition of several professional sports teams can be explained only through historical and sociological analysis. Now, let's ask another question: Why do we care so much? Why do we continue to come back to this age-old question? Why do we desire so much to know if blacks are innately superior athletes?

Do we care so much because blacks are perhaps "obviously" better at, say, track and field than everyone else? This cannot be the case. At the 2008 Summer Olympic Games, gold medals in track and field events were awarded to athletes from Portugal, Panama, Russia, Jamaica, Great Britain, Romania, Italy, Kenya, Ethiopia, the United States, and Bahrain. Maybe we care so much because blacks are "obviously" better at jumping? This doesn't seem to wash out either, for it would be easy to argue the opposite, that whites are actually better at jumping. For "proof," consider volleyball. The skills involved in basketball and those of volleyball are nearly identical: talented players must exhibit highly attuned hand-eye coordination, superior jumping ability, and quick reflexes. Yet volleyball leagues continue to be dominated by white athletes. And those who claim that "white people can't jump" must have overlooked Andrey Silnov, the Russian Olympian who won the gold medal in men's high jump at the 2008 Summer Games, and Tia Hellebaut, the Belgian who won the gold medal in women's high jump.

Thus, white people are naturally superior at jumping. "Our evidence does not prove this," you might say. "You cannot make sweeping generalizations about all white people based on the spectacular performance of a few." We agree! But why, then, is it socially acceptable to make such sweeping generalizations about black people based on the spectacular performance of a few? Why, upon observing the play of Kobe Bryant, Allen Iverson, Sheryl Swoopes, or Yolanda Griffith—or even the entire NBA and WNBA rosters—do we feel justified in making far-reaching statements about *all* African Americans? After all, we don't subject white people to the same false logic. After watching Wayne Gretzky, Matt Cullen, or Jagr Jaromir perform their magic on the ice rink, do we conclude that *all* white people are good at hockey? Rugby and football require the same types of players: tough, fast, hard-hitting, and team-oriented. If this is the case, then why have people pointed to black NFL players and declared that blacks are better athletes when they could just as easily have pointed to the scores of white rugby players and made the same proclamation for white people?

Questions such as these urge us to reevaluate how we form conclusions about African Americans, and other people of color, based on one-sided and casually collected observations, while we tend not to form such conclusions about white people. If we *question* the question about natural differences in athletic prowess, we soon discover that it only serves to perpetuate stereotypes about nonwhites and whites alike and makes into something real "natural differences" that simply do not exist.

More important, perhaps, when it comes to sports, notions of racial superiority and inferiority are not innocent ideas. The idea that blacks are better athletes rarely exists in isolation. It is often connected to another idea. Inherent athletic superiority is usually thought to be negatively correlated with inherent intellectual superiority. When two things are negatively correlated, this means that as the one thing increases, the other decreases. Here is the real danger in making claims about race-based athletic ability: Those claims insinuate that groups that are good at sports are bad at thinking. This brings us to the next assumption about biological differences between races: inequalities in IQ levels.

Intellectual Ability. Another stereotype that rests on assumptions of biological differences is that certain races of people are naturally more intelligent than others. "Asians are better at math." "Whites excel in the humanities." Statements such as these can be heard on many college campuses around the country.

IQ testing is a mechanism through which racial hierarchies are reinforced. IQ stands for intelligence quotient. First developed in 1905 by French psychologist Alfred Binet, who developed the device in order to locate children with special needs, IQ is a measure of general intelligence computed by multiplying the ratio of one's "mental age" and one's chronological age by a number representing average intelligence, in this case, 100. Binet fervently rejected the interpretation that IQ was dictated by heredity. That interpretation came to prominence in America at the conclusion of World War I. The idea resurfaced in 1969 when educational psychologist Arthur Jensen published an article, now generally viewed as infamously misleading, that emphasized innate differences in IQ levels between whites and blacks. And, most recently, in 1994, Americans witnessed the resurgence of ideas of inherent intellectual inequalities, with the publication of Richard Herrnstein and Charles Murray's *The Bell Curve*, a book 845 pages from bow to stern that claimed, among other things, that whites had higher IQ levels than blacks; that, for the most part, these differences were genetic; and that these intractable differences could explain all kinds of social ills and inequalities.[22]

Immediately after publication, *The Bell Curve* became a target of criticism from intellectuals belonging to several disciplines. Biologists rallied against the idea that IQ even could be measured as a single number extracted from a person's head and placed in a linear ranking. They also criticized the notion that IQ was genetically based and therefore immutable. IQ is much better understood as a panoply of capabilities used creatively to adapt to complex problems; it cannot be reduced to a unitary, unwavering, and quantifiable thing. Statisticians, for their part, discovered that Herrnstein and Murray displayed their findings in a manner that obscured their analyses and hid results that contradicted their central claims regarding racial differences in intelligence levels. For example, a statistic demonstrating the strength of many of their findings was excluded from the text because most of the findings on which their arguments actually rested were embarrassingly weak. Finally, social scientists pointed to countless studies that demonstrate that IQ differences cease to matter once social and historical factors are taken into consideration. These studies show that assumed natural differences do not exist at the aggregate group level and that they do nothing to explain inequality in America. What does explain such inequality are social conditions, historical contexts, and state policies. Today, the overall scientific

"What argument against social change could be more chillingly effective than the claim that established orders, with some groups on top and others at the bottom, exist as an accurate reflection of the innate and unchangeable intellectual capacities of people so ranked?" —Stephen Jay Gould

consensus is that *The Bell Curve* is a deeply flawed work (at best) or racist propaganda masquerading as science (at worst).[23]

Arguments that suppose that social and economic differences between races are the result of immutable, inherited, and inborn distinctions are grouped under the rubric **biological determinism**. As the preceding two sections have shown, biological deterministic arguments that attempt to separate races according to innate, genetic properties do not hold water. Biological determinism is nothing new. On the contrary, and as we will see in the following chapter, this train of thought has been around since the invention of race. But despite being an outdated mode of thinking, and despite being proven wrong, biological determinism refuses to go away. Why is this?

American biologist and historian of science Stephen Jay Gould provides an insightful answer. Writing specifically about IQ, Gould argues that "resurgences of biological determinism correlate with episodes of political retrenchment, particularly with campaigns for reduced government spending on social programs, or at times of fear among ruling elites, when disadvantaged groups sow serious social unrest or even threaten to usurp power. What argument against social change could be more chillingly effective than the claim that established orders, with some groups on top and others at the bottom, exist as an accurate reflection of the innate and unchangeable intellectual capacities of people so ranked?"[24]

When American psychologists first used the IQ test to rank the intellectual capacities of races, America had just emerged from World War I and was involved in an energetic campaign to develop a foreign policy based on principles of isolationism, patriotism, and "national purity." When Arthur Jensen revisited biological deterministic arguments in 1969, America's racial tensions and political unrest were boiling over: Martin Luther King, Jr., had been assassinated a year earlier, the Black Power Movement was gaining steam, and thousands of people were protesting the Vietnam War. And with what social change did the publication of *The Bell Curve* coincide? In the mid-1990s American social policies underwent a drastic transformation. Social services were slashed, and welfare spending was rolled back and reorganized, ushering in "the age of austerity"; and, more and more, the poor were viewed not as troubled citizens in need of help but as perverse problems in need of discipline.[25] Thus, in times when the social status quo has been met with a severe challenge—either by subordinated groups who lash out at the snares of their subordination or by dominant groups who look to ratchet up their own power by further exploiting the powerless— biological determinism is often to be found, reassuring people that social inequalities are really natural inequalities.

But biological determinism is bad science. More importantly, biological determinism has been used to justify injustices and to naturalize inequalities. Gould knew well of the pitfalls of such thinking: "Few tragedies can be more extensive than the stunting of life, few injustices deeper than the denial of an opportunity to strive or even to hope, by a limit imposed from without, but falsely identified as lying within."[26]

Race Is a Social Reality

James Baldwin, the great American novelist, poet, and social critic, once observed, "Color is not a human or personal reality; it is a political reality."[27] Baldwin was correct: Race, as we have just seen, is not a biological reality. It is a political reality, or what we might call a social construction. ***Race*** *is a symbolic category, based on phenotype or ancestry and constructed according to specific social and historical contexts, that is misrecognized as a natural category.* This definition deserves to be unpacked.

Symbolic Category

A symbolic category belongs to the realm of ideas, meaning-making, and language, as opposed to the realm of nature and biology. It is something that is actively created and recreated by human beings rather than pre-given. (By pre-given, we mean something that objectively exists and has simply to be assigned a name.) Symbolic categories mark differences between grouped people or things. In so doing, they actually bring those people or things into existence.[28] (Emphatically, this does not mean that refusing to recognize racial groups created in the course of centuries of oppression, colonialism, and scientific manipulation will somehow lead those races—and racial inequality—magically to disappear.)

For example, the term "Native American" is a symbolic category that encompasses all peoples indigenous to America. But the term "Native American" did not exist before non-Native Americans, Europeans, came to the Americas. Choctaws, Crows, Iroquois, Hopis, Dakotas, Yakimas, Utes, and dozens of other people belonging to indigenous tribes existed. "Native American" is a category that subsumes all these tribes under one *homogenizing heading*. (Homogenizing means combining different things into the same category.) Thus, the term "Native American" flattens out the immensely different histories, languages, traditional beliefs, and rich cultural practices of various indigenous tribes. The term transforms the multitude of indigenous people into one single category of people. Similarly, people have traveled from one geographical territory to the next since the beginning of humanity; however, it was not until national borders were erected and strictly enforced that such people became known through the symbolic categories of "immigrants" or "refugees."

The same is true of other racial categories. In naming different races, racial categories create different races. In the United States, the current **racial taxonomy**, or race-based classification system, delineates five major groups: Native American and Alaskan Natives, Asians and Pacific Islanders, Africans Americans (or blacks), Hispanics (or Latinos), and Caucasians (or whites). This taxonomy is imposed by nearly all the institutions in the United States—from political institutions like the U.S. Bureau of the Census, which asks citizens to check one or more boxes next to racial categories, to educational institutions like universities, which carry out surveys to obtain the racial composition of their schools.

The racial taxonomies that powerful institutions impose sometimes conflict with other racial taxonomies, including those embraced by people in their everyday lives.[29] An institution, such as the university, might assign you a racial or ethnic label that may not align with the racial or ethnic label you have assigned yourself.[30] This certainly happens to multiracial people, for whom "checking a single box" simply does not accurately reflect their full sense of who they are. In the 2000 Census, biracial citizens who checked white as well as another nonwhite category were categorized as belonging only to the nonwhite group, an outcome that certainly conflicted with their own self-identity.[31]

Now, if racial categories create different races, then would eradicating those categories—refusing to recognize racial groups that were created through centuries of oppression, colonialism, political discourse, and scientific manipulation—result in those races (and racial inequality) magically disappearing? Of course not. The process of racial misrecognition is found both at the structural and individual levels and, most important, is a historical process. It follows, then, that the practice of refusing to recognize the misrecognition, as with France's aversion to acknowledging racial categories or the prematurely celebratory declaration of a "color-blind" or "race free" America, is an ineffective and wrongheaded response to a world itself not color-blind. In many cases, the refusal to recognize race, social construction though it is, only exacerbates racial inequalities by rendering antiracist programs impossible.

Phenotype or Ancestry

Race, then, is a symbolic category. It is also based on phenotype or ancestry. A person's **phenotype** is her or his physical appearance and constitution, including skeletal structure, height, hair texture, eye color, and skin tone. A person's **ancestry** is her or his family lineage, which often includes tribal, regional, or national affiliations. The symbolic category of race organizes people into bounded groupings based on their phenotype, ancestry, or both. It is difficult to say which matters more, phenotype or ancestry, in determining racial membership in the United States. In some settings, ancestry trumps phenotype; in others, the opposite is the case.

Recent immigrants often are pigeonholed into one of the dominant racial categories because of their phenotype; however, many resist this classification based on their ancestry. Upon arriving in the United States, many first generation West Indian immigrants, quite familiar with racism against African Americans, actively resist the label "black." Despite their efforts, many are considered African American because of their dark skin (that is, they "look" black to the American eye). The children of West African immigrants, many of whom are disconnected from their parents' ancestries, more readily accept the label "black."[32] Moreover, many individuals with mixed heritage often are treated as though they belong only to one "race." For instance, many people think superstar golfer Tiger Woods is African American because of his darker skin tone. Woods, however, does not identify as African American, since he is part white, part black, part American Indian, part Thai, and part Chinese. In fact, as a child, Woods called himself a "Cabalinasian," a term he invented to reflect his multiracial roots.[33]

Tiger Woods constructs his racial identity through his ancestry, regardless of the assumptions people make about him based on his phenotype. Some people, however, rely on their phenotype to form a racial identity, though they often are grouped in another racial category based on their ancestry. Susie Guillory Phipps, a blond-haired blue-eyed woman who always considered herself "white," discovered, upon glancing at her birth certificate while applying for a passport, that her native state, Louisiana, considered her "black." How could this be? The reason was that Louisiana grouped people into racial categories according to the "one thirty-second rule," a rule that stated that anyone who was one thirty-second black—regardless of what they looked like—was legally "black." In 1982, Susie Guillory Phipps sued Louisiana for the right to be white. She lost. The state genealogist discovered that Phipps was the great-great-great-great-grandchild of a white Alabama plantation owner and his black mistress and, therefore (although all of Phipps's other ancestors were white), "black." (This outlandish law finally was erased from the books in 1983.) In this case, Phipps's ancestry was more important in determining her race, as identified by the state, than was her phenotype.[34]

Social and Historical Contexts

Race is such a fundamental part of American life that we tend to think of it as a natural boundary, one that has existed in the same form throughout history and across all other societies. But this is not true. Racial taxonomies are bound to their specific social and historical contexts.

The racial categories that exist in America are nonexistent in other parts of the globe. In South Africa, racial groups are organized around three dominant categories: white, black, and "coloured." The coloured category was designed during apartheid—South Africa's system of legalized segregation, now abolished—to include all "mixed-race" people. In Brazil, five racial categories are employed in the official census: *blanco* (white), *pardo* (brown), *preto* (black), *amarelo* (Asian), and *indígena* (indigenous). However, in everyday usage, many Brazilians identify themselves and one another through several other racial terms—including *moreno* (other type of brown), *moreno claro* (light brown), *negro* (another type of black), and *claro* (light)—which have much more to do with the tint of one's skin than with one's ancestry. Before racial language was outlawed by the Communist regime, Chinese racial taxonomies were based first and foremost on blood purity, then on hair, then odor, then brain mass,

U.S. Census Race Categories, 1790–2000

1790—Free white males; free white females; all other free persons; slaves
1800—Free white males; free white females; all other free persons, except Indians not taxed; slaves
1810—Free white males; free white females; all other free persons; except Indians not taxed; slaves
1820—Free white males; free white females; free colored persons, all other persons, except Indians not taxed; slaves
1830—Free white persons; free colored persons; slaves
1840—Free white persons; free colored persons; slaves
1850—Black; mulatto[a]
1860—Black; mulatto; (Indian)[b]
1880—White; black; mulatto; Chinese; Indian
1890—White; black; mulatto; quadroon; octoroon; Chinese; Japanese; Indian
1900—White; black; Chinese; Japanese; Indian
1910—White; black; mulatto; Chinese; Japanese; Indian; other (+ write in)
1920—White; black; mulatto; Indian; Chinese; Japanese; Filipino; Hindu; Korean; other (+ write in)
1930—White; Negro; Mexican; Indian; Chinese; Japanese; Filipino; Hindu; Korean; (other races, spell out in full)
1940—White; Negro; Indian; Chinese; Japanese; Filipino; Hindu; Korean; (other races, spell out in full)
1950—White; Negro; Indian; Japanese; Chinese; Filipino; (other race—spell out)
1960—White; Negro; American Indian; Japanese; Chinese; Filipino; Hawaiian; part Hawaiian; Aleut Eskimo, etc.
1970—White; Negro or black; American Indian; Japanese; Chinese; Filipino; Hawaiian; Korean; other (print race)
1980—White; Negro or Black; Japanese; Chinese; Filipino; Korean; Vietnamese; American Indian; Asian Indian; Hawaiian; Guamanian; Samoan; Eskimo; Aleut; other (specify)
1990—White; black or Negro; American Indian; Eskimo; Aleut; Chinese; Filipino; Hawaiian; Korean; Vietnamese; Japanese; Asian Indian; Samoan; Guamanian; other API (Asian or Pacific Islander); other race
2000—White; black, African American, or Negro; American Indian or Alaska Native; Asian Indian; Chinese; Filipino; Japanese; Korean; Vietnamese; Native Hawaiian; Guamanian or Chamorro; Samoan; other Asian (print race); other Pacific Islander (print race); some other race (print race)

SOURCE: U.S. Bureau of the Census.
NOTE: Categories are presented in the order in which they appeared on schedules.
[a]In 1850 and 1860, free persons were enumerated on schedules for "free inhabitants"; slaves were enumerated on schedules designated for "slave inhabitants." On the free-inhabitants schedule, instructions to enumerators read, in part: "In all cases where the person is white leave the space blank in the column marked 'Color.'"
[b]Although "Indian" was not listed on the census schedule, the instructions read: "'Indians'—Indians not taxed are not to be enumerated. The families of Indians who have renounced tribal rule, and who under State or Territorial laws exercise the rights of citizens, are to be enumerated. In all such cases write 'Ind.' opposite their names, in column 6, under heading 'Color.'"

Brazilian Color Questions and Categories, 1872–2000

1872—White (*branco*), black (*preto*), mixed (*pardo*), *caboclo* (Mestizo Indian)

1880—No census

1890—White (*branco*), black (*preto*), *caboclo* (Mestizo Indian), *mestizo*

1900—No color question

1910—No census

1920—No color question, but extended discussion about "whitening"

1930—No census (Revolution of 1930)

1940—White (*branco*), black (*preto*), yellow (*amarelo*)[a]

1950—White (*branco*), black (*preto*), mixed (*pardo*), yellow (*amarelo*)

1960—White (*branco*), black (*preto*), mixed (*pardo*), yellow (*amarelo*), *Índio* (Indian)

1970—No color question

1980—White (*branco*), black (*preto*), mixed (*pardo*), yellow (*amarelo*)

1991—White (*branco*), black (*preto*), brown (*pardo*), yellow (*amarelo*), *Indígena* (indigenous)

2000—White (*branco*), black (*preto*), brown (*pardo*), yellow (*amarelo*), *Indígena* (indigenous)

SOURCE: Instituto Brasileiro de Geográfia e Estatística.

FROM: Melissa Nobles, "History Counts: A Comparative Analysis of Racial/Color Categorization in U.S. and Brazilian Censuses," *American Journal of Public Health* 90 (2000): 1738–1745, pp. 1743, table 2.

[a]If the respondent did not fit into one of these three categories, the enumerator was instructed to place a horizontal line on the census schedule. These horizontal lines were then tabulated under the category *pardo*.

---

then finally, and of least importance, skin color, which, according to the taxonomy, was divided into no less than ten shades ("pure Chinese" identified by "pure yellow"). And in Japan, a group called the Burakamin are considered "unclean" and are thought to constitute a separate race, although it is impossible to distinguish someone with Burakamin ancestry from the rest of the Japanese population.[35]

Cross-national comparisons, then, reveal that systems of racial classification vary greatly from one country to the next. (The same cannot be said of systems of natural classification.) Racial categories, therefore, are *place-specific*, bound to certain geographic and social contexts.

Racial categories are also *time-specific*, changing between different historical time periods. Historians have found that the in times of antiquity, the historical period before the Middle Ages, the main social division for Greeks and Romans was not between people of different skin color, or even between men and women. During that time, the key social division was between masters and slaves. To us, a master and slave of antiquity would look nearly identical, sharing similar skin color, hair color, and body build; however, to the Greeks and Romans of those days, masters and slaves almost were different species.[36] And although most

Americans of European ancestry today would be considered white, their admittance into the "white race" was much less certain only one hundred years ago, when ethnic distinctions amongst European immigrant groups—Poles, Germans, Italians, Russian Jews—were much more pronounced and consequential than they are today.[37] That is why many social scientists have asserted that we must grapple with "the historical specificity of race in the modern world" in order to gain an accurate understanding of racial phenomena.[38]

Misrecognized as Natural

The last part of the definition we have been unpacking has to do with a process of **naturalization.** This word signifies a metamorphosis of sorts, where something created by humans is mistaken as something dictated by nature. Racial categories are naturalized when these symbolic groupings, the products of specific historical contexts, are wrongly conceived of as natural and unchangeable. We misrecognize race as natural when we begin to think that racial cleavages and inequalities can be explained by pointing to attributes somehow inherent in the race itself (as if they were biological) instead of understanding how social powers, economic forces, political institutions, and cultural practices have resulted in these divisions.

Naturalized categories are powerful, for they are the categories through which we understand the world around us. Such categories divide the world along otherwise arbitrary lines and make us believe that there is nothing at all arbitrary about such a division. They convince us that otherwise illegitimate boundaries erected between groups of people actually are legitimate. What is more, when categories become naturalized, alternative ways of viewing the world begin to appear more and more impossible. Why, we might ask, should we have only five main racial groups? Why don't we have ninety-five? Why should we divide people according to their skin color? Why not base racial divisions according to foot size, ear shape, tooth color, arm length, or height? Why is ancestry so important? Why not base our racial categories on regions—north, south, east, and west? You might find these suggestive questions silly, and, indeed, they are. But they are no sillier than the idea that people should be sorted into different racial groups according skin color or blood composition. To twist French sociologist Pierre Bourdieu's phrase, we might say, "when it comes to race, one never doubts enough."[39]

The system of racial classification at work in America today is not the only system imaginable, nor is it the only system that has existed in the young life of the United States. Race is far from fixed; rather, its forms have shifted and fluctuated over time, depending on the social, economic, political, and cultural pressures of the day.[40] Indeed, a multiracial movement today is challenging America's dominant racial categories (which remained relatively stable during the latter half of the twentieth century), as people of mixed race heritage refuse to accept as given the state's racial classification system.[41]

Race is not natural in the slightest respect. In fact, we can regard race as a *well-founded fiction*. It is a fiction because it has no natural bearing, but it is well-founded since most people in society provide race with a real existence and have come to see the world through its lens. Racial taxonomies often lead us to conclude that we are inherently different from one another, that nature dictates the separation of people. In truth, only society can be blamed for that. Race is social through and through.

This section opened with a quotation from James Baldwin, and it is fitting that it close with one as well: "For the sake of one's children, in order to minimize the bill that they must pay, one must be careful not to take refuge in any delusion—and the value placed on the color of the skin is always and everywhere and forever a delusion. I know that what I am asking is impossible. But in our time, as in every time, the impossible is the least that one can demand—and one is, after all, emboldened by the spectacle of human history in general, and American Negro history in particular, for it testifies to nothing less than the perpetual achievement of the impossible."[42]

Ethnicity and Nationality

The categories of **ethnicity** and **nationality** are intrinsically bound up with race. Ethnicity refers to a shared lifestyle informed by cultural, historical, religious, and/or national affiliations. Nationality is equated with citizenship—membership in a specific politically delineated territory controlled by a government.[43] Like race, both ethnicity and nationality are symbolic categories.

Race, ethnicity, and nationality are overlapping symbolic categories that influence how we see the world around us, how we view ourselves, and how we divide "us" from "them." The categories are mutually reinforcing: each category educates, upholds, and is informed by the others. This is why these three categories cannot be understood in isolation from one another.[44] For example, if one identifies as ethnically Norwegian, which, for them, might include a shared lifestyle comprising Norwegian history and folklore, language, cultural rituals and festivals, and food (such as meatcakes, lamb and cabbage stew, potato dumplings, cod, and lutefisk), they may also reference a nationality, based in the state of Norway, as well as a racial group, white, since nearly all people of Norwegian descent would be classified as white by American standards. Here, ethnicity is informed by nationality (either past or present) and signifies race.

Ethnicity often carves out distinctions and identities within racial groups. Ten people can be considered Asian American according to our modern racial taxonomy; however, those people might have parents or grandparents who immigrated to the United States from ten different countries, including Thailand, Vietnam, Cambodia,

Singapore, China, South Korea, North Korea, Japan, Indonesia, and Laos. They might speak different languages, uphold different traditions, worship different deities, enjoy very different kinds of food, and go through diverse experiences. What is more, many Asian countries have histories of conflict (such as China and Japan, and North and South Korea). As such, we cannot assume that a Chinese-American and a Japanese-American have similar lifestyles or see the world through a shared vision simply because both are classified as "Asian" under American racial rubrics. Therefore, just as race, ethnicity, and nationality cannot be separated from one another, neither can all three categories be collapsed into one.

Although ethnic affiliations often are informed by national affiliations, ethnicity can also transcend national borders. Jewish ethnic affiliation encompasses a wide array of people who vary in terms of nationality (from those living in the United States and Canada to those living in Israel, Eastern Europe, Argentina, or Mexico), political commitments (from the far right to the far left), languages (from English to Hebrew to Polish), and religious beliefs and practices (from Easter Orthodox to Hassidic to atheist). Despite these differences—which cut across national and religious boundaries—many Jews see themselves as bound together in a group, sharing a common history, culture, and ethnic identity.

Ethnicity is a very fluid, layered, and situational construct. One might feel very American when voting, very Irish when celebrating St. Patrick's Day, very Catholic when attending Easter mass, very "New Yorker" when riding the subway, and very Northern when visiting a relative in South Carolina. Race, too, can be performed to varying degrees.[45] One might act "very black" when celebrating Kwanza with relatives but may repress her blackness while in a business meeting with white colleagues. As we explain in more detail in Chapter 10, race and ethnicity are both marked and made. We may create, reproduce, accept, or actively resist systems of racial classification; we may choose to accentuate our ethnicity or racial identity. But in many cases, our choices, our racial or ethnic performances, will have little impact on how we are labeled by others. A person born to Chinese parents but adopted, at infancy, by a Jamaican-American couple might identify as ethnically Jamaican. She might enjoy Jamaican cuisine, read Jamaican literature, listen to Jamaican music, and study Jamaican history. However, although her adopted parents may be classified as racially black, she would be classified as Asian, her race decided for her.[46]

The degree to which an individual can slip and slide through multiple ethnic identities—this point is crucial—depends on the degree to which those identities are stigmatized. White Americans typically enjoy a high degree of fluidity and freedom when self-identifying ethnically. They can choose to give equal weight to all aspects of their ethnicity or to highlight certain parts while deemphasizing others. The same person could identify as either "half-Italian, quarter-Polish, quarter-Swiss," or "Polish and Italian" or just "Italian," for instance.

Many people of color do not enjoy the same degree of choice. Someone whose father is Arab American and whose mother is Dutch American could not so easily get away with ethnically identifying only as "Dutch."

In some instances, nonwhites may perform ethnicity in order to resist certain racial classifications (as when African migrants teach their children to speak with an accent so they might avoid being identified as African Americans); in other instances, they might, in an opposite way, attempt to cleanse themselves of all ethnic markers (be they linguistic, religious, or cultural in nature) to avoid becoming victims of discrimination or stigmatization. Either way, their efforts may prove futile since those belonging to dominated racial groups have considerably less ethnic agency than those belonging to the dominant (and hence normalized) racial group. (This is why some scholars have observed that, in its popular usage, the term "Hispanic" is deployed much more often as a racial, not ethnic, classification, while Hispanic subcategories, such as "Mexican" or "Cuban," are treated like ethnic markers.[47]) In fact, Americans tend to focus on ethnic differences within the white race while treating blacks, Latinos, and Asian Americans as if they had no ethnicity and minimizing cultural or historical differences between (for black Americans) Haitians, Jamaicans, Ethiopians, Trinidadians, Angolans, or Nigerians, or between (for Latinos) Puerto Ricans, Cubans, Mexicans, Peruvians, or Dominicans, or between (for Asians) Laotians, Indonesians, Cambodians, Vietnamese, Chinese, and Japanese people.[48]

One reason why race and ethnicity are relatively decoupled for white Americans but bound tightly together for nonwhite Americans is found in the history of the nation's immigration policies and practices. Until the late nineteenth century, immigration to America was deregulated and encouraged (with the exception of Chinese exclusion laws). However, at the turn of the century, native-born white Americans, who blamed immigrants for the rise of urban slums, crime, and class conflict, began calling for immigration restrictions. Popular and political support for restrictions swelled and resulted in the development of a strict immigration policy, culminating in the Johnson-Reed Act of 1924.

America's new immigration law, complete with national quotas and racial restrictions on citizenship, would fundamentally realign the country's racial taxonomy. "The national origins system classified Europeans as nationalities and assigned quotas in a hierarchy of desirability," writes historian Mae Ngai in *Impossible Subjects: Illegal Aliens and the Making of Modern America*, "but at the same time the law deemed all Europeans to be part of a white race, distinct from those considered to be not white. Euro-American identities turned both on ethnicity—that is, a nationality-based cultural identity that is defined as capable of transformation and assimilation—and on a racial identity defined by whiteness."[49]

Nonwhites, however, either were denied entry into the United States (as was the case for Asian migrants) or were associated with illegal immigration through harsh border-control policies (as was the case for Mexicans). Indeed, the immigration laws of the 1920s applied the newly formed concept of "national origin" only to European nations; those classified as members of the "colored races" were conceived as bereft of a country of origin. The result, Ngai observes, was that "unlike Euro Americans, whose ethnic and racial identities became uncoupled during the 1920s, Asians' and Mexicans' ethnic and racial identities remain conjoined."[50]

The history of America's immigration policy underscores the intimate conception between race, ethnicity, citizenship, and national origin. Racial categories often are defined and changed by national lawmakers, as citizenship has been extended or retracted depending on one's racial ascription. The U.S. justice system has decided dozens of cases in ways that have solidified certain racial classifications in the law. During the nineteenth and twentieth centuries, legal cases handed down rulings that officially recognized Japanese, Chinese, Burmese, Filipinos, Koreans, Native Americans, and mixed-race individuals as "not white." In 1897, a Texas federal court ruled that Mexicans were legally "white." And Syrians, Arabians, and Indian Americans (individuals who immigrated from India or who are of Indian descent) have been classified as "white" at some points in time and "not white" at other points.

For instance, Indian Americans were deemed white by law in the case of *U.S. v. Dolla* in 1910. Abdullah Dolla emigrated from Calcutta to New York City. A businessman, he worked in Georgia selling Indian merchandise. While applying for citizenship, Dolla argued that he was white because he was accepted as such by fellow Georgia citizens. He was found to be white and granted citizenship, and this ruling set a precedent, legally classifying Indian Americans as white. However, that ruling was challenged thirteen years later in *U.S. v. Bhagat Singh Thind*. Bhagat Singh Thind was an immigrant from Punjab, India, who paid his way through the University of California–Berkeley by spending his summers working for a lumber mill in Oregon. When World War I broke out, he joined the U.S. Army and was honorably discharged in 1918. Nevertheless, Thind was denied citizenship because the court found him (and therefore other Indian Americans) "not white."

The United States often has been thought of as a country of immigrants, a country that asks for "your tired, your poor, your huddled masses yearning to breathe free," as inscribed in Emma Lazarus's famous poem, "The New Colossus," and displayed on a plaque at the Statue of Liberty. Yet, for over one hundred fifty years, the United States denied citizenship—and all the rights that came with it—to thousands of hopeful immigrants because they were not white. As law professor Ian Haney López has observed in his book, *White by Law*, "in its first words on the subject of citizenship, Congress in 1790 restricted naturalization to 'white persons.' Though the requirements for naturalization changed frequently thereafter, this racial prerequisite to citizenship endured for over a century and a half, remaining in force until 1952. From the earliest years of this country until just a generation ago, being a 'white person' was a condition for acquiring citizenship."[51]

Citizenship is accompanied by many social privileges, such as the right to vote when one is so inclined, the right to own property when one has the means, the right to legal protection when one is victimized, the right to receive medical treatment when one is sick, and the right to receive an education when one is young. Because they could not obtain citizenship, many nonwhites lacked access to these basic privileges. If a white woman was married to a nonwhite man, she could not obtain citizenship. More shockingly, if a white woman who already was a U.S. citizen married a man considered nonwhite by law, she was treated like a traitor, her citizenship revoked.

Blacks were granted the right to naturalize (meaning, in this context, admittance to citizenship) in 1870. However, that right was denied other nonwhites until the 1940s, when Congress began granting it in piecemeal fashion. In 1952, Congress passed the *Immigration and Nationality Act*, which reorganized U.S. naturalization law and forbade denying citizenship on the basis of race. While the Immigration and Nationality Act abolished race-based restrictions on citizenship, it did retain a quota system that limited the number of people who could immigrate to America from certain countries.

Briefly examining how the legal definitions of white and nonwhite have changed over the years demonstrates the unstable and fluid nature of racial categories. It also shows how our legal system helps to construct race. Legal cases that determined peoples' race in order to determine their eligibility for U.S. citizenship—what were known as prerequisite cases—had poisonous symbolic consequences. Deemed worthy of citizenship, white people were understood as upstanding, law-abiding, moral, and intelligent. Conversely, nonwhite people, from whom citizenship was withheld, were thought of as base, criminal, untrustworthy, and of lesser intelligence. For most of American history, courts determined race, and race determined nationality; thus, nationality can only be understood within the context of U.S. racial and ethnic conflict.[52]

Today, many foreign-born residents still face great barriers when applying for U.S. citizenship. Compare U.S. naturalization rates with those of Canada. Around the time the Immigration and Nationality Act was signed into law, Canadian and U.S. naturalization rates were identical: approximately 80% of foreign-born residents were granted citizenship in each country, and both countries opened their doors to immigrants from Asia, the Caribbean, and Latin America. However, since that time, U.S. naturalization rates have declined rapidly, while Canadian rates have experienced little change. In 1980, only 50% of foreign-born residents were naturalized in the United States, while 70% were naturalized in Canada. In 1990, U.S. naturalization rates fell to 40%, while Canadian rates remained the same. And in 2000, Canadian rates climbed to 75%, while U.S. rates remained around 40%. Over the past three decades, Canada has awarded most of its foreign-born population citizenship, while the U.S. has not naturalized the majority of its foreign-born population.[53]

American Racism in the Twenty-first Century

Pace University is a comprehensive university with over 14,000 students, spread out over six campuses in and around New York City. The student body is diverse, and the university has prided itself on maintaining an accepting and welcoming environment. But in the fall of 2006, several incidents led many students to question how welcome they really were on campus. First, a student discovered a copy of the Koran—the Holy book of Islam—discarded in the toilet of a library bathroom. A few weeks later, a second Koran was given the same maltreatment; this time, the book was desecrated with hateful slurs. Then, a racial slur targeting African Americans was traced in the dew on a car window parked on campus. Shortly after that, swastikas and dozens of racial epithets were found scrolled on a bathroom wall. These events led Muslims and many students of color to fear for their safety. As Ashley Marinaccio, a senior at Pace, confessed, "when one minority is the victim of a hate crime, it certainly provokes fear in other groups, because you cannot help but think, 'Am I next?' I've had discussions with quite a number of people who are worried and do not feel safe because of these incidents."[54]

That these incidents were explicitly hateful and racist in nature, few would dispute. And that they occurred on a college campus is not very unusual. Many of the perpetrators and victims of hate crimes are young adults. In fact, 29% of hate crime offenders are between the ages of 18 and 24, and 11% of documented hate crimes occur in schools and college campuses.[55]

Although the historical period when all people of color, and African Americans in particular, were terrorized by whites—a period that spans a full *two-thirds* of U.S. history—seems far behind us, individuals still carry out overt acts motivated by racial hatred. These acts range in intensity from vandalism to murder. As we will discuss in more detail in Chapter 10, hate groups, such as the Ku Klux Klan, neo-Nazis, and skinheads, are still found all around the United States. According to the Southern Poverty Law Center, there are hundreds of active hate groups across the country. These groups are mostly found in the Southern states—Texas, Georgia, and South Carolina have over 40 active groups per state—but California ranks highest in the nation, housing within its borders 53 groups.[56] Members of hate groups cultivate explicitly racist biases against members of other races, ethnicities, or religions and act on those biases through incidents of violence, harassment, and intimidation.

For some people, this is what racism amounts to: intentional acts of humilia-tion and hate. Although such acts undoubtedly are racist in nature, they are but the tip of the iceberg as to what constitutes racism. To define racism only through extreme groups and their extreme acts is akin to defining weather only through hurricanes. Hurricanes are certainly a type of weather pattern—a most harsh and brutal type—but so too are mild rainfalls, light breezes, and sunny days. Likewise, racism is much broader than hate groups, racial slurs, and defiled Korans. It also comes in much quieter and what one might call everyday-ordinary forms.[57]

Five Fallacies about Racism

There are many misconceptions about the character of racism. Americans are deeply divided over its legacies and inner workings, and much of this division is due to the fact that many Americans understand racism in limited or mis-guided ways.[58] We have identified five fallacies about racism—logical mistakes, factual or logical errors in reasoning—that are recurrent in many public debates, fallacies one should avoid when thinking about racism.[59]

1. *Individualistic Fallacy.*   Here, racism is assumed to belong to the realm of ideas and prejudices. Racism is only the collection of nasty thoughts a "racist individual" has about another group. Someone operating with this fallacy thinks of racism as one thinks of a crime and, therefore, divides the world into two types of people: those guilty of the crime of racism ("racists") and those innocent of the crime ("nonracists").[60] Crucial to this misconceived notion of racism is intentionality. "Did I intentionally act racist? Did I cross the street because I was scared of the Hispanic man walking toward me, or did I cross for no apparent reason?" Upon answering "no" to the question of intentionality, one assumes they can classify their actions as "nonracist," despite the character of those actions, and go about their business, as innocent.

This conception of racism simply won't do, for it fails to account for the rac-ism woven into the very fabric of our schools, political institutions, labor mar-kets, and neighborhoods. Conflating racism with prejudice ignores the more systematic and structural forms of racism; it looks for racism within individuals and not institutions.[61] Labeling someone a "racist" shifts our attention from the social surroundings that enforce racial inequalities to the individual with biases. It also lets the accuser off the hook—"He is a racist, I am not"—and treats rac-ism as aberrant and strange, whereas American racism is quite normal.

Furthermore, intentionality is in no way a prerequisite for racism. Racism is often habitual, unintentional, commonplace, polite, implicit, and well-meaning.[62] Thus, racism is not only located in our intentional thoughts and actions; it also thrives in our dispositions and habits, as well as in the social institutions in which we are all embedded.

2. *Legalistic Fallacy.*   This fallacy conflates *de jure* legal progress with *de facto* racial progress. *De jure* and *de facto* are Latin expressions meaning, respectively, "based on the law" and "based in fact." Thus, one who operates under the legalistic fallacy assumes that abolishing racist laws (racism in principle) automatically leads to the abolition of racism writ large (racism in practice).

This fallacy begins to crumble after a few moments of critical reflection. After all, we would not make the same mistake when it comes to other criminalized acts: Laws against theft do not mean that one's car will never be stolen. By way of tangible illustration, consider *Brown v. Board of Education*, the landmark 1954 case that abolished *de jure* segregation in schools, making it illegal to enforce racially segregated classrooms. Did that lead to the abolition of *de facto* segregation? Absolutely not. Fifty years later, schools are still drastically segregated and drastically unequal.[63] In fact, some social scientists have documented a nationwide movement of educational resegregation, which has left today's schools even more segregated than those of 1954.[64]

3. *Tokenistic Fallacy.*   One who is guilty of the tokenistic fallacy assumes that the presence of people of color in influential positions is evidence of the complete eradication of racial obstacles. This logic runs something like this: "Many people of color, such as Barack Obama, Condoleezza Rice, Colin Powell, Carol Mosely Brown, and Alberto Gonzales, have held high-ranking political posts; therefore, racism does not exist in the political arena. Many people of color, such as Bill Cosby, Oprah Winfrey, Jennifer Lopez, and Lucy Lu, are celebrities and multimillionaires; therefore, there is no racial inequality when it comes to income and wealth distribution. Poor people of color (not society) are to blame for their own poverty."

Although it is true that many people of color have made significant inroads to seats of political and economic power over the course of the last fifty years, a disproportionate number of them remain disadvantaged in these arenas.[65] We cannot, in good conscience, ignore the millions of African Americans living in poverty and, instead, point to Oprah's millions as evidence for economic inequality. Instead, we must explore how Oprah's financial success can coexist with the economic deprivation of millions of black women. We need to explore, in historian Thomas Holt's words, how the "simultaneous idealization of Colin Powell [or, for that matter, Barack Obama] and demonization of blacks as a whole . . . is replicated in much of our everyday world."[66]

Besides, throughout the history of America, a handful of nonwhite individuals have excelled financially and politically in the teeth of rampant racial domination. The first black congressman was not elected after the Civil Rights Movement but in 1870! Joseph Rainey, a former slave, served in the House of Representatives for four terms. Madame C. J. Walker is accredited as being the first black millionaire. Born in 1867, she made her fortune inventing hair and beauty products. Few people would feel comfortable pointing to Rainey's or Walker's success as evidence that late-nineteenth-century America was a time of racial harmony and equity. Such tokenistic logic would not be accurate then, and it is not accurate now.

4. *Ahistorical Fallacy.*   This fallacy renders history impotent. Thinking hindered by the ahistorical fallacy makes a bold claim: most United States history—namely, the period of time when this country did not extend basic rights to people of color (let alone classify them as fully human)—is inconsequential today. Legacies of slavery and colonialism, the eradication of millions of Native Americans, forced segregation, clandestine sterilizations and harmful science experiments, mass disenfranchisement, race-based exploitation, racist propaganda distributed by the state caricaturing Asians, blacks, and Hispanics, racially motivated abuses of all kinds (sexual, murderous, and dehumanizing)—all of this, purport those operating under the ahistorical fallacy, does not matter for those living in the here-and-now. This idea is so delusional that it is hard to take seriously. Today's society is directed, constructed, and molded by—indeed grafted onto—the past.[67] All that is socially constructed is historically constructed; and since race, as we have seen, is a social construction, it, too, is a historical construction.

A "soft version" of the ahistorical fallacy might admit that events in the "recent past"—such as the time since the Civil Rights Movement or the attacks on September 11, 2001—matter but things in the "distant past"—such as slavery or the colonization of Mexico—have little consequence. But this idea is no less fallacious than the "hard version," since many events in America's "distant past"—especially the enslavement and murder of millions of Africans—are the *most* consequential in shaping present-day society. In this vein, consider the question French historian Marc Bloch poses to us: "But who would dare to say that the understanding of the Protestant or Catholic Reformation, several centuries removed, is not *far more important* for a proper grasp of the world today than a great many other movements of thought or feeling, which are certainly more recent, yet more ephemeral?"[68] We would not dare. (Additionally, any historian would remind us that, since America is just over 200 years old, *all* American history is "recent history.")

5. *Fixed Fallacy.*   Those who assume that racism is fixed, that it is immutable, constant across time and space, partake in the fixed fallacy. Since they take racism to be something that does not develop in any way, those who understand racism through the fixed fallacy are often led to ask such questions as "Has racism increased or decreased in the past decades?" And because practitioners of the fixed fallacy usually take as their standard definition of racism only the most

heinous forms of racism—racial violence, for example—they confidently conclude that, indeed, things have gotten better.

It is important to trace the career of American racism and to analyze, for example, how racial attitudes or measures of racial inclusion and exclusion have changed over time. Many social scientists have developed sophisticated techniques for doing so.[69] But the question "Have things gotten better or worse?" is legitimate *only* after we account for the morphing attributes of racism. We cannot quantify racism in the same way that we can quantify, say, birthrates. The nature of "birthrate" does not fluctuate over time; thus, it makes sense to ask "Are there more or less births now than there were fifty years ago?" without bothering to analyze if and how a birthrate is different today than it was in previous historical moments.

American racism assumes different forms in different historical moments. Although race relations today are informed by those of the past, we cannot hold to the belief that twenty-first-century racism takes on the exact same form as twentieth-century racism. And we certainly cannot conclude that there is "little or no racism" today because it does not resemble the racism of the 1950s. (Modern-day Christianity looks very different, in nearly every conceivable way, than the Christianity of the early church. But this does not mean that there is "little or no Christianity" today.) So, before we ask "Have things gotten better or worse?" we should ponder the essence of racism today and how it differs from racism experienced by those living in our parents' or grandparents' generation. We should ask, further, to quote Holt once more, "What enables racism to reproduce itself after the historical conditions that initially gave it life have disappeared?"[70]

Racial Domination

We have spent a significant amount of time talking about what racial domination or racism is not. We have yet to spell out what it is. We can delineate two specific manifestations of racial domination: institutional racism and interpersonal racism. **Institutional racism** is systemic white domination of people of color, embedded and operating in corporations, universities, legal systems, political bodies, cultural life, and other social collectives. The word "domination" reminds us that institutional racism is a type of power that encompasses the *symbolic power* to classify one group of people as "normal" and other groups of people as "abnormal," the *political power* to withhold basic rights from people of color and marshal the full power of the state to enforce segregation and inequality, the *social power* to deny people of color full inclusion or membership in associational life, and *economic power* that privileges whites in terms of job placement, advancement, and wealth and property accumulation.

Informed by centuries of racial domination, institutional racism withholds from people of color opportunities, privileges, and rights that many whites enjoy.

With *Mimic*, a staged photograph, Canadian-born artist Jeff Wall recreated an incident he had once witnessed when a white man, with this small, but deeply powerful gesture, mocked an Asian man walking past.

Examples of institutional racism include the tendency of schools and universities to support curricula that highlight the accomplishments of European Americans, ignoring the accomplishments of non-European Americans; the disproportionate numbers of white people in high-ranking political, economic, and military posts and the ongoing exclusion of people of color from such posts; and the prevalence of law enforcement practices that target people of color, especially African Americans and Arab Americans, as criminals or terrorists. In all three of these examples, racial domination is carried out at the institutional level, sometimes despite the motives or attitudes of the people working in those institutions. Because institutional racism operates outside the scope of individual intent, many people do not recognize institutional racism as racism when they experience it.

Below the level of institutions, yet informed by the workings of those institutions, we find **interpersonal racism.** This is racial domination manifest in everyday interactions and practices. Interpersonal racism can be *overt;* however, most of the time, interpersonal racism is quite *covert*: it is found in the habitual, commonsensical, and ordinary practices of our lives. Our racist attitudes, as Lillian Smith remarked in *Killers of the Dream*, easily "slip from the conscious mind deep into the muscles."[71] Since we are disposed to a world structured by racial domination, we develop racialized dispositions—some conscious, many more unconscious and bodily—that guide our thoughts and behaviors.

We may talk slowly to an Asian woman at the farmer's market, unconsciously assuming that she speaks poor English. We may inform a Mexican woman at a corporate party that someone has spilled his punch, unconsciously assuming that she is a janitor. We may unknowingly scoot to the other side of the elevator when a large Puerto Rican man steps in, or unthinkingly eye a group of black teenagers wandering the aisles of the store at which we work, or ask to change seats if an Arab American man sits down next to us on an airplane. Many miniature actions such as these have little to do with one's intentional thoughts; they are orchestrated by one's practical sense, one's habitual know-how, and informed by institutional racism.

"Can people of color be racist?" This question is a popular one in the public imagination, and the answer depends on what we mean by racism. Institutional racism is the product of years of white supremacy, and it is designed to produce far-reaching benefits for white people. Institutional racism carries on despite our personal attitudes. Thus, there is no such thing as "black institutional racism" or "reverse institutional racism," since there is no centuries-old socially ingrained and normalized system of domination designed by people of color that denies whites full participation in the rights, privileges, and seats of power of our society.[72] Interpersonal racism, on the other hand, takes place on the ground level and has to do with attitudes and habitual actions. It is certainly true that members of all racial groups can harbor negative attitudes toward members of other groups. An African American may hold ill feelings toward Jews or Koreans. An Asian American may be suspicious of white people. And such prejudiced perceptions are often rampant *within* racial groups as well, as when a Cuban-American feels superior to a Mexican-American, a Japanese-American feels uncomfortable around Chinese-Americans, or dark-skinned African Americans profess to being "more authentically black" than light-skinned African Americans. Indeed, some nonwhite groups have a deep, conflict-ridden history with other nonwhite groups. One thinks here of the Black-Korean conflict, the so-called Black-Brown divide, bitter relations among Latino subgroups, and animus among various American Indian Nations.

People of color, then, can take part in overt and covert forms of interpersonal racism. That said, we must realize that interpersonal racism targeting dominated groups and interpersonal racism targeting the dominant group do not pack the same punch. Two young men, one black, the other white, bump into each other on the street. The black man calls the white man a "honky." In response, the white man calls the black man a "boy." Both racial slurs *are* racial slurs and should be labeled as such, and both reinforce racial divisions. However, unlike "honky," "boy" connects to the larger system of institutional racial domination. The word derives its meaning (and power) from slavery, when enslaved African men were stripped of their masculine honor and treated like children. "Boy" (and many other epithets aimed at blacks) invokes such times—times when murdering, torturing, whipping, and raping enslaved blacks were not illegal acts. Epithets toward white people, including "honky," have no such equivalent. ("Honky" comes from derogatory terms aimed at Bohemian, Hungarian, and Polish immigrants who worked in the Chicago meat-packing plants.) "Boy" also reminds the black man how things stand today: If the confrontation escalates and the police are called, the black man knows that the police officers will probably be white and that he might be harassed or looked on as a threat; if the two men meet in court, the black man knows that the lawyers, judge, and jurors will possibly be mostly (if not all) white; and if the two men are sentenced, the African American man knows, as do many criminologists,[73] that he will get the harsher sentence. "Boy" brings the full weight of institutional racism—systematic, historical, and mighty—down on the African-American man. "Honky," even if delivered with venomous spite, is powerless by comparison.

Moreover, sociologists have shown that, unlike white people, people of color are confronted with interpersonal racism on a regular basis, sometimes daily. For people of color, there is a cumulative character to an individual's racial experiences. These experiences do not take place in isolation. Humiliating or degrading acts always are informed by similar acts that individuals have experienced in the past. To paraphrase sociologist Joe Feagin, the interpersonal events that take place on the street and in other public settings are not simply rare and isolated events; rather, they are recurring events shaped by social and historical forces of racial domination.[74]

Symbolic Violence

Elaborating on the nature of "unconscious racism," law professor Charles Lawrence has observed: "Americans share a common historical and cultural heritage in which racism has played and still plays a dominant role. Because of this shared experience, we also inevitably share many ideas, attitudes, and beliefs that attach significance to an individual's race and induce negative feelings and opinions about nonwhites. *To the extent that this cultural belief system has influenced all of us, we are all racists.* At the same time, most of us are unaware of our racism. We do not recognize the ways in which our cultural experience has influenced our beliefs about race or the occasions upon which those beliefs affect our actions. In other words, a large part of the behavior that produces racial discrimination is influenced by unconscious racial motivation."[75] Take note of the italicized sentence. Why didn't Lawrence write, "To the extent that this cultural belief system has influenced all of us, *all white people are racists?*" The answer is because such a statement would be inaccurate.

Racism surrounds us. To borrow an analogy developed by Beverly Tatum, racial domination is like polluted air. Some days, the pollution is weighty and visible, while, on other days, it is virtually invisible—"but always, day in and day out, we are breathing it in."[76] Because racism infuses all of social life, nonwhites and whites alike develop thoughts and practices molded by racism; nonwhites and whites alike develop stereotypes about other racial groups.

In fact, people of color may internalize prejudice aimed at their own racial group, unintentionally contributing to the reproduction of racial domination. Psychologists have labeled this phenomenon "internalized oppression" or "internalized racism." Following the work of Pierre Bourdieu, we label it "symbolic violence": "violence which is exercised upon a social agent with his or her complicity."[77] In the case of racial domination, **symbolic violence** refers to the process of people of color unknowingly accepting and supporting the terms of their own domination.[78] "So we learned the dance that cripples the human spirit," laments Smith, "step by step by step, we who were white and we who were colored, day by day, hour by hour, year by year until the movements were reflexes and made for the rest of our life without thinking."[79]

A good example of symbolic violence is the nearly worldwide acceptance of European standards of beauty. The false aesthetic separation between "white beauty"—epitomized by long, straight, blonde hair, blue eyes, and pale skin—and "black ugliness"—epitomized by short, curly, black hair, brown eyes, and dark brown skin—grew out of slavery. Features associated with the African-American phenotype were demonized. Since the "Black Is Beautiful" movement of the 1960s, many African-American women have resisted such standards, taking pride in their curly hair and their ebony-colored skin. Nevertheless, many others have internalized white standards of beauty, using costly and painful methods to straighten and dye their hair and, less frequently, to lighten their skin. In fact, Madame C. J. Walker, the first black millionaire mentioned earlier, made her fortune developing a product to straighten black women's hair! Today, many black women, to borrow a philosopher's line, have been "poisoned by the stereotype others have of them."[80]

Symbolic violence operates by virtue of the fact that the dominated perceive and respond to the structures and processes that dominate them through modes of thought (indeed, also of feeling) that are themselves the products of domination. The racial "order of things" seems to them natural, self-evident, and even legitimate. Such an insight neither grants everything to structural forces somehow detached from human volition nor blames the hapless victim. "The only way to understand this particular form of domination is to move beyond the forced choice between constraint (by forces) and consent (to reasons), between mechanical coercion and

THE BOONDOCKS · BY AARON McGRUDER

"It is the peculiar triumph of society—and its loss—that it is able to convince those people to whom it has given inferior status of the reality of this decree." —James Baldwin

voluntary, free, deliberate, even calculated submission."[81] This in turn has an important practical implication. What is required is a radical transformation of the social conditions that produce embodied habits, dispositions, tastes, and lifestyles that lead people to become actively complicit in their own domination. The only way to bring about change that does not entail merely replacing one modality of racial domination with another is to address specifically and to undo the mechanisms of dehistoricization and universalization—"always and everywhere it has been this way"—whereby arbitrary workings of power are enabled to continue.

Intersectionality

Racial domination does not operate inside a vacuum, cordoned off from other modes of domination. On the contrary, it *intersects* with other forms of domination—those based on gender, class, sexuality, religion, nationhood, ability, and so forth. Social scientists have evoked the term **intersectionality** to explain the overlapping systems of advantages and disadvantages that affect people differently positioned in society.

The notion that there is a monolithic "Asian experience," "African-American experience," or "white experience"—experiences somehow detached from other pieces of one's identity—is nothing but a chimera, an illusion. Researchers have labeled such a notion "*racial essentialism*," for such a way of thinking boils down vastly different human experiences into a single "master category": race.[82] When we fail to account for these different experiences, we create silences in our narratives of the social world and fail to explain how overlapping systems of advantages and disadvantages affect individuals' opportunity structures, lifestyles, and social hardships. When we speak only of "Hispanic people," for instance, we overlook how Latinas (Hispanic women) confront not only racism but sexism in their day-to-day lives. We also overlook how poor Hispanic families must struggle against poverty and worker exploitation whereas more well-off Hispanic families may not be confronted by such obstacles. And we overlook how Hispanics with disabilities and those whose faith would not be considered mainstream are disadvantaged in ways that able-bodied Hispanics and those who practice mainstream religion are not. Finally, we overlook the ways in which gay Hispanics face ridicule, discrimination, and violence that heterosexual Hispanics do not, as well as the fact that Cubans, Puerto Ricans, Mexicans, and Dominicans—all of whom would be classified as Hispanic—have very different cultures and experience life in the U.S. in very different ways.

The idea of intersectionality implies that we cannot understand the lives of poor white single mothers or gay black men by examining only one dimension of their lives—class, gender, race, or sexuality; no, we must explore their lives in their full complexity, examining how these various dimensions come together and structure their existence. When we speak of racial domination, then, we must always bear in mind the ways in which it interacts with masculine domination (or sexism), heterosexual domination (or homophobia), class domination (poverty), religious persecution, disadvantages brought on by disabilities, and so forth.[83]

In addition, we should not assume that one kind of oppression is more important than another or that being advantaged in one dimension of life somehow cancels out other dimensions that often result in disadvantage. Although it is true that poor whites experience many of the same hardships as poor blacks, it is not true that poverty somehow de-whitens poor whites. In other words, though they are in a similarly precarious economic position as poor blacks, poor whites still experience race-based privileges, while poor blacks are oppressed not only by poverty but also by racism. In a similar vein, well-off people of color cannot "buy" their way out of racism. Despite their economic privilege, middle- and upper-class nonwhites experience institutional and interpersonal racism on a regular basis.[84]

But how, exactly, should we conceptualize these intersectional modes of domination? Many scholars have grappled with this question, and we do so here, if only in the most provisional way.[85] The notion of intersectionality is perhaps as old as the social problems of racial, masculine, and class domination, but in recent memory it has been popularized by activists who criticized the feminist and Civil Rights movements for ignoring the unique struggles of women of color. The term itself is credited to critical race scholar Kimberlé Crenshaw,[86] who imagined society as divided every which way by multiple forms of inequality. In Crenshaw's view, society resembles an intricate system of crisscrossing roads, each representing a different social identity (for example, race, gender, class, religion, age). Your unique social position (or structural location) is identified by listing all the attributes of your social identity and then pinpointing the nexus (or intersection) at which all those attributes converge. This conception of intersectionality has been the dominant one for many years, leading scholars to understand overlapping modes of oppression as a kind of "matrix of domination."[87]

Recently, however, scholars have criticized this way of thinking about intersectionality, claiming that it reproduces, in minimized form, the very essentialist reasoning it sought to dismantle.[88] For example, those who have concentrated on the ways "class intersects with race" largely have bifurcated racial groups (especially African Americans) into two classes—the middle class and the poor (or "the underclass")—attributing to each certain social characteristics, principles, and practices. Thus, instead of Black Culture, we now have two distinct black cultures; instead of the Black Community, we think in terms of two subcommunities. When scholars divide racial groups into a set number of classes, genders, sexualities, and so forth, the end result is not a critique of essentialism but a new, softer kind of essentialism. At best, an approach that represents society as a hierarchy of culturally discrete boxes encourages us to conceptualize oppression through a simple additive model (one often hears of a "double jeopardy" or "triple oppression"). At worst, it replaces larger homogenizing rubrics ("Hispanic") with smaller ones ("Hispanic women") and offers little conceptual refuge from essentializing tendencies.

A better metaphor for intersecting modes of oppression might be, not crisscrossing roads, but a web of relations within which struggles over opportunities, power, and privileges take place.[89] One implication of this new theoretical development is the realization that racial domination is deeply implicated in the perpetuation of other forms of domination—and vice versa. Systems of domination, in other words, are mutually reinforcing: to flourish, each system relies on the logic and ramifications of others. Dissecting the details of this process—uncovering, for example, precisely how racial domination supports and is supported by masculine domination—is crucial for developing effective strategies to combat all kinds of social suffering. The result of intersectional thinking, in other words, should not only be a picture of your complex identity, however important that may be; it should also entail a thorough understanding of the ways in which intertwined modes of domination rely on one another for survival.

Whiteness

As should be clear from the preceding examples, the United States, since its inception, has been a nation that placed supreme value on whiteness. During its early stages, American democracy—which prided itself on liberty and valued freedom from oppression—did not cover nonwhite people. On the contrary, America was built on the backs of Native Americans, millions of whom were killed and uprooted, and on the backs of African Americans, kidnapped, enslaved, and forced to toil for their white owners. The original section of the U.S. Capitol building, which still stands today in Washington, D.C. and houses a predominantly white Congress, was erected by black slaves. It was also slaves who, in 1860, placed the statue *Freedom* atop the Capitol Dome—a statue of a helmeted Native American woman.[90]

Whiteness is a term we do not use much. Perhaps this is because many people have the tendency to assume that race is about people of color. But race is a fundamentally relational concept: We cannot understand the meaning of Hispanic, Asian, Native American, or black without simultaneously understanding the meaning of white. But white is not simply "just another" racial category; it is the *dominant* category, that with which all other categories are compared and contrasted. **Whiteness,** then, is *racial domination normalized.* This normalization produces and reproduces many cultural, political, economic, and social advantages and privileges for white people and withholds such advantages and privileges from nonwhite people.

The Race That Need Not Speak Its Name

Think, for a moment, about who you are. What qualities are most salient to your identity? Perhaps think about three characteristics that best describe your makeup.

Chances are that if you are white, you probably did not list your race as one of the characteristics most important to you. You might have listed your ethnicity—Irish, Italian, Jewish—religion, gender, sexual orientation, or political affiliation. On the other hand, if you are not white, there is a good chance that you listed your race as an important characteristic. You might have identified yourself as a "Black woman Christian" or as an "Asian-American gay man."[91]

What explains this difference? Why are white people more unlikely than people of color to identify themselves in racial terms? Sociologists have shown that many white people have a hard time coming to terms with their whiteness. In fact, many white people seem to believe they do not belong to a racial group. They see themselves, simply, as "normal."[92] And herein lies the power of whiteness. By refusing to speak its own name, whiteness presents itself as normality.

In our popular culture, history books, and political discussions, whiteness is treated as the standard. For instance, if you are wandering the aisles of your local bookstore searching for titles by Ralph Ellison, Toni Morrison, or Richard Wright—three of America's most accomplished novelists—you probably will not find what you are looking for in the "Literature" section. Ellison, Morrison, and Wright are most likely to be found in the "African-American" section. There, too, you will find historical treatises on slavery, segregation, and the Civil Rights Movement. Novelist Leslie Marmon Silko and Pulitzer Prize winning poet N. Scott Momaday are probably shelved in the "Native-American" section; and there, too, you will find historical books on the creation of reservations and tribal culture. In the "Literature" section, you will find shelves full of white authors: Jack Kerouac, Jane Austen, Herman Melville, and so forth. And in the "History" section, you will find book after book about white people: this one about Benjamin Franklin; that one about the Dust Bowl of the 1930s. Why, then, are not these sections respectively labeled "White Literature" and "White History"?

Consider some other examples of how whiteness is held up as the status quo:

- We often hear of "black churches." Seldom do we hear churches described (or describing themselves) as "white churches," even though their congregations are primarily white. These are simply "churches."

- Certain television shows, like the *George Lopez Show,* are considered "Hispanic television." Popular shows, such as *Seinfeld, Sex in the City,* and *C.S.I.* are made up of majority or all white casts, but those shows are not called "white television."

- Many African-American artists are said to produce "black music"; many African-American comedians are said to write "black jokes." But when is the last time you heard pop, rock, or country songs sung by white artists described as "white music"? Are the jokes written by Dane Cook, Jon Stewart, or Larry the Cable Guy called "white jokes"?

- There are "black ghettos," "Mexican barrios," "Chinatown," and "Native American reservations"; but gated suburban communities, many of which are nearly all white, are simply referred to as "gated communities" or "suburbs."

- "Asian culture" might be located in a piece of artwork or a type of fashion. The "Hispanic influence" might be pointed out in architecture or cuisine. Someone might be said to have "black style." But "white culture," "white influence," and "white style" are seldom uttered phrases.

- Many colleges and universities across the U.S. are majority-white campuses, but while these institutions are simply called colleges and universities, majority-black campuses are called "historically black colleges." Similarly, college courses that focus on Anglo-European history, literature, music, art, or architecture are not called "white studies," but many courses are listed under "African-American studies," "Chicano studies," or "Asian-American studies."

These examples demonstrate how whiteness surrounds us though it often goes unnamed. Whiteness positions itself against blackness, indigenousness, Asianness, Hispanicness, and Arabness; in so doing, it fades into the background by highlighting the differences of nonwhites. This is what we mean when we say that whiteness is racial domination normalized.

White Privilege

If whiteness is normal, then nonwhiteness is abnormal. Owing to centuries of racial domination, whiteness is infused with an essence of the positive; and this essence can exist only through its negation: an essence of the negative that marks nonwhiteness.[93] Look up "white" in any dictionary, and you will learn that the term means "the absence of color," as well as "free from spot or blemish," "innocent," "not intended to cause harm" (as in a white lie), "favorable," and "fortunate." According to the most recent version of the *Merriam-Webster English Dictionary,* white can also mean "marked by upright fairness," as in "that's mighty white of you." Under the antonyms for white, we find black. Upon looking up "black," we see that it means "very dark color" as well as "dirty," "soiled," "wicked," "indicative of condemnation," "Satanic" (as in black magic), "calamitous," "marked by the occurrence of disaster," "sullen," and "grotesque" (as in black humor).

Although whiteness permeates all areas of society—we breathe it in every day—it seems weightless to many of us. Like fish in the ocean, who fail to feel the weight of the water, whites tend to take their whiteness for granted. Conversely, for many who are not white, whiteness is very much a visible reality. As one sociologist has put it, "whiteness, as a set of normative cultural practices, is visible most clearly to those it definitively excludes and those to whom it does violence. Those who are securely housed within its borders usually do not examine it."[94]

Though they may not notice it, many white people benefit from belonging to the dominant race. **White privilege** is the collection of unearned cultural, political, economic, and social advantages and privileges possessed by people of Anglo-European descent or by those who pass as such. Social scientists have amassed a significant amount of evidence that demonstrates how white people, strictly because of their whiteness, reap considerable advantages when buying and selling a house, choosing a neighborhood in which to live, getting a job and moving up the corporate ladder, securing a first class education, and seeking medical care. That whites accumulate more property and earn more income than members of minority populations, possess immeasurably more political power, and enjoy greater access to the country's cultural, social, medical, legal, and economic resources, are well-documented, and indisputable, historical and sociological facts.[95]

Consider the links between race, neighborhoods, and safety. Even after adjusting for income and occupation, whites are far less likely to be exposed to toxic chemicals and pollutants than are Latinos or African Americans. One reason for this is that white neighborhoods are far less likely to house institutions of pollution, such as garbage dumps, trash incinerators, and chemical plants. (In Houston, Texas, 100% of the city's garbage dumps are located in black neighborhoods!) We can also see white privilege at work within the criminal justice system. Although most drug addicts are white, African Americans are four times more likely to be arrested on drug charges than whites. In the federal prison system, whites enjoy sentences that are, on average, 20% shorter than those given African Americans guilty of the exact same crime.[96] We will explore in detail how white privilege pervades other realms of social life in subsequent chapters.

If white people benefit from their skin privilege, people of color are disadvantaged by it. Whites have accumulated many opportunities due to racial domination, but people of color have suffered from disaccumulation. If we talk about "black poverty," then we must also talk about white affluence; if we speak of "Hispanic unemployment," then we must also keep in mind white employment; and if we ponder public policies for people of color, then we must also critically examine the public policies that directly benefit white people. In all cases, one group's privilege results in other groups' disadvantage.[97] It is precisely for this reason that, when asked by a reporter his views on America's "Negro problem," African-American novelist Richard Wright replied: "There isn't any Negro problem; there is only a white problem."[98]

White Antiracists

Some white people are fully aware of how the current system of racial domination benefits them and work to uphold such a system; they intentionally invest in their whiteness. Many others, who do not recognize their privilege, unknowingly support a system of racial domination that disadvantages people of color, unintentionally investing in their whiteness. Important here is the ideal of **color-blindness.** While some confuse physical differences with obvious racial differences, as we discussed earlier, others err in the opposite direction by claiming to ignore all racial markers. "I don't see color at all," they declare. "I'm color-blind!" Such avowals usually are well intentioned—indeed, many of us have been taught, since childhood, to "ignore race"—but, upon closer inspection, we realize that color-blindness is an illogical proposition. For it requires the simultaneous recognition and nonrecognition of racial markers (such as skin color). As law professor Neil Gotanda has pointed out, color-blindness "is self-contradictory, because it is impossible not to think about a subject without having first thought about it at least a little. . . . To be racially color-blind . . . is to ignore what one has already noticed. The medically color-blind individual never perceives color in the first place; the racially color-blind individual perceives race and then ignores it."[99]

Color-blindness would be the ideal response to a society unaffected by racial domination.[100] But, sadly, ours is not such a society. Accordingly, color-blindness is not only a self-contradictory code—"At once I see and fail to see your blackness"—but it is also a fundamentally wrong response to racial injustice, one that "fosters the systematic denial of racial subordination and the psychological repression of an individual's recognition of that subordination, thereby allowing it to continue."[101] We will have more to say about color-blindness in ensuing chapters, but a final thought deserves mention. The opposite of color-blindness is not a kind of racial exaggeration, where all you notice about a person is her or his race. Nor is it a demobilizing sense of racial guilt, where you wallow in the stereotypes you harbor. The opposite of color-blindness, rather, is simple honesty: honesty about our modes of perception and racialized ways of thinking, as well as about the true nature of our world, a world rife with racial inequality. Noticing race means observing a long history of misery, exploitation, and inequality; recognizing systems of social meanings that have affixed themselves to different skin pigments; and perhaps confronting stereotypes and misunderstandings we hold deep inside.

And still other whites recognize their own white privilege and disavow—in some cases, actively struggle against—the racial structures from which they draw their privilege. In fact, they leverage their very advantages in the fight to dismantle racial domination. As one sociologist has aptly said with **white antiracists** in mind: "We do not choose our parents, but we do choose our politics."[102] Throughout the history of the United States, some whites have fought racism. Charles Sumner was one such person. Sumner served in the U.S. Senate in the mid-nineteenth century and was recognized widely as a powerful orator and a radical abolitionist. Advocating a civil rights bill that sought to ensure equal treatment for African Americans after the fall of slavery, Sumner once addressed the Senate with these stirring words: "There is beauty in art, in literature, in science, and in every triumph of intelligence, all of which I covet for my country; but there is a higher beauty still—in relieving the poor, in elevating the downtrodden, and being a succor to the oppressed. There is true grandeur in an example of justice, making the rights of all the same as our own, and beating down prejudice, like Satan, under our feet." The civil rights bill did not succeed, but Sumner doggedly pursued his mission. On his deathbed, surrounded by friends and fellow politicians, Sumner repeated an urgent message three times over: "You must take care of the civil rights bill—my bill, the civil rights bill—don't let it fail!"[103]

There was also Bill Moore, a white postman working in Baltimore during the Civil Rights Movement. When the governor of Mississippi, Ross Barnett, refused to desegregate the University of Mississippi, Moore staged a one-man march from Chattanooga, Tennessee to Jackson, Mississippi. Playing up his identity as a letter carrier, Moore sought to "deliver a letter" arguing for integration to Governor Barrett. Wearing two placards on his back and chest—one reading "Equal Rights for All: Mississippi or Bust," the other, in reference to segregated diners, reading, "Black and White: Eat at Joe's"—Moore began his march on April 21, 1963.[104]

He was murdered three days later. Found dead and abandoned next to a northern Alabama highway, Moore had been shot twice in the head and once in the neck at point-blank range. He was thirty-three and a father of three. Likewise,

Charles Sumner paid dearly for threatening white supremacy. In 1856, two days after delivering a speech that criticized proslavery groups in Kansas, Sumner was beaten unconscious by Preston Brooks, a congressman from South Carolina. Brooks approached Sumner as he worked at his desk in the nearly empty Senate chamber and smashed his thick wooden cane over Sumner's head. Brooks continued to assault Sumner until his cane broke. Sumner suffered massive head trauma and would not return to the Senate for three years.

The sacrifices made by Sumner and Moore should not overshadow the sacrifices borne by hundreds of nonwhite women and men who fought against slavery, segregation, and other racist structures. For every white person beaten or killed for fighting against racism there are hundreds of people of color who suffered equally. We speak here of the passion of Charles Sumner and Bill Moore only to illustrate that, throughout the history of the United States, white people have aligned with people of color to struggle against racial domination.

Thinking Like a Sociologist

Understanding race in the complex world in which we all live does not simply mean memorizing certain terms, statistics, and historical events. It means breaking with commonsense comprehensions of the world, apprehending society with a sophisticated mindset that takes into account economic, political, cultural, and social forces that operate on a national and global scale. It means approaching the world skeptically and critically, rejecting overly simplified explanations, and evaluating and reevaluating the nature of things with a new outlook. It means, in a word, cultivating a **sociological imagination.**

American sociologist C. Wright Mills coined the term "sociological imagination" in 1959.[105] By this, he meant one's ability to understand everyday life not through personal circumstances but through the broader historical forces that structure and direct it. The sociological imagination allows its possessor to discover larger forces at work in the smallest of social scenarios—in one's home life, one's romantic adventures, even in one's innermost thoughts; thus, it unearths "the social at the heart of the individual, the impersonal beneath the intimate, the universal buried deep within the most particular."[106] As a result, individuals who think with the sociological imagination can perceive how their choices, and the choices of others, are constrained and enabled by social structures and processes. Once this is accomplished, they can transform personal problems into public issues.

Racial Terminology

Perhaps the single most dangerous threat to developing a sociological imagination is our failure to put aside our self-centeredness. It is a perplexing and powerful truth that to fully understand ourselves we must get over ourselves. In particular, conversations about race too often are encumbered by proverbial and petty debates over terminology. Countless conversations about race remain on a superficial level because someone focuses on a *word* rather than on the *thing*. Thus, some indigenous people prefer the term "Native American"; some prefer "American Indian"; and some say they belong to a "tribe," others to a "nation." Some people of European descent prefer the term "white"; others say "European American" or "Caucasian." Some people of African descent refer to themselves as "black"; others prefer "African American"; and still others use variants such as "Afro-American" or "Black American." Some Hispanic Americans prefer "Latino/a" to "Hispanic," "Mexican American," or "Chicano/a"; others feel differently. Some are offended at the use of "Americans" (as opposed to "North Americans") to refer to all people living in the United States. Some say "minorities," others "people of color," "nonwhites," or "underrepresented groups." Some hyphenate terms; others do not. Some capitalize Black and White; others do not. Some place the word "race" inside quotation marks; others do not. You probably have opinions about many or all of these choices. Some have very strong opinions backed by thoughtful justifications. But it's not about you.

In truth, there is no right or wrong racial label. Indeed, ten Hispanic Americans might offer ten different racial labels for themselves. If there is no superior racial terminology—and we aren't speaking here of hateful epithets, which should never be used—it is because the foundation on which this terminology rests, race, is nothing more than a well-founded fiction. Arguing with each other about racial terminology breeds a spirit of uncertainty and fear, a spirit that forces mouths—and minds—to close. If so many people stutter nervously when talking about race, it is because they do not want to say the wrong thing and have someone pounce irritably on a phrase they used, declaring "That term offends me!" Let us choose wisely the battles in which we engage. There are times to grow outraged and to make our outrage known. But rather than waste our energy on racial labels and on what offends us, let us instead channel our outrage to bigger problems. Let us grow outraged at racial domination, white supremacy, and rampant inequality. If we grow offended at a racial term, let us evaluate the system that created it, picking a fight with the system, not with the word itself—or with the one who uttered it. Changing words, after all, doesn't amount to much. W. E. B. Du Bois knew well this fact. Writing in 1928 to a young reader who objected to Du Bois's use of the term "Negro," a common term for African Americans at the time, Du Bois advised, "Do not . . . make the all too common error of mistaking names for things. Names are only conventional signs for identifying things. Things are the reality that counts. If a thing is despised, either because of ignorance or because it is despicable, you will not alter matters by changing its name. . . . It is not the name—it's the Thing that counts. Come on, Kid, let's go get the Thing!"[107]

Pursuing the thing, we use many different racial labels throughout this book and encourage you not to get hung up on any one of them. It is true, of course, that words—labels—do help to create the very things they "identify" or describe. Words do matter in social life. But to become heavily, one-sidedly, invested in words is self-defeating. In your conversations, we encourage you to think beyond yourselves and to reach through the words to a deeper engagement with the thing itself: the complex system of racial domination.

Reflexivity, Relationality, and Reconstruction

Crucial to developing a keen sociological imagination are three equally important modes of thinking we call "The Three Rs": *Reflexivity, Relationality, and Reconstruction. Reflexivity* means turning the instruments of social science—especially critical evaluation carried out with a sociological imagination—back on oneself. The reflexive thinker looks within herself to uncover taken-for-granted ways of thinking that influence how she understands the social world. Before we can know something, we must scrutinize our thoughts to understand how we know it. Or, to put it another way, if we wish to study society, then we must first study ourselves. How has my thinking been affected by racial domination and the naturalization of whiteness? How am I privileged or disadvantaged because of my race or, for that matter, my gender, class position, nationality, religion, or sexual orientation—and how might this bias my thinking? How has my thinking about race been affected by my education? Where do my own—and my society's—ideas of race come from? Part One of this book, "Reflexivity," allows us better to address these questions by historicizing the concept of race.

Relationality means that the building blocks of society are unfolding relationships. In this view, an individual or group is best examined by exploring the networks of relationships, or **fields of life**, within which that individual or group is embedded. These fields of life have their own inner logics—each operates in part according to its own internal principles—but they also are affected by larger societal forces. In America, every field of life is saturated with the realities of race. Part Two of this book, "Relationality," examines how society's major fields of life are penetrated by racial dynamics. Moving from large, impersonal fields to smaller, more intimate ones, it explores the political, economic, and residential fields before examining how America's legal field is affected by race. It analyzes the educational, aesthetic, and associational fields, then concludes with an examination of race and intimate relationships.

You will find that one surprising consequence of our relational perspective in this book is that the discussions that follow do not proceed, as is common in sociological writing on the topic, one racial or ethnic group at a time. We do not make the mistake of treating racial or ethnic groups as the starting points of our analyses. Proceeding in such a fashion not only reifies race—treating as real groups that, in truth, are based on a well-founded fiction—it also gives off the impression that each racial group is fundamentally different from the next. If you are looking for separate chapters on African Americans, Native Americans, and the like, you will not find them in this book. Nor, for that matter, will you find that equal space is given each racial or ethnic group in each and every chapter. In some chapters, one set of groups receive more attention; in others, other groups. *Our thinking in this book centers on relations, not groups.* It is organized around particularly important fields of life in our society, and it seeks to understand how race works in and across those different fields. We are more concerned with imparting a method for thinking about racial structures and dynamics in these fields of life than we are with telling you about specific racial groups.

If reflexivity pushes us to interrogate—that is, to ask hard questions about—our own thought and to search for unnoticed blind spots, and if relationality pushes us to understand how race works in multiple fields of life, then *reconstruction* pushes us to take our new-found knowledge and use it to change the world in which we live. It involves using the knowledge we have acquired about racial domination to fight it. It means reconstructing how we think about race in our own lives, then using our sharpened analysis to reconstruct how race is discussed elsewhere. This work can be carried out in many different ways and in different settings, from our family's dinner table to Washington, D.C. In the final chapter of this book, located in Part Three, "Reconstruction," we explore how people, whites and nonwhites alike, are striking out against racism.

CHAPTER REVIEW

A BIOLOGICAL REALITY?
biological determinism

RACE IS A SOCIAL REALITY
race, racial taxonomy, phenotype, ancestry, naturalization

ETHNICITY AND NATIONALITY
ethnicity, nationality

AMERICAN RACISM IN THE TWENTY-FIRST CENTURY
individualistic fallacy, legalistic fallacy, tokenistic fallacy, ahistorical fallacy, fixed fallacy, institutional racism, interpersonal racism, symbolic violence, intersectionality

WHITENESS

whiteness, white privilege, color-blindness, white antiracists

THINKING LIKE A SOCIOLOGIST

sociological imagination, fields of life

FROM THEORY TO PRACTICE

1. How do you identify racially and ethnically? How did you learn to identify in such a way? Critically evaluate how your racial composition might advantage or disadvantage you in your daily life.

2. Now that you have done that, think about all the other aspects of your identity, your gender, religion, nationality, and so forth. What part of your identity is most salient to you? Explore, in a reflexive fashion, why this is, paying close attention to how your multiple identities intersect with one another. What does intersectionality mean to you? Can you think of ways in which you do not identify with some members of your race (or ethnicity, gender, religion, etc.) because of another aspect of your identity? For example, perhaps many members of your racial group fail to tolerate your religious preference, or, maybe, some members of your gender just do not understand your sexual orientation.

3. While watching television, reading the newspaper, attending classes, taking in a sporting event, attending religious services, keep an eye out for whiteness. How does whiteness influence the classes you attend or your social circles? Identify examples of whiteness in the movies you watch and the music you listen to. Can you pinpoint some of the ways in which whiteness goes unnoticed?

4. Keep an eye out for one or more of the five fallacies about racism. Analyze a conversation, newspaper article, movie, play, everyday interaction, or any other object or event with respect to the five fallacies. Did you spot a fallacy? If so, which one? Or, did the people you observed avoid all the fallacies, and, if so, how did they pull it off? In either case, use the object you analyze to reflect on how you might avoid the fallacies when thinking about racial domination.

RECOMMENDED READING

- Pierre Bourdieu and Loïc Wacquant, *An Invitation to Reflexive Sociology* (Chicago: University of Chicago Press, 1992).

- Michael Brown, Martin Carnoy, Elliott Currie, Troy Duster, David Oppenheimer, Marjorie Shultz, and David Wellman, *White-Washing Race: The Myth of a Color Blind Society* (Berkeley and Los Angeles: University of California Press, 2003).

- Joe R. Feagin, Hernan Vera, and Pinar Batur, *White Racism: The Basics*, Second Edition (New York: Routledge, 2001).

- Stephen Jay Gould, *The Mismeasure of Man* (New York: Norton, 1996).

- C. Wright Mills, *The Sociological Imagination* (New York: Oxford University Press, 1959).

- M. F. Ashley Montagu, *Man's Most Dangerous Myth: The Fallacy of Race*, Third Edition (New York: Harpers, 1952 [1942]).

- Beverly Daniel Tatum, *"Why Are All the Black Kids Sitting Together in the Cafeteria" and Other Conversations about Race* (New York: Basic Books, 1997).

PART ONE

REFLEXIVITY

THERE ARE TWO LEVELS OF REFLEXIVITY. THE FIRST HAS TO DO WITH OUR position in society. This level of reflexivity pushes us to consider ourselves not as free-floating individuals for whom the playing field is equal but as people shaped, privileged, and disadvantaged by a society in which racial domination is rampant. You may very well be an intelligent, creative, and driven individual, but social scientists have amassed enough evidence to fill libraries to show how your intelligence, creativity, and work ethic cannot fully account for your personal successes and failures. Society matters. So, in order fully to understand where we have been and where we stand today, we must acknowledge how we benefit and suffer from racial domination, as well as the ways in which we are shaped by intersecting systems of oppression based on class, gender, sexuality, and religion.

The second level of reflexivity has to do with our education. In this case, education encompasses a broad array of activities, both formal (high school, religious schooling) and informal (parents, friends, media). We must scrutinize our educational experiences and determine how whiteness has informed those experiences. Did our high school or college education teach us much about Asian American history? If our friends and lovers are primarily the same race as we are, then with what kinds of life experiences might we be unfamiliar? It is only by asking ourselves such questions that we will be able to cast light on the unquestioned assumptions lurking in the shadows of our thinking, assumptions that tend to impede critical thought.

Along with these two levels of self-analysis, we add another dimension: all reflexivity must be historical. Our thinking is in no way produced strictly by present-day events and conversations. Quite the contrary: Our thinking—and especially our taken-for-granted, habitual thinking—is the product of hundreds of years of thought. Our thinking about race is conditioned by what the Spanish and English thought when they were colonizing the "New World," by what slaves and slave masters were thinking during the early years of America, and by what all Americans were thinking during the Indian Wars or during the era of Jim Crow. Since much of our thinking is internalized and forgotten history, through repeated acts of reflexivity we must strive to historicize our thinking. The most fundamental aspect of such an exercise is the historicization of the meaning of race itself.

Reflexivity should not be confused with relativity. The too-often-repeated mantra, "it's all relative," strikes us as a shortcut to thinking. Relativity implies that reality somehow only exists in your mind. We reject this notion, as do the millions and millions of people suffering from the inflictions of racial domination, injustice, and poverty, people who know that social realities are far too real. Reflexivity does not reduce reality to your own point of view; rather, it suggests that your point of view must be studied, questioned, and picked apart for you truly to know the realness of reality. A thorough understanding of ourselves is a prerequisite to a thorough understanding of the world in which we live. Nor is the point of rigorous reflexivity to discover if you are a "racist" or a "nonracist," for such a limited choice harkens back to the individualistic fallacy. The point, rather, is to uncover unconscious assumptions and inaccurate perceptions that produce blind spots in our thinking about race. And, like it or not, we all have blind spots.

Chapter 2

The Invention of Race

Recovering Our Inheritance

You do not come into this world African or European or Asian; rather, this world comes into you. You are not born with a race in the same way you are born with fingers and eyes and hair. Fingers and eyes and hair are natural creations, whereas race, as we learned in the previous chapter, is a social fabrication, a symbolic category misrecognized as natural. And if it is misrecognized as such so frequently, it is because we fail to examine race as a historical product, one that, in the larger scheme of things, is quite new.

White, African, Hispanic, Asian, American Indian—it wasn't always this way. Before the sixteenth century, race, as we know it today, did not exist. Does this mean that antiquity and the Middle Ages were periods of peace and harmony? Certainly not. Prejudices were formed and wars were waged against "other" people. But those "other" people were not categorized or understood as people of other races. Instead of the color line, the primary social division in those times was that between the "civilized" and the "uncivilized." Since religion greatly influenced this division, at least in the Middle Ages, we might say that the world at that time was divided between "sophisticated Christians" and "barbarous heathens."[1] The racial categories so familiar to us began to calcify only around the beginning of the nineteenth century, a mere two hundred years ago. In fact, the word "race" has a very recent origin; it obtained its modern meaning only in the late 1700s.

But racial domination survives by covering its tracks, by erasing its own history.[2] It encourages us to think of the mystic boundaries separating, say, West from East, white from black, black from Asian, or Asian from Hispanic, as timeless separations—divisions that have always been and will always be. This is a distortion of the truth. Struggling against racial domination requires us to struggle against the temptation to rid race of its history. As reflexive thinkers, we must examine race as a historical invention. And we must do so, if for no other reason, than because the project of exploring the history of race is, at the same time, one of uncovering the reasons behind our everyday actions. We cannot stand outside history and watch far-off lands and peoples of old with detached bemusement. Far-off lands, peoples of old—we have inherited them; they are inside us.

This chapter, then, aims to uncover the methods by which our current racial taxonomies came to be. We must start from the beginning, traveling backward in time some six hundred years to a world without race. This world would soon find itself turned inside out. A "New World" would be discovered and, in it, a "new people." At the same time, a new economic system—capitalism—would emerge, as would a new political arrangement: nations. Science and "rationality," too, would flourish. Amid such revolutionary transformations, race would emerge as a new way of viewing and ordering the world. This chapter explains how that happened. How, it asks, was race socially and historically constructed? It surveys six centuries of history—from Columbus's voyage to the twentieth century—focusing on the invention of race in the Americas.

Modernity Rising

More than any others, two European countries, two political and economic powerhouses of the early modern world, would give birth to the system of racial classification we know today: England and Spain. Before the European discovery of the Americas, England, like all of Northern Europe, was virtually shut off from the rest of the world.[3] There was, however, one piece of land the English coveted since the middle of the twelfth century: Ireland. Over and over, England invaded Ireland, labeling the Irish "rude, beastly, ignorant, cruel and unruly infidels."[4] In a phrase popularized in the fourteenth century: "it was no more a sin to kill an Irishman than a dog or any other brute." The Irish were regarded as nothing short of "savages" in the English mind, and this mindset—that the Irish were wild, evil, polluted, and in need of correction (if not enslavement)—would greatly influence how the English would come to view America's indigenous peoples. In fact, the cruel saying that circulated in North America during the nineteenth century—"The only good Indian is a dead Indian"—first circulated in England as "The only good Irishman is a dead Irishman."[5]

While England was fighting for control of Ireland, Spain, a kingdom loyal to the Catholic Church, was contemplating what to do about the Jews and Muslims who populated the Iberian Peninsula—a stretch of land that Spain had wrested from the Moors (Muslims who inhabited the region). Under Moorish control, the peninsula had developed into a pluralistic society, one marked by a fair amount of religious and cultural tolerance and frequent intermarriage.[6] But

Spain would have none of that. Ferdinand and Isabella, the king and queen, sought homogeneity—their subjects had to be of one mind, one religion, and one culture. The crown offered Jews and Muslims three choices: leave, convert, or die. Many, especially the economically privileged, converted to Catholicism to escape persecution. The newly converted, or *conversos*, soon began gaining economic standing, and some even began acquiring influence in the church. But this did not last long, as church leaders began to question the sincerity of the *conversos*, asking, "Were these people Christians by day but Jews by night?" Thus, in 1478, the Spanish Inquisition began in earnest. Family ancestries were interrogated for "religious contamination," and many Spaniards began to purchase certificates of ancestral purity, issued by the Catholic Church, to affirm their religious wholesomeness. Soon enough, interest in religious purity morphed into an obsession with blood purity.[7]

In fifteenth-century Spain, then, we can witness, in embryonic form, what we now call *nationalism*. A brand new identity was being fashioned, one based not on religion, family, or trade but on national affiliation. Newly formed nations were beginning to create a "people," an "imagined community," bound together inside artificially created political borders.[8] Political leaders initiated new ways to tie together the population they governed. Spain did so through religious repression; other nations would do so through racial repression. In fact, race soon would come to guide the emergence and development of many modern states, and these states would, in turn, serve as key actors in the development and maturation of modern systems of racial classification.[9]

As Europe's political landscape was undergoing massive reorganization, so, too, was its economic system. *Capitalism* was on the march. The medieval workshop was transformed into the capitalist factory. Products were manufactured ever more quickly and cheaply. And products began to be developed, not to meet needs but to make profits. Economic markets began to swell; money gained in importance; an elite class, one that accumulated wealth, property, and factory ownership, began to form; an entrepreneurial spirit captured ambitious hearts. Even more importantly, a new tide swept across the rural landscape. Social relations in the countryside became transformed into relations based on the exploitation of agricultural labor for the sake of profits. And capitalism also increasingly drove the extraction of materials from beneath the earth's surface: ores, minerals, and, especially, precious metals such as silver and gold.

Since new trading routes and economic partnerships were being sought to satisfy Europe's growing capitalist enterprise, expeditions began to set off for new corners of the globe ("new" by European standards, of course). The so-called **Age of Discovery** commenced as Spanish and Portuguese explorers traveled south to Africa and east to Indochina. (A more accurate label might be the "Age of Colonialism" or, from the standpoint of the indigenous peoples of Africa and the Americas, the "Age of Terrorism.") Travelers' accounts began to trickle back to Europe, narratives in the tradition of *The Travels of Marco Polo*, composed in the thirteenth century. These narratives preferred fantasy to fact, legend to observation. One German text of the period asserted: "In Libya many are born without heads and have a mouth and eyes. . . . In the land of Ethiopia many people walk bent down like cattle, and many live four hundred years."[10] Such tall tales gave rise to fantasies about non-Europeans in general, and people of the Orient in particular. As a result, Europe, a region once divided by internal strife and warfare, a landmass with no obvious geographic claim to the status of "continent," began to congeal around a shared identity. A new and powerful division entered the world, one separating "the West" from "the Rest."[11]

At the same time, people began to reject superstition and myth. They began to explain the world, not in terms of magical or religious forces but in terms of rational forms of thought. (Sociologists call this the *disenchantment of the world*.) This was the age of great intellectual revolutions in science, economics, political theory, philosophy, religion, and art. In 1492, Leonardo da Vinci, the Italian artist/inventor/mathematician, was forty and enjoying widespread fame; Niccolò Machiavelli, the influential Italian philosopher and author of *The Prince*, was twenty-three; and Thomas More, the English cleric and humanist scholar who coined the term "utopia," was twenty-nine. Copernicus, who would forever change the face of science with his finding that the Earth rotated around the sun, not vice versa, was concluding his adolescent years, while the monk who would spark the Protestant Reformation, Martin Luther, was a child of eight.[12]

Christopher Columbus was forty-one. A ruddy, red-headed sailor, Columbus, with the support of Queen Isabella of Spain, set sail in August in search of a western trade route to the riches of China and the East Indies. Approximately one month later, he stumbled on an island in what are now the Bahamas. Columbus named the island San Salvador, but the island's original inhabitants called it Guanahan. He then sailed to the second-largest island in the Antilles, an island that today is shared by Haiti and the Dominican Republic. The island's indigenous people, the Taíno, called their homeland Haití and Quizqueia, among other things; Columbus would christen it La Española, or Hispaniola, meaning "the Spanish island." Columbus sailed back to Spain with several kidnapped Taínos, captives whom he would present to the Spanish royal court and, afterward, train as translators.[13] Although figures vary widely, it is estimated that, at that time, the Americas were populated by 50 to 100 million indigenous people.[14]

The old world was passing away, and to replace it, a new modernity was rising. **Modernity** refers to the historical era marked by the rise of nations and nationalism, the development of capitalism, global expansion and the European discovery of "the New World," the disenchantment of the world, and rapid growth of scientific knowledge. The world was changing. A new worldview would be needed for a world itself quite new. And race would soon emerge as an important element in that worldview.

Colonization of the Americas

Contrary to popular belief, Columbus was not the first European to have encountered the Americas (that title usually is reserved for Leif Ericson, a Norse explorer who is said to have set foot in modern-day Newfoundland as early as 1001 C.E.). But Columbus's voyage was the most influential. News of it spread across Europe, sparking a rush of expeditions to the Americas. In short order, much of the "New World" would come under Spanish colonial rule, followed by English colonization of parts of North America. (The French and Dutch colonized still other parts of North America. We focus on Spain and England here because we are attempting not to provide a comprehensive history of European colonization, but to tell the story of the emergence of the U.S. racial classification system, a story for which the histories of Spanish and English colonization are most relevant.)

Colonialism occurs when a foreign power invades a territory and establishes enduring systems of exploitation and domination over that territory's indigenous populations. Through violent and mighty military acts, supported by technological superiority, as well as through organized deception and malevolence, the foreign power appropriates the resources and lands of the conquered territories for its own enrichment. In doing so, it destroys indigenous ways of life (social organization, tribal sovereignty, cultural and religious beliefs, family structures) and obliterates indigenous economies. Colonizers justify their oppression through belief systems that humiliate indigenous peoples, robbing them of their honor and humanity.[15]

The Spanish Conquest

The Spaniards were the first to colonize the Americas. Hungry for gold and silver, eager to claim the land for the Spanish Crown, and compelled to convert unbelievers to Catholicism, Spanish explorers descended on modern-day Cuba, Hispaniola, and the east coast of Mexico.[16] (They would also move into South America.) One of the most famous explorers was Hernán Cortés. In 1519, Cortés led a band of *conquistadores*, mercenary soldiers licensed by the Spanish Crown to capture the lands and riches of the New World, as well as the souls of its inhabitants. In search of a city that, rumor had it, was overflowing with wealth, Cortés resolutely marched inland. He and the *conquistadores* soon arrived at the capital of what today we call the Aztec empire (its inhabitants most likely referred to themselves with several different names)—a city called Tenochtitlán (present-day Mexico City)—a sight beyond their wildest imaginations.

Tenochtitlán was an engineering marvel, a beautiful city constructed in the middle of a lake, accessible only through a complex system of causeways. (The lake—and its causeways—are no longer.) And the city was enormous, booming with a population of 250,000 inhabitants. (At that time, London was but a city of 50,000 and Seville, the largest city in Spain, was home to only 40,000.[17]) Bernal Díaz del Castillo, a *conquistador* alongside Cortés, describes the stunning city: "With such wonderful sights to gaze on we did not know what to say, or if this was real that we saw before our eyes. On the land side there were great cities, and on the lake many more. The lake was crowded with canoes. . . . We saw *cues* and shrines in these cities that looked like gleaming white towers and castles: a marvelous sight. . . . Some of our soldiers who had been in many parts of the world, in Constantinople, in Rome, and all over Italy, said that they had never seen a market so well laid out, so large, so orderly, and so full of people."[18]

The ruler of the Aztec empire, Motecuhzoma (also known as Xocoyotzin or, in its anglicized form, Montezuma), welcomed Cortés and his men, hosting them in Tenochtitlán. The friendship was short-lived, however, for Cortés and his followers soon laid siege to Tenochtitlán, killing Motecuhzoma and thousands of Aztecs.[19] To the Spaniards went the spoils of war: Aztec land was given the *conquistadores* by the Spanish Crown in the form of large agricultural estates; the *conquistadores* captured gold, silver, gems, animals, textiles, and artwork; and Aztec women were baptized and presented by Cortés to his captains as wives. Indeed, *miscegenation,* or intermarriage and intercourse between people with different skin tones, was prevalent in the Spanish colonies. Spaniards, indigenous men and women, and Africans (who were brought *en masse* to the Caribbean and Latin America through the Atlantic slave trade) married each other and raised children. (The Spanish crown even encouraged intermarriage between *conquistadores* and indigenous women, a practice they thought would help stabilize the region.[20]) The territories soon were populated by children of mixed heritage. Systems of racial classification began to take shape, but miscegenation resulted in the categories becoming blurry and numerous. Indeed, dozens of racial categories began to develop, categories still employed today throughout Latin America.[21]

After the fall of the Aztec empire, the Spaniards quickly colonized the lands it had encompassed, ushering in an era of brutality and exploitation. Aztecs and other indigenous people of the region were forced to work as farmers, miners, builders, and servants on land that was once theirs.[22] But the Spanish oppression of indigenous peoples did not go without reproach. Bartolomé de Las Casas, a Spanish bishop, tirelessly spoke out against his kingdom's abuses. "From the very beginning," he once wrote, "Spanish policy towards the New World has been characterized by blindness of the most pernicious kind: even while the various ordinances and decrees governing the treatment of the native peoples have continued to maintain that conversion and the saving of souls has first priority, this is belied by what has actually been happening on the ground."[23]

Along with other clergymen, Las Casas would rally the church to protect native populations and to outlaw indigenous slavery (which took placed under a different guise, a system of trusteeship and forced labor known as the *encomienda* system). Finally, in 1542, Spain handed down a set of reforms known as *Leyes Nuevas,* or "The New Laws," which were designed to curb the exploitation of indigenous peoples and outlaw their enslavement. The New Laws, however, never took hold, as Spanish colonizers refused to loosen their grip on the indigenous people. Their disdain for the reforms was so pronounced, in fact, that messengers who delivered the New Laws to the colonies were shunned, beaten, and, in the case of modern-day Peru, even killed.

However, the New Laws said nothing about the abolition of African slavery in the Spanish colonies. In fact, Las Casas and other "protectors of the Indians" often "called for the sparing of Indian lives, especially in the mines, by importing many more African slaves." The result was the "slow but almost universal replacement of Indian slaves with black Africans." As would occur in North America, slavery would transform from a multiracial institution, which placed in bondage a wide variety of racialized groups, to one that reserved the shackle primarily for Africans.[24]

The English Conquest

Although the English began colonizing North America a full century after the Spaniards—the first permanent British colony was founded in Jamestown in 1607—the English influence on American racial classification is felt powerfully today. Unlike the Spaniards, the English were not keen on intermarrying with Native Americans. In fact, English settlers erected firm boundaries between themselves and indigenous populations, upheld by segregation statutes, and frowned on sexual relations between Native Americans and the English.[25] Nor were the English very interested in "converting the lost." What mattered to them were not the natives' souls so much as their resources and their land.

When settling the eastern coast of North America, the English created something that had never before existed in that part of the world: "the Indian." This was accomplished in two major steps. First, all the indigenous people—who practiced different systems of government, employed different economies, spoke different languages, observed different religious traditions, and participated in different styles of life—were lumped together under a single rubric: Indian. Tribes that had fought one another for decades and even centuries, tribes different in every conceivable way, were suddenly the same thing through English eyes. And what was that thing? It was the "savage," the mirror opposite of the civilized Englishman. It was the barbarous Other, a description the English had once reserved for the Irish and were now employing for the Native American.[26]

Whereas the first step entailed broad-sweeping *homogenization*, the second step involved a process of *polarization*. The category "Indian" was split into two: the good and the bad. On the one hand, the Indian was seen as unadulterated humanity, as simple, innocent, and peaceful. Here is the "noble savage"—child-like yet pure, primitive yet one with nature. (Fundamental to this image of the Indian was the misconception that indigenous populations lived without orga-nized government, the marker of "civilization" to the European. Such a picture could hardly have been more distorted; in fact, it was from the Iroquois that some of America's core democratic values, such as a devotion to individual rights, federalism, and participatory politics, were adopted by our Founding Fathers.[27]) On the other hand, the Indian was depicted as a beast, a brute, a bloodthirsty monster. Here, then, is the "ignoble savage"—wicked and fear-some.[28] In these two contradictory guises, the "Indian" thus came into this world, a European invention.

As the English began to thrive in North America, the land's indigenous pop-ulations began to die off at alarming rates. The Europeans had brought to the "New World" Old World diseases—such as smallpox, measles, the bubonic plague, cholera, typhoid, diphtheria, and malaria—to which Native Americans had little immunity.[29] Death swept across the native population, rendering some tribes extinct. Just in the English-colonized regions alone, between 1630 and 1730, European-introduced diseases killed off nearly 80% of the indigenous population of New England and 98% of the Western Abenaki, who inhabited the lands that are now New Hampshire and Vermont. In five deadly years, between 1615 and 1620, 90% of the indigenous population of Massachusetts died of the plague.[30] Millions of Native Americans perished, resulting in "the greatest human catastrophe in history, far exceeding even the disaster of the Black Death in medieval Europe."[31]

These deadly diseases spread so quickly across the Native American popula-tion, not only because indigenous populations had little to no inborn resistance to such biological threats but also because of large-scale changes brought about by English colonization. The English introduced domesticated animals, which spread disease. The relocation and concentration of indigenous communities made it more likely that infected individuals would come into contact with other members of the population. Many Native Americans' diets were flipped upside-down, as their normal means of sustenance, such as traditional crops and the buffalo, were eradicated.[32] More heinously, historians have documented a hand-ful of cases in which British soldiers intentionally infected Native Americans with diseases. In 1763, the commander-in-chief of the British army, Sir Jeffrey Amherst, facing an indigenous uprising, sought ways to introduce smallpox to

American Indian Population Decline and Recovery in the United States Area, 1492–1980

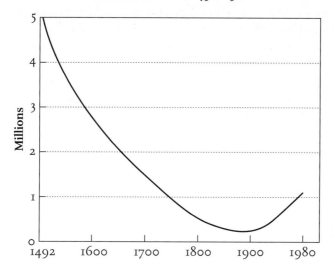

Non-Indian Population Growth in the United States Area, 1492–1980

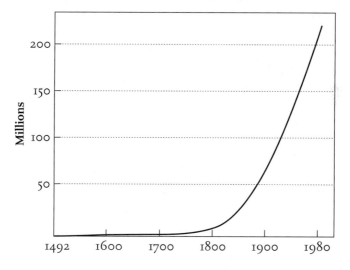

the dissonant rebels. One of his officers came up with the plan: "I will try to inoculate the bastards with some blankets that may fall into their hands, and take care not to get the disease myself." Pleased with the plan, Amherst penned the following reply: "You will do well to inoculate the Indians by means of blankets, as well as every other method that can serve to extirpate this execrable race." That year, a smallpox epidemic broke loose, spreading rapidly through the Ohio Valley.[33]

Many Native Americans who escaped disease would succumb instead to warfare. Colonialism is always, everywhere, and above all, violent. The first major outbreak of organized violence against Native Americans occurred in 1622. After English settlers murdered a respected leader, natives attacked Chesapeake Colony, leaving nearly 350 settlers dead. The English retaliated with vengeance, killing entire tribes and enslaving others. Their methods were vicious and, at times, deceitful. On one occasion, the English lured some 250 Native Americans to a meeting where a peace treaty would be signed. During the signing ceremony, English settlers poisoned their guests' share of the liquor, used in a ceremonial toast, killing 200. The remaining 50 were butchered by hand.

The events of 1622 unleashed a flood of violence against North America's indigenous population, a flood that only added to the military atrocities already being carried out by Spaniards. Historians call this violence the **Indian Wars.** They usually point to the 1540 Spanish subjugation of the Zuni and Pueblo (who occupied lands in modern-day Arizona and New Mexico) as the starting point of the Wars. The end would not come until 350 years later, at a massacre called Wounded Knee, which we shall discuss later.

America's indigenous population eventually was brought under the heel of European colonization. Native Americans were killed by disease and by the sword; they were starved, relocated, and enslaved. As a result, at the beginning of the twentieth century, the entire indigenous population of Canada, the United States, and Greenland combined numbered only 375,000.[34] From 1600 to 1900, 90% to 99% of America's indigenous peoples died as a direct result of European colonization. Never before has our world witnessed such massive loss of human life in such a short period of time. Noting this, historian Francis Jennings wrote, "The American land was more like a widow than a virgin. Europeans did not find a wilderness here; rather, however involuntarily, they made one."[35]

The Invention of Whiteness and Blackness

Encouraged by the swiftly advancing global capitalist economy, powerful English settlers sought to exploit the land and riches of the "New World" and grow wealthy. But they could not do it alone. An "exploitable people" was needed to exploit the resources of America, to cultivate the tobacco and corn fields, to mine for precious stones, to trap animals whose pelts could be shipped back to Europe. To meet this need, **indentured servants**—laborers who were bound to an employer for a fixed amount of time, after which they were freed—began pouring into North America by the shiploads.

Where did these people come from? Many were individuals who had bartered their passage to America in exchange for years of labor; others were ex-prisoners who had been released from English jails; still others were impoverished English men, women, and children, kidnapped from the streets of London and Liverpool; some were Native Americans, stolen from their tribal homelands; some were Africans brought to America by the slave trade, which began in the mid-fifteenth century; and hundreds were the "savage Irish," conquered in war and sold through the "Irish slave trade" into bondage.[36] By the 1620s, a **plantation system,** comprising dozens of large settlements organized around agricultural production for profit and reliant on coerced labor, had been set up. In such settlements, servants lived in separate and substandard housing and were often whipped or maimed if they disobeyed orders or failed to please their masters.[37]

As colonization pushed forward—as more land was captured, more resources discovered, and more settlements erected—the demand for servants increased and the conditions under which servants toiled grew ever harsher. Indentured servants were stripped naked and sold at auctions, and many were worked to the bone, dying long before they were able to earn their freedom. *Indentured servitude* in America steadily evolved into *slavery.* Workers became bound to their masters, not for a set period of time but for life.[38] Suffering through abysmal working conditions, some servants openly rebelled against the system. In 1676, an uprising called Bacon's Rebellion broke out in Jameson. Bonded laborers of African, English, and Irish descent rose up against wealthy plantation owners (also called planters), as well as against the colonial government that supported worker exploitation. The rebellion was no small matter: It was supported by most settlers, the majority of whom were poor, and it threatened the very existence of the system of involuntary servitude on which the planters relied. The rebellion was finally put down by armed soldiers from England, but it greatly disturbed the planters.

Soon, however, white servants would refuse to reach across the color line when struggling against labor exploitation. What changed? Nothing short of the fundamental way the mass of poor whites understood their lot in life. If enslaved whites struggled hand in hand with enslaved blacks during Bacon's Rebellion, it was because they *imagined themselves as slaves.* But in the decades following the Rebellion, the majority of free Americans began to view white servants as people who could be assimilated into American citizenry and black servants as slaves for life. In the years leading up to the American Revolution, "freedom" took on a whole new meaning for poor whites. The American military offered freedom to white indentured servants in exchange for their service, and the latter, starved of liberty and therefore hungry for it, took up arms by the droves. As the War of Independence unfolded, they began to see themselves as slaves no longer: They were "freemen"; that is, they were nonslaves, nonblack.[39]

As poor whites gained their freedom, enslaved blacks descended into a state of permanent **chattel slavery:** Africans were treated as any other piece of property, bought and sold at owners' discretion. While the Constitution secured whites' freedom, granting them access to "life, liberty, and the pursuit of happiness," it legalized black slavery. Revolutionary thinkers, even the most radical of the bunch, such as Benjamin Franklin and Thomas Paine, understood black slavery to be a "necessary evil," a compromise that would secure (white) American freedom.[40] Stunned at this hypocrisy, David Cooper, a leading writer of the revolutionary period, observed that "our rulers have appointed days for humiliation, and offering up of prayer to our common Father to deliver us from *our* oppressors, when sights and groans are piercing his holy ears from oppressions which we commit a thousandfold more grievous."[41] Indeed, freedom came into the world on the scarred backs of slaves. As one sociologist has argued, "Before slavery people simply could not have conceived of the thing we call freedom."[42]

What is more, black slavery provided wealthy planters a new and powerful system of labor exploitation, one that was permanent and durable.[43] But why weren't Native Americans permanently enslaved? For one thing, their numbers already were decreasing rapidly; soon, they would not be able to meet the needs of plantation capitalism. Second, Native Americans, who were familiar with the land, could easily escape their captors and find refuge in surrounding tribes. And third, Native Americans were relied on as guides and trappers in the fur trade, a lucrative business that lasted through the seventeenth and eighteenth centuries.[44] What about the "savage Irish"—could they be permanently enslaved? Not likely. Primarily pastoralists—who tended to animals on open pastures—the Irish knew little about farming and agriculture. And, upon escaping, an Irish slave could blend in with the English population.[45] The enslaved African, in contrast, could not blend in with the white population, nor was she or he accustomed to the American landscape, as was the Native American. Kidnapped and transported to a strange land, isolated, alienated, and shackled Africans had no refuge other than those provided them by their masters. They were also immune to Old World diseases and were used to a tropical climate similar to the one found in the American South. Finally, many were farmers, who knew how to rear a crop. Africans soon came to be seen as "the perfect slaves"—but note that it was *not* strictly because of their blackness that they were viewed as such.

Thus, as white servants were winning their freedom, not only from their old masters but also from the British, blacks were losing theirs. And so, whiteness and blackness, unformed and unsure of themselves, entered the world. Twins birthed from the same womb, that of slavery, whiteness and blackness were new creations whose very essences were defined by and through one another. The white race began to be formed "out of a heterogeneous and motley collection of Europeans *who had never before perceived that they had anything in common.*"[46] Blacks, too, who beforehand had belonged to hundreds of different tribal and ethnic groups, were at once brought together under a single racial category and brought low, into bondage, through the might of European domination. America, and all the world with it, awoke to a new era, not one separating Christian from heathen, nor gentleman from barbarian (though these recalcitrant rifts never fully vanished), but a world separating people of different "races."

Africans Enslaved

The transition from multicultural indentured servitude to permanent black slavery did not happen overnight. Black slavery would become **institutionalized** (meaning it would be incorporated into American society as a formalized and normalized establishment) through a series of social and legal changes that took place between 1660 and 1860. Rights began to be stripped from Africans, specifically, and nonwhites, in general. When Virginia introduced laws in the early 1660s that defined Africans as lifelong servants, it became the first colony to legalize chattel slavery.

The Atlantic Slave Trade

Africans were brought to America through the **Atlantic slave trade,** an economic system that relied on transporting kidnapped Africans from their homeland to the Americas. The Atlantic slave trade had been in operation since the mid-fifteenth century, and several countries, including Portugal, Spain, England, France, the Netherlands, and America, participated in the trade. Africans participated in the slave trade as well, kidnapping men, women, and children from various tribes and selling them into bondage for European goods, such as cloth, guns and gunpowder, tobacco, and liquor. Kidnapped slaves were shackled together and marched, under the sting of the whip and the barrel of the gun, to the African west coast, where they were imprisoned until being sold to European captains and loaded onto ships.[47]

Why did Africans sell fellow Africans into slavery? This popular question assumes there was such a thing as "Africa" and "Africans" during the slave trade, whereas, in fact, the notion of "Africa" as a continent inhabited by people, who, to varying degrees, understand one another as "Africans," came about only in modern times. Before the slave trade, many African communities were disconnected from one another. What bound the people of Africa together were not national or regional affiliations—and especially not racial markers—but kinship ties.

It is inaccurate to suggest that Europeans and Africans somehow were equal players in the Atlantic slave trade. The trade was driven by Europeans' desire to colonize and develop the Americas. Moreover, Europeans wielded great influence on the African Coast, erecting slave forts and prisons and organizing raiding parties, whereas Africans had no influence in Europe. Nevertheless, Africans did play an active role in the slave trade, and they did so for the same reasons as Europeans: to get rich. Many African societies that participated in the slave trade did get rich, at least for a short while. In the long run, however, the slave trade "underdeveloped" Africa as a whole, depleting its population (especially of young men), directing its attention away from other potentially more productive economic activities, and, perhaps most destructively, constructing Africans as an inferior people, and Africa as an exploitable land, in the minds of Europeans.[48]

The voyage from the west coast of Africa to America, across the broad waters of the Atlantic, was called the Middle Passage. It lasted two to three months, although, depending on the characteristics of the vessel and the weather, it could take several times as long. Conditions upon the slave ships were horrific. Africans were packed into the bowels of ships by the hundreds, sometimes after being stripped naked. Men and women were separated, to be shelved, like cargo, next to one another in spaces seldom larger than a coffin. One historian notes that British and French traders "would hold their captives in a space five feet, three inches high by four feet, four inches wide."[49] In some cases, slaves were packed into every crevice of the ship, including under the captain's bed. A first-hand description of the conditions of a slave ship from the late seventeenth century reads as follows: "If anyone wanted to sleep, they lay on top of each other. To satisfy their natural needs, they had bilge places over the edge of the sea but, as many feared to lose their place, they relieved themselves where they were, above all the men cruelly pushed together, in such a way that their heat and the smell became intolerable."[50]

As massive overcrowding left little room for food and water, many slaves died of malnutrition and dehydration. Others perished from diseases, such as dysentery and smallpox, which flourished under such putrid conditions. While some captains attempted to preserve the lives of as many slaves as possible, others were tyrannical, abusing and raping slaves throughout the voyage. Many slaves died at the hands of the ship's crew. And still others died, it seems, from sheer depression: naked and captive, surrounded by cruelty and disease, some slaves committed suicide by starving themselves to death. Eager to preserve their "shipment," some shipmen force-fed slaves, breaking their teeth and forcing their mouths open if necessary. Shipmen even took to carrying a special device designed explicitly for this purpose. A scissor-like instrument would be forced into the lips of the recalcitrant slave, and his or her jaws would then be forced open by the turn of a thumbscrew.[51]

It was not uncommon for slaves to rise up against their captors; in fact, it has been suggested that one out of eight to ten voyages experienced an insurrection.[52] Few rebellions were successful, however, as mutinying slaves, unorganized, starved, and powerless, were put down with brutality. After a slave revolt was squelched on a Danish ship sailing in 1709, the insurrection leader's right hand was chopped off and displayed to every slave on the ship. The following day, his left hand was severed and exhibited in a similar fashion. The day after that, the rebel's head was cut off and his torso was hoisted onto the mainsail, where it hung for two days. Those who participated in the rebellion were flogged, and their wounds were rubbed with salt, ashes, and pepper.[53]

Fifteen to thirty percent of slaves died aboard slave ships—and the longer the journey, the higher the death rate. In 1717, only 98 slaves out of 594 survived the voyage on a ship named *George*. In 1805, the citizens of Charleston refused to eat any fish, since so many dead bodies were tossed, like trash, into the harbor from the decks of slave ships.[54] Despite such massive loss of life, the slave trade flourished. A profit still could be made even if 45% of the slaves died during the voyage.[55]

The enormity of the Atlantic slave trade has been called "immeasurable" and is a matter of historical debate.[56] Most historians estimate that, from 1450 to 1850, 10 to 15 million Africans were transported to the Americas. Other historians, however, remind us that this figure is but a fraction of total lives lost, since it does not include those who died on slave ships, on forced marches in Africa, in villages in defiance of would-be captors, or in cages on the west coast. According to one study, of 100 people captured in Africa, 64 would arrive at the coast alive, 57 would live through coastal imprisonment to be packed onto ships, 48 would survive the journey to be placed on the auction block, and only 28 of the original 100 would survive the first few years of slave labor. In other words, for each enslaved African bent over in the plantation fields, there were three others who perished en route.[57]

The Rise of the Cotton Kingdom

From 1640 to 1700, slaves made up 61% of all transatlantic migrants who arrived in the Americas; in the following fifty years, that percentage increased to 75%.[58] The Atlantic slave trade gained momentum during the eighteenth century, but most slaves were transported to the British West Indies and Cuba to work in the booming sugar plantations. Relative to the slave labor force of the Caribbean, that of North America grew slowly during this time period; in fact, in 1700, Africans in the British Caribbean outnumbered those in the North American colonies by a ratio of six to one. The majority of slaves in North America worked in the areas of small-scale farming, domestic service, and craft manufacturing, though, by mid-century, tobacco, indigo, and rice began to be produced in the Southern plantations, a shift that increased the demand for slave labor.[59]

However, it was only at the start of the nineteenth century, a few years after Eli Whitney invented the cotton gin (1793), that the dynamics of slavery in North America transformed dramatically. The cotton gin—a simple enough contraption made of a wooden box, a set of hooks that pulled cotton through a wire mesh, and a crank—deseeded cotton with speed and efficiency. By hand, one could clean a pound of cotton in a day; using the gin, one could clean fifty pounds of cotton in a day. Suddenly, the production of cotton was made simple, the price of cotton fell, and cotton plantations emerged. Cotton quickly surpassed tobacco as America's leading cash crop. In 1790, America produced 140 thousand pounds of cotton; by 1800, it would be producing 35 million pounds. Cotton became king—with black slaves doing its bidding. As the demand for cotton increased in Europe, North American slavery was reinvigorated.

By 1865, it is estimated that there were close to 4 million slaves in America.[60] Plantation owners oversaw them with sharpened eyes, implementing strict disciplinary regimens to govern their labor. Maximization of productivity was the overarching goal, and the planters had this down to a science. Every slave was utilized, including pregnant women who were forced to work in the fields until the final week before giving birth—and then forced to return only two weeks thereafter. On average, slaves worked "sunup to sundown," as the old spiritual goes, for six days (or approximately sixty hours) a week. The cotton flowed, making plantation owners, on the eve of the Civil War, some of the richest men in the world.[61]

But we would do well to remember that most whites during this period were not plantation owners. In fact, most whites were poor—too poor to purchase large pieces of land, let alone slaves. Of the 2 million slaveholders living in the South in the mid-nineteenth century, the vast majority owned a very small number of slaves, while an elite group of planters owned slave armies. At the height of slavery, there were over 5 million whites in the South who did not own slaves.[62] Poor whites, especially unskilled laborers, fared poorly during slavery, since free labor naturally pulled down the price of all labor.

In relation to the rich white planter and the enslaved black, poor whites were more like the latter; however, they identified only with the former. They were white, after all. They were poor, but they were free—and in their mind they could someday, by a stroke of luck perhaps, come to own slaves themselves. They worked as the planters' overseers, patrolled the planters' fields with their "cats of nine tails" (that is, whipping devices made of thongs of braided cord), and served as the planters' police force, chasing down runaway slaves. To quote a keen observation made by W. E. B. Du Bois, "It must be remembered that the white group of laborers, while they received a low wage, were compensated in part by a sort of public and **psychological wage.** They were given public deference and titles of courtesy because they were white. They were admitted freely with all classes of white people to public functions, public parks, and the best schools. . . . Their vote selected public officials, and while this had small effect upon the economic situation, it had great effect upon their personal treatment and the deference shown them."[63]

Yes, poor whites lived in squalor; they went hungry; they labored for low payment; but, at the end of the day, their skin was the same color as that of the planters. To create a cheap labor force, white landowners worked to convince poor whites to ignore how they, too, were exploited by the slave economy and, instead, to take pride in their whiteness. As Pem Davidson Buck puts it in *Worked to the Bone*, to thwart the formation of interracial coalitions between poor whites and enslaved blacks, white elites had to "teach Whites the value of whiteness."[64]

The Horrors of Slavery

During slavery, blacks in bondage soon came to be regulated under a set of laws called **slave codes.** The codes denied blacks citizenship and governed even the most intimate spheres of their lives. Slaves were not allowed to own or carry arms, trade goods, possess land, leave their master's property without permission, or venture out at night. They were forbidden to socialize with free blacks, and a marriage between two slaves went unrecognized as an official union. Since slaves could not marry, slave families did not exist in the eyes of the law. Children were snatched from the arms of their mothers; wives were torn from the embrace of their husbands; families were scattered: a sister sent to Mississippi, a brother sold to a man in Kentucky.

It was illegal for a slave to testify in court against a white person, and a slave who argued with or struck a white person was punished severely. In Washington, D.C., for instance, slaves who hit white persons would be mutilated, their ears cut off. In some states, even free blacks could not lay a hand on whites, not even in self-defense. In Virginia, free blacks who defended themselves against the assaults of whites received thirty lashes. During this time, the rights of free blacks were eroded alongside those of enslaved blacks. By 1723, the right to vote was withheld from all blacks residing in the Southern colonies, free or not.[65]

Laws also were put in place that broadened the scope of slavery to include children of mixed heritage, thereby expanding the very definition of blackness. Sexual unions between free white men and enslaved black women, many of which were rapes, produced biracial children. Were they to be considered slave or free? "Slave," answered the codes. In 1662, Virginia legally defined the children of a slave mother, regardless of the status of the father, as slaves: "Whereas some doubts have arisen whether children got by any Englishmen upon a Negro shall be slave or Free, Be it therefore enacted and declared by this present Grand assembly, that all children born in this country shall be held bond or free only According to the condition of the mother."[66]

This law foreshadows a peculiar trend in the career of blackness as it was (and, for the most part, continues to be) defined in the American context. Since its inception, blackness always has been defined through the **one-drop rule**, which renders "black" anyone with any amount, no matter how miniscule, of African blood. More than a social convention, this "rule" was given legal existence through several statutes enacted during and after the time of slavery. For instance, in 1896 the U.S. Supreme Court, in *Plessy v. Ferguson*, a case to which we will return later, ruled that Homer Plessy, a light-skinned man who was one-eighth black, was "black" and therefore not entitled to rights reserved for whites. (And recall that, in the previous chapter, we saw how the legacy of the one-drop rule continued through the late twentieth century in the case of Susie Guillory Phipps, the fair-skinned woman who was classified as black by the state of Louisiana.) Blackness, then, was regarded as a mark, a blemish, whereas whiteness, by implication, was constructed as the essence of racial purity. In its ideal form, whiteness was unpolluted by Africa.[67]

Not only did the slave codes rid blacks of rights, but they also attempted to wrench from blacks their honor, dignity, and humanity. Slaves were denied access even to the most basic education. Some states made it illegal to teach a slave to read or write. Others forbade slaves from practicing religious worship and expression. Slaves were denied access to their African roots. They were forbidden to speak in their native tongue and were forced to dress in the style of their captors. Their names were changed, sometimes to insulting nicknames, such as Monkey or Villain. These nicknames were similar to those of livestock. Slaves were given "marks of servitude." Their ears were cropped, and they were tattooed and branded (sometimes with the same iron used to brand an owner's cattle) on the breast or forehead. Runaways were marked with clear identifiers, such as the letter "R" branded on their cheek.[68]

Runaways were not the only slaves punished. Slave codes secured slave masters' absolute power. Under the codes, white masters lived in a world typified by the absence of restraints. The whip was the master's favorite weapon of correction. In the Southern colonies, thirty-nine lashes often were given to offending slaves, the same prescription stipulated in Roman law. Though it was illegal for masters to murder a slave, they committed no crime if they "accidentally" killed a slave while punishing him or her.[69] Elizabeth Keckley, a slave separated from her parents at a young age, recalls a time when she was flogged, for no apparent reason, at the age of eighteen. Keckley tells us she was stripped naked and bound; she continues: "Then he picked up a rawhide, and began to ply it freely over my shoulders. With steady hand and practiced eye he would raise the instrument of torture, nerve himself for a blow, and with fearful force the rawhide descended upon the quivering flesh. It cut the skin, raised welts, and the warm blood trickled down my back. Oh God! I can feel the torture now—the terrible, excruciating agony of those moments."[70] Much thought and creativity was devoted to the question of how best to torture slaves. Slaves thought to be indolent were placed in stocks and pillars and displayed in the town square; slaves thought to be high-spirited were mutilated or castrated; slaves thought to be ill-mannered were forced to wear iron masks and collars.[71]

Sexual Exploitation and Dehumanization

Both men and women slaves lived in fear of such abuse, but women slaves disproportionately lived in fear of another sort of violation: that of sexual exploitation. Slavery "is terrible for men; but it is far more terrible for women," wrote Harriet Jacobs.[72] Since slave children increased a master's wealth, slave women were forced to copulate with whomsoever the master chose. Black women's wombs, their sexual freedom and their reproductive rights, were at the mercy of their masters, white men who often prided themselves on owning a good "breeding woman." In large part, slavery rested on the control of black women's bodies.[73] "Here," writes Dorothy Roberts, "lies one of slavery's most odious features: it forced its victims to perpetuate the very institution that subjugated them by bearing children who were born the property of their masters."[74]

Slave women also lived in constant fear of rape. In her slave narrative, *Incidents in the Life of a Slave Girl*, published in 1861, Harriet Jacobs describes her "trials of girlhood": "But I now entered my fifteenth year—a sad epoch in the life of a slave girl. My master began to whisper foul words in my ear. . . . Soon she [the slave girl] will learn to tremble when she hears her master's footfall. She will be compelled to realize that she is no longer a child. If God has bestowed beauty upon her, it will prove her greatest curse. . . . I cannot tell you how much I suffered in the presence of these wrongs, nor how I am still pained by the retrospect. My master met me at every turn, reminding me that I belonged to him, and swearing by heaven and earth that he would compel me to submit to him."[75]

The rape of a slave woman was not recognized as a crime. The black female body was not a body to be protected but one to be abused and molested. White masters used rape as a technique of terror, one that degraded both black women and men, since the latter could not keep their sisters, mothers, and wives safe from violation. If a child grew in the womb of a slave woman as a consequence of a white man's rape, that child would bear the "condition of the mother," becoming not the white man's son or daughter but a slave—one who increased the value of the master's estate.[76]

As a result of this rampant sexual exploitation, black women's bodies came to be constructed as objects to be treated with indignity, abused with cruelty, and raped with impunity. Nor were their children theirs to own and cherish; rather, the children belonged to, and were controlled by, the slaveholder. What is more,

"Soon she will learn to tremble when she hears her master's footfall." —Harriet Jacobs

since the dominant image of femininity, at least in well-to-do white culture, was based on leisure and luxury, black women, who knew neither leisure nor luxury, were understood to lack femininity. Thus, in the words of one historian, whites understood black women "as a sort of female hybrid, capable of being exploited like women but otherwise treated like a man."[77]

At the same time, whites were creating a distorted image of black masculinity, one that hinged on two widespread themes. On the one hand, the black male slave was a non-man, emasculated and infantilized since he lacked that supreme value on which masculine honor rests: unchained independence. He could not provide for or protect his loved ones (only the master could do that); in most cases, he could not even defend his own body from the scourges of whites. As such, he could lay no claims to manhood. On the other hand, in the white imagination the black slave embodied the most primordial essence of manhood; he was thought to be a lascivious creature, quick to give in to base and carnal urges. While black female slaves were understood to be asexual, their libido nonexistent, black male slaves—indeed, all black men—were stereotyped as hypersexual. Whites came to think of black men as sexual predators, who longed to have their way with white women. Thus, while white men, who often raped black women, were regarded as "Southern gentlemen," black men, who rarely molested white women, often were deemed rapists.[78]

Slavery also encouraged the creation of debasing stereotypes and degrading images targeting Africans. The Sambo character—an ignorant, silly, dishonest, and childlike plantation slave, completely dependent on his master—emerged as the dominant stereotype of the enslaved African. This cruel caricature was so widespread that one historian observed that, for most Southerners in the nineteenth century, "it went without saying not only that Sambo was real—but also that his characteristics were the clear product of racial inheritance."[79] Daily, the black slave was debased in popular language, in commonplace phrases, songs, children's games, and nursery rhymes: *Eeny, meany, miney, mo; Catch a nigger by the toe; If he hollers, let him go.*

Gradually, then, enslaved Africans were reduced to "socially dead persons," and blackness became associated with inferiority in relation to whiteness.[80] Out of slaves' social death grew American prosperity. While blacks lost their freedom, honor, and lives, the United States' economy grew exponentially, becoming what it is today: the most powerful economic force in the world. One sometimes hears commentators remark that American prosperity is due to the special "ingenuity and hard work of Americans" or that this nation is uniquely "blessed." In truth, the foundation of our nation's wealth rests on two hundred fifty years of free labor.

Resistance, Large and Small

Slaves fought back. Sometimes their methods of resistance were quiet and subtle. In public, slaves seemingly accepted the terms of their domination; in private, however, they criticized white supremacy, often in clandestine and creative ways. They sang of the fall of slavery, as well as of an afterlife in which there would be no more tears; jokes were made at whites' expense; poems were penned that rejoiced in the deaths of masters. Slaves learned to live a double life, one that required them to sling their heads low under the master's gaze but to raise them high and wink once the master's back was turned.[81] In addition, if whites thought of blacks as unintelligent and lazy, some blacks often acted as such to affront their masters. Tools were left out in the rain; plows were mishandled; shovels and hoes were sabotaged; livestock "escaped." Slaves worked lethargically and clumsily. They misunderstood instructions; got lost on the way to town; oversalted the dinner; made the coffee scalding hot. Everyday forms of resistance, whispered "nos" amidst the roar of racial domination, demonstrate that slaves did not believe of themselves what the whites told them to believe. They found ways to retain their honor.[82]

Sometimes, slaves' resistance was not so subtle. Dozens of **slave rebellions** took place over the course of American slavery. Slaves took up arms against their masters, burning buildings and crop fields and engaging whites in bloody warfare. When news of the Haitian Revolution—an enormously successful slave revolt that overthrew French colonialism and emancipated the entire Haitian slave population—reached America at the beginning of the nineteenth century, it inspired many American slaves to risk their lives to break the chains of tyranny. One of the most significant revolts occurred in 1831, when a man by the name of Nat Turner, a slave and fiery preacher, led some sixty slaves in open revolution. Turner and his followers marched defiantly from farm to farm throughout Virginia, fighting and killing whites and recruiting other slaves. The rebellion eventually would be put down, and Turner hanged, but not until after it had left almost sixty whites dead in its path.[83] Admiring the courage of slave revolutionaries, American historian Herbert Aptheker would observe, "They were firebells in the night; cries from the heart; expressions of human need and aspiration in the face of the deepest testing. They manifest that victimization does not simply make victims; it also produces heroes."[84]

Flight was yet another form of resistance. Slaves could run north to freedom, and to help them do so, there was a network of secret routes on land and water, safe-holds, and allies to fugitive slaves—collectively known as the Underground Railroad. The Underground Railroad helped thousands reach freedom in large part because of its brave and brilliant leaders. There was William Still, a black man called "the father of the Underground Railroad," who hid some sixty fugitive slaves in his home. There was Harriet Tubman, too, an ex-slave who would return to the South time and again to guide hundreds of slaves to freedom without losing a single one along the way. Tubman was so effective that whites offered a $10,000 reward for her capture. And there was William Garrett, a white Quaker, who, though arrested and fined to such a degree that he nearly met financial ruin, thought that freeing slaves was one's Christian duty.[85]

Whites and blacks worked side by side in the Underground Railroad, and, indeed, since the beginning days of American slavery, whites and blacks, together, called for its abolition, thus earning the name **abolitionists.** The abolitionist movement was strong in the North, which is in part why all the Northern states had abolished slavery by 1804. In the years leading up to the Civil War, the abolitionist movement gained steam, and slavery was decried from all corners of the country. From Massachusetts, it was criticized by William Lloyd Garrison, a white journalist and founder of the first abolitionist newspaper called *The Liberator*, who would write, "I accuse the land of my nativity of insulting the majesty of Heaven with the grossest mockery that was ever exhibited to man." From Kansas, it was

challenged by John Brown, a white man who organized several armed insurrections in the name of black liberation and who eventually was found guilty of
treason against (white) America and executed. From South Carolina, it would be
called "despotic," "sinful," and a "violation of the natural order of things" by Sarah
and Angelina Grimké, sisters ostracized by their white family for arguing that
"the white man should take his foot off the Negro's neck."[86]

And, perhaps most powerfully, slavery was condemned from the mouths of
former slaves. Frederick Douglas was one of them. Douglas taught himself to
read and write while a child in bondage. He later escaped slavery at the age of
nineteen and went on to become one of the most influential African Americans
of his day. A skilled writer and an orator of the highest caliber, Douglas launched
many pointed assaults on the institution of slavery, including a famous address
given on July 5, 1852 in Rochester, New York. Addressing an audience of influential white politicians, Douglas boomed: "This Fourth [of] July is *yours*, not
mine. You may rejoice, *I* must mourn. . . . Fellow citizens; above your national,
tumultuous joy, I hear the mournful wail of millions! whose chains, heavy and
grievous yesterday, are, today, rendered more intolerable by the jubilee shouts
that reach them. . . . What, to the American slave, is your 4th of July? I answer:
a day that reveals to him, more than all other days in the year, the gross injustice
and cruelty to which he is the constant victim."[87]

Whereas Douglas's voice was commanding and elegant, that of another black
abolitionist spoke with weather-worn wisdom and without sentiment. Sojourner
Truth has been described as "an unsmiling sibyl, weighted with the woe of the
world."[88] This tall, slender grandmother cast a powerful shadow over both the
abolitionist and women's rights movements (at this time, women, most of them
white, were fighting for the right to vote). Disappointed with the suffrage movement
for overlooking the plight of black women, and highlighting the intimate ties
between racial and masculine domination, Truth once addressed the white audience
gathered for a Women's Rights convention with these stirring words: "Dat man
ober dar say dat woman needs to be helped into carriages, and lifted over ditches,
and to have the best place eberywhar. Nobody eber helps me into carriages, or ober
mud-puddles, or gives me any best place. And ar'n't I a woman? Look at me, look
at my arm! I have plowed and planted and gathered into barns, and no man could
head me—and ar'n't I a woman? I could work as much and eat as much as a man
(when I could get it), and bear de lash as well—and ar'n't I a woman? I have borne
thirteen chillen, and seen 'em mos' all sold off into slavery, and when I cried out
with a mother's grief, none but Jesus heard—and ar'n't I a woman?"[89]

From Emancipation to Jim Crow

Sojourner Truth gave this address in 1851. Ten years later, on a still April morning, fifty confederate cannons opened fire on Fort Sumter, marking the beginning

of the Civil War. In 1863, President Abraham Lincoln issued the Emancipation Proclamation, an executive order that manumitted all slaves in the Confederacy (that is, released them from bondage). In 1865, the Confederate Army would be defeated by the Union, and more slaves would be freed. At the end of that year, the Thirteenth Amendment was ratified, permanently abolishing slavery in the United States. As the cannon smoke cleared, all black men and women stood legally free upon American soil.

But, in reality, what leg did they have to stand on? Here stood millions of blacks who, for two hundred fifty years, had endured kidnapping, torture, and rape, who had been denied education, property, and wealth, who, surrounded by powerful whites who ground their teeth at emancipation, had no place to turn, least of all to their families, who had been scattered throughout the country. Recognizing the slaves' poverty, and eager to punish the rebellious South, William Sherman, a general in the Union Army, issued a decree (Special Fields Orders, Number 15) in January 1865 that allotted forty acres of land to recently freed heads of households as well as to slaves who had fought in the Union Army. This policy came to be known as **Forty Acres and a Mule** (the beast would be used to pull a plow) and was the nation's first and only attempt at offering reparations for slavery.[90]

It is estimated that some 40,000 freed slaves saw Sherman's policy fulfilled. However, later that year, President Andrew Johnson, Lincoln's successor, overturned Sherman's order, returning the property to former Confederates who swore an oath to the Union. Having working their land for only one season— digging in *their* soil with hands unshackled!—blacks were dispossessed of it. The promise of Forty Acres and a Mule was never fulfilled, leaving the freed slave in a state of utter destitution. Du Bois's words ring true here: "To emancipate four million laborers whose labor had been owned, and separate them from the land upon which they had worked for nearly two and a half centuries, was an operation such as no modern country had for a moment attempted or contemplated. The German and English and French serf, the Italian and Russian serf, were, on emancipation, given definite rights in the land. Only the American Negro slave was emancipated without such rights and in the end this spelled for him the continuation of slavery."[91]

The period from 1863 to 1877 is known as **Reconstruction,** a time when the nation put itself back together, reincorporating the Southern states and reinventing American citizenry, white and black alike. Immediately after the fall of slavery, Southern states began implementing "black codes," variants of the slave codes that restricted the rights of newly freed blacks. Many blacks would be forced back onto the plantation fields, as black codes severely limited other employment opportunities. At the national level, however, freed blacks were winning rights. The ratification of the Fourteenth Amendment came in 1868 and extended citizenship rights to blacks. The ratification of the Fifteenth Amendment came two years later and gave black men (but not other non-whites or women) the right to vote. Some black men went to the polls, and some were even elected to public office. But white supremacy would not yield so easily. By and large, blacks were neither treated as American citizens nor respected as voters, for violence was the true law of the land. After the Civil War, whites lashed out at freed blacks, first through sporadic, unorganized hostility, then through organized terror, especially through the founding of the Ku Klux Klan in 1865.[92]

Dressed as ghosts of dead Confederate soldiers, the Klan terrorized not only blacks but all nonwhite persons, as well as Jews and Catholics. Barbarism and lawlessness reigned, as Klansmen whipped, tarred, raped, and murdered their victims. Their violence was an explicit attempt to uphold white supremacy and to bar blacks from any political or economic advancement. If a black man voted, he risked his life in doing so. Some ballot boxes even were patrolled by armed white men. And behind everything—behind the Constitution and all its new Amendments, behind black "freedom," behind all the changes of Reconstruction—lurked the threat of the lynch mob. Thousands of blacks were lynched during Reconstruction and on up through the mid-twentieth century. Far from being erratic acts of mob aggression, lynchings were preplanned events, bloody rituals that drew large crowds of onlookers of all ages. Often the victim would be tortured, his limbs severed, his flesh impaled with hot irons, and his body strung up a tree or burnt alive. Many victims accused of raping white women—indeed, the "rape complex" was the warrant most often marshaled for lynching—would be castrated. The victim would be mutilated after his death, parts of his body sold to spectators as macabre souvenirs. Often, whites would dance and sing around the corpse, carrying on in a festive spirit.[93] It was of lynchings that jazz great Billie Holiday sang in her famous 1939 recording of "Strange Fruit": "Southern trees bear a strange fruit/Blood on the leaves and blood at the root/ Black body swinging in the Southern breeze/Strange fruit hanging from the poplar trees."[94]

As Reconstruction came to a close, the era of **Jim Crow** segregation began in earnest. The name derives from a song called "Jump Jim Crow" (1828), by Thomas "Daddy" Rice, a white man who popularized minstrel shows. (Minstrelsy was a form of popular entertainment in which performers using makeup known as blackface invoked racist stereotypes and caricatures to portray black people in a degrading light.) By the late 1830s, the term "Jim Crow" had become associated with strict racial segregation reinforced under the terms of law. Nearly all aspects of everyday life were governed by Jim Crow laws, as whites and blacks were forced to use separate water fountains, parks, and bathrooms. It was illegal for blacks to attend white schools, to sit in railroad cars designated for white patrons, or to use white libraries. These laws were supported with the full weight of the Supreme Court in *Plessy v. Ferguson* (1896), the case mentioned earlier, which ruled that racial segregation was constitutional, since black and white facilities were "separate but equal." Of course, they were anything but, as facilities designated for blacks usually were in far worse shape that those allotted to whites. Jim Crow would command American life—in the South through formal law, in the North through custom, equally efficient—from the late nineteenth century up until the 1960s.[95]

If we have devoted a considerable amount of attention to slavery and its aftermath, it is because, more than any other institution, slavery has dictated the career of American racial domination. American slavery emerged to meet the needs of colonial exploitation and capitalist expansion. Before slavery, what we now know to be whiteness and blackness did not exist. After slavery, whiteness and blackness were understood as durable and everlasting features of nature. Capitalist colonization encouraged the rise of slavery, and slavery shaped the very contours of racism.[96]

Manifest Destiny

Conquering Mexico and the Invention of the Mexican American

Let's back up and cast our gaze further southward. While the U.S. cotton kingdom reigned supreme during the beginnings of the nineteenth century, wars were raging throughout the lands colonized by the Spaniards. Inspired by the successful American Revolution, many people oppressed by Spanish colonization (some of whom even fought with Washington's rebels) were fighting for their independence. America, thought the Latin American patriots, can identify with our struggle; it fought and won its freedom from European monarchs, and it will support us. The patriots, however, were wrong. The United States, eager to expand westward, thought of Latin America as land that could later be exploited, not as a country bravely wrestling for democracy. In fact, President James Monroe, when signing the Adams-Onís Treaty of 1819, a treaty that Spain gave the U.S. lands that are now Florida, promised the Spanish Crown that he would withhold support from Latin American rebels. More importantly, to support Latin American independence was to support rebel armies that enlisted and emancipated slaves. Latin Americans were fighting for their independence from Spain *and* for freedom from bondage. A wave of emancipation was sweeping the Spanish colonies, and American slaveholders trembled at the thought of that wave crashing over northern borders and washing across the cotton kingdom. Accordingly, America watched from a high perch, but did not extend its hand, as Latin American rebels fought for independence.[97]

And fight they did. The Mexican War of Independence began in September 1810, when a parish priest, Padre Miguel Hidalgo, sounded the church bells and led an insurrection of indigenous peasants and miners against Spanish colonialism. The bloody conflict lasted eleven years, claiming over 600,000 lives—over 10% of the country's population. (By contrast, only 25,000 died fighting for American independence.) In 1821, Mexico rested, having established itself as an independent nation whose borders included modern-day Texas, Arizona, New Mexico, California, Nevada, Utah, and Colorado.[98]

A year later, President Monroe seemed to have a change of heart. Having held nothing but contempt for Latin American independence, he recognized Mexican independence, becoming the first world leader to do so, and announced that the Americas were "henceforth not to be considered as subjects for future colonization by any European powers." Monroe's declaration, which later became known as the Monroe Doctrine, was praised by Mexican leaders. "America for the Americans!" became the slogan that emerged from the Monroe Doctrine. That Latin America should not belong to Europe, few Americans disputed. However, many began asking, "Should Latin America belong to the Latin Americans?" Many North Americans answered: "No, it should belong to us!" Thus, the Monroe Doctrine simultaneously outlawed the European conquest of Latin America and invited the American conquest of that land. A new slogan emerged: "**Manifest Destiny!**" In other words: "The western frontier, all of North America and the lands of Mexico—yes, this is God's will—is ours for the taking!"

Americans respected neither Spanish nor Mexican claims to land. From the beginning of the nineteenth century up until the Civil War, Americans would cross into Spanish and Mexican territories, capture a town, and declare independence. These buccaneering antics (called filibusters) usually drew the support of the U.S. military and increased the presence of white Americans in Mexican land. (In the popular American imagination, the brave white cowboy with his covered wagon stabs westward into land unoccupied and unsettled, no-man's land. We would do well to remember that these cowboys were, in fact, *stealing* land, upon which over half a million Mexican rebels fell dead while fighting for independence.) In 1845, the United States forced Mexico to relinquish the lands that are now Texas, the end result of an uprising started by white settlers who had illegally immigrated to Mexico.[99] With the annexation of Texas, the battle cry "Manifest Destiny!" grew ever louder. Consider one declaration, that of a politician named William Wharton, reflecting the public sentiment of white America: "The justice and benevolence of God will forbid that . . . Texas should again become a howling wilderness trod only by savages, or . . . benighted by the ignorance and superstition, the anarchy and rapine of Mexican misrule. The Anglo-American race are destined to be forever the proprietors of this land of promise and fulfillment. Their laws will govern it, their learning will enlighten it, their enterprise will improve it. . . . The wilderness of Texas has been redeemed by Anglo-American blood and enterprise."[100]

A year after annexing Texas, the United States declared war on Mexico. The Mexican-American War was fought between 1846 and 1848. Over 100,000 United States troops descended upon Mexican soil. Mexico, a country of only twenty-five years and still exhausted from its devastating war of independence, did not stand a chance, especially considering that most of the fighting done on the borderlands was carried out by untrained civilians. General Ulysses S. Grant, the most important Union general of the Civil War and eighteenth president of the United States, would call the Mexican-American War "one of the most unjust ever waged by a stronger against a weaker nation."[101] Mexico was defeated in 1848, and, through the **Treaty of Guadalupe Hidalgo**, the United States acquired the land that today is New Mexico, California, Utah, Nevada, parts of Arizona, and disputed areas of Texas. But why, we must ask, did the United States stop there? Why did this superior military power show restraint instead of claiming all of Mexico? The answer lies in the ways white Americans racially constructed the people of Mexico.[102]

Recall that the Mexicans were a people of mixed heritage, a people birthed from the unions of Spaniards, Africans, and Native Americans. Not surprisingly, white Americans understood Mexicans to be inferior people. Thus, when U.S. troops marched on Mexico City, America's leaders had a decision to make: Should they lay claim to the entirety of Mexico, and thus absorb millions of "inferior" Mexicans into their borders, or should they capture only a portion of Mexico, the portion populated with the least numbers of Mexicans? So as not to threaten America's white majority, political leaders chose the latter option.[103]

The Treaty of Guadalupe Hidalgo promised citizenship rights to Mexicans in ceded lands; however, that promise was never fulfilled, as the U.S. refused to extend full rights to nonwhites. Mexicans were constructed in American law and policy as belonging to an inferior race, one distinct from Native Americans of the Southwest. Mexican identity was determined by blood quantum. Those with one-half or more of Mexican blood were classified as Mexican. In turn, those classified as Mexican were then brought under the governance of race-based law, which denied them special privileges enjoyed by whites. Mexicans were not allowed to vote. And under the Homestead Act of 1862, many Mexicans were dispossessed of their land, which Congress promised to citizens of the United States or immigrants eligible for naturalization—read: white settlers.[104] As a result, "Mexican Americans of the Southwest became a foreign minority in the land of their birth."[105] As the United States grew richer off the land, off gold and silver acquired through the Mexican-American War, as well as off the cattle and sheep ranching industries blossoming throughout the Southwest, Mexicans, denied citizenship rights, descended into poverty. With the construction of the political border separating the United States from Mexico came the construction of a racial border, one separating whites from Mexicans, Mexicans from "Indians," and Mexicans from Africans. This was also an economic border, separating landowners from landless, and a psychological border, separating "superior" from "inferior."[106]

Citizenship rights finally would be extended to Mexicans born in the United States in 1898. Mexicans who immigrated to the U.S., however, could not apply to become citizens. Until 1940, that right was extended only to "free white immigrants." If Mexican immigrants wanted to naturalize, they would have to prove they were "white." Meanwhile, all Mexicans within American borders were subjected to Jim Crow segregation. In the Southwest, Mexican students would attend segregated, rundown schools until legal segregation was outlawed in the middle of the twentieth century.[107]

"The Indian Problem"

Shouts of "Manifest Destiny" were not only directed at Mexico; they also echoed across Native American land as well. While the United States was supporting filibusters into Spanish and Mexican territories, it also was contemplating new strategies for dealing with its indigenous population. Before the nineteenth century, American business relied on Native American labor to carry the fur trade. By 1800, the fur trade had bottomed out, and what mattered to America's swelling capitalist economy was not Native Americans' labor but Native America—the land. The question as to what would be done with tribes and their valuable land came to be known as "the Indian problem."

Broadly speaking, two strategies for acquiring tribal land, for solving "the Indian problem," were put forth: assimilation and removal. *Assimilation* required the dashing out of indigenous ways of life. Native Americans would be taught to treat the land the way white people treated it—that is, to parcel up the land into homesteads "owned" by individuals (not by tribal communities), to develop that land for profit (not for sustenance), and to abandon vast hunting grounds. *Removal* simply meant that tribes would be kicked off their land at gunpoint. Although many Americans favored a plan that combined both strategies—a destruction of Native American culture *and* white acquisition of tribal property—assimilation proved costly and time-consuming. Removal, then, would solve "the Indian problem."[108]

A series of harsh laws, passed between 1830 and 1890 and enforced by military action, created what was called **Indian Territory**, or land allotted by the U.S. government for tribal use. The Indian Removal Act of 1830, signed into law by President Andrew Jackson, permitted the forcible removal of Native Americans occupying fertile lands east of the Mississippi River. (The cotton kingdom needed room to grow.) Native Americans were pushed west into "the Great American Desert," as it was then known, a land thought to be worthless, invaluable, and barren, "which white men would never covet since it was thought fit mainly for

Eurocentric and Native American Views of Expansionism

Eurocentric View

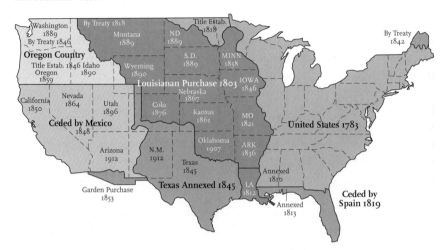

Native American View

Students typically are presented with a view that the United States gained its lands through settlement and from Mexico, Spain, France, and Great Britain. This depiction glosses over the land held by tribal groups.

horned toads and rattlesnakes."[109] Over the next fourteen years, over 70,000 Native Americans were driven from their homes and marched west of the Mississippi. As many as one third of those removed from their land died before reaching their new "homes." A particularly violent removal took place in 1838, when the U.S. military rounded up approximately 17,000 Cherokees from Georgia, Tennessee, North Carolina, and Alabama. Corralled into camps with only the possessions they could carry, the Cherokees were transported to Oklahoma and the western edge of Arkansas, a 1,200-mile journey. They traveled by foot, on horse, and by wagon, forever leaving behind the land of their ancestors. Along the way, between 4,000 and 8,000 died, which is why the Cherokees refer to this ordeal as *nunna dual Isunui*: "The Trail where we Cried," or The Trail of Tears.[110] "People feel bad when they leave Old Nation," observed one Cherokee exile. "Women cry and make sad wails. Children cry and many men cry, and all look sad when friends die, but they say nothing and just put heads down and keep on going towards West."[111]

Other laws would come crashing down on Native Americans. The Indian Intercourse Act of 1834 further delineated the boundaries of Indian Territory and ordered several tribes to relocate themselves within these boundaries. What was the punishment for refusal? Nothing short of the death sentence. At all costs, nomadic tribes were imprisoned within the confines of land set forth by Congress. By the mid-1800s, the reservation system we know today began to crystallize. And in 1887, the two strategies to solve "the Indian problem," assimilation and removal, were brought together under the **Indian Allotment Act.** The Act dissolved tribal landholding by allotting certain pieces of land to *individual* Indians residing on reservations: Heads of households were allotted 160 acres, single individuals a smaller parcel. "The General Allotment Act of 1887," writes one sociologist, "marks the acme of U.S. political control over Native Americans. . . . Indians were to be incorporated *as individuals* into both the economic and political structures of the larger society. It was the ultimate form of control: the end of the tribe itself as a political and social entity."[112]

The Indian Allotment Act was the brainchild of Northern abolitionists who sought to humanize Native Americans by giving them that which, in the white imagination, made one human: land and property. America's indigenous people would be saved by Anglo-American culture; they would be turned into farmers and incorporated into the American mainstream. But the Act resulted in the opposite outcome. Indigenous farming declined under the Act, since many of the most fertile parcels of tribal land were claimed by whites. Nor did the allotted land remain in Indian hands for long. Between 1887 and 1934, 90 million acres passed into white hands. How did this happen? First, the Allotment Act did not "allot" Native Americans any additional land; rather, it dispossessed tribes of land already in their possession. The allotment of 160 acres per Indian household freed a surplus of tribal land for white settlers. (It was as if you owned a large mansion, then, one day, the government knocked on your door and declared it was giving you a bedroom and bathroom to live in. The rest of your mansion was up for grabs.) Second, a significant amount of Native American land was sold or leased to non-Indians, since Native Americans were accused of failing to develop the land "up to white standards."

For these reasons, the Allotment Act proved an effective mechanism for dispossessing Indians of more than 60% of their remaining landholdings.[113] Author

Vine Deloria has observed: "Often when discussing treaty rights with whites, Indians find themselves told that 'We gave you the land and you haven't done anything with it.' . . . The truth is that practically the only thing the white men ever gave to the Indian was disease and poverty. . . . Never did the United States give any tribe any land at all. Rather, the Indian tribe gave the United States land in consideration for having Indian title to the remaining land confirmed."[114]

Such government policies crippled Native American economies and cultures. The policy of Indian removal forced tribes off land that could be developed and placed them on land thought to be worth little to nothing. Tribes that occupied land rich in minerals, such as coal or copper, were dispossessed of these resources by white-owned corporations. The destruction of the buffalo left plains tribes without their most valued economic resource. Theft of grazing grounds left pastoral tribes without a way to feed their herds. The horticultural tribes of the South were dispossessed of their rich soil and placed in land where crops could not grow. Moreover, Native Americans, like all people, had formed a special relationship with their land. This was the land of their childhood and of their fathers and mothers, a land of burial grounds and sacred sites, a land that gave meaning to the tribes that lived upon it. With Indian land loss, therefore, came not only economic strangulation and political powerlessness but also the decay of tribal identity.[115]

Like enslaved Africans, Native Americans resisted in large numbers. One form of resistance melded anguished cries for help with indigenous spirituality. In 1889, a Paiute spiritual leader named Wovoka claimed to have experienced a powerful vision during a solar eclipse. The walls of heaven were open before him, revealing God and the Paiute, living in paradise. Wovoka urged his people to live in peace with the whites, since their rewards would come in the afterlife. He also developed a dance that would uplift the Paiute, the Ghost Dance. News of the Ghost Dance spread throughout the west, and tribes incorporated it into their traditional belief systems. While Wovoka was, by and large, a pacifist, other tribes interpreted Wovoka's prophesies as foretelling the destruction of the whites. The Lakota, in particular, believed that the Ghost Dance would usher in a new era, one marked by the return of the buffalo and the fall of the whites.

Reservation agents and white settlers soon grew fearful of the Ghost Dance movement. As tensions mounted, U.S. troops were mobilized to suppress the dance. These tensions finally exploded on a cold December morning in 1890. Troops were ordered to disarm the Lakota, and as they did so, a shot was fired, sparking a massive shoot-out that felled 25 troopers and over 150 Lakota, a third of whom were women and children. This bloody event, known as the Wounded Knee Massacre, marked the gruesome finale to the 350-year-old Indian Wars.[116]

The nineteenth century witnessed the virtual destruction of tribal sovereignty, massive loss of Native American life, and near-total dispossession of tribal land.

At the beginning of the nineteenth century, much of the land that now makes up the continental United States had still been in tribal hands. By the end of the century, nearly all that land was controlled by whites. For the American Indian, therefore, white colonialism in the Americas brought a threefold infliction: an infliction of the body, in the form of bullet wounds, beatings, and disease; an infliction of the spirit, in the form of cultural re-education, religious suppression, and Anglo-American assimilation; and an infliction of the land, in the form of environmental devastation and the eradication of tribal property.

Immigration from Asia and Europe

During the mid-nineteenth century, immigrants flocked to America by the millions. The 1830s witnessed a swell of German immigrants, while the 1830s–1840s saw over 2.5 million Irish move to America, more than a million of them between 1845 and 1849, the years of the Irish Potato Famine. Approximately 200,000 German Jews also immigrated to the United States, and the California gold rush of the late 1840s drew many immigrants from Asia. Between 1850 and 1882, the Chinese population in the United States would grow to 100,000.[117] We can now understand why, in 1855, American poet Walt Whitman penned the following words: "Here is not merely a nation but a teeming nation of nations."[118]

When discussing the motivations of immigrants, we tend to explain migration patterns at the level of the individual. That is, we usually suggest that people were *pushed* out of their home countries by economic decline and *pulled* to America with hopes of making an honest dollar. This kind of interpretation unveils only half the story, however, because it fails to tell us why immigrants' home countries descended into poverty in the first place. To understand this, we need briefly to study how global capitalism works.

At the end of the nineteenth century, American capitalism was barreling forward at breakneck speeds. California and the Southwest had been "acquired," so to speak, and with this land came new riches: gold, silver, copper, cattle. And American business was flourishing. This did not happen in isolation, however. American fur traders relied on European and Chinese interests in fur; American miners depended on the worldwide interest in fine jewelry. American producers relied on consumers in other parts of the world, as capitalism developed as a global enterprise.

But what happens when capitalist development advances much more swiftly in one part of the world than in others? Answer: more developed countries drain resources and labor power of less developed countries. As a result, countries such as America overdevelop economically while so-called Third World countries underdevelop. Why is this? Because in the context of European colonization, less developed countries usually did not have complete control of their own economies. Think, for example, of the Atlantic Slave Trade: because

Immigration from South, Central, and Eastern Europe, 1820–1919

Decade	All South, Central,[c] and Eastern Europe	Italy	Greece	Eastern European Jews
1820–1829	3,343	430	17	
1830–1839	5,758	2,225	49	
1840–1849	4,275	1,476	17	7,500[a]
1850–1859	20,063	8,110	25	
1860–1869	26,522	10,238	n.a.	
1870–1879	172,655	46,296	209	40,000
1880–1889	836,265	267,660	1,807	200,000
1890–1899	1,753,916	603,761	12,732	300,000
1900–1909	5,822,355	1,930,475	145,402	
1910–1919	3,937,395	1,229,916	198,108	1,500,000[b]
1920–1924	1,114,730	460,644	52,144	

SOURCES: Carpenter, 1927, pp. 324–325; Rischin, 1962, p. 20; Willcox, 1929, p. 393.
[a]Between 1800 and 1869.
[b]Between 1900 and 1914.
[c]Persons born in Germany are not included.

Europeans controlled the trade, they (and America with them) prospered, while, by and large, Africa suffered.

As less developed countries plummet into poverty while more developed countries grow more powerful, a labor vacuum is created. In other words, as concentrated areas of capitalist growth pull resources from other parts of the world, they also pull workers from less developed countries—workers needed to mine gold, build railroads, and till fields. These workers respond to this pull out of necessity, since their country, underdeveloped by capitalism in America, can offer little. Thus, immigrants flock to areas of concentrated capitalism, and business owners welcome them, since they can be easily exploited. American workers, however, loathe them, for cheap immigrant labor can (like slave labor) drive down the price of all labor.

If tectonic plates shifted, resulting in an enormous opening at the bottom of the ocean—an opening that sucked down surrounding water, plant varieties, and fish—then sea life would be forced to relocate in that opening. They would migrate there because the new opening fundamentally altered the composition of their old eco-systems, draining from them food and nutrients. The same pattern occurs within social ecologies where certain structural conditions (like slavery) foster economic openings that drain resources and workers from other parts of the world. Because, like ecosystems, societies are intimately connected, abundance in one area usually causes paucity, a lack of abundance, in others. There is, therefore, a complex relationship between the wealthy country that receives immigrants and the underdeveloped country that sends them. We should bear this in mind when discussing American immigration, including and especially Asian immigration.[119]

The Invention of the Asian American

Until this point, we have said nothing about Asian Americans. This is because Asians did not begin to migrate to the United States in large numbers until the end of the nineteenth century. Asians, however, were already well "known" in the West. Recall that, during the so-called Age of Discovery, Europeans were defining themselves as a collective group against the "strange" peoples of the East, peoples described in travelers' tales as fearsome and otherworldly. Overlaid upon the dichotomy of Christian West and non-Christian East were several other oppositions giving charged meaning to, and increasing the distance between, West and East. As Edward Said has said, "On the one hand there are Westerners, and on the other there are Arab-Orientals; the former are (in no particular order) rational, peaceful, liberal, logical, capable of holding real values, without natural suspicion; the latter are none of these things."[120] Thus, people from China, Japan, and other Asian countries, as well as those from the Middle East, came to the United States already "othered." (We will have more to say about Arab Americans in a later chapter.) The West was "us," the East was "them"—and when "they" attempted to join "us," "they" encountered firm resistance.

Of course, **the term "Asian"** is a European invention, a kind of racial shorthand that subsumes under a single homogenizing category the peoples of China, Japan, Korea, India, Nepal, Bangladesh, Burma, Hawaii, the Pacific Islands, and all of Southeast Asia, including the Philippines, Cambodia, Vietnam, Indonesia, Thailand, Laos, Malaysia, and Singapore—peoples with immensely different and sometimes conflicting cultures, languages, and histories. These peoples of Asia had intermingled and traded with Europeans practically since the beginning of humanity; some even manned slave ships, while others came to the North American colonies as indentured servants. European contact with native Hawaiians is thought to have begun when Captain James Cook, a British sailor, landed on the islands in 1778. Because of its fertile climate, Hawaii soon was overrun by American and European planters, eager to develop sugar plantations on the islands. Like the indigenous peoples of America, many Hawaiians died from warfare and disease as a result of European contact. It has been estimated that Hawaii's population numbered between 200,000 and 800,000 when James Cook "discovered" the islands; only one hundred years later, the population had plummeted to less than 48,000. Hawaii lost most of its native population as well as its sovereignty, which was chipped away throughout the nineteenth century and dissolved in 1893, when the American military overthrew the Hawaiian monarchy and annexed the islands.[121]

Chinese laborers were imported to work the sugar fields of Hawaii. Around the same time, gold was discovered in California, and Chinese laborers flocked to the West coast, selling their labor on the cheap to mining companies. The influx of Chinese laborers sparked a powerful anti-Chinese movement. Starting in 1850, all foreign miners in California were forced to pay an extra tax, one that fell most heavily on Chinese workers. Chinese were also prevented from testifying against white people in court, and, since Jim Crow segregation was enforced, Chinese children were also forced to attend separate schools.[122]

Chinese people were distorted in the popular press as parasitic, soulless, and criminal. A newspaper announcing an "Anti-Chinese Meeting" in 1877 read: "Whereas, the Chinese as a class are a detriment and a curse to our country . . . they have supplanted white labor and taken the bread out of the mouths of the white men and their families, and Whereas, it is a well known fact that the Chinese as a class are notorious thieves and sluice robbers, and have within the last few months robbed the industrious miners and others in this vicinity, of anything and everything within their reach; therefore be it Resolved, That we, the citizens of Gold Run, do hereby declare the presence of Chinese in our midst a great nuisance. . . . Resolved, That as we are citizens and workingmen, and have the interests of our common country at heart, we do not approve of the destruction of property or violence to the Chinese, but pledge ourselves to use our united endeavors to free our country from Chinese labor without violence, if possible."[123]

The nonviolent option, it seems, was not always "possible." Many Chinese laborers were the victims of mob violence. In 1871, a white mob lynched, shot, and torched twenty-one Chinese immigrants in Los Angeles; in 1880, Denver's Chinatown was burnt to the ground, a laundryman beaten to death; in 1885, white workers killed twenty-eight Chinese men employed by the Union Pacific Railroad. Just as many poor whites during black slavery and Reconstruction blamed their poverty on African Americans, white workers during the nineteenth century saw Chinese immigrants as thieves who took "the bread out of the mouths of the white men and their families." The real culprit—an economic system that flourished by keeping labor cheap and pitting white worker against nonwhite worker—went without reproach.[124]

At the same time that American capitalism was encouraging the immigration of an expendable labor force from China and other parts of Asia, America was regulating Asian immigration and denying Asian immigrants the right to naturalize. In 1875, the Page Law, intended to bar Chinese prostitutes from the U.S., had the effect of barring virtually all Chinese women from American shores. Chinese men were needed to dig for gold and hammer railroad spikes, but Chinese women could bear children who, under the Fourteenth Amendment, would become American citizens. A permanent Asian community, populated with voting citizens, could not be tolerated, even if American business was growing rich on the labor of Chinese men. It was not long (1882) before *all* Chinese immigrants, men and women, were forbidden entry into the United States.

Peoples of West, South, and Southeast Asia suffered the same fate under the Immigration Act of 1917, as did nearly all Asian groups under the Immigration Act of 1924.[125] And, of course, the task of defining citizenship eligibility led courts to construct Asians as a nonwhite group. From 1878 to 1941, Chinese, Hawaiians, Burmese, Japanese, Filipino, and Korean immigrants were deemed "not white," while the whiteness of Indian Americans, as we learned in the last chapter, was a matter of great debate and legal uncertainty.[126]

Immigrants from the Old World

America at the end of the nineteenth century was shaped, not only by immigrants from Asia, but also (and especially) by immigrants from European countries. Focusing upon these new arrivals, Ellwood Cubberley, a social scientist, observed in 1909, "About 1882, the character of our immigration changed in a very remarkable manner. Immigration from Northern Europe dropped off rather abruptly, and in its place immigration from Southern and Eastern Europe set in and soon developed into a great stream."[127] Between 1886 and 1935, some 13 million immigrants from countries such as Austria, Hungary, Italy, and Russia flocked to America, 70% of them between 1901 and 1915. How were these **"new immigrants,"** as they were called, accepted? Professor Cubberley effectively answers our question by echoing a widely shared sentiment of the period: "These southern and eastern Europeans are a very different type from the north European who preceded them. Illiterate, docile, lacking in self-reliance and initiative and not possessing Anglo-Teutonic conceptions of law, order and government, their coming has served to dilute tremendously our national stock, and to corrupt our civic life."[128]

Jews, Poles, Slavs, Hungarians, Ukrainians, Armenians, Greeks, Italians, and Irish immigrants generally were not welcomed by native-born white Americans. In some circles, new immigrants were framed as members of "inferior races," "lesser breeds," "scoundrels," and "thieves," who had contributed considerably less to civilization than the upstanding people of the "English race."[129] Some even considered new immigrants "not white."

For the most part, new immigrants did not face the extreme levels of racial hatred and brutality that blacks, Asians, and Mexicans had to endure; but neither were they fully accepted into the (white) American mainstream. On the one hand, they enjoyed a fair amount of white privilege. For example, full citizenship rights were granted to Irish immigrants after they naturalized; and the causes of Irish immigrants were championed by two of America's most powerful institutions: the Catholic Church and the Democratic Party.[130] On the other hand, new immigrants were not looked on as the racial equals of Northern Europeans or other native-born Anglo-Saxons. The Irish were degraded in the popular press and by America's elites, and they quickly became among the poorest immigrant groups in the country.

Characteristics of Old and New Immigrant Groups at Time of Arrival, 1910

Origin	Percentage Illiterate	Percentage with Less than $50
Old		
Dutch and Flemish	2.7	65
English	0.5	49
French	10.8	52
German	5.7	66
Irish	1.4	81
Scandinavian	0.1	86
Scottish	0.4	56
Welsh	0.6	47
New		
Bohemian and Moravian	1.1	82
Croatian and Slovenian	33.5	96
Dalmatian, Bosnian, and Herzegovinian	39.3	93
Greek	24.0	93
Hebrew	28.8	87
Italian (north)	7.2	84
Italian (south)	51.8	92
Lithuanian	50.0	95
Magyar	11.8	90
Polish	35.0	97
Romanian	36.5	94
Russian	38.1	93
Slovak	21.3	94

SOURCE: Lieberson, 1963a, Table 16.

New European immigrants, then, were caught between violent exclusion and complete inclusion, between racial domination and white privilege. These "in-between people," to use the label developed by the eminent historian John Higham, struggled to find their place in America, battling poverty, ridicule, and violence along the way.[131] The swelling waves of immigrants from Southern, Eastern, and Central Europe resulted in a kind of fracturing of American whiteness. Ethnic hierarchies were established within the white race, with landowning, native-born Anglo-Saxons occupying the highest positions and impoverished new immigrants demoted to the status of "low-ranking members of the whiteness club."[132] The Irish—the "savages" of the Old World (sometimes referred to as "blacks turned inside-out," while blacks were sometimes called "burnt Irish"[133])—were understood as belonging to an "inferior white race," the so-called "Celtic race."[134]

Ethnic hierarchies were established within the white race, with landowning, native-born Anglo-Saxons occupying the highest positions and impoverished new immigrants demoted to the status of "low-ranking members of the whiteness club."

By the 1920s and 1930s, however, white ethnic hierarchies began to fade. How, we may ask, did these despised new immigrants, these "dark whites," as they were sometimes called, become, simply, white? Social scientists have offered four complementary answers to this question. The first has to do with the development of "ethnicity" as a concept. Around the beginning of the twentieth century, "race" and "ethnicity" were used interchangeably and in a loose fashion; there was no sharp distinction between the two. This began to change as scholars and policy makers began assigning the term "ethnic" to new immigrants from Europe, while "race" was used to differentiate blacks, Mexicans, or Asians from the white population. This implied that the distance between new immigrants and native-born whites was the result of *social and cultural differences*, which could be "solved" through education and would fade over generations, while the distance separating blacks, Mexicans, and Asians from white Americans was *natural and fixed*. In the words of one commentator writing in 1932, the "white immigrant [is] patently handicapped by foreign language and tradition," while the "Negro . . . is . . . more of a biological problem."[135] New ideas of socially constructed "ethnicity" were advanced by intellectuals belonging to the new immigrant groups. For example, Jewish intellectuals such as Horace Kallen and Isaac Berkson, both philosophers, attempted to lay claim to whiteness by identifying themselves as "white ethnics," even as they sought to preserve the distinctive cultural, linguistic, and religious heritage that signified their Jewishness.[136]

There was a second way in which new immigrants pulled themselves more fully into the white race. When impoverished newcomers from Ireland, Italy, Hungary, and other European lands arrived in America in search of work, they found themselves in competition with blacks, who had gained emancipation less than half a century earlier. Many new immigrants worked side by side with blacks and lived in the same dilapidated areas as black families. Soon enough, however, the new immigrants began to sense that they could gain an advantage over black workers by tapping into white employers' racial prejudices. "We deserve the best jobs," they clamored, "because we are hard-working white people! Hire us over those good-for-nothing blacks!" The rise of unions in the early decades of the twentieth century provided new immigrants with a space to articulate this platform, to mobilize as "whites," and thereby to exclude blacks, Mexicans, and Asians from their ranks. These nonwhite groups had little opportunity to retaliate, and by asserting their right to employment on the basis of their whiteness (instead of, say, their "Irishness" or "Italianness"), new immigrants avoided a nativist backlash by native-born white Americans.[137]

New immigrants quickly learned to use racial domination to their advantage. Far from wrestling against white supremacy to win honor, rights, and employment, new immigrants colluded with white supremacy, stepping up into whiteness on the backs of blacks, Mexicans, and Asians. Therefore, the third way new immigrants became white was by lashing out against nonwhites, chiefly blacks. New immigrants, especially the Irish, led anti-black propaganda campaigns and terrorized the black community through mob violence.[138] To transform themselves from "lazy Irish," "lying Italians," or "pitiful Greeks" into "entitled whites," new immigrants learned the ropes of racial contempt. In the elegant words of Toni Morrison, "Whatever the lived experience of immigrants with African Americans—pleasant, beneficial or bruising—the rhetorical experience renders blacks as non-citizens, already discredited outlaws. . . . [T]he move into mainstream America always means buying into the notion of American blacks as the real aliens. Whatever the ethnicity or nationality of the immigrant, his nemesis is understood to be African American."[139]

All these transformative changes took place within the framework of Jim Crow segregation, the fourth mechanism by which new immigrants became more fully white. Racial segregation, accompanied by white on nonwhite violence, solidified a culture of whiteness throughout the United States. Because new immigrants by and large were not subjected to the same painful processes of segregation as nonwhites, they could take advantage of the benefits of whiteness, from restaurants and restrooms to neighborhoods and schools.[140]

By distinguishing between race and ethnicity, asserting their whiteness to win jobs, participating in acts of racial hatred against nonwhites, and taking advantage of the perks of whiteness legitimated by Jim Crow, new immigrants chipped away at ethnic hierarchies within the ranks of whiteness.[141] To escape racial persecution, new immigrants joined the persecutors, thereby broadening the definition of whiteness and further strengthening the might of white supremacy. As James Baldwin has lamented with soft anger, "the Irish became white when they got here and began rising in the world, whereas I became black and began sinking. The Irish, therefore and thereafter . . . had absolutely no choice but to make certain that I could not menace their safety or status or identity: and, if I came too close, they could, with the consent of the governed, kill me. Which means that we can be friendly with each other anywhere in the world, except Boston."[142]

Racial Discourses of Modernity

If the "Middle Ages regarded skin color with mild curiosity," as Du Bois has observed, then the modern age defined itself on this very thing.[143] Between the European discovery of America and the early twentieth century, new **racial discourses**—collections of ideas about race that were developed by secular authorities such as philosophers, writers, and scientists—rose to prominence and helped to form classification systems riveted in white supremacy.[144]

Philosophers such as Hobbes, Locke, Voltaire, Montesquieu, Hume, and Kant justified slavery and racism in their writings.[145] "I am apt to suspect the negroes," wrote Hume, "and in general all other species of men (for there are four or five different kinds) to be naturally inferior to the whites."[146] Novelists and poets did their part as well, culminating in the late nineteenth century with Rudyard Kipling, a British poet and supporter of his country's colonial conquests, whose famous work, "The White Man's Burden" (1899), began with the lines, "Your new-caught, sullen peoples/Half-devil and half-child."

However, of all the secular authorities, the group that proved most influential in solidifying racial taxonomies was the natural historians, precursors to modern-day biologists and physical anthropologists. The natural historians were interested in classifying plants, animals, and so-called people groups. It was through their endeavors that, in 1624, the term "race" was first used—by François Bernier, a

French physician—to label and separate human bodies.[147] Others followed suit, including a Swedish botanist named Carolus Linnaeus, who developed one of the first major human taxonomies, dividing humanity into four separate groups:

Americanus: reddish, choleric, and erect; hair—black, straight, thick; wide nostrils, scanty beard; obstinate, merry, free; paints himself with fine red lines; regulated by customs.

Asiaticus: sallow, melancholy, stiff; black hair, dark eyes; severed, haughty, avaricious; covered with loose garments; ruled by opinions.

Africanus: black, phlegmatic, relaxed; hair—black, frizzled; skin—silky; nose—flat; lips—tumid; women without shame, they lactate profusely; crafty, indolent, negligent; anoints himself with grease; governed by caprice.

Europeaeus: white, sanguine, muscular; hair—long, flowing; eyes—blue; gentle, acute, inventive; covers himself with close vestments; governed by laws.[148]

Note that this list, published in 1735, attributes different personality traits, and even fashion senses, to each race. Forty years later, another typology of humanity was put forth by a German medical researcher named Johann Blumenbach. Blumenbach divided humans into five groups that correspond to different geographical areas—Caucasians, Mongolians, Ethiopians, Americans, and Malays—and held that Caucasians exemplified the standards of "pure beauty" in human form.[149] And how did Linnaeus and Blumenbach gather data to support their typologies? They did not travel the world; they, like other European scientists, relied on the accounts of European planters, travelers, missionaries, and soldiers—accounts that, as we have already seen, were highly fallacious.

Typologies such as those proposed by Linnaeus and Blumenbach (and *all* such typologies were developed by European scientists) presented distinct racial groups as fixed and immutable. They also attached behavioral traits to physical characteristics, claiming, for example, as Linnaeus did, that Europeans were naturally ingenious while Africans were naturally lazy. And, perhaps most harmfully, racial classifications justified racial inequality by suggesting that such inequality was natural—a divine ordering of the world.[150]

Two other "scientific" disciplines emerged that served the ends of white supremacy—phrenology (the study of skull shape and size) and physiognomy (the study of facial appearance)—each of which has now been discredited as pseudoscience. Both disciplines claimed that one's internal character could be determined by one's external features—by the shape of one's head (phrenology) or the shape of one's face (physiognomy)—and both attributed negative character traits to those not of European descent. Phrenology and physiognomy gave rise to a kind of scientific stereotyping, expressed most influentially (and, we now know, ludicrously)

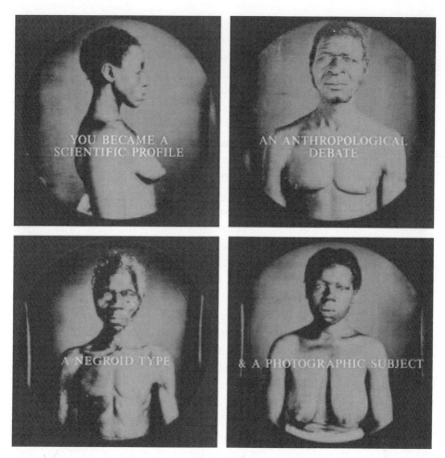

YOU BECAME A
SCIENTIFIC PROFILE

AN ANTHROPOLOGICAL
DEBATE

A NEGROID TYPE

& A PHOTOGRAPHIC SUBJECT

Racism did not naturally flow from systems of racial classification; rather, systems of racial classification flowed from racism.

in "criminal anthropology," an approach that held that lawbreakers were evolutionary throwbacks, that their vice was explained by their natural inferiority and affinity with beasts. Cesare Lombroso, an ambitious Italian doctor, popularized this idea around the late nineteenth century. "Born criminals," argued Lombroso, could be identified by their physical features. And we should not be surprised to learn that many of Lombroso's telling features were those of non-European peoples. For example, the inability to blush was associated with vice and dishonesty.[151]

As Lombroso's theories gained prominence, Francis Galton, a wealthy cousin of Charles Darwin, was hard at work on a theory that suggested that all human behavior was hereditary. Levels of intelligence and creativity, diligence and determination, moral fortitude and uprightness—they were all linked to heredity. To squeeze the best possible traits out of the human line, Galton suggested that marriage be regulated and child rearing modulated, according to the genetic giftedness of parents.[152] Eager to set this plan in motion, he coined the term **"eugenics"** to refer to a program that would ensure genetic purity. To its founder, eugenics was "the science of improving stock, which is by no means confined to questions of judicious mating but which, especially in the case of man, takes cognizance of all influences that tend in however remote a degree to give to the more suitable races or strains of blood a better chance of prevailing speedily over the less suitable than they otherwise would have had."[153] From this definition, we notice that Galton imagined a world of "superior" and "inferior" races and dreamt of a time when the former would overrun the latter.

With eugenics, science became a program; that is, "solutions" were advanced for the "natural inferiority of the lower races." One cruel solution was forced sterilization. From the end of the nineteenth century and *up until the 1970s*, thousands of Native Americans and African Americans, as well as people deemed mentally retarded or criminal, underwent surgical procedures against their will, sometimes without their knowing, that resulted in permanent infertility.[154]

Scientific theories that supported white supremacy were more likely to be backed by politicians, financed by business elites, and popularized by journalists— all of whom sought to uphold the white power structure—than theories that challenged racial domination. It is important to note that a good number of scientists criticized racist pseudoscience and eugenics. For example, in *Man's Most Dangerous Myth*, Ashley Montagu would chastise eugenicists, writing, "Our troubles, it must be repeated, emanate not from biological defectives but from social defectives; and social defectives are produced by society, not by genes. Obviously, it is social, not biological, therapy that is indicated."[155] Nevertheless, the doctrine of eugenics spread throughout the world, as did its "solutions," such as force sterilization, only to die out within the past forty years.

Science authoritatively legitimated that which had been developing throughout Europe's colonial conquests and America's enslavement of Africans: the notion that nonwhite people were naturally inferior in nearly every conceivable way. We should bear in mind that scientific taxonomies of racial groups were not based on biological evidence but were adaptations of social categories developed to help make sense of a world otherwise "opaque, unpredictable, and inchoate."[156] Nevertheless, scientific notions about race joined with other notions advanced by secular authorities, grounding racial differences in nature. From then on, racial differences did not belong to the realm of culture (manifest, say, through different lifestyles); rather, they were understood as part of the biological fabric of life.[157]

More pointedly, these social classifications masquerading as scientific "truth" made the horrors done to nonwhite people easier to swallow. Racial categories have never been "equal," since they were created to divide, dominate, and exploit different people. Racism did not naturally flow from systems of racial classification;

rather, systems of racial classification flowed from racism. Race was not, and never has been, an innocent description of the world. No, race came into this world a murderer, thief, and trickster.

America's Racial Profile Today

We have covered a lot of ground, from the discovery of "the New World" to the early twentieth century. To summarize: race did not always exist. The Indian was invented within the context of European colonization, as indigenous peoples of the Americas were lumped together under one rubric to be killed, uprooted, and exploited. Whiteness and blackness were invented as antipodes within the context of English, and later American, slavery. Blackness became associated with bondage, inferiority, and social death; whiteness with freedom, superiority, and life. The Mexican was invented within the context of the colonization of Mexico. At the end of the nineteenth century, the Asian was invented as a response to immigration from the Far East. Whiteness expanded during the early years of the twentieth century as new immigrants from Southern, Central, and Eastern Europe transformed themselves from "lesser whites" to, simply, "whites." All the while, white supremacy was legitimated by racial discourses in philosophy, literature, and science. The history of racial struggle in America was a history of domination, exploitation, enslavement, and murder of nonwhites by whites, horrors always accompanied by firm and costly resistance.

This chapter has demonstrated that we cannot hope to understand the history and dynamics of racial domination if we apprehend racial groups as individual cases with semi-autonomous histories and lifestyles. A relational perspective encourages us to study different racial actors in a state of mutual dependence and struggle, instead of focusing narrowing on, say, African-American history, Asian-American history, or European history. As race scholars, the thing we study—the object of our socioanalysis, if you will—should be the space of interracial conflict itself, not a single racial group.

By the middle of the twentieth century, the racial categories so familiar to us today were firmly established. Although the second half of the twentieth century would bring great changes in the realm of race, including the rise of the Civil Rights Movement and the fall of Jim Crow, the racial categories that emerged in America over the course of the previous three hundred years remained, for the most part, unchallenged. Americans, white and nonwhite alike, understood themselves as raced and accepted the dominant racial classification system even if they refused to accept the terms of racial inequality. That is why this chapter, one concerned with the genesis and historical development of racial categories, has not ventured too deeply into the mid- and late-twentieth century. We take up this task in the chapters ahead.

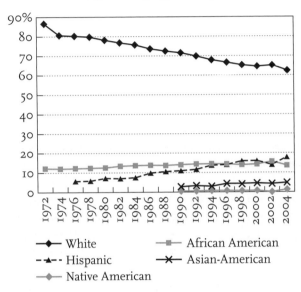

Changing Racial and Ethnic Composition of Young People,
Ages 18–24, 1972–2004

Before moving on to that task, however, let us take up one final issue. Having examined both the genesis and historical development of racial categories, on the one hand, and the historical transformation of American society itself, on the other, what can we say about what American society looks like today, in terms of the racial categories we have inherited? As of 2005, whites made up 67% of the population, Hispanics made up 15%, and blacks made up 13%. Asians made up 4%, and Native Americans and Native Hawaiians made up the remaining 1%.[158] Many Americans misperceive these percentages and make assumptions about the size of their country's racial groups that are far from accurate. In a recent study, 40% of white and nonwhite Americans significantly underestimated whites' majority status and overestimated the size of nonwhite populations. In other words, they thought that whites were a minority when compared to the Hispanic and black populations combined. Another study found that "the average American thinks that America is 32% black, 21% Hispanic, and 18% Jewish."[159]

Why do so many Americans think that whites are outnumbered by nonwhites even though whites outnumber Hispanics and blacks by a rate of nearly 6 to 1 and Asians by a ratio of approximately 17 to 1? The mainstream media's obsession with documenting the growth of immigrant and nonwhite populations is one reason. Dozens of news stories and hundreds of statistical reports have been dedicated to outlining the population of America's immigrants, the percentage of African Americans living in some city, or the growing Hispanic population. Recently, a white anchor on Fox News concluded a segment that linked the growing nonwhite population to birthrates by saying, "To put it bluntly, we need more babies."

Another reason people perceive America as a country where whites are not a numerical majority is that they base their judgments on certain areas of the country that have high concentrations of immigrant and nonwhite populations. Certain nonwhite populations are represented in significant numbers in some areas of the country but not in others. Hispanics make up 35% of Californians and Texans but only 8% of all people who live in Washington and 1% of those living in Maine. Likewise, blacks are numerous in the Deep South—constituting roughly one third of the population in Louisiana, Mississippi, and Georgia—but make up less than 1% of the population in Wyoming, Montana, and North Dakota.[160] Sometimes people, white and nonwhite alike, who live in areas with a high percentage of nonwhites believe that the rest of the country resembles their region.[161]

More important, perhaps, is the fact that white Americans who overestimate nonwhite populations are more likely to harbor negative views about immigrants and blacks than are those whose perceptions are more accurate. Compared to whites with accurate perceptions, whites who think they already number in the minority are more likely to believe that immigration will lead to more crime, national disunity, and the loss of American jobs. And those who think that blacks and Hispanics outnumber whites are likely to claim that the former two groups are threatening and violent.[162] These findings support Herbert Blumer's **theory of social position**, which hypothesizes that interpersonal racism will increase in one group the more it feels threatened by another. As Blumer put it, "A basic understanding of race prejudice must be sought in the process by which racial groups form images of themselves and of others. . . . It is the sense of social position emerging from this collective process of characterization which provides the basis for race prejudice."[163] Because people reify races—understanding them as distinct groups that compete for resources—their hostility toward other racial groups increases as does their perception of that group's size.[164]

Even though whites still constitute a considerable majority of America's population today, it is undeniable that things will look differently in the future. In many metropolitan areas, such as Houston, Los Angeles, New York, and Miami, whites are numerically outnumbered, as they are in some states, such as California, in which the white population dropped from two-thirds to less than half between 1980 and 2000.[165] By 2002, immigrants and their children living in America numbered 66 million, roughly 23% of the country's population.[166] However, even if the population of America's fastest growing nonwhite group, Hispanics, were to triple by 2050, they would still constitute but a quarter of the total population—a significant number, yes, but a far cry from a majority.[167]

As America grows more diverse, racial markers themselves seem to be growing more porous and fluid. A racial taxonomy comprised of five major groups

Faces in the Crowd

Women (51%) slightly outnumber men (49%).
Here's how race and ethnicity break down:

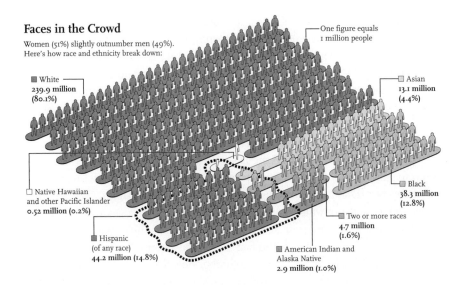

One figure equals
1 million people

White
239.9 million
(80.1%)

Asian
13.1 million
(4.4%)

Native Hawaiian
and other Pacific Islander
0.52 million (0.2%)

Black
38.3 million
(12.8%)

Two or more races
4.7 million
(1.6%)

Hispanic
(of any race)
44.2 million (14.8%)

American Indian and
Alaska Native
2.9 million (1.0%)

Who's Having Babies

Hispanics are the only group having more than enough children to replace themselves in the population.
More unmarried women are giving birth, but births by teenage girls are at their lowest rate.

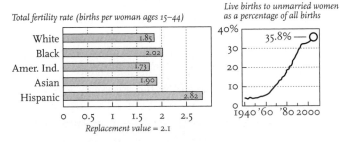

Total fertility rate (births per woman ages 15–44)

White	1.85
Black	2.02
Amer. Ind.	1.73
Asian	1.90
Hispanic	2.82

0   0.5   1   1.5   2   2.5
Replacement value = 2.1

*Live births to unmarried women
as a percentage of all births*

35.8%

40%
30
20
10
0
1940 '60 '80 2000

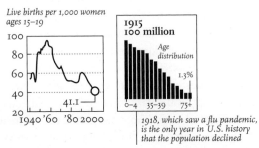

*Live births per 1,000 women
ages 15–19*

100
80
60
40
20
41.1
1940 '60 '80 2000

**1915
100 million**

Age
distribution

1.3%

0–4   35–39   75+

*1918, which saw a flu pandemic,
is the only year in U.S. history
that the population declined*

now seems more inadequate than ever. Today, 1 in 40 people claim **multiracial heritage**—that is, to belong to two or more racial groups—but that ratio jumps to 1 in 20 for people under the age of 18. By some projections, as many as 1 in 5 Americans will identify as multiracial by 2050. After asking multiethnic readers to contribute nicknames that describe their mixed heritage, a California newspaper compiled a list of terms. A half-Canadian, half-Mexican reader referred to himself as "Canexican"; a half-Pakistani, half-Mexican, as "Mexistani"; a half-Scottish, half-Mexican, as "McRiguez."[168]

Who claims multiracial heritage? Asians and Latinos have the highest proportion of people identifying as biracial or multiracial. And because whites far outnumber other groups, most of those who claim multiracial identity report being white plus something else. Blacks have the lowest proportion of people who claim multiracial identity.[169] This is not necessarily because there actually are fewer multiracial people of African ancestry but because, in the eyes of many, blackness remains a totalizing racial category. That is, to many (black and nonblack alike) one cannot be "black and Asian" or "black and white": all such people are simply black. The legacy of the one-drop rule continues to classify citizens with African heritage—be it one-tenth or nine-tenths African—singularly as African American.[170]

The rise of American multiracialism is due to several factors, including post-1965 immigration from Latin America and Asia and the recent rise in marriages that traverse the color barrier—both of which we will discuss at length in ensuing chapters. However, by themselves, changes in the population cannot fully account for the rise of multiracial identification. We must also explore symbolic changes to the racial order. After all, recalling the definition of race offered in the opening pages of this book, we know the boundaries surrounding certain racial populations are not natural or unalterable but are fundamentally symbolic in nature. If we look far enough back in our family trees, most of us will discover we are "mixed" ethnically or racially. And if we think about how racial categories have changed over the years, most of us who would not necessarily think of ourselves as multiracial or multiethnic today—Russian Jews or those of Italian and Irish descent, for instance—will realize that, had we been born in a different era, we might well have identified differently.

Thus, if multiracial identification is on the rise, especially among the youth, it is because many people find it necessary to transcend the limits of an overly simple and rigid racial classification system, preferring to locate their sense of self in two, three, or four histories, cultures, and heritages, rather than in one dominant racial label. And the United States government, by allowing for the first time citizens to check multiple racial boxes on the 2000 Census, has encouraged (or at least officially permitted) multiracial identification. If America is becoming more and more the multiracial nation, it is not only because racial populations have moved across national borders (immigration) but also because racial borders have moved across populations (racial reclassification).[171]

Before concluding, it is worth pausing a moment to ask: How do you feel about what you have just read? When you learned that several of America's major cities are majority nonwhite, how were you moved? Did such news startle or scare you? Did it excite or uplift you? When you tell your friends what you have just learned, what tone of voice will you use? That of the dispassionate observer, the elated messenger, the bearer of bad news? With these questions, we hope to encourage you to examine your gut reactions to news of America's morphing color lines, reactions that can serve as a barometer of your racial attitudes, your position on the racial hierarchy, and perhaps even your unspoken and unexamined—not to mention unintentional—connection to a culture of whiteness.

We, the Past

Having followed this story of the emergence of race, we citizens of the twenty-first century might now ask, "So what? What does any of this have to do with me?" The answer is: *Everything*. Having finishing this chapter, you should have little doubt about the historical and social nature of race. In the last chapter, we defined race as a symbolic category, one based on phenotype or ancestry, constructed according to specific social and historical contexts, and misrecognized as a natural category. In this chapter, we drew your attention to the specific "social and historical contexts" by which race entered the world. To think of race as a biological entity, as something that never has and never will change, is to forget the history of race. If we think reflexively about race, if we historicize it, we come to the conclusion that race is neither an innocent nor an obvious part of humanity but a European invention, forged in the context of colonization and slavery.

Moreover, a thorough understanding of the past enhances a thorough understanding of ourselves. We do not exist in a vacuum, magically undisturbed by historical and social forces. Rather, we are the products of history. The contours of our society—our current institutions, our schools, our neighborhoods, and our prisons—have been designed by the hands of history, as have our social sufferings and inequalities.

It is striking how much racial progress has been made in the United States since its founding. The changes that have taken place in the last sixty years, in particular, are simply unparalleled in the worldwide history of racial domination.[172] That the majority of Americans today consider wicked practices that were widely accepted a mere century ago—from racial violence and legalized segregation to laws against intermarriage and discourses that claimed the "natural superiority of the white race"—is remarkable. But it is perhaps equally striking how similar our fears of today are to those of yesterday. At the end of the nineteenth century, white Californians complained, "The Asians are stealing our jobs!" Now that scapegoat has morphed into Mexican form. At the end of the nineteenth century, American faced a severe "immigration problem," as millions of immigrants from Asia and new parts of Europe flocked to America. Today, politicians continue to worry about whom to let into the country, whom to naturalize, and whom to expel. The stereotypes and prejudices we carry with us, perhaps articulated fully only in the quietude of our living rooms or in our innermost thoughts, are nothing more than the imprints of a historical stamp. "It is history," wrote Émile Durkheim, "which is the true unconscious."[173]

When we look each other in the eye, we must look *past* the person standing before us, comprehending her or him not simply as a flesh-and-bones figure but as an individual who has been historically and socially constituted. This individual does not lack in freedom, but she or he *is* partly conditioned by the actions of those who came before. We inheritors of history should bear this in mind as we turn our attention now to unpacking how race works in society's different fields of life.

CHAPTER REVIEW

MODERNITY RISING
"Age of Discovery," modernity

COLONIZATION OF THE AMERICAS
colonialism, the Indian Wars

THE INVENTION OF WHITENESS AND BLACKNESS
indentured servants, plantation system, chattel slavery

AFRICANS ENSLAVED
institutionalization, Atlantic slave trade, psychological wage, slave codes, one-drop rule, slave rebellions, abolitionists, Forty Acres and a Mule, Reconstruction, Jim Crow

MANIFEST DESTINY
Manifest Destiny, Treaty of Guadalupe Hidalgo, Indian Territory, Indian Allotment Act

IMMIGRATION FROM ASIA AND EUROPE
the terms "Asian," "new immigrants"

RACIAL DISCOURSES OF MODERNITY
racial discourses, eugenics

AMERICA'S RACIAL PROFILE TODAY

theory of social position, multiracial heritage

FROM THEORY TO PRACTICE

1. Identify three ways in which present-day society mirrors seventeenth-, eighteenth-, or nineteenth-century America. Look for parallels in the realm of culture (recycled ideas, stereotypes, fears), politics (similar issues, agendas, practices), and everyday life (job competition, romantic relationships, recurrent social problems).

2. How have the people with whom you identify been systematically privileged or disadvantaged racially over the course of American history? How do you think your own life is privileged or disadvantaged because of this? In other words, how is your own social position shaped by historical forces?

3. History is a battleground. That is, people often fight about what history should be taught and how it should be taught. In light of this, how does the history reviewed in this chapter compare to the history of early America that you learned elsewhere? Meditate on the reasons for such similarities and differences.

4. Of the history reviewed in this chapter, which parts do you feel are often forgotten by the people in your life? Why do you think that is? What do you think would change if this history was remembered?

RECOMMENDED READING

- W. E. B. Du Bois, *Black Reconstruction in America* (Cleveland: Meridian, 1935).

- Stuart Hall, David Held, Don Hubert, and Kenneth Thompson, eds., *Modernity: An Introduction to Modern Societies* (Malden: Blackwell, 1996).

- Orlando Patterson, *The Ordeal of Integration: Progress and Resentment in America's "Racial" Crisis* (New York: Basic Civitas Books, 1998).

- David Roediger, *Working toward Whiteness: How America's Immigrations Became White, The Strange Journey from Willis Island to the Suburbs* (New York: Basic Books, 2005).

- Edward Said, *Orientalism*, 25th Anniversary Edition (New York: Vintage, 1994 [1978]).

- Audrey Smedley, *Race in North America: Origin and Evolution of a Worldview*, Second Edition (Boulder: Westview, 1999).

- Ronald Takaki, *A Different Mirror: A History of Multicultural America* (Boston: Little Brown, 1993).

PART TWO

RELATIONALITY

WE NOW TURN TO EXPLORING HOW RACE WORKS IN A NUMBER OF SOCIETY'S fields of life. Recall from Chapter 1 that by "field of life," we mean a realm of social life that follows its own basic principles. We shall examine how race directs the worlds of politics, economics, and residence; we shall continue by investigating the legal, educational, aesthetic, associational, and intimate fields. This organization will allow us to come to grips with the dynamic nature of racial domination in present-day America: how each aspect of our lives is somehow touched by the realities of race.

We can fully understand our lives only by examining how they are shaped by larger structural powers and enduring historical forces. Relational thinking means approaching the world with an outlook that is large and long. Large, because it is aware of the ways in which structural processes found in fields of life condition people's everyday actions. Long, because it bears in mind how history determines modern life. Thus, a relational thinker does not understand social problems simply by thinking in terms of individuals and groups—"unmarried teenage mothers," "welfare recipients," "suburbanites," or "urban gangs"—, treating groups (and their problems) as if they existed in isolation from the rest of society. Rather, the relational thinker recognizes the deep connections that make up society: connections between individual and institution, past and present, and the powerful and the powerless.

Relational thinkers also pay attention to the ways in which different fields of life are connected to one another. Although we have divided the following nine chapters into separate fields of life, we know that, in reality, each field influences the others. For example, if we wish to learn about the ghetto, we must simultaneously bring to mind the suburbs, since these two residential neighborhoods were formed in relation to each other through processes of migration, gentrification, and white flight. We must also examine the ghetto's relationship to the economic field (joblessness, urban decay), the political field (disenfranchisement, diminished social movements in the post-Civil Rights Era), the legal field (the rise of prisons, the war on drugs), and the educational field (the sorry state of urban schools, school violence). Further, we must analyze how cultural producers, such as the record and movie producers, turn out exaggerated images of the ghetto, especially through "Gangsta Rap." And how can we fully understand the ghetto without viewing it historically, grasping it in relation to slavery, Reconstruction, and legally enforced segregation?

As you can see, the ghetto, like all other aspects of race, cannot be analyzed in isolation. It must be apprehended in its full complexity, as a creation of intersecting fields of life, all of which are informed by a history of racial domination. Overwhelming? Indeed. But since race is perhaps the most complex of all social phenomena, it deserves an equally complex mode of thinking. The task is big, intimidating—like eating an elephant. And how do we do that? One bite at a time.

Chapter 3

Politics

Is This America?

She was the daughter of black sharecroppers, a woman who had worked a Mississippi plantation all her life. At the age of six, she started picking cotton. Because her family needed her in the fields, she received only six years of formal schooling. But when Mrs. Fannie Lou Hamer took the front seat at the 1962 Democratic Convention Credentials Committee hearing, she arrested the country's attention. After explaining to the committee the widespread disenfranchisement of southern blacks and recounting a brutal beating she and other women had been given by police officers for trying to order food at a segregated restaurant, Mrs. Hamer concluded: "All of this on account we want to register, to become first-class citizens. . . . I question America. Is this America, the land of the free and the home of the brave, where we have to sleep with our telephones off the hooks because our lives be threatened daily because we want to live as decent human beings? In America?"[1]

That's the question, a question that cuts to the quick of the matter: the drastic disconnection between the lofty ideals of American democracy and American democracy in practice, the simultaneous inclusion of "the people" in the high halls of governance and the exclusion of "certain people" from full citizenship. It is the contradiction of penning, "We hold these truths to be self-evident: That all men are created equal," while sponsoring a system of slavery and colonialism. It is criticizing the Nazi Holocaust while, fearing espionage, imprisoning thousands of Japanese American citizens in internment camps.

Who gets to feast at the bounty of American democracy, and who goes hungry? The previous chapter made clear that, for most of America's history, "democracy" was meant only for white people (primarily, white men). "The broad sweep of U.S. history," observe the authors of *Racial Formation in the United States*, "is characterized not by racial democracy, but by racial despotism, not by trajectories of reform, but by implacable denial of political rights, dehumanization, extreme exploitation, and policies of minority extirpation. Democracy has never been in abundant supply where race is concerned."[2]

Things have changed since Mrs. Hamer questioned America. The Civil Rights Movement arose in response to racial terrorism, segregation, and disenfranchisement, as people of color organized and fought for full citizenship rights. We begin this chapter by exploring how the Civil Rights Movement changed the face of American politics, concentrating, too, on the white backlash that emerged, eventually overpowering the movement. We then turn toward today, examining how race works in the political field. In so doing, we focus on partisanship and representation, voting, elections, and civil society. As we will see, racial divides play a defining role in American politics. Although the United States no longer legally supports racial segregation, racial domination persists, though in a less visible form. If this is true, then we, too, might question America to better America. If institutional racism is built into the foundations of our political system, then has American democracy lived up to its full potential?

The Civil Rights Movement

One hundred years after the Emancipation Proclamation, freedom had not come to African Americans. In the Southern states, Jim Crow laws institutionalized social practices that attempted to deny blacks their humanity. Black children often played in the streets, since designated "Colored" parks were in disrepair, and they could not relieve themselves from the summer heat in the white swimming pool or educate themselves in the white library. Separate schools were anything but equal. Consider Yazoo City, Mississippi, which, in the late 1950s, dedicated $245 per white child for educational expenses and only $3 per black child.[3] If a black woman went shopping, she was forbidden to try on her new dress, since storeowners thought white shoppers would not want clothes worn by blacks. If a black father sought food for his family, he would have to enter the restaurant through the back door, out of sight. Black men and women, even great-grandparents, were never greeted with the respectful titles of Southern politeness: instead of "Mr. Nelson" it was "Billy," instead of "Mrs. Mayberry," it was "Jan."

Where slavery reigned before the Civil War, a new form of racial despotism reigned after. Unable to obtain jobs elsewhere, blacks were forced back onto southern plantations through a new system of (informal) slavery called sharecropping. White planters gave blacks a small piece of land on which to grow crops and live (often in squalid shacks). In return, blacks gave white planters a portion of their crop. In most cases, the planters left black sharecroppers only with enough crops on which to survive, not enough to profit, and blacks were kept in dirt-floor poverty through a system of unending debt.

What is more, whites withheld from blacks the most basic right of American citizenship: the vote. Although black men won the right to vote with the ratification of the Fifteenth Amendment in 1870, and women won suffrage rights in 1920, black women and men were disenfranchised by dozens of backhanded tactics. When blacks went to the courthouse to register, they were told that they had to own property or that they needed to be accompanied by whites, who could vouch for their character. Some were forced to take complicated literacy tests requiring them to copy down and explain portions of the state's Constitution. Others were posed more humiliating questions: "How many feathers are on a chicken?" "How many bubbles are on a bar of soap?" As a result, most southern blacks were not registered to vote. To take but one example, in 1960 fewer than 2% of Mississippi's black adults were registered to vote.[4]

This system of racial domination was safeguarded by ongoing, systematic, and virtually unchallenged white terrorism. Blacks literally were beaten, raped, and strangled into submission. Between 1930 and 1950, thirty-three blacks (that we know of) were lynched in Mississippi. There was Henry Bedford, a seventy-two-year-old tenant farmer beaten to death for apparently speaking disrespectfully to a white man; there was J. B. Grant, a seventeen-year-old shot over one hundred times by a lynch mob and hung on a railroad trestle (for what, we do not know); there were Charlie Lang and Ernest Green, both fourteen, tortured, castrated, and murdered for allegedly raping a young white girl. It would later be discovered that the boys and the white girl, all childhood friends, were simply playing together.[5]

Then there was Emmett Till, a fourteen-year-old from Chicago who had traveled to Mississippi to visit relatives. Till, a teenage prankster making good on a dare, whistled at a white woman in a country store on August 24, 1955. He would be dead two days later, as white men broke into his relative's home, kidnapped Emmett, beat him, cut off his testicles, shot him, and tossed him into the Tallahatchie River. After seeing her son's mutilated body, Emmett Till's grieving mother allowed photographers to take pictures so that others might see what had been done. Till's bludgeoned body was put on display in magazines and television broadcasts around the United States, exposing millions of people to the racial violence ravaging the South.

It has been said that Emmett Till's murder galvanized and energized many Americans, black and white, to participate in the **Civil Rights Movement**, that collection of organizations and people who carried out political acts aimed at dismantling the white power structure by abolishing racial segregation, non-white disenfranchisement, and economic exploitation. Although this is certainly true for some, we must remember that the Civil Rights Movement really began when the first enslaved African on the first slave ship bound for the "New World" raised her head, looked her captor in the eye, and said, "no." What we know to be the modern Civil Rights Movement drew inspiration, strength, and strategy from what historian Charles Payne calls the "black organizing tradition," one that runs from slave revolts (large and small), through Reconstruction, through the tumultuous sixties.[6] During the 1950s and 60s, a fire first ignited by revolting slaves, tended by everyday black people struggling against racism during Reconstruction, and rekindled by those who refused to lower their eyes when met with Jim Crow's icy stare, roared up in combusting waves. In the words of civil rights veteran Fred Shuttlesworth, it was "a fire you [could not] put out!"[7]

"We know through painful experience," wrote Martin Luther King, Jr., from a Birmingham jail cell, "that freedom is never voluntarily given by the oppressor; it must be demanded by the oppressed."[8] To this we add: oppression exists nowhere without the consent of the oppressed. During the Civil Rights Movement, blacks demanded their freedom from whites. They found courageous ways to withdraw from their oppressors their cooperation.

The NAACP

The **National Association for the Advancement of Colored People (NAACP)** was the dominant black protest organization that preceded the modern Civil Rights Movement. Founded in 1909 by black and white intellectuals, the NAACP was a formal bureaucratic organization based in New York that did battle with racial domination primarily in the courts. Soon after its founding, the NAACP proved itself a force with which to be reckoned, winning several Supreme Court cases that dismantled legal barriers preventing blacks from voting. The organization also launched education programs targeting white America. Working on the assumption that white racism was rooted in ignorance of nonwhite peoples, the NAACP produced press releases, speeches, pamphlets, and a magazine (*The Crisis*), depicting nonwhite people as realistic, reasonable, and intelligent human beings. In direct opposition to the mainstream press, which depicted nonwhites as evil, crafty, and dim, the NAACP supported works that displayed and praised the accomplishments of nonwhite scholars, artists, and writers.[9]

As the NAACP grew stronger, incorporating more members and winning more court battles, so, too, did the opposition to it. At mid-century, precisely the time when the NAACP began fighting for the integration of public schools, whites launched a coordinated attack that would eventually bring the organization to its knees (for the time being). In 1956, most Southern state legislatures demanded that the NAACP release its membership lists. Observing that this was a strategy aimed at crippling the organization, sociologist Aldon Morris writes, "The intention was clear. If the NAACP yielded to this pressure and revealed its members' addresses, the members would suffer economic reprisals, violence, and other forms of repression. It was clear that the organization could be destroyed by exposing its members."[10] The NAACP refused to capitulate and, as a result, was outlawed in several Southern states. And cruel acts of terror were visited on NAACP leaders, such as Medgar Evers, Mississippi's first NAACP field secretary, who was fatally shot in the back on the steps of his home.

The white power structure was crippling the NAACP, but it could not subdue the black organizing tradition. The weakening of the NAACP seemed to strengthen a new kind of political protest, one that involved not just intellectuals and lawyers but ordinary people: sharecroppers, teachers, students—even children. This new movement was based in the South, where racial domination was most overt and bloody; and it waged its wars, not only in the courtrooms, but also in the streets, at segregated lunch counters, and from the inside of jail cells. Thus, civil rights organizing shifted from a model based on legal action to one based on direct action, from a bureaucratic organization to community-based groups. The result was the modern Civil Rights Movement.[11]

SCLC and Church-Driven Direct Action

Although blacks had engaged in direct action against white domination since the slave revolts, this form of political protest was revisited and reinvented in earnest after World War II. Black veterans who fought Hitler's armies returned to America only to ask, "How can my country criticize racism abroad but not at home? Why is it that America rightly defends Jews from Nazi violence but fails to defend blacks from white terrorism?" Many black soldiers, among them Medgar Evers, returned to their communities determined to stand up against racial injustice. They found support in the Double-V Campaign—"Victory at Home; Victory Abroad"—that was launched by a black newspaper, the *Pittsburgh Courier*.

Along with military veterans, black preachers and their congregants played a vital role in steering and energizing the Civil Rights Movement. More than any other institution, the black church would serve as the institutional hub of the movement. The church was relatively isolated from the white power structures that gripped the rest of society. It housed a mass base of blacks, who, under its roof, could voice their problems and needs in a safe space. And because it was financially independent, preachers did not have to worry about losing their jobs if they caused a stir; they answered only to the congregation. Thus, the black church would produce some of the most outspoken critics of white domination. There was Reverend T. J. Jemison, who led a boycott against segregated buses in Baton Rouge years before the better-known Montgomery bus boycott; there was Reverend Fred Shuttlesworth, who, having been whipped and beaten with chains for trying to enroll his children in an all-white public school and having his Birmingham house bombed one Christmas Eve, was fond of quoting

Jesus's injunction that "one must lose his life to find it"; and there was a young preacher from Atlanta, the son and grandson of preachers, bearing the name of a revolutionary who had come before him: Martin Luther King, Jr.[12]

One of the first major demonstrations of the Civil Rights Movement was the **Montgomery Bus Boycott,** which began a few days after December 1, 1955, when Rosa Parks, in defiance of Alabama segregation laws, refused to relinquish her bus seat to a white man. (Nine months earlier, a fifteen-year-old woman named Claudette Colvin had been expelled from a bus under similar circumstances. Soon thereafter, however, she became pregnant and was deemed by black clergy and other organizers an unfit face for the movement.[13]) Parks was bailed out of jail by E. D. Nixon, who, along with members of the Women's Political Council and the black clergy, had worked with Parks to organize the boycott. (In fact, the Women's Political Council had first conceived of the boycott and had been planning it for months. In popular historical accounts, the faces of the Civil Rights Movement typically belong to men, but the truth is that women also provided committed leadership as well as thankless labor throughout the struggle.[14]) It was soon decided that a new organization must be formed to support the boycott; hence, the Montgomery Improvement Association (MIA) was born. Nixon was nominated as head of the MIA but declined, keenly observing that a minister, who had his fingers on the pulse of and was greatly respected in the black community, would be better suited for the job. Nixon volunteered King, who had just arrived in Montgomery months earlier and whose oratorical skills Nixon greatly admired. King accepted.

Hundreds of Montgomery's blacks supported the boycott, refusing to ride on the segregated buses. The MIA organized carpools, funded primarily by black churches, to transport women and men to and from work. Mass meetings were held in churches, and pamphlets were distributed throughout the city's black community, discouraging citizens from riding the bus. As the boycott spread, whites flocked to organizations determined to maintain the racial status quo, organizations such as the White Citizen Counsel and the KKK. Some reacted with violence, firebombing black ministers' churches and houses. Nevertheless, the boycott persisted for more than a year, testifying to the determination and endurance of these civil rights activists.

By all standards, the Montgomery Bus Boycott was successful. For one, it helped to bring about a Supreme Court ruling, handed down on November 15, 1956, outlawing racial segregation on buses. What is more, the boycott trained hundreds of black activists in the teachings and tactics of nonviolent resistance, a form of weaponless warfare, inspired by Jesus and Gandhi, that encouraged people not only to resist striking back when struck but also to focus their energy on systematic racism, embedded in social institutions, rather than on individual people with racist beliefs. Next, news of the boycott was broadcast around the country, and this inspired other blacks to engage in direct confrontation with

racial domination through public and persistent protest. Finally, the boycott organized black clergy as a political force. The MIA would soon give way to a larger
and more powerful organization—the **Southern Christian Leadership Conference (SCLC)**—which was founded in 1957.[15]

The SCLC would serve as the key organization of the civil rights struggle. It
would organize many mass demonstrations, marches, boycotts, and rallies.
Under the encouragement of Ella Baker, it would also help to run Citizenship
Schools, that is, mini-courses (held in the backs of stores and the basements of
churches) that taught blacks to read so they could pass restrictive voting tests.
Miss Baker, as she was called, believed deeply in the goals of the SCLC but was
very critical of the style of charismatic (masculine) leadership that soon emerged
within the organization. She once stated, "I have always felt it was a handicap
for oppressed people to depend so largely on a leader. . . . Such people get so
involved with playing the game of being important that they exhaust themselves
and their time and they don't do the work of actually organizing people."[16] Miss
Baker reminds us that it is a mistake—we might call it the messiah myth—to
assume that the heart of the Civil Rights Movement beat within the chest of a
single person or of a select core of magical personalities, no matter how courageous or brilliant they might have been. King was a powerful leader, it is true;
but far greater was the power of the people. (Malcolm X was another powerful
leader of the black liberation struggle. He and the Black Panthers are discussed
at length in a later chapter.)

SNCC and Youth-Driven Direct Action

Miss Baker also was instrumental in the formation of the **Student Nonviolent
Coordinating Committee**, or **SNCC** (pronounced "snick"). Students had proven
themselves a powerful force in the movement, and Miss Baker suggested they
could benefit from collective coordination based on local leadership. Hence,
just as SCLC was formed out of preexisting networks made of black clergy
engaged in political action, SNCC (founded in 1960) incorporated into one
organization hundreds of politically mobilized young people, many of whom
were college students.

Students and young people had been involved in the modern Civil Rights
Movement since its inception. Among the first major demonstrations invented
and orchestrated by students were **sit-ins.** On February 1, 1960, four black freshmen at Greensboro's North Carolina Agricultural and Technical College took
seats at a "whites-only" lunch counter at the local Woolworth department store.
They were not served, though they repeatedly (and politely) asked for a menu
and remained on their stools until closing time. Word got out, and the following
day, twenty-four students took seats at the counter. By the end of the week, there
were more students who wanted to sit-in than there were seats to hold them.

The Greensboro events sparked a national movement. Hundreds of high school and college students staged sit-ins all around the South. The sit-ins captured the nation's attention and, in so doing, exposed the absurdity of Jim Crow laws. Here were American citizens, money in hand, simply asking for a cup of coffee or a turkey sandwich but being denied even these things. More: many were jailed and beaten for doing so. But the sit-ins persisted, and Jim Crow finally buckled. By the summer of 1960, many cities had desegregated their lunch counters. The sit-ins also reinvigorated the Civil Rights Movement by demonstrating the power of student-led public demonstrations and by drawing many white and nonwhite college students into the movement.[17]

Another key event initiated by young people was the **Freedom Rides** of 1961. The Supreme Court had just outlawed racial segregation in interstate bus terminals, and a small group of activists, made up of white and black members of a group called the Congress of Racial Equality (CORE), decided to "test" the new ruling. The group decided to charter two buses and to ride, white and black side-by-side, from Washington, D.C. to New Orleans. They got as far as Birmingham, the city King called "the country's chief symbol of racial intolerance,"[18] where the activists were beaten so severely by a white mob that the Freedom Rides were put on hold. Members of Nashville's SNCC chapter stepped in, offering replacement riders and encouraging the rides to continue. If the white mob was successful in stopping the Freedom Rides, it was argued, then violence would be seen as an effective weapon against the movement. The buses rolled out of Birmingham and made it to Montgomery, where riders were pulled from the buses and beaten again. As these violent scenes made front-page news, President Kennedy sent in federal marshals to protect the riders, who would eventually make it as far as Jackson, Mississippi. Freedom Rides would continue throughout the summer of 1961, further calling national attention to the plight of blacks in the South.

That same year, SNCC found itself in somewhat of a crisis. The organization was being pulled in two competing directions. One group of activists wanted SNCC to continue engaging in direct action aimed at desegregation, while another wanted it to focus on voter registration. At the very moment when it seemed SNCC would split, Miss Baker stepped in, speaking against disunity and urging the organization to form two arms—one focused on direct action and another on voter registration. SNCC followed Miss. Baker's advice, and the voter registration arm began devoting intense energy to confronting one of the biggest challenges facing the Civil Rights Movement: black disenfranchisement.[19]

Freedom Summer

Until now, we have concentrated primarily on large-scale demonstrations— dramatic, public, and relatively short-term. But from the Civil Rights Movement (and SNCC in particular) there emerged another kind of protest tradition, one

"Ordinary people who learn to believe in themselves are capable of extraordinary acts, or better, of acts that seem extraordinary to us precisely because we have such an impoverished sense of the capabilities of ordinary people." —Charles Payne

based in local organizing, long-term investment in community leaders, and very specific practical goals.[20] Miss Baker called the latter kind of tradition "spadework," referring to the nitty-gritty, tiresome, and unglamorous labor of chipping away at the white power structure day-by-day and door-to-door. Recognizing the importance of this kind of work, SNCC in 1961 deployed to the South a collection of grass-roots organizers determined to bring the vote to disenfranchised blacks living in rural poverty.

The situation was bleak. In several Mississippi counties, only one or two blacks out of a thousand were registered; in some counties the electorate was 100% white.[21] The SNCC workers knew they needed some help; so, in the summer of 1964, 1,000 volunteers, most of them white college students, were trained in nonviolent tactics and sent to Mississippi in a massive project known as **Freedom Summer.** The volunteers lived with black families, who cooked and looked after them, and worked toward two important goals. The first was increasing voter registration, a task that entailed building relationships with residents of the community and urging them to register. The second was bringing quality education to Mississippi's poorest areas (neglected by white society) through the establishment of Freedom Schools. These schools intended to teach black children not only reading, writing, and arithmetic but also self-worth, critical thinking, and leadership.[22]

Whites terrorized black families throughout the South, many committing acts of violence that went unpunished.

Freedom Summer was highly successful by many measures. Many blacks registered to vote, and the Freedom Schools attracted between 3,000 and 3,500 students, three times the number for which volunteers originally had hoped.[23] However, these victories came at a cost. White Mississippi did not yield easily. Just ten days into Freedom Summer, three volunteers, all in their early twenties—James Chaney, Michael Schwerner, and Andrew Goodman— set out to Mt. Zion United Methodist Church, which had been firebombed. Authorities found their bodies weeks later. The two white men, Goodman and Schwerner, had been shot, while Chaney, the black volunteer, was tortured before being shot three times. By the end of Freedom Summer, another volunteer had been killed, four critically wounded, eighty beaten, and one thousand arrested; thirty-seven churches had been bombed; and thirty homes had been burned.[24]

Many young white people sacrificed themselves for the sake of the civil rights struggle. This was certainly the case in Freedom Summer, when white participants repeatedly faced situations of mortal danger. But, more broadly, whites sacrificed all throughout the Civil Rights Movement. Recall, for example, Bill Moore, the white postman of whom we spoke in Chapter 1, who was murdered for his efforts on behalf of integration. And think, too, of Viola Liuzzo, a white woman (and mother of four), who was instrumental in organizing the Selma to

Montgomery March (discussed in the subsequent section) and who was killed by Klansmen on the final day of the march. Without the support of at least a significant number of antiracist whites, the cause of civil rights would never have made the gains it did. Blacks, of course, sacrificed even more.

The volunteers of Freedom Summer came face-to-face with the violence and hatred that had victimized Mississippi's black population for years. This was quickly realized when law enforcement officials, searching for the bodies of Chaney, Schwerner, and Goodman, dragged the Pearl River and discovered eight other bodies of murdered black men. One of the men had been decapitated. Reflecting on this macabre discovery, one volunteer wrote, "Mississippi is the only state where you can drag a river any time and find bodies you were not expecting. . . . Negroes disappear down here every week and are never heard about. Things are really much better for rabbits here. There is a closed season on rabbits when they may not be killed. Negroes are killed all year round. So are rabbits. The difference is that arrests are made for killing rabbits out of season."[25]

The Selma to Montgomery March
Although SNCC and SCLC had their differences, the two organizations often worked together. This was the case with the Freedom Rides and sit-ins, both supported by SCLC, and it was the case with the famous **Selma to Montgomery March.** The white power structure was firmly entrenched in Alabama, the state where four black girls were murdered when whites bombed the Sixteenth Street Baptist Church in Birmingham (a city that had grown so used to such attacks that it was nicknamed "Bombingham"), where police chief Eugene "Bull" Connor ordered firefighters to aim their water cannons at the legs of demonstrating black children, as the cannons were known to break legs, and where in Lowndes County—the stretch of land that activists would traverse during the Selma to Montgomery March—not a single black voter was registered. Local residents, determined to secure for blacks the right to vote, decided to stage a massive demonstration, a fifty-four mile trek from Selma to the steps of Alabama's capitol building.

On March 7, 1965, less than a month after a Selma police officer shot and killed Jimmy Lee Jackson during a mass gathering, hundreds of activists lined up in pairs and began the march. They never made it out of Selma, as sheriff deputies and state troopers, using billy clubs and tear gas, attacked the peaceful marchers, forcing them to retreat into town. So many demonstrators were injured that the black hospital soon overflowed with victims. Churches had to be turned into ad hoc hospitals. Because of this, the event is remembered as Bloody Sunday.

But the activists were determined to march. Immediately, SCLC leaders began organizing another march. King issued a press release, calling all American citizens who supported the Civil Rights Movement to join him in Selma, and hundreds responded to the call. At the end of the month, thousands of marchers set off again.(This was actually the third march. In a second go, the SCLC had conducted a partial march that amounted to a brief prayer gathering on Selma's Edmund Pettus Bridge.) Amidst hecklers who lined stretches of the highway waving Confederate flags and yelling racial slurs, they traveled fifty-four miles over the course of four days. On being asked about her weariness, one elderly woman marcher reflected, "My feets is tired, but my soul is at rest."[26] At the conclusion of the march, a crowd 25,000 strong gathered at the capitol building. King stood at the top of the steps and boomed to the swelling crowd, "Yes, we are on the move and no wave of racism can stop us. . . . The burning of our churches will not deter us. The bombing of our homes will not dissuade us. We are on the move now. The beating and killing of our clergymen and young people will not divert us. We are on the move now. The wanton release of their known murderers would not discourage us. We are on the move now. Like an idea whose time has come, not even the marching of mighty armies can halt us. We are moving to the land of freedom. . . . I come to say to you this after-noon, however difficult the moment, however frustrating the hour, it will not be long, because 'truth crushed to earth will rise again.' How long? Not long, because 'no lie can live forever.'"[27]

Roughly five months later, President Johnson signed into law the **Voting Rights Act of 1965**—one of the most significant victories of the Civil Rights Movement. The act prohibited voter discrimination, outlawed literacy tests, and gave the federal government power to oversee voter registration. As a result, for the first time in their lives—a full century after the fall of slavery—blacks were able to participate in American democracy. The results speak for themselves: Whereas only 5% of black Mississippians were registered voters in 1964, 24% were registered in 1968—a 380% increase.[28] Today, major Southern cities—even Birmingham and Selma—have had black mayors, and Southern states can boast of having the most black elected officials in the nation. The Civil Rights Move-ment had scored another major legislative victory a year earlier with the passage of the **Civil Rights Act of 1964.** That act cracked legal segregation, outlawing discrimination on the basis of race, religion, sex or national origin in hotels, theaters, transportation, restaurants, and the workplace.

Other Ethnic Movements

In addition to these legislative victories, the African American Civil Rights Move-ment inspired other marginalized groups to engage in similar tactics while fight-ing for deeper inclusion in American society.[29] The movement showed the nation that collective mobilization and enduring protest could bring about significant social change. Accordingly, other racial groups began to rise up and challenge white racism.

Just as African American political protest was rooted in the black organizing tradition, American Indian activism drew on a long legacy of Indian rebellion and resistance, symbolized by important figures, such as Geronimo and the Ghost Dancers, and key events, such as the defeat of Custer. However, American Indian activism was reenergized during the 1950s and 60s, not only by the Civil Rights Movement but also by its direct response to federal policies aimed at eroding tribal sovereignty and reservations. American Indians, from dozens of tribes, organized together against federal encroachment on Indian rights, the failure of government organizations (such as the Bureau of Indian Affairs) to address the needs of indigenous people, and the economic hardships that were wracking Native America. Tribes in the Pacific Northwest staged "fish-ins" in tribe-owned rivers and lakes that were being overrun by local and state officials; pan-Indian organizations, such as the **American Indian Movement** (founded in 1968) were formed, along with Indian newspapers; and between 1969 and 1978, American Indian activists participated in acts of civil disobedience that involved over seventy property seizures, including, in 1972, a week-long takeover of the Bureau of Indian Affairs headquarters. Like the black organizing struggle, many of these actions and demonstrations were organized and led by young people, especially American Indian college students.[30]

One of the most important demonstrations, one that drew the country's attention to the plight of American Indians and would spur on further activism, was the occupation of Alcatraz Island in November 1969. The protesters—including Wilma Mankiller, later to become the first woman Chief of the Cherokee Nation—wanted the federal government to release the island to Indians for the explicit development of Indian education. Indeed, the island belonged to them anyway, according to an 1868 Sioux treaty stating that all abandoned federal land that was once Sioux would be given back to the Sioux people. Federal marshals eventually removed the protesters, but not until June 1971—nineteen months after the occupation began. Although the protesters' formal demands went unmet, the Alcatraz standoff, and similar demonstrations, did raise people's awareness of the struggles of indigenous Americans and resulted in an American Indian cultural revival—manifest in the National Museum of the American Indian, dozens of university-sponsored American Indian Studies programs, and efforts aimed at preserving indigenous culture, religion, and language.[31]

Mexican-American-led movements emerged alongside those led by African Americans and American Indians. One of the most powerful protest movements addressed the pressing problems of migrant farm workers. César Chávez, a migrant worker from southern Arizona, emerged as an outspoken critic of migrant worker exploitation. Chávez organized workers, leading fasts, strikes, demonstrations, and nationwide boycotts to win contracts for poor migrant workers who picked grapes, berries, lettuce, and other crops under oppressive conditions.

"What really counts is labor: the human beings who torture their bodies, sacrifice their youth, and numb their spirits to produce this great agricultural wealth—a wealth so vast that it feeds all of America and much of the world. And yet the men, women, and children who are the flesh and blood of this production often do not have enough to feed themselves." —César Chávez

Chávez later cofounded the **United Farm Workers of America,** a labor union dedicated to "provide farm workers and other working people with the inspiration and tools to share in society's bounty." Through their organizing efforts, the United Farm Workers won many rights for migrant farm workers, Mexican American and otherwise, including union contracts that secured fair working conditions such as rest periods, access to clean water, and pension plans.[32]

As with the black liberation struggle, the battle against oppressive labor conditions on farmlands dotting the U.S.-Mexican border was bloody. Protestors were fired, beaten, and killed. After Rufino Contreras, a twenty-seven-year-old farm worker protesting the dreadful work conditions of lettuce pickers, was shot and killed in February 1979, Chávez, standing on top of a flatbed truck, delivered his eulogy to thousands of fellow farm workers: "What is the worth of a farm worker? Rufino, his father, and brother together gave the company twenty years of their labor. They were faithful workers who helped build up the wealth of their boss, helped build up the wealth of his ranch. What was their reward for their service and their sacrifice? When they petitioned for a more just share of what they themselves produced, when they spoke out against the injustice they endured, the company answered them with bullets; the company sent hired guns to quiet Rufino Contreras."[33]

Chávez continued, exhibiting keen sociological insight: "Capitol and labor together produce the fruit of the land. But what really counts is labor: the human beings who torture their bodies, sacrifice their youth, and numb their spirits to produce this great agricultural wealth—a wealth so vast that it feeds all of America and much of the world. And yet the men, women, and children who are the flesh and blood of this production often do not have enough to feed themselves. . . . If Rufino were alive today, what would he tell us? He would tell us, 'Don't be afraid. Don't be discouraged.' He would tell us, 'Don't cry for me, organize!'"[34]

Arab Americans—people who immigrated (or whose relatives once immigrated) to the United States from Arabic-speaking regions of the Middle East, including Algeria, Bahrain, Egypt, Iraq, Jordan, Kuwait, Lebanon, Libya, Mauritania, Morocco, Oman, Palestine, Qatar, Saudi Arabia, Sudan, Syria, Tunisia, United Arab Emirates, and Yemen—would also organize during the 1960s.[35] People of Arab descent had immigrated in large numbers since the 1870s (mostly in search of economic prosperity and religious freedom) and immediately had been met with white racism. They were depicted in the popular press as violent and malicious and in the popular media as conniving and wicked.[36] Although bound together by a common language, cultural practices, and lifestyles, many Arab Americans did not view themselves as such until the 1960s. During that time, the Middle East was undergoing major transitions owing to the creation of the Israeli state and the Six-Day War of 1967, a brief yet consequential conflict between Israel and Egypt, Jordan, Iraq, and Syria. Many Arabs felt that America's unwavering support of Israel was unfair and generated anti-Arab sentiment in the States. Arabs reacted by mobilizing politically, combating stereotypes, and urging U.S. politicians to seek more balanced solutions to Middle East conflicts. Lebanese, Iraqis, Syrians, and others of Middle Eastern heritage began viewing one another as a people with similar interests and struggles. They began referring to themselves as "Arabs."[37] Thus, the very term "Arab American" came about because people of Middle Eastern descent decided to mobilize around this pan-ethnic rubric.

Asian Americans, too, organized during this time, speaking out against racial domination, economic exploitation, and racial segregation. Some of their most vibrant and effective demonstrations took place in California. Within San Francisco's Chinatown, for example, political organizations were formed and peaceful demonstrations were carried out to protest city officials' neglect of their Chinese citizens. And college campuses all across the Golden State erupted with Asian-American activism.[38]

Asian-American student activists played a key role in forming the Third World Liberation Front, a multiracial organization founded on the campuses of the University of California—Berkeley and San Francisco State College. The Third World Liberation Front challenged these campuses' Eurocentric curricula, which distorted the histories and cultures of people of color. Seeking a "relevant education," as one of their posters declared, the Third World Liberation Front went on strike at both sites between 1968 and 1969. "Shut it down!" was their rallying cry, as student protestors formed picket lines, blocked campus entrances, disrupted classes, and marched on the president's office with a list of demands. Their demands included additional support for underrepresented students, the hiring of faculty of color, and the establishment of an Ethnic Studies College designed to help nonwhite students use their education to better their communities. The strike that took place at San Francisco State College was especially tumultuous, lasting five months and resulting in protestors being beaten and arrested by police officers. In the end, however, the university capitulated to many of the demands of the Third World Liberation Front, which is why, today, the College of Ethnic Studies at San Francisco State College—home to four departments: Asian American Studies, Africana Studies, Raza Studies, and American Indian Studies—is the largest in the nation.[39]

"To Stand in the Bright Sun and Cast a Long Shadow"

If we have devoted a fair amount of pages to the Civil Rights Movement, it is because the movement reshaped the fundamental meaning of American democracy and political engagement, changing the nature of race relations in America in multiple and momentous ways. Had it not been for the Civil Rights Movement, many of you would not be able to vote, to gaze out into your future and see unlimited possibilities, or even to enroll in the college you are at right now. And before we move to the next section, it is worth repeating that the backbone of the movement was the youth. It was young people who risked their lives during Mississippi's Freedom Summer, who sat silently at the lunch counters as mobs jeered and spat at them, who marched out of school and into jail cells when their parents could not. College students just like yourselves, women and men willing to "stand in the bright sun and cast a long shadow," in SNCC activist Bob Moses's elegant words, carried the Civil Rights Movement to its successful conclusion.

Were these young people an especially courageous lot, fearless and full of extraordinary virtue? "There are heroes and, emphatically, heroines enough in this history," answers Charles Payne. "Yielding to the temptation to focus on their courage, however, may miss the point . . . that ordinary people who learn to believe in themselves are capable of extraordinary acts, or better, of acts that seem extraordinary to us precisely because we have such an impoverished sense of the capabilities of ordinary people. If we are surprised at what these people accomplished, our surprise may be a commentary on the angle of vision from which we view them. That same angle of vision may make it difficult to see that of the gifts they brought to the making of the movement, courage may have been the least."[40]

White Backlash

Why did the Civil Rights Movement stop? It would be incorrect to assert that the movement ended because it had fulfilled all its goals. Neither the Civil Rights Act nor the Voting Rights Act fixed everything. If we were to assume that legal changes, no matter how significant, automatically change people's beliefs and practices—conditioned by hundreds of years of racial domination—we would be guilty of the legalistic fallacy. Many employers forced to take down their "Blacks Need Not Apply" signs simply continued their discriminatory practices more covertly. Recognizing this, civil rights activists sought to change not only the law but the very structures of society that perpetuate poverty, exploitation, and racial domination. Since these social ills are still with us today, we must admit that the Civil Rights Movement, for all its triumphs, ended with many goals unfulfilled.[41] So, why did the movement stop short? The answer lies in the **white backlash** that mounted in direct response to the Civil Rights Movement, a backlash fueled by conservatives and liberals alike.

The political right gained a new identity—and a new constituency—through their reaction to the Civil Rights Movement. When Alabama governor George Wallace stood in 1963 on the steps of the University of Alabama to block the entrance of two black students to the all-white university, he taught Republican politicians two strategic lessons. The first was that politicians who opposed racial justice could garner great support from white voters. Wallace discovered this himself. After receiving over 100,000 telegrams and letters commending him for his stand against racial integration at the university, he exclaimed, "The whole United States is Southern!"[42] Indeed, Wallace never lost an election in Alabama after 1963 and, though he was unable to win the presidency, he made a shockingly strong showing, winning 12.5% of the vote running on a third party ticket in the 1968 election. That means one out of every eight Americans voted for a man whose most famous line was "Segregation now! Segregation tomorrow! Segregation forever!" While running (oddly enough) in the Democratic primaries in 1972, Wallace reaped overwhelming support in several states, southern and northern: in Florida he captured 42% of the vote; in Michigan, he secured 51%.

The second lesson can be stated as an injunction: "Promote white supremacy, but never do so explicitly." When Wallace took his stand on the university steps, he claimed to do so, not because he opposed racial integration (although he said as much a few months earlier in his inaugural address) but because he opposed "illegal usurpation of power by the Central Government." By cloaking a race-specific issue (segregation) in race-neutral language (states' rights), he was able to win support from white Americans who were willing to endorse policies promoting racial inequality but would rather not get behind an overtly racist politician. As one Alabama senator said of Wallace: "He can use all the other

issues—law and order, running your own schools, protecting property rights—
and never mention race. But people will know he's telling them: 'A nigger's
trying to get your job, trying to move into your neighborhood.'"[43]

Other right-wing politicians would follow suit, using **coded language** to defend
the white power structure, though never explicitly. Richard Nixon appealed subtly
to racial stereotypes and fears, vowing to confront problems (like crime and moral
failure) that many white Americans wrongly assumed were nonwhite problems.
In 1969, Nixon's Chief of Staff, H. R. Haldeman, penned the following words in
his diary: "President emphasized that you have to face the fact that the whole
[welfare] problem is really the blacks. The key is to devise a system that recognizes
this, while not appearing to. . . . Pointed out that there has never in history been
an adequate black nation, and they are the only race of which this is true."[44]
Additionally, one of Nixon's top aides, Kevin Phillips, author of *The Emerging
Republican Majority*, convinced Republicans to work to expand black voting rights
in the South, "not as a moral issue, but because such a stratagem would hasten
the departure of southern whites into the Republican Party."[45] The strategy
worked, helping to polarize the electorate around racial politics and to recruit
masses of southern whites, who had been loyal Democrats since Reconstruction,
into the Republican Party (a shift known as the partisan realignment).

Ronald Reagan used racially coded language as well. While governor of
California, he opposed the Civil Rights Act of 1964 as well as the Voting Rights
Act of 1965, calling the latter "humiliating" to Southerners. In 1980, he opened
his campaign for the presidency with a speech in—of all places—Philadelphia,
Mississippi, the small town where Goodman, Chaney, and Schwerner had been
murdered. As one journalist observed, "It was at that sore spot on the racial map
that Reagan revived talk about states' rights and curbing the power of the federal
government. To many it sounded like code for announcing himself as the candidate for white segregationists."[46] While in the White House, Reagan, like
Nixon, grew adept at criticizing antipoverty programs, such as welfare, by drawing on whites' inaccurate assumption that most recipients of welfare were nonwhite and lacking in moral uprightness.

The ascendancy of the new conservatism—one overtly concerned with preserving "moral values" and "law and order" and covertly with pandering to the
white majority at the expense of racial justice—was a direct response to the Civil
Rights Movement. By opposing racial equality while never admitting doing so,
the right staged a successful counterrevolution against the Civil Rights
Movement—but not without help from the left. White liberals who supported
the Civil Rights Movement were faced with a fact many found unsettling: guaranteeing nonwhites freedom from discrimination and disenfranchisement meant
little if those laws were not accompanied by programs that attempted to compensate victimized groups for years of suffering. "Freedom is not enough,"

announced President Lyndon Johnson. "You do not take a person who, for years, has been hobbled by chains and liberate him, bring him up to the starting line of a race and then say, 'you are free to compete with all the others,' and still justly believe that you have been completely fair. . . . We seek not just freedom but opportunity—not just legal equity but human ability—*not just equality as a right and a theory but equality as a fact and as a result.*"[47] Past wrongs had to be redressed through reparatory action—a reality many liberals did not want to face.

White liberals feared that compensatory programs, such as affirmative action (which we discuss at length in the next chapter), would fracture the Democratic Party, allowing Republicans to gain political power. For that reason, they struck a devil's bargain with white supremacy, telling nonwhites that much progress had been made and that it was time to support a broader liberal agenda, one that focused, not on the wounds inflicted by racial domination, but on general social uplift. Thus, liberals mirrored their supposed political opposites by refusing to confront racism head on. They mirrored Republicans in another way as well: they sought to account for problems ravaging many nonwhite communities, not by examining the historical career of racial oppression or by investigating systematic forms of discrimination, but by blaming the failures on nonwhites themselves.[48] As Daniel Patrick Moynihan wrote in *The Negro Family*, a controversial report that located blame in the individual, not the system that created him, "at the center of the tangle of pathology is the weakness of the family structure. Once or twice removed, it will be found to be the principal source of most of the aberrant, inadequate, or antisocial behavior that did not establish, but now serves to perpetuate, the cycle of poverty and deprivation."[49]

Thus, in the mid-1960s, most white liberals joined their conservative counterparts in what sociologist Stephen Steinberg has called "a retreat from racial justice in American thought and policy."[50] One reason these politicians could so easily turn their backs on race was that they learned to bend the weapons of the Civil Rights Movement against the Movement. Most important, they learned to *appropriate the language* of the Civil Rights Movement while promoting agendas aimed at dismantling the movement—a process captured by the term **discursive co-optation.** Here, "discursive" refers to language, ideas, and meaning-making, whereas "co-optation" signals the strategic act of borrowing, manipulating, and deploying terms and ideas originally developed by political opponents.

On the right, politicians took from the Civil Rights Movement the notion that racial discrimination used to uphold the white power structure was unjust and, through an act of abstraction that involved a good deal of historical amnesia, distorted it into the concept of "color-blindness": the notion that public policies that address social problems created by centuries of racial domination are unjust.[51] (Audaciously, right-wing politicians criticizing affirmative action often summoned King's famous line that people should be judged "not by the color of their skin but by the content of their character," forgetting that King also believed that "America must seek its own ways of atoning for the injustices she has inflicted upon her Negro citizens."[52]) On the left, politicians invoked the language of racial equality but refused to support bold programs that had a fighting shot at achieving that goal. Instead, they maintained that real change would come about only through universal policies—"a rising tide lifts all boats," as President Kennedy once said—and advised nonwhites to stop fighting for systematic change and to start "fixing" their families.[53]

When it came to racial politics, most conservatives and liberals were hard to distinguish, joining voices to declare, "Let us speak of race no longer, for it is no longer significant. Let us, instead, champion the cause of universalism. After all, have we not made great progress?" And many nonwhites, abandoned and "hobbled by chains" of racial oppression, shook their heads and replied with a heavy voice: "Yes, progress has been made. But the promise of freedom—real freedom for people of color and poor whites alike—remains unfulfilled. There are fewer lynchings now than there were thirty years ago, but we all must bear in mind, as James Baldwin reminded us to do, that 'there are a great many ways to lynch a man.'"[54]

Partisanship and Representation

Having reviewed the arc of social movements led by people of color fighting for full inclusion in American society, as well as the white backlash that came in the wake of those movements, we might now ask, how do things stand now? Are people of color full citizens in American society, represented fairly, elected proportionately, and treated justly? In the remaining sections of this chapter, we shall address how race works in the present-day political field. As we shall see, American politics—as they have been since the Declaration of Independence— are conditioned by racial domination.

Partisanship and Racial Polarization

Let us begin by describing the racial demographics of political parties. Since the partisan realignment in the 1970s, most white voters have supported the Republican Party. In the last seven presidential elections, the majority of whites voted Republican; in fact, since 1960, in 10 out of 11 elections, most whites have backed the GOP ticket.[55] As one analyst put it, "if the electorate were entirely white, the GOP would always win the presidency."[56] Not only this, but many white Democrats, when given the choice between a white Republican and a nonwhite Democrat, have voted against their party. For instance, although New York City, by and large, has supported the Democratic Party, when David Dinkins, a black man, ran for mayor on the Democratic ticket in 1989, he received only

Party Identification Trend, by Demographic Groups

| | 2000 | | 2002 | | 2004 | | Minimum |
	Rep %	Dem %	Rep %	Dem %	Rep %	Dem %	N
White	32	29	35	27	34	29	15,613
Black	6	65	6	63	6	65	2,038
Hispanic	21	42	22	36	20	40	1,284

SOURCE: Pew Research Center, "Party Identification Trend, by Demographic Groups," http://people-press.org/commentary/pdf/95.pdf.

a minority of white votes. Over 70% of the city's whites, most of whom were registered Democrats, voted for the Republican candidate.

Most nonwhites, however, remain loyal Democrats. In the four national elections that took place between 2000 and 2006, most nonwhite voters cast their ballots for Democratic candidates. Exit polls from the 2006 elections, for instance, showed that 77% of nonwhites voted Democratic. In 2000, only four out of ten registered white voters were Democrats, whereas eight out of ten registered black voters backed the party. Since the presidential election of 1936, African Americans have proven to be a mainstay of the Democratic Party. Although Republicans enjoyed an increase in support after September 11, 2001, most African Americans did not partake in this shift. What is more, black loyalty to the Democratic Party remains virtually unaffected by socioeconomic standing; that is, poor, middle-class, and wealthy blacks alike pledge their support in equal numbers to the Democrats.[57]

Although some Hispanic voters did shift to the right after the September 11 attacks, most Hispanics voted Democratic. Upper-class Hispanics, however— unlike their lower-income counterparts—were more likely to register as Republicans, although they did so in far lower numbers than whites with similar incomes. We must not forget, moreover, the intraracial differences often overshadowed by the homogenizing header "Hispanic." While Puerto Rican Americans and Mexican Americans usually voted blue, most Cuban Americans, who since the 1970s generally have felt that Democrats cut Fidel Castro too much slack, stood by the Republican Party.[58]

These partial exceptions notwithstanding, the trend toward racial polarization continued in the 2008 election won by Barack Obama. Not surprisingly, black voters voted for the Democratic nominee in overwhelming numbers—95%— while Obama lost among white voters by a margin of 12%. (White men voted against him by a margin of 57% to 41%.[59]) Latino support for Obama also increased by 14% over the level of support given the Democratic nominee in

Party Affiliation among African Americans Sept. 2001–Oct. 2003

	Rep %	Dem %	N of cases
Total	7	64	5,406
Men	8	56	2,284
Women	6	69	3,122
18–29	9	53	1,342
30–49	6	66	2,224
50+	5	71	1,654
< $20k	8	63	1,145
$20–$30	6	66	749
$30–$50	6	69	1,007
$50–$75	6	66	531
$75–$100	7	66	273
$100k+	10	61	239

SOURCE: Pew Research Center, "Party Affiliation among African Americans," http://people-press.org/display.php3?PageID=750.

2004, Latinos preferring Obama over John McCain, the Republican nominee, by a margin of 67% to 31%.[60] (However, "South Florida's large Cuban-American population remained dependably Republican," according to election researchers.[61]) Overall, white voters accounted for no less than 90% of the Republicans' support, while nonwhites accounted for only 8% (1% black, 6% Hispanic, 1% Asian). The Democratic nominee, meanwhile, derived only 62% of his total support from whites, nonwhites contributing nearly all the rest (23% black, 10% Hispanic, 2% Asian).[62]

It appears, then, that the American electorate is **racially polarized:** the majority of whites tilt toward the GOP, while the majority of nonwhites lean in the opposite direction, offering solid support for the Democratic Party. This does not mean, however, that the Republican Party accurately represents the interests of America's white masses, nor does it mean that the Democratic Party pays much attention to issues that concern its nonwhite constituents. Indeed, our two-party system offers voters a very limited set of choices, and when the race is tight, candidates usually ignore their loyal supporters and cater to the swing voters in the middle. Thus, Republicans do not exert much effort crafting policies that will help poor whites, since they know most of these voters will back their platform regardless. Likewise, Democrats often ignore the interests of their nonwhite supporters, because they know most blacks and Hispanics will cast votes in their direction. Since the two-party system encourages candidates to pander to the white middle-class, nonwhite voices often go unheard, outright rejected by the party of Lincoln and quietly pushed aside by the party of Kennedy.

Political Representation?

In a society that praises its color-blind constitution and race-neutral political process, how can we make sense of such obvious racial polarization? The answer, of course, is that, far from being color-blind, American politics are deeply affected by racial domination. More than that: mainstream American politics actively *promote* racial domination by disadvantaging and silencing people of color. We need only look at how poorly nonwhites are represented by our elected government to justify this claim.

At the national, state, and local levels, who gets elected? The answer comes back: very few nonwhites. Over the entire span of U.S. history, 1,895 people have been elected to the Senate, of which only 19 (or 1%) were nonwhite. From 1966 to 2007, only one Native American has been elected to the Senate, along with four Hispanics, four Asian Americans, and three African Americans; the rest were white. Between 1966 and 2002, of the 316 people who served as state governors, 307 were white, 4 were Asian American, 4 were Hispanic, and 1 was African American. In other words, since the passage of the Voting Rights Act, 97% of these two high-ranking political positions have been held by whites. In the same time period, of the 6,667 House elections that took place in majority-white districts, Africans Americans clenched only 35 spots, less than 1%.[63]

Nonwhites do not fare much better in appointed positions, especially when Republicans are in power. Together, Ronald Reagan and George H. W. Bush appointed 558 judges to the federal bench, constituting 60% of the federal judiciary. Of those judges, most were young white men who identified as conservatives and generally were hostile to policies designed to dismantle racial inequality. Reagan went so far as to appoint William Rehnquist—an outspoken supporter of school segregation, who once expressed in a memo to another judge, "The Constitution does not prevent the majority from banding together. . . . It is about time the Court faced the fact that the white people in the South don't like the colored people"[64]—to the county's highest juridical post: Chief Justice of the Supreme Court. Although George W. Bush has appointed more nonwhite and women judges to the federal bench than any other Republican president, when it comes to ruling on civil rights legislation, his appointed cohort, too, has proven among the most conservative on record. With respect to issues pertaining to affirmative action, civil liberties, freedom of speech, and discrimination suits, an overwhelming majority of judges appointed by Bush (72%) voted against legislation that would extend citizens' civil rights.[65]

Just as the Civil Rights Act did not wipe out de facto racial discrimination in employment opportunities (we speak more about this in the next chapter), the Voting Rights Act did not automatically kick open the gates of political power. In the years following 1965, whites have maintained a virtual monopoly over seats of high political influence. But, you might ask, why does this matter? Do not whites, especially white Democrats, represent nonwhite voters just as well as would nonwhite politicians? This is an empirical question—one verified or denied only by examining social-scientific data—and researchers who have investigated this question have found that, unlike many nonwhite elected officials, white officials often do not work to meet the needs of their nonwhite constituencies.

Researchers have documented how, compared to white Democrats, nonwhites of the same party are more likely to represent the interests of their nonwhite constituents, to draft policy that matters to many nonwhites, and to sponsor bills and make speeches about racial justice.[66] In one such study, political scientist David Canon demonstrated that white members of Congress elected from districts with sizeable black populations were far less knowledgeable and attentive to the needs of their black constituents than were black legislators elected from similar districts. Does this mean that black elected officials only care about "black issues"? Canon found the opposite to be true. Although white legislators often do a poor job of representing black interests, black legislators often are proficient at representing the needs of their white constituencies.[67]

Put simply, many nonwhite politicians who are familiar with the unique hardships experienced by many nonwhite Americans, whose close friends and family members are nonwhite, and who have experienced American racism firsthand, seem able to marshal their political influence on behalf of nonwhite voters much more effectively than their white counterparts belonging to the same party. Many nonwhite voters are fully aware of this fact. In one survey, about two-thirds of blacks polled stated they believe black politicians are better at representing their needs than white politicians.[68] Perhaps now we can now understand why, once Senator Barack Obama, whose father is Kenyan and whose mother is white, tossed his hat into the presidential race leading up to the 2008 election, many African Americans began asking, "Is he black enough?"

Superficial versus Substantive Representation

That said, we must be wary of committing the tokenistic fallacy, mistakenly assuming that, say, all Latinos holding political positions care about the needs of Latino citizens or even are aware of those needs. Many prominent nonwhite politicians refuse to lobby for policies that promote racial justice or equality; in fact, some have been the most outspoken supporters of systems that uphold racial domination! Just as corporations tend to promote workers who are content with the status quo, workers who will not shake things up too much, houses of political power have preferred appointing to seats of influence nonwhites who do not pose much of a threat to white privilege.

Thus in 1991, when Clarence Thomas, an African American, was nominated to the Supreme Court by George H. W. Bush, major civil rights organizations, such as the NAACP and the Urban League, protested because Thomas opposed many policies designed to bring about racial equality. Thomas was appointed to the bench nonetheless, and, since then, he has become one of the most conservative voices on the Court, exerting no energy to intervene on behalf of African Americans. When reporters asked the retiring Justice Thurgood Marshall, whom Thomas replaced on the court, if he thought a black judge should take his place, Marshall replied, "My dad told me long ago, 'There's no difference between a white snake and a black snake. They'll both bite.'"[69]

Thurgood Marshall knew that one's race does not guarantee one's political convictions. We would be well served to remember this, noting, too, that some nonwhites have ascended to high posts precisely because they have colluded with racial domination. Thus, when it comes to nonwhite political leadership, we should distinguish between **superficial representation** and **substantive representation.** Superficial representation speaks to the process of appointing to political positions nonwhites disconnected from the needs and problems of most nonwhite citizens. Thus, because Secretary of State Condoleezza Rice and Attorney General Alberto Gonzales did not leverage their political clout to dismantle racial domination, we might consider their appointments examples of superficial representation. By contrast, Thurgood Marshall, a great-grandson of a slave and the first African American to serve on the Supreme Court, was very concerned about the liberties and lives of nonwhite Americans. Marshall's appointment to the bench was an example of substantive representation, genuine political representation marked by a correspondence between the goals of nonwhite representatives and those of nonwhite citizens. Superficial representation cares only about diversity in skin color, not diversity in political conviction. Substantive representation is not satisfied until both these requirements are met; it requires not only that political representatives be drawn from nonwhite communities but also that they be committed to working on behalf of those communities.[70]

Gerrymandering

We cannot conclude our discussion of political representation without unpacking the complicated system of political maneuverings known as **gerrymandering.** The word was coined around the beginning of the nineteenth century when American statesman Elbridge Gerry (who would serve as the country's fifth Vice President) created an irregularly shaped political district to secure his reelection. Many thought Gerry's district resembled a salamander. Hence: Gerry + salamander = gerrymander.[71] Thus, gerrymandering is the processes by which elected politicians redraw and manipulate the borders of political districts to secure political advantage.

Here is how it works: Pretend you are a Republican elected to Congress. To secure an easy reelection, one with the least amount of competition possible, you gather sympathetic state legislatures and begin thinking of ways to redraw your state's congressional districts. Further pretend that your state is made up of four electoral districts, each of which has an equal number of white and nonwhite voters. Because you know that most of the white voters in your state will vote Republican, while most of the nonwhite voters will vote Democratic, you use two strategies to dilute the nonwhite vote. First, you *pack* as many nonwhite voters as you can into one district. Republicans will lose the next election in this district, but it is no matter, for you know your party will win the remaining three districts. Why? Because you have successfully *cracked* the nonwhite vote, spreading it thinly over the three redrawn districts and thus severely limiting nonwhites' ability to vote as a group (what is known as bloc voting). If you are successful, you will have created a political arrangement where many nonwhite votes are wasted. They are wasted in the packed district, because their candidate of choice will easily win the race by receiving an overwhelming amount of support. In the cracked districts, however, nonwhite votes are wasted, because they are drowned out by the white majority. They have little influence, since they constitute such a small percentage of the constituency.

Many civic leaders seeking to increase the political representation of nonwhite groups actually have favored "majority-minority districts," which purposefully are created to promote minority bloc voting. Arizona's second Congressional district was redrawn to ensure that the Navajo Nation and the Hopi Tribe—two tribes that have an antagonistic history—are represented by different congresspersons. That way, Hopi concerns are not overlooked by a representative pandering to the Navajo majority. Because the Hopi reservation is enveloped by the larger Navajo reservation, the oddly shaped district surrounds the Hopi reservation before snaking west, following a chain of rivers for hundreds of miles, before broadening out to cover the northwest area of the state. Similarly, Illinois's fourth Congressional district was designed to join two Hispanic areas separated geographically. Thus, the district surrounds one neighborhood before making its way west, narrowly following Interstate Highway 294, then circling back east to surround the other Hispanic area.

Because it is very difficult for nonwhite politicians to get elected in majority white districts, and because (as we have already seen) most nonwhite legislatures better represent the interests of nonwhite voters, some have argued that drawing districts in which nonwhites can exhibit significant influence over the election helps to secure nonwhite representation. Others, however, have pointed out that this form of packing the vote concentrates nonwhite influence in a single district and can diminish Democratic power writ large since reorganized electoral boundaries remove nonwhite voters from white Democratic districts.[72]

In the early nineties, the Supreme Court set down rulings in *Shaw v. Reno* (1993) and *Miller v. Johnson* (1995) that deemed race-based gerrymandering unconstitutional. In both cases, plaintiffs took issue with newly created black-majority districts redrawn in North Carolina and Georgia, respectively. The Court did not outlaw the practice of gerrymandering in general, just gerrymandering based on race. Writing for the majority, Justice Sandra Day O'Connor argued: "Racial classifications of any sort pose the risk of lasting harm to our society. They reinforce the belief, held by too many for too much of our history, that individuals should be judged by the color of their skin. . . . Racial gerrymandering, even for remedial purposes, may balkanize us into competing racial fractions."[73]

If we carefully consider the Court's decision, we can witness how whiteness works in the highest echelons of political power. In these rulings, the Court adopted a definition of race that pertained only to nonwhite people. White majority districts were treated as raceless, normal, and perfectly legal; but black majority districts were considered raced, harmful, and illegal. By outlawing race-based gerrymandering while allowing for political gerrymandering, the Court failed to recognize white majority districts *as white districts*. Whiteness was thus rendered invisible, while "race" came to mean "not white." As some social scientists have put it, "Whites who insist on color-blind redistricting are really demanding an electoral system that acknowledges *their* majority status. Their objection is to districts where they are not the majority, where they might have to relinquish the privileges of their racial status."[74]

What we must not fail to realize is that for all the sacrifices and struggles borne by those thousands of civil rights warriors who organized and marched and died to win full inclusion in white-dominated America, just and fair political representation has not yet arrived for people of color. The issue is no longer whether nonwhites have equal access to the voting booth. The issue is whether their votes matter as much as white votes, whether the demands of nonwhite citizens effectively can influence the course of this country, and whether their lives demand the attention of the political leaders of our democracy or are muted by the white majority.

Alexis de Tocqueville worried about this. The author of *Democracy in America* (1835) observed that our political system often is steered by majority interests that overrun minority rights and concerns, a problem he called the **tyranny of the majority.** "What is a majority," he asked, "in its collective capacity, if not an individual with opinions, and usually with interests, contrary to those of another individual, called the minority? Now, if you admit that a man [or a woman] vested with omnipotence can abuse it against his adversaries, why not admit the same concerning a majority? . . . My greatest complaint against the democratic government as organized in the United States is not, as many Europeans make out, its weakness but rather its irresistible strength."[75]

Voting

If we explore today's voting patterns, we quickly observe that race plays a decid-ing role in determining voter turnout and political preferences. Repeatedly, stud-ies have shown that both nonwhites and whites will rush to the polls in larger numbers if the ticket is racially mixed than during elections when all candidates are of the same race. If, say, a Hispanic woman is running for city council, Hispanic voters, knowing that this candidate is more likely to represent their interests than her white counterpart, will do their best to see that she is elected. That logic is straightforward, but it is not immediately clear why white voters will turn out in larger-than-usual numbers when the ticket is mixed. Not only this, but white voters are much more politically mobilized in communities that are racially integrated than in homogeneous ones. For decades, social scientists have documented that, as the size of the nonwhite population increases, so too does white voter turnout.[76] What could explain this trend?

The answer begins to materialize once we examine how whites in racially mixed areas tend to vote. Overwhelmingly, these whites exhibit more racially conservative opinions than whites living in majority-white communities. To put it another way, as the nonwhite population increases, so, too, do white voter turnout *and* whites' levels of racial intolerance. Political scientists have explained this relationship through the **threat hypothesis**, which holds that, compared to whites who live in racially homogeneous areas, whites who live near nonwhites are more likely to develop racist attitudes about nonwhite people. Accordingly, whites in these areas are prone to oppose public policies designed to combat racial inequality.[77] This is as true today as it was during 1968, when George Wallace ran for president. In the Northern states, Wallace received the most votes in white neighborhoods that adjoined black enclaves.[78]

The Effects of Racial Attitudes on Voting Behavior

Once we examine how policy and candidate preferences vary across racial groups, we are immediately struck by obvious and substantial differences. Although no racial group should be treated as a unified mass—there is great variation among Asians, whites, Arab Americans, and other racial groups along all lines, political and otherwise—it is nonetheless true that racial groups, to varying degrees, exhibit a coherent set of political persuasions. In the post-Civil Rights Era, class-based voting has decreased, whereas race-based voting has increased. That is, all else equal, working-class and middle-class citizens do not vote very differently from one another; however, white and nonwhite citizens (again, all else equal) exhibit very different voting patterns.[79]

With respect to race-specific policies (for example, civil rights, equal economic opportunity, affirmative action), whites and nonwhites, in aggregate, hold drastically different stances. Consistently, whites disapprove of policies aimed at improving nonwhites' quality of life. Consider these statistics from the National Election Study: 90% of blacks polled thought "the government should ensure fair treatment of blacks," whereas only 46% of whites felt the same way; 50% of whites thought that securing fair treatment for blacks "was not the government's business," while only 7% of blacks felt the same way. Over 74% of blacks and 18% of whites believed that "federal spending on programs that assist blacks should be increased." By contrast, 20% of whites and 3% of blacks thought it should be decreased. When it came to affirmative action, 50% of blacks strongly favored policies promoting employment hiring and promotional preferences, while only 5% of whites felt likewise.[80]

Are these differences strictly race-based, or can they be explained by other factors? That is, what is more important in determining voters' opinions about racial politics, one's racial attitudes or her education, political party, religion, or other qualities? Several studies have demonstrated convincingly that racial attitudes are the single most important factor when it comes to determining opinions about public policies promoting racial equality. As David Sears and colleagues discovered through several statistical tests, for white Americans, racial attitudes—measured by one's opinions about continuing discrimination, positive or negative emotions toward nonwhites, and stereotypes of nonwhites—are more important than political ideology, party identification, educational level, and demographic variables (like one's sex and age) in predicting one's evaluation of race-specific policies and political candidates.[81] In another study, Martin Gilens evaluated whites' views of welfare. Since the Reagan years, welfare has emerged as a program that many associate with poor black women (even though most welfare recipients are white). But do many whites oppose welfare because of their dislike of blacks or for other reasons dissociated from race? Gilens provides strong evidence that whites' perception of blacks as "lazy" has a more powerful effect on their evaluations of welfare policy than anything else, including their political party, financial interests, or beliefs about American individualism.[82]

Principle-Implementation Gap

Since the Civil Rights Movement, opinion polls have shown that most white Americans increasingly have accepted the *principle* of racial inclusion while rejecting, time and again, any sort of *policy measures* designed to carry this out. For instance, between 1963 and 1986, white attitudes in favor of school integration increased by 30%, but white support for federal programs intending to do just that declined by 9%.[83] The same is true across a wide range of issues: whites seem to disapprove of discrimination in housing and racial segregation but are unwilling to support federal programs aimed at combating these problems; and

Attitudes toward Principle of School Integration and toward Federal Implementation of School Integration

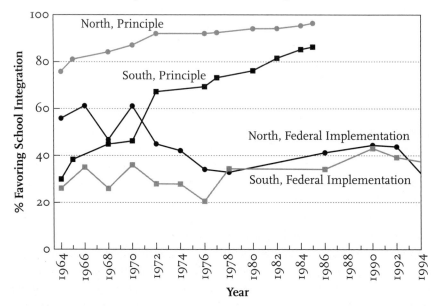

SOURCE: Howard Schumann et al., *Racial Attitudes in America: Trends and Interpretations,* Revised Edition (Cambridge: Harvard University press, 1997), p. 126, fig. 3.8

most whites claim to disapprove of racialized poverty, though they also disapprove of most race-based antipoverty programs. Social scientists have referred to this disconnect as the **principle-implementation gap.**[84]

The principle-implementation gap can be explained by examining whites' ideas about how race works in the world. According to a recent poll, 34% of whites believe that racial inequalities are caused by systematic discrimination, whereas 52% believe that they are brought about because nonwhites "lack motivation." Informed (knowingly or unknowingly) by ideas that emerged from the white backlash following the Civil Rights Movement, most whites today explain racial disparities by blaming the victim, just as Moynihan did in his scathing report. They suggest that, if nonwhites want full inclusion into American society, all they need to do is to work hard.[85] As a matter of fact, whites committed to the norm of individualism—the very American idea that social problems and achievements can be explained solely by examining individual-level characteristics (for example, talent, drive, intelligence)—are very likely to reject policies aimed at uplifting disadvantaged racial groups.[86]

This view of the world rests on a double rejection, one that, on the one hand, participates in the ahistorical fallacy by forgetting the history of racial

domination—years and years of economic deprivation, psychological humiliation, social exclusion, and political domination—and, on the other hand, refuses
to acknowledge modern-day discrimination, proof of which we offered in the
first chapter and offer throughout this book. If these opinion polls are correct
in their finding that the majority of white Americans participate in this double
rejection, then we must conclude that the majority of white Americans fundamentally misunderstand how race works in contemporary society. "But we are
all entitled to our own opinion about this," one might reply. Opinion has nothing to do with it. Questions about the causes of racial inequality are scientific
questions, exclusively satisfied by scientific proof. And in this case, social science
disconfirms the idea that discrimination and history do not matter. You very well
might be of the "opinion" that individual failings, and individual failings alone,
account for racial inequalities, just as you might be of the "opinion" that the sun
revolves around the Earth.

Voter Intimidation and Felon Disenfranchisement

Today, almost a half-century after the passage of the Voting Rights Act of 1965,
many people of color still face modern-day voter intimidation, which mirrors, in
a softer and shrewder form, techniques deployed by southern whites during the
mid-twentieth century. Less than a month before the 2008 presidential election,
a supporter of the Republican ticket displayed in several of Philadelphia's black
neighborhoods fliers "warning that people with outstanding warrants or unpaid
parking tickets could be arrested if they show up at the polls on election day." In
2006, a congressional campaign worker for California's Orange County Republican Party circulated a letter, written in Spanish, to roughly 14,000 Hispanics,
threatening them with arrest if they voted. "You are advised that if your residence
in this country is illegal or you are an immigrant," the letter warned, "voting in
a federal election is a crime that could result in jail time." (It goes without saying
that naturalized immigrants older than eighteen have voting rights.) That same
year, Native American voters attempting to participate in South Dakota's primary
were asked to show a valid photo ID at the polling place—a mandate not required
by either federal or state law. Those who did not have such an ID were not given
a ballot. In 2003, black Philadelphians systematically were targeted and challenged at the polls by "official looking" men who carried clipboards and drove
sedans doctored up (with magnetic signs) to look like law enforcement vehicles.
A year before that, hundreds of fliers were displayed in African-American neighborhoods in Louisiana explaining that citizens could vote on December 10. The
polls closed on December 7. In 1998, a South Carolina state representative distributed 3,000 brochures to African-American communities, warning voters that
police officers would be "working" the polls and advising them that "this election
is not worth going to jail."[87] These examples (but a few of many) demonstrate

that Jim Crow, though driven underground by the Civil Rights Movement, lives on in twenty-first-century America, working to secure white political power by tried-and-true strategies of voter intimidation and suppression.

Many democratic elections across the globe are tainted by some form of voter intimidation (race-based or otherwise). However, America is unique in another practice that disproportionately strips the right to vote from nonwhites. The United States is the only democracy that disenfranchises felons *as well as ex-felons*. Sociologists estimate that 5.3 million American citizens (1 adult in every 40) are denied the right to vote because of felony convictions. Most of these people are ex-felons, individuals who have served their time. In the abstract, **felon disenfranchisement** has nothing to do with race; however, on closer inspection, we discover a clear connection between felon disenfranchisement and racial domination. For one, when we examine when states adopted laws denying felons voting rights, we notice that many states did so after the ratification of the Fifteenth Amendment, which gave black men the right to vote. From inception, felon disenfranchisement was conceived as an effective way to diminish nonwhite political power. This was especially true for newly manumitted slaves. As the prison emerged to replace the slave plantation as the major social institution used to disempower African Americans, blacks would be imprisoned, and therefore disenfranchised, at much higher rates than would whites. Indeed, as Jeff Manza and Christopher Uggen demonstrate in *Locked Out: Felon Disenfranchisement and American Democracy*, states where blacks constituted a significant proportion of the prison population were more likely to adopt and expand felon disenfranchisement laws than states where the black prison population was relatively small.[88]

On this account, things have not changed much. Because the criminal justice system, which we discuss at length in Chapter 6, is guided by, and works to reinforce, racial domination, blacks and Hispanics are imprisoned at disproportionately high rates. Just as they were a century ago, nonwhites, and blacks in particular, are the people most severely affected by today's felon disenfranchisement laws. Nationwide, suffrage rights have been denied to at least one in seven black men. In the states with the highest black disenfranchisement rates, as many as *one in four* black men cannot vote.[89] These are troubling statistics for a democracy that prides itself on the principle of universal suffrage. And lest we think the proportion of disenfranchised felons and ex-felons is inconsequential, we need only remember the 2000 presidential race. To win, the Republican nominee, George W. Bush, had to carry Florida—the country's leader in felon disenfranchisement with over 1.1 million citizens (10% of the constituency) denied the right to vote. Like in other states, a disproportionate number of these disenfranchised citizens were African American: 293,000, to be exact, of whom 205,000 had completed their sentences. This amounted to 19% of the black electorate. Political analysts estimate that, had these former felons been allowed

Timeline of Statehood and Disenfranchisement, 1787–1864, 1865–1899

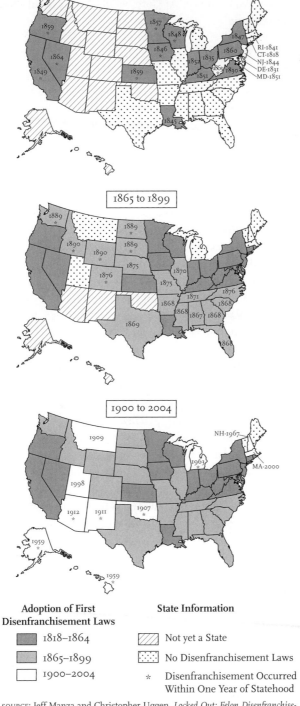

1787 to 1864

1865 to 1899

1900 to 2004

Adoption of First Disenfranchisement Laws

■ 1818–1864
■ 1865–1899
□ 1900–2004

State Information

▨ Not yet a State
⠿ No Disenfranchisement Laws
* Disenfranchisement Occurred Within One Year of Statehood

SOURCE: Jeff Manza and Christopher Uggen, *Locked Out: Felon Disenfranchisement and American Democracy* (New York: Oxford University Press, 2006) pp. 50–51, fig. 2.2.

to vote, the Democratic nominee, Al Gore, would have carried Florida, thereby clinching the presidency.[90]

Elections

It was 1988, and, according to all the polls, Massachusetts governor Michael Dukakis would be the next president of the United States. Dukakis was pummeling his Republican opponent, George H. W. Bush. The Republicans needed something to sink Dukakis, and they would find it after assembling a thirty-person focus group of swing voters, people who had voted for Reagan but were planning to vote for Dukakis in the upcoming election. The moderator began reviewing the governor's political record, asking for participants' reactions, and, eventually, he hit on an issue that struck a nerve with the focus group. A young black man named Willie Horton, a convicted murderer serving a life sentence in a Massachusetts prison, had escaped while on a weekend furlough. Ten months later, Horton had broken into the home of a white couple, beating and stabbing Cliff Barnes and raping his fiancé, Angela Miller. On hearing this story, focus group participants recoiled in disgust. Fifteen of the thirty voters changed their minds: they would no longer support Dukakis. The Republicans had found what they were looking for.[91]

Bush soon began repeating Horton's story, using it to accuse Dukakis of being "soft on crime." Bush mentioned Horton during speeches, and the news media covered the story heavily, repeatedly displaying Horton's picture: a large, cold-faced black man with a mature afro. Television and radio ads featured the story. One television ad displayed a picture of Horton's mug shot as a voice intoned, "Dukakis not only opposed the death penalty, he allowed first-degree murderers to have weekend passes from prison." A radio commercial featuring Cliff Barnes was perhaps even more damaging. Barnes voice's echoed over the radio waves: "Mike Dukakis and Willie Horton changed our lives forever. . . . For twelve hours, I was beaten, slashed, and terrorized. My wife, Angie, was brutally raped. . . . Dukakis simply looked away."[92] Republicans repeated Horton's name so much that, years after 1988, polled voters would report remembering three names about the election: Bush, Dukakis, and Horton.[93]

Bush began gaining ground. He caught up to Dukakis, and, in early October, when the story was receiving the heaviest news coverage, he took the lead. During this time, no one—not the media or either political party—mentioned race. Instead, the Horton story was about crime and liberal policy. This changed in late October, when Jessie Jackson, who had been the runner-up for the Democratic nomination, accused the Bush campaign of tapping into whites' fears of blacks, especially their fear of the black male rapist and his white women victims (an image, as we have already learned, rooted in the ritual of lynching that came to prominence after Reconstruction). Once race was mentioned, Bush's ratings began to drop, but it was too late. In an upset victory, Bush won the presidency, and, in the end, all parties involved admitted that he would not have prevailed without the help of the heinous acts of Willie Horton.[94]

Implicit Racial Appeals

There is substantial evidence that Bush's campaign intentionally used Horton's image as a racially motivated appeal to garner white votes. From day one, Bush aides were fully aware of Horton's race.[95] Indeed, several other white criminals had escaped from the Massachusetts furlough program and had committed violent crimes, yet they were never mentioned by the Republicans.[96] Even the name "Willie Horton" was a Republican creation, coined by Bush's campaign manager, Lee Atwater—a southern white accustomed to referring to black men with emasculating labels—who changed William Horton (the name Horton went by) into the boyish "Willie."[97] This does not mean that all right-wing political appeals are racially motivated. Had the Bush campaign featured one of the white furlough escapees to criticize Dukakis and to promote Bush as a "law and order" candidate, it would not have been a racial appeal. But this strategy would not have packed the same punch. Bush was able to beat Dukakis—who, pre-Horton, was ahead by no less than twenty percentage points—only because his use of racial imagery connected with the racialized dispositions of a mass of white voters.

As we have already seen in this chapter, this country's political system is deeply divided by race. Since the partisan realignment, our two-party system has been driven and organized around issues of race: the Democratic Party has secured loyalty from most nonwhites, while the Republican Party has become virtually an all-white organization. Thus, Republicans have much to gain by ignoring nonwhite citizens and attracting white voters through racial appeals. However, since the Civil Rights Movement, racism has been outwardly decried by most Americans. In these times, nobody wants to be labeled a racist or to get behind a politician who is labeled as such. Today's politicians no longer can employ explicit racist appeals to win support in the ways they could forty years ago. (During the 1970 Alabama gubernatorial race, a group called Committees for [George] Wallace displayed newspapers ads with a young blond girl sitting on a beach surrounded by seven grinning black teenage boys, accompanied by the caption: "This Could be Alabama Four Years From Now."[98]) Those who do—as Pat Buchanan did in his 1996 bid for the presidency, advocating strict immigration, because most immigrants "are not English-speaking white people from Western Europe [but] Spanish-speaking brown and black people from Mexico, Latin America, and the Caribbean"[99]—usually do not ascend to the highest posts. This fact testifies to the attenuation of racial domination in American politics.

Thus, the American political field is characterized by a fundamental tension: on the one hand, deep racial cleavages split the electorate and its political parties;

on the other hand, most Americans and their representatives support (at least publicly) racial equality. As a result, politicians hoping to secure whites' support by "playing the race card" must do so through **implicit racial appeals.** In the words of political scientist Tali Mendelberg, "The power of implicitly racial appeals today is due to the coexistence of two contradictory elements in American politics: powerful egalitarian norms about race, and a party system based on the cleavage of race. Politicians convey racial messages implicitly when two contradictory conditions hold: (1) they wish to avoid violating the norm of racial equality, and (2) they face incentives to mobilize racially resentful white voters."[100]

White voters need not be outspoken racists for implicit racial appeals to resonate with them. Indeed, research suggests that implicit racial appeals can backfire when they are rendered explicit, when voters recognize the appeals as fundamentally racial in content.[101] (Recall that George H. W. Bush dropped in the polls once people began noticing the racial intent of the Willie Horton story.) What implicit racial appeals rely on are white voters' deep-seated racialized dispositions—habits, feelings, and convictions that sometimes rest beneath the level of consciousness. These dispositions are conditioned by major social institutions (schools, families, religious institutions), which themselves are products of a history of racial domination. Our racialized dispositions may lie relatively dormant until triggered by suggestive images (a mug shot of a black man) or coded language ("welfare queen," "urban unrest," "illegal immigrants," "Islamic terrorists") that lead us to alter our political persuasions. But implicit racial appeals must be made with great precision and sophistication; our racial resentment must be awakened without our knowledge. And those who use racial appeals must always have a way of denying they are doing so.

Bush was not the first politician to use implicit racial appeals—nor was he the last. During Tennessee's 2006 Senate race, the Republican National Committee released a commercial targeting the Democratic nominee, Harold Ford, who would have been the first southern black man elected to the Senate since Reconstruction. At one point in the ad, an attractive white woman with blonde hair giggles, "I met Harold at the Playboy party!" The commercial ends with the white woman winking at the camera and whispering suggestively, "Harold, call me." The commercial tapped into an enduring taboo—sexual relations between black men and white women—one seen as especially scandalous in Southern states. Ford lost the election.

The Role of the Media

Journalists and reporters can prime our racial dispositions just as effectively as politicians. Indeed, by displaying Willie Horton's face on nightly news programs and in newspaper stories, the media played a deciding role in carrying out the Republicans' strategy. With the rise of twenty-four-hour news networks and their accompanying political pundits, the news media has asserted itself as a powerful force in our society. Media spokespersons often summon up racial cues and coded language when reporting a story or debating an issue. This can be done in multiple ways. Reporters can overemphasize some details and underemphasize others. For instance, leading up to the 2008 presidential elections, some reporters, over and over, pointed out that Barack Obama's middle name is Hussein, thereby linking him to Saddam Hussein and growing anti-Arab sentiment. News stations can also hand-select guest "experts" to comment on a developing story. During a recent Fox News program, a guest named Mark Fuhrman, a former detective for the LAPD, commented on the O. J. Simpson case, saying, "I dealt with people like this every day for twenty years. They will get up every day. They will kill somebody and go have some chicken at KFC."

But just how much influence do the media have over our thinking about race? A substantial amount, according to recent research. Consider an experiment designed by Nicholas Valentino in 1996, when Bill Clinton was running for reelection against Bob Dole. Valentino showed the participants a video clip of a local news station reporting a crime. The video was manipulated such that some participants watched a crime story where no suspects were implicated, while others were shown the same story with suspects: some saw white suspects, others saw nonwhite suspects. Another group of participants was the control group: they were not shown a video at all. When Valentino asked participants to evaluate Clinton and Dole, he discovered sizable differences between the groups. Clinton was highly favored by the group who did not watch the video, but his percentage lead over Dole dropped by twenty points when Valentino polled the group that was shown the crime story with no suspect as well as the one that watched the story with a white suspect. Clinton fared worse with the group that viewed the crime story with a nonwhite suspect. In this case, his percentage lead over Dole dropped by a startling forty percentage points as compared to the control group. This experiment demonstrated at least two things: (1) voters' approval of a Democratic candidate drops steeply when they are shown images that link nonwhites with crime; and (2) the media wield impressive power over our thinking.[102]

Civil Society

In a democracy such as America's, politics is not only about those who hold political office; it is also about ordinary citizens, who, collectively, hold the power to change society. Hence, a chapter on politics and race cannot end without a discussion of the everyday interactions and exchanges that constitute democratic life. That area of social life where we find public debate, community organizing, and citizen-led political mobilization is called **civil society**.[103]

Coded language and implicit racial appeals are not limited only to politicians and media representatives. In everyday talk, we use communicative cues (verbal and nonverbal) to articulate our opinions about racial groups and racial issues, sometimes through understated and inarticulate language. *"I'm not racist, but I think a lot of Native Americans would be better off if they started working harder and stopped their, well, addictions."* Here, the speaker distances herself from racism while advancing a racial claim. *"I have a lot of black friends, so I can make this joke."* In this case, the speaker believes he is permitted to crack an offensive joke about blacks simply because he knows a few. *"Why don't I have any Mexican friends? They keep to themselves. I think they're prejudiced against us."* Through an act of projection, this speaker fails to recognize how her racialized dispositions influence her friendship circles, blaming her Mexican peers for self-segregation. *"Racially profiling Arabs in airports is not about race. It's about national security."* This speaker deracializes a clearly racial issue, refusing to see how strategies that claim to protect all Americans seem to have the opposite effect for Americans of Arab descent. *"Compared to us, Asians have it easy."* This speaker, absorbed only by the problems affecting the group with whom she identifies, fails to notice injustices affecting Asian Americans; unintentionally, she supports racial domination by pitting nonwhite groups against one another in a kind of "suffering competition." In each of these statements—based on interviews of college students and middle-aged adults[104]—the speaker manipulates her or his speech in such a way as to avoid being labeled a racist while advancing ideas that collude with racial domination.

Sometimes, however, racial discourse in civil society is anything but implicit. During a speech in 2006, George Allen, who was then running for a Virginia Senate seat, pointed to S. R. Sidarth, an audience member of Indian descent, and said, "This fellow here . . . macaca, or whatever his name is." (Macaca is a racial slur meaning monkey.) Attempting to mimic a Chinese broadcaster, Rosie O'Donnell on *The View* uttered, "You know, you can imagine in China it's like: 'Ching, chong. . . . ching, chong, chong, chong.'" And then there was radio host Don Imus, who, during a live broadcast on April 4, 2007, referred to the Rutgers women's basketball team as "nappy-headed hos." All three of these comments relied on degrading stereotypes of the groups they targeted, and all three were widely denounced. However, in all three cases, some people rushed to defend Allen, O'Donnell, or Imus—or at least to defend their *right* to use racist speech in civil society—transforming the perpetrators of the insult into "victims of censorship."[105]

Does Racist Speech Deserve First Amendment Protection?

Incidents such as these raise an important question: Should racist speech be protected by the First Amendment? Most Americans would answer "yes," especially those who are rarely on the receiving end of racial slurs; however, some activists and legal scholars disagree. In *Words That Wound,* four law professors argue that racist speech does not deserve constitutional protection.[106] Their argument, in abridged form, runs as follows. First, racial slurs are harmful. They inflict serious emotional (anger, depression), psychological (stigmatization, self-hate), and even physical (hypertension, stroke) damage on their victims. Second, racist language does not endorse, but discourages, the primary goal of the First Amendment, which is to promote speech. When one is attacked with a racial epithet—or with an epithet that is sexist, homophobic, or xenophobic in nature—one usually can marshal only one of two responses: silence or violence. After all, what could we possibly say to someone who tells us, as Mel Gibson recently told a Malibu police officer, "Fucking Jews . . . the Jews are responsible for all the wars in the world"?[107] On these two grounds, the argument goes, racist speech should not find refuge in the First Amendment; rather, it should be subject to punitive measures, such as court-ordered fines.

"But the First Amendment protects all speech!" the critic replies. This is not true. Much speech does not enjoy constitutional protection. Examples include a CEO lying to investors about the strength of a company, a mob boss asking one of his men to kill a rival, or a preschool teacher telling her students about sexual acts. Slander, defamation, bomb threats, forgery, inciting a riot, and obscene phone calls are all forms of speech that are not covered by the First Amendment and that can result in legal reprimand.[108] These kinds of speech are outlawed precisely because they inflict harm. Likewise, since racist slurs are harmful, should they not be added to the list of criminalized speech?

On the flip side, some people, who themselves might never use racial slurs, argue that racist speech must be protected by the First Amendment. Democracy exists only in a society where freedom of expression is allowed to flourish. That freedom must be extended to all ideas, no matter how reprehensible those ideas might be. Although racist speech is harmful, the greater harm is to give the government the power to censor our speech.

Whatever camp with which you align in this debate—and we leave that decision to you—it is worth recognizing that those who believe that racist speech does not deserve constitutional protection can teach us all an important lesson. That lesson has to do with how white privilege works in civil society. When racially derogatory language enters into public discourse, either through widely publicized utterances like the ones listed above or in more everyday occurrences that do not make the nightly news, whites can go about their lives unaffected. But members of marginalized groups targeted by such language, reminded through such violent words of their own domination, can be deeply wounded. Because racist speech does not exist in a vacuum but is emboldened by a history of racial domination as well as by present-day racial inequalities, such speech is never innocent, no matter the speaker's intent. Rather, it is a powerful mechanism through which racial domination is supported and reproduced. If this is the case, shouldn't our first concern be with the victims of racist speech—those who have been defamed, shamed, and hurt—not with the speakers or even with civil society as a whole? Stanford Law professor Charles Lawrence would answer "yes": "Whenever we decide that racist hate speech must be tolerated because of the importance of tolerating unpopular speech," writes Lawrence, "we ask Blacks and other subordinated groups to bear a burden for the good of society—to pay the price for the societal benefit of creating more room for speech. And we assign this burden to them without seeking their advice or consent. This amounts to white domination, pure and simple."[109]

Social Movements Today

It is within civil society that we also find social movements. Although this generation has not borne witness to antiracist movements as large or vibrant as those of the 1950s, 1960s, and 1970s, today there are many social movement organizations working to dismantle racial injustice. Some are more institutionalized and bureaucratized, as was (and is) the NAACP. These include the National Council of La Raza, a civil rights organization focused on the problems facing Hispanic Americans; the Anti-Defamation League, an organization dedicated to fighting anti-Semitism; the Native American Rights Fund, a nonprofit law firm "dedicated to asserting and defending the rights of Indian tribes, organizations and individuals nationwide"; the Japanese Americans Citizen League, which played a pivotal role in the movement seeking reparations for victims of Japanese internment camps; and the Arab-American Anti-Discrimination Committee, among many others. American Indian governments—such as the Navajo or Ho-Chunk Nations—who fight for tribal sovereignty, land and water rights, and the preservation of traditional culture and language, should also be included here. These organizations tend to focus their efforts on educational programs, community service, and legal change.

Other movements are more community-based and focus on direct action. Here, one thinks of the bold women of color feminist movements (which broke with the majority-white women's movements in the 1960s and 1970s) that have called attention to the ways in which racism and sexism intersect in the lives of black women, Latinas, and other women of color. In addition, many **pan-ethnic movements**—movements based on a unified racial identity that transcends ethnic, national, or religious differences—are active today. Asian-American pan-ethnic movements, for example, look to bind together people of Asian descent, including Chinese, Vietnamese, Cambodian, Korean, and Japanese Americans, around common political programs.[110]

Community-based intergroup coalitions have formed to battle poverty, crime, and racism. One such group, Direct Action for Rights and Equality (or DARE), reaches across racial lines while mobilizing families to revitalize inner-city neigh-borhoods.[111] Multiracial cultural movements—such as spoken word poetry, break dancing, and hip-hop—have arisen as one of the most exciting and energetic movements of our time. Indeed, some commentators have argued that socially conscious hip-hop (*real* hip-hop, as some might say) holds the keys to unlocking a modern-day civil rights agenda.[112] We discuss this possibility more in Chapter 8, but it is worth mentioning in passing that many people agreed with Lauryn Hill when she said, "Hip-hop isn't just music, it is a spiritual movement. . . . You can't just call hip-hop a trend!"

Multiracial social movements have also galvanized around specific issues, such as affirmative action, the death penalty, and protecting indigenous peoples' sovereignty around the world. Consider, for example, movements fighting for **reparations** for past wrongs. These movements recognize the deciding role his-tory plays in modern life—or, to quote Boots Riley of the hip-hop group, The Coup, "Every slave story present tense, Every uprise a consequence"[113]—and struggle to obtain some sort of recompense from countries that benefited from past forms of racial oppression, whether that be monetary reparations for slavery or presidential apologies for the Native American genocide. Although some believe the reparations movement is shooting for unachievable goals, we should remember that reparations are not without precedent. The most generous reparations given by America were those that atoned for imprisoning Japanese citizens without due process in internment camps after the bombing of Pearl Harbor. Under Franklin D. Roosevelt's Executive Order 9066, American troops rounded up over 120,000 Japanese Americans, imprisoning them in the camps or expelling them to Japan. Japanese Americans—classified as anti-American threats, terrorists, and spies—suffered dearly, losing their jobs and welfare, their homes and property, and, for some, their lives. America eventually would come to see the injustice of Executive Order 9066. In 1980 (almost forty years after Executive Order 9066 was issued), a formal apology was offered by Congress along with reparations in the form of $20,000 for each Japanese American who had been confined in the camps.[114]

Another fast-growing social movement is that of white antiracists. Groups such as Antiracist Action (ARA) and the People's Institute for Survival and Beyond encourage white people to divest their white privilege and to take intentional steps toward eliminating racism in their communities.[115] White anti-racists believe that, since racism is embedded in the inner burrows of our minds and bodies, whites must practice a kind of reflexive vigilance, examining how their everyday actions support and are supported by racial domination. It is not enough that whites remain on the sidelines, simply showing kindness to non-whites. Racism often sneaks through the door that kindness opens. Rather, whites must be active participants in the fight against racism, using their race-based privileges to pick apart the very system that confers on them these privileges. In other words, white antiracists take to heart Paulo Freire's injunction that "'washing one's hands' of the conflict between the powerful and the powerless means to side with the powerful, not to be neutral."[116]

Some of the most outspoken white antiracists are those who encourage whites to become "race traitors" in order to "abolish the white race." As the coeditors of the journal *Race Traitor* explain, "When we say we want to abolish the white race, we do not mean we want to exterminate people with fair skin. We mean that we want to do away with the social meaning of skin color, thereby abolishing the white race as a social category. Consider this parallel: To be against royalty does not mean wanting to kill the king. It means wanting to do away with crowns, thrones, titles, and the privileges attached to them. In our view, whiteness has a lot in common with royalty: they are both social formations that carry unearned advantages."[117]

But most whites are not antiracists; neither are they, in the main, members of hate groups such as the KKK. The majority of whites sit in the middle between these two camps, apparently members of no social movement. However, this appearance is itself a product of whiteness's invisibility, for, as we have seen throughout this chapter, when whites' racial interests are threatened, they can act as a **social movement that need not speak its name.** When faced with legislation that promotes racial equality, most whites come together to oppose such measures, thereby acting as a solidified political force that usually dissipates once the threat is eliminated. A white man might not belong to any political organization, but when state representatives begin considering using tax money to offer reparations for slavery, he might join other whites in writing letters to his congressperson, signing petitions, and attending demonstrations against reparations. In doing so, this man participates as a member of a mass-based social movement, one without a name or structure but able effectively to mobilize, nonetheless, to uphold the status quo. Once state representatives drop the reparations idea, this man can go back to his daily life, never knowing all the other people like him who joined together to block the legislation.

The Longing for Color-Blind Politics

America—it is undeniable—is better off because of the Civil Rights Movement. The Movement pushed the nation, kicking and screaming, several steps closer to the dream of establishing a democracy without racial hypocrisy and injustice. The gains of the movement, and the sacrifices of its champions, cannot be ignored. Because of them, racial domination has been dealt a massive blow.

The political field is complex and many-sided, however, and, despite the ongoing work of many social movements struggling for civil rights, the worldwide fight against racism has run into new obstacles in recent years. One reason for this is the changing nature of raced politics. Specifically, states once built on racial domination are now claiming to be rid of race. "The successes of antiracist and anticolonialist movements in recent decades are being transformed into new patterns of racial inequality and injustice," writes sociologist Howard Winant. "The 'new world racial system,' in sharp contrast to the old structures of explicit colonialism and state-sponsored segregation, now presents itself as 'beyond race,' 'color-blind,' multicultural, and postracial."[118]

This seems strange since, as we have seen throughout this chapter, American politics are racial through and through. Indeed, there is no other divide in electoral politics—not gender, class, or religion—that is as extraordinary as that of race.[119] And policies designed to confront racial issues are "hot issues," ones that garner much attention and debate. Although you might not have an opinion about social spending or free trade, you probably have one about affirmative action. So, we know race is important in the political field, and yet, many of us wish to conceive of politics as "beyond race." What could explain this apparent contradiction?

If color-blindness is such a widespread and deeply rooted doctrine in (white) American politics today, it is because color-blindness is, in fact, the ideal response to skin differences is a world without race. As political theorist Amy Gutmann explains, "The principles that most of us learn, from childhood to maturity, are therefore color-blind not because color-blindness is the right response to racial injustice but rather because color blindness is the ideal morality (for an ideal society)."[120] What Gutmann means is that, in a perfect world—a world without a history of colonization, genocide, slavery, and systematic degradation, a world without present-day racial inequalities, institutional and interpersonal racism, and racial domination—color-blindness would be the appropriate ethical code. But we have not inherited such a world. As such, color-blindness is an inappropriate way of thinking about our world.

Color-blindness is an ineffective mode of response to a world itself not color-blind. The politician who boasts of a color-blind society boasts of a world that has yet to arrive. This person is like a man who stands on his front porch and waves off firefighters as his house ignites behind him. "No need for water here, my friends. Everything is fine." Now, this response would be normal and acceptable if his house were not on fire; but since things stand otherwise, this response is wrongheaded and dangerous. The same is true of the code of color-blindness. "No need for policies designed to combat racial inequalities, fellow citizens. Everything is fine." A house on fire will collapse if the owner, refusing to recognize the smoke and flames, turns off the water hose. And the foundations of "the house that race built"—American democracy—are threatened if we, its caretakers, fail to recognize and to remedy racial domination in our political processes.[121] To borrow one of Abraham Lincoln's favorite sayings, "If we turn our backs on the fire and burn our behinds, we will just have to sit on our blisters."

CHAPTER REVIEW

THE CIVIL RIGHTS MOVEMENT

Civil Rights Movement, National Association for the Advancement of Colored People (NAACP), Montgomery bus boycott, Southern Christian Leadership Conference (SCLC), Student Nonviolent Coordinating Committee (SNCC), sit-ins, Freedom Rides, Freedom Summer, Selma to Montgomery March, Voting Rights Act of 1965, Civil Rights Act of 1964, American Indian Movement, United Farm Workers of America

WHITE BACKLASH

white backlash, coded language, discursive co-optation, racially polarized, superficial representation, substantive representation, gerrymandering, tyranny of the majority

VOTING

threat hypothesis, principle-implementation gap, felon disenfranchisement

ELECTIONS

implicit racial appeals

CIVIL SOCIETY

civil society, panethnic movements, reparations, social movement that need not speak its name

FROM THEORY TO PRACTICE

1. Today, some commentators argue that many of the problems facing black Americans are due to the failure of black leadership. "If African Americans only had a leader like Martin Luther King, Jr., things would be different." In light of what you have just read about the Civil Rights Movement, do you agree or disagree with this claim? Does the claim rest on the messiah myth? Name three important lessons the Civil Right Movement teaches us about how everyday people can enact significant social change.

2. Who is your congressperson? What is her or his stance on policies designed to promote racial equality? How might you better understand her or his stance in light of what you have learned in this chapter?

3. Looking back on the last election (local, state, or national), how was race mobilized by different candidates? In your view, did some candidates make implicit racial appeals? If so, explain.

4. Coded racial language surrounds us. Think of a time when you have heard someone use coded racial language. Identify what was said; then unpack the utterance, explaining how the speaker was able to collude with racial domination without explicitly doing so. How should we respond when met with coded racial language?

5. Identify a recent occurrence where racist speech made its way into public discourse. Analyze this occurrence by scrutinizing the utterance and by paying attention to the public reaction. What makes this incident of racist speech so powerful? That is, what historical patterns and present-day injustices does it rely on for meaning? How did various publics react to this speech? What became the object of attention: the thing said, the speaker, or the group it targeted? Finally, should such speech be protected by the First Amendment? Why or why not?

RECOMMENDED READING

- Adam Fairclough, *Better Day Coming: Blacks and Equality, 1890–2000* (New York: Penguin, 2001).

- Donald Kinder and Lynn Sanders, *Divided by Color: Racial Politics and Democratic Ideals* (Chicago: University of Chicago Press, 1996).

- Martin Luther King, Jr., *Why We Can't Wait* (New York: Signet, 2000).

- Tali Mendelberg, *The Race Card: Campaign Strategies, Implicit Messages, and the Norm of Equality* (Princeton: Princeton University Press, 2001).

- Aldon Morris, *The Origins of the Civil Rights Movement: Black Communities Organizing for Change* (New York: Free Press, 1984).

- Alexis de Tocqueville, *Democracy in America* (New York: Perennial Classics 2000 [1835 and 1840]).

Chapter 4

Economics

Inequality in the Promised Land

America, it is often said, is the most affluent nation on the planet. If we define affluence by a country's Gross National Income, the sum of the country's total value of goods and services and of funds garnered from other countries, then there is no questioning America's dominance. America's Gross National Income weighs in at 9.7 trillion dollars. The second wealthiest country, Japan, is not even close with 4.5 trillion. Germany comes in third with 1.9 trillion, lagging far behind America. In fact, if we add up the Gross National Incomes of the third through the tenth wealthiest nations—Germany, Britain, France, China, Italy, Canada, Spain, and Mexico—we arrive at the sum of 7.2 trillion dollars, a full 2.5 trillion dollars behind America. In a world of money, America reigns colossus.[1]

However, if we define affluence not by the accumulation of wealth but the distribution of wealth, America ranks far from the top. The numbers are startling. In the 1950s, the top 4% of American wage earners made, cumulatively, the same total as the bottom 35% of the country's workers. Today, the top 4% brings in the same amount as more than 50% of the country's lowest-paid workers, while the bottom 20% of earners collects only 4% of the country's income. According to the Internal Revenue Service, 50% of Americans report an income under $30,000, while the top .05% of Americans earn over $500,000 a year. With respect to wealth, the top 20% of American households control 68% of the country's net worth and an impressive 87% of the country's net financial assets. America's elite of the elite, the top 1%, control one-third of the country's estates. If money is time, consider this: while it takes a chief executive of a U.S. company an average of 3 hours to make $1,000, it takes the janitor who cleans that executive's office roughly 103 hours to earn the same amount. It would take the waitress who serves the executive dinner and the cashier who rings up his groceries even longer.[2]

America's accumulation of riches, therefore, is matched only by the drastically uneven ways those riches are distributed.[3] Here, luxurious abundance and abundant destitution, the sublime and the slum, coexist in bright contrast. And what role does racial domination play in creating and maintaining such economic inequality? A lead role—and why shouldn't it? As we saw in Chapter 2, race was sprung into existence by the motors of modernity, one of the most powerful of which was the development of a new economic system we now know as capitalism.

This chapter concentrates on the workings of race in the economic field. It begins by analyzing changes that took place during the twentieth century, changes that systematically excluded people of color from American prosperity. Turning its attention to the present day, it then examines income and wealth disparities by race before investigating racialized poverty and affluence. Next, it focuses on labor market dynamics, concentrating on hiring practices, labor organizing, promotions, and the multicultural workplace. It concludes with an extended discussion of policy measures designed to confront racialized economic inequality: welfare and affirmative action. We issue to you a friendly warning before we begin. A fair amount of data lie ahead—facts and figures—plus a wide range of terms and concepts. If you are not careful, you will easily get lost in the details. Try always to focus on the big picture; the basic arguments are what count.

Economic Racism from the New Deal to Reaganomics

American Indians never received compensation for being uprooted from their land, for being imprisoned on reservations, or for having their indigenous economies gobbled up by white settlers. Mexican Americans were never compensated for being deported to Mexico during the late nineteenth and early twentieth centuries, nor were they repaid for being dispossessed of their homes and land through the 1862 Homestead Act. Some Japanese-American victims of internment camps received monetary reparations but were never allowed to claim rightful ownership of lands stripped from them in the wake of the Pearl Harbor bombings, lands that, today (especially in California), are among the most wealth-producing in the nation. And African Americans were denied reparations for slavery promised them. As freed Mississippi slave Isaac Stier once observed, "De slaves spected a heap from freedom dey didn' git. . . . But dey sho' got fooled. Mos' of 'em didn' fin' deyse'ves no better off. Pussonally, I had a harder time after de war dan I did endurin' slav'ry. . . . Dey promised us a mule an' forty acres o' lan'. Us aint seen no mule yet."[4] Consequentially, as America rolled into the twentieth century, the vast majority of its nonwhite citizens struggled through poverty, trying to make a life amidst the rubble left from years of economic warfare.

Things were better for most whites, but not radically so. The Great Depression began in the fall of 1929, ushering in a period of severe economic deprivation. From the stock market crash of 1929 to America's entrance into the Second World War in 1941, thousands of Americans, of all colors, lost their jobs, their homes, their families. When Japan bombed Pearl Harbor, most whites stood a far throw from middle-class security. But the clouds soon began to lift. As the country marched into war, unemployment almost disappeared, as new manufacturing jobs were developed. With thousands of white men fighting overseas, women and nonwhites were allowed to work in positions previously denied them. Many have claimed that during the war women entered the workplace for the first time. Such a statement applies primarily to middle-class white women, for poor white women and women of color always had worked.

World War II revived the American economy and launched the country into the roaring fifties. Many Americans prospered; however, they did not prosper equally. During these times of economic uplift, the economic gap between whites and nonwhites did not shrink, nor did it maintain its shape (which would imply that all people rose at the same pace). Instead, the racial gap increased—and substantially.[5] What happened? The answer is to be found in government programs that lifted thousands of whites into the ranks of the middle class, while denying nonwhites this advantage.

When Affirmative Action Was White

Responding to the Great Depression, President Franklin D. Roosevelt initiated several programs dealing with welfare, work, and war designed to uplift Americans. Together, these programs came to be known as the **New Deal**. To date, no anti-poverty program in the history of America has come close to matching those of the New Deal, which birthed unemployment insurance, the minimum wage, workday limitations, and veteran assistance. And yet, these programs were crafted to accommodate racial domination. During the development of New Deal policies, the southern arm of the Democratic Party was a force with which to be reckoned in the House and Senate. These white men acted as a separate party within the Democratic Party, a party that was willing to back New Deal policies only if they did not threaten the racial hierarchy of the south. By securing a disproportionate number of committee seats and flexing their political muscle, southern Democrats forced northern Democrats into a devil's bargain: "Either you design New Deal policies in such a way that Jim Crow remains perched atop his roost, or we will align with the Republicans and veto them." Northern Democrats gave in, barring nonwhites access to social spending programs.[6]

Thus, many nonwhites were denied access to old age insurance, aid to dependent families, and unemployment insurance—collectively known as welfare— ushered in by the Social Security Act of 1935, one of the country's most significant pieces of social legislation. This was accomplished by disqualifying certain jobs, those dominated by nonwhite workers, from the policy. For instance, many southern black men, who constituted a full 40% of southern agricultural workers during the 1930s, could not benefit from these programs, because farm workers did not qualify. Neither did maids, a profession dominated at that time by black women. As a result, the majority of blacks—65% nationwide and up to 80% in some parts of the South—could not take advantage of the benefits offered by the Social Security Act.[7] The act was designed to discriminate; it functioned, in the words of NAACP spokesperson Charles Houston, "like a sieve with holes just big enough for the majority of Negroes to fall through."[8]

Besides giving us welfare, the New Deal also provided work and wage regulations. It mandated a standardized minimum wage, imposed work hour limitations, and provided a climate in which unions could flourish. But, again, southern Democrats refused to extend these rights to blacks and other nonwhite citizens. James Mark Wilcox, a representative from Florida, spoke for his fellow white southerners when he said, "We may rest assured, therefore, that when we turn over to a federal bureau or board the power to fix wages, it will prescribe the same wage for the Negro that it prescribes for the white man. Now, such a plan might work in some sections of the United States, but those of us who know the true situation know that it just will not work in the South. You cannot put the Negro and the white man on the same basis and get away with it."[9] So, again, farm workers, maids, and other nonwhite jobs were excluded from the benefits.

During the Second World War, the labor force began to change. Nonwhites made inroads into manufacturing jobs dominated by white men. And many southern blacks did not have to migrate north to work in a factory, as the South was becoming more industrialized. This meant that many nonwhites for the first time had access to New Deal work policies. This worried southern Democrats, who responded by backing Republican-led antilabor legislation. This new alliance led to the passage of the 1947 Taft-Hartley Act, which greatly diminished union power and the ability to organize workers. To the southern Democrats, their unflinching desire to maintain the racial caste system of the old Confederacy trumped their commitments to working-class Americans.[10]

The Second World War rearranged American racial dynamics in several ways. It ignited anti-Asian, particularly anti-Japanese, sentiment—a process encouraged by government-sponsored racist propaganda and internment camps. At the same time, it allowed Jews and white Catholics, groups that previously had been ostracized from the American mainstream, to move closer to the center of American whiteness. As anti-Semitism raged horrifically in Europe, it began quieting down in America. Jews began enlisting in the military in record number and, for the first time, were treated to the perks of first-class citizenship. Thousands of other nonwhite men also attempted to enlist. Many, however, were denied strictly on the basis of their race. It was only during the final throes of the war, when the American military found itself desperately short of manpower, that it began admitting nonwhites into its ranks in substantial numbers.[11]

With respect to widening racial inequalities, more important than the war itself was the New Deal legislation that followed it, legislation designed for veterans returning home. By all standards, the Selective Service Readjustment Act—or, more popularly, the **GI Bill of Rights**—was massive. In the three decades that followed the war, the United States spent more than 95 billion dollars on the bill, making it the single most comprehensive set of social benefits ever issued by the federal government under a unified initiative. Using the GI Bill, millions of veterans bought homes, went to college, got by on unemployment insurance, financed small businesses, and bought farmland. College enrollment shot through the roof, nearly tripling between the beginning of the war and the 1950s. Accordingly to one source, America "gained more than 400,000 engineers, 200,000 teachers, 90,000 scientists, 60,000 doctors, and 22,000 dentists."[12] And the dream of buying a home, which before the war was a luxury enjoyed only by the wealthy, became a reality for everyday Americans. In the decade that followed the war, over 13 million new homes were erected, nearly 40% of which were funded by veteran mortgages.[13] The GI Bill, more than any other program, forged the American middle class.

But, again, these benefits were not extended with equal generosity to nonwhites. As white veterans were propelled into the good life with the help of the GI Bill, nonwhites were excluded. The drafters of the GI Bill, many of whom were southern Democrats, left the administration of the bill up to state and local authorities. This meant that the distribution of veteran benefits (including loans, job placement, unemployment assistance, college tuition aid, and vocational training) was left in the hands of local Veteran Affairs offices, private banks, or universities—all of which were staffed by white people who doggedly upheld the racial order. Many banks made it a policy to deny black and Latino veterans loans to start up small businesses and home mortgages. Major colleges and universities barred black veterans from entry, leaving historically black colleges—which during that time, were underfunded and struggling—to shoulder the burden. Nearly all black veterans who used the GI Bill's educational benefits did so at these segregated institutions. And nonwhite veterans who applied for job assistance were channeled into menial and unskilled professions. Of the jobs filled by Mississippi veterans by 1946, 86% of skilled and semiskilled posts were taken by whites, while 92% of the unskilled jobs were staffed by blacks.[14]

Why did economic and educational inequalities between whites and nonwhites increase rather than decrease during and after World War II, a time when the country was lifting itself out of the Great Depression and flourishing economically? Because, answers political scientist Ira Katznelson, "at the very moment when a wide array of public policies was providing most white Americans with valuable tools to advance their social welfare—insure their old age, get good jobs, acquire economic security, build assets, and gain middle-class status—most black Americans were left behind or left out. Affirmative action then was white."[15]

The End of Industrialization

It would be a mistake to assert that nonwhites did not benefit from New Deal programs. The standard of living for many nonwhites improved considerably thanks to these programs. However, if nonwhites benefited slightly, many whites benefited enormously. While the New Deal enabled whites to advance to middle-class status, the majority of America's nonwhites were locked into low-wage work. Although nonwhite affirmative action programs launched in the 1960s and 70s allowed people of color to make inroads into white-collar professions, many remained at the bottom rungs of the labor market. During the 1980s, the upward economic momentum propelled by industrialization that following the Second World War came slowly to a halt. Manufacturing jobs began disappearing from the Northeast and Midwest, a process known as **deindustrialization**.[16]

The factory was giving way to a service economy, one based on finance, sales, transportation, personal care, and technical advances. This process would widen the already impressive racial gap left by unequally distributed New Deal policies. Deindustrialization was particularly hard on blacks and Puerto Ricans. To take but one example, between 1979 and 1984, half of all black men working in durable-goods manufacturing in major Midwest metropolises lost their jobs.[17] And out-of-work blacks often had a difficult time finding work in the service sector; in fact, whites were four times more likely to be employed full time in service industries than blacks.[18]

The economy was not the only thing changing. Federal assistance was also being altered dramatically under the leadership of Ronald Reagan. If Roosevelt opened the floodgates of federally mandated social benefits, Reagan built a dam. A staunch individualist, Reagan felt that the government should not interfere in the workings of the economy. The market should rule itself, he believed, which meant that all forms of social benefits—especially liberal policies ushered in by the New Deal—should be dismantled. A "politics of austerity," to borrow a phrase from Paul Pierson, was the result: welfare spending was rolled back.[19]

Reagan championed the doctrine of **supply-side economics**, or Reaganomics, as it came to be known. The chain of reasoning ran like this: once the government pulls out of the market—primarily by cutting taxes to the wealthy—the wealthy will invest the money they usually dedicated to taxes into new capital ventures, which in turn will lead to cheaper production, which in turn will lead to lower prices and increased demand, thereby expanding the economy. Tax cuts will leave the federal government worse off, decreasing its ability to carry out antipoverty programs; however, this is of no matter, since low and moderate income workers will profit alongside the wealthy. How so? New capital investments developed by wealthy beneficiaries of tax cuts will create jobs, thereby allowing the riches at the top level to "trickle down" to the less fortunate at the bottom.[20]

What was the result of Reagan's new economic strategy? Unsurprisingly, the wealthy prospered under the program: the top 10% profited from a 5% tax cut, while the top 1% enjoyed a 15% cut, which brought about a lavish 60% income increase. The rest of the country, however, did not fare so well. Those in the middle—between the 50th and 90th income percentile—were relatively unaffected. But the bottom 50% actually suffered from tax *increases,* and the poorest fifth of Americans watched their incomes drop an average of 10%. Poor people of color were among the hardest hit. In the early 1980s, the poorest black families lost 18% of their family income. Many had to get by on less than $100 a week.[21] As a result, the distance separating America's elites from its poor increased substantially, as did the wage gap between nonwhites (namely, blacks and Hispanics) and whites.[22]

Tracing America's economic development from Reconstruction to Reaganomics, we witness the emergence of white economic privilege. Despite advances made by all Americans during the last one hundred and fifty years, whites were pulled farther ahead by government-sponsored programs that institutionalized, at the highest and lowest levels, systems of exclusion and exploitation. The tendency to forget this history, to assume that the white middle class somehow made itself through pure determination and gumption, is pervasive. In reality, the white middle class emerged only with the government's help. To declare dead the American past, to refuse to account for the genesis of racial disparities in the economic field, is to misunderstand modern society in deep and profound ways.

Income and Wealth Disparities

We can observe how this history of race-based exclusion hatched a society laden with economic inequality by examining the most recent data on income and wealth disparities. By **income**, we mean wages and salaries earned from employment, retirement, or government aid. By **wealth**, we mean owned assets that yield monetary return, such as stocks and bonds, savings accounts, houses and real estate, and business and farm ownership. You use your income (your paycheck from work) to buy groceries, diapers, and school supplies. You use your wealth (the funds accrued from your money-generating assets) to wield political influence and to secure a desired standard of living for you and your family.

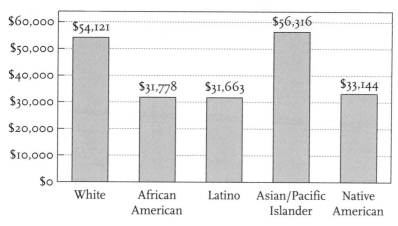

Median Family Income, 1999

Income comes from your job, while most wealth comes from intergenerational transfers (that is, passed down from one generation to the next). With income, you work for your money; with wealth, your money works for you.[23]

Income Inequality

Between 1998 and 2000, the median household income of Hispanics and Native Americans was $32,000. It was $29,000 for black households and $45,500 for white households. A median is the middle number in a set of ranked numbers. (The median of the set 1, 2, 3 is 2.) So, if you made every American family line up by race (a Native-American line, a white line, and so forth) and income earnings (richest to poorest), and if you picked the family exactly in the middle of the white line, that family would be $13,500 richer than the families in the middle of the Hispanic and Native American lines and $16,500 richer than the family in the middle of the black line. If we look at individual (not household) income, we observe a similar trend. In 2006, whites on average made $38,253 a year, and Asians on average made $40,511 a year. Blacks, however, averaged only $26,919 a year, while Hispanics made even less: an average income of $25,674. According to this estimate, blacks and Hispanics earn roughly 33% less than whites. But some estimates place the percentage even lower, finding that blacks and Hispanics earn 55% less.[24]

Although Asian workers seem to be leading the pack, with average earnings exceeding those of all other groups, a closer analysis suggests that their high earnings average is due to the fact that a significant percentage of Asians are very well off (about 7% of Asians make over $100,000 a year, whereas only 5% of whites and 1.5% of blacks and Hispanics rake in comparable salaries). Indeed, according to a nationwide study, for every dollar a white man makes, Asian men, on average, make 89 cents. Comparable gaps are observed between black and white women as well as between Hispanic and white women. The largest gap was observed between black and white men: on average, for every dollar a white man earns, a black man earns 75 cents. These gaps narrow considerably when we account for important characteristics, such as education, employment experience, immigrant status, and hours worked; however, the gaps do not disappear. This means that on average a white man will make more than a black man, a Hispanic man, or an Asian man, even if all these men work exactly the same hours, possess exactly the same work experience, and hold exactly the same college degrees.[25]

Several explanations have been offered for racialized income inequality. We highlight some here and take up others later. One explanation claims that high levels of immigration lead to racial disparities in income levels. The idea runs as follows: Immigrants from poor countries flock to the United States searching for a better life. Because they came from poverty, they are willing to work for substandard wages. This attracts employers longing for the cheapest labor available. Soon, employers replace native-born workers with an immigrant labor force. This leaves many workers unemployed and drives down wages on the bottom rung of the income sector, thereby widening the gap between the working poor (many of whom are nonwhite) and the well off (many of whom are white). It also sours relations between nonwhites and immigrant groups.[26]

Although some employers will pass over native-born workers for immigrant workers, researchers have found that immigration has little effect on income inequality. Because the labor force is racially segregated, immigrants primarily compete with other immigrants for jobs in immigrant-dominated labor sectors (like domestic service), not with poor blacks or poor whites.[27] For example, Mexican immigrants who work in Nebraskan meatpacking plants primarily contend for jobs, not with semiskilled native-born Americans but with immigrants from Somalia, recruited by employers because of their willingness to work for substandard wages and on account of their status as political refugees not subject to immigrant raids, unlike many undocumented Mexican workers.[28] In fact, some studies have shown that the influx of Mexican immigrants in some metropolitan areas actually increases the wages of blacks and whites.[29]

The history of racial domination in the United States economy has left us with a highly **segregated labor force**. According to one study, 48% of Hispanics work in mostly Hispanic jobs, while 44% of blacks work in mostly black jobs. The same is true of whites: 25% of workplaces are exclusively white, whereas a significant proportion employs fewer than 10% nonwhite workers. Now, job segregation would help to explain income inequality across race only if wages were lower in majority-nonwhite jobs than in majority-white jobs. This is precisely what research has found. Whites earn 9% more per hour than blacks and, stunningly, 28% more per hour than Hispanics. Mapped onto the racial segregation of the labor force is an unequal distribution of earnings, one that privileges majority-white jobs and disadvantages majority-black and, to a greater extent, majority-Hispanic jobs.[30]

Many nonwhites are working in jobs that offer not only lower pay but also lower prestige. In fact, some sociologists have connected job status, wages, and race in a single equation, claiming that when a job becomes associated with a dominated racial group—just as domestic service is equated with Latinas or New York City taxi driving is equated with Arab-American men—that job loses status. Owing to the normalization of whiteness, majority-white jobs are simply "jobs," whereas majority-nonwhite jobs are "black jobs" or "immigrant jobs." There is more: since whiteness is infused with the essence of the positive, majority-nonwhite jobs are given a lower placement on the status hierarchy. Once a job's status declines, so, too, does its wages. The influx of nonwhites into certain sectors of the labor market pulls down both wages and status.[31] Certain jobs become connected with certain racial groups and often become the subject of ridicule and humiliation. For proof of this, we need look no further than our own college campuses, where recently, white students attending *Cinco de Mayo* parties have dressed up like Mexican janitors and gardeners. At one party thrown at the University of Delaware, white students dressed as Mexican landscapists, wearing shirts with the names Pedro or Julio on the front, and, on the back: "Spic and Span Gardening."[32]

Wealth Inequality

Although racialized income inequality is still with us, the gap between white wages and nonwhite wages has narrowed over the last twenty years. The same cannot be said of wealth inequality. Compared to income disparities, racialized wealth inequalities are much starker. The statistics speak for themselves: The average black family is completely without wealth. Black middle-class workers earn roughly 70 cents for every dollar earned by white middle-class workers; however, they possess only 15 cents for every dollar of wealth possessed by white middle-class workers.

If we compare whites' and blacks' net worth (total assets minus debt) and their net financial assets (total assets excluding home and auto equity), we are met with striking differences. On average, white married couples have access to $65,024 of net worth and $11,500 of net financial assets. By comparison, black married couples have access to only $17,437 of net worth and no net financial assets. Single white people, on average, possess $20,083 of net worth and $2,400 of net financial assets. Single black people, in contrast, possess only $800 of net worth and not a single penny of financial assets. Poor whites possess *equal*

America's accumulation of riches is matched only by the drastically uneven ways those riches are distributed.

amounts of wealth as well-off blacks. Whites living in poverty had an average of $28,683 of net financial assets from which to draw, whereas high-income blacks (doctors, lawyers, professors) had an average of $28,310. Poor blacks, by contrast, had a measly $184 in net financial assets, suggesting that white poverty and black poverty are not the same thing.[33]

Perhaps blacks and other people of color do not have as much wealth as whites, because they do not have the same levels of education, salaries, jobs, or family status. But substantial racialized wealth inequality remains after these characteristics are accounted for. Whites in white-collar professions hold an average of $56,487 in net worth, whereas blacks in similar professions hold only $8,299. And the average net worth of college-educated whites is $74,922, but the average net worth of blacks with the same education is only $17,437. If drastic disparities exist despite one's education, then perhaps education is not the end-all-be-all solution for America's racial cleavages.[34]

To understand wage disparities across race, we must look first to the past. Recall what we said in Chapter 1: racial advantages and disadvantages accumulate over generations. This means that today's wealth inequality is a concrete result of yesterday's racism. In whites' healthy assets, as compared to the sparse wealth of most people of color, we see the legacies of slavery, colonization, and "the Indian Problem"; we see the hundred years that ran from the Civil War to the Civil Rights Movement, during which people of color were barred from participating completely in business or commerce; we see government policies that uplifted poor whites while leaving poor nonwhites behind; and we see decades of meager wages, bad schools, and sharecropping.[35] For most of its history, the American market has been anything but "free."

This is especially important since most wealth is passed down from one generation to the next. This is truer today than ever before. In 1900, 39% of America's wealthiest people came from wealthy families, whereas another 39% fought their way there from humbler beginnings. By 1950, 68% of the richest people came from wealthy backgrounds, and by 1970, it was nearly impossible to work your way into wealth, since 82% of the wealthiest were born into fortune, and only 4% climbed up from the lower rungs of the social ladder.[36] Nevertheless, most Americans, white and nonwhite alike, seem to believe that wealth is a result of hard work, pluck, personal drive, or superior talent. In a recent survey, the most popular response to the question "What makes someone wealthy?" was "Hard work and initiative."[37] Hard work can pay off, to be sure—but rich families tend to pay better. "It is not usual," remarked the American sociologist C. Wright Mills, "and it never has been the dominant fact, to create a great American fortune merely by nursing a little business into a big one. It is not usual and never has been the dominant fact carefully to accumulate your way to the top in a slow, bureaucratic crawl. It is difficult to climb to the top, and many who try fall by the way. It is easier and much safer to be born there."[38]

Past forms of domination are not the only explanation for today's racialized wage disparities. Present-day institutional racism also plays a large part. First, banks are more likely to offer credit to whites than to nonwhites. According to a study conducted by the Federal Reserve, commercial banks turn down black and Hispanic applicants two to three times more often than white applicants. In fact, the study concluded that the poorest white applicant has a better chance of getting her or his mortgage application approved than the highest paid black applicant! Creditworthiness, the essential element needed to purchase a house— and, for most of us, a house is the most important generator of wealth—seems to be calculated not only on the basis of one's income and past credit history but also on the basis of one's skin color.[39]

Second, nonwhites who do manage to secure a mortgage loan often pay higher interest rates than whites. During the housing spike, nonwhites were more likely to be offered high-interest subprime mortgages than whites, and when the housing bubble burst and foreclosures began sweeping the nation in 2007, they were disproportionately affected, losing their homes at extremely high rates, their credit scores plummeting.[40] On the whole, blacks pay half a percentage point more on loans than whites do. Although this may not look like much, it amounts to blacks who take out a twenty-five-year mortgage being deprived of $4,000. This adds up. Social scientists predict that the current generation of black homeowners will pay an extra 21.5 billion dollars to banks—the penalty one pays for being black.[41] Columbia law professor Patricia Williams learned this the hard way. An African-American woman with impeccable credit and a high-paying job, Williams applied for a home loan and was immediately approved. However, once the bank discovered she was black, it asked for a larger down payment and increased Professor Williams's interest rate. "The reason the bank gave for its new-found recalcitrance was not race," Williams remembers. "The reason they gave was that property values in that neighborhood were suddenly falling. . . . [But] the house was in a neighborhood that was extremely stable. . . . And even though I suppose it was a little thick of me, I really hadn't gotten it: For of course, I was the reason the prices were in peril."[42]

Professor Williams brings up yet another way in which institutional racism hinders nonwhites from obtaining wealth: housing prices. Put bluntly, homes of a given size, design, and age in nonwhite or racially integrated communities do not accrue as much value as similar homes in white communities. Between 1967 and 1988, the United States enjoyed a boom in the housing market. During this period, the average white-owned home increased in value by an average of $53,000; the average black-owned home increased by only $31,000. In fact, there is evidence that some banks refuse to offer loans for homes in nonwhite neighborhoods, a discriminatory practice known as redlining.[43]

As we have just seen, banks impede nonwhites' access to home ownership through three mechanisms: by disproportionately denying loans to nonwhite applicants, by charging nonwhites higher interest rates, and by devaluing homes in nonwhite neighborhoods. It is noteworthy that, because some banks refuse to do business with well-qualified nonwhite homebuyers, they work against their economic interests. Denying nonwhites home loans simply because they are nonwhite is not a strategy dictated by the logic of the market; it makes sense only according to the reasoning of racism. Consider the fact that in twenty-seven years only 10 applicants out of 3,900 who secured loans through the Nehemiah Homes—a program in New York's outer boroughs that constructs and sells homes to working poor people, a disproportionate number of whom are nonwhite—have defaulted on their loans.[44] Responding to accusations that nonwhites somehow were to blame for the collapse of the 2008 subprime mortgage industry, one journalist observed, "Lending money to poor people and minorities isn't inherently risky. . . . On the other hand, lending money recklessly to obscenely rich white guys, such as Richard Fuld of Lehman Bros. or Jimmy Cayne of Bear Stearns, can be really risky. . . . Lending money to poor people doesn't make you poor. Lending money poorly to rich people does."[45]

Things of economies—credit, risk, value—do not transcend the bounds of white privilege. This raises an important, and more general, point. Some have postulated that market activity can only be explained by market forces, that the economy is somehow set apart from society and governs itself with its own laws. However, as the example of racialized practices in bank lending demonstrates, economic action is often steered by forces beyond the boundaries of the abstract (and color-blind) logic of commerce. The economy, in other words, is **embedded** in society—its history and culture, its cleavages. Karl Polanyi, author of *The Great Transformation*, took pains to press this point: "Man's economy, as a rule, is submerged in his social relationships. He does not act so as to safeguard his individual interest in the possession of material goods; he acts so as to safeguard his social standing, his social claims, his social assets."[46] In other words, to quote Bourdieu, "it is not prices that determine everything, but everything that determines prices."[47] If this is true, and if our society is gripped by racial domination, then our economy is far from color-blind and does not exist in its own world, somehow cordoned off from the realities of race. Class cannot be understood apart from race; and race cannot be comprehended apart from class.

Chasing the American Dream: Poverty and Affluence

With nearly 39 million Americans living in poverty, and another 12 to 24 million teetering dangerously close, America's poor population is far greater than that of other developed countries.[48] Some estimates find that roughly 20 percent of American citizens live below the **poverty line.** This means that their income is not enough to sustain a decent standard of living, what is called a poverty threshold. According to the U.S. Bureau of the Census, in 2006 the poverty threshold for a single person under the age of 65 was $9,669; it was $20,444 for a family made up of a couple and their two children.[49] If these people earned less than their respective thresholds, they are said to be below the poverty line. One in five Americans struggles through such hardship.

Things may be worse. Some researchers have found that poverty thresholds underestimate the needs of the poor—sometimes by as much as 25%. Additionally, income statistics sometimes fail to capture the material hardships of poverty, such as "how many Americans are going to bed hungry, how many have had their gas or electricity cut off, how many have been evicted from their homes, how many live in housing that their fellow citizens judge unacceptably crowded or dilapidated, how may think they need medical care they are not getting, or how many have untreated toothaches."[50]

Most poor Americans are white. Forty-five percent of poor Americans are white; a quarter is black, and a quarter is Hispanic. But if we compare proportions by race, we see that only 10% of whites are poor, while 25% of Hispanics, American

Indians, and blacks live below the poverty line. Between 12 and 18% of Asians live in poverty.[51] Thus, Asians are roughly 1.5 times more likely to be poor than whites, while African Americans, Hispanics, and American Indians are twice as likely. When we explore ethnic variation in poverty levels within racial categories, we notice marked differences. Of Hispanics, Mexican Americans and Puerto Ricans are much more likely to be poor than Cuban Americans. Of Asians, Southeast Asians are much more likely to live down-and-out than Filipinos, Japanese, or Indian Americans. In fact, first-generation Laotian and Cambodian families have a 61% poverty rate, first-generation Chinese and Vietnamese families have a 25% rate, and first-generation Filipino families have only a 10% rate.[52]

The Causes of Poverty

What causes poverty? "The poor themselves," some answer back. Many Americans rationalize poverty in their midst by attributing it to negative characteristics of poor people: their laziness, incompetence, or lack of education.[53] At least since medieval times, people have blamed the poor, and especially the so-called undeserving poor (able-bodied people out of work), for their plight. Americans are no different in this respect.[54]

We even have invented a slew of pejorative labels that downgrade and stigmatize poor people. "White trash" is an epithet reserved for impoverished, rural (and usually southern) whites that began circulating in northern newspapers and books in the 1850s. Recently, it has regained popularity, along with "hick," "hillbilly," and "redneck."[55] "Underclass" was coined in 1962 by Gunnar Myrdal, a Swedish economist who used the term to describe the throngs of "unemployed unemployables" pushed out of work by the motors of deindustrialization. But journalists and popular writers quickly picked up the term, racializing it by applying it to poor inner-city blacks.[56] "White trash" brings to mind something that is dirty and polluted, something that does not belong in a safe and clean society. Trash should be buried or burned. "Underclass" conjures up a group of people below (or under) society, a group that should be cordoned off, kept low, and ostracized.[57] Both epithets evoke the idea of a threat—the backwards, backwoods white family (portrayed in *To Kill a Mockingbird* or *Deliverance*) or the murderous black gangstas (portrayed in the lyrics of Ludacris or 50 Cent)—precisely because these labels speak to behavioral traits more than economic ones do. "Most interpreters of the 'underclass,'" writes historian Robin Kelley, "treat behavior as not only a symptom from culture but also as the determinant for class. In simple terms, what makes the 'underclass' a class is members' common behavior—not their income, their poverty level, or the kind of work they do. It is a definition of class driven more by moral panic than by systemic analysis."[58]

Poverty cannot be explained solely by concentrating on the behavior of those suffering through it. Of course, we all make bad decisions. For some those

Uninsured Children by Poverty Status, Age, and Race and Hispanic Origin: 2006

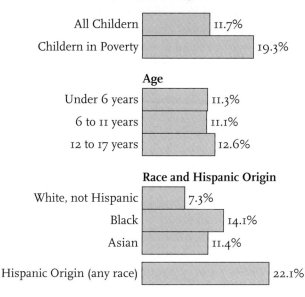

All Childern — 11.7%
Childern in Poverty — 19.3%

Age
Under 6 years — 11.3%
6 to 11 years — 11.1%
12 to 17 years — 12.6%

Race and Hispanic Origin
White, not Hispanic — 7.3%
Black — 14.1%
Asian — 11.4%
Hispanic Origin (any race) — 22.1%

decisions can be rather costly. The man who loses his job for sexually harassing a coworker must accept responsibility for his own economic hardship. But the farther you climb up the social ladder, the farther you have to fall before you land at the bottom. The surgeon who sexually harasses his nurses can afford to hire a well-trained lawyer should a suit be leveled against him; the priest who abuses an altar boy can find refuge in his host organization. But the janitor who cracks a crass joke about a coworker might find herself fired and with no place to turn. Privilege might best be defined as one's ability to screw up and get away with it.

Therefore, to understand the causes of poverty we must deploy a sociological imagination, taking into account things that are bigger than individuals, things such as social structures and historical changes. "True compassion," said Martin Luther King, Jr., "is more than flinging a coin to a beggar; it understands that an edifice which produces beggars needs restructuring."[59] Social scientists have identified many structural causes of poverty. We highlight three here. First, modern-day capitalism produces a pool of unemployed laborers. A natural side effect of market capitalism is the fact that the number of people willing to work far exceeds the number of job vacancies. Economists call it "natural unemployment." In 2007, America's unemployment rate fluctuated around 4.5 percent—that's 6.8 million people. Many people are unemployed due to outsourcing, downsizing, and layoffs.[60]

Second, deindustrialization made conditions of poverty worse. Mid-level occupations, such as factory work, have all but disappeared, resulting in an economy shaped like an hourglass, with opportunities at the very top (in professional posts) and at the very bottom (in the low-wage service sector) but little sustainable work in the middle.[61] As a result, millions of Americans are counted among the working poor: people who have secured regular work that does not provide them with the means to lift themselves out of poverty. Here we find the garment worker who cannot afford the dresses she sews, the maid who will never be able to stay in the hotel she cleans, the medical transcriptionist who has not been to a doctor in years, the bank clerk whose balance is in the red. Today, fully one-third of the breadwinners of American families make less than $10 an hour; 20% make less than $8, and 12% make less than $6 an hour.[62] With wages like these, they cannot hope to pull their family out of poverty. Getting by is hard enough.

The third structural origin of American poverty is found in the country's austere welfare state. Social spending in America dedicated to lessening economic difficulty—food stamps, housing subsidies, aid to needy families, Medicaid, Social Security—has been rolled back in recent years. In fact, with the exception of Japan, America dedicates a smaller percentage of its wealth to antipoverty programs than any other developed country.[63] Studies have shown that such programs drastically reduce a country's poor population. If Germany, the Netherlands, and the United States did not offer any assistance to the poor, all three countries would have a 30% poverty rate. After assistance, both Germany and the Netherlands have a 7% rate. American welfare programs, meager in comparison, bring about only a 12% drop, resulting in an 18% poverty rate—more than double that of Germany and the Netherlands.[64]

Black Poverty, Black Affluence

Today, central cities house 40% of America's poor. Poor whites are captured in this percentage, but most of them do not live in neighborhoods with high concentrations of poverty. A study of the five largest cities in the U.S. found that 68% of poor whites live in areas where the majority of their neighbors are not poor. The same is true for only 15% of poor blacks and 20% of poor Hispanics. Conversely, whereas only 7% of poor whites live in extremely impoverished areas (with poverty rates at or above 40%), 32% of Hispanics and 40% of blacks live in such neighborhoods.[65] Another study finds that the number of social establishments—such places as banks, grocery stores, pharmacies, restaurants, and childcare centers—increase as a neighborhood's poverty level increases but decrease as a neighborhood's proportion of blacks increases. In other words, it is not poor neighborhoods that are lacking these establishments but poor *black* neighborhoods.[66] "To be a poor man is hard, but to be a poor race in a land of dollars is the very bottom of hardships."[67]

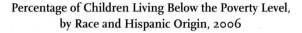

Percentage of Children Living Below the Poverty Level,
by Race and Hispanic Origin, 2006

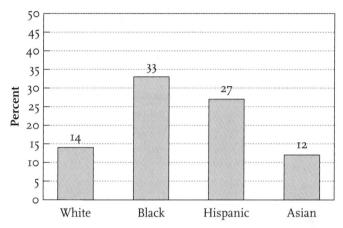

In the **black ghetto**—a racial institution marked by social isolation and economic vulnerability first formed when blacks emigrated north during the early twentieth century—poverty is more concentrated and everyday establishments are scarce. What is more, its isolated residents suffer from pandemic unemployment and are cut off from social networks of working people who could tell them about employment opportunities and help them get jobs. People who live outside the ghetto, and who are connected to job networks, often find out about jobs in the inner city faster than the people who actually live there.[68]

During the latter decades of the twentieth century, inner-city poverty in ghetto neighborhoods became more severe and more concentrated.[69] Why? Social scientists have advanced three interlocking explanations.[70] The first, often referred to as the **spatial mismatch thesis**, holds that jobs that employed large numbers of semi-skilled black workers—manufacturing jobs—were moved in large numbers from the central city to the suburbs at the end of the twentieth century. From the end of the Second World War until the beginning of the 1970s, central cities in the biggest metropolitan areas lost 880,000 manufacturing jobs and 867,000 positions in retail and wholesale trade, while these cities' suburbs gained millions of jobs in these industries. Large cities began to look like donuts with job opportunities concentrated in the (mainly white) suburbs and a drastic dearth or absence of opportunities in the (mainly nonwhite) central city. This resulted in massive unemployment rates and concentrated poverty.[71]

The second explanation has to do with **residential segregation**, a topic to which we shall return in Chapter 5. Many blacks who wanted to leave the ghetto, and who had the means to do so, simply couldn't because of entrenched racial segregation and the virtual absence of fair housing policy enforcement. Writing in 1945, St. Clair Drake and Horace Clayton, authors of *Black Metropolis*, summed up the problem concisely: "The impecunious immigrant, once he gets on his feet, may . . . move into an area of second-settlement. Even the vice-lord or gangster, after he makes his pile, may lose himself in a respectable neighborhood. Negroes, regardless of their affluence or respectability, wear the badge of color. They are expected to stay in the Black Belt."[72] What is more, housing policy financed the suburbanization of America—offering large tax breaks for businesses relocating to the suburbs and subsidizing suburban housing developments—but by and large restricted these boosts to white citizens. Indeed, the Federal Housing Association operated under the assumption that integrated neighborhoods would drive down property values. Hence, we read in its *Underwriting Manual* from the period, "If a neighborhood is to retain stability, it is necessary that properties shall continue to be occupied by the same social and racial classes."[73]

As a result, during the first half of the twentieth century, many black neighborhoods were integrated along class lines: the educated were neighbors to the uneducated, the white collar home abutted the blue collar lawn. However, the Civil Rights Movement broke down legally enforced barriers to residential mobility, and many middle-class black families moved out of the central city. This is the third explanation for the concentration and exacerbation of racialized poverty in the ghetto. Black inner-city neighborhoods experienced a kind of **brain drain**, where the more educated, wealthy, and privileged left behind families who constituted "the truly disadvantaged," to borrow a phrase from sociologist William Julius Wilson.[74] The declining presence of middle-class blacks, writes Wilson, "deprives ghetto neighborhoods of key resources, including structural resources (such as residents with income to sustain neighborhood services) and cultural resources (such as conventional role models for neighborhood children)."[75] Recently, however, researchers have challenged this point, arguing that most middle-class blacks live, not interspersed throughout predominantly white suburbs, but in predominantly black middle-class neighborhoods usually positioned between black ghettos and white neighborhoods. (We will return to this point in Chapter 5.) "The ghetto . . . is not bereft of role models and institutions," observes sociologist Mary Pattillo-McCoy. "What is missing are jobs that pay a decent wage, health care, decent affordable housing, and effective educations."[76]

The black middle class receives much less attention from journalists, reporters, and scholars than do the black poor, despite the fact that the majority of blacks are not poor. Seventy-five percent of blacks belong to the middle and upper classes. Although a black elite has existed since slavery and Reconstruction, the black middle class did not begin to flourish until the 1960s, after the Civil Rights Movement. Like the white middle class, the black middle class largely was formed through government programs: civil rights legislation that eroded legally enforced barriers to upward advancement as well as the de-whitening of affirmation action programs.

Before 1960, less than 10% of the black population could be considered middle class, with only 385,586 black women and men in the entire country working as business owners, professionals, or officials. By the end of the 1980s, that percentage had grown to 45%, with over a million blacks employed in such professions.[77] Over the last thirty years, black enterprises have multiplied at an impressive rate. In 1973, the combined sales of the top 100 black-owned businesses came to $473 million; in 2007, that total amounts to over $27 billion. Between 1999 and 2002, black-owned firms grew by 45%; and today there are over 1.3 million black-owned businesses in the U.S. Black-owned banks, such as OneUnited Bank and Broadway Federal, have prospered and are reaching out to black neighborhoods, as are black-owned insurance companies, newspapers, and computer industries. Over 200 black women and men have ascended to the upper ranks of Fortune 500 companies.[78]

Despite these impressive gains, we must not make the mistake of thinking that black affluence is identical to white affluence. The bulk of the black middle class belongs to the *lower* middle class. Although there are successful black surgeons and stock brokers aplenty, most black middle-class women and men work in sales or as clerks or public-service workers, garnering much lower wages than professionals belonging to the upper middle class.[79] And, as we have already seen, white middle-class families tend to have much more wealth than black middle-class families—even if the families have similar incomes. One study compared white and black middle-class families and found, should they need to dip into their reserves to make ends meet—say, a company goes out of business—the typical white family could survive at the poverty line for a whole year. The typical black family would not last a month.[80]

Just as black poverty is accompanied by disadvantages that do not trouble many poor whites, black middle-class families must confront challenges that many white middle-class families do not. Some have argued that while poor blacks suffer from economic exploitation and social isolation, middle-class blacks suffer "in a spiritual sense," as E. Franklin Frazier put it in *Black Bourgeoisie*.[81] Affluent blacks, having succeeded in life—having graduated from college, secured a stable job, purchased a home, and stored some money away in savings—continue to be met at every turn by racial domination.

Since the fall of slavery, some blacks have held tight to the belief that, once they obtain some professional and financial success, whites will extend to them their respect and friendship. Booker T. Washington, a powerful black political leader who gained fame around the turn of the twentieth century, once addressed a crowd saying that whenever he had "seen a black man who was succeeding in business, who was a taxpayer, and who possessed intelligence and high character, that

Neighborhood Social and Economic Characteristics of the Average Middle-Class Black and White Person in Metropolitan Philadelphia, 2000

Neighborhood Indicator	Average Middle-Class White Philadelphian	Average Middle-Class Black Philadelphian
Neighborhood median income	$53,195	$34,741
Neighborhood poverty rate	7.4%	20.4%
Percent college educated	28.3%	16.5%
Percent professionals	37.4%	28.4%
Neighborhood unemployment rate	4.8%	11.4%
Neighborhood housing vacancy rate	4.6%	10.6%
Homeownership	72.0%	60.5%
Percent "own group"	83.8%	60.9%

SOURCE: Compiled from data reported in *Separate and Unequal: Racial and Ethnic Neighborhoods in the 21st Century*. http://browns4.dyndns.org/cen2000_s4/SepUneq/PublicSeparateUnemqual.htm. Accessed Jan. 7, 2005.

individual was treated with the highest respect by the members of the white race."[82] But blacks soon came to realize the hollowness of such statements. Now they could afford a home, but realtors refused to show them properties outside the black area of town. Now they had earned a college degree, but companies would not hire them. Now they had worked diligently and loyally, but the promotion was offered to someone else. Cut after cut after cut—these everyday acts of violence can result in a spiritual suffering brought on by the realization that something as unreasonable as racism cannot always be won over by reason. Something that seeks to dehumanize a people does not routinely wither and die when those people assert their humanity. Middle-class blacks have learned that money can help them ascend to very high places, but it cannot lift them above the veil of racism.

American Indian Reservations

The central city is not the only site of American destitution; poverty also is pervasive in many rural communities. Since their creation, American Indian reservations have been wracked by extreme rural poverty. The median household income for American Indians on reservations is less than half the U.S. average, and the poverty rate is 3.5 times the national average. The unemployment rate on reservations fluctuates around 50%, and the number of homes lacking complete plumbing is 19 times the national average. The Pine Ridge Indian Reservation in South Dakota has a shocking 75% unemployment rate, and its per capita income is only a quarter the national average. Although the Crow Reservation houses one of the largest coal reserves in the world, most of those living on the reservation face bleak economic conditions: over 50% of tribal members receive some public assistance. By and large, American Indian reservations are plagued by dire poverty, joblessness, and poor living conditions.[83]

Some tribes, however, are prospering. With a popular golf resort, developed construction industries, and flourishing plastic, automotive, and electronics manufacturing plants, the Choctaw tribe is the second largest employer in Mississippi, generating over $170 million dollars in annual wages and supplying 12,000 jobs. Not only are most Choctaws employed, but the tribe provides jobs for over 6,000 black and white workers in surrounding counties. Northern Arizona's White Mountain Apache Tribe runs a ski resort, manages prime logging forests, employs hundreds of workers at a busy sawmill, and brings in revenue with hunting and fishing tourism. Like the Choctaw, the Apache's economic prosperity has spilled over into non-Indian communities, benefiting those in surrounding areas. And the Salish and Kootenai Tribes, living on Montana's Flathead Reservation, have built up successful tourism, agricultural, and retail enterprises. The tribes' unemployment rate is lower than the state's average, and non-Indians seeking a solid education often apply to the tribal college.[84]

So why are some tribes beating poverty while others are beaten by it? Indian gaming is a popular answer. Since 1998, roughly 200 of the 559 federally recognized tribes have ventured into gaming, and some tribes have profited considerably. But this is rare. The top 13% of Indian casinos account for 60% of Indian gaming revenue, which means that an elite group of tribes—namely, those with prime locations—are doing well, while most are drawing in unimpressive profits. Indian gaming is not a viable economic strategy for isolated tribes located in the backcountry, and some Indian Nations, such as the Navajo Nation, have outlawed casinos on their land for fear that they would erode traditional culture and breed gambling addiction. And Indian gaming usually comes with a high cost: it tends to chip away at tribes' political sovereignty. This is a serious drawback because sovereignty seems to be connected directly with Indian economic sustainability and advancement.[85]

Tribal sovereignty means the power of Indian tribes to act as semi-autonomous states, designing and running their own system of governance. Since 1970 the federal government, responding to American Indian political resurgence, began recognizing tribes' right to self-rule. "Indian Peoples are nations, not minorities," David Wilkens once asserted.[86] Tribal sovereignty, or "Indian self-determination," allowed many tribes to chart their own course on matters of economic development, political decision making, and the management of natural resources. As a result, several tribes exercising their sovereignty have developed new economic initiatives and have invested in reservation communities, ensuring that American Indian resources benefit American Indian people instead of outside investors. And tribal sovereignty works best, studies have demonstrated, when Indian Nations develop proficient institutions rooted in the cultural foundations of the tribe. Indian culture is itself a valuable resource to Indian Nations working toward independence, because tribes that align their political governance with their heritage seem to be the most successful.[87]

The Pueblo de Cochiti of New Mexico is one such tribe. Operating under a traditional form of rule, the tribe's top six positions are chosen every year by the Cochiti chief spiritual leader, the Cacique. Though this form of government operates without a constitution, it does include a very sophisticated system of checks and balances. If the lieutenant governor finds that spiritual leaders are abusing their power, he can exercise immediate impeachment rights. Policy development is guided by the Pueblo Council, made up of forty male tribal members. And the Cacique himself—who, though he is the most powerful member of the tribe, often occupies a more humble position in the economic sector—is forbidden to use any Cochiti money for his own enrichment. This system of governance serves the Cochiti well today, as the tribe is a paragon of economic success. Operating a retirement community, a marina, a golf course, and a number of other profitable enterprises, it boasts of one of the lowest unemployment rates in all of Indian Country.[88]

Some American Indian tribes are beginning to overcome poverty that has riddled reservations since their inception. Much work, however, remains to be done. In the final analysis, the economic problems in Indian Country are best confronted by political solutions—not the "quick fix" of Indian gaming, despite all the glitter and controversy. "Economic development on Indian reservations is first and foremost a political problem," write sociologists Stephen Cornell and Joseph Kalt. "At the heart of it lie sovereignty and the governing institutions through which sovereignty can be effectively exercised. . . . It is increasingly evident that the best way to perpetuate reservation poverty is to undermine tribal sovereignty. The best way to overcome reservation poverty is to support tribal sovereignty."[89]

The Struggles of Immigrants

Immigrants are another group disproportionately affected by poverty. Over the last thirty years, the poverty level for children of immigrants—who make up no less than one in five U.S. children—has increased, rising from 12% in 1970 to 21% in 2000. Some estimates conclude that one in three children of immigrants live in poverty. And things are markedly worse for those who do not carry naturalization papers.[90]

As we discussed in Chapter 2, the United States maintained strict limitations on immigration throughout most of the twentieth century. Certain groups—such as Italians—came under quota restrictions, while other groups—namely, people from Japan, China, Korea, and other parts of Asia and the Pacific Rim—were barred from entry altogether. The **Immigration and Nationality Act of 1965,** drafted in the wake of the Civil Rights Movement, changed all this by abolishing national-origin quotas. Although the Act established limitations on the number of visas allotted each year to most immigrants (distributed on a first-come, first-served basis), it did not limit family reunification visas, which allowed immigrants with family members in the U.S. to be admitted. Fifteen years later, the 1980 Refugee Act was ratified. This act provided political asylum for refugees and asylees victimized on the basis of their race, religion, nationality, political affiliation, or group membership.

These two acts drastically changed immigrant flows to America. Immigrants from Latin America (Mexico in particular) and Asia began coming to America in large numbers, as did refugees, asylees, and undocumented migrants from many parts of the globe. Many immigrants from Mexico, finally reunited with their families, came with little education and little money in their pockets. Today, Mexican immigrants rank among the poorest immigrant groups with a 36% poverty rate for first-generation children. Vietnamese, Hmong, Cambodian, and Laotian families fled their countries during the Vietnam Wars and the subsequent American bombings of Cambodia. In 1975, roughly 150,000 refugees were airlifted out of Vietnam, and over 85,000 were relocated to the United States. Many of these refugees' homes had been firebombed and their property burned or stolen—and in America most remained in poverty.[91]

Note that there is no monolithic "immigrant experience" or natural sequence through which those fresh off the boat assimilate to American society, politics, and culture. Rather, immigrants are absorbed into different segments of the American landscape. Some assimilate into the upper classes, some into the lower classes. The body of thought that explores these processes is called **segmented assimilation theory.** Sociologists Alejandro Portes and Min Zhou describe three common pathways through which immigrants adapt to American society. "One of them replicates the time-honored portrayal of growing acculturation and parallel integration into the white middle-class; a second leads straight into the opposite direction to permanent poverty and assimilation into the underclass; still a third associates rapid economic advancement with deliberate preservation of the immigrant community's values and tight solidarity."[92] In other words, new immigrants either join the ranks of the economically privileged, the economically downtrodden, or the moderately prosperous ethnic economy. There is no so-called "Middle America" into which immigrants enter after a process of assimilation. Because American society is divided along all sorts of lines, on arrival new immigrants are met with a range of divides and are sorted into them accordingly. The important question is this: What determines their American experience? Why do some immigrants climb upward while others slide down into the depths of poverty?

To answer this question we must look first to the shape of the American economy, just as we did when examining the causes of American poverty in general.

Immigration Border Control and Its Unexpected Consequences

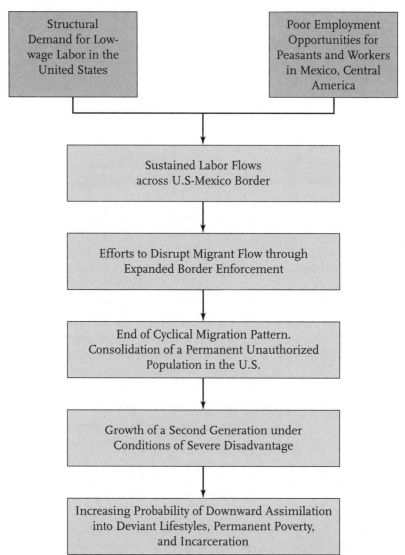

Stable blue-collar jobs with decent wages, jobs that traditionally have been attractive to newly arrived immigrants, are now scarce. And the gap between dream jobs in the professional sector and nightmare jobs in the service sector continues to widen, such that workers on the bottom of the market have virtually no chance of climbing upward. Mobility ladders simply don't reach that high. Consequentially, many immigrants who come without college degrees, let alone high school diplomas, must work in low-wage industries offering little opportunity for eco-nomic advancement. That idea so cherished in the American imagination—the poor immigrant working her or his way to a life of comfort—is becoming less and less a reality in America's hourglass-shaped economy.[93]

However, for those elite immigrants who arrive with wealth, college degrees, and specialized skills, lucrative jobs often await. Thus, to understand divergent immigrant trajectories, we must examine not only the shape of the U.S. econ-omy but also the skills, education, training—in a phase, the **class privileges**—immigrants bring with them. Speaking generally, immigrants from India, China, Africa, Western Europe, and Canada tend to be well educated and to have a higher proportion of professionals and managers in their midst. Those from the Caribbean, El Salvador, Mexico, and other Latin American countries tend to have little education and are represented disproportionately in low wage work. Once they master the English language (if they haven't done so already), highly skilled immigrants who received an education in their mother country usually have little trouble securing professional posts as engineers, mathematicians, scien-tists, and teachers.[94] We should point out, however, that a college degree from a foreign country is not as valued as a U.S. education. A recent study found that similarly educated native-born whites, Asian Americans, and Asian immigrants educated in the United States have similar incomes, but Asian immigrants edu-cated in their home countries earn 16% less than do these three groups.[95]

To the job opportunities found at the very top and the very bottom of the labor market, immigrants have added a third option: employment in the ethnic enclave. An **ethnic enclave** is a semi-autonomous economy, large or small, that is owned, operated, and managed by members of the same immigrant or ethnic commu-nity. In New York City, Dominican immigrants have created an entrepreneurial enclave complete with its own restaurants, travel agencies, and Spanish-speaking newspapers. Here one also finds informal finance agencies called *financieras* that allocate loans and grant credit to Dominicans who are not able to secure them through mainstream banking channels. *Financieras* award loans, which usually are accompanied by low interest rates, based on a person's reputation in the com-munity and her or his personal and familial connections. The same is true in the Cuban enclaves of Miami, where many Cuban-owned businesses were started from "character loans," loans made by agencies in the Cuban community to other Cubans. Salvadoran immigrants in Los Angeles and Washington, D.C. have cul-tivated a growing ethnic enclave as well, one based on transnational enterprises: American goods are shipped to El Salvador, while Salvadoran food, clothing, music, and cultural goods are transported to the United States.[96]

Immigrant women are key players in enclave economies. Seventy-three percent of foreign-born Chinese women are employed—24 percentage points higher than foreign-born European women and 16 points higher than native-born white women.

This is not because Chinese immigrant women have an abundance of class privileges but in spite of this: they have drastically low levels of education (with less than half completing high school) and low English proficiency. Many first-generation Chinese women work in Chinatown-based jobs, such as New York City's garment industry, which employs over half of all working Chinese women in the city. In fact, roughly 70% of all garments sewn in New York City were sewn by the hands of immigrant Chinese women. Many of these women work six days a week for less than minimum wage, bending over machines and, paid by the piece, working as fast as they can. Garment workers often compare their wages, not to those of other Americans, but to what they would earn in China for comparable work. Since their exploitative wages in the United States are higher than Chinese wages, and since few economic opportunities are available beyond the enclave, Chinatown's garment industry is not in want of eager workers. On top of working in the garment shops, immigrant Chinese women are expected (and expect of themselves) to support their husbands and to raise their children. They are responsible for the bulk of the domestic labor—cooking, cleaning, grocery shopping, childcare. First-generation Chinese women, like many immigrant women, are expected to work not one but three full time jobs: wife, mother, and worker. Doubly disadvantaged, these women hold in one hand the demands of a menial job and in the other the demands of a family. Their shoulders must grow weary.[97]

Some studies have shown that immigrants who work in ethnic enclaves earn more money than those with similar education and skills employed in the mainstream economy. For instance, self-employed Asian immigrants earn $6/hour more than other immigrants with similar education and skills.[98] And low-interest character loans requiring little collateral, a creation of the ethnic enclave, have been used by hundreds of immigrants to start their own bookstore, restaurant, or bodega. These findings lead some researchers to conclude that "enclaves are no mere ghetto where foreigners huddle together eking out a living from marginal activities. Instead, ethnic enterprise can be an effective avenue for economic mobility."[99]

Some studies, however, argue that ethnic enclaves impede immigrants' upward mobility. Finding that enclave-employed immigrants are not better off than those working elsewhere, earning low wages and sometimes facing unfair working conditions, some scholars have labeled enclaves "ethnic mobility traps." Researchers have observed that San Francisco's Chinatown is controlled by a small group of elite clans who often bar from their enterprise immigrants unwilling to adopt their conservative political opinions. Others have noted that the Cuban enclave in Miami benefits men more than women.[100] Social scientists have not yet resolved what has come to be known as the "enclave economy debate." At best, we can conclude only that ethnic enclaves seem to offer newly arrived immigrants looking for reliable work a mixed bag of advantages and disadvantages.

Roughly 70% of all garments sewn in New York City are sewn by immigrant Chinese women.

Besides the structure of the economy, the class privileges (or lack thereof) of immigrants, and ethnic enclaves, there is a final mechanism that determines how well immigrants fare in America: racial privileges.[101] On coming to America, immigrants immediately are confronted with its racial order. They are branded with foreign racial classifications—Indonesians, Cambodians, and Koreans become "Asian"; Russian Jews, Croatians, and Germans become "white"—which affects their economic trajectories. Plainly, taking into account class privileges, such as education and job training, immigrants classified as white and Asian tend to do better than immigrants classified as Hispanic or black. Recently, researchers found 21% of first-generation immigrants classified as white to be poor; the same was true of 24% of those classified as black, 27% of those classified as Asian, and 41% of those classified as Hispanic. When they looked at the economic standing of the children of immigrants, "the second generation," they noticed that many were not as poor are their parents. But they also noticed that some racial groups fared better than others. For whites and Asians, the poverty level dropped more than a half, whereas it declined less than a third for blacks and Hispanics. When the researchers observed the economic conditions of the children of children of immigrants, "the third generation," they were confronted with a shocking finding: the poverty rate for Asians declined further; it remained the same for whites and Hispanics; but it *increased* by 26 percentage points for blacks. By and large, third-generation black immigrants were poorer than were their grandparents, who emigrated from Haiti, the West Indies, or South Africa.[102] The American dream of poor immigrants carving out a better life, if not for themselves then at least for their children, comes more easily to those classified near the privileged end of America's racial hierarchy.

Racial privileges shape economic privileges. They make it harder for immigrants of color to cash in on their education, to find stable and well-paying jobs, and to gain economic security. Recognizing this, many immigrants resist Americanized racial classification by emphasizing their "immigrant-ness." For instance, West Indian parents often cultivate in their children an island accent so they might take advantage of employment opportunities not offered their African American peers.[103] Such adaptive strategies are rewarded by employers, many of whom would rather hire immigrants than native-born Hispanics or blacks. The irony of this racialized process is that immigrants who refuse to assimilate are rewarded, while immigrants who assimilate with racial groups are punished. This is why sociologist Mary Waters observes that "we should not just be asking as a society, 'How can we structure our immigration policy and our institutions to facilitate immigrants adopting our civic culture and becoming American?' We should also be asking, 'What can we do about the pervasive inequalities in American life that often mean that becoming black American or Mexican American leads to a less bright future than remaining an immigrant?'"[104]

Labor Market Dynamics

Getting a Job

The unemployment rate has fluctuated greatly over the past fifty years. It decreased from 1950 to 1960, only to increase sharply through the 70s, peak in the early 80s, and climb slowly down until 1990. It increased slightly in the early 90s but decreased for the remainder of the decade. Despite all this fluctuation, one thing has remained the same: the nonwhite unemployment rate consistently has been double that of whites. If you remove blacks from the equation, the difference shrinks considerably. In 2006, the unemployment rates by race were as follows: whites 4%, blacks 9%, Hispanics 5.5%, and Asians 3%. What can explain these racial disparities—and blacks' high rates of unemployment in particular?

Americans debating this question have divided into two camps. On one side there are those who believe that "impersonal market forces" explain racial inequalities in the labor force. "It's not racism per se," argues this camp. "Nonwhites are disadvantaged in terms of lower wages and higher unemployment rates because they don't have the necessary schooling or skills to compete in today's economy. If nonwhites had the same training as whites, things would even out." On the other side are those who explain racial inequalities by institutional racism.

Although the labor market continues to be marred by racial inequality, nonwhites have made impressive advances in the professional realm.

"Blacks and Hispanics have higher unemployment rates, because they are denied job opportunities solely on the basis of their skin color," argues this camp. "To understand racial cleavages in the workforce, we must pay attention to persistent discrimination." Because each camp sees the world differently, each has its own policy recommendations. Those who believe that the problem lies in impersonal market forces hold that the solution lies in job training programs and inner-city education. Those who believe that discrimination is the problem claim that education is not enough; they advocate civil rights legislation, affirmative action programs, and "diversity education" in the workplace.[105] Which camp is right?

Those who point to the persistence of institutional racism have mountains of evidence to back them up. Social scientists have amassed libraries full of data that conclusively and convincingly show how qualified Hispanics and blacks seeking jobs are passed over for white applicants. One study found that employers were three to four times more likely to offer whites a job than equally qualified blacks or Hispanics. In another study, nearly half of employers interviewed in four major cities criticized blacks' skills and work ethic, while Hispanics and Asians, praised for their "immigrant work ethic," were not evaluated nearly so negatively.[106] As we mentioned in the preceding section, some employers would rather hire immigrants than native-born people of color. A white supervisor who oversees the hiring procedures for a service firm confessed to one interviewer: "The Polish immigrants that I know and know of are more highly motivated than the Hispanics. The Hispanics share in some of the problems that the blacks do."[107] Some firms recruit directly from white immigrant populations, advertising openings in German- or Polish-language papers instead of in the local English paper.

In another study, 185 employers based in Chicago were asked if they believe different racial groups have different work ethics. Half claimed they noticed no difference or refused to categorize their workers in such a fashion. But 38% claimed that blacks have the weakest work ethic out of all groups, and 8% placed both blacks and Hispanics at the bottom of the ranking. No employer reserved this demeaning evaluation for whites.[108] And studies have found that employers stereotype black men as poor, from the ghetto, and belligerent—and black women as single mothers living (welfare) paycheck to paycheck.[109]

Audit studies are an especially powerful way to determine if and how discrimination affects hiring decisions. These studies send paired actors to apply for real jobs. The actors are equal in every way aside from race.[110] In one experiment, economists Marianne Bertrand and Sendhil Mullainathan responded to 1,300 help-wanted ads by submitting résumés from phantom job applicants. The résumés reported similar skill levels, education, and experience but differed on one account: the names. Some were assigned names common among blacks (like Lakisha and Jamal); others were assigned names common among whites (like Emily and Greg). The results? Compared to applicants with black-sounding names, those with white-sounding names were 50% more likely to be called for an interview.[111]

In another creative audit experiment, sociologist Devah Pager sent four men to apply for 350 low-skill jobs in Milwaukee. Two white men made up one pair, two black men formed another. Within each pair, one applicant reported having been convicted of a felony drug charge. Besides race and criminal record, the actors as applicants were identical on all other measures. Pager found that 34% of whites without a criminal record received callbacks from the employer, but the same was true of only 17% of whites with a criminal record. And only 14% of black applicants without a criminal record, and 5% with a record, received callbacks. In other words, whites convicted of selling drugs were more likely to land a job than were blacks with no criminal history![112]

Taken together, these studies offer irrefutable evidence that institutionalized racism denies qualified blacks and Latinos job opportunities. The "discrimination matters" camp is right. Does this mean that the "impersonal market forces" camp is wrong? Yes and no. They are wrong to think the market is detached from society. Since the economy is embedded in social relations, as we have already seen, an argument touting the explanatory superiority of class instead of race is flawed from the get go. However, this camp is right to stress how a good education, networks of employed friends and family members, and skill training disproportionately are denied to nonwhites. Thus, the division between the

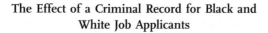

The Effect of a Criminal Record for Black and
White Job Applicants

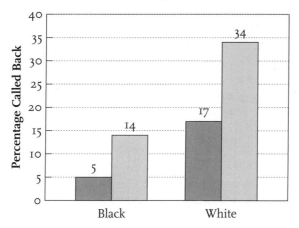

"market forces" camp and the "discrimination" camp in fact is a *false division*. It is a non-debate, one that signals not a bona fide point of dispute but racial domination manifest in multiple fields of life (for example, the educational, associational, political fields).[113]

Institutional racism in hiring decisions compounds with institutional racism in other points of time and in other sectors of society. Whites in America have a history of hording opportunities. **Opportunity hoarding**, according to sociologist Charles Tilly, occurs when members of one race "acquire access to a resource that is valuable, renewable, [and] subject to monopoly" and guard that resource from members of other races.[114] The resource that many whites obtained during the middle to late decades of the twentieth century was nothing less than a hearty slice of the American pie. In the words of one historian, the story of America in the mid- to late-twentieth century "is a history of the ways that whites . . . were able to hoard political and economic resources—jobs, public services, education, and other goods—to their own advantage at the expense of the urban poor."[115] This gross imbalance of opportunities directly affects labor market dynamics today.

What is more, **disadvantage breeds disadvantage.** Since blacks and Latinos are discriminated against when applying for jobs, many have a spotty work history. Since they have a spotty work history, they are less attractive to employers. Again, if institutional racism channels many blacks and Hispanics into periods of unemployment or low-wage work, then they will have a difficult time cultivating within their children a middle class disposition—those ineffable "soft skills" such as social graces and professional communicative styles, often bound up with white privilege—for which employers often look.[116] And they will not be able to help their family and friends secure employment in good-paying work, which is precisely what social scientists have found.[117]

We cannot understand racial inequalities within the workforce without accounting for the pernicious fact of discrimination. But neither should we forget that racial domination, having a long and established career, has robbed many nonwhites of opportunities to build up class privileges: education, soft skills, job training, connections to powerful people. The source of the problem is threefold: a history of opportunity hoarding; modern day racial discrimination at the point of hiring; and institutional racism at work in other fields of life.

Racial Antagonism and Interracialism in a Split Labor Market

In the industrial northern cities of the 1920s and 30s, blacks, many of them men who had recently emigrated from the South, began securing jobs as meatpackers, steel workers, bricklayers, and carpenters. By some estimates, the black unemployment rate in northern and western cities at this time was significantly lower than the white rate. Why were black workers more attractive to employers? Because they were more exploitable. Compared to whites, blacks worked longer hours for lower wages. During this time, many "whites only" unions barred blacks from membership, and some spokespeople in the black community, persuaded by capitalists who owned the factories, became ministers of symbolic violence and discouraged blacks from organizing as workers. The result was the weakening of black militant labor. Unorganized, black workers had no bargaining power. They could not demand from their employers better wages or improved working conditions, nor could they strike if their employers paid them no mind.[118]

Always seeking the cheapest labor available, employers often replaced white workers with blacks, who came to be known as "strike insurance" to some company owners.[119] And when white workers went on strike, blacks often were used as strikebreakers. During the Great Steel Strike of 1919—when over a quarter million steel workers walked out of their jobs when their companies refused to raise their wages and shorten their workday—some 40,000 black workers were brought in to weaken the strike. Many were imported from the rural South. In large part because of this, employers crippled the strike, forcing the steel workers to return to the same dangerous conditions for the same meager wages.[120] Racialized strike breaking occurs to this day. In 2004, when workers at the Tyson Foods meat processing plant in Jefferson, Wisconsin were forced to strike when the company initiated wage cuts and withdrew benefit packages, African Americans from the nearby town of Beloit were bussed in to replace the striking workers.

Employers use blacks and other racially and economically dominated groups to weaken union mobilizing, drive down wages, and maintain oppressive working

That some employers would rather hire undocumented workers on the cheap than native-born union members helps to stir up anti-immigrant sentiment.

conditions, because America has a **split labor market.** "To be split," writes sociologist Edna Bonacich, "a labor market must contain at least two groups of workers whose price of labor differs for the same work, or would differ if they did the same work."[121] According to Bonacich, a split labor market is steered by the struggles of three groups: the business elite, higher paid labor, and cheap labor. The business elite own and run the companies and seek the cheapest labor possible. The higher paid labor work in these companies and, through union organizing, have secured a decent wage and fair working conditions. However, higher paid labor lives in constant threat of cheap labor, which the business elite can hire to cut costs. Because the division between higher paid labor and cheap labor corresponds to racial divisions, competition between the two labor groups can heighten racial antagonism. Today, for instance, the fact that some employers would rather hire undocumented workers on the cheap than native-born union members helps to stir up anti-immigrant sentiment.

At the same time, some unions have begun actively recruiting Mexican immigrants, documented or otherwise. After losing many jobs to nonunionized workers, a significant number of whom were undocumented immigrants, the United

Brotherhood of Carpenters and Joiners have started to reach out to immigrants. "If you want [your union] to grow, you have to represent the people who are doing the work," said one Colorado union leader.[122] Thus, just as competition for jobs can lead to racial antagonism, organizing across the color line to secure fair and honest working conditions can lead to **interracialism**: the process of forming a racially integrated political community that works toward a common goal.[123]

The formation of Hawaii's racially diverse working-class movement provides a unique glimpse into the process of interracialism. After the islands of Hawaii were colonized, white settlers from Britain and America sought a cheap labor force to work the sugar plantations. They found it in native Hawaiians and migrants from China, Japan, and the Philippines. However, by 1870 the American-led anti-Chinese movement pressured Hawaii's business elite to abandon their Chinese laborers and whiten their workforce. The elites gave in and began importing workers from Portugal. Although the Portuguese workers were not granted complete admission into Hawaii's *haole* race—the Hawaiian word (literally "foreigner") used to describe European immigrants to the islands—they were considered whiter than workers from Asia. Japanese workers were considered racially inferior and, especially after the bombing of Pearl Harbor and the ensuing construction of Japanese internment camps, were seen as anti-American. But Filipinos were thought to sit lower still than the Japanese, occupying the lowest point in Hawaii's racial hierarchy. So, the *haole* worked to uphold white supremacy; the Portuguese hoped to be admitted to the privileged race, deriding Asian immigrants; and the Japanese joined other groups in disdaining Filipinos.[124]

But in the 1930s, things began to change. Union campaigns began to organize workers around one central idea: the fight is not against one another but against white supremacy and worker exploitation. As one labor organizer put it, "We want you in [this union] where all brothers are alike . . . Japanese, Filipinos, Portuguese, *haoles,* and all are the same."[125] Union meetings were held in multiple languages—English, Japanese, and Ilocano—and affirmative action policies were put in place such that each racial group was well represented in union leadership. Hawaii's working class began to recast the racial system, blaming the *haole* business elite, not only for exploiting their labor but also for reinforcing racial divides.

Hawaii's interracial working-class movement was tested in 1946, when sugar workers called for an all-industry strike. The business elite wouldn't budge at the bargaining table, figuring a strike would rekindle old racial divisions and smother the interracial unions. The strike, however, had the opposite effect. Workers demanded not only better pay but also antidiscrimination guidelines, a radical proposition twenty years before the Civil Rights Act. Drawing strength and identity from their newly formed intergroup alliances, workers walked the picket lines for seventy-nine days. The employers finally conceded to their demands. Summing up the victory, a union leader declared, "It is the first time in the history of Hawaii that a strike of sugar workers on the plantations of Hawaii has ever been won. The first time in history that a strike of sugar workers has been conducted where there has been no split along racial lines."[126]

In the split labor market, the business elite can employ racial domination on behalf of worker exploitation, pitting one group against another to thwart interracial worker solidarity and to keep the price of labor as low as possible. If workers participate in these racial struggles, forming prejudices against Chinese workers (as in the late nineteenth century), black workers (as in the early twentieth century), or Mexican workers (as in the present day), they tend to blame other exploited workers for their exploitation, instead of focusing on the real source of the problem: the business elite. In so doing, they unknowingly inflict upon themselves a form of symbolic violence, forging the chains that weigh them down. If, however, workers refuse to play by the rules of this game and instead build interracial coalitions, as did the Hawaiian working class, they can commit their energies to confronting the structural conditions that produce economic vulnerability and hellish working conditions. The key point, therefore, is that a split labor market dependent on racial cleavages disadvantages *all* workers—white and nonwhite, documented and undocumented—alike.

By exploring the racial dynamics of a split labor market, we are better able to understand one of the causes of interpersonal racism. Interpersonal racism shapes and is shaped by institutional racism in the economic field. In the words of Herbert Blumer, "race prejudice exists basically in a sense of group position rather than in a set of feelings which members of one racial group have toward the members of another racial group. This different way of viewing race prejudice shifts study and analysis from a preoccupation with feelings as lodged in individuals to a concern with the relationship of racial groups."[127] Specifically, racial antagonism is heightened when we begin to believe that in order to grasp hold of society's resources—jobs, safe neighborhoods, good education—we must engage in a competition with other racialized groups. And if we perceive those resources to be scarce, studies have shown, we are more likely to harbor racial resentment toward other groups.[128]

When we begin speaking in terms of "our" jobs or "our" neighborhoods being threatened by "them," we fall prey to a sociological shortsightedness that encourages us to blame exploited people, instead of scrutinizing the structures that create such exploitation in the first place. In today's working-class America, Mexican immigrants are perhaps the group most often blamed for "stealing our jobs." But listen to the poet, Jimmy Santiago Baca: "So Mexicans are taking jobs from Americans. O Yes? Do they come on horses with rifles, and say, *Ese*, gringo, gimme your job? . . . Below that cool green sea of money, millions and millions of people fight to live, search for pearls in the darkest depths of their dreams, hold their breath for years trying to cross poverty to just having something. The children are dead already. We are killing them, that is what Americans should be saying. . . . Mexicans are taking our jobs, they say instead. What they really say is, let them die, and the children too."[129]

Power and Privilege in the Workplace

Since the Civil Rights Movement, nonwhite women and men, as well as white women, have climbed the corporate ladder, earning seats of power previously reserved for white men. However, entrenched barriers of white male privilege have proven themselves resilient, as the workplace continues to be infiltrated by racial and masculine domination. Recent studies exploring middle-class occupations have found that blacks are nearly twice as likely to be laid off than whites, a difference that could not be explained by conventional measures, such as seniority or education. In other words, race is the main explanation as to why blacks working in white-collar professions are the first to be fired.[130] With respect to promotions, women and people of color—with similar years of schooling and similar years working for a company—are less likely to hold positions of authority than their white male counterparts. In fact, relative to blacks and Hispanics, whites are twice as likely to be supervisors—controlling budgets, wielding power over hiring and firing decisions, instructing subordinates—while Asians seem to be on par with whites on this score.[131]

Many nonwhites who have ascended to positions of authority tend to be low-level supervisors overseeing other nonwhites and, relative to white men, are cut off from social ties and communication channels that could otherwise connect them to opportunities, resources, and influential people.[132] Standing out against other (mostly white male) supervisors, nonwhites in positions of power, especially those placed there as racial tokens, often are subjected to intense monitoring and scrutiny. Many feel isolated and weighted down by performance pressures. They are cut off from other nonwhite workers because of their superiority and cut off from other superiors because of their race.[133]

Hindered by intersecting modes of domination, women of color are doubly disadvantaged in the workplace. In general, black, Latina, and Asian women fill low-status and low-paying positions relative to white women and nonwhite men. And women of color are rewarded less for their education and job experience than are white men, white women, or men of color. In fact, if black women were paid as much as white men with similar credentials, they would earn on average $7,000 more per year![134] Just as a country's financial exchange rate fluctuates depending on its position in the global economy, so, too, one's human capital exchange rate is determined by one's position in the American racial and gender orders.[135]

Thus, on entering the workplace, white women, men of color, and women of color (to varying degrees) are met with **glass ceilings**—unspoken obstacles to advancement designed to handicap members of dominated groups.[136] Glass ceilings seem more prevalent (and thicker) the further one climbs up the corporate hierarchy. Although there are some exceptions to this rule, the highest positions of power continue to be dominated by white men.[137] It goes without saying that glass ceilings result in serious consequences. One study estimated that barriers to career promotion account for one-third of the income gap between black and white men.[138]

So what keeps glass ceilings in place? Sociologists have identified a process known as **homosocial reproduction.** Put simply, authorities tend to fill positions of power with people like themselves. As Rosabeth Moss Kanter put it in *Men and Women of the Corporation,* organizational rules are much more formalized and clear at the bottom of the organizational hierarchy.[139] Things are murkier at the top. For instance, if you work at a software company, they might guarantee you will advance to a managerial position after five years of work. There are no such guarantees when it comes to appointing the company's vice president. Because of this, high-level supervisors can show great discretion in staffing supervisory positions, and as dozens of studies have demonstrated, they often do so by excluding qualified candidates whose gender or racial identity differs from their own. A white man's chances of securing a supervisory position are doubled if his supervisor (the one doing the promoting) is also a white man. The same pattern holds for nonwhites. For instance, the odds of a black woman advancing to a high-level supervisory position increase dramatically if her supervisor is black. Homosocial reproduction is practiced by whites and nonwhites alike. However, because they are disproportionately represented in positions of power, only white men can do so with some regularity. In other words, "ingroup favoritism may be universal, but opportunities to practice it are not."[140]

Welfare

The final two sections of this chapter take up two policies that greatly affect racial dynamics in the economic field: welfare and affirmative action. With these topics, there has been more ranting than reason, more uninformed guesses than educated evidence. The purpose of these last two sections, then, is to see what social science has to say about welfare and affirmative action in employment. (We review the literature on affirmative action in education in Chapter 7.) With respect to welfare, we address three questions: Why is American welfare so skimpy? Who's on welfare? And does welfare lead to dependency?

By **welfare,** we mean government provisions intended to help disadvantaged people, including those who are poor, elderly, war veterans, unemployed, and disabled. In-kind welfare programs allocate resources for specific needs, such as food, medical care, or housing. These include food stamps, Medicaid, and housing subsidies. Cash programs, on the other hand, provide recipients with regular income. These include Temporary Assistance for Needy Families, Social Security, and general assistance.

Why Is American Welfare So Skimpy?

Above we compared American social spending to that of other developed countries and discovered that Japan is the only industrialized country that devotes a smaller portion of its wealth to welfare programs. Why does America lag behind other industrialized nations in welfare spending? Historians have found that America's skinny welfare state can be understood only when we explore the relationship between the development of social spending programs and the career of racial domination. Because New Deal programs only worsened racial inequalities, President Johnson hoped to initiate new welfare programs that promoted racial equality. Through his War on Poverty, launched in the 1960s, Johnson began targeting inner-city ghettos by implementing school improvements, housing allowances, job training, and community action programs. These initiatives were taken up by leaders involved in the Civil Rights Movement, who recognized that racial justice had to be accompanied by economic justice. "What good is it to be allowed to eat in a restaurant if you can't afford a hamburger?" King once asked.[141] When antipoverty programs became intertwined with antiracism movements—and especially after affirmative action was legislated—whites (including working-class and poor whites) began turning away from the Democratic Party and their new policies. The white backlash mounted as suburban homeowners resisted integration and beat back fair-housing laws.

On accepting the White House, Nixon sought to cater to the growing white hostility aimed at nonwhites and antipoverty programs, to reach the "forgotten Americans," as he liked to call them. He shifted the welfare focus away from programs that targeted America's urban poor. Although the far-reaching programs of the War on Poverty would have helped many poor people, white and nonwhite alike, they were thwarted by racial divisions and white backlash. "The long-term legacy of coupling social policy to racial issues has diminished America's ability to stem the decline of the inner cities and to protect the family," laments Jill Quadagno in *The Color of Welfare*.[142]

Since the War on Poverty, welfare spending has continued to be rolled back. In 1996, President Clinton, making good on his promise to "end welfare as we know it," ended America's largest cash assistance program, Aid to Families with Dependent Children (AFDC), replacing it with Temporary Assistance for Needy Families (TANF). TANF placed strict restrictions on how long recipients could collect welfare: two years while unemployed and only five years over a lifetime. Clinton's act, tellingly titled the Personal Responsibility and Work Opportunity

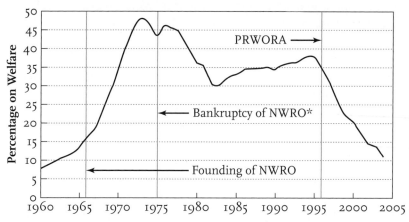

Poor Families Receiving AFDC or TANF, 1960 to 2005

*National Welfare Rights Organization

Reconciliation Act (PRWORA) stressed individual responsibility, moral upright-ness, and a good work ethic.[143]

TANF has pushed many single mothers into the swelling ranks of the work-ing poor. Its supporters have understood this trend as a success, touting a decline in welfare rolls and poverty levels.[144] But if we look beyond the raw numbers, we notice that things have gotten worse for America's poor families. For example, many poor single mothers pressed into low-wage work through the welfare-to-work programs earned more income than they did while on wel-fare. Their official poverty levels *decreased,* but their material hardship *increased.* Single mothers returning to work had to pay for childcare and transportation; and most lost Medicaid benefits and had their food stamps and housing subsi-dies cut. As a consequence, single mothers working in the service sector found themselves worse off than those relying primarily on welfare, even if their incomes were larger.[145]

Before we turn to exploring who's on welfare, we must briefly discuss another form of welfare: that of the corporate variety. If, by welfare, we mean government provisions intended to help disadvantaged people, then, indeed, the American welfare state is anemic. If, however, by welfare we have in mind government provisions reserved exclusively for corporations or industries, payments and ben-efits including grants, contracts, subsidies, tax relief, low-interest loans, and gov-ernment services—in a phrase: **corporate welfare**—then the American welfare state is quite generous. Analysts estimate that, annually, the federal government spends between $90 and $125 billion on corporate welfare. By comparison, in 2008 the federal budget allocated only $16.5 billion in TANF funds.[146]

In the case of corporate welfare, which is usually masked by euphemisms like "economic development" or "public-private partnerships," tax dollars are dedicated not to providing a single mother and her children money to survive on but to providing companies money to build sports stadiums and corporate offices, or to advertize their wares, train workers, or conduct product research.[147] Proponents of these provisions claim that they help the federal government to create jobs; however, studies have found otherwise. In the 1990s, for example, the biggest beneficiaries of corporate welfare slashed roughly a third of a million jobs.[148] And the price tag of some corporate welfare programs was so costly that it is questionable whether taxpayers ever reaped a return on their investment. For example, in 1993 Alabama used $253 million in economic incentives to coax Mercedes-Benz into building an assembly plant near Tuscaloosa, one that would employ 1,500 workers; this amounted to a subsidy of $169,000 for each job. In 1997, Pennsylvania gave $307 million in incentives to a Norwegian engineering company to open a shipyard that would employ 950 workers; this amounted to a subsidy of $323,000 per job.[149]

Who's on Welfare?

Depending on your socioeconomic background, you might be surprised to learn that most Americans have benefited from welfare during some point in their lives. This statement holds true even if we forget about the more universal welfare programs such as Social Security and veterans' assistance (which are not based on recipients' incomes) and concentrate solely on means-tested programs such as food stamps, TANF, and Medicaid (which are income-based). Two-thirds of all Americans collect means-tested public assistance during some point in their lives, 63% of them receiving Medicaid, 52% food stamps, and 13% cash assistance (now TANF).[150] Far from being a crutch only for the poorest of the poor, welfare programs are something most Americans will use.

Many people receive assistance through TANF, including single mothers, refugees, recently unemployed workers, new immigrants, and poor families living in urban and rural areas. Of those receiving TANF aid, 40% are black, 30% are white, 26% are Hispanic, 2% are Asian, and 2% are Native American. Given the historical legacy of economic racism and present-day processes of discrimination, we should not be surprised to learn that blacks and Hispanics are over-represented on welfare lists, accounting for nearly half of all first-time TANF recipients.[151] What is more, several studies have shown that black and Hispanic women were just as (or more) likely to hold continual employment after leaving welfare, yet were more likely to return to welfare than white women.[152]

Social scientists have provided four reasons for this discrepancy. First, poor black and Hispanic women are less likely to have a solid education and to cohabitate or marry than white women are, characteristics associated with longer welfare assistance.[153] Second, and more important, however, is the fact that the networks enveloping white women, supportive family and friends, usually are more privileged than those enveloping nonwhite women. Accordingly, white women looking to lift themselves out of poverty are better able to take advantage of their "private safety net"—money from parents, lovers, or friends—than are women of color, whose social resources are less bountiful.[154]

Third, studies have shown that white single mothers receive assistance from several different kinds of programs (including Social Security, veteran's payments, and unemployment compensation) at much higher rates than single mothers of color, who rely heavily on TANF. White single mothers are better able to beat poverty by drawing on resources offered by a diverse portfolio of programs.[155] The fourth explanation has to do with obstacles women of color face in the labor market. As we have already described, nonwhites face racial discrimination and unequal access to good wages and positions of power. One study found that the average salary of a black woman with a college degree is $25,914, while it is $28,266 for a white man with only a high school diploma![156] If college-educated black women face such unfair discrimination in earnings, imagine the bleak prospects facing black women with little education.

Does Welfare Lead to Dependency?

Much public debate on welfare has revolved around this question. Clinton seemed to think that welfare made people dependent on the government, as do many Americans today. In fact, studies tracing media coverage on social spending since the 1930s have concluded that the concept of dependency has played a leading role in structuring the welfare debate, with concerns about women's dependency ballooning in recent years as concerns about men's dependency fade into the background.[157] Does welfare deplete one's drive to work? On the contrary: studies have shown that most welfare recipients work while on welfare and after welfare. Indeed they must, as one cannot survive by relying on welfare alone. The vast majority of single mothers on welfare must supplement their TANF benefits with other income to make ends meet.[158] Many do so through "care work," watching over children or taking in an ailing friend or family member.[159] Contrary to popular belief, most people on welfare want to work and do work.

Although some evidence suggests that members of the inner-city poor experience a difficult time transitioning from welfare to work,[160] most people collect welfare only for short periods of time. One study found that the majority of welfare recipients do not stay on welfare for more than one year. Another study conducted before TANF (when one could stay on welfare for longer periods of time) concluded that only 30% of recipients stayed on welfare for more than two years. The uncertainty and skimpy pay of low-wage work does force many poor families to return to welfare after having left it—90% of those who use welfare during some point in their life will do so again—but this pattern is explained less by the supposed psychological state of welfare dependence than by the realities of living and laboring at the bottom of the income ladder. Far from being a means whereby people can eke out an existence without working, most families rely on welfare between jobs or when struggling through a family emergency.[161]

The failure of social scientists to document "welfare dependency" has led some to treat it as a demeaning label for the poor, much like "white trash" or "underclass."[162] Welfare recipients long have been slandered by politicians and the popular press. When Clinton's welfare reform act was being debated on the floor of Congress, two Congressmen made speeches comparing welfare recipients to wild animals who had lost their ability to survive in the wild. And President Reagan often spoke of Cadillac-driving "welfare queens" with "a tax-free income of over $150,000."[163] When politicians discuss welfare, especially if they are toeing an antiwelfare line, they often evoke racially coded language. For instance, when David Duke, former Grand Wizard of the KKK, won a seat in the Louisiana House of Representatives, he announced, "This . . . is a victory for those who . . . choose to work hard rather than abuse welfare."[164] Many of Duke's constituents were fully aware of who the ex-Klansman had in mind when he spoke of welfare abusers. For their part, media reporters have portrayed welfare recipients in an unflattering light, as lazy and lascivious. Some have blackened the welfare rolls, as if African Americans were the only beneficiaries of social spending.[165]

Many Americans see welfare as a racialized policy. In his book *Why Americans Hate Welfare*, Martin Gilens marshals an impressive amount of data to demonstrate that most whites hate welfare, because they assume that the majority of welfare recipients are "lazy blacks," undeserving of the government's help. Another study found that in states with large white populations, whites who stereotyped blacks and Hispanics as lazy were less willing to spend money on welfare than those who did not. And according to a large social survey, 59% of whites polled believed that most blacks would rather collect a welfare check than work for a living. Forty-six percent felt the same way about Hispanics, while 18% characterized Asians in this light. Only 3% believed that, given the chance, most whites would choose welfare over work.[166] These startling statistics reveal that many white Americans not only consider blacks and Hispanics to be welfare dependent but incorrectly assume that welfare is a policy that benefits only nonwhites.

When Affirmative Action Wasn't White

A recent study reported that one-third of those polled admitted they did not know the meaning of affirmative action; and we have strong reason to believe the other two-thirds were overconfident.[167] Affirmative action has been misconstrued in the media and distorted by politicians, who disparage the controversial program to court voters. What are the realities of affirmative action? Below we address four key questions: What is affirmative action? Does it help those it was intended to help? Does it hurt white men? And, finally, is affirmative action an affront to the American ideal of meritocracy?

Before we march forward we should pause and look back. Affirmative action is not new. As we learned at the beginning of this chapter, white affirmative action was instituted with the New Deal. And some have rightly pointed out that it is much older than that: "It is strange and peculiar, arbitrary and incorrect, to suggest that affirmative action began in the summer of 1963 when President John F. Kennedy issued Executive Order 10925. . . . The more accurate beginning date for this legal and public policy is 1641. This is when the fledgling jurisdictions that would later become the first states began to specify in law that rights to property, ownership of goods and services, and the right to vote would be restricted by race and gender. In 1790, Congress formally restricted citizenship via naturalization to 'white persons,' a restriction that remained in place until 1952. Understood in this way, affirmative action has been in effect for 360 years, not 39."[168] What is new, then, is nonwhite and nonmale affirmative action.

What Is Affirmative Action?

Affirmative action (in its current nonwhite and nonmale form) is an umbrella term referring to a collection of policies and practices designed to address past wrongs, institutional racism, and sexism by offering people of color and women both employment and educational opportunities. Such policies and practices encourage employers seeking to create integrated institutions to consider race, ethnicity, and gender in their hiring, admittance, and other decisions. In so doing, they seek proactively to redress historic patterns of domination, to combat present-day discrimination, and to ensure equal access to opportunities.[169]

School busing, race-based outreach, setting aside contracts for nonwhite- and female-run firms, and monitoring workforces' underrepresentation of people of color and women are all programs that can be classified as affirmative action. It is helpful to conceptualize affirmative action policies on a continuum, where on one end are rigid quotas (extremely rare) and on the other end are companies that have taken positive steps against discrimination. Between these extremes is where most affirmative action programs lie. Here we find "preference systems," or systems of "social restitution," that give qualified white women and nonwhite women and men a slight advantage over equally qualified white men in hiring and promotion. Here we also find recruitment strategies that target underrepresented groups, and self-examination programs, where employers scrutinize their workplace representation. Affirmative action programs differ from antidiscrimination laws in that the former are proactive—they attempt to prevent discrimination from occurring—while the latter are reactive: they redress specific people who have been victimized by discrimination.[170]

Modern-day affirmative action programs can be traced back to 1941, when President Franklin D. Roosevelt criminalized racial discrimination in government and war industries. His executive order largely was ignored, because it carried no sanctions for violators. That changed in 1961, when President John F. Kennedy, through Executive Order 10925, mandated that federal contractors take proactive steps—that is, "affirmative action," a term he coined—to treat prospective and current workers equally, regardless of race, color, or national origin. The Civil Rights Act of 1964 came three years later; its Title VII forbade employers from discriminating on the basis of race, sex, religion, color, or national origin. President Johnson followed Kennedy's lead one year after that with Executive Order 11246, which added women to the list of protected groups and created the Office for Federal Contract Compliance (which would later become the Office for Federal Contract Compliance Programs, OFCCP). President Nixon contributed as well, requiring firms with at least $50,000 in federal contracts and at least 50 employees to submit written affirmative action plans accompanied by benchmarks and timetables.[171]

None of these legal policies defined affirmative action as quota systems. In fact, quotas are illegal under OFCCP guidelines: "In seeking to achieve its goals, a [contractor] is never required to (1) hire a person who does not have the qualifications needed to perform the job successfully; (2) hire an unqualified person in preference to another applicant who is qualified; (3) hire a less qualified person in preference to a more qualified person."[172] Despite popular opinions to the contrary, affirmative action required of federal contractors does not allow quotas or the hiring of unqualified applicants.

Importantly, federally mandated affirmative action rules apply only to companies that conduct a fair amount of business with the federal government, about 3% of American firms. Captured in this small percentage are relatively large firms employing about 20% of the country's workforce. But there are other types of affirmative action programs, including policies regulating public employees and court-ordered affirmative action. With court-ordered affirmative action, federal courts can require companies found guilty of practicing discrimination to implement affirmative action programs. If the company's practices are excessive, courts can order the company to develop and monitor quotas, although this is very uncommon. Finally, some companies, hoping to allay the threat of litigation or to promote good business practices, voluntarily enforce on themselves affirmative action guidelines. It is hard to say how many of America's corporations have adopted affirmative action. By some estimates, 71% of firms have some sort of affirmative action plan, while others have found that less than half practice affirmative action. We might conclude that, although some companies voluntarily practice affirmative action, many have shifted to a less aggressive "diversity management" model, which we discuss in a later chapter.[173]

Does Affirmative Action Help Those It Was Intended to Help?

Affirmative action significantly has increased the representation of white women and nonwhite women and men in employment. It has created inroads to professions previously reserved for white men. And it has decreased the levels of occupational segregation by impressive margins. Firms that contracted with the federal government in 1980 (and thereby were subjected to federally mandated affirmative action programs) increased their nonwhite workforce by 25% more than firms who did not. Big-city firms that took affirmative action measures in hiring were 10% more likely to hire women and 20% more likely to hire black men than firms who did not. Affirmative action has increased the representation of nonwhite women and men and white women in the public service sector as well. The military carried out a successful affirmative action campaign to recruit nonwhites into commanding ranks. And between 1970 and 1990 the number of nonwhite men and women and white women in the police force rose dramatically: from 10,000 to 97,000 for nonwhites, and from 2,000 to 20,000 for women.[174]

What is more, affirmative action seems to have benefited, not only members of disadvantaged communities, but the disadvantaged communities themselves. Affirmative action programs have helped to produce hundreds of nonwhite doctors, who are much more likely to practice in nonwhite communities than their white counterparts. Graduates admitted to one medical school under affirmative action guidelines were more likely to serve patients living in communities largely abandoned by professional medicine—the inner city and poor rural areas—than students who were not.[175]

Despite these gains, some have wondered whether affirmative action comes at too high a cost: namely, that it imprints on its recipients a stigma of self-doubt. Such reasoning would only hold if the majority of white women and nonwhite women and men believed they had benefited from affirmative action. But the opposite is true: over 90% of women and 75% of blacks feel that affirmative action has not played a role in their employment opportunities. And some evidence suggests that affirmative action has helped, not handicapped, the self-esteem of nonwhite women and men as well as white women. By expanding their occupational opportunities, affirmative action has raised the aspirations of those previously relegated to menial work. If nonwhite women and men and white women are wracked by self-doubt, the source is most likely not affirmative action but centuries of white supremacy and patriarchy, durable systems that have sought to force a mark of inferiority upon those not white and male.[176]

This does not rule out that some coworkers, operating under the assumption that a white man is always better qualified for the job, might stigmatize their nonwhite and female peers as "affirmative action hires." But research has found that most white women and nonwhite women and men do not feel their coworkers doubt their abilities because of affirmative action. Only 1% of women executives felt their experience with affirmative action was completely negative, while 22% felt it affected their careers in both positive and negative ways.[177] And, again, the realities of racial and masculine domination would lead us to conclude that many white men would look down on nonwhite men and women and white women even if affirmative action did not exist.

Some have argued that those hired and promoted by affirmative action are unqualified. What does social science say? Several studies examining job performance evaluations have concluded that affirmative action hires do just as well as those not hired by affirmative action. In fact, some have found that black women consistently outperform white males working in similar positions. One study of police officers hired through affirmative action found that they perform at the level of white male officers. And firms operating with affirmative action protocols perform no differently (in terms of profit margins, growth, and so forth) than firms that do not. Indeed, some research suggests that companies with solid affirmative action plans reap bigger profit margins than companies with poor records of recruiting women and nonwhites.[178]

Not only is the practice of hiring unqualified workers through affirmative action disconfirmed by research, but it is also illegal. (See the OFCCP guidelines above.) Passing over a qualified white candidate for an unqualified nonwhite candidate is discrimination and punishable under federal law. Affirmative action does not work like this. Rather, affirmative action encourages employers to take race and gender into account when choosing from a pool of qualified applicants. Or, to put it another way, it encourages employers not to discriminate against qualified white women and nonwhite men and women.

Far from suggesting that affirmative action reserves job positions for unqualified individuals, some social scientists have argued that the policy selects out the most privileged members of disadvantaged populations. "It is important to recognize," writes William Julius Wilson, "that in modern industrial society the removal of racial barriers creates the greatest opportunities for the better-trained, talented, and educated segments of the minority population—those who have been crippled the least by the weight of past discrimination."[179] If this is true, then the problem is not that unqualified people are staffing positions but that a large proportion of nonwhites lacking qualification—a good education, job-training, network connections—virtually are unaffected by affirmative action. Those who advance this line of argument can marshal some evidence to support their point, but more research is needed. If it is the case that poor and uneducated members of disadvantaged populations are passed over by race- and gender-based affirmative action, then these policies may need to be complemented by class-based programs.[180]

Does Affirmative Action Hurt White Men?

Affirmative action has helped nonwhite women and men to secure employment opportunities previously denied them; and it has certainly helped white women, who, by some accounts, are its biggest beneficiaries. But has it done so at the expense of white men? Many white Americans believe this to be true. When asked who was most likely to face discrimination at work, survey respondents picked whites over blacks by two to one. And 40% of people participating in a recent poll thought whites being disadvantaged by affirmative action was a bigger problem than blacks being disadvantaged by race-based discrimination.[181] Are these fears justified?

The evidence suggests they are not. First, as we have already seen, racial discrimination unfairly targeting nonwhites continues to influence hiring and promotion decisions. The findings from social-scientific studies demonstrate that employers regularly pass over equally or better qualified nonwhites to hire whites. Second, compared to nonwhites, whites are much less likely to believe they were denied a job or promotion on account of their race. One study found that 16% of blacks and 8% of Hispanics claimed to have been refused pay increases or promotions because of their race; only 3% of whites felt likewise.[182] Third, whites rarely file complaints citing "reverse discrimination." Of the nearly half a million complaints filed with the Equal Employment Opportunity Commission between 1987 and 1994, only 4% were reverse discrimination cases. Between 1990 and 1994, there were 100 claims of reverse discrimination filed by white men; there were over 150,000 claims filed by women and nonwhites in 1994 alone. Courts reject most reverse discrimination cases. Indeed, between 1990 and 1994, district and appellate courts rejected *all* reverse discrimination cases as without merit. Perhaps we see such a small number of reverse discrimination cases, because white men do not report being victimized. If this were true, we would expect whites to under-report instances of other forms of discrimination too. But this is not the case. With respect to discrimination cases based on age or AIDS status, whites file complaints in impressive numbers.[183]

Affirmative action may not only cost most white men nothing, it might actually help them. This is because affirmative action provides discipline and structure to employment practices that previously operated willy-nilly, relying heavily on personal connections. In the words of sociologist Barbara Reskin,

"White men are helped by affirmative action more often than they are hurt. It encourages employers to formalize hiring and to move away from the old boy network when thinking about people for jobs."[184] Affirmative action does provide a boon to qualified white women and nonwhite men and women over equally qualified white men. However, it also gives qualified white men a fighting chance against less qualified applicants who previously would have landed the job through cronyism.

Is Affirmative Action an Affront to American Meritocracy?

Many have argued that affirmative action threatens an important American value: that of meritocracy, the notion that one succeeds only on the basis of her or his own abilities. This idea relies on three assumptions. The first is that people get ahead in life solely by virtue of their own talents, skills, and work ethic. Our analyses of white affirmative action and racial inequalities in wealth show that this is rarely the case. (Many of us who have received some sort of help practice a self-imposed amnesia, reassuring ourselves that we got to where we are solely by our own merits.)

The second assumption is that race and gender preferences are the only kinds of preferences in the world. In truth, the preferences advanced by affirmative action, which seeks to redress past and current wrongs, join hundreds of other kinds of preferences in employment—many of them, to be sure, justified by less admirable reasons. One thinks of sons who inherit their father's business; legacies admitted to Ivy League universities because their parents are contributing alumni; or homeowners who enjoy tax breaks. What bothers many Americans, it seems, are not preferences but preferences based on race and gender.[185]

The third assumption holds that employment practices without affirmative action are more merit-based than those with it. But evidence documenting ongoing racial discrimination challenges this assumption. Here is yet another instance when whiteness (and masculinity) operates as an invisible norm. When a well-qualified white man lands a job, it is because he is well qualified. When a well-qualified Arab-American woman lands a job, it is because of her race and gender. Too often we forget that white men—qualified or otherwise—sometimes receive jobs, promotions, and pay raises precisely because of *their* race and gender.

Affirmative action does not threaten meritocracy; it strives to protect it by replacing a system rife with race and gender biases with a system that rewards one's skills, abilities, education, and talent regardless of race or gender. To quote Reskin once more: "An essential part of affirmative action is the replacement of subjective and biased personnel practices with practices that treat all prospective and actual workers uniformly. . . . Although many Americans would prefer a labor market that never takes race or gender into account, as long as employers and employment practices routinely discriminate against minorities and women, the choice is not between meritocracy and affirmative action, it is between discrimination and affirmative action."[186]

The Value of Inconvenient Facts

Some of you—especially those who come from white middle-class homes—might find all of this hard to believe, or at least hard to swallow. (Indeed, a recent poll reported that half of white Americans believe the average black American is financially as well off as the average white.[187]) Hard facts can strain when they are piled, brick-heavy, on our shoulders. The temptation to shrug is great, especially for those who doubt the realities of racial domination and think that America offers each of us an equal shot at success. This is why social science can be so very helpful. It disillusions us of long-held assumptions and makes us better aware of life circumstances we previously had been inclined to deny.

To be sure, as all of you who have worked through this chapter can attest, social science is also difficult and challenging. It means paying attention and working carefully through lots of data and complex arguments. It means striving to take in the big picture while also mastering a good deal of highly detailed information. It is important, however, that we make the effort, for there is certainly a great deal at stake: nothing less, in fact, than a correct understanding of the economic world in which we live, the racial problems that have long plagued it, and what remains to be done to overcome them.

CHAPTER REVIEW

ECONOMIC RACISM FROM THE NEW DEAL TO REAGANOMICS
New Deal, G.I. Bill of Rights, deindustrialization, supply-side economics

INCOME AND WEALTH DISPARITIES
income, wealth, segregated labor force, embeddedness

CHASING THE AMERICAN DREAM: POVERTY AND AFFLUENCE
poverty line, black ghetto, spatial mismatch thesis, residential segregation, brain drain, tribal sovereignty, Immigration and Nationality Act of 1965, segregated assimilation theory, class privileges, ethnic enclave

LABOR MARKET DYNAMICS
opportunity hoarding, disadvantage breeds disadvantage, split labor market, interracialism, glass ceilings, homosocial reproduction

WELFARE

welfare, corporate welfare

WHEN AFFIRMATIVE ACTION WASN'T WHITE

affirmative action

FROM THEORY TO PRACTICE

1. Think about how you and your family have benefited—or been disadvantaged—by the processes and mechanisms discussed in this chapter. What do these large-scale economic forces and developments have to do with your own life? Think about this not only in reference to recent times but also in light of longer-term trajectories. For instance, we covered a history reaching back at least a hundred years. Probe your family histories to determine how, if at all, the laws and policies we have discussed affected your family's fortunes.

2. What have been your own experiences in the labor market and at the workplace? How might you better explain them in light of what you have learned in this chapter? In other words, using your sociological imagination, explain your personal problems (or successes) by thinking about them as belonging to larger historical, economic, and social processes.

3. Think of a work of popular culture or literature that somehow addresses the economic issues we have discussed in this chapter. Which issues does it touch on, and how does it affect your thinking about those issues? And how, in turn, is your thinking about that work altered, now that you have read through this chapter and learned what social scientists have to say about the same issues?

4. Interrogate your preconceptions about the causes of poverty. What do you believe? How did you come to hold these beliefs? How do your beliefs compare to the social-scientific explanations reviewed in this chapter?

5. American writer Susan Sontag once observed, "All possibility of understanding is rooted in the ability to say no." How has this chapter urged you to say no to things you previously believed about the racial dynamics of the economic field? Has it encouraged you, for instance, to see the immigrant experience or American meritocracy in a different, more complex, way? How, why, or why not?

RECOMMENDED READING

- Martin Gilens, *Why Americans Hate Welfare: Race, Media, and the Politics of Antipoverty Policy* (Chicago: University of Chicago Press, 1999).

- Ira Katznelson, *When Affirmative Action Was White: The Untold History of Racial Inequality in Twentieth-Century America* (New York: Norton, 2005).

- Leslie McCall, *Complex Inequality: Gender, Class, and Race in the New Economy* (New York: Routledge, 2001).

- Melvin Oliver and Thomas Shapiro, *Black Wealth/White Wealth* (New York: Routledge, 1997).

- Alejandro Portes and Josh DeWind, eds., *Rethinking Migration: New Theoretical and Empirical Perspectives* (New York: Berghann Books, 2007).

- Barbara Reskin, *The Realities of Affirmative Action* (Washington, D.C.: American Sociological Association, 1998).

- William Julius Wilson, *The Truly Disadvantaged: The Inner City, the Underclass, and Public Policy* (Chicago: University of Chicago Press, 1987).

Chapter 5

Housing

White America

One of the most pernicious images of America is that the country is white. We notice this image when someone asks a Korean American, "How long have you been in this country?" She answers: "For five generations." We notice it, too, in our stories of who settled America, stories that often recall the adventures of European pioneers and forget the Mexican homesteaders who helped to develop the Southwest, Chinese trailblazers who pounded out the transcontinental Central Pacific Railroad, and enslaved Africans on whose backs America was built.[1] Often overlooked is the fact that a great number of European migrants returned to their native countries—between 1885 and 1918, 55% of Englishmen returned to their homeland, as did 40% of Poles and 50% of Italians—while many migrants from Africa and Asia made homes in America.[2] Indeed, the very phrase "settled America" suggests that America was an empty landmass waiting to be settled, not an area already settled by millions of indigenous people who would be robbed of their land through violence and trickery. The image of white America is there, too, in every news story and statistical report about the rising population of Hispanic Americans. When was the last time the birth rate of white babies was deemed newsworthy?

In an imagination conditioned by racial domination, nonwhites always come to, but never are from, America. Perpetual aliens, strangers, they invade but never are invaded. Strangers, German sociologist Georg Simmel reminds us, are not people who are far away from us but people within our midst who are never fully accepted. They are at the same time intimate and remote, familiar yet foreign.[3] Such has been the condition of America's nonwhite populations. And it has been that way since colonial times, when citizenship was restricted to "free white persons," and since antebellum America, when prominent whites poured hundreds of hours—and thousands of dollars—into a plan to transport blacks back to Africa.

To attribute to whites a certain ownership over America, even if it isn't done on purpose, is to amputate from our collective memory the fact that nonwhites have always belonged to America—to its industry and progress, its culture and spirit, its suffering and celebration. Just as it is a mistake to think of America as a giant melting pot, where hundreds of different cultures melt into one, so it is a mistake to ignore how each of us has been engaged by, and engages with, people of different backgrounds. American culture is black just as much as it is white; its history is indigenous just as much as it is colonial; its progress borne out by Mexican farmers just as much as by Greek meatpackers, Persian bankers, and Jewish scientists.

The duty of the sociological thinker, therefore, is to denaturalize racist modes of thinking, to deconstruct America as a white country. Nowhere is this more important than in the careful analysis of how racial domination works within the residential field—for it is only through the study of residence that we can fully understand how whiteness infuses our conceptions of who owns America and who "belongs" here. This chapter takes up such a task. It begins with a historical overview of the racial struggles over housing that took place during the twentieth century, explaining the changing demographic contours of cities, the origins of black ghettos, and white flight from the inner city. It then moves into the present day by discussing the causes and consequences of racial segregation before analyzing how race works in four major residential areas: ghettoes, cities, suburbs, and rural areas. A home, we know, is more than bricks and mortar. It is the cultural and spiritual center of the family, a dwelling steeped in significance and meaning. Where you live is intimately connected to thoughts of who you are. And in America, the geography and dynamics of the residential field—which side of the tracks your house is located on, gated communities, the pride you take in your hometown—are in part driven by, and drive, racial domination.

Racial Struggles over Residence in Twentieth-Century America

If they had to guess, many Americans, operating under the accurate belief that their country's acceptance of nonwhites has improved over the years, would claim that America was more racially segregated at the conclusion of the Civil War than it is today. In fact, the opposite is true. Throughout the nineteenth century, whites and nonwhites lived relatively close together, interacting with one another on a daily basis. In northern cities, whites and blacks lived side by side; in southern cities, black servants and sharecroppers lived close to their white employers, either on their land on in alleys connected to main streets. By and large, there were no "black areas of town" before the 1900s. To be sure, many nonwhites excluded from participating fully in the labor market tended to live in the poorest areas of town, but so, too, did poor whites and new immigrant groups from Eastern Europe. The segregation levels in major cities during the nineteenth century, however, were less than half of what they are today. In 1890, the average black person living in Milwaukee resided in a neighborhood that was 1% black; today, the average black person living in Milwaukee resides in a neighborhood that is over 70% black. In 1860, only 40% of St. Louis's black population would have to move into predominantly white neighborhoods to achieve a perfectly integrated city; today, that number exceeds 80%. At the beginning of the twentieth century, most blacks residing in northern cities lived in neighborhoods that were majority-white; by the end of the century, most lived in neighborhoods that were majority-black.[4] What happened in between is the subject of the ensuing sections.

The Racialization of Neighborhoods

The racial and economic landscape of American cities underwent dramatic changes as the twentieth century unfolded. The rise of industrialism, which facilitated the rise of cities, attracted thousands of people—immigrants, blacks, Mexicans, whites, Asians—to roiling metropolises. As they poured into cities, some ethnic groups tended to cluster together in neighborhoods, many living in crowded, dilapidated slums. Irish, German, Polish, Swedish, Persian, Italian, and Hungarian families lived in cordoned off areas with such names as the Irish Kilgubbin, Polish Hamtramck, and Hungarian Delray. Chinatowns emerged in some cities, as did black belts, where African-American families did live together. As groups grew in numbers and moved into different neighborhoods, ethnic conflict sparked up between Greeks and Persians, blacks and Sicilians, Chinese and Germans, to name just a few. As Harvey Zorbaugh described it, writing in 1929, "While the Irish and Swedish had gotten on well as neighbors, neither could or would live peacefully with the Sicilian. There was considerable friction, especially among the children of the two races. The play parks were the scenes of many a 'battle' when the Irish boys would attempt to run out the Italian, and alley garbage cans were stripped of their covers which served as shield in these encounters."[5]

But as the twentieth century marched forward, prosperous European immigrant families were able to move out of the slums and to assimilate into the white American mainstream. Meanwhile, those who wore the badge of otherness—the "racial uniform," in the words of American sociologist Robert Park—were forbidden by law and custom to live anywhere else.[6] As European Americans of the "new immigration" were further enveloped by whiteness, ethnic distinctions between Italians, Irish, Hungarians, and so forth became less salient. So, too, did ethnic distinctions among neighborhoods, such that by the 1920s many neighborhoods based on close-knit ethnic affiliations gave way to urban divisions based on race and class. Little Italy, Hungarian town, and the Norwegian village melted into white sections of town, a transition that made the racial contrast between nonwhite and white neighborhoods even more stark.[7]

Migration and Urbanization

At the same time, cities were growing and becoming more racially diverse. Employment opportunities in manufacturing and in agriculture (especially sugar beet farming) inspired many Mexican families to move north. In fact, the U.S. government endorsed Mexican migration, and factory employers actively recruited Mexican Americans and Mexican immigrants, who by and large could be hired at cheaper rates than whites.

However, as the economy began to take a turn for the worse, a turn that resulted in the Great Depression of the 1930s, whites started blaming Mexicans for widespread unemployment and economic scarcity. White anger targeting Mexicans soon materialized into government policy. In what became known as **Mexican Repatriation Programs,** thousands of Mexican families were rounded up and sent via train back to Mexico. All too often, those who conducted the roundups did not bother to differentiate between Mexican Americans and Mexican nationals: more than half the people shipped back to Mexico were United States citizens. Repatriation proved an especially painful experience for Mexican families, who lost their jobs, property, and livelihood. Families were separated, and many were forced to live in poverty-stricken borderlands. By the end of the 1930s, roughly 2 million people—over one third the overall population of people of Mexican heritage—forcibly were removed from American soil.[8] Recognizing the suffering induced by repatriation programs, the state of California, which alone deported roughly 400,000 American citizens and legal residents of Mexican ancestry, offered an official apology in 2005. "The state of California," the act read, "apologizes . . . for the fundamental violations of . . . basic civil liberties and constitutional rights during the period of illegal deportation and coerced emigration."[9]

If Mexican Repatriation Programs were intended to evict Mexicans *en masse* from America, policies targeting Native Americans were designed to have the opposite effect: to advance programs of assimilation and tribal dissolution. During the Great Depression, poverty crushed many families living on reservations, and it continued to do so during the World War II years. To combat this suffering, policy makers advanced programs to relocate thousands of Native Americans to urban centers, hoping they could prosper from the economic uplift that took hold after the war. They also hoped that indigenous peoples, once removed from their respective reservations, would shed their "Indianness" and be fully incorporated into (white) mainstream American society. From 1950 to 1970, thousands of indigenous people moved to Detroit, Seattle, Chicago, and other metropolises. Los Angeles served host to the largest American-Indian population, with 60,000 indigenous residents. By 1990, more than 60% of American Indians were residing in cities.[10]

American Indian urbanization proceeded in lockstep with processes of **tribal termination.** In 1953, Congress enacted legislation that divested the federal government of trust responsibilities to Indian country. State governments were given legal jurisdiction over Indian reservations and, between 1953 and 1973, 109 tribes were terminated in the eyes of the federal government. Over 1 million acres of land entrusted to tribes were left unprotected. And thousands of Native Americans were stripped of their (legally recognized) tribal affiliations, including those people who belonged to Wisconsin's Menominee tribe and Oregon's Klamath tribe. Tribal termination policies were slowed during the Kennedy years and abandoned by the Nixon administration in the wake of the American Indian Movement; yet the effects of twenty years of wiping out political sovereignty and tribal ownership of economic resources are still felt today in Indian Country.[11]

The beginning of the twentieth century also was witness to a massive movement of blacks from the rural South to the urban North. As southern slavery gave way to sharecropping, Jim Crow segregation, and racial terrorism, many blacks sought to escape to better conditions. A decline in the price of cotton resulted in job shortages in southern agriculture. At the same time, the First World War sharply reduced European immigration, cutting off Northern industry's main source of cheap labor, and created massive job vacancies in growing Midwest metropolises. These two economic shifts encouraged many blacks to head north to Chicago, New York, Cleveland, Detroit, and other cities in search of better work and a safer life for their children. In his poem, "The South," Langston Hughes effectively captured the sentiment of many African Americans during this period. Referring to "The lazy, laughing south with blood on its mouth," he wrote: "And I, who am black, would love her, but she spits in my face; and I, who am black, would give her many rare gifts, but she turns her back upon me. So now I seek the North—the cold-faced North. For she, they say, is a kinder mistress. And in her house my children may escape the spell of the South."[12] Like Mexicans, blacks were urged by employers to head north. In search of honest work, they came by the droves. Between 1910 and 1930, over 1.5 million African Americans traveled north; another 3 million followed between 1940 and 1960—a movement known as the **Great Migration.**[13]

But these sojourners encountered a new face of racism, one enforced not so much by the mob violence of the Ku Klux Klan as by the antiseptic arm of the law. Blacks were cordoned off to restricted districts, rundown slums that quickly became overcrowded. Isolated from the surrounding city, these slums began to see more crime and disease, as well as poverty, since most blacks who managed

"The lazy, laughing south with blood on its mouth. And I, who am black, would love her, but she spits in my face; and I, who am black, would give her many rare gifts, but she turns her back upon me. So now I seek the North—the cold-faced North. For she, they say, is a kinder mistress." —Langston Hughes

to secure jobs were forced to work in menial and dangerous positions with little hope for advancement. Blacks constituted a cheap and expendable labor force, the kind dreamed of by employers profiting off the North's booming industrial economy; but they were kept a safe distance from the surrounding white population, whose antislavery sentiments during the Civil War in no way translated into pro-integrationism after the fall of the Confederacy.[14] As the folk saying went, "The South doesn't care how close a Negro gets just so he doesn't get too high; the North doesn't care how high he gets just so he doesn't get too close."[15]

Tensions between blacks and whites heated up, sometimes exploding into **racial uprisings**—popularly referred to as "race riots"—that were a recurrent feature of the first half of the twentieth century. One of the worst uprisings took place in Chicago during the summer of 1919. One hot July day, a seventeen-year-old black teenager swam to the "white side" of a bathing beach and was pelted with rocks by white swimmers. In the altercation that ensued between black and whites, the teenager—his name was Eugene Williams—drowned. This sparked a week-long uprising that left 38 people dead (23 blacks and 15 whites), 500 injured, and 1,000 homeless. The Chicago uprising was just one of many that took place during the summer of 1919, a summer that would later aptly be called The Red Summer. Uprisings continued throughout the interwar years. And during World War II, white mobs attacked Mexicans and blacks in Los Angeles and Chicago. Racial uprisings also would erupt in Harlem, Mobile, and Brownsville, Texas. One of the bloodiest uprisings of the century took place in Detroit during June 1943. Fights between white and black youths escalated into three days' fighting, shooting, and looting. When things died down, 34 people lay dead, most of them black.[16]

The Origins of the Ghetto

Major U.S. cities experienced housing shortages lasting from the Great Depression to the mid-1940s. While these shortages were painful for many whites, they were downright intolerable for nonwhite populations who were forced to live in slums teeming with people. Simply put, most houses were built strictly for white inhabitants. In 1947, 92% of Detroit's housing units were for whites only, and only 1% of new homes constructed in the city in 1951 were open to nonwhites.[17] Federal law not only permitted racial segregation, it encouraged it, since lawmakers feared that integrated neighborhoods would result in unrest that would drive down property values. The Federal Housing Administration denied loans to many nonwhites, regardless of their financial or veteran standing, and real-estate brokers refused to show nonwhites homes outside "designated areas."[18] According to one analyst, "the Federal Housing Administration and the Veterans Administration financed more than $120 billion worth of new housing between 1934 and 1962, but less than 2% of this real estate was available to nonwhite families—and most of that small amount was located in segregated areas."[19] By 1940, thanks to the discriminatory efforts of the federal government and the housing market, racial residential segregation was widespread.

For their part, white home sellers made matters worse by including in the deeds to their property **covenants**, which sought to uphold the "desirable residential characteristics" of a neighborhood. Covenants could restrict the purchase of land or property to certain religious or racial groups. "This property shall not be occupied by any person expect those of the Caucasian race," a typical covenant might read. Although covenants were rendered legally unbinding in 1948, they still could be included in property deeds—indeed, they are still used today—and remained effective. Even if the courts no longer enforced covenants, banks refused to subsidize contractors looking to build homes for nonwhites on land deemed "for whites only," and realtors who violated racial covenants risked being boycotted by whites.[20] Nonwhites were not only denied a place to live beyond majority nonwhite areas, but they were also systematically denied the ability to purchase homes within those areas. Lenders refused to offer mortgages and home loans in nonwhite neighborhoods through a discriminatory practice known as **redlining.** The word derives its name from lenders' practice of taking a city map and drawing in red ink a border around nonwhite neighborhoods, marking them as too risky for loans or subsidies.[21]

There was good money to be made in the exclusion of nonwhites from the private housing market. To save money, slumlords ignored housing repairs and building occupancy codes, a combination that proved deadly during times when faulty electric wiring could set ablaze a house swelling with people. Landlords also divided their properties into multiple apartments, charging their nonwhite occupants inflated rents. In 1960, the median black rent payment was $76 per month, whereas the median white rent payment was $64 per month, even though whites were living in much better conditions.[22] "The process of housing segregation set into motion a chain reaction that reinforced patterns of racial inequality," observes historian Thomas Sugrue, speaking of blacks in postwar Detroit. "Blacks were poorer than whites, and they had to pay more for housing, thus deepening their relative impoverishment. In addition, they were confined to the city's oldest housing stock, in most need of ongoing maintenance, repair, and rehabilitation. But they could not get loans to improve their properties. As a result, their houses deteriorated. City officials, looking at the poor housing stock in black neighborhoods, condemned many areas as blighted, and destroyed much extant housing to build highways, hospitals, housing projects, and a civic center complex, further limiting the housing options for blacks. Moreover, the decaying neighborhoods offered seemingly convincing evidence to white home-owners that blacks would ruin any white neighborhood that they moved into. Finally, neighborhood deterioration seemed definitive proof to bankers that blacks were indeed a poor credit risk, and justified disinvestment in predominantly nonwhite neighborhoods."[23]

Housing opportunities for nonwhites were strained even further by urban development projects undertaken after World War II. Cities' infrastructure was ill suited to accommodate their steady growth. Highways had to be installed; hospitals to be erected; sewage processing plants to be built. City planners in Detroit, Milwaukee, New York and other major cities were careful not to interfere with middle-class white neighborhoods; instead they destroyed entire nonwhite communities, complete with mass eviction orders. In fact, some saw highway development as "a handy device for razing slums."[24] Most of those who owned property in areas designated for highway construction were forced to leave before selling their property, for who would want to buy a house that would be bulldozed in a week's time? And dozens of African American and Puerto Rican neighborhoods were razed, not to make way for a new expressway but in the name of **"urban renewal."** As Robert Caro has noted, urban renewal was unique, not only in scope—an enormous venture with costs soaring in the billions—but in philosophy, because it was the first time in the country's history that the "government was given the right to seize an individual's property not for its own use but for reassignment to another individual for *his* use and profit."[25] Publicly, proponents of urban renewal programs were motivated by a desire to breathe new life into the ailing inner city and to better the living conditions of slum dwellers; privately, they were driven by large profits to be made by the erection of luxury apartments, art museums, and toll roads.[26]

The mid-twentieth century was the age of the wrecking ball, which crashed through windows and walls that once housed families struggling against the big city and smashed the hearts of tight-knit neighborhoods that had stood for generations. Urban renewal programs obliterated entire blocks of slum areas—most of them occupied by nonwhites—and millions of people lost their homes. In New York City alone, between 1946 and 1953, Robert Moses, the powerful and infamous city planner, evicted "not thousands of people or ten thousands but hundreds of thousands, from their homes and tore the homes down."[27] Overwhelmingly, Moses, and dozens of city planners like him—planners who, in fact, flocked to Moses's table to learn how to toss people out of their homes to make way for this stadium or that expressway—replaced the housing he destroyed not with apartments for the poor but with high-rises for the rich. Residents of areas marked for destruction—the cities' most economically vulnerable and racially marginal—were expected to find another place to live, sometimes with, but more times without, the government's help. In a tight housing market in which only a handful of neighborhoods were open to nonwhites, slum dwellers did the only thing they could: they packed themselves into other racial slums, worsening the already poor living conditions there.[28]

White Fight and White Flight

Disadvantage bred disadvantage to create the America ghetto. But as the Civil Rights Movement gained steam and racial segregation lost its legal foothold, nonwhites with some resources and savings accounts began moving out of slum areas into neighborhoods traditionally reserved for white people. Nonwhite communities previously segregated by race soon became segregated by race and class, as economic fault lines within black, Asian, and Hispanic communities were made more salient. In many respects, the liberation of middle-class nonwhites from segregated areas resulted in the decay of tightly knit, economically diverse nonwhite communities. Those left behind in the corroding slums represented such communities' poorest of the poor.

Whites did not take these changes lightly. Many thought that nonwhites would bring drugs, sexual immorality, and crime into their neighborhoods and would cause property values to plummet. Some whites described the migration of nonwhites into their neighborhoods with the language of war. They spoke, that is, of being "invaded," "taken over," or "threatened," as well as of the need to "defend" and "protect" their homes, families, and livelihoods.[29] Testifying in front of a Senate committee in 1963, a local politician captured the sentiment of many white families: "When integration strikes a previously all-white neighborhood . . . there will be an immediate rise in crime and violence[,] . . . of vice, of prostitution, of gambling and dope. . . . [Racially mixed neighborhoods] will succumb to blight and decay, and the residents will suffer the loss of their homes and savings."[30]

Broadly speaking, whites reacted to the racial integration of their neighborhoods in two ways: by picking up and moving or by slugging it out with newcomers, that is, by fleeing or fighting. Fearing racial integration, many whites who had the means to do so sold their houses in the city and fled to the suburbs, a migratory process known as **white flight.** White flight had begun in the 1950s, spurred on by deindustrialization. Whites who could afford it followed factory jobs as the latter relocated from the city center to the suburbs and surrounding small towns. But white outward migration grew massive in the wake of the Civil Rights Movement—migration spurred on, not by job loss, but by racial fear.

This fear was exploited by real estate agents who spotted a chance to cash in on neighborhood integration. "Blockbusting" agents, as they became known, learned to stir up whites' fear of integration. They might pay a black woman to walk her baby through a white neighborhood, giving off the image that she lived there. Or they might sell a house to an Asian family and publicize it widely. Once word spread that the neighborhood was being "taken over," agents would post fliers and call homeowners, encouraging them to sell their homes before things got worse. One especially crafty blockbuster paid a pair of black children to travel door to door in a white neighborhood delivering fliers that read, "Now is the best time to sell your house—you know that."[31] As a result, many panicking whites sold their homes to real estate agents at below-market rates. The agents, in turn, would sell that house to nonwhite families hungry for decent housing at above-market rates, thereby collecting a large profit and exacerbating whites' fear. And if nonwhite families could not secure a home loan, blockbusting agents would often step in, offering loans at inflated interest rates.

As blacks and Asians moved in, whites moved out and were welcomed in small towns and suburban communities. In fact, the federal government endorsed white migration to the suburbs through loan programs developed during the New Deal and administered through the Federal Housing Administration and the Veterans Administration. As discussed in Chapter 4, these programs provided, for the first time in American history, the opportunity for working white families to own a home. In fact, for many it became cheaper to buy a house in the suburbs than to rent one in the central city.[32] When we consider this fact, as well as rampant white fear of nonwhites' "taking over" cities, we should not be surprised to learn that neighborhoods changed rapidly in their racial composition, from completely white to completely black in only a few years. Whites poured out of Atlanta so quickly that the city, once nicknamed "The City Too Busy to Hate," earned a new title: "The City Too Busy Moving to Hate."[33] As whites fled, they took their accumulated wealth with them, depleting the cities' tax base. Soon, city centers, spaces that just a few decades before had housed massive factories and bustled with the vibrancy of urban life, were hollowed out and abandoned by factories, by thousands of white homeowners, and by well-off nonwhite families. In 1940, only one third of all metropolitan residents lived in the suburbs; by 1970 the majority of them did.[34]

But not all white people left their neighborhoods during this time. Working-class white homeowners and European immigrants, who had poured their life savings into their homes and whose grasp on homeownership was more tenuous than that of their middle-class counterparts, could not afford to flee the city. Instead, on facing racial immigration, they chose to ward off nonwhite families through intimidation tactics, protests, and violence—a strategy that can be labeled **white fight.** Neighborhood homeowners' associations were employed as political vehicles through which white homeowners could "defend their property" from encroaching nonwhite populations. Signs were posted throughout neighborhoods reading "Whites Only" or "All White." In 1945—the year American soldiers liberated Jewish concentration camps throughout Germany and Poland—white homeowners in one Midwestern city hung signs that read, "Negroes moving here will be burned. Signed, Neighbors."[35]

When a nonwhite family moved into a previously all-white neighborhood, white residents often reacted with protests and organized violence. Whites picketed houses, carried signs, and shouted racial slurs at their new neighbors. When that did not work, protests often escalated into vandalism, and vandalism escalated into terrorism. Whites threw rocks through windows, poured gasoline on front lawns, dumped rotting garbage on porches, and pulled down fences. In some cases, they lit newly purchased houses on fire or planted a burning cross—the terrifying emblem of the KKK—on the front lawn. Sometimes, the houses of new nonwhite residents, as well as the offices of their real-estate officer, were firebombed. Young people regularly participated in these acts; in fact, they played a key role in upholding white supremacy through such neighborhood-based violence. In most cases, they were responsible for spreading the word about events and for adding a special dose of verve and spit to the white rallies. They were also quick to hurl the first firecracker, to spatter a house with black paint, or to torch an effigy in the tree of a newly arrived nonwhite family.[36]

Not all whites reacted with such vehemence. Some sold their homes to nonwhites, despite their neighbors' pleas and threats. Compared to other whites, those belonging to Jewish communities were far less likely actively to resist nonwhite "intrusion."[37] White antiracists fought for racial integration and against the white backlash. They worked for the multiracial NAACP to dissolve the legal standing of segregation and formed new organizations, like the Detroit Interracial Committee, that urged whites to "join the fight against religious and racial hate."[38] Some white religious leaders, like Milwaukee's James Groppi, a Catholic priest who organized several protests against residential segregation in one of

EMERGENCY MEETING

SAT., MARCH 11, 1950 - 7 P. M.

All Residents on Streets - Dequindre
Marx, Orleans, Riopelle, Greeley and
all streets up to Oakland
6 Mile to 7 Mile Roads

NEIGHORHOOD INVADED BY COLORED PURCHASE ON ORLEANS & MINNESOTA

EVERY RESIDENT ASKED TO BE PRESENT TO VOTE ON MEASURES TO BE TAKEN, SIGN PETITIONS, AND ELECT BLOCK CAPTAINS

PLACE - LAZAR HALL

Dequindre and Minnesota

On facing racial immigration, some whites chose to ward off nonwhite families through intimidation tactics, protests, and violence.

the nation's most segregated cities, stood up against white resistance.[39] And we should not forget that some whites—those in interracial marriages—were victimized by neighborhood-based white terrorism.[40]

In many other cases, however, whites fought tooth and nail, risking prison time to preserve the color line.[41] Although some nonwhite families stood firm and brave in the face of such harassment, in many cases whites' efforts drove nonwhites back to the slums. Like most people during the Civil Rights Movement, the majority of nonwhites simply wanted to live a "normal life." They did not want to pit their families against whites' racial hatred, and rather than put up a fight, many victims of racial violence returned to run-down neighborhoods.

Urban Unrest

By the 1960s, American cities had undergone rapid transitions—economic, racial, and political. Not only were native-born nonwhite populations growing and expanding out of concentrated slum areas, but the abolition of national-origin quotas (as discussed in the previous chapter) resulted in immigrants from Asia and Latin America streaming into the country by the thousands. American Indians continued to relocate to the cities, and so did Mexican Americans, settling primarily in border towns and urban areas of the Southwest. But despite these changes, racial segregation remained stubbornly entrenched. The expansion of nonwhite neighborhoods did not translate necessarily into integrated neighborhoods. As one group moved in, the other group moved out—if not to the suburbs, then to another area of the city. And many nonwhite city dwellers— victims of years of economic exploitation, housing discrimination, and the compounding effects of racial domination—remained trapped in their respective ghettos, areas that had deteriorated only because of the flight of jobs and the middle class to the city's outskirts. Sociologists writing in 1962 observed that many blacks living in northern cities "live[d] in essentially the same places that their predecessors lived during the 1930s—the only difference [was] that[,] due to increasing numbers, they occup[ied] more space centered around their traditional quarters."[42]

The violent enforcement of racial segregation and degradation continued to relegate nonwhites to neighborhoods stripped of city services, bereft of jobs, ignored by politicians, and simmering with a sentiment of discontent. In the mid-1960s, many of these neighborhoods exploded. The majority of these racial uprisings took place in poor black neighborhoods and, unlike the uprisings that took place earlier in the century, was started by black residents. Harlem, which, according to one of its residents at the time, "needed something to smash,"[43] hosted a racial uprising in 1964; a year later, the week-long Watts uprising of Los Angeles resulted in the deaths of 34 people (25 of whom were black) and over 1,000 injuries; and Detroit served host to a vicious uprising in 1967, one that left 43 dead (most of them shot by police) and over 2,500 buildings looted and burned. After Martin Luther King, Jr., was assassinated in 1968, uprisings erupted all across the nation. Throughout the mid to late 1960s, in one major city after another, black neighborhoods went up in flames. Many Americans were certain that in these uprisings a second civil war was brewing.

If whites rebelled earlier in the century to preserve racial domination, blacks rebelled in the 1960s to dismantle it. Uprisings were not merely criminal or destructive acts; they were expressions of rage and suffering caused by a racist system. Many uprisings started as protests against police action within the black community. And insurgents did not go about destroying buildings arbitrarily; rather, they targeted for destruction white-owned businesses in black neighborhoods, stores that refused to hire blacks, and institutions that mistreated blacks.[44] The majority of surveyed whites felt the uprisings mainly were caused by "looters and undesirables." Nearly half of all blacks surveyed in 1968, however, believed the uprisings were a reaction to "discrimination and unfair treatment."[45]

While many blacks disagreed with the uprisings, arguing that racial progress would best be achieved by more conventional means, others felt that conventional approaches took too much time and that more radical action was needed. A growing sense of black militancy was taking hold in urban black communities, or what came to be known as the Black Power Movement (which we discuss in more detail in Chapter 9). Many insurgents, the majority of whom were young black men, were driven by its new spirit of militancy; but more than that, they were fed up with white supremacy. "People keep calling it a riot," recalls Tommy Jacquette, who at twenty-one years of age participated in the Watts revolt. "But we call it a revolt because it had a legitimate purpose. It was a response to police brutality and social exploitation of a community and of a people, and we would no more call this a riot than Jewish people would call the extermination of the Jewish people 'relocation.' . . . People said that we burned down our community. No, we didn't. We had a revolt in our community against those people who were in here trying to exploit and oppress us. We did not own this community. We did not own the businesses in this community. We did not own the majority of the housing in this community. Some people want to know if I think it was really worth it. I think any time people stand up for their rights, it's worth it."[46]

The racial uprisings not only brought the plight of the urban black poor to the forefront of American discourse, they also directly resulted in policies aimed at improving conditions in the ghetto. Government programs such as welfare payments, low-income housing subsidies, and job programs were initiated, as were summer programs for young people, often referred to as "riot insurance." And police officers received training on how better to interact with the black community.[47] The uprisings brought about another consequence as well: the ratcheting up of police repression in the black community, a topic we take up in the next chapter.

In their song, "Loaded Gun," American Steel, the Oakland-based punk band, scream: "I didn't see Watts burn, but I felt the embers." So it is for us today. Our cities and suburbs—as well as our small towns—have been forged in the fires of Watts, Harlem, Detroit, and other cities that hosted racial uprisings, as they have by white flight and fight, immigration patterns, housing discrimination, and urban renewal. After reviewing the racial history of the residential field, we better understand why many nonwhites today harbor a distrust of mainstream white institutions like banks, police forces, and local political organizations. And we see the roots of a new kind of conservative ideology, one based on anti-government intervention, free enterprise, and the privatization of public services, an ideology that would help such politicians as George Wallace, Richard Nixon, Ronald Reagan, and George W. Bush get elected.[48]

In the history of American housing, we see, too, the origins of present-day racial segregation and disadvantage. Because of the intimate connection between home ownership and wealth accumulation, the unequal distribution of wealth discussed in the previous chapter is explained in large part by the housing struggles reviewed here. Because many assets, especially those rooted in real estate, are passed down from one generation to the next—property usually is inherited—the wealth and financial security many whites enjoy today are a direct consequence of government restrictions and business practices that systematically excluded nonwhites from stable homeownership during the second half of the twentieth century.

Throughout the twentieth century, many whites blamed nonwhites for their problems, allowing the real culprits—job loss brought on by deindustrialization, the housing shortage that came after World War II—to escape scrutiny. Casting a backward glance at the history of housing in twentieth-century America reveals, not a smooth transition or a "natural" progression but a bloody struggle over the right to live where one wishes—the very ownership of America. And at the plinth of this struggle lies the color line, pitting the principles of American democracy against the practices of white supremacy.[49]

Racial Segregation

How racially segregated are America's neighborhoods today? To answer this question, we need a good measure of segregation. Racial segregation can be measured by the degree to which certain racial groups are distributed throughout the city. For instance, if a city had a 20% Asian population, then in a city with no racial segregation, each neighborhood would be 20% Asian. The degree of segregation, therefore, can be gauged by the percentage of a certain racial group that would have to move into other neighborhoods to obtain zero segregation. If in our city of 20% Asians a neighborhood is 40% Asian, then to achieve perfect integration, 20% of those people would have to move into a neighborhood where the Asian population is below 20%.[50] Imagine that a city is a grid of boxes, each box representing a neighborhood. Now imagine that you are given a bag of multicolored marbles: white marbles represent your white population, black marbles your black population, and so forth. To model perfect integration, you would need to gather all your white marbles and drop then, one by one, into each box until they run out, repeating this step with your other marbles. If you did that, your segregation level would be 0. If, however, you decided to dump all your black marbles into a few connected boxes and all your white marbles into different boxes, you could model a very high level of *segregation. Which model does America resemble?*

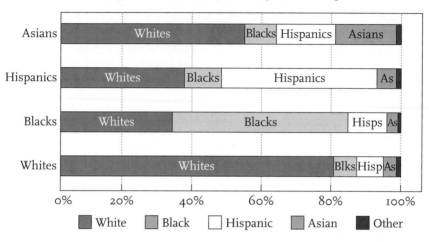

Diversity Experienced in Each Group's Typical
Neighborhood—National Metropolitan Average

Without a doubt, American neighborhoods—especially those in its Midwestern and Eastern cities—are severely segregated along the color line. Although segregation has declined in some metropolitan areas (mostly in multicultural cities of the West and Southwest) and smaller towns since the 1970s, most Americans live in racially segregated neighborhoods. In many areas, more than 60% of the entire black population would have to move into different neighborhoods to achieve perfect integration. Northern cities, such as Detroit, Chicago, Milwaukee, and Gary are the most segregated in America, where our segregation measure reaches 80%–90%.[51] If blacks are segregated to such a severe degree in cities, then so, too, are whites. Many times when people speak of segregation, they speak of neighborhoods with a high concentration of blacks or Hispanics, failing to realize that those neighborhoods exist only because there also are neighborhoods with a high concentration of whites. An all-white section of the city is no more "natural" than an all-black one: each exists because of the other.

The segregation rates of African Americans are much higher than those of Hispanics or Asians. According to one study, blacks are twice as likely to be isolated from other racial groups as, and are nearly 60% more segregated than, Hispanics and Asians. In fact, the average Hispanic and Asian family living in a city is more likely to have white neighbors than Hispanic or Asian neighbors.[52] However, this might change in the near future, as demographers are beginning to document a steady rise in Hispanic and Asian segregation, a rise connected, many argue, with a strong stream of immigration from Latin American and Asian countries.[53]

We should also be mindful that different Hispanic and Asian ethnic groups experience different levels of segregation. Filipinos, Vietnamese, and Indian

The Most Segregated Large Metropolitan Area for Blacks or African Americans in 2000: Milwaukee-Waukesha, WI

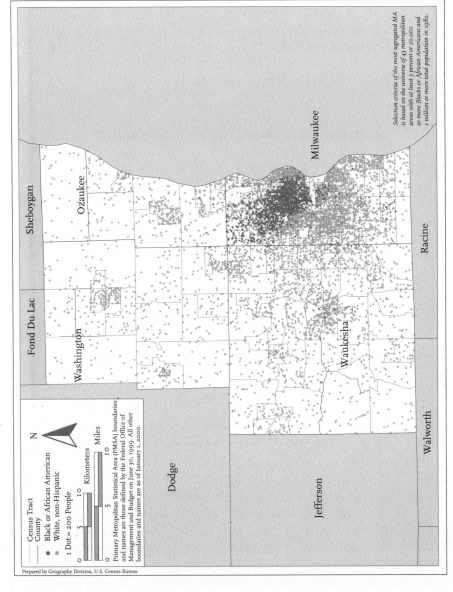

Prepared by Geography Division, U.S. Census Bureau

Americans are more segregated and live in poorer neighborhoods than do Chinese, Japanese, and Korean Americans.[54] And the degree to which Hispanics are segregated depends in large part on the color of their skin. Focusing on Caribbean Hispanics, such as Puerto Ricans, Dominicans, Cubans, and Panamanians—groups that share many cultural characteristics (such as religion and Spanish proficiency) but vary greatly with respect to skin tone (from very light to very dark)—researchers have found that dark-skinned Hispanics are much more segregated than light-skinned Hispanics. In ten metropolitan areas, 52% of light-skinned Hispanics would have to move to achieve perfect integration. That percentage jumps to 72% for brown-skinned Hispanics and soars to 80% for black Hispanics.[55] And many black Hispanics, especially those of Puerto Rican descent, live in poorer neighborhoods than light-skinned Hispanics.[56]

The fact that Asians and Hispanics are less segregated than African Americans reflects, not so much the former two groups' extreme integration into white neighborhoods, but the extreme segregation of African Americans. In twenty-nine cities, which contain no less than 40% of the entire black population, blacks are isolated to such an acute degree that most of them live only within "black areas of town."[57] The segregation of black Americans living in these cities is so severe that Douglas Massey and Nancy Denton, authors of *American Apartheid*, refer to it as "hypersegregation," a term describing the observation that "black Americans in these metropolitan areas live within large, continuous settlements of densely inhabited neighborhoods that are packed tightly around the urban core. . . . No other group in the contemporary United States comes close to this level of isolation within urban society."[58]

The Role of Economic Factors

What causes racial segregation? Perhaps what on the surface looks like racial segregation is segregation based on **economic factors**. That is, because on average whites are more wealthy than nonwhites, perhaps racial segregation is due, not to mechanisms of racial domination, but to class-based inequalities. If this is true, then racial segregation would disappear the higher one climbed up the economic ladder. The idea, however, is not borne out by evidence. In northern cities, blacks, regardless of income, remain highly segregated from whites. Blacks making minimum wage are just as segregated as those making more than $50,000 a year. Middle-class Latinos are slightly less segregated than poor Latinos: in Los Angeles, for instance, 64% of the poor Latino population would have to relocate to achieve perfect integration, while only 50% of the middle-class Latino population would have to do so. It is clear that economic inequalities alone cannot explain racial segregation. In fact, class-based explanations do nothing to explain the hypersegregation of African Americans—the most affluent of whom are more segregated than the poorest

Hispanics in the country's largest Latino barrio—or the fact that racial segregation persists in affluent suburbs.[59]

The Role of Personal Choice

What about **personal choice?** In a recent survey, two-thirds of Milwaukee residents claimed that the reason their city was so segregated was because "people of different races choose to live in communities with people of their own race."[60] To what extent were they right? Are black people segregated simply because of their desire to live in black neighborhoods? By and large, the answer is no. Most African Americans strongly endorse the ideal of integration. Consider the findings of the Detroit Area Survey. In this study, white and black people were shown maps of hypothetical neighborhoods that varied in terms of racial composition: dwellings that housed black families were colored black; those that housed white families were colored white. Those who participated in the study were asked how they felt about the different neighborhoods and in which neighborhoods they would choose to live. The majority of blacks said their ideal neighborhood was 50% black and 50% white; when asked about their preference, many emphasized the importance of racial cooperation and collaboration. However blacks showed a strong aversion to segregated neighborhoods: 30% would not move into an all-black neighborhood and, fearing they would be unwelcome (or, worse, would be met with hostility), 60% were unwilling to move to an all-white neighborhood.[61]

While blacks are strong proponents of integration, whites are advocates of segregation. A quarter of whites who participated in the Detroit Area Survey reported that a single black neighbor would make them uncomfortable. Regarding a neighborhood that was one-third black, 73% of whites would refuse to travel there, 57% would feel uncomfortable, and a full 40% would move away if they lived there. When shown a neighborhood that was 50% black and 50% white, 84% of whites would not enter that area, while 64% would move away, and 72% would feel uncomfortable. In other words, the neighborhood that most blacks would want to move to—one with an even balance of black and white folks—is the one that whites would want to move away from. These whites, echoing the sentiments of whites across the twentieth century, feel that having even a handful of black neighbors would drive down property values and increase neighborhood crime.[62]

Therefore, racial segregation in part is caused by personal choice: not the choices of Puerto Ricans to live with other Puerto Ricans, or blacks with other blacks, but the choices of whites to live with other whites. Just as they did in the twentieth century, some whites will go to great lengths to avoid racial integration at the neighborhood level, from lashing out in violence at their nonwhite neighbors—roughly half of all Chicago's hate crimes occur in white neighborhoods undergoing a process of integration—to paying outlandish mortgages and suffering lengthy commutes to live in predominantly white suburbs.[63] This is why observers have claimed that ending America's racial segregation will require, not a recasting of the personal choices of nonwhites—the majority of whom, as we have just seen, overwhelmingly value integration—but "a moral commitment that white America has historically lacked."[64] It will require a moral commitment to render hollow and worthy of reproach the joke that circulates in segregated white neighborhoods: "What is a word that starts with 'n' and ends with 'r' that you should never call a black person? . . . 'Neighbor.'"[65]

Although the majority of nonwhites favor integration with whites, some nonwhites—those who can exercise a fair amount of choice about where to live—deliberately choose to stay in poor, majority-nonwhite neighborhoods rather than move into the suburbs. Indeed, some researchers have observed a small-scale reverse migration on the part of upper- and middle-class blacks who are moving back to inner-city neighborhoods, choosing Harlem over the Hamptons, Oakland over San Francisco, Southeast Washington, D.C. over Richmond, Virginia. Rather than live in the suburbs, where much of life is structured by white privilege and interracial ignorance, a committed cadre of affluent blacks prefer life in the inner city, where they are surrounded by people who, while generally poorer, understand their history, their jokes, their struggles.[66] "Who said, after all," asks Mary Pattillo, "that residential integration with whites is still the preeminent goal to which blacks (and whites) should aspire?"[67]

We should interpret these facts from a sociological point of view. This is what sociology teaches: personal choice does not exist in a vacuum somehow unaffected by historical and social forces. Rather, a person's choices are deeply influenced by structures much larger, older, and more powerful than the person herself, including and especially structures of racial domination. Thus, the housing choices of both whites and nonwhites are affected by the legacy of white supremacy: whites who work to keep white neighborhoods white strive to uphold it; whites who choose to move into integrated neighborhoods, and nonwhites who choose to move into white neighborhoods, struggle against it; and nonwhites who prefer nonwhite neighborhoods try to avoid it. If our choices are conditioned to varying degrees by racial domination, then some nonwhites' preference for segregated nonwhite neighborhoods might reflect their unknowing acceptance of the terms of their own domination, just as whites' preference for segregated white neighborhoods might reflect their unknowing acceptance of a system that profits them.

The Role of Housing Discrimination

Social scientists also have explained racial segregation by analyzing the mechanisms of **housing discrimination**.[68] Through the employment of audit studies, where paired actors, equal in every way aside from race, approach a realtor as prospective homebuyers or renters, researchers have gathered conclusive evidence documenting compounding and multisided discrimination against nonwhites. According to a massive audit study conducted by the U.S. Department of Housing and Urban Development, Hispanics and blacks looking for housing faced high levels of discrimination (which occurred in 50% of their interactions with realtors and landlords), as did Asians (who faced discrimination in 20% of cases) and Native Americans (who faced discrimination in 30% of cases).[69] Although housing discrimination has been outlawed since the Fair Housing Act of 1968, it is clear from such studies that it continues, albeit in more covert and underhanded ways. As sociologist Nathan Glazer once observed, racial segregation persists "despite the many state laws, and the national legislation, which make discrimination in rental and sales of housing illegal."[70]

How, exactly, are nonwhites discriminated against? Over and over again, audit studies document the practice of realtors falsely informing prospective nonwhite clients that the houses or apartments they noticed in an advertisement have just been rented or sold. One study documented the practice of a Chicago-based developer who worked only with whites; blacks were *always* told no properties were available, whereas whites were shown properties the majority of the time.[71] According to another study, prospective black homebuyers were informed of 65 homes for every 100 shown to whites, and they inspected only 54 homes for every 100 shown to whites.[72] Yet another study found that between 60% and 90% of houses and apartments displayed to whites are never shown to blacks.[73] In addition, a good number of realtors often show nonwhites only those homes located in nonwhite or integrated areas, leading them away from majority-white neighborhoods—a practice known as "steering" that may be on the increase.[74] One analyst found that Hispanic and black homeseekers encounter steering between 30% and 40% of the time, while white homeseekers are often discouraged from buying in integrated neighborhoods.[75] Real estate offices advertise homes in majority-nonwhite or integrated neighborhoods at far lower rates than they do homes located in middle-class white neighborhoods, a pattern that persists even after taking into account the economic profile of the neighborhoods.[76] Added to these modes of discrimination are the all too familiar subtle snubs experienced by nonwhite clients: realtors who never return your calls, who never discuss with you multiple financing options, who reportedly are always too busy to schedule a meeting with you, who quote you higher prices than they do for whites, or who generally treat you badly, hoping you will take your business elsewhere.

Social scientists also have documented gender discrimination in housing, a dynamic that makes things especially difficult for women of color. Not only are women sometimes denied loans or charged higher rents on the basis of their sex, but they are also disproportionately victimized by sexual harassment. Landlords and building managers may agree to fix a repair or wave a late fee in exchange for sexual favors or may threaten a tenant with eviction unless she "is nice to him."[77] What is more, on learning that a woman is in an abusive relationship, landlords have been known to reject her rental application or evict her. In fact, housing discrimination against abused women is enough of a problem that the National Law Center on Homelessness and Poverty has created an informational brochure on this topic.[78]

For their part, banks and loan companies, as we learned in the previous chapter, also help to reinforce racial segregation. Regularly, nonwhites, even those with impressive financial portfolios, are denied mortgage loans and receive poor credit ratings. One study found that, even "after controlling for all objective indicators for applicant risk, lenders still rejected minorities 56% more often than otherwise identical whites."[79] According to political scientist Karen Orren, since the 1960s, life insurance companies virtually have abandoned the city, choosing instead to offer mortgage loans almost exclusively to suburban properties.[80] And many banks, continuing a more clandestine kind of redlining, refuse to finance homes in nonwhite and integrated neighborhoods. Interestingly, banks seem most hesitant to invest in areas undergoing racial change—distributing loans at high volumes in majority-white areas, moderate volumes in majority-black areas, and low volumes in racially mixed areas—a practice directly at odds with the principle of racial integration.[81]

The Costs of Segregation

The **consequences** of segregation are multisided and complex, as they are grim and troubling. First, racial segregation takes an economic toll on its victims. Because banks often deny qualified nonwhites home loans, nonwhite home seekers must secure mortgages with inflated interest rates and high monthly payments. And because realtors steer nonwhites away from affluent white neighborhoods, many nonwhites end up purchasing homes that are not worth as much as comparable homes in white neighborhoods. In fact, studies have shown that black homeowners actually are penalized for purchasing a home: the average black homeowner resides in a neighborhood that is more segregated and less prosperous than that of the average black renter.[82] And in his study of housing discrimination, John Yinger estimates that each time a black or Hispanic person looks for housing, she or he, met with all the mechanisms of discrimination discussed earlier, pays an average "discrimination tax" of $3,000.[83]

Added to the economic disadvantages attached to housing in segregated neighborhoods are the disadvantages associated with one's proximity to well-paying jobs. Opportunities for work are abundant in some areas—namely, booming suburbs that have flourished since the white flight of the 1960s—and virtually nonexistent in others. Nonwhites clustered together in isolated city centers live in gutted-out areas cut off from the economic mainstream. Not only

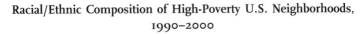

Racial/Ethnic Composition of High-Poverty U.S. Neighborhoods, 1990–2000

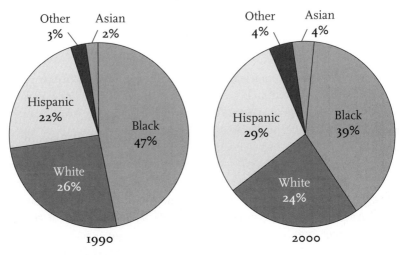

this, but social scientists have learned that employers often use an address as a proxy for identifying an applicant's race in order to discriminate against non-whites. In other words, even if a job application does not ask you to list your race, the person doing the hiring has little trouble figuring out if you are black, white, or Asian simply by determining if you live in a black, white, or Asian neighborhood.[84] In many overlapping ways, therefore, racial segregation directly reproduces racialized poverty.

Racial segregation also affects people's living conditions. Forced to endure life in neighborhoods bereft of normal institutions (like grocery stores and banks), housed in old, dilapidated structures in a state of disrepair—infected with rats and bugs, overcrowded, leaky and stuffy and cold—and miles away from the nearest hospital or medical clinic, residents in poor, nonwhite neighborhoods experience a quality of life resembling nothing like the American ideals of comfort and security. To a lesser degree, this is true even of many middle-class black families, forced to live in neighborhoods with higher crime rates and lower property values than those of their white counterparts who earn the same amount of money.[85]

Racial segregation also has political consequences. If nonwhites are clustered only in certain areas of the city, they can be more or less ignored by political representatives who focus their energies on other areas. Although segregation can help nonwhites elect nonwhite representatives, as we learned in Chapter 3, by the same token it marginalizes nonwhites in the political arena. The segregation of nonwhites therefore erodes hope of coalition building and interracial collaboration in the political field, both on local and national levels.[86]

Students' performance in school does not go unaffected by racial segregation. Children and young people living in run-down segregated neighborhoods must attend poor schools with teaching shortages and few resources. Roughly half of all property tax revenue is used for public elementary and secondary education.[87] Because property tax is dictated by property values, affluent neighborhoods with soaring property values will enjoy a plump tax base from which schools can draw, while poor neighborhoods with abysmal property values will have a paltry tax base. This means that schools that service students in nonwhite low-income areas necessarily will be forced to operate with a much smaller budget than will schools housed in affluent white neighborhoods; they will have less money for field trips, textbooks, computers, and competitive teacher's salaries. It is small wonder, then, that black and Latino students living in highly segregated ghettos perform worse in school than black and Latino students from poor families living in more affluent neighborhoods. For many students living in racially isolated neighborhoods, doing well in school takes a back seat to staying safe, avoiding street crime and gangs, navigating the drug scene, and making ends meet.[88]

Besides such material consequences, racial segregation also brings about symbolic consequences. By dividing cities along racial dimensions, racial segregation gives off the appearance that racial divisions are real, natural, and unchanging. The geographic segregation in cities encourages a kind of mental segregation, one that reinforces and reifies the racial order. As one historian has put it, "in the very act of defining the boundaries of the 'ghetto,' whites also continually defined and reinforced the boundaries of race."[89] French sociologist Pierre Bourdieu takes pains to remind us there exists an intimate connection between "objective divisions of the social world" and "the principles of vision and division that agents apply to them."[90] By this, Bourdieu means that the way the world looks powerfully influences the way we look on the world; the social divisions that exist within society, those separating white from nonwhite, men from women, rich from poor, and so forth, wield great influence over the cognitive maps directing our thinking. And, with racial segregation, how could it be otherwise?

And, last, we cannot forget the deep emotional costs of racial segregation. "The people of Harlem know they are living there because white people do not think they are good enough to live anywhere else," wrote James Baldwin in 1960. "No amount of 'improvement' can sweeten this fact. . . . A ghetto can be improved in one way only: out of existence."[91] When a white family leaves a neighborhood to which Arab Americans have moved, or when a realtor refuses to show a newly married black couple homes in areas outside the black ghetto, a message, clear and cutting, is delivered: "You are not good enough to live near white people." "Housing is no abstract social and political problem, but an extension of man's personality," remarked American sociologist Kenneth Clark in 1965. "If the Negro has to identify with a rat-infested tenement, his sense of personal inadequacy and inferiority, already aggravated by job discrimination and other forms of humiliations, is reinforced by the physical reality around him. . . . A house is a concrete symbol of what the person is worth."[92] Indeed, as anthropologist John Hartigan has observed, the closer whites live to blacks, the higher their chances of being labeled "poor white trash." Just as politicians' ties with lobbyists or unpopular public figures can cause their political capital to plummet, whites' racial capital, the very value of their whiteness, seems to decrease the closer they live to populations denigrated within the American racial order.[93]

Economic, material, political, educational, symbolic, and emotional—the consequences of racial segregation are mighty and many. But if racial segregation disadvantages some, it advantages others. If inner-city blacks are cut off from well-paying jobs, whites living in the suburbs are well connected to corporate America; if Mexicans living in crowded barrios are ignored by their political representatives, whites throughout the suburbs, with their healthy tax base, can more easily catch hold of the prince's ear; if Native Americans relegated to isolated and impoverished reservations are burdened by a sense of inferiority, whites living the good life might come to possess, perhaps without their knowledge, a sense of superiority, of entitlement. It is incorrect to assume that every white gain translates into nonwhite loss—or, conversely, that for nonwhites to get ahead whites must suffer. However, it is equally inadequate to speak of the disadvantages faced by people of color living in segregated neighborhoods without at the same time calling to mind the advantages enjoyed by whites living in equally segregated communities.

The City

Immigration has been and remains an urban phenomenon. Of the thousands of immigrants who come to the United States each year, most settle in large "receiving cities" or "gateway cities," such as Miami, Los Angeles, New York, Dallas, Chicago, Houston, and San Francisco. Through international communication channels, immigrants in the sending countries learn where pockets of immigrants from their country have settled. In fact, Armenians hoping to emigrate to the United States tend not to say they are moving "to America" but "to Hollywood," referencing the Armenian enclaves of Los Angeles. Although not as segregated as African Americans—or, for that matter, European immigrants of the nineteenth century—today's immigrants are a fairly segregated lot, many clustering together in ethnic enclaves.[94]

Are ethnic enclaves transitional neighborhoods in which new immigrants live until they gain enough footing in American society to move out, or are they more established communities, where multiple generations of immigrants live even though they do not have to? The answer, social scientists have learned, is "both." According to the **spatial assimilation thesis**, advanced by American sociologist Douglas Massey, new immigrants self-segregate in enclaves and rely on the enclave economy for their start.[95] After some time in the enclave, immigrants, having acquired savings and improved their English skills, look for a new place to live, one that can offer a higher standard of living. In this view, ethnic enclaves are a stopping point for immigrants on their way to economic and cultural assimilation.

According to another view, the **ethnic community thesis**, ethnic enclaves are sought out by immigrants who could afford to live elsewhere. Some immigrants prefer living in areas where a good number of their neighbors eat the same food, celebrate the same holidays, and speak their native language.[96] Although most ethnic neighborhoods are underprivileged, some are quite well-off. The Vietnamese and Japanese enclaves of inner-city Los Angeles, for example, are at least as affluent as the other neighborhoods where Vietnamese and Japanese families live. The same is true of New York City's Afro-Caribbean, Filipino, and Indian-American enclaves.[97]

Added to these two patterns is a third: racial segregation. Some ethnic groups—first-, second-, and third-generation immigrants alike—are victimized by housing discrimination at alarming rates. According to one audit study, Koreans in Los Angeles regularly face extreme discrimination.[98] These three patterns are not mutually exclusive; that is, all three have been verified by social-scientific research. Within ethnic enclaves—indeed, within neighborhoods of all varieties—we find those who could live elsewhere but who, attracted to its cultural life, choose not to; those who wish to live elsewhere but are trapped within it; and those who use the enclave as a launching pad from which to ascend.[99]

Interracial Conflict: Blacks and Koreans

Immigrants always have added to the pulse and vibrancy of American urban life. This is especially true of today's Korean immigrants, the immigrant group with the highest rate of self-employment in the United States. Many cities owe their affordable dry cleaners and nail salons, fish markets and fresh-flower stands, and neighborhood grocery stores to Korean entrepreneurs. For over a hundred years, immigrant groups have established businesses in the inner city. Throughout the twentieth century, Jewish shopkeepers were a regular fixture in the center of town. But as their children inherited not just the opportunities their parents had worked so hard to provide but also the opportunities involved in being welcomed deeper into the ranks of whiteness, they took leave of their shops, opening up in turn new opportunities for streams of other ethnic immigrants. Koreans have filled the business niche left by

Jewish shopkeepers, and many have opened up shop in the black ghetto, because they can afford to live there and because they do not have to compete with large corporations, which are much more interested in the deeper pockets of suburban residents.[100]

Many black ghetto residents, however, view Korean shopkeepers with a fair degree of animus and resentment. Although blacks and immigrants by and large compete for different jobs, as we learned in the previous chapter, many poor blacks feel that Koreans entrepreneurs have stolen their jobs, while others feel generally mistreated and disrespected by shopkeepers. We are met with this tension when Ice Cube raps, "Every time I want to go get a fucking brew, I gotta go down to the store with the two Oriental one-penny-counting motherfuckers; They make a nigga mad enough to cause a little ruckus"; or when comedian Dave Chappell jokes, "Now I would never say I hate all Korean people. I haven't met all Korean people. That hate talk's for savages. But even though I don't generalize, I do do percentages and averages. So far I hate one out of five Koreans I've met." Conflicts between black patrons and Korean storeowners often are colored by racist language, with each party exchanging epithets. Black-Korean conflict boiled over in the early nineties. In 1991, a Korean merchant shot and killed a black teenager in South Central Los Angeles. A year later, Los Angeles went up in flames as insurgents of all racial identities took to the streets after four white police officers, who had been caught on videotape beating a twenty-five-year-old motorist named Rodney King, were acquitted. As the smoke settled from the country's first multiethnic uprising, fifty-two had been killed and millions of dollars worth of property had been destroyed. Korean storeowners were hit the hardest, suffering almost half the total property damage—roughly $400 million.[101]

Black-Korean conflict reminds us how racial domination can occlude and distort, how it can hide the real causes of human misery under false arguments that attribute those causes to certain dominated racial groups. Instead of examining processes of disinvestment and deindustrialization that hollowed out the city's core, ongoing modes of capitalist exploitation that keep plump the unemployment rolls, or America's skimpy welfare state and the retreat of state involvement from poor urban areas, the mind clouded by racial domination prefers to blame immigrants or blacks. The distrust and fear that different racial and ethnic groups living in poor urban neighborhoods harbor toward one another is matched only by the interests and struggles shared by these groups.

Gentrification

All those living in poor inner-city neighborhoods, blacks and whites and immigrants alike, are affected by **gentrification.** A term coined by British sociologist

Ruth Glass, gentrification refers to a process of neighborhood change by which relatively affluent people move into an area populated by poorer residents. Unlike the urban renewal programs of the twentieth century, gentrification usually is not motivated by the government or accompanied by mass eviction notices and a wrecking ball. Rather, it is initiated by middle-class people, who, by their own volition, begin to move into an area of the city that, although run down and home to many poor residents, is attractive: maybe its architecture suddenly has roared back into style, or it is located near a fashionable art district. These privileged newcomers begin to fix up the neighborhood, improving its housing stock and opening up quaint coffee shops and restaurants. Bit by bit, the neighborhood grows more attractive and hip; it quickly becomes the place everyone wants to live. Lawyers, doctors, artists, and young professionals begin moving in. This causes the property values and taxes to spike, forcing the landlords to raise the rent. Before you know it, an area that once was known as a slum district is now a middle-class borough, and many of the poor families who once made a home there—indeed, who were vital to the neighborhood's history and revitalization— are forced to find cheaper housing elsewhere.

In many cases, gentrification results in poor nonwhites being displaced by privileged white residents. Recently, this has occurred in northwest Fort Lauderdale, where whites are buying most of the houses in predominately black neighborhoods, moving into streets named after African-American families who settled the areas; gentrification is taking place in the East Austin blue-collar Hispanic barrio, too, where, after a new condominium development raised land values by more than 50%, someone hung signs that read, "Stop gentrifying the East Side"; and the residents of New York City's Harlem and Chinatown are trying to dam up a wave of gentrification that is threatening to wash over these historic neighborhoods.[102]

There are many social mechanisms propelling the motors of gentrification, including the erratic course of the housing market and recent campaigns to lure affluent people back to city centers. An especially important mechanism, one we highlight here, has been a change in the dynamics of racial segregation. Since segregation's heyday during the first half of the twentieth century, nonwhites and immigrants have been able to move out of segregated areas, decreasing landlords' abilities to make money by avoiding property maintenance, transforming one apartment into several, or charging inflated rent. Because the fast dollar can no longer easily be made from racialized ghettos, landlords now welcome gentrification, a process that increases their property values and their rent collections. Their financial incentive, which once was to tighten the grip of isolated nonwhite slum neighborhoods, so as to better exploit their residents, has now given way to the incentive to push poor nonwhite residents out.[103]

Advanced Marginality: The Ghetto

It is fitting to end our section on race in the city by returning to the ghetto, that institution, formed by fear and racism, in which the metropolis's "urban outcasts" live. In the previous chapter, we defined the ghetto as a racial institution marked by social isolation and economic vulnerability first formed when blacks migrated North during the early twentieth century. To this we might add Massey and Denton's observation that "a ghetto is a set of neighborhoods that are exclusively inhabited by members of one group, within which virtually all members of that group live." By this definition, African Americans are the only group in the history of the United States that have experienced ghettoization.[104] Even early European immigrants, who clustered together in Germantowns and Little Italys, did not experience ghettoization to the degree that blacks experience it today. There are poor white neighborhoods, Hispanic barrios, and Chinatowns aplenty. But a ghetto is not defined exclusively by its poverty, nor, as we have already seen, are all kinds of poverty the same.

The defining characteristic of a ghetto is not economic destitution but advanced marginality. **Advanced marginality** refers to the severe spatial and social segregation of the ghetto's residents, marked by their amputation from America's economic prosperity, national security, collective imagination and memory, and welfare state services.[105] The ghetto first originated in medieval Europe as an area of the city where Jews were cordoned off from the rest of the population. In fact, the word "ghetto" comes from an Italian word meaning "the part of a city to which Jews are restricted."[106] And it is this restriction, this social isolation, which is the essence of the ghetto.

Throughout the ghetto's sordid history, **public housing**—government-owned units provided at low rates to poor residents—has always played a large part in reinforcing and reproducing conditions of advanced marginality. Public housing arose after World War II as a response to the country's housing shortage. At first, many white and black families stayed in public housing units for short periods of time. However, as urban renewal projects were visited upon ghetto areas and thousands of poor blacks, evicted from their homes, were channeled into already swelling slum areas, public housing "was now meant to collect the ghetto residents left homeless by the urban renewal bulldozers."[107] To make room for these displaced newcomers, cities erected towering public housing units—Chicago's Robert Taylor homes once housed as many as 20,000 tenants—always in the isolated ghetto and, more often than not, "bleak, sterile, and cheap—expressive of patronizing condescension in every line."[108] Unlike many European states, which provide public housing in the form of financial housing subsidies to poor families, American public housing tends to consist of these inner-city projects.

Public housing residents (among whom over 1 million people count themselves), lacking many of the basic necessities many Americans take for granted,

Perhaps no other American is burdened with so demeaning a stigma attached to her place of residence as the tenant of the public housing project.

have struggled to create a community within the bleak, looming projects.[109] This has involved struggling against gang violence, forming more productive and understanding relationships with the police, and petitioning the city for social services and economic opportunities. America remains uneasy about its projects. Concluding that public housing units were a failure in social policy, the wrecking ball has once again come to the ghetto. Many inner-city projects have been demolished, with their residents, once again, forced to relocate within the ghetto's borders.[110]

Consider New Orleans, a city that, before Hurricane Katrina, housed 500,000 people, 67% of whom were black, and that had the second-highest concentration of poverty in the nation. A full decade before 2005, New Orleans housing authorities had sought ways to dismantle the city's public housing. After Hurricane Katrina ravaged the city that year, closing down 80% of its public housing, some public officials secretly rejoiced. Congressman Richard Baker, a Republican from Baton Rouge, told a group of lobbyists, "We finally cleaned up public housing in New Orleans. We couldn't do it, but God did."[111] Although the U.S. Department of Housing and Urban Development pledged $154 million to rebuild public housing in New Orleans, it remains to be seen if the money will be used to restore the old structures or to replace them with new privatized developments that charge higher rents. Some of the city's African-American residents fear that city planners responsible for rebuilding New Orleans will neglect housing for the poor or, more insidiously, will "see the disaster as a glorious opportunity to engineer poverty out of the city altogether." They worry, in other words, that "Hurricane Katrina will prove to be the biggest, most brutal urban-renewal program black America has ever seen."[112]

Perhaps no other American is burdened with so demeaning a stigma attached to her place of residence as the tenant of the public housing project. For this citizen, a *"blemish of place* is thus superimposed on the already existing stigmata traditionally associated with poverty and ethnic origin."[113] On meeting a new acquaintance, the tenant of the projects dreads the otherwise ordinary question, "Where do you live?" For she fears her address will cause the new acquaintance to look upon her as a failure. We should resist making the same mistake and, instead, should approach the public housing complex as "a contemporary mirror for American self-examination," viewing it with a historically informed and politically attuned sociological imagination.[114] In the end, we all play a small part in maintaining the advanced marginality of the ghetto. To quote the authors of the Kerner Commission, a 1968 group charged with researching race riots, "What white Americans have never fully understood—but what the Negro can never forget—is that white society is deeply implicated in the ghetto. White institutions created it, white institutions maintain it, and white society condones it."[115]

The Suburbs

America's sprawling suburbs originated as a racial creation, and they remain one today. Suburban development was fueled by white fear: fear of racial integration, of plummeting property values, and—most of all—of violent crime. In their distance from city centers, their cul-de-sacs and dead-end roads, their stringent zoning laws, and their lack of public transportation, the suburbs purposefully are constructed to promote isolation from city-dwellers and their "vices." Nowhere is this better exemplified than in **gated communities**, which have flourished since the 1970s. As their name suggests, gated communities, where nearly 8 million Americans reside, are residential areas fortified by high walls and security forces. To enter, pedestrians, bicyclists, and motorists must pass through a large gate, sometimes enabled by round-the-clock guards and surveillance cameras. No longer only a luxury of the elite, middle-class gated communities are now springing up all over suburbia.[116]

Overwhelmingly, gated communities attract affluent whites who believe violent crime is on the rise and who want to avoid being victimized by it. And many gated community residents' fear of crime is directly connected to poor nonwhite populations living in the inner city. What happens, then, when poor nonwhites enter gated communities, most regularly as service sector workers, landscapers, nannies, pool cleaners, gardeners, and housekeepers? According to recent eth-nographic research, gated community residents often are suspicious of, say, a truck-full of Mexican landscapers driving around their community. And many associate service workers with crime. Dependent on low-paid service workers to maintain their high standard of living at cheap rates, yet wary of the presence of nonwhite or immigrant groups in their majority-white haven, gated commu-nity residents' fears are heightened, making their motivations for living in a gated community that much more powerful.[117]

Americans often view urban life, in fact, as made up of "chocolate cities and vanilla suburbs," as funk master George Clinton once put it, and associate multiracial cities with poverty and crime and white suburbs with affluence and safety. After eating at Sylvia's, a famous soul food restaurant located in the heart of Harlem, Fox News commentator Bill O'Reilly announced that he "couldn't get over the fact" that Sylvia's was like any other restaurant. "It was like going into an Italian restaurant in an all-white suburb in the sense of people were sitting there, and they were ordering and having fun," O'Reilly said. "And there wasn't any kind of craziness at all."[118] Embedded within this comment is the implica-tion that black city areas are distinctly different, especially in terms of order and civility, from all-white suburbs.

The suburbs, however, are neither all affluent nor all white. In fact, since the 1990s, poverty has been on the rise in many suburbs. Between 1990 and 2000, suburban poverty levels rose an astonishing 21% (rising only by 8% in cities). Indeed, many cities have attempted to entice upper-class individuals to newly renovated central-city areas by pushing out poor families, who in turn have relocated to the inner-rings of the suburbs. The result has been the beginnings of "suburban ghettos," areas with extremely high poverty and unemployment rates, detached from social services and employment opportunities.[119]

In 2000, 70% of whites, 60% of Asians, 50% of Hispanic Americans, and 40% of African Americas lived in the suburbs. Most nonwhites migrating to the suburbs moved into areas already populated by nonwhites and areas undergoing racial change. Suburban areas with small nonwhite populations experienced higher levels of integration, while segregation is more trenchant in areas with large nonwhite populations. Typically, black Americans with ample bank accounts do not move from segregated urban areas to integrated suburbs but from one black neighborhood to another. To pluck one statistic from many: 60% of black households earning over $75,000 live in majority-black neighborhoods. The same is true, though to a lesser extent, of Hispanic and Asian Americans.[120]

Because many middle-class black neighborhoods abut poor black neighbor-hoods, middle-class residents often shop at the same stores, play in the same parks, and walk down the same streets as poor blacks living a few blocks away. Some middle-class blacks attempt to erect clear boundaries between themselves and their downtrodden neighbors (and hence have been labeled "buppies," a combination of black and yuppie). Others, however, have forged alliances with poor members of the black community, together participating in church fund-raisers or community education projects. Accordingly, many of the social problems that fester in the ghetto have crept into middle-class black neighborhoods, which are less affluent and have higher crime rates than middle-class white neighborhoods (or even many poor white neighborhoods). On the whole, the black middle class are just as segregated from whites—and, in turn, from good schools, well-funded social service agencies, and grocery stories with fair prices and fresh produce—as are poor blacks.[121]

At the same time, middle-class black families often oscillate between black and white communities, navigating racial boundaries at different times and for different reasons. Career-driven blacks may work in a majority-white corporate world but worship in a majority-black church. Black children from well-off families may attend a majority-white prep school during the weekday and play on a majority-black inner-city little league team on the weekends.[122] However, other middle-class black families, especially those sprinkled across majority-white suburbs, may remain culturally and spatially isolated from other black families. Black adolescents brought up in such areas often describe themselves as "raised white," such that they do not identify with African-American history, culture, or communities. Indeed, biracial adolescents raised in white suburbs often identity as white until they get to college, where they undergo a re-racialization orchestrated by their peers, professors, and guidance counselors. As one biracial woman attending the University of California–Berkeley explained, "Before I came to Cal I was white. I was all white culturally. . . . Here I am perceived as black. I'm treated as black so I don't have a problem with being black. . . . But it's a difficult situation. It's really hard."[123] Comments like these attest to the fluidity of racial categories, as well as to the importance of place in molding those categories.

Growing numbers of immigrant families live and work in the suburbs. In fact, almost half of new immigrants who arrived in the 1990s settled in suburban areas. In Los Angeles, which, along with New York, is home to the largest and most diverse collection of immigrant communities in the nation, there are more Mexican, Chinese, Filipino, Korean, Japanese, and Vietnamese citizens and immigrants living in the suburbs than in the inner-city. Large Cuban communities thrive in the suburbs of New Jersey; Salvadoran enclaves are nestled beyond the city limits throughout southern California; and the Chinese section of San Gabriel, a suburb of New York City, is called "suburban Chinatown." Although not as affluent as many white suburbs, suburban ethnic communities provide a higher standard of living than do inner-city ethnic enclaves and other urban neighborhoods.[124]

One of the largest and most diverse Asian-American communities is found in the suburban cities that made up the San Gabriel Valley, east of Los Angeles.

First settled by Asian workers in the mid-nineteenth century, the San Gabriel Valley is home to the eight cities in the United States with the highest proportions of Chinese Americans as well as to thousands of Japanese, Filipino, South Asian, and Japanese Americans. Public libraries and schools in the area have embraced Asian cultures as well as the principles of multilingualism and multiculturalism, with some high schools incorporating Mandarin language courses into their curriculum. As one observer has commented, many Asian-American youth living in San Gabriel Valley "do not know they are 'supposed to' major in engineering and not in sports," and a significant number of the area's young people, Asian and non-Asian alike, are "multilingual, multiracial, and multicultural . . . [and] comfortable in diversity."[125]

Rural America

Most of this chapter has focused on urban life, and for good reason: most Americans—over 80%, in fact—live in metropolitan areas.[126] However, racial dynamics also affect the lives of millions of people living in rural areas, the residents of American Indian reservations, farmlands, and small towns. In fact, many rural areas are just as racially segregated as their urban counterparts, and, what is more, many rural nonwhites live "in close proximity to the historical remnants of institutions explicitly created to conquer, oppress, and maintain their subordinate position in society."[127] For this reason, the remainder of this chapter is devoted to unpacking the racial dynamics of residence in rural America.

Colonias and Bordertowns

Since the early 1900s, American agriculture has relied on the busy hands and sturdy backs of migrant laborers, who were willing to work for below-market wages. In fact, between 1942 and 1964, the U.S. government recruited Mexican nationals for agricultural work through the Bracero program, which granted them temporary residence in the U.S. Over 4.5 million Mexicans worked in the United States through this program, willing to bend and sweat and pick in the fields for substandard wages. They often lived in crowded and hot dwellings, with bunkbeds stacked on top of one another. Called "legalized slavery," the Bracero program was outlawed the same year the Civil Rights Act was ratified; however, the working and housing conditions for today's migrant workers—the overwhelming majority of them are Mexican immigrants who work in the rural West—have not improved much.[128]

Between 1990 and 2000, the proportion of Mexican immigrants working in agricultural fields nearly doubled.[129] Small settlements, called *colonias*, have sprung up around the fields where migrant workers toil. Many *colonias* are made up of low-cost housing, or, in some cases, lines of dilapidated shacks built of pieces of discarded sheet metal, old tires, and scrap wood. Their residents are isolated—culturally, linguistically, economically, and politically—from the neighboring white communities, including the farmhouses of their employers; and many suffer from a lack of social services and basic medicine. Although *colonias* house significant numbers of Mexican immigrants, many are made up of native-born Mexican Americans. In south Texas, for instance, roughly two-thirds of *colonia* residents are American citizens.[130]

The desolate towns nesting against the 2,000-mile border separating the United States from Mexico are some of the poorest areas in the country. Star County, Texas, has the highest poverty rate in the nation. Mexican Americans and Mexican immigrants who populate the borderland face limited economic opportunities and must accept positions in America's growing low-wage market. To survive, more and more family members are pushed into the workforce. And many Mexican-American families have moved north, to the upper Midwest and other parts of the country, in search of a better life.[131]

Since the Treaty of Guadalupe, the U.S.-Mexican border has been hotly contested, and, in this respect, today is no different. Sprinkled along the border are anti-immigrant signs, planted on ranchland or near the highway, reading, "Terrorists love open borders. Remember 9-11," or "Help Save America." Fearing an "invasion" of Mexican immigrants who illegally cross the border, hundreds of white men and women, many of them retired veterans, have organized vigilante groups who voluntarily patrol the border. The Minuteman Civil Defense Corps and other such "do-it-yourself" patrols spread volunteers along the border and ask them to "monitor and report the locations of migrants" to U.S. Border Patrol officers. Many Minuteman volunteers dress in paramilitary clothes and carry loaded pistols on their belts. Minuteman troops often find themselves in confrontation with volunteers who staff assistance camps along the border, providing migrants with food, water, and medical supplies. According to Chris Simcox, the founder and president of the Minuteman Defense Corps., his group is "helping out the Department of Homeland Security, being their eyes and ears, spotting and reporting."[132]

But many have wondered whose security the Minuteman intend to protect. Small shops that rely on the business of Mexican families who cross the border to buy this or that have suffered considerable losses because of the Minutemen. Their heavily armed, military-like presence has heightened the area's racial tensions. And anti-immigration groups have reinvigorated not only antigovernment militias (which had been in decline since the mid-1990s) but also hate groups, such as the neo-Nazis and the KKK. Speaking at a white-power rally in 2006, New Jersey-based radio talk-show host Hal Turner implored his audience to "clean your guns, have plenty of ammunition . . . and then do what has to be done" to undocumented immigrants.[133] Racist diatribes such as this create a nationwide environment of fear for people of Mexican descent, American citizens and undocumented immigrants alike.

Life on the Reservation—and Environmental Racism

A large proportion of America's indigenous population lives on reservations.[134] These are anything but one-dimensional settings. They vary along economic, cultural, religious, linguistic, and political lines. There is also immense variation within Indian Nations, caused (among other things) by differentiation built into tribal structure: separate clans, traditions, and villages. On examining the history of the Cherokee Nation, one sociologist noted that because the tribe's language changed from village to village, as did its customs, rituals, and everyday practices, it is more accurate to speak of "many different Cherokee populations," as opposed to a single, monochrome tribe.[135]

Those who have never set foot on an American Indian reservation might carry in their minds a great many misconceptions of reservation life. Indeed, many non-Indian Americans seem to view Indians as somehow locked in time, living on reservations the same way their ancestors lived centuries ago. Reacting to the frequency of these stereotypes, a joke circulated on an Indian listserv in 2002 that read, "Things Native Americans Can Say to a White Person upon First Meeting One: (1) Where's your powdered wig? (2) Do you live in a covered wagon? (3) What's the meaning behind the square dance? (4) What's your feeling about riverboat casinos? Do they really help or are they just a short-term fix? (5) I learned all about our people's ways in the Boy Scouts."[136] Just as it would be absurd to ask a white person these questions, it would be equally absurd to ask a resident of an Indian reservation, "Where's your headdress?" or "Do you live in a tepee?" More accurately, like most other Americans, many Native Americans live with one foot in the present and the other in the past. Many members of the Navajo Nation, for instance, live in modern homes decorated with traditional hand-woven rugs, pottery, and sand paintings; in their back yards, next to the trampoline and propane grill, sits a hogan, a small, dome-shaped wood and mud structure, which serves as a sacred ceremonial site.

Among the many problems facing American Indian reservations in the twenty-first century, environmental racism ranks among the most pressing. **Environmental racism** can be defined as any policy, practice, or directive that disproportionately disadvantages (intentionally or unintentionally) nonwhite communities.[137] Native American lands have been targeted for radioactive dumpsites, incinerators, and erosive mining operations. According to one source, over 300 reservations are threatened by environmental hazards, from chemical waste to dangerous air emissions, clear-cutting, and strip-mining. Faced with stringent environmental regulations, waste disposal firms have looked to Native American reservations, which are not subject to state laws regarding dumping. Hoping to buy off corrupt tribal leaders or to exploit the economic vulnerability of reservation inhabitants, these firms have offered thousands, even millions, of dollars for the right to pollute Indian Country.[138]

Consider the case of the Skull Valley Band of Goshutes, located on reservation land in northern Utah. Only a couple dozen tribal members live on the impoverished reservation, and it is not hard to see why. "To the southwest lies the Dugway Proving Ground, where the U.S. government develops chemical and biological weapons. To the east is one of the world's largest nerve-gas incinerators. To the north is a giant magnesium plant, a major polluter. To the northwest sit a hazardous-waste incinerator and a toxic-waste landfill. The tribe's only profitable business is a municipal garbage dump serving Salt Lake City."[139] In 2006, tribal members were approached with a proposition by Private Fuel Storage, a consortium representing nuclear utilities. In exchange for $100 million in fees to be dished out over a span of forty years, the Skull Valley reservation would agree to store nearly all the country's radioactive waste, roughly 44,000 tons. The payoffs were obvious, as were the risks—nothing short of the permanent poisoning of their lands—and tribal members disagreed on the plan and finally rejected it, for the time being. To debate whether or not residents of the Skull Valley reservation should have taken the deal is an important exercise. Equally important, however, is a sociological exercise that forces us to question why these Native Americans must choose between rural poverty and radioactive waste. What past and present economic, social, and political forces combine to produce this devil's bargain?

American Indians living on reservations are exposed to some of the worst air and water pollution in the country. As a result, they are at high risk of contracting cancer and lung diseases, of dying at a young age, and of giving birth to babies with defects. Compared to the national average, Native Americans living on reservations are 1.2 times as likely to die of a heart attack or stroke and are 3.5 times more likely to die of diabetes. When we learn that doctors can identify industry pollutants in the milk of nursing mothers living on the Akwesasne Mohawk reservation in upstate New York, we begin to understand one reason why many Indian babies are born prematurely and weigh less than the national average—and why the infant mortality rate on reservations is 1.5 times the national average and why the SIDS (Sudden Infant Death Syndrome) death rate is 2.5 times the national average.[140]

Native Americans have formed coalitions to resist environmental racism. In 1999, residents of the Eastern Navajo reservation appealed to the Nuclear Regulatory Commission to put an end to ongoing uranium mining. California's Mohave Nation and Nevada's Western Shoshone battled against proposals to build radioactive waste dumps on tribal land. And interracial coalitions aimed at combating such problems have emerged since American Indians are not the only group that suffers from environmental racism. After taking economic attributes into account, Latino and black urban neighborhoods are far more likely to experience environmental hazards than their white counterparts. The majority of large hazardous waste landfills are located in nonwhite neighborhoods; as many as three out of five African Americans live in areas with toxic waste dumps; and more than 46% of all public housing units are located within a mile's radius of factories emitting toxic gases.[141]

Poor rural black communities, especially those located in the Deep South, also have been sacrificed to house the nation's waste. In a document prepared for the United Nations, sociologist Robert Bullard wrote, "The Lower Mississippi River Industrial Corridor has over 125 companies that manufacture a range of products including fertilizers, gasoline, paints and plastics. Environmentalists and local residents have dubbed this corridor 'Cancer Alley,' and tax breaks given to polluting industries have created few jobs at a high cost. This is particularly true in Louisiana. . . . In the 1990s, Louisiana wiped off the books $3.1 billion in property taxes to polluting companies. The state's top five polluters have received $111 million over the past decade."[142] Over thirty petrochemical and industrial plants are located within a two-mile radius of Mossville, Louisiana, a rural black community. According to a 1999 study carried out by the United States Department of Health and Human Services, dioxin levels in Mossville residents are extremely high. A deadly substance, dioxin can cause cancer, hormone disruption, and severe birth defects.[143]

We now know who suffers from environmental racism. But who benefits from it? Companies that profit directly from creating pollution (such as chemical or plastic manufacturers) or by disposing of it (such as those involved in the waste processing industry)—as well as corrupt politicians more interested in funding their campaigns than in the livelihoods of their most vulnerable constituents—undeniably are beneficiaries of environmental racism. But there is another beneficiary as well. If you live as the average American does, you use up roughly twenty tons of raw materials each year, consuming ten times more than the average Chinese citizen and thirty times more than the average person living in India.[144] Where did all your garbage go? Is the place you now live powered by coal or nuclear energy plants? If so, who is forced to breathe the coal emissions that power your television set? Where does the radioactive waste from your nuclear energy plant get buried? If you are privileged enough to live in a neighborhood that does not house garbage incinerators or sewage plants, an area that does not abut nuclear waste dumps or factories spouting toxic gasses into the air, but you continue to gobble up resources, then, when asked, "Who benefits from environmental racism?" you must answer: "I do."

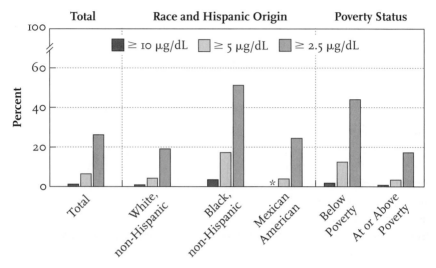

Percentage of Children Ages 1–5 with Specified Blood Lead Levels by Race and Hispanic Origin and Poverty Status, 2000–2004

* Data not shown. Estimate is considered unreliable (relative standard error is greater than 40 percent).
NOTE: Data for 2001–2004 are combined. The symbol µg/dL refers to blood lead level.

The Changing Face of Rural White America

Poor, rural white communities face many of the same problems that affect poor nonwhite communities. Small villages throughout Kentucky and Virginia have been victimized by environmental devastation, including illegal dumping and strip mining that has caused flash flooding. Poor whites living in rural America often are isolated from mainstream economic opportunities, over-looked by their government leaders, and constrained to live in inadequate housing. Like poor blacks living in the projects, poor rural whites living in trailer parks are marked with a stigma, a "blemish of place," which threatens to erode their sense of self-worth and dignity.[145] Trailer parks, it is commonly held, are where "rednecks," "hicks," and "white trash" live; they are breeding grounds for deviant behavior, poor hygiene, and lazy talking. And poor, rural whites—especially those of the Deep South—often are stereotyped as bitterly intolerant, harboring violently racist attitudes associated only with zealots of the KKK. This is an old belief, one that existed before the Civil War, and it divides rich from poor, civil from uncivil, North from South. As W. J. Cash wrote in 1960, there exists among ordinary people, from North and South, "a profound conviction that the South is another land, sharply differentiated from the rest of the American nation, and exhibiting within itself remarkable homogeneity."[146]

The world of poor, rural whites has been turned into a kind of backward and bigoted world, one that outsiders enjoy pointing to with a smirk or a condescending shake of the head. In debasing poor, rural whites, other Americans—affluent and city-dwelling whites and nonwhites alike—can conveniently avoid inspecting their own racist attitudes and dispositions. "I'm not a racist," they say. "If you want to see racism, talk to a redneck." This is not to say that many poor, rural whites do not embrace white supremacy. Many do, but no more than the rest of society. If poor, rural whites have been pegged the "most racist" of all Americans (and we know that quantifying racism is an exercise doomed from the start), it is not necessarily because they actually possess more bigoted views, but because they have not adapted ways of hiding their views behind coded language as have many middle-class urbanites. In truth, interpersonal racism is not concentrated in backwoods white towns but is found throughout America, in all communities, white and nonwhite alike. And as long as we peg the poor, rural white as the American bigot, we can avoid the painful exercise of asking how racial domination thrives in our own communities, and families, and even in our own thinking.[147]

Today, many rural middle-class white communities no longer are able to avoid confronting their own racial modes of thinking and acting, primarily because immigration patterns are transforming the racial landscape of previously majority-white towns. Some small towns that only ten years ago hosted small pockets of nonwhites now are adjusting to growing nonwhite populations as well as to cultural change. Grocery stores are beginning to stock Chinese food; Wal-Mart is beginning to follow English announcements with ones in Spanish; Middle-Eastern restaurants are appearing on Main Street. The reactions from white residents have been diverse and, at times, disquieting.

Lewiston, Maine, an inland town of 36,000 located in the whitest state in the union, recently has experienced an influx of Somali immigrants. Between 2001 and 2002, roughly 1,200 Somalis moved to Lewiston; that number doubled over the course of the next five years, until Lewiston had the highest per capita Somali concentration in the United States. The Somalis, many of whom were refugees, were attracted to Lewiston's low cost of living, its tradition of racial and religious tolerance (most were practicing Muslims), its good schools, and its hearty welfare benefits. But some of Lewiston's white residents resented the immigrants, assuming they were disproportionately draining the town's resources. This sentiment was made official in a letter, penned by the town's mayor, asking the elders of the Somali community to discourage their friends and family members from moving to the city. "The Somali community must exercise some discipline and reduce the stress on our limited finances and our generosity," the mayor wrote. "Our city is maxed-out financially, physically, and emotionally." The Somali residents of "Little Mogadishu" felt unfairly blamed for the town's financial hardships, responding to the mayor's letter with reminders of their own contributions to Lewiston.

The mayor's letter, however, began a string of events—including a rally held by a white supremacist group and a man rolling a severed pig's head down the center isle of a local mosque during an evening prayer service—that stoked the coals of racial hostility, dividing Somali residents from their white neighbors.[148] But even in this charged atmosphere, non-Somali antiracists, nonwhite and white alike, took stands against interracial hostility and intolerance. While the hate group rally drew only 30 people, roughly 5,000 turned out for the counter-protest held on a same day, a "diversity rally" that condemned racial hatred.[149]

Like Lewiston, the 37,000-person town of Carpentersville, Illinois, has experienced drastic changes in its racial demography. In 1990, Hispanics made up 17% of the town's population; in 2007, that number jumped to 40%. Although most of the town's Hispanic families are American citizens, some of Carpentersville's white residents have reacted to their rising Hispanic population by voicing opposition to illegal immigration. In a recent election, candidates calling themselves "The All American Team" won seats to Carpentersville's board of trustees by vowing to penalize landlords who rented to undocumented workers, as well as businesses that employed them. Before the election, a flier printed by a supporter of the All American Team was circulated throughout the town. It read: *"Are you tired of waiting to pay for your groceries while Illegal Aliens pay with food stamps and then go outside and get in a $40,000 car? . . . Are you tired of reading that another Illegal Alien was arrested for drug dealing? Are you tired of having to push 1 for English? . . . Are you tired of not being able to use Carpenter Park on the weekend, because it is overrun by Illegal Aliens? Are you tired of seeing the Mexican Flag flown above our Flag? If you are as tired as me then let's get out and Vote for the: All American Team."*[150]

In 2007, the newly elected All American Team passed an ordinance making English the official language of Carpentersville. This ordinance forbids the printing of various city notices, including warning signs and local regulations, in both Spanish and English, and would discourage city employees, including police officers, from speaking Spanish. As a result of these moves, the racial climate in Carpentersville has grown more toothy and intolerant. Many of the town's Hispanic residents feel unwelcome and under attack. For them, white residents are not taking on illegal immigration but are mounting an assault on Hispanic culture and language. Indeed, after entering Carpentersville's village hall to attend a meeting on illegal immigration, a second-generation Mexican American was told by a white resident, "This is a white's man's meeting." Many whites, however, feel that the town's Hispanic population is not assimilating fast enough. "They want the American dream, but they don't want to assimilate," declared one member of the All American Team. "Immigrants are what made this country great, but the immigrants of yesterday and the immigrants of today are totally different people. They don't have the love of this country in their hearts."[151]

Carpentersville is not alone. In establishing English as the town's official language, it joins thirty-five other municipalities and counties that have passed or proposed English-only resolutions, as well as forty other state and local governments that have passed laws designed to "make life miserable for illegal immigrants in the hope that they will have no choice but to return to their countries of origin."[152] And, indeed, many of these laws are having their desired effect. Undocumented immigrants, many of whom have worked in the town for years, are leaving Carpentersville, because they fear deportation more than ever before. And Mexican-American citizens are leaving, because they feel unwanted and victimized by cold intolerance. In this way, English-only ordinances and other laws targeting the Hispanic population can be interpreted as a new tactic of white fight. This time the battle is waged, not through violence and protests, but by the strong arm of the law.

Analyzing Immigration in Small Town U.S.A.

Baruch Spinoza, the Dutch philosopher, once said, "Do not weep. Do not wax indignant. Understand." By this, he meant that the student of society should hold in abeyance her or his opinions on political matters until she or he has properly analyzed them. This is sound advice for us sociologists of race as we try to make sense of how Carpentersville, Lewiston, and other small towns have reacted to their shifting color line. First and foremost, we must scrutinize how the debate is framed. In many cases, if we dig a little deeper, we realize that the opponents in a debate need not be opponents after all and that the foundation on which the debate rests is unsound. Ordinances consecrating English as a town's official language tend to present a picture of society in which people who advocate such ordinances are for learning English and those who are against them oppose learning English. But this is a distorted picture of the world, for all parties in Carpentersville—whites, third-generation Hispanics, and undocumented immigrants alike—agree that, without English proficiency, one has little hope of climbing the economic ladder or of participating fully in civil society. This is why each year thousands of immigrants—in Carpentersville and elsewhere—enroll in introductory English courses.

A sociological analysis of immigration patterns in small towns would also marshal social-scientific data in order to verify or rebuff assumptions about the immigrant experience. Are Mexican immigrants failing to assimilate? Most sociological research on the subject leads us to answer no. Noting, first, that assimilation is a complicated and fragmented process, as we learned in the previous chapter, we can assert with confidence that the children of immigrants obtain higher levels of education and higher English proficiencies than their parents, the hallmarks of traditional assimilation. In fact, most grandchildren of Mexican immigrants (two-thirds of third-generation Mexicans, to be exact) do not speak any Spanish.[153]

Because the racial dynamics of Carpentersville and Lewiston cannot be fully understood outside their historical contexts, our sociological analysis must cast a backward glance. Are "the immigrants of yesterday and the immigrants of today totally different people," as the Carpentersville politician holds? Hardly: in the beginning of the twentieth century, many white Americans feared that the newly arrived Italian immigrants would never learn English and would refuse to integrate fully into American society. "That the Mediterranean peoples are morally below the races of Northern Europe is certain as any social fact," wrote one commentator of the time. As time passed, however, these fears dissipated. Italians mastered English, influenced American culture, and, indeed, were welcomed into the same ranks as the "races of Northern Europe."[154]

But we cannot stop there, for the very term "assimilation" deserves a rigorous unpacking. What does it mean to become an American? Does it mean obeying American laws? If so, do all the rule-breakers in this country, including all who break speed limits, consume illegal substances, and fudge on their taxes, forfeit their American status? Certainly not. Does becoming an American mean speaking English? The white residents of Carpentersville seem to think so. But one wonders why an English-only ordinance has not been proposed in Lewiston, where a quarter of the town's white citizens speak French at home, where the local Catholic Church gives mass in French, and where local doctors and dentists advertise their services in French.[155] These are the kinds of questions propelled by the sociological imagination.

Digging deeper, we come to realize that the desire for assimilation is necessarily ethnocentric.[156] **Ethnocentrism** is the practice of intentionally or unintentionally evaluating another culture in terms of your own culture's assumptions and viewing the other culture as inferior to your own. The process of assimilation seeks to produce immigrants that are "just like us," on the assumption that the immigrant has little to offer the host culture but that the host culture has much to offer the immigrant. The assimilated immigrant is expect to dissolve—to "melt"—into the American whole, a process that requires shedding virtually all markers of one's homeland: language, religion, clothing, and so forth. This requirement rests on the ethnocentric assumption that the American culture to which one assimilates is superior to the immigrant culture that one must leave behind.

And here we come full circle, returning to the idea that opened this chapter: the American version of ethnocentrism assumes that American culture is white. American culture, it is often assumed, is rooted in the English culture and language imported by the Pilgrims. Indeed, four of the sample questions on the

United States naturalization test ask about Pilgrims; no questions ask about American life before the Mayflower sailed in 1620. But a quick flip through the history books forces us to realize that early American history is just as Spanish as it is English. It was a Spaniard, Juan Ponce de León, who first landed on what is now the mainland of the United States, naming the shore he discovered La Florida; Spanish explorers were the first Europeans to reach the Appalachian Mountains, the Mississippi River, and the Grand Canyon. A full two hundred fifty years before Lewis and Clark set off on their expedition, four Spanish explorers traveled from Florida to the California coast; and the first European settlement in America was not Plymouth but St. Augustine, Florida, founded by Spaniards in 1565. When politicians warn that Latino immigrants will erode American culture, as Arizona Representative J. D. Hayworth recently did, they forget the rich Hispanic history and culture that helped to make America what it is today.[157]

If we reflect on immigration in the context of colonial history, we add still another layer to our analysis of immigration. Colonizing powers force assimilation onto native populations. Then the ancestors of that native population, pushed to the borders of the colonial territory, accept the terms of assimilation for a chance to reap some of the colonizers' bounty.[158] What does this mean in terms of American immigration? "The Hispanic world did not come to the United States," writes Mexican novelist Carlos Fuentes. "The United States came to the Hispanic world. It is perhaps an act of poetic justice that now the Hispanic world should return."[159]

Last, and very importantly, the sociologist attempting to make sense of small town immigration must never get too far removed from people's real life experiences, emotions, and struggles. By altering the composition of rural, white America, immigrant waves are causing all members of the national body to experience growing pains. As Algerian anthropologist Abdelmalek Sayad has advised, "The most important thing is that we have to be wary of imagining that this process [of immigration] is perfectly harmonious or devoid of all conflict. That is an illusion we like to sustain."[160] The people of Carpentersville and Lewiston know well the unsettling sound of the noisy gears of change. As sociologists of race, we have the opportunity to offer these people, and each other, a deeper and fuller understanding of this painful process, assuming that, before we pick a side, we subject the issue to rigorous sociological examination. "Do not weep. Do not wax indignant. Understand."

Toward an Integrated America

Focusing on the workings of racial domination in the residential field, this chapter has underscored the continuing persistence of racial segregation, as well as problems and privileges unequally distributed to different communities on the basis of their racial makeup. These social ills are old and established, but, as we have learned, they have not been with us forever. Nor must they remain this way. Although racial residential segregation is a basic fact of life for most Americans, segregation levels have decreased in recent years. Today, roughly 10 million Americans live in racially integrated neighborhoods. Although that figure amounts to only 3% of the total population, it does provide some evidence that racial segregation's grip might be loosening. Even more encouraging is the finding that 75% of neighborhoods that were integrated in the 1980s remained so a decade later. In other words, in these neighborhoods whites did not flee to the suburbs when nonwhite families began moving next door. Whites and nonwhites committed to the principles of integration have helped to build up stable, multiracial neighborhoods.[161]

But arriving at an America that is truly integrated will take many more committed individuals, for we still have a long way to go. When imagining the promise of multiethnic neighborhoods, we must resist assuming that integration necessarily will cause whites to suffer. Nonwhite gain does not necessitate white loss, because racial domination does not function under such zero-sum conditions. More realistic is the notion that "racism legitimates the squandering and dissipation of an important *surplus* of societal resources and human talents."[162] Working toward a more integrated society means attempting to reclaim the human surplus that racial domination wastes and to decrease the human misery that racial domination creates. Whites and nonwhites, then, can benefit from integration. Listen to James Baldwin once more: "It is a terrible, and inexorable, law that one cannot deny the humanity of another without diminishing one's own: in the face of one's victim, one sees oneself. Walk through the streets of Harlem and see what we, this nation, have become."[163]

CHAPTER REVIEW

RACIAL STRUGGLES OVER RESIDENCE

Mexican repatriation programs, tribal termination, great migration, racial uprisings, covenants, redlining, urban renewal, white flight

RACIAL SEGREGATION

economic factors, personal choice, housing discrimination, consequences of segregation

THE CITY

spatial assimilation thesis, ethnic community thesis, gentrification, advanced marginality, public housing

THE SUBURBS

gated communities

RURAL AMERICA

colonias, environmental racism, ethnocentrism

FROM THEORY TO PRACTICE

1. Using the "Fact Finder" feature on the United States Census Bureau's website, determine the racial composition of the ZIP code in which you grew up. Compare the makeup of your ZIP code to that of the entire U.S. population. Using your sociological imagination and what you have learned in this chapter, explain the disparities you notice.

2. In this chapter we quoted the Kerner report as claiming that "white society is deeply implicated in the ghetto." To this we might add that all society is implicated in the creation of the ghetto. Reflecting on your upbringing, how might this statement apply to you? That is, how might you be contributing to racial segregation and the reproduction of the ghetto?

3. How might you be contributing to the problem of environmental racism? What are some things you could do to combat this problem?

4. Gustavo Arellano, author of the satirist column "¡Ask a Mexican!," once responded in this way to a reader who claimed that, instead of immigrating to America, Mexicans should try to better their native country: "Gracias for illustrating the great double standard in America's immigration policy. Centuries of immigrant waves chose not to improve their homelands and to try their luck in a new land, and we rightfully celebrate their pluck as pioneers. Yet when Mexicans follow in the footsteps of our *gabacho* forefathers, we accuse them of lacking self-motivation and want to shut down the border."[164] Do you agree or disagree with Mr. Arellano's point? More important, given what you have learned thus far, how might you analyze the immigration debate with historical insight and sociological sensitivity?

5. Where have you always wanted to live? What, in other words, is your ideal living arrangement? Would you like to live in the city or in the country; in a house or a condominium; in what kind of a neighborhood? Reflect on these questions with an eye toward racial dynamics. How might racial domination in the residential field condition your ideas? Have you thought about the racial composition of your dream neighborhood? How—and why (or why not)?

RECOMMENDED READING

- St. Clair Drake and Horace Clayton, *Black Metropolis: A Study of Negro Life in a Northern City*, Revised and Enlarged Edition (New York: Harbinger, 1962 [1945]).

- Douglas Massey and Nancy Denton, *American Apartheid: Segregation and the Making of the Underclass* (Cambridge: Harvard University Press, 1993).

- Thomas Sugrue, *The Origins of the Urban Crisis: Race and Inequality in Postwar Detroit*, Princeton Classic Edition (Princeton: Princeton University Press, 2005).

- Sudhir Venkatesh, *American Project: The Rise and Fall of a Modern Ghetto* (Cambridge: Harvard University Press, 2000).

- Loïc Wacquant, *Urban Outcasts: A Comparative Sociology of Advanced Marginality* (Cambridge: Polity Press, 2007).

- Roger Waldinger, *Still a Promised City? African Americans and New Immigrants in Postindustrial New York* (Cambridge: Harvard University Press, 1996).

Chapter 6

Crime and Punishment

Toward a Rational Assessment of Crime

No subject requires a higher level of critical thinking, a more unwavering commitment to rational assessment, than the subject of crime. Talk of crime and punishment often summons from us all sorts of visceral reactions and hasty declarations that, on closer inspection, do more to assuage our anxieties than to contribute useful and complex insights. When discussing race and the legal field—that realm of social life that consists of all the forces of law, lawbreaking, and the punishment of lawbreakers—we must take special precautions to suspend judgment, to search through our innermost fears, and to subject popular pronouncements and political propositions to rigorous scrutiny founded on social-scientific evidence. "To turn the thing over in mind, to reflect," wrote American philosopher John Dewey, "means to hunt for additional evidence, for new data, that will develop the suggestion, and will either, as we say, bear it out or else make obvious its absurdity and irrelevance. . . . To maintain the state of doubt and to carry on systematic and protracted inquiry—these are the essentials of thinking."[1]

If we wish to think deeply about crime—and to develop effective ways of addressing it—we must resist accepting as truth the prepackaged collection of assumptions, statements, and beliefs Americans commonly (and sometimes carelessly) attach to issues of illegal behavior and punishment. This requires reevaluating those dangers that seem to trouble us the most and taking note of all the other dangers we dismiss because of our selective focus. It also means rethinking the very essence of "crime" and evaluating why, although many things inflict harm, only some are outlawed. Likewise, the way we fight crime must be denaturalized and evaluated. "Getting tough on crime" has been the primary solution to lawbreaking presented to many of you; as such, this approach might appear natural and obvious. But a thorough analysis, one that includes historical reflection, reveals that this approach is relatively new and that, of the many methods designed to decrease crime, it might be among the least effective. We must also develop complex, not simplistic, appraisals of all the actors found in the legal realm—lawyers, police officers, victims, criminals—and even force ourselves to construct multidimensional depictions of those who have committed terrible crimes. For carrying out monstrous deeds does not necessarily make one a monster; to paraphrase Helen Prejean, everyone is more than the worst thing they have ever done.[2]

Finally, to comprehend fully the criminal justice system, we must set ourselves the task of uncovering how the legal field is deeply embedded in society—and how society's problems are embedded in it. The phrase "justice is blind" suggests that the legal field is somehow detached from normal society, that it floats, lofty and remote, above society's prejudices. As critical thinkers, we are forced to reject this notion as a happy myth and instead to focus our attention on the multiple ways in which race—as well as class and gender—operates as a central organizing principle of the criminal justice system. Let us, therefore, approach the hot topic of crime with cool heads, denying ourselves the indulgence of easy answers and using our minds "historically and rationally for the purpose of reflective understanding and genuine disclosure."[3] Thoughts of crime grip the American mind, but arriving at a more rational and rigorous understanding of race, crime, and punishment can help liberate our thinking from the clutches of fear, thereby helping us to make better decisions as we work to create a more just democracy.

Toward such an end, this chapter starts with a historical overview that traces the development of America's prison boom. After that, it explores the workings of race in the legal field in three related sections: fear, crime, and punishment.

The Rise of the American Prison

Early conceptions and practices of justice, crime, and punishment were formed under conditions of colonialism and slavery. Indigenous systems of justice were overshadowed by European ones, which criminalized tribal practices. (Not even certain dances and idioms were exempt from such criminalization.) Enslaved Africans were excluded from the protection of the law, which did not recognize as rape the sexual assault of a slave girl by a white man or classify as murder the "accidental" killing of a slave at the hands of his master. Americans often remember the legal system birthed by the American Revolution as a paragon of freedom and justice. We would do well also to remember, however, that, from

Between 1880 and 1930, lynch mobs murdered over 2,300 black men, women, and children that we know of.

its inception, American law permitted nonwhites to be brutalized, dehumanized, and killed. It is within this contradiction—the simultaneous extension of liberty and the retrenchment of justice, the exaltation of freedom for most but at the expense of some—that the American justice system was forged.

The Lynch Mob and the Prison Labor Camp

After the fall of slavery, two juridical institutions—that is, institutions having to do with the creation of laws and the meting out of punishment—arose to control and confine nonwhites, and African Americans in particular. The first was the **lynch mob.** Sometimes the lynch mob operated in cahoots with local law enforcement; other times its rabid masses simply overpowered sheriff's deputies attempting to protect their captives long enough that they might receive a fair trial. The mob would break into the jail cell, dragging the trembling black man outside, and, with complete impunity, torture him to death. Between 1880 and 1930, lynch mobs murdered over 2,300 black men (and women and children) that we know of.[4] The broader white public justified the practice of lynching in a number of ways, one of which was by arguing that it kept white women safe

Photograph of a lynching made into a postcard that one white
onlooker mailed home to his parents.

from the black male rapist. "There is only one crime that warrants lynching,"
declared Bill Tillman, Senator of South Carolina, "and Governor as I am, I would
lead a mob to lynch the negro who ravishes a white woman."[5] Of course, the
vast majority of black men accused of rape, castrated and hung from Dogwood
limbs, were innocent. A good number of accusations were brought forth, not by
the supposed victim of rape, but by her husband or brother or someone in the
community. Indeed, many white women, constrained by southern manners,
were told to keep quiet as others used these women's bodies as a pretext for
leveling a scourge against black men.

Although many whites believed lynch mobs were carrying forth swift and
effective justice on the body of a rapist, most lynch mobs were not motivated by
this crime. Or, to put it another way, the southern white man's definition of
"rape," as it applied to black men, hardly could have been broader. As W. J. Cash
has observed, "What Southerners felt . . . was that any assertion of any kind on

the part of the Negro constituted in a perfectly real manner an attack on the Southern woman. What they saw, more or less consciously, in the conditions of Reconstruction was a passage toward a condition for her as degrading, in their view, as rape itself."[6] Accordingly, when Ida B. Wells, a black woman who defiantly and indefatigably stood up against the institution of the lynch mob, researched southern lynchings, she found that most black men were killed not because they had been accused of rape but because they had been found to be too "uppity." They refused to take their hat off in front of a white woman; they winked at her; they laughed behind her back.[7] Nonetheless, the lynch mob thrived on the widespread fear that black men were violent, lecherous predators, a fear that spread during Reconstruction and is with us still. The lynch mob upheld white supremacy by letting blacks know they could not find refuge in the law. And it upheld white patriarchy—a racialized system of masculine domination—by cultivating within white women a dread of the black male rapist, a dread that increased white women's dependency on their white male protectors.[8]

Alongside the lynch mob, a second juridical institution arose after emancipation: the prison. Although prisons long had been a feature of American society, they took on a new function after the fall of slavery, namely, to re-enslave thousands of black workers recently released from bondage. New laws were drafted to target poor blacks, ensuring that they would be segregated from white society. **Vagabond laws** were adopted in state after state after the Civil War. These laws outlawed begging and loitering. In short, they transformed the poor into the criminal, who, for simply panhandling—or even looking for work—could be sent to jail or a hard labor camp. Under many vagabond laws, a panhandler could be imprisoned for six months and was not offered the right to a jury trial.[9]

Like sharecropping, post-emancipation prisons facilitated a kind of neoslavery. Formerly institutions that warehoused mostly white offenders, prisons began teeming with black exslaves, many of whom were arrested under vagabond laws or for no longer submitting to white supremacy.[10] To meet the labor shortage once filled by enslaved workers and poor whites (many of whom perished in the Civil War), and to uphold an economic system built on racial domination, southern prisons introduced "convict leasing" programs, which forced prisoners to work for no pay. Once again, black men returned in shackles to the cotton fields, the swamps, the roadsides, sometimes chained to white prisoners. As state treasuries and prison wardens grew rich off convict labor, prisoners literally were worked to death. Historians have found that prison labor camps were just as inhumane as were conditions under slavery. At Mississippi's Parchman Prison Farm, for instance, one out of every six prisoners died under the cruel work conditions; in fact, according to historian David Oshinsky, "not a single leased convict ever lived long enough to serve a sentence of ten years or more."[11] Such harsh conditions were remembered in Johnny Cash's song, "Going to Memphis":

"Well I brought me a little water in a Mr. Prince Albert can; But the bossman caught me drinkin' it, and I believe he broke my hand; Another boy is down, the shovel burned him out; Let me stand on his body, to see what the shoutin's about."

The Prison Boom

As the twentieth century rumbled forward, lynching and racialized terrorism died down and convict labor was curtailed, mainly because of protests by unions, who could not compete with prisoners' cheap labor. The prison, of course, remained. But in the 1970s, experts began to question incarceration as an effective way of fighting crime and reducing recidivism (repeat offending). A growing consensus among experts in the legal field was that more rehabilitative measures needed to be put in place—and that an effective anticrime strategy must attack the problem at its roots, focusing on social conditions that foster deviant behavior, such as poverty and institutional racism.[12] The prison was coming under strict criticism as an expensive, unhelpful, and inherently racist institution. It is curious, then, that during this time, America's prison population did not shrink but grew—and by leaps and bounds. In fact, the rapid expansion of American incarceration, which began in the early 1970s and continues to this day, can only be described as a **prison boom.**

The numbers are unprecedented. Between 1925 and 1975, the prison population remained the same, fluctuating between 100,000 and 200,000 prisoners. But around 1975, the prison population began to skyrocket and, by 2000, had reached 1,400,000. From 1970 to 2003, moreover, the number of state and federal prisons did not double or triple or even quadruple; it grew *sevenfold*. In 2003, over seven million people—what amounts to the entire population of Switzerland—were under the supervision of the criminal justice system (on probation or parole, or in jail or prison).[13]

Although America does not suffer from higher crime rates than other industrialized countries, it was the only country to experience a prison boom of this magnitude. Between 1983 and 2001, the prison population in several other industrialized countries grew only marginally. The United Kingdom's prison population per 100,000 citizens increased from 87 to 126; in Italy it increased from 65 to 95, in Sweden from 65 to 68. In some countries, such as Germany, Denmark, and Austria, the prison population decreased. In the United States, however, the prison population grew from 275 per 100,000 citizens in 1983 to 686 per 100,000 in 2001. California alone houses more inmates than France, Great Britain, Germany, Japan, Singapore, and the Netherlands *combined*.[14] Today, with a prison population of over 2 million—and, for the first time in U.S. history, more than 1 in 100 adults behind bars—the United States incarcerates more of its citizens than any other nation on earth.[15] China has the second

Incarceration in the United States and Europe

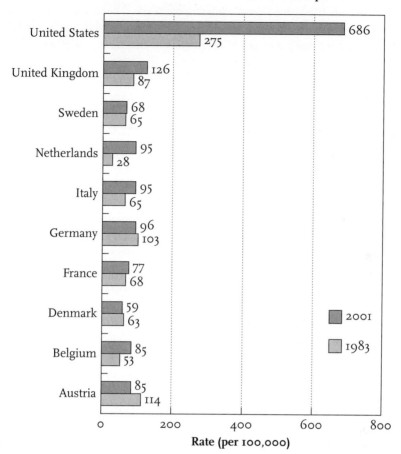

highest number of people incarcerated. But compared to the United States' prison population, China's is smaller by half a million, even though its general population exceeds ours by more than one billion.[16]

The Color of America's Incarcerated

By international standards, American women are incarcerated at a very steep rate. In fact, between 1977 and 2004, the number of women behind bars jumped from 11,212 to 96,125—a 750% increase! The U.S. incarcerates women of color, and poor black women in particular, at disproportionate rates. In California, for example, black women make up 7% of the general population but 33% of the state's prison population. And, according to recent research, "women [today] are the fastest-growing segment of the prison population."[17]

Although women are being incarcerated at historically high rates, they still account for only 6% of the nation's prison population. The vast majority of those behind bars are men. Relative to other countries, America's white male population is incarcerated at a steep rate, one that exceeds the total incarceration rate of most industrialized countries. But the brunt of the prison boom has been borne by America's nonwhite male populations—namely, by its poor, undereducated black and Hispanic men. Blacks and Hispanics account for 28% of the U.S. population but over 66% of all prisoners. Hispanic men are three times—and black men nearly eight times—more likely than white men to be in prison. According to sociologist Bruce Western, if white men were incarcerated at the same rates as blacks, the prison population would jump from 2 million to 6 million.[18] America imprisons 1.6% of its white men between the ages of twenty and forty, 4.6% of its Hispanic men that age, and 11.5% of its black men that age. For poor, young black men, the prison cell has become an all too familiar institution—just as familiar, in fact, as the college campus, the military base, or the factory floor.

The imprisonment rate for young men of color who drop out of high school is especially high. In 1980, 2% of all white male dropouts between the ages of twenty and forty were in prison or jail; in 2000, that number jumped to 7%. For Hispanics, 3% of male high school dropouts between the ages of twenty and forty were in prison or jail in 1980, and 6% were incarcerated in 2000. For African Americans, the percent increase is breathtaking: In 1980, one of ten high school dropouts between the ages of twenty and forty were in jail or prison. In 2000, *one of three* black male dropouts that age was behind bars. The incarceration rate of young black men who dropped out of high school was nearly fifty times the national average.[19]

By the end of the twentieth century, hundreds of thousands of America's poor had passed through the prison system. A white man born after World War II (that is, around 1945–1949) who later dropped out of high school had a 4% chance of serving time in prison sometime in his life; however, a white man born after the Civil Rights Movement (that is, around 1965–1969) who later dropped out of high school had an 11% chance of doing time. By contrast, a black man born after World War II who later dropped out of high school had a 17% chance of serving time in prison, whereas a black man born after the Civil Rights Movement who later dropped out of high school had nothing short of a 60% chance of being locked up at some point in his life.[20] If these statistics have not alarmed you, we suggest you go back and read them again.

Did Crime Increase?

Why did America's prison population multiply so quickly and by such an enormous measure? "Because crime increased," one might reasonably reply. Is this the case? Rising crime rates certainly are part of the answer. Between 1965 and 1980, the homicide rate in America doubled before generally following a downward trend between 1981 and 2000.[21] However, most of the prison boom cannot be explained by rising crime rates. There are two main reasons for this. First, most people incarcerated during the prison boom were nonviolent offenders. That is, most were sent to prison for possessing or selling drugs, not for murder. Although there was a spike in murder rates after 1965, the prison boom is not a reflection of a significant increase of convicted murderers. Second, for the most part, overall crime rates remained the same, and even decreased, during the prison boom. America's youth from poor neighborhoods were not committing more crime in 2000 than they were in 1980. In a 1980 survey, 18.5% of poor white male teenagers and 17.5% of poor black teenagers confessed to having attacked someone with the intention of seriously injuring or killing them that year. In 2000, only 17% of poor white teenagers and 14% of poor black teenagers confessed to doing so. In the same way, people were stealing, selling drugs, and damaging property at lower rates in 2000 than in 1980. However, as time passed, more people were being locked up in newly erected prisons.[22]

It is clear that the prison boom—and the disproportionate number of black men incarcerated as a result of it—cannot be explained by a surge in crime during the last quarter of the twentieth century. It is commonplace to conceive of crime in America as something that is perpetually worsening. But we must reject this notion as inaccurate. Indeed, the chances of being murdered were far greater during several points in the nineteenth century than at the height of the prison boom. One study has concluded that only 12% of the rise of incarceration rates between 1980 and 1996 was driven by increases in the crime rate; the other 88% was caused by changes in sentencing policies.[23] To understand how policies shifted to create an era of mass incarceration, we must examine the rise of a new political philosophy—a "tough on crime" stance—and its connection to the racial order and the Civil Rights Movement.

Severe Sentencing

What changed during the prison boom was not so much the crime rate but the way crime was punished. Namely, it was punished more harshly. Arrest rates climbed at record pace, and sentences grew more severe. Although violent crime fell between 1990 and 2001, the chances a suspect would be arrested for a violent crime doubled during that decade. Between 1965 and 2001, drug arrests quadrupled, hitting black and Puerto Rican men especially hard. In the 1970s, black men were twice as likely to be arrested on drug offenses as white men. Does this mean that drug use increased between 1965 and 2001 and that black men were more likely to use and sell drugs? The evidence leads us to answer no to both questions. Between 1979 and 2000, drug use among young adults declined by 10%, and, according to surveys of high school seniors, white students during this time reported using more drugs than black students. In fact,

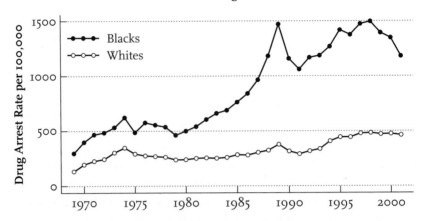

Black and White Drug Arrest Rates

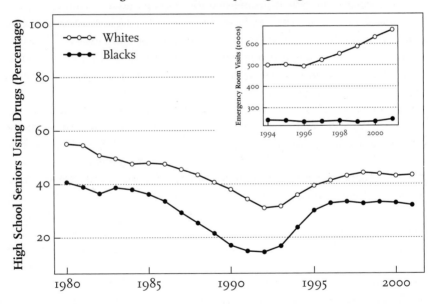

High School Seniors Reporting Drug Use

scholars who have analyzed emergency room records have discovered that, compared to blacks, whites were two to three times more likely to be rushed to the emergency room for drug-related problems.[24]

Not only did arrest rates, especially for drug-related offenses, shoot upward during the prison boom, but several other changes were put into effect to harshen criminal sentencing. Parole was limited severely or abolished entirely. Mandatory minimum sentences, which did not allow offenders—including those convicted of nonviolent crimes—an early release until a set time was served, were enforced. During the 1970s, several laws were passed attaching a life sentence to those found guilty of selling hard drugs, as well as to those possessing more than an ounce of cocaine or heroine. Draconian sentencing policies continued through the 1990s, most notably with **three-strikes laws.** Three-strikes laws intensified punishment for repeat offenses, with many such laws imposing a life sentence for the third offense. California's 1994 three-strikes law doubled the sentence for the second offense and mandated life in prison for the third, even for non-violent crimes such as minor fraud and drug possession. By 2000, twenty-four states had adopted three-strikes laws similar to California's.[25] Why did criminal sentencing take such a mean turn? The answer lies in the rise of the "law and order" politician.

The Rise of the "Law and Order" Politician

It might be hard for many of us to believe, but opinion polls from the mid-1960s show that most Americans did not list crime as among the nation's most press-ing concerns. The Vietnam War and civil rights were what occupied most Americans' minds at the time. Nevertheless, the Republican Party, beginning with Barry Goldwater's 1964 presidential bid, started to focus on crime as a central issue. "Tonight there is violence in our streets," Goldwater boomed during his acceptance speech as the Republican nominee. "History shows us that nothing prepares the way for tyranny more than the failure of public officials to keep the streets safe from bullies and marauders."[26] Although Goldwater was defeated, he planted a seed among Republicans, a seed that would soon blossom into a new kind of politics. The Republican Party latched onto an issue that before had been only of marginal concern to most Americans. In so doing, it helped to create America's "crime problem."

Richard Nixon launched a "war on crime" to protect Americans from those who "increasingly threaten our cities, our homes, and our lives." Ronald Reagan followed by initiating a "war on drugs," introducing harsher penalties for those found guilty of possessing and selling drugs. And George H. W. Bush won the White House after exposing his opponent, Michael Dukakis, as "soft on crime," marshalling the infamous Willie Horton case to drive home his point. States with the steepest growth in prison populations and the sharpest decreases in social welfare spending were governed by Republicans. To take but one example: when Republican John Ashcroft was governor of Missouri between 1985 and 1993, the state's prison population increased by a whopping 80%. Ashcroft slashed state services by over one billion dollars, while allocating over $100 mil-lion to new prison construction.[27]

Rapidly, the terms of political debate were altered in such a way that "tough on crime" stances, which called for repressive punishments, were counterposed to more rehabilitative stances, which focused on the root causes of crime. In fact, many conservative politicians argued that social welfare programs actually helped to cause crime. "The solution to the crime problem," Nixon would declare, "is not the quadrupling of funds for any governmental war on poverty but more convictions."[28] With this **bipolar discursive frame**—an exaggerated way of thinking that relies on two paired opposites, in this case "tough on crime" versus "soft on crime"—America's concern with rehabilitation and the war on poverty became eclipsed by a war on crime and an ardent pursuit of punitive measures. Once this frame took root in public thought and debate, it became virtually impossible for candidates—Democrats included—to get elected to public office without promising to crack down on crime. President Clinton became an avid supporter of three-strikes laws, and his Violent Crime Control and Law Enforcement Act of 1994 allocated nearly $10 billion for the construction of new prisons and mandated life sentences for third-time offenders.[29]

Alongside the "law and order" politician rose another important player: the "law and order" entrepreneur, who discovered there was big money to be made from the prison boom and even helped contribute to the boom. Prisons have transformed regional economies by employing thousands of correctional officers, wardens, prison chaplains, and other workers. They also have expanded America's cheap labor force, as inmates are put to work at third-world wages, making everything from clothing to be sold at Nordstrom department stores to graduation caps and gowns.[30]

The prison industry has ballooned into a multibillion-dollar industry, complete with its own online community of corrections vendors—"The Corrections Connection" is the largest—selling everything from barbed wire, cell padding, and handcuffs to metal detectors, inmate clothing, and security cameras. Plumbing companies bid for lucrative prison jobs; catering companies profit handsomely from supplying daily meals to millions of inmates; and some of the nation's largest architectural and construction firms make billions off the construction of new prisons. Telephone companies cash in on the prison boom as well; supplying telephone service to women and men in jail and prison has become a money-spinning enterprise. Prisoners are ideal customers, one analyst has observed, because "phone calls are one of their few links to the outside world; most of their calls must be made collect; and they are in no position to switch long-distance carriers. . . . It is estimated that inmate calls generate a billion dollars or more in revenues each year. The business has become so lucrative that MCI installed its inmate phone service, Maximum Security, throughout the California prison system at no charge."[31] Indeed, entire prisons now are operated by private companies. Private prisons have been on the rise since the mid-1980s, and, today, over half the states rely on for-profit prisons, where roughly 90,000 inmates are housed each year.[32]

Pointing to the uneasy alliance between government and private industry, analysts have coined the term **"prison-industrial complex."** In a seminal article, Eric Schlosser defined this "complex" as "a set of bureaucratic, political, and economic interests that encourage increased spending on imprisonment, regardless of the actual need. . . . It is a confluence of special interests that has given prison construction in the United States a seemingly unstoppable momentum. It is composed of politicians, both liberal and conservative, who have used the fear of crime to gain votes; impoverished rural areas where prisons have become a cornerstone of economic development; private companies that regard the roughly \$35 billion spent each year on corrections not as a burden on American taxpayers but as a lucrative market; and government officials whose fiefdoms have expanded along with the inmate population."[33]

More than any other set of policies, those introduced by the **war on drugs** helped to feed the prison-industrial complex, bring about the prison boom, and wreak devastation on African-American communities. Between 1981 and 2001, national drug control spending increased from less than \$2 billion to over \$18 billion. More and more police officers were dispatched to poor, nonwhite communities to arrest street-level dope slingers—despite the fact that drug use declined during the 1980s and whites were more likely to use drugs than were nonwhites. Thousands of young nonwhites from poor communities were arrested for drug-related offenses. Law enforcement officers targeted ghetto neighborhoods because there drug transactions often took place in public areas—street corners, public parks—and were easier to spot than drug transactions in more affluent neighborhoods, which often occurred in private settings.

Nonwhite neighborhoods also were targeted because of America's established tradition of linking nonwhites with drug use. As Michael Tonry writes in *Malign Neglect*, "Through [the twentieth century] in periods of high intolerance of drug use, minority group stereotypes have been associated with deviant drug use. Early in this century, even though mainstream women were the model category of opiate users, Chinese opium smokers and opium dens were among the images invoked by opponents of drug use. . . . In the 1920s, it was blacks and cocaine. In the 1930s, images of Mexicans and marijuana were prominent in the antimarijuana movements that culminated in the Marijuana Tax Act of 1937 and the many states prohibiting marijuana use. In the antidrug hysteria of the 1980s, crack cocaine, the emblematic drug of the latest 'war,' is associated in public imagery with disadvantaged minority residents of the inner cities."[34]

Repressing the Civil Rights Movement

Two questions remain unanswered. First, why did Republican politicians focus on crime as the main problem plaguing America when most Americans did not view it as a major problem? Second, why did the focus on crime resonate with so many Americans once it was introduced? The answer to both these questions lies in the white backlash against the Civil Rights Movement. It is no coincidence that the prison boom began shortly after the main thrust of the Civil Rights Movement came to an end. In fact, the former fact helps explain the latter.

Often, when Republican politicians mentioned "violence in the streets," they were not speaking of mugging and assault (which had not increased dramatically) but were using coded language to decry civil disobedience tactics of civil rights activists. Since the beginning of the Civil Rights Movement, politicians criticized protesters as "criminals," "hoodlums," and "troublemakers."[35] In a real sense, such labels were accurate, for activists often got their point across by breaking laws, such as by refusing to follow segregation regulations. By dismantling systems of racial domination that had structured American society for years, the Civil Rights Movement made many whites uneasy. This unease intensified as legalized racial segregation fell, causing whites to cross paths more frequently with nonwhites, and peaked during the racial uprisings of the late 1960s. Unlike many African Americans, most white Americans did not understand the uprisings as political acts against demoralizing ghetto conditions but as criminal acts of vandalism and violence.[36] As a result, when politicians began speaking against crime in the streets, many whites knew precisely to what they were referring and enthusiastically endorsed platforms promising to "punish criminals" and "restore order to our troubled society."

Many racial uprisings began as a response to police brutality and unfair treatment, and the police responded in kind. Expenditures for "riot control" and domestic surveillance programs expanded once the uprisings got underway. Studies have shown that, during the 1970s, police funding increased dramatically in cities with large black populations and those that had hosted major uprisings and strongly supported the Civil Rights Movement.[37] To suppress the uprisings, law enforcement officers began to treat poor, black communities as "danger zones," subjecting those neighborhoods to a high level of surveillance. However, after the riots quelled, police presence did not die down but remained steady and even increased. Instead of arresting rioters, police officers began arresting *potential* rioters, that is, young black men.[38]

Thus, perhaps the primary, if unspoken, intent of law and order policies was to repress the Civil Rights Movement, especially potential rioters. On that score, these policies had their desired effect. As for their more overt motives—to decrease crime and the distribution of drugs—law and order policies had only a trivial effect.[39] The war on crime and on drugs, it seems, defeated something—but not criminal activity or drug trafficking. This goes to show that, to quote the French philosopher Michel Foucault, "we must first rid ourselves of the illusion that penalty is above all (if not exclusively) a means of reducing crime. . . . We must analyze rather the 'concrete systems of punishment,' study them as social phenomena that cannot be accounted for by the juridical structure of society alone, nor by its fundamental ethical choices."[40]

Fear

America is a nation gripped by fears: of crime, illegal immigration, and terrorist attacks, just to name a few. Of course, crime, illegal immigration, and terrorism ought to concern us; but often our fears escape the confines of reasonableness. How accurately does our fear of crime square with reality? By and large, the answer to this question is "not very much." Although crime rates fell during the 1990s, six out of ten Americans believed they were rising. And although drug use dropped among high school students during that decade, most Americans listed drugs as the greatest danger threatening the country's youth. And with a rampant fear of crime came a call for harsher penalties. According to a national survey, 85% of Americans feel that current sentencing guidelines do not deal "harshly enough with criminals," and 70% feel that the country should spend more money on the crime problem.[41] This section explores some of the causes and consequences of America's fear of crime, analyzing how these fears are informed by racial domination and, by marshalling recent social-scientific evidence, holding these fears up to the light of rational assessment.

Criminalizing Darkness

Numerous studies have shown that one's fear of crime is strongly connected to one's racial identity, racial attitudes, and the racial makeup of one's neighborhood. After surveying undergraduate students at two Midwestern universities, one criminologist concluded that, compared to their nonwhite counterparts, white students were more likely to list crime among the nation's most serious problems and to fear being victimized by a crime.[42] Time and again, studies have produced convincing evidence of a robust link between the proportion of blacks and Hispanics in a neighborhood and fear of crime.[43] If fact, social scientists have found that the racial composition of a neighborhood—as well as the perceived composition of a neighborhood (that is, how many nonwhites people think live nearby, regardless of how many actually do)—are more powerful predictors of one's fear of crime than actual crime rates.

After comparing neighborhoods with identical crime rates, sociologists Lincoln Quillian and Devah Pager concluded that people who lived in areas with a higher proportion of young black men thought their neighborhood was plagued with more crime than those who lived in majority-white areas.[44] Another study demonstrated that whites living in a multicultural section of the country, and Hispanics living in a predominately white section, were more likely to fear being victimized by a crime when they thought blacks and Hispanics lived nearby.[45] This study reminds us that a racialized fear of crime does not affect whites alone. Members belonging to racial groups feared by the larger white society can adopt the attitudes of their host society and come to fear members of their own group.

Given America's history of bestowing on nonwhites the stain of villainy, it should not be surprising that Americans' fear of crime is deeply connected to the career of white supremacy. But besides historical forces, what else explains these racialized fears? The media is a popular answer—and for good reason. When asked why they felt America had a crime problem, over 75% of survey respondents referred to stories they had seen in the media. Between 1990 and 1998, America's murder rate fell by 20%, but one wouldn't have known this by watching the news, for during this time, the number of stories about murder airing on network newscasts increased by 600% (excluding all stories on O. J. Simpson).[46] And although young black men are far more likely to be victims of murder than other groups are, often the media portrayed young black men only as perpetrators of violence, focusing a disproportionate amount of attention on white and female victims. The same is true in the news coverage of rape. Carrying out America's enduring fixation of the rape of white women by black men, studies have shown that rapes of this nature garner a significant amount of media attention, even though such cases are relatively rare.[47]

Although the media certainly bear some responsibility for promoting a fear of blacks and Hispanics, the media also have played a large role in debunking such fears. What is more, the media are in the business of spreading all kinds of fears (for example, the obesity epidemic, deadly bacteria strains, school shootings, poisoned Halloween candy), but only a handful of scares stick.[48] Why are some fears fleeting while others are stubbornly durable? Mary Douglas, the British anthropologist, points out that all societies have at their disposal a vast array of threats on which to focus, and in most cases, the threats to which a society directs its attention do not necessarily carry the highest degree of objective danger. (After all, Americans wring their hands over avian flu, which has killed a total of zero Americans, but worry little about the common flu, which kills an average of 36,000 Americans each year—so little, in fact, that many forget to get their annual vaccination.[49]) Certain threats are overlooked, while others receive a great deal of attention, either because they offend the fundamental values of society or because they facilitate the continued stigmatization and exclusion of marginalized groups.[50] The fear of being victimized by nonwhite men fulfills both those requirements.

The stigmatizing of Hispanics and, especially, of blacks as criminals is deeply entrenched in America's collective consciousness, so much so that Americans' fear of crime has more to do with *blackness* than with crime itself. Indeed, survey data have shown that Americans, whites and nonwhites alike, believe blacks to be more prone to violence than nonblacks.[51] Because Americans so often comprehend crime through blackness, and blackness through crime, blackness, as conceived by nonblack America, is in a sense itself a crime—not in the metaphorical sense but in the very literal sense of something that "offends strong and definite states of the collective conscience," to borrow Émile Durkheim's definition.[52] Richard Wright, the great American novelist, understood this. Of America's black men, the novelist wrote: "Excluded from, and unassimilated in our society . . . every sunrise and sunset makes him guilty of subversive actions. Every movement of his body an unconscious protest. . . . Every glance of the eye is a threat. *His very existence is a crime against the state!*"[53]

With this in mind, we can now understand why many whites, especially those who harbor antiblack and anti-Hispanic prejudices, are avid supporters of law and order policies. Compared to their nonwhite peers, white undergraduates are more likely to support harsher punishments for criminals. According to one study, only half of white students felt that rehabilitation should be a main goal of the criminal justice system, but two-thirds of nonwhite students felt this way. The same study reported that 50% of white students support the death penalty, whereas only 29% of their nonwhite peers do.[54] And several studies have concluded that, as whites' interpersonal racism against blacks and Hispanics grows, so too does their support of punitive policies. Holding constant other important measures, whites' prejudice has been linked to their support of the death penalty, excessive force used by police officers, longer prison sentences, warrantless searches of young men of color, and spending tax dollars to fight crime.[55]

In some cases, the pervasive phobia of black men has brought about tragic consequences. In 1984, Bernhard Goetz, a middle-aged white man, boarded a New York City subway car and was approached by four young black male teenagers. What happened next remains a matter of dispute. By some accounts, the teenagers simply asked Goetz for five dollars; by other accounts, they intended to rob him but brandished no weapons. Goetz responded by pulling out an unregistered .38 caliber pistol and shooting all four teenagers. In court, Goetz claimed he shot in self-defense, even though none of the teenagers was packing a gun. The jury agreed, charging Goetz with criminal possession of a weapon but not multiple counts of attempted murder. (In a 1996 civil trial, however, a jury ordered Goetz to pay $43 million for paralyzing Darrell Cabey, one of the four black youths.[56])

For a claim of self-defense to pass muster, the defendant must prove he or she reacted in a "reasonable" way. In *People v. Goetz*, the point-blank shooting of four young, unarmed black men was deemed a reasonable act. Such a verdict was only possible because the jury—and the general public—shared Goetz's fear of young black men.[57] As law professor Jody Armour points out, a nonblack person who harms a young black man and later claims self-defense can marshal one of three arguments to defend the reasonableness of his actions. First, he can claim that, although he acted out of prejudice, his actions were reasonable because most Americans fear young black men and, had they found themselves in a similar situation, they would have acted in a similar fashion. Because what is widely accepted is not necessarily reasonable, especially when it comes to racism, this argument fails. Second, the defendant can claim he holds no ill will against young black men but acted in self-defense, because, statistically speaking, young black men commit more crime than anyone else. But this defense fails the test of reasonableness simply because black men who commit crimes make up less than 2% of the entire black population.[58]

If neither of these arguments works, the defendant can find refuge in the claim that he has a psychological disorder: an inherent fear of black men triggered by a prior assault by a black man. This defense successfully has been used before. After being mugged by a black man, Ruth Jandrucko, a white woman, claimed she had developed a phobia of black men and therefore could not work around them. The court—and every appellate court that later reviewed the case—agreed and awarded her worker's compensation. But this argument is no more reasonable than the previous two. It is unreasonable to view all black men as criminals because of the actions of one. Had Ms. Jandrucko claimed she developed a fear of all white men because of a previous mugging, her case most certainly would have been tossed out of court. Thus, on no grounds is the widespread fear of black men reasonable. Believing otherwise, writes Armour, sends a message that "your dread of blacks is a valid excuse for taking the life of an innocent black person."[59]

Do Immigrants Increase Crime?

On the morning of April 16, 2007, students at Virginia Tech awoke to the sound of gunfire. Seung-Hui Cho, a 23-year-old English major armed with a .22 caliber semiautomatic handgun and a 9 millimeter Glock, marched onto campus and began a shooting rampage. When it was over, 33 people lay dead, as did Cho, having committed suicide as the police approached. To date, this massacre is the deadliest school schooling in American history.[60]

Despite the fact that the vast majority of school shootings in the U.S. are carried out by young white men, in the aftermath of the Virginia Tech shooting some Americans attempted to make sense of this seemingly senseless event by focusing not only on Cho's access to firearms or his mental state but also on his immigrant status. Noting that Cho had emigrated from South Korea at the age of eight, some asked, "Would the Virginia Tech killings have occurred if America's immigration laws were stricter?" Patrick Buchanan, a conservative spokesperson, drew a direct connection between the Virginia Tech shooting and immigration: "Cho was among the 864,000 Koreans here as a result of the

Immigration Act of 1965, which threw the nation's doors open to the greatest invasion in history, an invasion opposed by a majority of our people. Thirty-six million, almost all from countries whose peoples have never fully assimilated in any Western country, now live in our midst. Cho was one of them. . . . What happened in Blacksburg [Virginia] cannot be divorced from what's been happening to America since the immigration act brought tens of millions of strangers to these shores, even as the old bonds of national community began to disintegrate and dissolve in the social revolutions of the 1960s. 'In our diversity is our strength!' So we are endlessly lectured. But are we really a better, safer, freer, happier, more united and caring country than before, against our will, we became what Theodore Roosevelt called 'a polyglot boarding house for the world[?]'"[61]

Although Buchanan's views are extreme, they resonate with a question that Americans have been asking for over a century: do immigrants make the country less safe? Many seem to think so. According to a recent poll, 73% of Americans believe that immigrants are "somewhat" or "very likely" to increase crime. President George W. Bush, considered liberal on issues of immigration by his Republican peers, declared in a 2006 speech that illegal immigration "strains state and local budgets and brings crime to our communities."[62]

Just as they helped to create a "crime problem," politicians recently have fashioned an "immigration problem," intensifying anti-immigrant sentiment that disproportionately targets those from Latin American, Asian, and Middle Eastern countries. (Immigrants from Croatia or Poland or Russia—those deemed white on arrival—generally are not thought of as threats.) Driven by the "tough on crime" logic applied to the criminal justice system, U.S. immigration policies have grown more punitive in recent years. Social rights and benefits have been withdrawn from undocumented immigrants, and immigration authorities have relied more heavily on the use of detention, just as juridical authorities increased their dependence on incarceration. Immigrant raids have increased as well, with some of the most extreme raids taking place in southwestern cities. In 2008, for example, Maricopa County sheriffs, along with volunteer members of the sheriff's "posse," carried out high-profile immigrant raids in Phoenix and its neighboring townships, arresting dozens of people at their homes and workplaces. One raid began at 2 A.M., when strike force members, armed with semiautomatic weapons and police dogs, stormed local businesses and government buildings, including the public library and the City Hall of Mesa, Arizona, looking for undocumented immigrants working as janitors.[63]

Punishments for violating immigration law have grown more severe. The 1996 Anti-Terrorism and Effective Death Penalty Act broadened the list of criminal acts that warranted deportation for noncitizens; the 1996 Welfare Reform Act denied even legal immigrants many public benefits; and the 2001 Patriot Act, discussed in detail in the ensuing section, denied noncitizens many basic

As immigration rates soared during the 1990s, crime rates plummeted.

civil rights. Today, those who reenter the United States after being deported are subject to two years' imprisonment; those who reenter after being deported for breaking the law are subject to ten years in prison; and those who have been convicted of an aggravated felony who reenter after being deported can be imprisoned for twenty years.[64]

Many of these policy shifts have been driven by the fear that immigrants, documented and undocumented, increase America's crime rate. However, social-scientific research has arrived at the opposite conclusion, finding that immigrants make America safer. After searching through homicide records in cities with large immigrant populations, criminologist Ramiro Martinez found that border cities, such as El Paso and San Diego, are some of the safest metropolitan areas in the country. Despite their high levels of poverty, many immigrant communities in large cities—Haitian neighborhoods in Miami, Mexican barrios in Houston—have incredibly low crime rates.[65]

Recent studies have concluded that youth of Mexican descent commit far less violent crime than do white or black youth, and analysts have attributed this gap to immigrants from Mexico. One study found that first-generation immigrants (that is, immigrants who were born in another country and who came to the U.S.) were 45% less likely to participate in a violent crime than were third-generation

Immigration Flows and Homicide Trends
(U.S. Totals in 3-Year Averages)

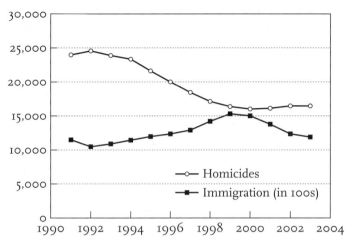

Americans (those born in the United States to parents who are U.S. citizens). Comparing immigrants to whites and blacks of similar class backgrounds, researchers have found that immigrants are less likely to participate in many different kinds of criminal behavior, from gang fights and selling drugs to arson and mugging. In fact, those who live in immigrant neighborhoods, regardless of racial identity or immigrant status, are less likely to commit crimes than those who do not.[66]

Noting these trends, some social scientists have argued that a sizable proportion of the crime drop that occurred in the 1990s can be attributed to the swelling immigrant population. As immigration rates soared during the 1990s, crime rates plummeted. Violent crime fell by 57%. As sociologist Robert Sampson has observed, "Consider that immigration rose sharply in the 1990s, especially from Mexico and especially to immigrant enclaves in large cities. Overall, the foreign-born population increased by more than 50% in 10 years, to 31 million people in 2000. . . . Immigration grew most significantly in the middle of the 90s and hit its peak at the end of the decade, when the national homicide rate plunged to levels not seen since the 1960s. Immigrant flows have receded since 2001, while the national homicide rate leveled off and seems now to be creeping up. . . . Perhaps the lesson is that if we want to continue to crack down on crime, closing the nation's doors is not the answer."[67]

To explain why immigrants commit so little crime, sociologists have pointed to their high rates of marriage and the presence of professionals in immigrant neighborhoods, as both factors are negatively associated with crime. They also have observed that immigrant neighborhoods often operate under a code of

informal social control, which encourages neighbors to watch out for one another and to be mindful of criminal activity.[68] In other words, members of immigrant neighborhoods have accepted as part of their civic duty the shared task of keeping their sidewalks safe. By casting "eyes upon the street," immigrants participate in what Jane Jacobs believed to be the best strategy for upholding safety in an urban environment. "The first thing to understand," wrote Jacobs, "is that the public peace—the sidewalk and street peace—of cities is not kept primarily by the police, necessary as police are. It is kept primarily by an intricate, almost unconscious, network of voluntary controls and standards among the people themselves, and enforced by the people themselves."[69]

Perhaps we have been asking the wrong question. Instead of asking, "Why do immigrants commit so *few* violent crimes?"—and thereby assuming that the uprightness of immigrants is curious and surprising—we should bend the question in the opposite direction, asking, "Why do Americans commit so *many*?" We will explore this question in more depth later on, but here it is worth underscoring a startling finding from studies of immigration and crime rates: Second generation immigrants are more likely to commit crimes than first-generation immigrants; and third-generation immigrants are more likely to do so than second-generation immigrants. For those concerned with America's crime rate, the problem seems to be the *successful* assimilation of second- and third-generation immigrants, not the *failed* assimilation of the first generation. A recent study concluded that second-generation Mexican Americans were eight times as likely to be incarcerated as first-generation Mexican immigrants and that second-generation Vietnamese Americans were ten times as likely, compared to those born in Vietnam. Most first-generation immigrants have a lower incarceration rate than whites born in the United States; however, the opposite is true of second-generation immigrants.[70] What these findings suggest, writes one commentator, "is that the cause of crime lies less with immigrants than with the country that they, like generations of new arrivals before them, are busily assimilating themselves into."[71]

Since so much evidence points to the conclusion that immigrants, documented and undocumented, make America safer, one must wonder why so many Americans fear an "immigrant invasion" and why politicians continue to draft laws designed to make immigrants' lives harder. If immigrants make things only better by reducing crime (not to mention also strengthening the economy, as a number of economists have demonstrated), then anti-immigration legislation is intended not to curb social problems associated with immigration, as is often thought, but to punish the immigrant herself. Like blackness, foreignness (and ethnic markers connected to foreignness, such as speaking Spanish) has become intimately intertwined with our notions of criminality, so much so that immigration itself is conceived as a criminal act, as something that offends the American consciousness. It is small wonder, then, that just as antiblack and anti-Hispanic prejudices are strongly associated with one's support of punitive policies, interpersonal racism directed at nonwhites, and at Mexicans in particular, is strongly associated with anti-immigration policies, such as California's Proposition 187, designed to deny undocumented immigrants access to education, emergency medical care, and welfare benefits.[72]

The Arabization of Terrorism

America, like many countries, has been the victim of numerous terrorist attacks. In 1993, terrorists attacked the World Trade Center, killing 6 people and wounding 1,000 more; in 1995, terrorists bombed the Federal Building in Oklahoma City, killing 168 people; and in 1998, the U.S. embassies in Kenya and Tanzania were firebombed, leaving 4,000 injured and over 200 dead. But for many Americans, the threat of terrorism became much more imminent and terrifying after the attacks on September 11, 2001, which sent the twin towers of the World Trade Center crashing to the ground in a cloud of gray ash and smoke. Nearly 3,000 people lost their lives, including 343 firefighters and 23 police officers.[73]

Anyone who has watched the footage of the September 11 attacks knows that terrorism is something to fear. The terrorists' prime objective, after all, is to draw blood. And immediately after the events, fear coursed quickly through the American body politic.[74] Arab Americans suffered from a double helping of fear, because not only did they join all Americans in worrying about repeat attacks, but they also dreaded repression from the American government as well as assaults from their fellow non-Arab citizens. Looking back, we know such fears were justified.

In the weeks following the attacks, men and women of Arab descent—as well as those perceived to be Arabs (Indian American Hindu Sikhs, for example)—were victims of workplace discrimination, racist threats, assaults, and even murder. In 2001, the FBI reported that crimes directed at Muslims increased seventeen-fold, while Arab groups registered over 2,000 events where Americans lashed out at "Arab looking" people after September 11. The American-Arab Antidiscrimination Committee reported that, in the nine weeks after September 11, over 700 violent attacks directed at Arab Americans took place. Of those events, 66% involved physical or psychological attacks, 27% consisted of acts of arson or vandalism; 22% included hate mail and bomb threats; 16% were beatings, and 1% entailed hate-motivated murder. (Many of the 700 total attacks included more than one of these elements, which is why the percentages add up to more than 100.) There was, for instance, Mark Stoman of Dallas, who walked into a line of convenience stores and shot clerks from Pakistan, India, and Bangladesh; there was James Herrick of Salt Lake City, who set ablaze a Pakistani restaurant; and there was Patrick Cunningham of Seattle, who opened fire on people worshipping in a mosque.[75] In the weeks following September 11, America was not safe for its Arab citizens.

In a very real sense, Arab Americans are invisible in discussions of the "war on terror."

Despite these violent outbursts, many Americans, according to opinion poll data, viewed Arab Americans with a fair degree of tolerance and understanding, acknowledging that an entire group of people could not be blamed for the actions of a few wrapped in similar-looking skin who lived on the opposite end of the earth. In the months and years following September 11, however, non-Arab Americans' interpersonal racism toward Arab Americans grew, and today, the average American is more likely to harbor anti-Arab prejudices than in 2001. According to recent polls, 25% of Americans harbor "unfavorable" views of Muslim Americans; 33% believe that Arab Americans are "more sympathetic to terrorists"; and 44% confess to having less trust in Arab Americans after September 11. However, many Americans continue actively to deny anti-Arab prejudice: 51% have "favorable" views of Muslim Americans, and as many as 80% believe that "Arab-Americans, Muslims, and immigrants from the Middle East are being singled out unfairly by people in this country."[76]

Nevertheless, it is clear that for a good number of Americans, the face of a "terrorist" is the face of an Arab and that anti-Arab prejudice has risen only since the September 11 attacks. Why did anti-Arab prejudice increase, rather than decrease, in the months following the attacks? The answer lies in the ways Arabs have been depicted in the political field as well as in the press. The categories of Arab, Muslim, and Middle Eastern have been rendered synonymous in modern representations, a maneuver that overlooks the fact that most Muslims around the world are neither Arab nor Middle Eastern (but reside in Southeast Asia), and that flattens the historical and cultural differences between Middle Easterners who do not consider themselves Arab (such as Turks or Persians) and Middle Easterners who do (such as Palestinians).[77] Scholars have concluded that Arabs often are portrayed in films as bestial, violent villains. One study analyzed more than nine hundred films and found that, with few exceptions, Arabs were represented as "Public Enemy #1—as brutal, heartless, uncivilized religious fanatics, and money-mad cultural 'others' bent on terrorizing civilized Westerners, especially Christians and Jews."[78] And politicians, for their part, often saddle Arabs with negative qualities.[79]

As a result, since September 11 a bipolar discursive frame has calcified, one that pits America against "the Arab world." Positive qualities are attached to the American side of the frame, while negative characteristics are assigned to the Arab side. In fact, in this polarized way of thinking, the positive qualities are set against (and gain their essence from) their mirror images, such that if the Arab world is violent, America is peaceful; if the Arab world is irrational, America is rational; if "they" are freedom-hating, "we" are freedom-loving.[80] Where, then, do Arab Americans fall in this schematic? Are they "we" or "they"? In a very real sense, Arab Americans are invisible in discussions of the "war on terrorism." One hears much of Americans and much of Arabs, but very little attention has been devoted to the nation's 3 million Arab American citizens.[81] Because of this—and because racial identities are so powerful, they often trump other identities (such as those based on nationality)—Arab Americans are stripped of their "Americanness" and associated with the Arab/terrorist side of the bipolar discursive frame.[82]

Profiling Arab Americans

Like Eastern European immigrants during World War I or Japanese Americans during World War II, Arab Americans often are treated like enemies within American borders. It is well documented that Arab Americans are profiled as terrorists, strictly on the basis of their appearance or last names. In the nine months following September 11, one antidiscrimination group documented over eighty cases of Arab Americans being illegally removed from planes after boarding but before takeoff.[83] Responding to calls of unfair treatment, the Department of Homeland Security enabled The Traveler Redress Inquiry Program (TRIP), an initiative that allows travelers to record their grievances. Since its inception, the TRIP system has received 600 to 800 complaints each week, many of them from Arab Americans who feel they have been mistreated by airport security or by border patrol officers.[84]

While many Arab Americans are experiencing an erosion of their civil liberties, a significant number of non-Arab Americans support profiling Arab

Americans in the name of national security. According to recent surveys, 75% of Americans believe that immigration from Arab countries should be restricted, and 40% feel that the U.S. government "should have more power to monitor Muslims legally living in the United States than it has to monitor other religious groups." Although African Americans know well the humiliation of being racially profiled, 71% of blacks polled favor profiling people of Middle-Eastern descent. One out of three Americans believes that the United States should subject Arab Americans to special surveillance; and one out of two believes that Arabs should carry special identification cards, like those carried by Jews during the years leading up to the Holocaust.[85] This is all the more disturbing given that Arab Americans were among those who served at Ground Zero as police officers, firefighters, doctors, and emergency workers—as well as among those who perished at the Twin Towers.

Although many Americans believe the racial profiling of Arab Americans is a necessary evil, one that helps to prevent future terrorist attacks, there is mounting evidence that profiling is ineffective—and that it may make matters worse. In a recent memo, a group of senior U.S. intelligence specialists argued that paying too much attention to people's outward appearance—their racial identity or their garments (a woman's burka, for example)—might distract security officers from noticing suspicious behavior. "If your goal is preventing attacks," the memo read, "you want your eyes and ears looking for pre-attack behaviors, not characteristics."[86] Indeed, as we learned in the aftermath of the Oklahoma City bombing, the deadliest terrorist attack on American soil before September 11, impulsively blaming Arabs is unsound and can prevent arrests of the real culprits. Although an Arab American man was arrested shortly after the bombing, and although a *New York Times* editorialist vented, "Whatever we are doing to destroy Mideast terrorism, the chief terrorist threat against Americans, has not been working,"[87] it was discovered that white men belonging to a militia were responsible for the tragedy.

Since September 11, Arab Americans, deemed a destructive force within "our" midst, have been exorcized from mainstream America and subjugated to a wide array of dehumanizing and violent acts, carried out by fellow citizens and government officials alike. The "communist," who quickly receded from our memory after the end of the Cold War, has been replaced by the "Arab terrorist" as the primary threat to American life. This shift has brought a considerable amount of suffering to Arab American communities. Indeed, medical researchers have discovered that, owing to intensified discriminatory practices that followed September 11, Arab-American women who gave birth six months after the attacks experienced higher risks of premature birth and low birth weight relative to all other women. The events of September 11 were traumatic for all Americans, but it was only within the bodies of Arab-American women that we observed an objective consequence of being both Arab and American during this crucial period in the nation's history.[88]

One final thought deserves mention. Today, Americans are told that the events of September 11 constitute the first time in history that a terrorist attack of that magnitude was visited upon American soil. Having surveyed the history of racial domination in America, we know better. America's indigenous peoples were brought mercilessly under the heel of Western colonizing forces over the course of 350 years of war. The Mexican Repatriation Programs could accurately be classified as organized kidnapping. Black America has been plagued by a most brutal and bloody terrorism, which has included the Middle Passage, slavery, and merciless lynch mobs. The Klu Klux Klan resembles a terrorist organization much as al-Qaeda does. Post-September 11 America is set apart not by the *presence* of terrorism but by the *victims* of it. Terrorism carried out by white Americans is nothing new; terrorism visited on white Americans is. As applied to modern times, the term "age of terror"[89] is historically inaccurate, for terrorism in America is anything but a modern development.[90] Perhaps the African-American comedian Earthquake put it best when he remarked, "Many people wonder why I'm not tripping after the terrorist attacks in New York and D.C. I'm a niggah—I've been dealing with terrorists all my life!"[91]

Crime

Having reviewed racialized fear of crime in America, we turn now to examining crime itself. We begin by discussing drug trafficking and street gangs. We then examine offenses often overlooked in public discussions of crime: white-collar crimes and crimes of corporations. Finally, we turn our attention to more violent crimes, including violence against women and homicide. Along the way, we offer explanations for crime by employing, as always, sociological analysis grounded in current research.

Drug Trafficking

The combined forms of enterprise classified as criminal under current law can be said to constitute the **underground economy.** By some estimates, each year four out of five Americans buy something through the underground economy, which employs somewhere between 15 and 25% of the U.S. labor force.[92] Without a doubt, the largest and highest yielding industry within the underground economy is the drug trade. It is estimated that the illegal drugs account for roughly 8% of worldwide trade, grossing between $300 and $400 billion every year, more than the combined global revenues of textiles, clothing, iron, and steel.[93]

According to the *National Survey on Drug Use and Health*, in 2006, 20 million Americans over the age of 12 used drugs each month. Of those, 72% (14.8 million people) only smoked marijuana. Five million people took painkillers, 2 million in-gested cocaine, 1 million took hallucinogens, and 300,000 shot heroin into their veins. American Indians had the highest rates of drug use, with 13% using drugs at least once a month. Whites and blacks had the second highest rate (9%), fol-lowed by Hispanics (7%), and Asians (4%). Drug use seems particularly high among Native-American youth between the ages of 12 and 17. Their rate of drug use is almost twice that of the national average (19% versus 10%).[94]

Many Americans associate drug trafficking with **urban street gangs**, the mem-bers of which are vital players in the underground economy. Because many gangs are based in racially segregated urban neighborhoods, they mobilize race as a principle for forming group boundaries and identities. Across America, one can find white gangs (including skinheads and biker gangs), black gangs (includ-ing those that gained wide recognition in the 1980s, such as Los Angeles's Bloods and Crips), Latino gangs (including Chicago's Latin Kings), Asian gangs (including the Chinese Mafia), and others. Modern cities are populated with equal numbers of black and white gangs.[95] Because immigrant youth often rely on gangs as avenues through which to carve out an American identity, we also find gangs in immigrant enclaves, including Salvadoran enclaves in San Fernando, Vietnamese communities in Southern California, the Kurdish section of Nashville, and the Italian and Irish sections of New York City.[96]

There are a number of reasons why people join gangs. For some, like the sons and daughters of immigrants, the gang is an institution in which they can ground their identity. For others, the gang offers economic opportunity, namely, through the drug trade. Most gangs, however, avoid the drug trade, as well as other entre-preneurial opportunities within the underground economy. For the most part, gang-driven drug trafficking operations are unorganized, small-scale ventures that rarely expand beyond the confines of a neighborhood.[97] They also do not pay well. After combing the books of a Chicago drug gang, a pair of scholars discovered that the average low-level dope slinger worked approximately twenty hours a week for $200 a week, a pay rate below the federal minimum wage.[98]

Still, for impoverished ghetto residents, the underground economy offers a viable way to earn a living, however meager, where few opportunities exist. Just as down-and-out Irish, Italian, and Jewish immigrants of the early twentieth century sold drugs and bootlegged alcohol to get by, some of today's most mar-ginalized citizens earn a buck the same way.[99] The underground drug economy provides economic livelihood in the desolate ghetto, an area abandoned by steady jobs and disowned by state services, and enables its employees to avoid the tedious (and often humiliating) work found in the licit low-wage service sector. After spending five years with crack dealers in New York's Spanish Harlem, anthropologist Philippe Bourgois asked, "Why should these young men and women take the subway to work minimum wage jobs—or even double minimum wage jobs—in downtown offices when they can usually earn more, at least in the short run, by selling drugs on the street corner in front of their apartment or school yard?"[100] That many more ghetto residents *do* take the subway to work at their minimum wage jobs testifies to their commitment, even while facing the meanest of conditions, to earn a living through means deemed upright by American society.[101]

The American ghetto has created a form of economic activity—"hustling"—of which selling drugs and gang activity are only a small part. "The demands of the ghetto require an economy utterly different from what most of America can imagine," writes sociologist Sudhir Venkatesh in *Off the Books*. "The barber may rent his back room to a prostitute; the mechanic works out of an alley; the preacher gets donations from a gang leader; and everyone has a hand in keeping the streets tolerable and keeping the goods and services flowing. . . . With few well-paying full-time jobs available in the neighborhood and with access only to the most menial jobs elsewhere in the city, [ghetto] resident may turn to hustling as a temporary means to keep food on the table, clothes on a child's back, and rent paid up."[102]

White-Collar Crime

Of course, illegal entrepreneurship is not specific to the ghetto. Technological crimes, such as computer hacking, fraud, identity theft, environmental law violations, tax evasion, bribery, counterfeiting, money laundering, and embezzling are found in affluent communities and wealthy corporations. Edwin Sutherland coined the term **"white-collar crime"** to refer to these illegal acts. "White collar crime," wrote Sutherland, is "crime committed by a person of respectability and high social status in the course of his occupation. . . . Persons of the upper socioeconomic class engage in much criminal behavior; [and] this criminal behavior differs from the criminal behavior of the lower socioeconomic class principally in the administrative procedures which are used in dealing with the offenders."[103] Sutherland advanced this definition to focus our attention on the upper echelons of the criminal world, illegal acts committed by more privileged members of society. Just as drug trafficking is not specific to the inner city, white-collar crime does not thrive only in the suburbs; however, because many white-collar crimes require a certain degree of expertise and education, most are committed by middle-class citizens. Relative to those who participate in street-level criminal behavior, white-collar criminals are three times more likely to have steady employment, five times more likely to own a home, and eight times more likely to have more than $10,000 in assets.[104]

White-collar crime has increased over the last thirty years. In 1970, crimes of fraud cost Americans around $5 billion; in 1990, they cost them around $100 billion. It is estimated that the white-collar crime industry grosses around $300 billion each year, far outpacing revenue gleaned from America's street crime.[105] Most people arrested for white-collar crimes are white. In fact, Americans seem to associate white-collar crime with whites and street-level crime with blacks and Hispanics. In studies simulating decisions made by jurors, psychologists have found that people presented with different criminal scenarios are more likely to favor harsher sentences for whites convicted of embezzlement than blacks convicted of the same crime but are more likely to prefer the harsher sentence for blacks convicted of robbery than for whites convicted of the same crime.[106] In other words, when our categories dividing crimes of privilege from crimes of poverty correspond to our racial categories separating racially privileged from racially dominated groups, we are more likely to punish crimes we understand to be "racially typical."

Thinking about white-collar crime brings to mind various acts perpetrated in corporate America that, although they inflict harm, remain perfectly legal or do not result in stiff penalties. Corporations, for example, are allowed to dump toxic waste in some communities and to emit toxic pollutants that can cause serious diseases. Drug companies are allowed to market pills whose side effects include stroke and loss of breath, but the possession of marijuana can fetch a prison term. Our energies expended on worrying about the murderer lurking in the night might be better directed to evaluating our workplace conditions, since Americans are three times more likely to die of occupational hazards than of homicide. Indeed, every hour, two Americans will be killed by a murderer, whereas three will be slain by their job. Why, we might ask, is the corporate supervisor who, by ignoring safety precautions in the name of profit, directly is responsible for a mine caving in and killing ten men merely fined or fired, but the crazed man, who guns down ten people in a shopping mall, receives the death penalty? Both actions, after all, resulted in the death of ten innocent people. Is corporate oversight that results in deadly consequences that much different than first-degree homicide? No corporation intentionally desires to kill its workers, of course; but organizations that bypass safety regulations know full well that they are playing with people's lives. Accordingly, is not the corporation's wager pitting profit against people akin to the murder's intent of inflicting harm?[107]

We commit these questions to you. As you grapple with them, we encourage you to call into question criminalization processes and their relation to systems of economic exploitation and racial domination. There is great power in the act of defining the crime, of labeling certain things criminal while overlooking others that are just as harmful. In recent years, social thinkers have documented the ascendancy of **neoliberalism,** a form of social organization in which the dynamics of the market are given priority over other concerns.[108] In a society governed by neoliberalism, all sorts of dehumanizing, harmful, and deadly acts can masquerade as legitimate or normal, hiding behind phrases such as "it's not personal, it's just business" or "the bottom line." Honoré de Balzac, the great French novelist, once wrote, "Behind every great fortune is a crime." Why then are not the crimes of capitalism considered as such? The words of Frederick Engels ring just as true today as they did when penned in 1844: "If one individual inflicts a bodily injury upon another which leads to the death of the person attacked we call it manslaughter; on the other hand, if the attacker knows beforehand that the blow will be fatal we call it murder. Murder has also been committed if society places hundreds of workers in such a position that they inevitably come to premature and unnatural ends. Their death is as violent as if they had been stabbed or shot. . . . Murder has been committed if society knows perfectly well that thousands of workers cannot avoid being sacrificed so long as these conditions are allowed to continue. Murder of this sort is just as culpable as the murder committed by an individual."[109]

Violence against Women

In recent years, Americans often have pointed out abuses against women in other countries (especially those in the Middle East, Africa, and parts of Asia), thereby giving the impression that women in the United States rarely are victimized by violence. Violence against women, however, is one of our nation's most pervasive crimes. Every fifteen seconds, a woman is beaten by her boyfriend or husband, making domestic abuse among America's most common acts of violence. Between 2 and 6 million women are abused by their partners each year, and in some studies as many as one in four women report being recently beaten. Every day, three women are killed by their husbands or boyfriends.[110] These numbers should chill us to the bone.

American women continue to be terrorized by rape. According to the U.S. Department of Justice, over 600 women are raped each day. It is estimated that one in eight women will be raped sometime in her life, and we have reason to believe that this ratio is underestimated, since as many as 60% of sexual assaults are not reported to the police. Half of all rape victims are assaulted before their 18th birthday, and college women are especially at risk, with 25% of all rapes taking place on college campuses. Far from being perpetrated by strangers, most rapes are committed by persons whom the victims know, their friends, boyfriends, husbands, or relatives.[111]

Although women throughout society suffer from violent attacks—and although researchers have found that, after accounting for income, race is not significantly correlated with rates of domestic abuse[112]—poor women, immigrants, and women of color are victimized at disproportionately high rates. Native-American women are abused at twice the rate of black and white women. And between 40% and 60% of Asian women are beaten at some point during their lives. Compared to black women, white women are nearly twice as likely to be killed by an intimate partner; however, the leading cause of death for black women between the ages of 15 and 24 is partner homicide.[113]

A woman's risk of partner abuse increases the more isolated she is from the wider society, and immigrant women are perhaps the most isolated in America. Often living thousands of miles away from their families, unfamiliar with American laws and customs, coping with limited English proficiency, and sometimes connected to their communities only through their husbands, abused immigrant women have few places to turn for help. (Indeed, some cultural traditions, like purdah—the strict segregation of the sexes that is observed in some immigrant and Muslim-American communities and that, in some cases, inhibits women from leaving the house—further isolates immigrant women.) Many cannot seek help from their in-laws, who tend to side with the husband or, worse, to perpetuate violence themselves. Sociologist Margaret Abraham has observed that, in South-Asian immigrant communities, older women are delegated the responsibility of "controlling young women." As such, wives are sometimes abused not only by their husbands but also by their mothers-in-law and other relatives.[114]

If they are undocumented immigrants, women may refuse to report their abuse to the authorities, because they fear that doing so would lead to their deportation. Moreover, American immigration law helps to trap in abusive relationships women who come to the United States to marry. To guard against fraudulent marriages, where an immigrant marries a U.S. citizen or permanent resident only to obtain citizenship, the Immigration and Naturalization Service (INS) does not allow immigrants even to apply for permanent residency until they have been married for a minimum of two years. Although this stipulation is waived for women who can prove their husbands are abusing them, many immigrant women do not have access to the kind of evidence required by the INS, such as police affidavits or reports from social workers.[115] And some domestic violence shelters, for their part, make matters worse by turning away abused women who cannot speak English. The fact that many shelters are located in white neighborhoods makes it that much harder for immigrant women, many of whom do not have driver's licenses (let alone a car), to seek refuge there.[116]

Like immigrant women, many physically and sexually abused American women of color do not have equal access to protection or justice. As we learned earlier in this chapter, the widespread fear of the black male rapist with the white female victim has resulted in black men being looked on as violent threats. However, that same trope also has facilitated the systematic disregard for black female rape victims. Law scholars who have sifted through sentencing records have found that men who rape black women are punished less severely than those who victimize Latina and white women. One study that evaluated sentencing decisions for rape cases found that black men convicted of raping white women received the harshest sentences, while black men convicted of raping black women received the lightest. According to another study, while men, nonwhite and white alike, found guilty of raping Latina women served an average term of five years, and men convicted of raping white women served an average of ten years, men convicted of raping black women served an average sentence of only two years.[117] In these sentencing discrepancies, we observe the American racial hierarchy and the systematic devaluation of black women victims.

We notice this, too, in the heightened media coverage white victims of rape receive, especially if their assailant is black, as compared to the relatively skimpy coverage of black victims. We might ask, for example, why the rape of a white female jogger, who was brutally beaten and raped in New York City's Central Park by a group of young black men, was national news, but the equally brutal gang rape of a young black woman, who, in the same week, was assaulted on top of a four-story building before being thrown off the roof, received little attention.[118] Moreover, even when cataloguing black-on-black violence, the media tend to highlight only the violence visited on black males and hence once again to overlook the abuses of black women.[119] This self-imposed blindness continues despite the fact that, in a significant proportion of cases, the victims of young men convicted of homicide actually happen to be men who had beaten the assailants' mothers.[120]

Not only are black women victims devalued in the courts and ignored by the media, they often are silenced by other members of the black community. Because women are abused more often than not by those they know, most black women are victimized by black men, just as most white women are victimized by white men, and Asian women by Asian men. Accordingly, black women often are faced with a difficult decision after being raped or beaten: should I speak out against my attacker and risk reinforcing the stereotype of violent black men, or should I remain silent and risk being abused again, while my attacker goes unpunished? "In all of their lives in America," writes Nellie McKay, "black women have felt torn between the loyalties that bind them to race on the one hand, and sex on the other. Choosing one or the other, of course, means taking sides against the self, yet they have almost always chosen race over the other: a sacrifice of their self-hood as women and of full humanity, in favor of the race."[121] Such are the workings not only of physical violence but also of the symbolic violence of which we spoke in an earlier chapter.

In many cases, when a black man is charged with violating a black woman, members of the black community rally around the black man under the banner of "racial solidarity"—or in the words of Katheryn Russell-Brown, "black protectionism"[122]—drowning out the lone voice of the victim with shouts decrying racial biases in the criminal justice system. When boxer Mike Tyson was accused of raping Desiree Washington, a young black woman, many prominent African Americans, eager to squash the "black male rapist" trope, rushed to Tyson's side, proposing that Washington "got what she deserved." Although black men continue to be falsely accused of rape, black women are far more likely to be raped than black men are to come under false allegations. Why, then, did so few voice support for Washington or, beyond that, speak out against the systematic oppression of women of color?[123] Cornel West has argued that "the idea of black people closing ranks against hostile white Americans reinforces black male power exercised over black women . . . in order to preserve the black social order under circumstances of white literal attack and symbolic assault."[124]

The bodies of women of color have been cheapened by the combined forces of racial domination and masculine domination. As a result, when these bodies are brutalized, society does not react with the same degree of righteous anger as it does when white women's bodies are victimized. Because women of color have been "chained, branded, burned, bought, sold, lynched . . . raped, beaten, stalked, and profiled" since the founding of the nation, violence afflicted on their bodies has been naturalized.[125] Add to this the relentless degradation of women of color in popular culture—especially in gangsta rap—and we might begin to understand how it is possible that young black women can be raped in public settings, like parties, in full view of others.[126]

Homicide

Although the United States' crime rate is not dramatically higher than that of other industrialized countries, its murder rate is. Between 16,000 and 17,000 Americans are murdered each year—that's around forty-five murders every day. Russia and South Africa have higher murder rates, as do Mexico and Poland, but when it comes to murder, the United States beats out India, France, Australia, Canada, Spain, and many other nations. The homicide rate rose steadily between 1965 and 1975, before dropping slightly during the late 1970s and spiking in 1980. The murder rate fell between 1980 and 1985, only to climb again until 1993, when it plummeted to levels not seen since the 1960s. Recently, however, homicide rates have begun to creep back up—not so much in large metropolitan areas such as Los Angeles or New York City but in midsize cities such as St. Louis, Milwaukee, and Charlotte. Some have attributed its rise to budget cuts caused by the war on terror. As federal funds have been directed toward beefing up homeland security and fighting the wars in Afghanistan and Iraq, midsize cities, which rely on federal funds more than large cities do, have experienced significant budget cuts in law enforcement.[127]

When we compare murder victimization rates by race, the differences are unsettling. Between 1980 and 2004, victimization rates for white adults (between

Violent crime thrives in neighborhoods wracked by compounding structural disadvantage.

the ages of 25 and 44) decreased steadily, as did the rate for Hispanic adults. By 2004, the victimization ratio per 100,000 people was 3 for whites and 7 for Hispanics. That rate was 25 per 100,000 for African American adults, whose victimization rates decreased in the early 80s, increased between 1985 and 1993, and decreased thereafter until 2003, when they began to rise again. Comparisons among young people (ages 12–24) reveal starker differences. The victimization rate for both white and Hispanic youth generally has declined during the last twenty-five years (although the rate went up for Hispanic youth between 1990 and 1995), and today, roughly 3 white youth, and 12 Hispanic youth, per 100,000 are murdered. The victimization rate for black youth rose sharply from 1985 to 1993, when the rate topped out at nearly 70 victims per 100,000. It dropped after that, only to creep back up again at the turn of this century. Today, 42 black youth in 100,000 are victims of homicide. In other words, black youth are 14 times more likely to be murdered than white youth and 3.5 more likely than Hispanic youth. Murder is the leading cause of death among black youth.[128] According to one study, "the murder rate for black men is double that of American soldiers in World War II."[129] Why?

Popular answers abound. Many people fear that violence in the media—on television, music, and video games—is directly linked to murder rates. They have good reason to be concerned. By the age of 18, the average American has viewed over 40,000 murders acted out on the television screen. But she also has been exposed to an equal number of kind and generous acts, as sitcom and movie characters are constantly involved in good deeds. Given this, shall we argue that the media encourages acts of benevolence? There is not much evidence that media violence causes actual violence. Nor can blood-soaked television or video games help explain racial disparities in murder rates (since there is no reason to believe that black youth watch more violent programming than nonblack youth) or, for that matter, the much higher homicide rate in the U.S. as compared to other countries, which air equally violent movies and television shows.[130]

Perhaps our answer lies in the fact that Americans own roughly a quarter of a *billion* guns and have more guns stolen each year (around 300,000) than many other industrialized countries have gun owners.[131] With the introduction of semiautomatic and automatic weapons, as well as high-caliber bullets, guns have grown more deadly in recent years, and firearm dealers are found in every corner of the nation. In fact, America, a nation of automobiles, has more licensed firearm dealers than gas stations.[132] There is little doubt that America's homicide rate would be lower if its citizens were not so well armed. In seven out of ten homicides, guns are used as the murder weapon; and 70% of victims are killed by a single gunshot, which suggests that, had the murderer been forced to use a less lethal weapon, many victims would still be alive today. The proliferation of guns might help explain why America's murder rate is high by international standards, but because there is no reason to believe that guns are more prevalent in black neighborhoods, access to firearms does little to explain racial disparities in murder rates.[133]

To understand why black youth fall victim to murder at such high rates, social scientists convincingly have shown that we must examine the brutal inequalities and overlapping hardships that define the African-American ghetto. The evidence points to a single, clear conclusion: Violent crime thrives in neighborhoods wracked by compounding structural disadvantages. What matters is not so much individual-level disadvantage—we gain little by comparing one poor individual with another, or one individual from a broken home with another—but structural disadvantage observed at the neighborhood level.[134] **Structural disadvantage** refers to the concentrated accumulation of overlapping and mutually reinforcing social problems in a single residential area. These problems include a disproportionate number of jobless adults, poor schools, and single-parent households, as well as high degrees of social isolation, racial segregation, and chronic poverty.

If the rate of murder is unparalleled within black communities, it is because so, too, is the level of structural disadvantage. Studies comparing black and Hispanic neighborhoods have shown that the latter are located closer to more prosperous white neighborhoods, have better relations with law enforcement officials, have fewer single-family households, and, overall, have lower levels of structural disadvantage.[135] Similarly, when researchers have compared black and white neighborhoods with equal levels of structural disadvantage, they have found no significant difference in homicide rates.[136] And because the discrepancies in homicide rates across race largely are explained by examining neighborhood-level differences—ecological dissimilarity, we might call it—we should hardly be surprised to learn that black youth who live outside majority-black neighborhoods have the same rates of offending as white youth.[137] "The combination of urban poverty and family disruption is so strong," write Robert Sampson and Lyndia Bean, "that the 'worst' urban neighborhoods in which Whites reside are considerably better off than those of the average Black community. . . . Racial segregation exposes African-American youth to neighborhoods with higher risk factors and fewer protective factors for violence than neighborhoods where youth from other groups live."[138] As a result, many poor whites who come from broken homes or who are unemployed (factors associated with violent crime) live in areas with steady levels of family stability and employment. The same is not true of poor blacks living in urban areas. As we have already learned, black poverty is not the same as white poverty; it is much worse.

Crime ridden streets have bred a spirit of fear and distrust in many black neighborhoods, a spirit that dissolves community relationships and modes of informal social control. Recall that informal social control can effectively attenuate violent crime by ensuring that little problems do not boil up into bigger ones and by encouraging neighbors to look out for one another. Although researchers have documented a high degree of social control in other poor neighborhoods, especially those of immigrants, they have observed that poor black inner-city dwellers often are isolated from one another, primarily because of a widespread fear of victimization.[139]

To adapt to the extreme structural disadvantage found within the ghetto, many young black teenagers develop cultural dispositions and attitudes that promote (and even normalize) violent crime. According to sociologist Elijah Anderson, black youth living in poor inner-city neighborhoods operate under a **"code of the street,"** which requires them to present themselves as aggressive, hard menaces who are not to be trifled with and who, at a second's notice, will "act a fool" and resort to violence.[140] Young people abiding by such a code earn respect from their peers through acts of courage and aggression. To the man who hits on a rival's girlfriend, throws the first punch, or pulls the trigger, go "the props," "the juice." Disrespected, in the fullest sense of the term, by mainstream white society, poor black youth create their own ways of allocating respect and honor; but these ways serve to breed only violence and to reproduce the conditions of their own domination—again, symbolic violence.[141] That said, we should bear in mind that the code of the street is not endorsed solely by black youth. "The important thing to note about the subculture that ensnares [young black men] is that it is not disconnected from the mainstream culture," writes sociologist Orlando Patterson. "To the contrary, it has powerful support from some of America's largest corporations. Hip-hop, professional basketball, and homeboy fashions are as American as cherry pie. Young white Americans are very much into these things, but selectively; they know when it is time to turn off Fifty Cent and get out the SAT prep book."[142]

The code of the street and the dissolution of informal social control both help explain why blacks, and young blacks especially, have such high rates of homicide; but both these factors must be understood, above all, as induced by the extreme structural disadvantage that makes the black ghetto distinct from other poor neighborhoods in America. Years of research have yielded the firm conclusion that social problems related to homicide are rooted in enduring systems of domination: notably, economic marginality and racial segregation. For example, people who were abused as children are far more likely to commit a violent crime than those who were not; but child abuse is prevalent in neighborhoods reeling from chronic poverty and endemic unemployment.[143] America—and Black America, in particular—has a violent crime problem. And because the problem is environmental, not individual, in nature, so, too, must be the solution. A weed will spring up again and again unless it is pulled up by the roots. Any crime-fighting proposal that fails to recognize this is bound to fall miserably short of the mark.

Punishment

The last major section of this chapter takes up punishment, the nation's reactions to crime and its methods of combating it. The ensuing discussions follow the process of punishment through the criminal justice system, beginning with policing strategies and with profiling and racial disparities in arrest rates and then moving into sentencing decisions. The section ends where the chapter began, namely, with prisons, exploring the high costs of mass incarceration and evaluating how effective prisons are when it comes to decreasing crime.

American Police State

It has been well documented that Hispanics and African Americans are arrested at much higher rates than whites. According to statistics released by the FBI, 13 blacks in 100 are arrested annually, whereas only 5 whites in 100 are. In some states, the difference is much more exaggerated. In Wisconsin, for example, where only 6 whites out of 100 are arrested each year, that ratio shoots up to 41 out of 100 for blacks.[144] What explains this wide discrepancy? Although some of the difference undoubtedly is attributed to the high rates of violent crime found in some nonwhite neighborhoods, a good proportion is caused by institutional racism operating at multiple levels of the criminal justice system.[145]

Ever since the racial uprisings of the 1960s, poor, nonwhite urban neighborhoods have been subjected to heightened surveillance and police repression. What held true for cities that experienced major uprisings in around the middle of the twentieth century remains true today: metropolitan areas with sizable black populations have larger police forces and bigger crime-fighting budgets than cities with fewer black residents. More detailed analyses have demonstrated that, on a national level, police forces grow in proportion to cities' level of racial residential segregation as well as to whites' fear of crime.[146]

Owing to the criminalization of dark skin, blacks, Mexicans, and Puerto Ricans are singled out as potential criminals at a much higher rate than Asians and whites. One study found that whites are six times less likely than blacks, and four times less likely than Hispanics, to be stopped by the police. Although whites constitute 43% of New York City's population, they account for only 13% of civilians stopped by law enforcement officers.[147] Compared to whites, African Americans and Hispanics are more likely to report being stopped, questioned, and frisked without due process by police officers.

African Americans have grown so used to being pulled over by the police that many refer to being stopped on account of DWB: "driving while black."[148] Perhaps more disconcerting is the fact that, once pulled over, black and Hispanic drivers are more likely than their white counterparts are to be fined, arrested, and searched. A New Jersey-based study found that the majority of cars searched during traffic stops belonged to nonwhite drivers (70%), and a high percentage of drivers searched subsequently were arrested. Many police officers, the study went on to say, intentionally targeted blacks and Latinos because, statistically, they have higher arrest rates.[149] Thus, through a self-reinforcing cycle of disadvantage, racial profiling results in more nonwhites being arrested, and high levels of nonwhite arrest rates are marshaled as evidence to justify racial profiling.

What some white people have a difficult time understanding is that, for many people of color, the police are anything but guardians. As African-American comedian Dave Chappelle has observed, "The premise of reasonable doubt for a Black person and for a White person are two separate things. For a White person, the idea that the police planted evidence is ridiculous: 'The police are here to serve and protect us!' Yeah *you*. But to a Black person, it's not ridiculous. The FBI followed Martin Luther King around! Was he a threat to America?"[150]

Many nonwhite Americans, especially those brought up in poor communities, are taught from childhood that the police—not to mention judges, lawyers, parole officers, social workers, prison guards, and all others in the legal field— bring violence and harm, unfair treatment and repression. The police, after all, historically have served as the primary guardians of white supremacy, called on to track down runaway slaves, to kill Native Americans who refused to stay cooped up in their reservations, to enforce Jim Crow segregation, and to unleash attack dogs on civil rights marchers. When, in 1989, rap group N.W.A. (Niggaz with Attitude) released their hit song "Fuck the Police," many white Americans recoiled in horror, although many nonwhite Americans, although they may have disagreed with the group's profanity and message, understood at a deep level the angst and anger fueling the song's lyrics.

According to the Bureau of Justice, police officers are more likely to use force on black and Hispanic citizens than on their white counterparts.[151] Police brutality has been inflicted on blacks and Hispanics—sometimes in lethal doses. In 1992, Malice Green, a black man, was beaten to death by two white police officers after he resisted arrest. In 1997, Abner Louima, an immigrant from Haiti, was arrested outside a Brooklyn nightclub and taken to a police station, where he was beaten, tortured, and sodomized with a broomstick by New York City police officers. In 1999, four plainclothes police officers fired forty-one shots at Amadou Diallo, a 23-year-old West African immigrant, who they believed to have been holding a gun. When they approached Diallo's bullet-ridden, dead body, officers discovered he had been gripping his wallet. In 2003, Ousmane Zongo, another unarmed young West African immigrant, stumbled upon a CD pirating sting operation and was shot four times—twice in the back—by a New York City police officer. And in 2006, undercover police officers unleashed a barrage of gunfire at Sean Bell, a 23-year-old African-American man, and two of his friends. The officers sprayed bullets into Bell's car and surrounding houses. Bell and his two friends, none of whom was armed, were leaving a strip club (one the police had been investigating), celebrating Bell's final hours of bachelorhood. Sean Bell never made it to the church the following morning. His bride-turned-widow accepted Bell's surname days after she laid him in the ground.[152]

How do we make sense of such killings? It is tempting to shovel blame solely on the shoulders of the police officers, calling them "racist" or "incompetent" and demanding their resignation. Police officers who kill innocent and unarmed people should be held accountable for their actions. But focusing only on the officers permits us to avoid examining the circumstances in all their complexity. Millions of people play a part in criminalizing darkness—from the elderly white woman terrified of her black neighbors to the young black teenager who refers to himself as a "thug"—which directly is responsible for racial disparities in arrest rates and the killing of innocent men of color. To blame "racist cops" is to blot out the many ways in which our complicity maintains a system of racial domination that facilitates racially motivated police brutality.

Likewise, to point our fingers solely at the victims, assuming they "must have done something wrong," is to misidentify the wrongdoer, to criminalize the innocent. Indeed, everyday citizens have not been the only victims of police shootings. Between 1941 and 1996, twenty black undercover police officers have been shot and killed by their white colleagues; however, no undercover white officer during these fifty-five years has been gunned down by a black cop.[153]

Unjust Sentencing

Scythian, an ancient Greek philosopher, once likened laws to spider webs, as "they catch the weak and the small, but the strong and powerful break through them."[154] Indeed, as it stands now, the American legal system is biased by design, heavily tilted against the poor. Because nonwhites from disadvantaged communities are arrested at higher rates relative to whites, and because most of these accused people are flat broke, they are forced to rely on public defenders, who tend to be overworked, underpaid, and unable to afford potentially useful resources such as DNA tests or expert witnesses. Public defenders have very poor records: whereas private attorneys win over half their cases, public defenders achieve a not guilty verdict only 11% of the time; and while private attorneys force the courts to dismiss 48% of their cases, public defenders get only 11% of their cases dropped.[155] Some public defenders, burdened by their caseloads, hastily push for plea deals, to which many defendants, seeing no better option, reluctantly agree. These facts remain even (and especially) in capital cases, forcing one journalist to quip, "some people go to traffic court with better prepared lawyers than many murder defendants get."[156]

The strong arm of the law often reserves its harshest blows for nonwhite offenders. Consider the sentencing disparities between crack and powdered cocaine. There is little difference between the two drugs. Both lead to a similar high, have similar health risks, and cost about the same (between $110 and $150 per gram). But powdered and crack cocaine are treated extremely differently under the law. Those caught with 5 grams of crack are sentenced to a minimum five years in prison, but one must be caught with 500 grams of powdered cocaine to receive the same minimum sentence. In fact, the *maximum* sentence for simple possession of powdered cocaine (anything under 500 grams) is one year, whereas the *minimum* sentence for possessing 5 grams or more of crack (that's five Sweet 'n' Low packets' worth) is five years in the pen.[157] Tellingly, most of those arrested for possessing or distributing crack are African Americans; whites and Latinos make up the majority of those arrested for possessing or selling powdered cocaine.

In 2007, the U.S. Sentencing Commission set out to address some of these disparities, taking on, for example, the troubling fact that street-level crack dealers are subject to the same sentence as powdered cocaine dealers selling 100 times as much product. The commission proposed new sentencing guidelines and, making its recommendations retroactive, gave roughly 20,000 inmates serving time on crack charges a chance at early release. It did not, however, recommend that the sentencing disparities be eliminated. It just reduced them. Instead of a 100-to-1 sentencing ratio, new ratios would vary from 80 to 1 to 25 to 1. What is more, federal judges dealing out the sentences were in no way bound by the commission's recommendations. They were, rather, bound by mandatory minimum sentences, which helped to drive the gross sentencing disparities between crack and powdered cocaine and were unaffected by the commission's recommendations. Only Congress could change the mandatory minimums and, so far, has not done so.[158] This meant that those who use and deal crack in poor, inner-city black neighborhoods continued to be sentenced to more years in prison than those using and dealing the exact same substance, only in powdered form, in affluent white and Latino communities. The only explanation for this discrepancy is persistent and blatant institutionalized racism in sentencing guidelines.

Consider Georgia law, which allows courts to hand down a life sentence for repeat drug offenses, even if both offenses are minor ones (such as simple possession). Between 1990 and 1995, 573 repeat offenders were sentenced to life under this law, but only 13 of them were white. Fifteen percent of black repeat offenders, but only 3% of white repeat offenders, were put away for life. Compared to whites who commit similar crimes, nonwhite juvenile offenders are more likely to be tried as adults; are more likely to receive tougher punishments; and are more likely to be viewed as "inherently criminal" by their parole officers. Blacks arrested for aggravated assault are jailed nearly a third longer than whites arrested for the exact same offense—a discrepancy brought to the nation's attention during the trial of six young black teenagers arrested for assaulting a white teenager in Jena, Louisiana.[159]

Outside the local high school in Jena (population 3,000), a tree once stood that was known as the "white tree," so named because, according to local convention, only white students were allowed to sit under it. The day after a black student defied the unspoken law in September 2007, white students hung three nooses on the tree, sending a threatening message to black students, one that harkened back to the days of white terrorism. Tension between whites and blacks mounted, and, later in the school year, when a young white high school student taunted black students with racial epithets and jeers, a group of black students beat him unconscious. The victim of the assault was taken to the hospital and released a few hours later. Six black male students were arrested and charged— not with assault but with attempted murder, a sentence grievously disproportional to the crime. Thousands of people descended on the little Louisiana town to protest, marching on behalf of "the Jena 6," as they came to be known. As a result, charges were scaled back to aggravated second-degree battery and conspiracy to commit aggravated second-degree battery. According to Louisiana law, what distinguishes "aggravated" battery from simply battery is employment of a weapon. The prosecutor in the Jena 6 case argued that the tennis shoes worn by one of the black assailants were dangerous weapons, and the jury accepted this argument.[160]

The Jena 6 still face prison time, and if they are tried as adults—as was one of the black youths, Mychal Bell, who was 16 at the time of his arrest—they will forever be plagued by a criminal record. The white students who hung the nooses on the tree were punished by only a few days' suspension.[161] The events of Jena, Louisiana represent but a small piece of a larger problem: that justice, far from being blind, systematically disadvantages poor nonwhites, and especially young black men, who come under the cold eyes of the law.[162]

Nowhere is institutional racism within the criminal justice system more cruel than in death penalty sentencing. After taking into account dozens of other factors (including previous offenses and the heinousness of the crime), numerous studies have concluded that, of all people accused of committing capital offenses, blacks are more likely to be sentenced to death than whites. Moreover, people accused of killing whites are four times more likely to receive the death sentence than those accused of killing blacks.[163] Since 1973, 130 people have been found innocent and released from death row. Of those, 66 are black, 50 are white, and 12 are Hispanic. This pattern mirrors that of all exonerations. Since 1989, 223 people have been found innocent based on DNA evidence, including the five blacks originally charged in the infamous Central Park jogger case, discussed earlier. Of the 223, 138 are black, 59 are white, and 19 are Hispanic.[164] These figures suggest that America is imprisoning—and even killing—innocent men and women, a disproportionate number of whom are black.

Because racial domination systematically tilts the scales of justice against people of color, many blacks and Hispanics, especially those living in poor neighborhoods, have little faith in the criminal justice system.[165] Some even feel that justice has a better chance of being served if community members dole it out, which explains "retaliatory killings" and the edict against "snitching" (for example, reporting crime) in high-crime neighborhoods.[166]

It is clear how nonwhites' views of the criminal justice system are affected by racial domination. But does racial domination affect whites' views? Absolutely. The very fact that many whites view the criminal justice system as unbiased and fair reflects their racial privilege, the privilege of knowing that in no time in American history has the system been used as a machine of oppression against people with their skin color; that people who look like them are not racially profiled; that whiteness is not riveted to images of violence and criminality, as is blackness; that most police officers are white and have good relationships with white communities; that, should they stand trial, their whiteness will not result in a harsher sentence; and that, in a jury trial, they can rest assured they will be judged by "a panel of their peers."

The Many Costs of Mass Incarceration

We began this chapter by discussing the prison boom and the racial imbalance of America's prison population, and we explored the social mechanisms that help account for this gross discrepancy. It is fitting, therefore, to conclude this chapter by examining the consequences of imprisonment, for offenders and ex-offenders, as well as for society as a whole.

For over fifty years, researchers have warned us about the negative psychological effects of incarceration. The experience of confinement, of caging, can exert very powerful effects on one's mental state. This is especially true of the 20,000 inmates imprisoned in super-maximum facilities. Living in a concrete 7-feet by 14-feet cell, the inmate held in supermax spends twenty-three hours a day locked down. He or she eats all meals in solitude and, although they may be dimmed, his or her cell lights are never shut off. Such conditions often drive prisoners to suicide or insanity. Medical researchers have demonstrated that prisoners subjected to solitary confinement can become delirious and hallucinatory in as little as 48 hours. Historian Alfred McCoy calls solitary confinement "no-touch torture," saying, "it sends prisoners in one of two directions: catatonia or rage."[167]

If they survive prison, offenders are met with a whole host of problems once released. There are, first, political consequences, as many no longer are allowed to participate in the most fundamental right of citizenship, the right to vote (as we discussed in Chapter 3). There are also severe economic costs of being branded with a criminal record. Many licensed or professional occupations in health care or the public sector disqualify all applicants with criminal records, and a good number of employers simply refuse to hire exconvicts, especially men of color with felony convictions. One study found that a criminal record reduces one's chances of landing a job by 50 to 60%.[168]

Because budgets for educational and vocational training have been rolled back in recent years, prisoners have little hope of gaining job skills while doing time. And because they are cut off from the larger society, prisoners' connections to stably employed friends and family members, people who could connect them to job opportunities, diminish the longer they are behind bars. As a result, many women and men with criminal records have a very difficult time securing well-paying, full-time jobs. Add to this the fact that ex-offenders are denied many types of social services, such as food stamps, public housing, Medicaid, and government-based financial aid for college, and we can begin to understand how difficult it can be for someone recently released from prison to turn her or his life around. We can thereby begin to grasp the direct connection between incarceration and chronic poverty.[169]

Compared to those who have never been incarcerated, exconvicts have lower wages, employment rates, and annual incomes. Incarceration results in a 15% reduction in hourly wage rates across the board, and those who have been incarcerated work an average of eight fewer weeks a year than if they had never been convicted. An exconvict earns 30% to 40% less each year than a person with the same job skills and education. A black man who dropped out of high school earns roughly $9,000 a year; but a black man who dropped out of high school and has a criminal record earns roughly $5,700 a year. Since the *majority* of black male dropouts will be incarcerated at some point in their lives, the economic consequences of incarceration are intimately linked to the persistence of racialized poverty. In fact, if no Hispanics or African Americans were incarcerated, the poverty rates for both groups would plummet by significant margins. Under such conditions, no less than one-fifth of all poor blacks would be lifted out of poverty.[170]

Incarceration also wreaks havoc on the family, as wives must cope without their husbands, children without their mothers. Incarcerated parents miss out on key events in children's lives—their first steps, major holidays, soccer games—which, research has shown, erodes the bond between parent and child. If it is the father who is incarcerated, the newly single mother often is forced to make ends meet by working several jobs and cannot afford to spend extended amounts of time supervising her children or helping them with homework. As a result, many children from single-parent homes fare worse in school and are at a higher risk of developing behavioral problems than their peers from two-parent households. If it is the single mother who is incarcerated, her parental rights may be revoked and her children may become wards of the state, shuffled through the foster care system.

Incarceration often tears families apart. Although the divorce rate for men inside and outside of prison is the same—50 percent—most marriages involving an incarcerated partner end in less than seven years, a full decade before the national rate of seventeen years. Couples with children are at a high risk of splitting if the father is locked up. By one estimate, America would enjoy 20% to 30% more marriages if it did not incarcerate a single person. And men with criminal records seem to have a difficult time getting married after their sentence expires. Just as they are "marked" by employers who refuse to hire them, they are "marked" by potential mates who refuse to marry them. By the age of 35, roughly 80% of men who have never been incarcerated are married; the same is true of only 40% of men with a record.[171]

Incarceration also comes with a hefty price tag. It costs approximately $27,000 a year to incarcerate one person. In a nation with a prison population exceeding 2 million, this amounts to over $50 billion a year. If we add in the costs of policing, legal processing, court fees, and all the other expenses of the criminal justice system, we are met with the realization that America spends an extravagant $100 billion a year to fight crime, money that could otherwise be directed at building schools, decreasing pollution, raising teachers' salaries, funding job skill programs in the inner city, or beefing up America's skinny welfare state. Indeed, as the prison system has swelled, the United States has rolled back social spending. In 1973, states spent 2% of their budgets on police and corrections and 5.5% on cash assistance to the poor; in 2003, cash assistance programs accounted for less than 1% of state expenditures, and police and corrections accounted for roughly 4.5%.[172]

Not only is incarceration incredibly costly, it also reproduces the racial order. That is, the prison can be understood as one of America's premier "race making" institutions. By supervising, punishing, and confining a disproportionate number of poor blacks and Hispanics, the prison imprints on dark skin the stamp of criminality with all the force of state power. As sociologist Loïc Wacquant has observed, "Indeed, when 'to be a man of colour of a certain economic class and milieu is equivalent in the public eye to being a 'criminal,' being processed by the penal system is tantamount to being made black, and 'doing time' behind bars is at the same time 'marking race.'"[173]

Do Prisons Make Us Safer?

However devastating the effects of incarceration on the lives and families of offenders, and however much damage the criminal justice system does to our strivings toward racial justice, and however high a price we all pay for having the world's largest prison population, many Americans would still approve of incarcerating thousands of people every year if that kept them safer. So, the million-dollar question is: do prisons decrease crime? The crime drop America has been enjoying for the last twenty-five years coincided with the prison boom. Did the boom cause the drop? The vast majority of research requires us to answer no. The most sophisticated research to date concludes that the prison boom can only account for 2% to 5% of the crime drop. In other words, "nine-tenths of the decline in serious crime through the 1990s would have happened even without the prison boom."[174]

Since the rise of "law and order" politics and the implementation of harsher sentences, prisons have abandoned their original mission—to rehabilitate those who have committed crimes—and instead have become punishing and warehousing institutions. Evidence suggests that rehabilitation programs reduce recidivism; however, since funding for such programs has been scaled back, there is little proof that prisons decrease crime by rehabilitating offenders.[175]

If prisons do not rehabilitate offenders, perhaps they decrease crime simply by taking criminals off the streets—that is, by incapacitating them. This line of reasoning would make sense if most people behind bars were career criminals responsible for multiple offenses. Although many prisoners have carried out dozens of crimes, a good number of them are first-time offenders. What is more, street-level drug dealers are easily replaced after they are arrested, resulting in an incapacitation effect of zero. For this reason, we must conclude that incapacitation decreases the crime rate by a modest, even marginal, degree.[176]

Lastly, we might argue that prisons function as a strong deterrent for would-be criminals. If prisons are to have a **deterrent effect**, someone contemplating a crime must weigh the rewards of the crime (say, $5,000 for stealing a car) against the punishment (say, three years in prison for grand theft auto) and decide against committing the crime specifically because the punishment outweighs the reward. There is no denying that prisons deter some people from committing a crime. But how strong is the effect? "Not very strong," is the answer from current research. Surveys of prisoners reveal that one in three people convicted of a felony confess to having never considered their punishment when committing their crime. Indeed, many offenders literally were out of their minds when they broke the law: 30% of state convicts confess to having been on drugs when they committed their crimes, and another 17% committed the offenses in order to get money for drugs. For this reason, it is safe to conclude that many, if not most, people do not even perform the mental cost-benefit analysis required by the deterrent effect.[177]

Not only this, but there is good reason to believe that prisons produce more crime. You may already have arrived at this conclusion, having learned that incarceration leads to poverty and family breakdown, both of which are correlated with crime. If an ex-offender cannot find steady work after her release, she might resort to stealing appliances or selling drugs to get by. If an ex-offender's marriage dissolved while he was in the pen, he might find community in the friends he socialized with before his arrest, friends perhaps involved in the criminal underworld. The criminal justice system spends far less money and effort reintegrating ex-offenders into society than it does punishing them. The result is that a good number of the 630,000 people released from prison every year "return to their old ways," so to speak.[178] And why should we expect otherwise? After all, they just left a parallel society filled with offenders, a place where first-time offenders were introduced to career criminals, where friendships between gang members and drug dealers were forged and solidified. A person might enter prison a man who committed a single crime and leave it a hardened criminal. In a sense, being released from prison is akin to graduating from crime school.

And poor nonwhite communities, from which most of America's convicts are pulled, suffer worst of all. By extracting from these communities' families hundreds of husbands and fathers, wives and mothers, and by removing scores of able-bodied workers, incarceration contributes to the reproduction of social marginality, racialized poverty, fractured families, and, ironically, high crime rates.

Incarceration fuels the structural disadvantage found in poor urban communities, which, as we have already seen, increases crime, which, in turn, results in more people going to prison, and on and on it goes—racial domination, economic destitution, and criminal persecution advancing in lockstep.[179]

Things Are Not What They Seem

A rational assessment of race and crime, one that marshals the power of social science to judge the validity of popular claims, often leads to surprising discoveries. By holding in abeyance the emotional reactions unleashed during discussions of crime and punishment, choosing, instead, to study the thing carefully and objectively, we are presented with facts that flip conventional wisdom on its head. Crime is not forever on the rise; immigrants do not cause crime but make the streets safer; we have more to fear from unsafe working conditions than from the crazed murderer lurking in the darkness; prisons do more harm than good when it comes to decreasing crime. Perhaps Gaston Bachelard was right in saying "the first impression is not a fundamental truth."[180]

If many things believed to be threatening (for example, immigrants) actually make us safer, and if many things believed to be protective (for instance, prisons) actually increase our risks of harm, then, as critically minded sociological thinkers, we are obliged to rethink the crime problem and its solutions. This requires, first, reconsidering the dangers to which our minds and money should be devoted. The high homicide rates in poor urban neighborhoods certainly deserve attention, but so, too, do rampant violence against women (and the system of masculine domination on which it relies) and offenses carried out by corporations (and the system of economic exploitation on which they rely). Indeed, the sociological thinker must be willing to question the very definition of "crime" itself.

Second, we must rethink conventional solutions to fighting crime, solutions, as we have just seen, that may bring about harmful unintended consequences. We must denaturalize incarceration as the one and only means of punishment.[181] This precisely has been the goal of the anti-incarceration movement. Thoroughly multiracial and made up of citizens of all ages, the anti-incarceration movement has criticized America's reliance on the prison as the primary method through which punishments are dealt. Those in the movement have emphasized many other ways of confronting crime—alternatives to incarceration—that are less costly and do not result in the harmful side effects of mass incarceration. They have also marshaled evidence, including some reviewed here, that demonstrates that proactive approaches to decreasing crime will yield higher payoffs than reactive ones. Building more prisons is a fundamentally reactive solution. Attacking the structural disadvantages of poor, inner-city neighborhoods—dismantling racial segregation, confronting widespread joblessness, fighting for a higher minimum wage, developing ways of making college tuition more affordable and available to exfelons—is a proactive solution, one that holds greater promise for making America safer.

Finally, we must examine how our racialized fears erode the hope of a multicultural democracy rooted in interracial alliances. The more we fear one another, looking on each other as potential threats, enemies, and terrorists, the slimmer are our chances of reaching out to one another to help build the society in which we wish to live. Fear causes us to lock our doors; it keeps us from walking across the block and introducing ourselves to our neighbors. It causes us to divert our eyes, to clutch our purses, to change seats on an airplane when confronted with people whose very skin tone marks them as criminals. Psychologists have shown that we pay a high price for racialized fear, the price of walking through life filled with unhealthy doses of guilt, shame, anxiety, and depression.[182] The nation as a whole pays a high price as well—for racialized fear withers away the promise of American community, and it makes a mockery of justice.

CHAPTER REVIEW

THE RISE OF THE AMERICAN PRISON

lynch mob, vagabond laws, prison boom, three-strikes laws, bipolar discursive frame, prison-industrial complex

FEAR

informal social control

CRIME

underground economy, urban street gangs, white-collar crime, neoliberalism, structural disadvantage, code of the street

PUNISHMENT

deterrent effect

FROM THEORY TO PRACTICE

1. Think about a police officer. Write down five adjectives you think accurately describe her or him. Having done that, reflect on how your views of a police officer are informed by America's racial past. Reflect, too, on how your upbringing might have informed your outlook.

2. In this chapter we learned that, in many cases, the voices of women of color are silenced in debates about crime, especially those concerning domestic

violence and rape. Reflecting on public discussions of crime and punishment, name another group whose voice is silenced. How is this group ignored? Why do you think this is so? How might fully including this group in public debate help us to reach new understandings?

3. After determining your congressperson's stance on crime and punishment, write to her or him, asking why she or he has chosen such an approach. If you agree with your representative, commend her or his approach by citing social-scientific evidence, found in this chapter or other sources, that supports her or his policies. If you disagree, however, suggest an alternative approach to fighting crime that *is* supported by social-scientific evidence. In each case, explain how the congressperson's approach ensures or denies people of color fair treatment.

4. Think of something that is harmful but not criminalized (for example, actions carried out by state officials). Offer a sociologically informed explanation for why these actions are not criminalized. When doing so, be sure to identify who is disproportionately affected by the harmful actions and who benefits from their not being criminalized. Additionally, determine how this helps to support systems of domination.

5. A young man is found guilty of possessing 5 grams of crack cocaine and is therefore eligible to serve a minimum sentence of five years in prison. This is his first offense. Assuming the role of the judge with absolute sentencing powers—and pretending for a moment that judges are not bound by draconian mandatory minimum sentences—offer an alternative to incarceration. That is, what other punishment, besides prison, might be suitable in this case? And why would it be preferable to the conventional sentence of incarceration?

RECOMMENDED READING

- Barry Glassner, *Culture of Fear: Why Americans Are Afraid of the Wrong Things* (New York: Basic Books, 1999).

- Mae Ngai, *Impossible Subjects: Illegal Aliens and the Making of Modern America* (Princeton: Princeton University Press, 2003).

- Devah Pager, "The Mark of a Criminal Record," *American Journal of Sociology* 108 (2003): 937–975.

- Michael Tonry, *Malign Neglect: Race, Crime, and Punishment in America* (New York: Oxford University Press, 1995).

- Bruce Western, *Punishment and Inequality in America* (New York: Russell Sage Foundation, 2006).

Chapter 7

Education

The Promise of Education

Study after study has concluded that individuals who have more education make more money, have more stable marriages, and live longer and healthier lives than those with little education. Education, it seems, increases one's chances of experiencing a thriving, successful life. Not only that, but education makes civic debate and democracy possible. That was as true in the mid-nineteenth century, when Alexis de Tocqueville wrote of America, "The first duty imposed on those who now direct society is to *educate democracy*. . . . A new political science is needed for a world itself quite new," as it is today, when in 2007 Harvard President Drew Gilpin Faust declared that "education is the engine that makes American democracy work."[1] It is no wonder, then, that when a despotic government overthrows a democratic state, one of its first acts is to close the doors of the university.

If a democratic society cannot function properly without education, it is because education provides us with tools to comprehend, and therefore to critically assess, the economic, social, cultural, and political forces that govern our lives. It also allows us to employ our sociological imagination to better understand ourselves—our innermost desires, passions, struggles, and hardships. Freedom, therefore—which for a society means unencumbered democracy and for an individual, the capacity for self-knowledge and self-mastery—arrives only on the back of education. "To be free," wrote C. Wright Mills, "the individual must become more rationally aware," and, we add, to become more rationally aware, the individual must be educated.[2]

But, today, education is not granted freely and equally to all citizens. Nor is education innocent of overlapping modes of domination, including racial domination. You can be educated to hate yourself and others, to prize certain cultures' accomplishments over others', to assume "your place" within the social hierarchy. Through education, truth can be buried under falsehoods and distortions. Education, then, can both liberate and constrain, it can both open doors and slam them shut. However, and here's the rub, it is only by further educating ourselves that we are able to distinguish between truth and falsehood and, therefore, to expose domination in the curriculum and classroom. Racist education must be beaten at its own game.[3] By evaluating the workings of racial domination in the educational field, this chapter contributes to this work.

The chapter begins with a historical overview of racial struggles over education across the twentieth century. Then, it turns to analyzing the many ways in which whiteness informs what and how we are taught. Next, it underscores racial inequalities in education, proposes sociological explanations for those inequalities, and evaluates a potential remedy for them: affirmative action. Racial domination within the educational field is a topic that should concern us all—for nothing short of our very minds and freedoms is at stake.

"I Have a Right to Think!" Racial Battles over Education, 1900–1970

It is perhaps more common today to hear students complaining about having to attend classes, to read books, to complete their assignments—that is, to engage in all those activities that enrich and stimulate the mind—than it is to hear them confess their gratitude for the right to learn. Perhaps their classes and textbooks do not challenge and inspire them. But perhaps, too, we have forgotten those who suffered in previous generations so that we—all of us—might pursue the journey of the mind to its furthest extent. This section serves as a reminder, however brief, of the racial struggles that took place within the educational field during the tumultuous twentieth century, a reminder that the right to think was something young people, like many of you, risked their lives for, a right we would do well not to take for granted.

The Colonizer's Education: Indian Boarding Schools

As we learned in Chapter 2, at the beginning of the twentieth century, whites sought new ways to "civilize"—that is, to Anglicize—America's indigenous people. Education would become a primary civilizing machine. American Indian parents were forced to send their children to boarding schools run by Christian missionaries and, later on, by the federal government. If parents refused (and many did), they were pressured by military power, threatened with imprisonment, or denied food rations. Hundreds of Indian children were sent to boarding schools, where their hair was cut and their traditional garb traded in for English-style clothes.[4] In her memoir, *The School Days of an Indian Girl*, Zitkala-Sa recalls the traumatic experience of having her long hair sheared: "Our mothers had taught us that only unskilled warriors who were captured had their hair shingled by the enemy. Among our people, short hair was worn by mourners, and shingled hair by cowards! . . . I was carried downstairs and tied fast in a chair. I cried aloud, shaking my head all the while until I felt the cold blades of the scissors against my neck, and heard them gnaw off one of my thick braids. Then I lost my spirit. Since the day I was taken from my mother I had suffered extreme indignities. People had stared at me. I had been tossed about in the air like a wooden puppet. And now my long hair was shingled like a coward's! In my anguish I moaned for my mother, but no one came to comfort me. Not a soul reasoned quietly with me, as my own mother used to do; for now I was only one of many little animals driven by a herder."[5]

A boarding school's primary objective was to strip American Indian students of all their Indianness, to force them to assimilate into Anglo-American society and culture through strict, military-style discipline. Schools often were built a good distance from reservations, and parental visits were discouraged. Students were forbidden to speak in their native tongue or to practice their religion. And the slightest infractions were subject to harsh punishment, as one former student remembered: "If everybody knew part of their language or even spoke any Indian terms you would be spanked for it. . . . You were brought in front of everybody and when you lined up in the morning before you go to breakfast, they would call you out, they would have you pull your pants down, grab your ankles and they would spank you in front of everybody so everybody could view it."[6] In some cases, American Indian students even could be punished for singing traditional songs. They were taught, day after day, that their way of life, and that of their parents and grandparents, was silly, backward—evil.

Many students were thoroughly indoctrinated into whiteness and, on returning home, appeared alien to their family members and others in the community. Others, however, resisted their cultural re-education. Students ran away from the schools, practiced outlawed ceremonies in secret, and whispered to one another in their native language. Some even mounted organized rebellions not only against schools' colonialist project but also against their pitiful conditions.[7] When government researcher Lewis Meriam published *The Problem of Indian Administration* in 1928, he brought to the public's attention what many American Indian students already knew: "that the provisions for the care of the Indian children in boarding schools are grossly inadequate."[8] In 2008—with the discovery of mass graves at former boarding schools located in Canada, containing hundreds if not thousands of bodies of children, some of whom, many believe, were punished to death—we learned what many American Indians long had suspected: that the abuses suffered by American Indian children at boarding schools were much worse than even those documented in Meriam's scathing report.[9]

Meriam's report—which, besides pointing out the sorry conditions of boarding schools, called attention to their inability to educate students—caught the government's attention, and things began to change. In 1933, John Collier, a white man, became the Commissioner on Indian Affairs and began reforming Indian education. Collier loosened the grip of Anglo-American colonialist education, encouraging bilingualism in boarding schools, replacing far-off schools with day schools on reservations, and making sure that schools provided students with a safe and healthy environment. He even introduced Native American literature, poetry, and philosophy into schools' curriculum through new textbooks written in collaboration with tribal elders.[10]

Despite these important changes, American Indians did not regain full control over the education of their children until the Civil Rights Era. In 1966, the first Indian-controlled school was established on the Navajo Reservation, and three years later (on that same reservation) the first tribal college, Navajo Community College, was founded. Whereas education historically had been "for Indians," these schools represented education "by Indians." Today, in many reservation schools, tribal language is taught beside English, and Native American folklore and literature is read along with the likes of Mark Twain and Jane Austen.[11]

The effects of colonialist education are still felt across Indian country, though, especially in tribes whose culture and language virtually were wiped out and whose religion and traditions continue to be viewed as primitive relics, things to be displayed in a museum. Indeed, many today point to misrepresentations of American Indians in textbooks and popular movies, as well as in national myths about the country's indigenous population, and justly claim that Indian education—in the broadest sense of the word—has not yet fully been wrenched from the colonizer's grip.

"Spoiling Field Hands": Early African-American Education

While American Indians were being forced to conform to white society at the beginning of the twentieth century, African Americans were being forcefully excluded from it. After Reconstruction, whites, especially southern whites, actively resisted educating the teeming black masses, who only a generation before had been released from bondage. The thought of even a negligible portion of their taxes being devoted to building black schoolhouses so infuriated many whites that they refused to approve *any* school taxes, strangling blacks' education even at the expense of their own children's. Whites worked to deny blacks education for at least two reasons. First, whites knew that if blacks were granted access to the world of learning, it would be difficult to exploit them as a cheap labor source. "Educate a nigger and you spoil a good field hand," the old saying went. Education would expand blacks' horizons; it would give them access to stable jobs, money, maybe even positions of power; it would, in short, allow them to seek out a livelihood other than the menial one they were forced to accept under sharecropping and other exploitative systems.[12]

Second, if blacks were educated, whites would incur a symbolic cost. Whites, especially poor whites, who constantly sought ways to distinguish themselves from blacks, understood, to quote the famous abolitionist and educational advocate, Horace Mann, that education was "the great equalizer." "The poorer classes of whites," Gunnar Myrdal observed in *An American Dilemma*, "are in competition with Negroes for jobs and for social status. One of the things which demarcates them as superior and increases the future potentialities of their children is the fact that white children in publicly supported school buses are taken to fine consolidated schools while often Negro children are given only what amounts to a sham education in dilapidated one-room schools or old Negro churches by underpaid, badly trained Negro teachers."[13]

As a result of whites' enduring and muscular opposition to educating blacks, "the question was not so much what kind of education blacks were going to receive but whether they would receive any education at all."[14] Recognizing the precarious state of black education, an African-American reformer by the name of **Booker T. Washington**, whom we met briefly in Chapter 4, offered whites a compromise. Born in a rundown Virginia shack to a slave mother and a white father he never knew, Washington climbed the rungs of the social ladder, becoming his era's most powerful black leader. His breakout moment came in 1895, when he delivered a famous speech at the Atlanta Cotton States and Industrial Exposition, his "Atlanta Compromise," as it came to be known. In this speech, Washington made two concessions. The first was that allowing blacks full access to political power, the fundamental idea of Reconstruction, had been a mistake; the second was that blacks did not strive to be equal to whites. He advised blacks to dedicate themselves to working hard, even in the lowest sectors of society, instead of fighting for equal rights. In turn, he asked whites to treat blacks fairly. The races, said Washington, were to be separate but cooperative: "In all things that are purely social we can be as separate as the fingers, yet as one hand in all things essential to mutual progress."[15]

Educating blacks, argued Washington, was not something whites should fear, for black education would not concern itself with creating black professors, doctors, and lawyers but would seek to develop better trained workers: skilled field hands, manual laborers, and domestic servants. Washington's compromise rang beautifully in whites' ears, and they rewarded him in kind by providing him with the philanthropic support and political backing necessary to institute his program of **"industrial education,"** which he did in earnest at Tuskegee

Institute, an all-black school he founded in 1880. Industrial education amounted to vocational training, as Washington—a man who pulled himself "up from slavery," as he liked to boast—believed that the solution to "the race problem" was for blacks to accept their dominated position and to work hard in jobs reserved for them.[16]

As soon as it was introduced, the doctrine of industrial education came under attack from black leaders. Many believed that Washington's program served racial domination and legitimized an unjust educational system, where whites received the best training while blacks were prepared for tedious and backbreaking work—slavery in new guise. Others pointed out the growing inequality between white and black schools. For example, blacks in North Carolina received 28% of school funds in 1900 but only 13% in 1915; their funding plummeted during Washington's prime. Still others worried about the psychological damage Washington was inflicting on the minds of black youth by, essentially, teaching them to accept white society's message about their inferiority.[17]

One of Washington's most outspoken critics was **W. E. B. Du Bois,** a thinker we have quoted on multiple occasions in earlier chapters. The first African American to graduate with a Ph.D. from Harvard, Du Bois was a scholar of deep erudition and passion, a prolific writer, who published works of history, sociology, poetry, and fiction, and a tireless political activist, who cofounded the NAACP and edited its magazine, *The Crisis.* An intellectual's intellectual, one who took great pleasure and inspiration from philosophy and literature, Du Bois believed that blacks were entitled to much more than what Washington's humble industrial education offered. He believed that black education should be no different from white education. In *The Souls of Black Folk,* Du Bois wrote, "Shall we teach them trades, or train them in liberal arts? Neither and both: teach the workers to work and the thinkers to think; make carpenters of carpenters, and philosophers of philosophers, and fops of fools."[18] By denying blacks access to higher learning, Washington was closing the black mind, robbing his students of the beauty of Blake or the brilliance of Hegel. Du Bois himself took great comfort in the fact that the life of the mind was not bound by color. "I sit with Shakespeare and he winces not," he once wrote. "Across the color-line I move arm in arm with Balzac and Dumas, where smiling men and welcoming women glide in gilded halls."[19]

Du Bois also chastised Washington for perpetuating a kind of symbolic violence, for failing to criticize white supremacy. "Mr. Washington represents in Negro thought the old attitude of adjustment and submission. . . . His doctrine has tended to make the whites, North and South, shift the burden of the Negro problem to the Negro's shoulders and stand aside as critical and rather pessimistic spectators; when in fact the burden belongs to the nation, and the hands of none of us are clean if we bend not our energies to righting these wrongs."[20]

To Du Bois, blacks would never arrive at freedom by toiling quietly in the lowliest parts of a society. Rather, the brightest and most talented members of the race— **"the talented tenth,"** he liked to call them—should educate themselves in order to uplift all blacks. "I freely acknowledge that it is possible, and sometimes best," argued Du Bois, "that a partially underdeveloped people should be ruled by the best of their stronger and better neighbors for their own good."[21]

Today, Washington's platform strikes many of us as inadequate. But we must remember the racial context in which he worked and recognize, too, that the words he uttered to white folks (especially those with deep pockets) most likely reflected a political strategy rather than his true feelings. After all, the students of Tuskegee Institute not only learned to work; they also learned to read. Washington accommodated white supremacy to save black education. Du Bois, however, refused to grant racial domination any such accommodation. Thus, the state of black education at the beginning of the twentieth century was defined by two opposing camps—industrial education and equal education—championed by two powerful black leaders.

Looking back, neither program provided the struggling black masses a means to organize against racial domination. Washington preached submission while Du Bois, who very much believed in fighting against injustice, advanced a program that was rather elitist in nature. All the while, African Americans were hungry for full access to education. Wrote one commentator at the time: "The eagerness of the coloured people for a chance to send their children to school is something astonishing and pathetic. They will submit to all sorts of inconveniences in order that their children may get education."[22] With the dawning of the Civil Rights Movement, blacks' yearning for education would be more fully realized.

"Separate Is Not Equal": School Desegregation

Both those striving to overthrow white supremacy and those struggling to uphold it recognized in education the potential to spark political protest. Of Northern capitalists funding black education in the South, one Southern Senator bemoaned, "What the North is sending South is not money but dynamite; this education is ruining our Negroes! They're demanding equality."[23] Education, thought many whites, threatened their way of life—and they were right. As nonwhite education coughed and sputtered along—teachers making due with beat-up and outdated textbooks, holding class in dilapidated and, of course, segregated, schoolhouses—voices of resistance began to ring out. A spirit of protest, one born during the earliest days of colonialism and the slave trade, was educated and given a voice loud and clear. "Education is the kindling of a flame," as Socrates had noted long ago.

Beginning in the 1930s, the NAACP launched an aggressive campaign against legalized segregation. Led by a forward-thinking and sharp-minded lawyer named Thurgood Marshall (who, as we know, would later become the first African American to sit on the Supreme Court), the NAACP won several legal victories. In the 1936 case *Murray v. Maryland,* Marshall successfully argued that the University of Maryland School of Law's practice of turning away black applications was unconstitutional and that black law schools did not offer the same resources as white ones. And in 1950, the U.S. Supreme Court ruled in favor of the NAACP in *Sweat v. Painter,* finding striking inequalities between the all-white University of Texas School of Law and law schools in Texas reserved for African Americans.[24]

Other organizations, too, would join the fight. In 1945, the League of United Latin American Citizens came to the aid of five families who, in **Mendez v. Westminster School District,** challenged the segregation of Mexican-American students in California. The U.S. District Court of Los Angeles ruled in favor of the families, and its decision was upheld in 1947 by San Francisco's Ninth District Court of Appeals. *Mendez v. Westminster* allowed Earl Warren—then governor of California and later to become Chief Justice of the U.S. Supreme Court and author of the *Brown v. Board of Education* decision—to sign into law a bill repealing the segregation of all students in the state, including African and Asian Americans. Additionally, the case provided a precedent for *Brown:* not only did a federal court rule that "the segregation of Mexican Americans in public schools was a violation of the state law," but also it impressed on NAACP lawyers the importance of marshalling social-scientific evidence to criticize the segregationists' key idea (and motto): "separate but equal."[25]

Using previous legal victories such as these as the building blocks of a larger case, the NAACP filed several lawsuits on behalf of black parents, whose children were denied entry to white schools throughout the country. In 1952, the Supreme Court agreed to hear five of these cases, consolidated under the lead case's title, **Brown v. Board of Education.** Employing strategies used in *Mendez,* the NAACP marshaled an impressive array of social-scientific evidence challenging the "equal" pillar of the "separate but equal" doctrine. Black and white schools were separate, but they were anything but equal, Thurgood Marshall argued—and the court agreed. In a unanimous decision handed down in 1954, the court ruled on behalf of the NAACP, dismantling the legal basis of racial segregation. "In the field of public education," read Chief Justice Warren, "the doctrine of separate but equal has no place. Separate educational facilities are inherently unequal."[26]

The Supreme Court's decision required segregated schools to be phased out. But instead of matching their strong ruling with equally strong benchmarks and timelines for change, the Court balked, vaguely suggesting that states comply with *Brown* with "all deliberate speed." This gave Southern whites time to mount a defiant backlash against school desegregation. They formed **Citizens Councils** in town after town and went on the offensive. They tried to abolish public education outright and encouraged whites to start private, all-white institutions. Once this unpopular strategy failed, they initiated a set of legislative acts dealing with "public placement." These acts permitted racial integration in theory but made actual integration almost impossible by erecting a maze of bureaucratic requirements and procedures through which nonwhite students had to navigate if they hoped to transfer to white schools. And, finally, Citizens Councils lobbied state legislatures to take down the NAACP, a strategy that was enormously effective, as we learned in Chapter 3.[27] Frustrated by the poor enforcement of *Brown,* a decision "heeded with all deliberate delay," Martin Luther King, Jr., would write, "The phrase 'all deliberate speed' did not mean that another century should be allowed to unfold before we release the Negro children from the narrow pigeonhole of the segregated schools; it meant that, giving some courtesy and consideration to the need for softening old attitudes and outdated customs, democracy must press ahead out of the past of ignorance and intolerance, and into the present of educational opportunity and moral freedom."[28]

And press ahead it did. In the face of white hostility, nonwhites persisted and, as in much of the Civil Rights Movement, change was carried forward on the shoulders of the youth. Nonwhite students across the nation gathered their courage and stepped into formerly white-only schools filled with hostile students, bitter teachers, and unforgiving principles. Among them were nine black teenagers selected by the NAACP (on account of their impressive academic records) to desegregate Little Rock Central High. Members of the Arkansas Citizens Council lined up and blocked the entrance, an act supported by the state's governor, Orval Faubus, who deployed the National Guard to aid the segregationists. This state-sponsored defiance of *Brown* emboldened whites, who formed mobs to intimidate black students attempting to integrate. The **Little Rock Nine**, as they came to be known, were able to set foot in Central High only when President Eisenhower provided them with an armed military escort, the 101st Airborne.[29] What followed was a year of terror for the Little Rock Nine, one defined by ongoing verbal and physical attacks, including acid being thrown in the face of fifteen-year-old Melba Patillo Beals, a brutal encounter Beals has recorded in her memoir, *Warriors Don't Cry.*[30]

School integration came slowly to the nation and more slowly still to the South. By one estimate, substantial integration did not occur in the South until ten to fifteen years after *Brown.*[31] But change did come. By 1975, the percentage of black children attending all-black schools in the South had dropped to 18%, and nearly half the black children of that region were enrolled in majority-white

Percentage of Black Students in Majority White Southern Schools, 1954–2003

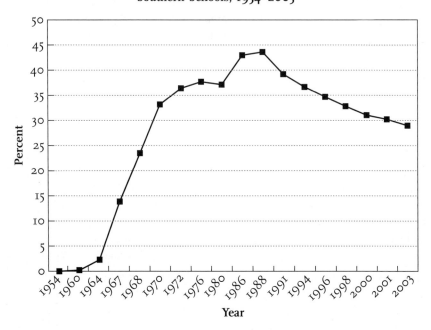

schools. These are impressive numbers by any measure, considering that just twenty years earlier, schools had been rigidly segregated.[32] That said, *Brown* did not, contrary to popular belief, plunge a stake in the heart of legal segregation; what it did was to outlaw the legal discrimination that was practiced in schools and universities. In fact, certain cases after 1954 actually legitimized and legalized segregation.

Because courts understood racial segregation as matter of discrimination (for example, where qualified nonwhite applicants are turned away strictly on the basis of their race), they failed fully to grasp the complexity of the problem and, therefore, did not develop effective and enduring desegregation initiatives. Operating under the individualistic fallacy, the courts outlawed intentional school segregation but not school segregation caused by systemic racial domination operating in other realms of social life—most consequentially, the residential field. This was most clearly seen in the 1974 case, *Millikin v. Bradley,* in which a divided U.S. Supreme Court ruled that integrating schools by busing students between the black inner city and the white suburbs was unacceptable and not mandated by *Brown*, since schools forced to participate had not violated the law by actively discriminating against students. The Court ruled, in other words, that racial school segregation attributed to intentional acts of discrimination was unlawful, but racial school segregation attributed to residential segregation was not.[33] Because America's neighborhoods remain segregated by race, and because school segregation is a direct reflection of residential segregation—you attend school wherever you happen to live—our schools today remain separate and unequal.

Whiteness in Education

Whiteness, as you might recall from our introductory chapter, is racial domination normalized. How, then, is racial domination normalized in the educational field? Where does whiteness lurk in our curriculum, classrooms, and campuses? This section takes up these questions, focusing on how certain racialized practices and bodies of knowledge camouflage themselves under the guise of normalcy. In doing so, it focuses primarily on college education, although the points advanced in the following pages certainly are applicable at the primary and secondary levels. (The noticeable *lack* of critical engagement with racial domination in elementary and high school classrooms itself is evidence that whiteness thrives in these arenas.) We have decided to focus on college education in order to highlight the world in which you are now a part and to help you critically to evaluate your classes, dorm rooms, and sorority parties with a fine-tuned sociological imagination, ferreting out racial domination wherever it may lie.

Whiteness in the Curriculum

Du Bois was an ardent critic of the many ways in which whiteness blunts scientific progress and distorts truths about the world. After reviewing the history of Reconstruction during the early twentieth century, Du Bois concluded that the literature on slavery and its fall, books and articles penned by white (male) authors, functioned "for our pleasure and amusement, for inflating our national ego, and giving us a false but pleasurable sense of accomplishment. . . . With a determination unparalleled in science, the mass of American writers have started out so to distort the facts of the greatest critical period of American history as to prove right wrong and wrong right." They did this, Du Bois continued, by bending historical facts to accommodate racial domination, so much so, in fact, that history became nothing more than propaganda for white supremacy. "The historian has no right, posing as scientist, to conceal or distort facts. . . . [He produces a work that] paints perfect men and noble nations, but it does not tell the truth."[34] As Du Bois feared, the distortions promoted by historians made their way into state-approved textbooks that justified slavery, criticized Reconstruction, and mourned the fall of the South, books that circulated well into the 1950s.[35]

Much has changed since Du Bois's time, but we still can detect the residue of racial domination within **Eurocentric historical accounts.** Such accounts consider the stories and experiences of Americans of European descent central to our knowledge of American history, while marginalizing the stories and experiences of non-European Americans. Thus fundamental to the historical account of the birth of the United States is the signing of the Declaration of Independence (but not the governance of the Iroquois Nation, from which many principles of democracy were borrowed by American statesmen); Abraham Lincoln's Emancipation Proclamation (but not slave revolts, led by insurgents such as Nat Turner); and the labor of white meatpackers, brewers, and stealers (but not that of Asian-American railroad workers, miners, and farmers).

Whiteness casts America as a white nation with a white history and blinds us to the ways in which nonwhite groups contributed to the development of the United States.[36] An accurate and comprehensive American history is thoroughly multiracial—hence the absurdity of shelving a book on the United Farm Workers under "Chicano Studies" but one on the Mexican-American War under "U.S. History." The history of immigration remains incomplete without a detailed account of how throngs of workers from China, Japan, and Southeast Asia crossed the Pacific and joined America's citizenry. The history of the Civil War is unfinished without a discussion of African-American soldiers, as would be a historical account of World War II that ignored the vital role of Navajo code talkers. When we search for the essence of modern American culture and practices, we find it in the nation's rich history of racial and ethnic diversity. American Indians taught European settlers how to cultivate corn and tomatoes, and the modern (and quintessentially American) word "okay" is derived from the Choctaw "oke," meaning "it is so." Blacks gave America jazz and blues; a Jewish immigrant by the name of Irving Berlin wrote "God Bless America." American cowboys learned how to herd cattle from Mexican *vaqueros*, adopting, too, the latter's style of dress (the cowboy hat is a variant of the sombrero) and language ("lasso" comes from *lazo*, "stampede" from *estampida*).[37] Multicultural American history notices these things. It casts a backward glance at American history and sees the nation in all its complex diversity: a panoply of people from all points of the globe toiling and suffering and persevering, each fully belonging to our past and present.

Eurocentric history not only silences the voices of nonwhites, it also tends to dull the sharp edge of past injustices. One need only read one of the many books on the Civil War published each year to discover how some historians gloss over the hell that was slavery, preferring to entertain a nostalgia for the South's "good old days"; one need only peruse one of the hundreds of books on American immigration to learn much of "immigrant gumption, hard work, and determination" and little of anti-immigrant violence and discrimination.[38] The fact that more Americans know of Martin Luther King, Jr., than of Emmett Till, or of

Thanksgiving dinner between pilgrims and Native Americans than of the Indian Wars, speaks to how whiteness in our historical imagination considers past wrongs something to be "forgotten, distorted, skimmed over."[39]

History is not the only discipline distorted by whiteness. Consider how whiteness informs the field of literature. Until very recently, the Western literary canon—the collection of works consecrated as "classics"—comprised almost entirely works by white men. Although works by white authors largely were considered universal, able to capture the experiences of all people, many works by nonwhites were considered works only for nonwhites. Indeed, the traditional English canon is so white that surveys have found that the push for multicultural curriculum has affected English literature more than any other field.[40] Today the battle still rages. Some scholars bar the entry of works by nonwhites into the canon, while others vie for their inclusion, arguing that literature cannot hope fully to reflect American life without the inclusion of voices echoing up from the "abused and scorned" corners of society.

An analysis of literary works themselves reveals that many white writers, of today and of past generations, normalize whiteness by treating white characters as de-racialized women and men and nonwhite characters as racially marked.[41] In *Playing in the Dark: Whiteness and the Literary Imagination,* Toni Morrison explores whiteness and the "racialized other" in the literary imagination, demonstrating how a fictionalized, nonwhite presence was essential to novelists' and poets' understanding of Americanness. She demonstrates how writers have depicted blacks as savage and dimwitted to create an image of whiteness as essentially civilized and intelligent—that is, as blackness's mirror image. It is only through Mark Twain's enslavement of Jim, a black slave, that Huck Finn is able to experience freedom. Ernest Hemingway makes white women pure and beautiful by depicting black women as predatory and inhuman, as in this passage from his *To Have and Have Not,* when Marie, a white woman, asks her lover:

> "Listen, did you ever do it with a nigger wench?"
> "Sure."
> "What's it like?"
> "Like nurse shark."[42]

Morrison's key insight is that many white American poets and novelists, who sit comfortably in today's canon and are read by thousands, glorified whiteness and denigrated blackness in their literary works; blackness was sullied to make whiteness shine clean and unblemished. "Africanism," she writes, "is the vehicle by which the American self knows itself as not enslaved, but free; not repulsive, but desirable; not helpless, but licensed and powerful; not history-less, but historical; not damned, but innocent; not a blind accident of evolution, but a progressive fulfillment of destiny. . . . The contemplation of this black presence is central to any understanding of our national literature and should not be permitted to hover at the margins of the literary imagination."[43]

Consider, too, how whiteness affects anthropology. The anthropologist's method—ethnography, the practice of embedding oneself in a foreign culture so as to learn about it—has helped to normalize whiteness. America's nonwhite groups traditionally have been treated as objects of study, as exotic cultures within our nation, worthy of observation and scrutiny. White communities, in contrast, communities from which many anthropologists come, have been considered uninteresting and domestic—in a word, normal. Anthropologists have treated Native-American communities as especially important settings for research. One can search the library to find hundreds of anthropological books on tribal communities. In many of these books, Native Americans are treated as vestiges of a bygone era, as "genuine" only if they uphold their ancestors' cultural practices and lifestyles. Of anthropologists, Vine Deloria, Jr., has observed, "Indians must be redefined in terms that white men will accept, even if that means re-Indianizing them according to a white man's idea of what they were like in the past and should logically become in the future. . . . [But] would [a school board] submit to a group of Indians coming to Boston and telling [Bostonians] what a modern Irishman was like? Expecting them to dress in green and hunt leprechauns so as to live on the leprechaun's hidden gold would hardly provide a meaningful path for the future."[44]

Whiteness even can be found in progressive intellectual movements, like feminism. Women of color feminists, for example, long have criticized the mainstream women's movement for claiming to speak for "all women" while ignoring the unique struggles of women of color. A defining characteristic of feminist discourse, women of color feminists have argued, is the assumption that all women experience the same troubles, regardless of race, class, or sexuality. However, to fully understand and combat sexism, we must explore how it intersects, and feeds on, other systems of domination, those grounded in racial difference, economic inequality, and heterosexism, for example. As Chandra Mohanty has noted in *Feminism without Borders,* mainstream feminist scholarship that fails to reflect on the ways whiteness influences its thought "inadvertently produces Western women as the only legitimate subjects of struggle, while Third World women are heard as fragmented, inarticulate voices in (and from) the dark."[45]

Recently, nonwhite and white scholars alike have taken steps to expose whiteness in our intellectual thought. And their efforts have yielded impressive results. Historians have produced some of the most influential works on whiteness, not to mention critical accounts of civil rights movements. Literary critics have advanced our thinking on racial domination as well; today some of the most carefully discussed and analyzed writers are women and men of color. Anthropologists, too, have subjected their traditions to careful scrutiny, criticizing established works influenced by racist or colonial modes of thought, and have been at the forefront of efforts to denounce racist scientific practices. And the influence of women of color feminists on the women's movement, and feminist scholarship in general, cannot be overemphasized. Because of the hard work of student and academic activists, many colleges around the nation house Ethnic, African-American, Chicano, Native-American, and Asian-American Studies departments. Certain canons, whose places of honor previously were reserved for white authors, have widened; nearly every university in the country has come to profess the value of multicultural education; and many have taken effective steps to promote racial diversity within their student bodies.

We should be greatly encouraged by the progress that has been made in our colleges and universities. But we also must remain vigilant, continually questioning how whiteness pervades our curriculum, from preschool to graduate school, in order to exorcise it from our scholarship and, thereby, to gain a firmer grasp on the truth.[46] The goal, to quote Mohanty once more, is to "decolonize our disciplinary and pedagogical practices" so that "education becomes the practice of liberation."[47] This requires paying special attention to how texts treat (or refuse even to talk about) race, how authors write primarily to a white audience, how scientists use metaphors that draw on the white (and male) experience, how philosophers flatten different racialized histories and struggles under the umbrella of "universal humanity," how intellectual accomplishments of Europeans, who rose to prominence in an age of violent racial domination, are still considered the standard against which all works must be measured, and so forth. It requires, in short, a critical eye trained on instances when racial domination is normalized and a sociological imagination poised to purge the Eurocentric vision from our thought.

Whiteness on College Campuses

Leaving family and hometown to attend college can be a painful and frightening experience, especially for first-generation college students and those from small towns or religious communities.[48] The transition to college can be doubly trying for students of color attending majority-white colleges or universities.[49] White students from rural America often view the college town as the most diverse place they have lived, whereas students of color from cities with sizeable non-white populations often view the same town as the whitest place they have lived. Many students of color feel unwelcome, isolated, and bereft of community on predominately white campuses—and experience a significant culture shock during their first year. For their part, white students, studies have shown, often feel uncomfortable around their nonwhite peers, a sentiment that can cause them to avoid interacting with students of color or, in some cases, to treat them with hostility.[50] A survey of students at a large Midwestern university discovered that two-thirds of students of color saw race relations as a serious problem on campus, but less than half of polled white students agreed with them. The same survey found that 16% of students of color reported being the victim of discrimination or racial harassment during the last year. Nationwide, one in four students of color report being victimized by racially motivated verbal or physical attacks sometime during their college careers.[51]

Universities often prioritize certain groups' history, culture, and needs over others. For instance, because most universities do not honor Jewish holidays, many Jewish students who wish to attend religious services are forced to miss class during Yom Kippur and other holy days during the Jewish High Holidays. And Jewish students who wish to remain kosher usually have to find their meals someplace other than the convenient cafeteria frequented by their non-Jewish peers.[52] Native Americans attending universities with Indian mascots, such as the University of Illinois (Fighting Illini), Florida State University (Seminoles), University of Utah (Utes), Southeastern Oklahoma (Savages), or Carthage College (Redmen), must put up with humiliating and contorted caricatures of Native Americans. Some colleges cancel classes in honor of Martin Luther King Day, but others refuse. "In this multicultural society, it's impossible to honor everyone's holidays," one might say. That may be true, but at the very least, we should pay attention to whose culture and traditions are honored by our universities and whose are brushed aside.

Some of you may already have picked up on certain ways whiteness helps guide your classroom discussions, especially those about race. Think about the class for which you are reading this book. In your classroom conversations, which students talk with confidence and which keep quiet? If your classroom is like others around the nation, then most likely there is a group of nonwhite students who do a good deal of the talking and a contingent of white students who don't seem to have much to say. On one end of the classroom, there sit the students of color, who carry the conversation; on the other end, there sit the white students, who observe quietly.[53] Why is this, and what does it do to the racial order?

While many nonwhite students grew up talking about race, many white students did not. Accordingly, white students sometimes find themselves uncomfortable in classroom discussions about race, fearing they will say something ignorant or offensive and hear it from their peers. Other times, white students, immersed in their assumed racelessness, are surprised to learn that they, too, can be the objects of stereotypes and narrow thinking. That is, white students do not find it hard to believe that other whites are raised to believe Latin Americans are overly emotional. However, many have a harder time facing up to the fact that some Latin Americans are raised to think whites are wicked and backstabbing. Reflecting

Native Americans attending universities with Indian mascots must put up with humiliating and contorted caricatures of Native Americans.

on her teaching experiences, educator bell hooks has written, "White students respond with disbelief, shock, and rage, as they listen to black students talk about whiteness, when they are compelled to hear observations, stereotypes, etc., that are offered as 'data' gleaned from close scrutiny and study."[54]

In many classrooms, nonwhite students are dubbed as (or, sometimes, dub themselves) the "real experts" on racism, as if whites—whose ancestors literally *invented* race—had nothing to do with it. This bias is manifest most obviously (and offensively) when a white professor asks a nonwhite student to speak for all members of his or her racial or ethnic group. "Samir, tell us," the professor might say. "How do Arab Americans feel about the war on terrorism?" If Samir is feeling feisty, he might reply, "I don't know. Why don't you go and ask America's 3.5 million citizens of Arab descent? I can, however, tell you what *I* think." Only whiteness allows the professor to pose such a question, to ask Samir to act as the voice of "his people," as if Arab Americans had but one voice, unified on every issue. A white student would never be asked to speak on behalf of all white students.

Research has shown that students of color receive differential treatment during their college careers, treatment that can have negative effects on their academic records. Educators asked to evaluate similarly performing white and nonwhite students often give nonwhite students lower marks. In one experiment, teachers were asked to examine the definitions students attached to words and to evaluate those students' verbal skills. Researchers did not vary the definitions but did vary the race of the students. Rating identical definitions, teachers attached poorer grades to black students.[55] Studies such as this (and many others with similar findings) suggest that, to use the language of economics, nonwhite students do not receive the same "returns" for their academic "investments," relative to their white peers. A Native-American student with the same ability and work ethic as a white student might be seen by the professor—the latter's thinking blurred (perhaps without his knowledge) by racial domination—as the less intelligent of the pair.

The situation is all the more unfair to women of color, because sexism often clouds educators' judgment of female students' potential. Many studies have found that educators view women as less intelligent than men. One experiment, for example, distributed résumés of young psychologists to established psychologists. Like the verbal skill experiment, the résumés were identical except that some were assigned male names, others female names. Overwhelmingly, the psychologists evaluated the male résumés more favorably.[56] Findings such as these should unnerve us, because they suggest that some people running postsecondary institutions, like the one you are attending now, still do not think nonwhites (and women) fully belong.

Whiteness not only informs classroom dynamics and academic evaluations, it also can be found in other aspects of college life. Many college students find dorm life to be stressful and uncomfortable, but the situation is intensified for nonwhite students in dorms with very few members of their ethnic or racial group. A black student skimming her college newspaper might run across lines such as these (which were printed in a column that appeared in the University of Wisconsin's student-run newspaper after the O. J. Simpson trial came to an end): "To believe that one cop led a multi-million dollar plot to execute or lock up one nigger (oops did I say nigger? . . .) is completely ludicrous."[57] A young Puerto Rican might be asked repeatedly on what sports teams he plays. A Hispanic student from the big city might be asked if she grew up in the projects. An Asian-American student struggling through his chemistry class might be told that Asians are supposed to be good at science. A Native-American student might join her friends at a Halloween party only to find that one partygoer is dressed like an "Indian" and talking in fragmented, half-English sentences, mimicking American Indian characters in old Western movies.

Indeed, an entire book could be written on how racial domination, stealthy and veiled during most days of the year, suddenly bursts confidently and clumsily to the surface in full view and ugly form on Halloween night and during other masquerade events. In 2007, white students attending California's Santa Clara University hosted a "South of the Border" party and dressed up as Hispanic janitors, gardeners, and pregnant teenagers. That same year, white students at Clemson University in Connecticut threw a "gangsta party," where white students dressed in blackface, drank 40 ounces, and spoke "black English."[58] Incidents such as these only widen the space between students of color and the larger (majority-white) student body, and they often make nonwhite students yearn for their community back home.[59]

And, as we have mentioned before, hate crimes are not uncommon occurrences on college campuses. According to one FBI report, half of all surveyed college and universities documented on-campus hate crimes during the previous year.[60] Recently, a white college student harassed three Jewish students attending a small college in Massachusetts, threatening to kill one of them and sending all of them photographs of Holocaust victims as a "reminder of what happened to [their] relatives." A former student of the University of California—Irvine sent nearly sixty students of Asian descent a threatening e-mail, chocked full of racial slurs. Three white students attending a Maine university left a sinister message on a black student's answering machine. "I wonder what you're gonna look like dead?" the message said. "Dead. I wonder if, when you die, you'll lose your color."[61] College campuses, revered for centuries as bastions of tolerance, understanding, and freedom, have not yet shaken loose the cords of racial domination.

And yet, college campuses precisely are where some of the best antiracist work is being carried on. For every unreflexive professor who asks a student to speak for her or his racial group, there are dozens of others who would never do such a thing. For every student who commits a racist hate crime on campus, there are dozens of antiracists who demonstrate against such events. If antiracist activism has slowed around the world in other fields of life, it seems in the last ten years or so to have proliferated on college campuses, thanks in large part to the leadership of students of color, the commitment of white and nonwhite antiracists, and the forging of multiracial alliances. Ms. Baker would be proud: "The tribe increases. . . . The struggle is eternal. Somebody else carries on."[62]

Educational Inequality

Compared to whites and Asians, blacks are more likely, and Hispanics and Native Americans *much* more likely, to drop out of high school. According to one study, only 14% of Asians and 17% of whites drop out of high school, compared to 24% of blacks, 26% of Puerto Ricans, 28% of Mexican Americans, and 29% of Native Americans. Another study found that, of adults between the ages of 16 and 24, 7% of whites and 13% of blacks were high school dropouts. That percentage jumped to 29% for Hispanics. Perhaps most disconcerting of all is the fact that, unlike other racial and ethnic groups, the *majority* of Hispanics do not graduate from high school.[66]

When it comes to applying to college, research has found that Asian, white, and black high school seniors are far more likely to submit applications than

Hispanic seniors. According to one study, only 47% of surveyed Hispanic seniors submitted an application, and a quarter of those, a group that included many high-achieving students, applied only to one college. Only 22% of Hispanics between the ages of 18 to 24 enrolled in college in 2000, compared to 39% of whites and 31% of blacks in this age bracket. Asians, in contrast, have very high rates of college enrollment, with 50% of adults aged 26–35 having received some college education—a full 20 percentage points above Native Americans and blacks.[67] Most Hispanics who enroll in college attend community and two-year colleges, not selective four-year universities. Hispanic students who do attend four-year universities are less likely to attend prestigious institutions, relative to Asian and white students; and those select few who enroll in four-year universities are more likely to drop out after their first year, with an attrition rate of 34%, a rate that far outpaces those of blacks (29%), whites (25%), and Asians (14%).[68]

College completion rates show equally alarming patterns. In 1980, only 8% of college graduates were Hispanic, and that percentage rose a mere two points by 2000, a paltry increase given the rapid demographic growth of Hispanic youth over the last two decades. In fact, Hispanic college attendance remains, as it did nearly forty years ago, the lowest in the country in relation to non-Hispanic whites, blacks, and Asians.[69] According to the National Center for Education Statistics, the proportion of Hispanic students graduating from college has not increased since 1990, despite the growth of Hispanics within the United States; as such, whites are over three times, and blacks nearly two times, as likely to complete college as Hispanics. By one estimate, while 49% of Asians, 30% of whites, and 16% of blacks enrolled in kindergarten today will grow up to earn a bachelor's degree, only 6% of Hispanics will obtain the same level of schooling.[70]

Importantly, there is also considerable variation within racial groups with respect to educational attainment and achievement. Research has concluded that Mexican Americans score lower on standardized tests, possess lower educational aspirations and expectations, and complete college at lower rates than do Cubans, Dominicans, or Puerto Ricans. Southeast Asians and Pacific Islanders lag behind their Korean, Japanese, Indian, and Chinese peers in all measures of educational success—a fact often lost on policy makers and school administrators, who tend to ignore disadvantaged Asian groups while implementing programs addressing racial inequalities. Gender differences persist as well, with women graduating from college at higher rates than men (accounting for nearly 60% of all awarded degrees). Black women, in particular, have made impressive strides in the educational field in the last twenty years, and today, they have more ambitious educational aspirations, graduate from college at higher rates, and earn higher marks than black men, a trend with enormous ramifications for African-American culture. By contrast, Mexican-American women, especially first-generation Americans, are among the nation's most undereducated groups.[71]

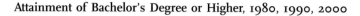

Attainment of Bachelor's Degree or Higher, 1980, 1990, 2000

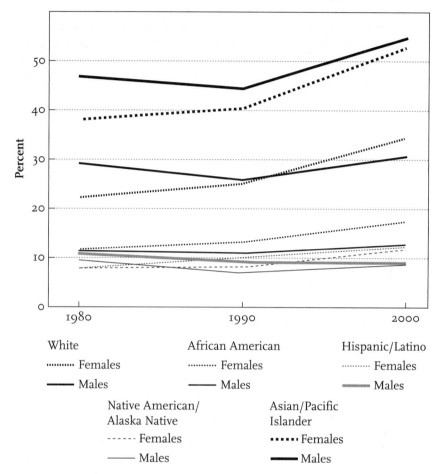

Even after accounting for these intraracial and gender differences, we still can accurately observe that in a nation where you can be confident that your financial prosperity, familial stability, and physical vitality will increase with educational attainment, blacks, Native Americans, and Hispanics lag considerably behind Asians and whites. In many ways, Hispanics—and Mexican Americans, in particular—who make up no less than one-fifth of U.S. public school students, seem to be falling through the cracks even as they are rising, *en masse,* at a population pace that is fundamentally altering the American landscape.[72]

What explains racial inequalities in education? "Poverty and the unequal distribution of wealth," you reply, offering an answer accurate and powerful. Indeed, economic inequality and educational inequality are wound tightly together, such that one helps determine the other and vice versa. Studies have shown that students with highly educated and wealthy parents are advantaged in the educational realm as compared to peers whose parents have little education and wealth. And, in many cases, racial disparities in education shrink considerably once researchers account for economic inequality. Thus, if Asian and white students outpace their Hispanic, black, and Native American peers, it is in part because the former tend to have parents with deeper pockets and more education. Parents' financial assets help students pay for school supplies, computers, field trips, private tutors, college tuition, and a whole gamut of things that constitute the ticket price of a solid education. (For example, only 20% of Hispanic students have more than one computer at home, compared to 27% of blacks, 42% of Asians, and 57% of whites.[73])

It is not that black and Hispanic parents invest less in their children's education relative to other groups. Research has shown that, after taking income differences into account, biracial, black, and Hispanic parents are just as likely (sometimes more likely) to save for their children's college education as are white parents.[74] It is that, because of racialized economic inequality, black and Hispanic parents have fewer resources to invest. The role of economic inequality in explaining racial disparities in education cannot be underestimated.[75] The economic explanation, however, is not the only one supported by research. And since we already have devoted an early chapter to explaining racialized economic inequality, we now focus on three other explanations that help us understand racial inequality in education, explanations that center on the family, culture, and schools.

Before we begin, we must remind ourselves that structural and historical forces, including economic domination, condition familial, cultural, and school-based practices. Sometimes one hears it said, "It isn't structure; it's culture," or vice versa. We believe that artificially divorcing structural explanations from cultural ones in the study of educational inequality—or of any other social problem—is thoroughly misguided, because it fails to appreciate the complexity of our social world.

The Role of the Family

A family can provide students not only with material resources but also with immaterial resources that help them get ahead in school. How do parents pass along to their children non-economic resources—skills, beliefs, knowledge, dispositions, network contacts—that advantage them in the educational field? And how might that help us better understand racial inequality?

Cultural Capital. If we refer to parents' financial resources as "economic capital," we can also refer to the degree to which they introduce their children to cultural information and practices that will advantage them later in life as "cultural capital." Your knowledge of cultural material (such as classical music or French Impressionism) and cultural practices (such as how to dress properly for a dinner party or how to sound confident and smart when discussing politics) can greatly benefit you in the educational realm. Just as one type of currency can be exchanged for another—dollars for Euros, yen for pesos—cultural knowledge can be exchanged for educational achievement (graduating from an elite school) or economic advancement (landing a dream job). In shorthand: cultural capital can be exchanged for educational capital or economic capital. **Cultural capital,** therefore, can be defined as the sum total of one's knowledge of established and revered cultural activities and practices.[76]

We say "established and revered cultural activities and practices," because not all cultural knowledge behaves as capital. You can be the foremost expert on punk rock and know just how to act at a NOFX concert, but that won't get you very far in college. Your knowledge of Greek philosophy and your ability to debate Plato, however, will. Cultural capital, therefore, has mostly to do with one's experience with and understanding of "high-brow" culture, such as opera, art, classical music, and canonical literature; it also has to do with one's facility in spoken and written English.[77]

Our ideas of how cultural capital contributes to social inclusion and exclusion— how social status and advantage get passed down through the generations—are owed in large part to the work of French sociologist Pierre Bourdieu. Bourdieu demonstrated that a person's class background provides her with different degrees of cultural capital, which, in turn, helps her to reproduce her class position. Many people from wealthy homes are endowed, from a very young age, with large amounts of cultural capital—they visit museums, are taught to play the piano, and learn the language and etiquette of the elite class—which allows them to access the upper echelons of society. And if those from more humble origins seem uncomfortable at black tie events or uncertain during classroom debates, it is because, unlike their more well-to-do peers, they have not inherited significant amounts of cultural capital. In Bourdieu's words, "Not only do the most privileged students derive from their background of origin habits, skills, and attitudes which serve them directly in their scholastic tasks, . . . they also inherit from it knowledge and know-how, tastes, and a 'good taste' whose scholastic profitability [and, we might add, profitability beyond the academic world] is no less certain for being indirect. 'Extra-curricular' culture . . . is very unequally distributed among students from different backgrounds, and inequality of income does not suffice to explain the disparities which we find."[78] Taste, then (or cultural capital)—far from being innocent—is a reflection of one's social upbringing. It not only helps one to navigate certain situations and to distinguish between "refined" and "vulgar" conduct; it also marks the person who does the navigating, indicating what sort of a person she is, how "well-groomed" or "well-bred" she might be. In Bourdieu's pithy formulation, one which we invite you to ponder, "Taste classifies, and it classifies the classifier."[79]

As Bourdieu's ideas have spread, researchers have devoted a significant amount of energy to analyzing the diffusion and cultivation of cultural capital. They have found that, even before children are out of diapers, they acquire certain advantages and disadvantages associated with their parents' social standing. Child psychologists Betty Hart and Todd Risley took a hard look at the way parents talk to their young children, and they discovered that middle-class parents direct an average of 487 utterances at their children per hour, whereas parents on welfare direct only 178 utterances per hour. Middle-class parents not only talk to their children more, they also are more encouraging. By age three, the average middle-class child has been offered roughly 500,000 encouragements and 80,000 discouragements. Those numbers are reversed for poor children, who, by age three, have heard roughly 75,000 encouragements and 200,000 discouragements. Hart and Risley went on to demonstrate that how frequently and positively parents converse with their children is tied not only to childhood language competence and intelligence—by age three, the average middle-class child knows 1,110 words and has an IQ of 117, while the average poor child knows only 525 words and has an IQ of 79—but also to subsequent success in school.[80]

Other studies have shown how parents consciously and unconsciously work to nurture within their children certain cultural competences. In her book, *Unequal Childhoods,* sociologist Annette Lareau argues that parenting styles unique to middle-class households better prepare children for success in the academic and business worlds. Working-class parents, she observes, set clear boundaries between adults and children and encourage long stretches of child-initiated play and leisure time, whereas middle-class parents tend to provide their children with several regimented activities (soccer practice, ballet lessons, choir rehearsal) and teach them to regard adults as their equals. The result? Middle-class children obtain a sense of entitlement and confidence, and they quickly learn how to question and challenge adults, qualities that greatly advantage them in the classroom.[81] Thus, "the disadvantages that poverty imposes on children aren't primarily about material goods. The real advantages that middle-class children gain come from more elusive processes: the language that their parents use, the attitudes toward life that they convey."[82]

A child in possession of large amounts of cultural capital becomes endowed with characteristics that encourage academic success, such as structure, openness, discipline, and maturity. She develops a disposition that evokes respect and admiration from teachers and peers—a certain way of standing and sitting, of talking and listening, a class-specific posture and essence. Not only this, but she has a well-tuned sense of informal practices, a certain know-how, that gives her a boost. She has better access to the **"hidden curriculum,"** that collection of unspoken "values, dispositions, social and behavioral expectations . . . essential to satisfactory progression through school."[83] The hidden curriculum comprises anything from knowing how to e-mail your professors to responding in class to a question to which you don't know the answer. A student with a middle-class sense of entitlement feels comfortable challenging her grade on a paper, but a student with a more working-class disposition perhaps thinks, "What you see is what you get."[84] More generally, a student with a great deal of cultural capital is able to be "recognized" by the teacher as someone cut from the same cloth—as "someone just like me"—since most teachers, after all, possess a good amount of cultural capital and are from middle-class backgrounds. It is small wonder, then, that studies have documented a direct correlation between cultural capital and academic achievement (test scores and grades).[85]

Because parents with more schooling and economic capital tend to have more cultural capital, and because white and Asian parents tend to have more schooling and economic capital than do black, Hispanic, and Native American parents, we can begin to understand how the unequal distribution of cultural capital helps to reproduce racial inequalities. However, the story is more complicated than that. It is not only the case that racial privilege is accompanied by economic capital, as we discussed in Chapter 4, and that economic capital begets cultural capital; it is also the case that the consumption of cultural activities varies by race. All families "do culture" in one way or another, but studies have shown that Asian, but especially white, families tend to participate in more activities that foster cultural capital. That is, white families are more likely than nonwhite families to attend classical music concerts and opera, to frequent museums, and to enroll their kids in ballet classes. Such variation remains even after accounting for differences in parental education.[86]

This provokes the question: Who gets to decide which cultural practices and knowledges can be cashed in as "capital" and which cannot? The answer, in brief, is that racial domination gets to decide. (Here we witness the three-way merger of cultural capital, economic capital, and what we might call racial capital—that is, white privilege—or, put simply, how the social order reproduces itself in such a way that those on top—those who occupy privilege posts in cultural, economic, and racial hierarchies—remain on top.) By and large, it is your familiarity with *Eurocentric* art, literature, language, and history that garners cultural capital. Whiteness educates cultural capital, and cultural capital upholds whiteness. Noting this does not make Picasso less brilliant or opera less beautiful. But it should make us appreciate why only specific kinds of cultural knowledge can be "cashed in" for other kinds of capital, such as economic or educational capital, thereby helping to produce racial inequalities in education.

Social Capital.   The family can be a key source of another type of capital as well: **social capital.** If cultural capital has to do with *what* you know, social capital refers to *whom* you know. It is, to paraphrase Bourdieu, the sum of all resources

Familism may be a double-edged sword, advantaging students in some respects while disadvantaging them in others.

one accrues by virtue of being connected to a network of people.[87] **Familism** is a specific variant of social capital having to do with one's attachment to, and reliance on, family-based relationships.[88]

Many researchers have explored the relationship between social capital, especially familism, and educational success. By and large, they have discovered that students benefit greatly from extended family ties. Psychologists have found that familism produces positive psychological effects, while educational scholars argue that familism can mitigate the negative experiences associated with belonging to a dominated racial group.[89] Several studies have documented a positive relationship between social capital and high school and college completion among at-risk youth. Others have noted that as students' social capital increases, so too do their educational aspirations and ambition.[90]

Familism, studies have shown, is an important component of Hispanic culture. Hispanics value interdependence, as well as family support and obligations, more than other racial or ethnic groups; they report higher degrees of familial cohesion and assist family members in instrumental ways to a greater degree than do other racial or ethnic groups; they also live in denser kinship networks than other racial or ethnic groups.[91] After examining how familism affects Hispanic students in school, researchers have documented a positive relationship. High academic performance of Hispanic students has been linked to social capital provided by family networks, as family members help students to complete their homework and to make informed educational decisions.[92]

But familism may also serve as an impediment to students' educational success. American sociologist Alejandro Portes, for example, has pointed out that families with dense network ties—who often place weighty demands on their talented and privileged members and value group conformity—can stifle high-achievers' motivation and accomplishments. Indeed, some researchers have attributed the poor performance of Hispanic students to the unique demands placed on them by their parents, demands that might include caring for their siblings or grandparents or working to help supplement the family income.[93] Others have found that Hispanic parents value the noncognitive and social aspects of intelligence as much as the cognitive and individualistic aspects, a preference that might result in Hispanic youth underperforming in (cognitive and individualistic) educational evaluations. Accordingly, some have found that strong bonds of familistic solidarity are associated with weak test scores and grades.[94]

Social capital—and familism, in particular—may be a double-edged sword with respect to its impact on school performance, advantaging students in some respects while disadvantaging them in others. It goes without saying that social capital works best when combined with other forms of capital. A student well-connected to economically downtrodden and poorly educated family members will benefit less than one connected to a network rich in cultural and economic capital. You know the game. If your uncle graduated from Harvard Business School and remembers his alma mater when donating money, the school's admissions board might take a long, hard look at your application. If your aunt is the CEO of an architecture firm, you might not have to worry about securing a good job after college. People belonging to racial groups that have been, and currently are being, excluded from elite networks might not receive much return from their familistic ties, while white students, connected to networks in which privilege has accumulated over generations, might reap healthy gains. Successful Americans often assure themselves that they "pulled themselves up by their own bootstraps," as the old saying goes. But if we look closer, we usually notice that many hands, at one time or another, have pulled at those bootstraps. How far one can ascend society's staircase of status and power depends, in large part, on whom one knows.

The Role of Culture

"Culture," an elusive concept if there ever was one, has to do with the realm of meaning-making, symbols, and traditions. "Cultural patterns," said the great American anthropologist Clifford Geertz, "provide a template or blueprint for the organization of social psychological processes, much as genetic systems provide such a template for the organization of organic processes. . . . The reason such symbolic templates are necessary is that, as has often been remarked, human behavior is inherently extremely plastic."[95] How, then, does culture affect racial inequalities in education—and how does it not?

The Fallacy of Undifferentiating Difference. Why are some nonwhite groups, such as Asians, excelling in school, while others, like Hispanics, are falling behind? A popular answer to this question is that the "culture" of some racial and ethnic groups facilitates educational failure or success. Some racial groups, the logic goes, have a kind of inherent zeal and respect for education, and this culturally specific disposition gives them an edge in the classroom. In many cases, a racial or ethnic group's success in the educational field is itself accepted as proof of their unique penchant for learning. We should regard this kind of thought with suspicion. As Steven Steinberg has written, "How do we know that some ethnic groups value education more highly? Because they have a superior record of educational attainment. Obviously, it is incorrect to infer values from the outcome, and then to posit these values as causal factors."[96] Just because the New York Yankees have won more World Series championships than any other Major League Baseball team does not mean the Yankees love the game more than the Philadelphia Phillies or the Seattle Mariners. To reason that Asians get good grades because they are an especially studious lot is to commit what psychologists call the "fundamental attribution error," which discounts the importance of structural factors and explains behavior solely on the basis of individuals' personalities.[97]

Let us take a further step back, questioning our question. What do we assume when wondering why one nonwhite group stands out in education when compared to other nonwhite groups? We assume (and erroneously so) that Native Americans, African Americans, Hispanic Americans, and Asian Americans have experienced similar histories of racial oppression—similar modes of exclusion from American society—and are affected in a similar way by institutional and interpersonal racism. A variant of the ahistorical fallacy, we might call this way of thinking **the fallacy of undifferentiating difference,** a fallacy that takes hold of all the extremely diverse histories and social experiences of nonwhite groups and flattens them. It is only after this flattening is executed that one can ask, "Why are Asians outpacing Hispanics and blacks in all measures of educational performance?"

A question that relies on the fallacy of undifferentiating difference is properly addressed only with a response that reverses the fallacy, a response, in other words, that pays attention to social and historical circumstances unique to different nonwhite groups. With respect to the question at hand, we must remember that, historically, certain racial groups were brought to the United States against their will—through the slave trade—or were rendered "minorities" through the workings of colonialism, while others voluntarily migrated here. This distinction between **"involuntary"** and **"voluntary minorities"**—and we note that some racial or ethnic groups fit snugly into neither of these categories—is key to understanding modern-day differences among nonwhite groups. Some have argued that because the relationship between white America and involuntary minorities traditionally has been one of abject domination, involuntary minorities (such as African Americans, Hispanics, and Native Americans) are more leery of the nation's mainstay institutions (like schools and courts) and tend to be less invested in them than voluntary minorities (like Asian and Jewish Americans), whose relationship with America, though not always positive, has never been one of the colonized within a colonizing country, or the slave within a slave society.[98] When we recall that, for years, many schools were designed to "civilize Indians," to strip them of all cultural honor, language, and religion, we may begin to comprehend why some Native-American students are more distrustful of the university than, say, their Asian-American peers.

Additionally, the economic privileges of voluntary minorities, privileges often accrued in immigrants' home countries, translate into other kinds of privileges, including educational success. A significant number of Asian and Jewish immigrants came to America with healthy amounts of economic and cultural capital. They had college degrees and savings accounts and applied for professional jobs. As a result, they were significantly advantaged relative to nonwhite groups that had been systematically excluded from the ranks of the American middle class. According to one estimate, between 1961 and 1977, some 40%–60% of all Asian immigrant workers were educated professionals, as compared to 20%–29% of all other immigrant groups. The vast majority of Chinese Americans serving on Fortune 1000 companies' boards of directors hail from wealthy families in China or Taiwan. And a recent study found that 85% of high-achieving Asian Americans were the children of fathers who had earned graduate degrees.[99] If we resist undifferentiating racial difference, we do not need to scratch our heads over the fact that Asian Americans are outperforming other nonwhite groups. Specific historical and social patterns have predisposed them to do so.

The Stereotype of the Model Minority.   It is indisputable that, by and large, Asian Americans are thriving in the educational field. Although they account for only 3% of the general population, Asian Americans account for over 5% of all college students. Chinese Americans, Indian Americans, and Korean Americans are twice as likely to attend college, compared to whites. As of 2003, 30% of whites held a bachelor's degree or higher, compared to 50% of Asian Americans.[100] Although not all Asian-American ethnic groups are excelling in school—immigrants and refugees from Asian countries, whose parents

Racial Composition of Schools Attended by the Average Student of Each Race, 2003–2004

	Racial Composition of School Attended by Average:				
Percentage Race In Each School	*White Student*	*Black Student*	*Latino Student*	*Asian Student*	*American Indian Student*
% White	78	30	28	45	44
% Black	9	53	12	12	7
% Latino	9	13	55	20	11
% Asian	3	3	5	22	3
% American Indian	1	1	1	1	35
Total	100.0	100.0	100.0	100.0	100.0

SOURCE: Common Core of Data, 2003–2004

Relationship between Segregation by Race and Poverty, 2003–2004

	Percentage Minority Students in Schools									
% Poor in Schools	0–10%	10–20%	20–30%	30–40%	40–50%	50–60%	60–70%	70–80%	80–90%	90–100%
0–10%	32	25	15	13	11	9	12	10	13	17
10–25%	23	25	23	14	8	4	3	2	1	1
25–50%	31	33	37	39	34	27	18	10	7	6
50–100%	15	17	25	35	48	60	67	77	78	76
% of Schools (Total)	40	12	8	6	6	5	4	4	4	10

SOURCE: Common Core of Data, 1991 and 2003

do not speak English, often lag behind their peers in language acquisition, and some Asian-American students, those of Vietnamese, Cambodian, and Pacific Island descent, for example, are disadvantaged with respect to educational attainment[101]—many Asian Americans appear at the head of the class.

Some people have attributed the educational success of Chinese, Indian, Korean, and other Asian-American students to their peer group culture, one that encourages studious behavior and collaborative homework sessions.[102] Others have suggested that Asian-American parents play a key role in imbuing their children with respect for education and a disciplined work ethic. Studies have found that, relative to other racial and ethnic groups, Asian-American parents expect more from their children, invest more resources in their education, and provide them with more structure, exercising strict control over their homework and recreational activities.[103] Standing alone, however, the parenting styles of Asian Americans cannot fully account for their children's academic success. After all, studies have shown that black parents have higher educational expectations for their children than white parents, but white students graduate from college at higher rates.[104] There is something more to the puzzle, and that "something" is the pressure to succeed placed on Asian Americans, not so much by their parents but by a much larger and more powerful force: American society.

Ever since the nineteenth century, white America has regarded its Asian inhabitants as constituting a "model minority." After the Civil War, a Baton Rouge newspaper compared Chinese immigrants to blacks, saying the former "were more obedient and industrious than the negro, work as well without an overseer, and at the same time are more cleanly in their habits." And around the same time a *New York Times* editorial derided Irish immigrants by declaring, "'John Chinaman' was a better addition to [American] society than was 'Paddy.'"[105] The model minority image was reborn after the Civil Rights Movement, when in 1966 William Peterson published an article in *The New York Times Sunday Magazine* entitled "Success Story, Japanese-American Style." "By any criterion of citizenship that we choose," he wrote, "the Japanese Americans are better than any group in our society, including native-born whites." Peterson referred to African Americans and Hispanic Americans, by contrast, as "problem minorities."[106] Peterson's article was widely read and circulated and, since then, Asian Americans have been depicted in the popular press as America's most successful nonwhite group. *Time, Newsweek,* and *Sixty Minutes* have dubbed Asians "model minorities"; *Fortune* magazine has called them "super-minorities"; and *The New Republic* claimed "the triumph of Asians" was "America's greatest success story." Journalists rave that Asian Americans are "winning all the science prizes," "outperforming others at school and work," and even "outwhiting whites."[107]

To think of Asian Americans in terms of the **stereotype of the model minority** is to think of them, first and foremost, as whiz kids, extremely gifted in school (especially when it comes to the more technical disciplines, such as physics, math, and computer science), disciplined beyond their age, geeky and quirky, quiet and polite. If anything, this description seems positive, even flattering. But we must remember—listen close—that there are no such things as "positive" stereotypes. There are only stereotypes, oversimplified ways of thinking that can result in harmful consequences for the people they target. For Asian Americans, the burden to succeed—and not just to succeed, but to ascend to the level of genius—can result in a lose-lose situation. If they succeed—if they claim the coveted science prize or win the spelling bee—some non-Asian Americans may

There are no such things as "positive" stereotypes. There are only stereotypes, oversimplified ways of thinking that can result in harmful consequences for the people they target.

think, "Well, of course they won. They're Asian." But if they lose, many people might think, "Why didn't they win? They're Asian." In both scenarios, Asians Americans' racial attributes take precedence over their personhood, eclipsing their unique personalities, intelligence, and drive.

What is more, every "positive" stereotypical statement invokes its antipode. The saying, "Blacks are good athletes," can mean, "Black aren't very intelligent." The claim, "Jews are excellent at managing money," can mean, "Jews are stingy and greedy." In the same way, all claims attaching a glorifying attribute to Asian Americans inevitably affixes a degrading attribute as well. In the words of Frank Wu, author of *Yellow*, "To be intelligent is to be calculating and too clever; to be gifted in math and science is to be mechanical and not creative, lacking interpersonal skills and leadership potential. To be polite is to be inscrutable and submissive. To be hard working is to be an unfair competitor for regular human beings and not a well-rounded, likable individual."[108]

For some Asian Americans, the pressure to live up to the model minority image is too heavy a cross to bear. Young Asian-American women—faced with parental and societal pressures to be perfect students as well as perfect women, girlfriends, and wives—commit suicide at alarmingly high rates. High school- and college-aged Asian-American women have the highest suicide rates of women in any racial group. In fact, suicide is the second leading cause of the death of Asian-American women between the ages of 15 and 24.[109] In some cases, behind those polished piano recitals and those flawless report cards sits a sad and still young woman, "buried above ground."[110]

Besides wreaking havoc on the psyches of many Asian Americans, the model minority stereotype exacerbates racial divisions. Fear of Asian-American overachievement has caused a good deal of anxiety on college campuses among non-Asian students, white and nonwhite alike. Students at MIT joke that the acronym of their university stands for "Made in Taiwan," not Massachusetts Institute of Technology. Some white University of California— Los Angeles students claim that UCLA stands for "United Caucasians Lost among Asians." Students at the University of California–Berkeley were greeted with the words, "Stop the Asian Hordes," spray-painted on the Engineering School's walls, while a former student body president of that university once remarked, "Some students say that if they see too many Asians in a class, they are not going to take it because the curve will be too high." A newspaper reporter quoted a non-Asian Yale student who advised, "If you are weak in math or science and find yourself assigned to a class with a majority of Asian kids, the only thing to do is transfer to a different section."[111] Because they view Asians—solely on account of their race—as brilliant and academically gifted, some non-Asian students treat them as a threat to their academic success and future prosperity.

More invidiously, the model minority stereotype is marshaled—with all careful subtlety—to oppress and humiliate other nonwhite groups. This stereotype and the fallacy of undifferentiating difference spring from the same foul soil: When American society looks at Asian Americans and exclaims, "You did it!," in the next breath it casts a sidelong glance at other nonwhite groups and chides, "Now, why can't you?" Asian Americans are treated as a kind of "middle-man minority," to borrow sociologist Hubert Blalock's term, whose accomplishments are used as proof that the reign of racial domination has come to a close and that other nonwhite groups, languishing in poverty or disproportionately imprisoned, have only themselves to blame.[112] Writer Michael Lind has observed, "In addition to fulfilling their immediate functions—selling egg rolls, measuring blood sugar—Vietnamese vendors and Filipino lab technicians serve an additional function for the white overclass: they relieve it of guilt about the squalor of millions of native-born Americans, not only ghetto blacks and poor Hispanics but poor whites."[113]

Oppositional Culture. The work of anthropologist John Ogbu has greatly influenced how social scientists conceive of the relationship between cultural practices and racial inequalities in education. Ogbu believed that many involuntary minorities have developed an **oppositional culture,** a collection of linguistic, behavioral, aesthetic, and spiritual attitudes and practices formed in direct opposition to mainstream white culture. Oppositional culture is structured by powerful historical forces. Black oppositional culture, for example, is rooted in slave times, when enslaved Africans developed a specific style of talking and joking, a repertoire of folkloric, musical, and religious practices that helped them cope with the pains of slavery. Savvy to the fact that whites, who denied them access to white culture and prohibited them from reading and writing, held to a set of assumptions about how blacks "should" talk and act, many enslaved Africans learned how to "code switch," how to exude a persona of servitude in front of whites, while, back at slave quarters, freely criticizing and mocking whites and their oppressive system.[114] As the Ethiopian proverb goes, "When the great lord passes, the wise peasant bows deeply and silently farts."[115]

After the fall of slavery, African Americans continued to navigate between the dominant white society and the marginalized black community. In the process, they formed a cultural identity that directly negated the mainstream white society, which had caused so much of their suffering. This oppositional culture, argue Ogbu and others, is a major part of African-American culture today and, what is more, might disadvantage blacks and other involuntary minorities in school. Specifically, Ogbu has argued that black and Latino students do not aspire to excel in school because, if they did, they would be viewed by their peers as "selling out" or "acting white." It is not so much that these students deny the importance of a good education as that they are unwilling to adopt certain behaviors, perceived as uniquely "white," which would allow them to do well in the white-dominated educational realm. As Ogbu has put it, "What the students reject that hurt their academic performance are "White" attitudes and behaviors conducive to making good grades . . . [,] [attitudes and behaviors such as] speaking standard English, . . . taking hard/advanced placement courses, acting like a nerd, taking mathematics and science classes, spending a lot of time in the library, and reading a lot."[116]

Thus some nonwhite students resist adopting "standard English," because they feel that doing so would mean speaking in the oppressor's tongue. And some contend that excelling in the classroom—with its Eurocentric curriculum— would require them to sacrifice their self-respect and racial pride.[117] For some blacks, Latinos, and Native Americans, to "act white," and thereby to please one's teachers, is to betray one's race. This ethic is upheld by peer groups. A Mexican American student who refuses to mix Spanish with English (that is, to talk "Spanglish") might face ridicule from his friends, and a black student who trades in her dark hoodie for a starched blouse from The Gap might find herself invited to fewer and fewer parties. According to a recent survey, 22% of Hispanic students polled claimed that "my friends make fun of people who try to do well in school," whereas only 13% of whites reported likewise.[118]

In reality, nonwhite students who believe they must choose between success in school and staying true to themselves and their "people" set for themselves a false bargain. These two goals can live side by side within the same person. Is not denying yourself the right to reach your full potential, to flourish and blossom as a student, nothing more than an act of symbolic violence, an acceptance of the terms of your own domination? Who is the real "sell out," we wonder, the student who drops out on account of a Eurocentric curriculum or the student who wades through it, graduates from college, returns to her home community, and secures a position on the school board where she is in a position to *change* that curriculum? Indeed, throughout history, many of the women and men who have been most effective in confronting and dismantling America's system of racial domination have been well educated and equipped with the competences and attitudes necessary to "dismantle the master's house with the master's tools" (to invoke the line so famously discussed by Audre Lorde—who, by the way, used it to arrive at conclusions somewhat different from our own).[119] Bartolomé de Las Casas, Fredrick Douglas, Simone de Beauvoir, Martin Luther King, Jr., Anna Julia Cooper, Samson Occum, Edith Maude Eaton, Thurgood Marshall: these persons who made a difference were all able to enact change only after they had educated themselves, appropriating the culture of the oppressive society in order better to understand how to change that culture.[120] (This is not to minimize, of course, the enormous contributions made by persons lacking in a formal education. During the Civil Rights Movement, for example, poor blacks with little schooling often made a huge difference in the struggle against racial domination.[121])

That said, Ogbu's theory of oppositional culture—first put forward in the 1970s—has amassed a long list of critics. Scholars have found that young nonwhites' identities simply do not hinge on an oppositional culture mindset, that blacks and Hispanics feel no pressure to reject so-called white values.[122] A recent study of over 11,000 students, for example, concluded that African Americans are just as engaged in school as are their white counterparts. Another discovered that pressures against "acting white" are found only in schools with a high percentage of nonwhites and low-income students enrolled in college preparation courses.[123]

In her recently published book, *Keepin' It Real: School Success beyond Black and White*, sociologist Prudence Carter developed a theory of race, culture, and schooling that modifies Ogbu's concept of "acting white." Drawing on ten months of in-depth study of high school students living in Yonkers, New York, Carter argues that some black and Latino students "perform blackness" or "act Spanish" but that doing so does not mean being apathetic toward school. "Resistance to 'acting white,'" she observes, "for many African-American students is about maintaining cultural identity, not about embracing and rejecting the dominant standards of achievement. . . . Resistance to 'acting white' refers to [students'] refusal to adhere to the cultural default setting in U.S. society . . . [,] the generic American, white, middle-class patterns of speech and mannerisms, dress and physical appearance, and tastes in music and art forms."[124]

However, problems arise for black and Latino students when their teachers do not deem their cultural attitudes and practices appropriate and positive. If modern-day educational institutions are steeped in whiteness—as we have demonstrated above—then those institutions will favor Eurocentric knowledge and cultural styles over non-Eurocentric ones, even if the latter are not avowedly anti-intellectual. Consider the example of a young black man from a poor, inner-city high school who excels in his classes and wins a scholarship to a top university. He is just as talented and smart as his classmates, and he works hard to finish all his homework. But he begins to feel alienated by much of the material assigned in class, Eurocentric material that does not resonate with his experience, spark his imagination, or incite his passion. He has been surprised and angered by some things his classmates have said about African Americans; troubled that his professors have relegated "the African-American experience" to only a single class week; and disappointed that he has not had the opportunity to read more black writers and poets. He begins to grow disillusioned with college, and the question, "How does this matter to my friends and family back home?" plagues him—but he puts his head down and tries to get through it.[125]

On campus, he dresses in the style of his home neighborhood—baggy jeans, an oversized t-shirt, a gold necklace, a clean baseball cap cocked to the side. His demeanor is the "cool pose" of the street, which he and his friends adopted as teenagers, and his language is sprinkled with slang. He sometimes finishes answering a question in class with "y'know what I'm sayin'?" Based on his expressions of blackness, as well as his lack of enthusiasm for the (Eurocentric) curriculum, his professors associate the young man's style and language with underperformance. Indeed, seated next to a young Asian-American woman who wears collared shirts, slacks, and glasses, who sits up straight and raises her hand confidently, who looks you in the eye, and whose father attended this university, our young black student "looks," to his professors, like a slacker. They evaluate him accordingly, giving him lower marks than if he had presented himself differently.[126]

Sadly he comes to believe that his low marks are accurate evaluations of his capabilities; that the problem isn't racial domination in the educational realm—whiteness in the curriculum and on campus—but his own inadequacies. "I guess I was wrong," he thinks. "I'm not cut out for this." A self-fulfilling cycle thus takes hold, as doubts about failure lead to actual failure, his acceptance of it reflecting James Baldwin's penetrating observation: "It is the peculiar triumph of society—and its loss—that it is able to convince those people to whom it has given inferior status of the reality of this decree; it has the force and the weapons to translate its dictum into a fact, so that the allegedly inferior are actually made so, insofar as the society's realities are concerned. . . . We find ourselves bound, first without, then within, by the nature of our categorization."[127]

In this example, it is not the student's cultural attributes per se that are the problem but the educational institution's *interpretation* of those attributes. Our student did not disengage from school; the school disengaged from him.

Stereotype Threat.   "If it is quite illusory to believe that symbolic violence can be overcome with the weapons of consciousness and will alone," Bourdieu observed, "this is because the effect and conditions of its efficacy are durably and deeply embedded in the body in the form of dispositions."[128] Your collusion with whiteness, in other words, need not be a matter of conscious decision, as in the choice to resist acting white. Racial domination can infect the unconscious—the domain of unreflective habits, tendencies, and dispositions—such that we end up reproducing racial inequality without even knowing it. This is precisely the finding generated by a collection of fascinating psychological studies that confirm the existence of what has been come to be known as "stereotype threat."

The notion of stereotype threat derives from the work of Claude Steele and Joshua Aronson. Steele and Aronson set out to determine how elusive and abstract stereotypes meted out very concrete consequences in the lives of members of stereotyped groups. They reasoned that a negative stereotype about your racial group makes you conscious of the fact that any of your actions that happen to align with that stereotype end up verifying the stereotype, making it more real in the eyes of others and, perhaps, even of yourself. **Stereotype threat**, therefore, "is being at risk of confirming, as self-characteristic, a negative stereotype about one's group."[129] Members of dominant groups rarely experience this threat, while it holds great sway over the conscious and unconscious behavior of members of marginalized groups.

For example, whenever black students undertake an intellectual task, they face the threat of confirming demeaning stereotypes about the intellectual capability of African Americans. This threat, hypothesized Steele and Aronson, can interfere with blacks' intellectual performance. To test this hypothesis, the psychologists developed a series of simple experiments. In one experiment, they gave black and white undergraduates at Stanford University a thirty-minute test based on questions drawn from the Graduate Record Examination (the test you take to get into graduate school). Steele and Aronson believed that telling students that the test measures intellectual ability would trigger in black students the stereotype threat, the anxiety that, should they do poorly, their results could be used to confirm the stereotype that blacks are intellectually inferior to whites. To find out if this really would happen, the researchers divided the students into two groups, both of which comprised white and black students. Group 1 was told that the test was "a laboratory problem-solving task," and Group 2 was told that it measured their "intellectual ability." The results were startling. In Group 1, black and white test scores were indistinguishable, as were the scores for whites in both groups. However, blacks in Group 2 scored much lower than did whites and blacks in Group 1. The conclusion was clear: "Making African-American participants vulnerable to judgments by negative stereotypes about their group's intellectual ability depressed their standardized test performance relative to White participants, while conditions designed to alleviate this threat improved their performance, equating the two groups."[130]

Steele and Aronson further verified the presence—and power—of stereotype threat in another experiment. This time, instead of manipulating what the test measured (for example, intelligence or not), they primed race by asking students in one group to list their race before taking the test and omitting this step for students in another group. When race was not primed, black and white test scores virtually were identical; but when race was primed, blacks scored significantly lower than whites. Simply reminding black students of their racial identity—and the negative stereotypes that accompany it—awakened stereotype threat and reduced their performance.[131]

Since the publication of Steele and Aronson's groundbreaking work, the stereotype threat hypothesis has been confirmed by hundreds of studies and has been applied to other groups. Medical researchers have concluded that blacks taking tests where stereotype threat was activated have higher blood pressure and lower scores than whites and blacks taking tests under conditions where the threat was not.[132] Hispanics, women, and students from poor families have been found to be subject to stereotype threat.[133] Even whites can experience stereotype threat, when comparing themselves to Asian students. In a recent study, Aronson found that white men taking a mathematics examination scored considerably worse when they were told prior to the examination that Asians typically outperform whites on such tests.[134] Collectively, these studies offer indisputable evidence that students, even if they fail to realize it, are corrupted by stereotypes others have of them. This is a burden disproportionately borne by African-American, Hispanic, and Native-American students—as well as by women. The crippling consequences of stereotype threat are yet another example of the role culture plays in reproducing racial inequalities in education.

The Role of Schools

Although one's family and culture can play a deciding role in broadening or narrowing one's educational horizons, schools themselves are perhaps the most powerful institution with respect to generating educational inequalities. The American school system is plagued by "savage inequalities," inequalities marked, on one end, by affluent schools that lavish their students with pedigrees, cultural capital, network connections, and the finest education, and, on the other, by ghetto schools, dilapidated, mired in poverty, and frequently vexed by violence.[135] Perhaps the situation is best captured in a two-line poem penned by a high school student attending one of New York City's poorest schools:

> America the beautiful,
> Who are you beautiful for?[136]

Students Advantaged, Students Betrayed.   Picture your high school. Perhaps you attended a state-of-the art suburban school, one, in fact, that prompted your parents to move to that new subdivision. Maybe you went to a small, rural high school with a graduating class of thirty. Perhaps you are from an inner-city school, or one on the U.S.-Mexican border, where the teachers looked tired and nothing—nothing—was new. Did your high school have new textbooks and nice laboratory equipment? Did it offer art classes with plenty of supplies and take you on field trips to museums and concerts and historical landmarks? Did your gym and weight room have new equipment? Were your teachers competent and qualified; did most have years of experience under their belts? Was it exceptional that you went off to college or did most of your classmates do that as well? Answering questions such as these will provide you with a glimpse into the educational advantages you acquired (or did not acquire) due to the kind of school you attended.

As we already have learned, *Brown v. Board of Education* did not abolish school segregation: fifty years later, schools are still drastically segregated and drastically unequal.[137] In fact, social scientists have documented a nationwide movement of educational re-segregation, which has left today's schools even more segregated than during the time of *Brown v. Board of Education*.[138] The average white student attends a school that is at least 80% white, and 7 out

Educational Attainment and Average Income of Asian-American Groups, 2005

Group	% of Adults With at Least 4-Year Degree	Average Income
Asian Indian	68%	$66,000
Korean	54%	$52,000
Pakistani, Bangladeshi, Sri Lankan	54%	$48,000
Chinese	53%	$56,000
Filipino	48%	$46,000
Japanese	44%	$59,000
Indonesian, Malaysian, Thai	44%	$40,000
Vietnamese	25%	$41,000
Native Hawaiian, Pacific Islander	17%	$38,000
Cambodian, Laotian, Hmong	13%	$32,000

Amount Set Aside for Higher Education by Asian-American Families, by Group

Group	None	Up to $10,000	$10,001–20,000	> $20,000
Southeast Asian	12%	73%	4%	8%
Filipino	3%	51%	10%	32%
South Asian	6%	34%	17%	22%
Korean	3%	40%	17%	42%
Chinese	9%	31%	22%	37%
Japanese	6%	41%	23%	27%

SOURCE: Scott Jaschik. The original story and user comments can be viewed online at http://insidehighered.com/news/2007/07/27/asians.

of 10 Latino and African-American students attend majority-nonwhite schools. In Texas, 65% of Mexican Americans and 50% of African Americans attend schools in which at least 70% of the students are nonwhite.[139] Like residential segregation, racial segregation in schools is connected to a whole host of social problems.

Many schools in predominantly nonwhite, low-income neighborhoods are staffed by unqualified teachers who are expected to work for meager wages and with little resources. Studies have shown that black and Hispanic students attending public schools are more likely to be taught by uncertified teachers than are their white counterparts. In some states, as many as 1 in 5 public school students are being taught by uncertified teachers. Uncertified teachers disproportionately are found in poor, majority-nonwhite schools. And such schools often have a difficult time retaining even those teachers (ghetto schools have remarkably high teacher turnover rate). By contrast, teachers who attended the most prestigious universities, who have more teaching experience, and who earn higher test scores primarily teach white, economically privileged students. One way the state of Illinois evaluates the quality of its teachers is by giving them a test, dividing the scores into four quartiles. In the state's majority-white schools, only 11% of teachers score in the lowest quartile, but in schools with virtually no white students, a full 88% of teachers rank in the lowest quartile.[140]

We can hardly blame the teachers for such discrepancies. The vast majority of states offer no incentives for teaching in poor, nonwhite schools. As a result, the nation's best teachers get hired where they are needed the least, accepting jobs in affluent, majority-white institutions. Teachers with lesser proven ability, experience, and credentials, in contrast, accept positions in run-down neighborhoods. In a nation that continually stresses the importance of education, teachers are among America's lowest paid professionals. And the situation is worse in poorer states with large nonwhite populations, states that allocate a pitifully low proportion of their annual budget to education. In fact, a recent report concluded that three of the nation's whitest states—Maine, Vermont, and West Virginia—spend the highest proportion of their gross state product on public education. Mississippi annually spends only $5,391 on each student; Connecticut, a state with far fewer poor and nonwhite children, spends $9,588. And because federal funding for education is dictated by how much the state dishes out, more affluent, whiter states (usually in the North), the ones that spend more on education, are given more federal funds than poorer states with large nonwhite populations (usually in the South). For example, each year the federal government awards Arkansas $964 per poor child but awards Massachusetts $2,048 per poor child.[141] It is not so much teachers who are to blame for the sorry state of America's poor nonwhite schools; the onus is on our government.

In some of the nation's worst schools, it is all teachers can do to maintain order. Keeping their students safe necessarily takes precedence over education, as the festering problems of the ghetto—its poverty and joblessness, its crime and violence—seep through the walls of the school. In her book, *The Failures of Integration,* Sheryll Cashin provides a snapshot of Ballou Senior High School, located in one of Washington, D.C.'s roughest neighborhoods: "The 2003–2004 school year has been hellish. Ballou was closed for a month in the fall when someone took mercury from a science classroom and spread it around the building. The day the school reopened, a gunman fired shots half a block from the premises just as classes were letting out. Since then, several fistfights have broken out among students involved in loosely organized gangs. The latest fistfight turned deadly. On February 2, 2004, one student, Thomas Boykin, fatally shot another student, James Richardson, a star football player, near the school cafeteria and wounded another in the leg."[142]

Bowen Paulle conducted participant-observation research in one of the toughest, most crime-ridden schools in the South Bronx (New York City) during the 1990s. He observed that the effects of school violence do not easily fade away once the outward violence is gone. "The anxiety related to threats and episodic outbursts of brutal violence," he wrote, "was always both 'out there,' in the educational settings, and 'in there,' beneath the flesh of the exposed." The violence gets under students' skins, into their very bones, and remains there as a depository of fear, insecurity, and intimidation, long outlasting the fights and stabbings, the shouting and gunshots.[143]

Author and teacher Jonathan Kozol set out to evaluate the state of education in inner-city America. He toured the country, talking with students and teachers in Camden, New Jersey, San Antonio, Texas, and other city centers. His discoveries were shocking. Kozol found schools whose gyms had been flooded with sewage because of broken plumbing and whose classrooms were sweltering owing to poor heating systems. He found ramshackle biology labs, supply closets without any paper, four computers in a school of 600, and a school so poor it could not afford to put goalposts on its football field. During a tour of East St. Louis, a young reporter told Kozol, "The ultimate terror for white people is to leave the highway by mistake and find themselves in East St. Louis. People speak of getting lost in East St. Louis as a nightmare. The nightmare to me is that they never leave that highway so they never know what life is like for all the children here. They *ought* to get off that highway. The nightmare isn't in their heads. It's a real place. There are children living here."[144] Given these conditions, should we be surprised to learn that a public school serving primarily wealthy, white students has a 1 in 4 chance of producing consistently high standardized test scores; but one serving primarily poor, nonwhite students has about a 1 in 300 chance?[145]

Far too many ghetto, reservation, and barrio schools—third-world institutions smack dab in the center of the world's wealthiest nation—do little to prepare their students for college or even for vocational training. Affluent schools, which include not only elite private institutions—some of which charge as much as $40,000 per year for tuition, are staffed by teachers holding Ph.D.s, and shuttle their students into Ivy League colleges at alarmingly high rates—but also public high schools in wealthy suburbs, open wide the doors of privilege.

Tracking. "American high schools are racist," declared Tom Vander Ark, Executive Director for Education at the Gates Foundation. "It's not that most teachers are; it's the institution—the basic architecture."[146] As we have learned throughout this chapter, in many ways schools are guided and conditioned by racial domination, and one more mechanism of inequality—one grafted into schools' very architecture—deserves mention here: tracking. **Tracking** is the practice of sorting students into different tracks, ostensibly according to their ability. A typical tracking system features four tracks: honors/accelerated, college preparation, vocational, and remedial. Students' future opportunities—the extent to which they will go to college, enroll in the Armed Services, find a job straight out of high school, or drop out—are determined largely by the track to which they are assigned.

Although some have argued that tracking has its advantages, studies have found tracking to be anything but an innocent practice but one that—intentionally or unintentionally—produces racial inequality. Researchers have found that whites and Asians disproportionately are represented in higher tracks (accelerated and college prep), while African Americans, Hispanics, and Native Americans disproportionately are clustered in lower ones (vocational and remedial). Racialized tracking remains even after students' cognitive ability and class backgrounds are taken into account. And studies have shown that, as a school's racial diversity increases, the chances that blacks and Hispanics will be assigned to higher tracks decreases. This suggests that, in schools with sizeable nonwhite populations, upper-level tracks function as a collection of "white and Asian classes," while lower-level tracks are reserved for blacks and Hispanics.[147]

How is this possible? How is it that nonwhite and non-Asian students are overrepresented in vocational and remedial tracks when schools have developed fairly objective measures to evaluate students' ability? One answer is that whiteness can muddy teachers' evaluations of Native-American, Hispanic, and African-American students. According to survey research, a significant proportion of white teachers harbor prejudicial attitudes, and some evidence suggests that white teachers often overlook Native-American, Hispanic, and African-American students' abilities, instead emphasizing their academic weaknesses and disciplinary infractions.[148] "Clearly," write sociologists Samuel Lucas and Mark Berends, "teachers are in a position to sponsor a child for upward mobility or to ignore evidence of a child's promise. . . . Teachers of different races [may] not only interpret students' performances differently but, in actuality, *literally see different performances.*"[149]

Accelerated and college prep classes not only groom students for college; they also stimulate and mature them intellectually.[150] But, again, we see an unequal distribution of opportunity—and the wastefulness of racial domination. When we consider the inequality *between* schools (inner-city schools versus suburban schools) and the inequality created *within* schools (maintained through tracking and other mechanisms) we cannot help but be overcome by all the potential and talent and ingenuity lost on account of racial domination. Think of all the spirit and passion snuffed out by the harsh realities of the reservation, the ghetto, the barrio, the trailer park; of all the bright and motivated students assigned to classes that do not enable them to reach their full potential; of all those dreams deferred.

> What happens to a dream deferred?
> Does it dry up, like a raisin in the sun?
> Or fester like a sore—And then run?
> Does it stink like rotten meat?
> Or crust and sugar over—like syrupy sweet?
> Maybe it just sags, like a heavy load.
> Or does it explode?
>
> —Langston Hughes, "Dream Deferred"

Combating Educational Inequality: The Case of Affirmative Action

The final section of this chapter is dedicated to a program designed to combat racial inequality in the educational field: affirmative action. We have already addressed at length affirmation action in employment in Chapter 4 and, accordingly, offer only a brief discussion here. This might disappoint you, especially because many of you are deeply invested in this issue and because, recently, courts have limited affirmative action as it pertains to college enrollment (especially in the U.S. Supreme Court case of *Gratz v. Bollinger*). But affirmative action is such a controversial program that often it overshadows other important issues pertaining to racial domination in the educational field, issues such as whiteness in the curriculum and the causes and consequences of racial inequality. We have given these issues priority in this chapter rather than obsessing over the debate around affirmative action, a debate that can do more to occlude the truth about racism, fairness, and opportunity than to reveal it.[151] We urge you, now and always, to approach affirmative action with an open mind and reasonable spirit; approach it with a desire to learn as much as you can about it before judging it. To this end, we pose three questions that any critical thinker must answer before arriving at a conclusion about affirmative action. First, are you sure you know exactly what affirmative action is? Second, does affirmative action unfairly handicap deserving whites and Asians? Third, does America still need a program designed to ameliorate racial inequalities in education and, if so, is affirmative action the best one for the job?

How Does Affirmative Action in Education Work?

In Chapter 4 we defined affirmative action (in its current nonwhite and nonmale form) as "an umbrella term referring to a collection of policies and practices designed to dismantle institutional racism and sexism by offering people of color and women employment and educational opportunities." Many Americans overestimate two features of affirmative action: its prevalence and its power. With respect to its prevalence, affirmative action is not used in all colleges and universities. Although the precise number of schools that employ some type of affirmative action program remains a matter of debate, what is certain is that a significant number of colleges—some 75% by one estimate—place no weight on race or gender as a positive criterion of admission. Most schools that do not employ affirmative action programs are nonselective institutions that accept most applicants. Selective institutions, in contrast, those with competitive admissions, are the schools most like to rely on some type of affirmative action.[152]

And how do colleges and universities "do" affirmative action? How much power does affirmative action have? First, bear in mind that affirmative action does not rely on quota systems, which, as we have learned, are illegal. Note, too, that affirmative action can take many different forms. When employed in college admissions, it means, simply, giving people who belong to groups that are disproportionately underrepresented—people who have suffered, and still suffer, from patriarchal and racial domination—an edge over members of groups who are not. This usually amounts to selecting a woman or nonwhite applicant from a pool of equally qualified applicants or, in a stronger version, selecting a woman or nonwhite applicant whose application is slightly weaker than those of her or his male or white counterparts. Affirmative action does *not* mean selecting a woman or nonwhite applicant over male or white applicants whose records are substantially better, nor does it mean choosing unqualified people over qualified ones. There may be sound reasons to criticize affirmative action, but suggesting that it admits into top universities unqualified applicants at the expense of qualified ones is not one of them.[153]

How Does Affirmative Action Affect Whites and Asians?

In some cases, giving "targeted minorities" an edge in admissions procedures only increases the scores of students who would have been accepted without affirmative action; in other cases, the edge is fundamental to students being accepted; and in still other cases, the edge is not enough. To be sure, elite schools with affirmative action policies reject large numbers of African Americans, Hispanics, and Native Americans, along with sizable numbers of Asian and white applicants. But what, more specifically, are the consequences of affirmative action for whites and Asians, who in most cases do not qualify for affirmative action programs? We know that, even after thirty years of affirmative action, whites and Asians apply to, enroll in, and graduate from college at higher rates than Native Americans, African Americans, and Hispanics and that such racial disparities only widen when we examine selective institutions. It is true that some whites and Asians who would have been accepted at certain colleges and universities are denied entry because of affirmative action policies; however, it is equally true that they make up a relatively small proportion of applicants. According to one account, "Very few white and Asian students are actually bumped [because of racial considerations], and many of them get into alternative elite institutions of equal stature."[154]

In fact, it is far more likely that a qualified white or Asian applicant will be rejected from a top university because her or his spot was reserved for an academically mediocre but socially privileged white applicant with ties to the university. Roughly 1 in 7 Ivy League students are **legacies**, children of alumni. And numerous studies have shown that legacies are significantly less qualified than other students (including affirmative action applicants) on virtually every measure of academic ability. No less than 15% of freshmen enrolled in America's top universities are white students who failed to satisfy their university's minimum requirements but were nonetheless accepted because they are children of professors, administrators, alumni, generous donors, or other people the university seeks to please. These unqualified white students are nearly twice as prevalent on college campuses as nonwhites who benefited from affirmative action. "Rather than promoting social mobility," observes Peter Schmidt, author of *Color and Money: How Rich White Kids Are Winning the War over College Affirmative Action,* "our nation's selective colleges appear to be thwarting it, by turning away applicants who have excelled given their circumstances and offering second chances to wealthy and connected young people who have squandered many of the advantages life has offered them."[155]

There are cases where a deserving student's spot at a prestigious university is given to a student much less deserving—but, in the vast majority of cases, this is not because of affirmative action but because of admissions policies that give legacies a boost. The "good old boys club" is much more powerful than a program aimed at remedying racial inequality. Hence, those who accuse affirmative action of "discriminating against whites and Asians" are harboring a kind of misplaced resentment. It is not affirmative action but legacy-favoring practices that deny a significant number of qualified students—white and nonwhite alike—a place at the table. Every university, it seems, has its price.

Is Affirmative Action the Most Effective Program?

After reading this chapter, you should have no question in your mind that racial domination in the educational field is still with us, that it runs deep, and that it will be vanquished only by enduring and toothy programs. Is affirmative action the most effective program? It is certainly helping. Women and nonwhites have made impressive gains in higher education as a direct result of affirmative action. According to one estimate, the percentage of black students at top universities would slip from 7% to 2% if affirmative action were removed from admissions policies. Indeed, when the University of California banned race-conscious admissions practices, the percentage of black freshman decreased by 50% in a single year.[156]

Affirmative action has been effective in combating past and present modes of gender- and race-based exclusion. But it is effective enough? As we mentioned in Chapter 4, some have argued that the biggest beneficiaries of affirmative action have been white women, followed by middle- to upper-class blacks and Hispanics. "Minority members from the most advantaged families . . . reap disproportionate benefits from policies of affirmative action based solely on their group membership," writes sociologist William Julius Wilson.[157] Although this claim has not gone unchallenged, there is good reason to believe that affirmative action programs do little to aid the thousands of nonwhites who each year are born into dire poverty.

Some policy makers have proposed a type of affirmative action based not on race or gender but on class. Because nonwhite populations disproportionately are victims of poverty, proponents of income-based affirmative action postulate that such programs will alleviate both class- and race-based inequality. The evidence, however, suggests otherwise. When schools have transitioned from race-based to class-based affirmative action programs, the racial diversity of their student body has declined. Why? Because there are many more poor whites than poor nonwhites (in raw numbers), even if the percentage of poor Africans Americans, Latinos, and Native Americans exceeds that of whites. This is why Harvard economist Thomas Kane has suggested that an income-based affirmative action program would have to be six times the size of current race-based programs to admit a similar number of African Americans.[158]

Others have suggested that what needs to change is not affirmative action but how colleges evaluate their applicants. As the number of college applications has skyrocketed over the years, selective universities have grown increasingly reliant on test scores to identify "good" students. Dependence on "test score meritocracy" has resulted in the simultaneous need for affirmative action because of the racial test score gap. As sociologist Jerome Karable has observed, a society's conception of "merit" tends to be defined by its dominant groups, who tender a definition that aligns with their interests.[159] When colleges and universities put special emphasis on test scores, they propagate a measure of merit that benefits economically privileged white and Asian students—students who are tracked in accelerated classes, who can afford SAT tutors and Kaplan courses, and who are virtually immune to stereotype threat. Accordingly, studies have suggested that placing more emphasis on performance-based measures of merit, such as class rank, would greatly alleviate colleges' reliance on race-based affirmative action programs while still allowing them to pursue diversity.[160]

More radical, still, is the call for a drastic overhaul of the entire educational system. Affirmative action benefits only the small percentage of students who have risen to the top and who feel confident enough to apply to selective universities. What about the thousands of others who fall through the cracks long before their senior year of high school? Affirmative action does little to combat the high drop-out rates of Native Americans, the low educational aspirations of Mexican Americans, or the unfair way African Americans are assigned to remedial tracks. Since racial domination penetrates our schools to the very lowest level, so, too, must our policies to combat it. This would require nothing short of a "revolution in public education," one accompanied by new facilities, new computers, racial audits on school tracking, longer school years, more federal funding for public education, full access to higher education, and impressive incentives for teachers who choose to ply their trade in the poorest schools.[161] Impossible, you say? Not so! In fact, other countries, all of them less wealthy than the United States, have taken bold steps in this direction. A big problem requires bigger solutions.

One last issue about affirmative action deserves mention. Some have suggested that affirmative action forces all nonwhite students, whether admitted under race-conscious admissions policies or not, to bear a heavy psychological burden. Their self-confidence might suffer as they consider the possibility that, perhaps, they are "not good enough" to be enrolled in their college. By and large, however, the evidence suggests that by providing nonwhites with access to higher education, affirmative action can boost their self-esteem. If we were truly worried about students' self-esteem, we might show greater concern for white students, whose racial privilege has, since they were children, provided them one unfair advantage after another, advantages much more powerful than any affirmative action program ever conceived or implemented.[162]

The Benefits of a Multicultural Learning Environment

If we hope to drive racial domination from the gates of our schools and universities, then we must continue the work of confronting whiteness in the curriculum, classroom, and college campus, and we must develop new, radical ideas for combating racial inequalities. We must do so, not only in the name of racial justice, but also because a multicultural learning environment, one that welcomes students from diverse backgrounds and encourages a wide variety of ideas, is beneficial to the intellectual development of all students.

Dozens upon dozens of studies have pointed to one clear conclusion: white and nonwhite students alike thrive in multicultural learning environments. Students' critical thinking skills are improved greatly by in-class and out-of-class interactions with students of different racial identities. Indeed, one study concluded that, compared to other students, those who interacted with racial and ethnically diverse peers demonstrated the largest improvement in academic skills, intellectual engagement, and motivation. Students who participated in programs developed to foster interracial campus community improved their cognitive skills and leadership abilities, and they were more satisfied with college life.[163]

Some critics of multicultural education have suggested it "lowers the bar." But all the evidence leads us to the opposite conclusion. Young men and women who engage actively with people from racial and ethnic groups other than their own, who are introduced to a variety of viewpoints on the world, who are taught how to identify and deconstruct racial domination, and who are exposed to intercultural training *make better students*. A college campus that encourages racial diversity within its student body is a campus that strives to shape students into mature, critical thinkers. Not only this, but multicultural education better prepares students to participate competently in America's multicultural workforce and democracy, both of which grow more racially diverse by the day.

CHAPTER REVIEW

"I HAVE A RIGHT TO THINK!" RACIAL BATTLES OVER EDUCATION, 1900–1970
Booker T. Washington, industrial education, W. E. B. Du Bois, the talented tenth, *Mendez v. Westminster School District, Brown v. Board of Education,* citizens councils, Little Rock Nine, *Millikin v. Bradley*

WHITENESS IN EDUCATION
eurocentric historical accounts

EDUCATIONAL INEQUALITY
cultural capital, hidden curriculum, social capital, familism, the fallacy of undifferentiating difference, involuntary and voluntary minorities, stereotype of the model minority, oppositional culture, stereotype threat, tracking

COMBATING EDUCATIONAL INEQUALITY: THE CASE OF AFFIRMATIVE ACTION
legacies

FROM THEORY TO PRACTICE

1. Identify at least one way whiteness informs your major field of study or one of the classes in which you are currently enrolled. Explain precisely how racial domination is normalized; offer at least one consequence of this normalization; and advance at least one suggestion for how whiteness might be effectively confronted.

2. Identify at least one way whiteness guides life on your college campus. Select an example from any aspect of college living, including everyday interactions on the quad or in the cafeteria, dorm life, classroom discussions, study

hall, athletic events, parties, and so forth. Explain how your example is an example of whiteness; speak to its consequences for white and nonwhite students; and think of at least one way it might be combated.

3. Think about your upbringing in terms of cultural capital. How did your family's cultural practices provide or fail to provide you with cultural capital? How has this affected your transition to college? And how might you analyze the cultural capital you did or did not inherit from your family in light of cultural capital's connection to Eurocentrism?

4. Think about your high school. How did it confer or fail to confer on you advantages that have helped in your transition to college? In light of what you have learned in this chapter, evaluate your high school experience, paying special mind to how racial domination may have informed your school and your experience.

5. Research your college or university's affirmative action policy. What is your institution's stance with respect to using race as a criterion in admissions? Write a letter to the administrator in change of affirmative action, explaining why you support or disagree with your college or university's policy. In your letter, be sure to justify your argument by drawing on what you learned in this chapter about affirmative action.

RECOMMENDED READING

- Prudence Carter, *Keepin' It Real: School Success beyond Black and White* (New York: Oxford University Press, 2005).

- W. E. B. Du Bois, *Souls of Black Folk* (New York: Dover, 1903 [1994]).

- Ruth Frankenberg, ed., *Displacing Whiteness: Essays in Social and Cultural Criticism* (Durham: Duke University Press, 1999).

- Jonathan Kozol, *Savage Inequalities: Children in American's Schools* (New York: HarperCollins, 1991).

- Kathryn Neckerman, *Schools Betrayed: Roots of Failure in Inner-City Education* (Chicago: University of Chicago Press, 2007).

- Claude Steele and Joshua Aronson, "Stereotype Threat and the Intellectual Test Performance of African Americans," *Journal of Personality and Social Psychology* 69 (1995): 797–811.

- Frank Wu, *Yellow: Race in America beyond Black and White* (New York: Basic Books, 2002).

Chapter 8

Aesthetics

Demystifying Art

"Aesthetic" (es-thét-ik) comes from the Greek word *aisthetikos,* meaning "sensitive" or "to perceive or feel." The word was popularized in the English-speaking world after the works of German philosopher Immanuel Kant were translated into English and today has come to mean "artistic" or "concerned with the appreciation of beauty or art." A chapter on race and the aesthetic field, therefore, has to do with racial domination in the artistic realm, that sphere of society where artistic goods, such as painting, photography, sculpture, dance, stage performance, literature, poetry, music, fashion, and cinema, are produced and consumed.

In 1926, Du Bois addressed the Chicago chapter of the NAACP with a speech entitled "Criteria for Negro Art." "I do not doubt," he began, "but there are some in this audience who are a little disturbed at . . . the subject I have chosen. Such people are thinking something like this: 'How is it that an organization like this, a group of radicals trying to bring new things into the world, a fighting organization which has come up out of the blood and dust of battle . . . can turn aside to talk about Art?' Or perhaps there are others who feel a certain relief and are saying, 'After all it is rather satisfactory after all this talk about rights and fighting to sit and dream of something which leaves a nice taste in the mouth.'" Having identified both types of audience member—one who held the topic of art to be an unwelcome distraction, the other who held it as a welcome one—Du Bois continued, "Let me tell you that neither of these groups is right. The thing we are talking about tonight is part of the great fight we are carrying on[,] and it represents a forward and upward look—a pushing onward."[1]

Likewise, this chapter is not a distraction from the rigorous study of racial domination, nor is it softer or less important than previous chapters on politics, economics, or education. Our understanding of racial domination would remain drastically incomplete without a serious examination of artistic works and performances—the collection of things that constitute what has come to be known as "culture." In today's media-connected world, television, movies, and music wield considerable power over our modes of thought. The television is everywhere—in buses, bars, and waiting rooms, in airport lobbies, elevators, and SUVs. According to one study, the average American home has more televisions than people, and in such a home, the television is turned on for more than one-third of the day.[2] And so-called "high art" (art that is found in museums and opera houses, not on your iPhone) influences our perceptions of brilliance and the beautiful, as well as our interpretations of the past, evidenced by the fact that more people get their history by visiting museums than by reading books.[3] When you consider the thousands of ways movies, photographs, music videos, and so many other cultural goods influence what we think about and how we think about it, the ways they open and close our minds to imaginative possibilities, how they represent our social world and its problems, and how they reproduce or challenge the norms of dominant groups, there is no denying the importance of aesthetics in the career of racial domination.[4]

How, then, should we sociological thinkers approach the study of art? For starters, we must resist "spiritualizing" art by treating it as somehow detached (and lifted above) social reality. Art must be situated within the social contexts in which it was created and scrutinized as a reflection of those contexts. "Flowers," wrote American philosopher John Dewey, "can be enjoyed without knowing about the interactions of soil, air, moisture, and seeds of which they are the result. But they cannot be *understood* without taking just these interactions into account."[5] Similarly, to understand art and its relation to the racial order, we must subject artistic practices to a **triple reading**.[6]

First, we should examine an artwork's properties in relation to other artworks in the aesthetic field. Here we pay attention to how the artist engages fellow artists. Let's call this the aesthetic reading. Second, we should examine an artwork's properties in relation to events and structures within society. Here we explore what the artist is trying to tell us about the nature of the social world, including the nature of racial domination. Let's call this the political reading. Third, we should examine the artwork in relation to specific racial or ethnic traditions. Here we account for the ways art builds on or breaks with aesthetic currents in, say, black, white, Jewish, or Vietnamese culture. Let's call this the racial reading. All three readings assume that the artist may have acted intentionally or unintentionally. To illustrate this triple reading, consider a Toni Morrison novel. The aesthetic reading would explore how the novel conversed with other poets and novelists (such as William Faulkner and T. S. Elliot); the political reading would examine how it commented on American society (its racism, poverty, and sexism); and the racial reading would analyze the degree to which the novel connected with trends in black culture (the Southern vernacular of the characters, African-American folklore and oral history).

Analyzing a wide variety of art forms, this chapter carries out this triple reading in order to examine how art influences the racial order and how the racial order influences art. It begins with a brief historical overview of the workings of racial domination in the aesthetic field during the last one hundred fifty years. It then turns to the modern day by exploring three rich topics: representation, racialization, and cultural appropriation. If "the job of the artist is always to deepen the mystery," as Francis Bacon once said, then the job of the sociologist is to demystify that mystery and, specifically, to unpack the multiple ways art fights for or against racial domination.

Race and Art in Nineteenth- and Twentieth-Century America

Throughout most of the nineteenth and twentieth centuries, the American and European aesthetic fields were dominated by whites. Art was associated with the white educated, leisure class. Indeed, some art forms—the novel, for instance— were invented during the eighteenth century to entertain the idle upper class, their ranks swelling on account of the advance of capitalism. Nonwhites, economically and socially dominated, were denied access to fine art. Most could not afford the entrance fee to museums, and, for those few who could, most museums were closed on Sundays, the only days off for many nonwhite laborers. Moreover, it was virtually impossible for a talented artist of color to be admitted to one of the nation's professional schools of art.[7] And most others—the would-be consumers of art, the art audience—were deprived of the sort of knowledge that would allow them to get much out of the art they experienced, even were they capable of spending their weekend days strolling leisurely through museum galleries.

The Reign of Minstrelsy

In past centuries, whites held a virtual monopoly over the dominant images of beauty, genius, and art. As a result, white artists could misrepresent nonwhites with impunity, portraying them in the most distorted ways. For example, throughout the eighteenth and nineteenth centuries, neoclassical European and American sculptors represented Cleopatra—the famous Egyptian queen—as a white woman. They also chose as their favorite medium white marble, an intentional (and racialized) choice that, in their eyes, served to exalt purity and fidelity.[8] Neoclassical painters, too, associated white skin with the beautiful and the good. Consider "The Great Bath at Bursa" (1885) by French artist Jean-Léon Gérôme, a contemporary (and critic) of Manet and other impressionist painters. In this painting, Gérôme depicted a Turkish bath house filled with nude white women. In the middle of the canvas, one such woman leaned elegantly on a partially clothed black woman, who

Jean-Léon Gérôme's *The Great Bath at Bursa* portrayed the sexualized racial order as personified in two women: the very presence of the black female body had the effect of sexualizing the white women, in the eyes of white viewers.

was guiding her. To its white viewers, the very presence of the black female body had the effect of sexualizing the white women, who, had the artist not inserted the black figure, might instead have evoked the essence of wholesomeness and cleanliness. To provide added emphasis to the contrast, Gérôme intertwined the two women: a white hand drapes softly on a black shoulder, and a black arm wraps gently around a white waist. And in this fleshly marriage, skin on skin, he portrayed the entanglement of pure with polluted, civilized with primitive—the sexualized racial order as personified in two women.

Particularly unsettling exhibits known as **human zoos** became immensely popular during the nineteenth and twentieth centuries. In these exhibits, which toured America and Europe and drew large crowds at World's Fairs, nonwhite people from so-called "primitive" cultures were put on display. The people were usually shown in their "natural habitat"—that is, in primitive surroundings white designers thought were most "authentic"—sometimes wearing very little or no clothing. The 1889 World's Fair, held in Paris and attended by roughly 28 million people, displayed no less than 400 Africans in a "Negro village," the Fair's most popular attraction.[9] Seven years later, a Congolese pygmy named Ota Benga was placed in a cage in New York City's Bronx Zoo alongside apes and chimpanzees. Outside the cage a sign was posted: "The African Pigmy, 'Ota Benga,' Age, 23 years, Height, 4 feet 11 inches, Weight, 103 pounds. Brought from the Kasai River, Congo Free State, South Central Africa, by Dr. Samuel P. Verner. Exhibited each afternoon during September." The day after the Ota Benga exhibit premiered, *The New York Times* reported, "Few expressed audible objection to the sight of a human being in a cage with monkeys as companions, and there could be no doubt that to the majority the joint man-and-monkey exhibition was the most interesting sight in Bronx Park." But the exhibit did draw controversy, especially from some outspoken black ministers, and was short-lived. Ota Benga, however, never returned to his homeland and, after being shuffled from one American institution to another, killed himself in 1916.[10]

Human zoos were intended to demonstrate the supposed natural superiority of the white race and, accordingly, their natural dominion over the world's nonwhite people. White exhibitors controlled the representation of whiteness as well as indigenous people's non-whiteness. Similarly, through the **minstrel shows**, which ruled the American stage between 1830 and 1910 (so much so that entire theaters, with names such as Ethiopian House, were dedicated solely to minstrelsy), whites controlled the dominant image of blackness. Performed by white actors in blackface (and, for a brief stint after the Civil War, by black actors as well), minstrel shows purported to represent authentic African-American life. Actors blackened their skin by applying burnt cork or shoe polish and enlarged their lips with red makeup. Minstrel shows featured a collection of stock characters that portrayed blacks as lazy, ignorant, subservient, buffoonish, and childish. There was the dandy—the presumptuous, "uppity" black—and his mirror image, the slave, happy and content in his chains. There was also the caretaking mammy figure (think Aunt Jemima), the lascivious mulatto seductress, and the "old darky," stupid but musical. As the abolitionist movement gained steam, minstrel shows became avowedly proslavery and portrayed black slaves as content and earnest, eager to please their white masters. Some minstrel songs even celebrated lynching and torture, as actors sang of blacks who were "roasted, fished for, smoked like tobacco, peeled like potatoes, planted in the soil, or dried up and hung as advertisements."[11]

Through an exaggerated way of speaking, costume, makeup, postures, and movement, the minstrel show became a grotesque mockery of blackness on which the white audience could project their anxiety and confusion, their patronizing affection and seething hatred. The minstrel show perfectly fulfilled the racist fantasy because it was nothing less than blackness under complete white control. It was blackness possessed by a white body; blackness excreted from the white (social) body in the shape of a minstrel.[12] Although minstrel shows died out after the early twentieth century, *minstrelsy*—white control of the representation of blackness in particular and non-whiteness in general—carried on throughout the twentieth century. Blacks continued to be depicted as ignorant and silly in radio and television shows like *Amos 'n' Andy*, a popular minstrel-inspired show (created by two white men) that made its television debut in the 1950s. Native Americans, for their part, were cast as cruel, savage, and primitive in American western movies and successful television shows, many of which still air on cable and satellite channels today; and South Asians were typed as erotic, spiritual, and irrational in children's books, vaudeville shows, circus acts, and movies (such as the 1942 version of *Jungle Book*).[13]

Voices from the Underground

But art cannot be colonized. Even under the most oppressive of conditions, dominated groups create and imagine; they sing and write, carve and dance. Jews played music within their dark and crowded chambers at Auschwitz and Dachau; America's indigenous people refused to put an end to the Ghost Dance, even after their white colonizers forbade it; and enslaved Africans wrote songs and folklore while bending and sweating in the cotton fields of Georgia and Mississippi. During the nineteenth and twentieth centuries, some nonwhite artists fled America's oppressive system in order to ply their trade. This was the case with Mary Edmonia Lewis, a sculptor of Native-American and African-American heritage, who exiled herself to Rome during the middle of the nineteenth century and went on to create classic works such as "Old Arrow Maker and His Daughter" (1866) and "The Death of Cleopatra" (1876).[14] But Lewis was the exception to the rule. Most nonwhites simply made do in America, which, try as it might, was unable to silence their voices.

Consider the career of African-American music. To express their anguish, enslaved Africans sang spirituals. Often slow and melodious, these dirges (Du Bois called them "sorrow songs") often cried out to God for deliverance:

> The blind man stood on the road and cried,
>
> The blind man stood on the road and cried,
>
> Cryin', "Oh, my Lord, save me,"
>
> The blind man stood on the road and cried.

Some heart-wrenching spirituals went so far as to present suicide as a quick way to escape the hell that was slavery. Others, however, were filled with hope as well as with calls for freedom (for example, "Go Down Moses"). "The Negro folk-song—the rhythmic cry of the slave—stands today not simply as the sole American music but as the most beautiful expression of human experience born this side of the seas."[15] So Du Bois wrote in 1903.

Spirituals fused despair with joy, pain with promise, and, taken together, constituted a birthed-from-suffering art form that spans the full range of human emotions. Indeed, spirituals expressed explicitly contradictory emotions. To be the victim of racial domination was to curse that domination's cruelty and, in the next breath, to laugh at its senselessness. Despair and hope, apathy and perseverance—these emotional states lived side by side in the spirituals and, indeed, are a unique characteristic of African-American music. Nowhere is this more apparent than in the **blues**, a musical form that evolved from spirituals in the early twentieth century. As James Baldwin teasingly said, "In all jazz, and especially in the blues, there is something tart and ironic, authoritative and double-edged. White Americans seem to feel that happy songs are *happy* and sad songs are *sad,* and that, God help us, is exactly the way most white Americans sing them. . . . Only people who have been 'down the line,' as the song puts it, know what this music is about."[16] One need only listen to the folk tunes of white America (those produced by country-western singers) next to those of black America (those produced by jazz and blues artists) to understand Baldwin's point.

It is often said that blacks gave America the blues. We must remember that it is the other way around. The blues represent a response to racial domination, a comingling of contradictory passions, a marriage of sorrow and laughter. Because whites as a group have not experienced the kind of racial oppression in which the blues are rooted, white America has produced no equivalent to the "blues impulse." It has no answer to Nina Simone's "Mississippi Goddamn," for example, a song that is completely comedy and completely tragedy from first note to last.[17]

In the mid-twentieth century, bebop arose as the dominant strain of jazz music. (Think Charlie Parker, Theolonius Monk, and Dizzy Gillespie.) As philosopher Cornel West observes, their music was "not only a reaction to the white-dominated, melody-obsessed 'swing jazz'; [it was also] a creative musical response to the major shift in sensibilities and moods in Afro-America after World War II."[18] Notice here the triple reading in which West engages: an aesthetic reading (black jazz as a response to white jazz); a political reading (the social currents that stirred after the defeat of Nazi Germany); and, implicitly, a racial reading (bebop as a distinctly African-American art form).

Meanwhile, the blues continued to gain in popularity, and such musicians as Louis Armstrong, Duke Ellington, and Miles Davis began playing to large audiences. As they did so, white musicians took notice and began to incorporate the blues into their repertoire. Soon, headlining musicians—from Bob Dylan to the Rolling Stones—were trying their hand at the blues, a musical appropriation that made some African Americans cringe. Poet Langston Hughes was one of them, bemoaning:

> You've taken my blues and gone.
> You sing 'em on Broadway
> And you sing 'em in Hollywood Bowl
> And you mixed 'em up with symphonies
> And you fixed 'em
> So they don't sound like me.[19]

In the minds of Hughes and others, the white appropriation of the blues disconnected the music from the social conditions—white racism—in which it was grounded and, in doing so, cheapened it. In the words of music historian Craig Werner, "When the Stones called out for satisfaction, they meant yesterday. When Otis Redding and Aretha Franklin covered the song, their responses carried the weight of hundreds of years."[20]

The white sanitation of the blues, some argued, dulled their jagged edge and glossed over past and present forms of suffering to which they spoke. Indeed, even if Dylan and the Stones did not see things this way, whites have a long history of borrowing art forms associated with nonwhites in the interest of white supremacy. As Dexter Hawkins, a white academic, put it in 1875, "The strength of [Anglo-Saxon] blood is manifest in the fact that it crosses with all cognate races, and takes up and absorbs their good qualities without losing its own identity."[21] As Hawkins's words attest, whites for centuries have been able to accept and appreciate nonwhite art forms without accepting and appreciating those who created them, resulting, as sociologist Black Hawk Hancock has observed, in a contradiction between the inclusion of nonwhite, especially African-American, *culture* and the simultaneous rejection and marginalization of nonwhite *people*.[22]

The Rise of Multiculturalism

As the twentieth century barreled forward and as the Civil Rights Movement rose up and changed the racial landscape of American politics, things began to shift within the aesthetic field. Specifically, nonwhite artists began to move from margin to center. For example, Spanish radio, which began in the 1920s, grew into a formidable enterprise serving the Southwest's growing Mexican-American population.[23] Asian-American painting—the works of Japanese-born Yasuo Kuniyoshi, for example—began appearing in art museums. And artistic movements—for instance, the blossoming of black literary and artistic life that took place throughout the 1920s and 1930s, known today as the Harlem Renaissance—challenged white domination within the aesthetic field. At first, many nonwhite artists had to rely on white sponsors for financial backing. Such uneasy collaboration often bridled nonwhites' artistic freedom and blunted their political edge. Not only this, but many a book publisher, movie producer, and theater owner shied away from avowedly antiracist works that, in their minds, would not turn a profit.[24] Under these limiting strictures, many nonwhite artists bleached their art, so to speak, conforming it to white tastes and prejudices.

Nonwhite artists were gaining admiration and acclaim, but because whites still controlled the levers of artistic production, many did not gain full control over their art or, for that matter, over their representations of racism or nonwhite groups. Bit by bit, however, nonwhite artists broke through artistic spaces that before had been virtually monopolized by whites. Asian-American musicians and conductors, such as Yo-Yo Ma, the highly acclaimed cello prodigy, and

Seiji Ozawa, who directed the Boston Symphony Orchestra from 1973 to 2002, shook up the world of classical music. African-American playwrights such as August Wilson (who won two Pulitzer Prizes) and Lorraine Hansberry (whose *Raisin in the Sun* was the first play written by a black woman to run on Broadway) emerged as respected dramatists whose plays confronted racism and plumbed the depths of Black America. (August Wilson's major work, a series of plays called *The Pittsburgh Cycle*, examined continuities and transformations in the black experience over the past hundred years, each of the ten plays in that series taking place in a different decade of the twentieth century.) Television sitcoms featuring Jewish characters and depicting Jewish life flourished in the 1970s and grew by leaps and bounds in the 1990s.[25] And in the realm of comedy, nonwhite comedians pushed the envelope and forced their audiences to confront racism. In the wake of the Civil Rights Movement, African-American comedian Richard Pryor made audiences laugh and squirm with his unapologetic, irreverent humor that found ample material in America's sticky "race problem." "The truth is gonna be funny," he wrote in his 1995 autobiography, "but it's gonna scare folks."[26]

It is undeniable that nonwhites have made considerable gains within the aesthetic field, but we must bear in mind that real progress is not measured simply by counting nonwhite bodies. In many cases, success comes with a price. The widely popular *The Cosby Show*, which aired from 1984 to 1992, introduced America to an upper-middle-class black family. The show refused to associate blackness with poverty and crime and, instead, presented a portrait of a family that many Americans, white and nonwhite alike, grew to respect and admire. As one commentator reflected, "It was impossible simply to laugh at these characters and make their blackness an object of derision and fascination."[27] But the show appealed to a significant slice of American viewers precisely because it neglected to confront racial domination or to grapple with problems facing many black Americans, such as racial barriers to economic advancement. One suspects that the show's ratings would have plummeted had it grappled with such controversial issues. Just as we must distinguish between superficial and substantive political representation (as we learned in Chapter 3), so we must abandon the assumption that the transference of nonwhite artists into mainstream "art worlds" (to borrow the well-known term of sociologist of culture Howard Becker) automatically results in the radical transformation of those worlds.[28]

Racial Representation in Art

Turning now to the present day, this section confronts the topic of racial representation in the aesthetic field. How does art represent racial groups and racial domination? How do fashion, television, music, photography, and other art forms present us with a racialized image of the social world? How might these images affect the racial order? These are the questions we address over the next several pages. As we will see, art can reflect, support, or challenge racial domination; it can be driven by white, racist, or antiracist aesthetics. As we navigate among the images and sounds that meet our eyes and ears on a daily basis, we should be diligent in deciphering how art represents racial domination and certain racial and ethnic groups. Is, for example, television programming defined more by the white, racist, or antiracist aesthetic? Certainly all three aesthetics are found on television, but which is more prevalent—and why?

The White Aesthetic

Detecting whiteness in art often means paying attention to absences. It means seeing the unseen, listening to silences. This requires our constantly asking ourselves on viewing a piece of art, "What—or who—is missing?" Images of whiteness often are understated and subtle. They rely on an unspoken edict that treats the white body and the white experience as normal, an edict that, for some of us, connects with our innermost presuppositions about the world. As art historian Martin Berger has observed, "Images do not persuade us to internalize racial values embedded within them, so much as they confirm meanings for which the discourses and structures of our society have predisposed us."[29] If this is the case, then our task should be to examine critically whiteness in art so as to better understand how our deep-seated racial dispositions fail to treat nonwhite experiences as a *central* part of American life.

Consider the world of *haute couture,* high fashion. When the spring 2008 collections of the Western world's most influential designers—from Prada and Balenciaga to Chloé and Chanel—premiered across America and Europe, the vast majority of the displayed clothing hung on the bodies of skinny, white blondes. More than one third of the fashion shows in New York City's runway season employed no black models, and most others employed just one or two. In fact, fashion agencies openly discriminate against nonwhites, sending modeling firms requests for "Caucasian models only." Because standards of beauty continue to be riveted to whiteness, white models often are much more sought after than nonwhite ones. Compare, for instance, Irina Kulikova, a young white Russian, and Honorine Uwera, a young black Canadian. Both women are "captivating beauties," as one observer put it, but while Uwera was hired for only five New York City runway shows during the spring 2008 season, Kulikova was hired for 24 in New York City, 14 in Milan, and 24 more in Paris. According to J. Alexander, a judge on *America's Next Top Model,* "Some people are not interested in the vision of the black girl unless they're doing a jungle theme and they can put her in a grass skirt and diamonds and hand her a spear."

Denying nonwhite women access to the runway strictly on the basis of their skin color is certainly unfair, but this kind of discrimination reaches beyond the models themselves to the dominant definition of beauty. In the words of one reporter, "It is not just a handful of genetically gifted young women who are hurt by this exclusion [that favors white models]. Vast numbers of consumers draw their information about fashion and identity from runways, along with cues about what, at any given moment, the culture decrees are the new contours of beauty and style."[30] The whiteness of *haute couture* is but one of a thousand mechanisms that bar nonwhiteness from our conception of the beautiful. Non-white children learn from a very young age that to be white is to be pretty and desirable, which is why, as psychologists have long shown, upon given the choice between a white doll and a black one, African-American preschool and elementary school children are more likely to choose the white one. And when asked to color a sketch of a person using a color that matches their own skin, these children frequently do not select an accurate match but a crayon a shade or two lighter than their own skin tone.[31]

These internalized biases—traces of symbolic violence—do not necessarily fade with age. According to the American Society of Plastic Surgeons, ethnic plastic surgery increased by 65% between 2000 and 2005, with nose jobs being the most common procedure among African Americans, Asian Americans, and Hispanics. Of the nearly half million Asian Americans on whom cosmetic surgery was performed in 2005, many underwent double-eyelid procedures meant to make their eyes look rounder—less "Asian."[32] "In the bathroom one night, I used a toothpick to push up my epicanthic folds," writes Vietnamese American Andrew Lam. "They held for a few seconds, giving me the appearance of rounder eyes, and a glimpse of what I might look like with double eyelids. I had contemplated cosmetic surgery, and for a few months, even saved money for the purpose." Lan never went through the surgery, although he was constantly bombarded with advertisements for such a procedure: "One only needs to open a Vietnamese magazine or newspaper in San Jose or Orange County to see the onslaught of ads for cosmetic surgery. . . . In the online business directory of the Southern California-based Nguoi Viet Daily News, where the largest Vietnamese population in the United States resides, there are more than 50 local listings for cosmetic surgery."[33] Millions of white Americans undergo cosmetic surgery as well—but not with the aim of inching closer to a white beauty standard—by altering, for example, their "black noses" or "Asian eyes."

Whiteness informs not only high fashion, which only an elite handful of people can afford, but also more everyday fashion—the kind of clothes worn by your classmates and, maybe, by you. Nowhere is this more obvious than in the marketing campaigns and hiring practices of Abercrombie and Fitch. A company that began supplying outdoor gear in 1892, Abercrombie and Fitch today is a

Abercrombie and Fitch has learned how to bottle up and sell white privilege by manufacturing a "look."

major fashion retailer targeting young consumers. The company owes its success less to the quality of its products than to its ability to peddle an image, to market a brand. And its success is attributed to tapping into young people's deep yearning to be included among "the beautiful people," who, in Abercrombie and Fitch's eyes, constitute the white leisure class. "Surely we know that people are not buying 'Abercrombie' for the clothes," writes Dwight McBride. "The catalogue isn't even about featuring those, after all. People buy 'Abercrombie' to purchase membership into a lifestyle. . . . In order for such a marketing strategy to work, in all of the diverse ways that this one clearly does, the consumer must necessarily bring to his or her understanding of A&F . . . a fundamentally racist belief that this lifestyle—this young, white, natural, all-American, upper-class lifestyle—being offered by the label is what we all either are, aspire to be, or are hopelessly alienated from ever being."[34]

If Abercrombie and Fitch continues to flourish, it is because it has learned how to bottle up and sell white privilege by manufacturing a "look." (Or, as *New York Post* fashion columnist Lisa Marsh has observed, Abercrombie and Fitch's "aggressive lifestyle marketing makes you feel like you're buying a polo shirt and getting the horse and summer house on Martha's Vineyard with it."[35]) This look can be spotted (in its catalogue, the enormously popular *A&F Quarterly*) in its larger-than-life posters featuring mostly (if not exclusively) white models, and even (and especially) in its store clerks, or "brand reps." Brand reps are hired only if they have the "A&F look," an embodiment of the celebration of whiteness on which the company thrives, and, indeed, they can be fired if they cease to embody it.[36] It should not surprise us that Abercrombie and Fitch's hiring practices long have discriminated against nonwhites, whose very presence affronts the "A&F look." For hard evidence, we need look no farther than the recent ruling of *Gonzalez v. Abercrombie & Fitch* (2005), which required Abercrombie & Fitch to pay $40 million to a group of African Americans, Asian Americans, and Hispanics who, together, filed a discrimination lawsuit against the retail giant.

Marketing research has found that nonwhites—especially Hispanics, Asian Americans, and Native Americans—consistently are underrepresented in commercials. And when nonwhites do appear in them, they often are typecast in stereotypical ways (for example, Asian Americans appear most frequently in ads for technological goods, like computers).[37] In the same way, some television shows and movies with all-white or majority-white casts have enjoyed enormous success. Think, for instance, of *Gossip Girl, Seinfeld,* or *Family Guy.* Consider as well comic strips, the vast majority of which feature exclusively white characters, from *Family Circus,* which represents a white middle-class worldview, to *Wizard of Id,* which depicts white characters fumbling about in the Middle Ages. Not a single frame in Bill Watterson's *Calvin and Hobbes,* which enjoyed a decade-long run as a syndicated daily from 1985 to 1995 and resulted in several book-length collections, featured a nonwhite character. Calvin met cranky teachers, mean babysitters, schoolmates, family members, aliens and monsters and dinosaurs— even rambunctious clones of himself—but never a Puerto Rican or an Indian American.

Art that fails to include nonwhites represents the world as a white world. And if nonwhites do not exist, then neither does racial domination. How, after all, could movies, television shows, and comic strips that exclude people of color ever hope seriously to wrestle with the topic of racial inequality? White artists, often unaware of the benefits they reap solely on account of their whiteness, often exert the privilege of pretending that race no longer matters. The Brady Bunch depicted an idyllic white family beset by the most minor problems—like finding a prom date—while black neighborhoods in major cities erupted in racial uprisings. The disconnection between the show's depiction of tranquil American life and the fires that burned through Watts and Harlem and Detroit is startling.

One thinks, too, of country music. Although country music long has marketed itself as the music of the "American working man," one is hard pressed to find a country ballad dealing with racial discrimination in the labor force, racialized wage inequalities, or the oppressive conditions under which migrant workers toil. On the contrary, we find songs that romanticize white racism. For example, Toby Keith's duet with Willie Nelson, "Beer for my Horses"—the video for which features only four people of color, including a black prostitute and a black homeless man urinating in public—glorifies lynching. (The company that owns the rights to this song, Tokeco Tunes, did not grant us permission to reprint the lyrics. However, we encourage you to log onto YouTube™ and watch the music video.)

As one journalist accurately has observed, "During the days when Toby Keith's 'Grandpappy' stalked the Jim Crow South, lynching was an institutional method of terror employed against blacks to maintain white supremacy." In the present day, the song has been so successful that it was made into a movie bearing the same title and starring Toby Keith as the bootstrapping hero. The villain? "A dark-skinned 'Mexican guy' who traffics drugs and kidnaps the girlfriend of Keith's character."[38]

Even less aggressive songs, ones that reminisce about "the good old days," are steeped in whiteness. The chorus of Rascal Flats's song, "Mayberry," the name of the fictional 1920s North Carolina town in which *The Andy Griffith Show* was set, nostalgically recalls a past era, in which life was simpler and better. But a song such as this (again, call up the music video online, and read the lyrics) prompts us to ask: for whom were the "good old days" good? Should we expect Asian Americans to long for this time, a time when Asian immigrants were barred entrance to the United States? Should we expect blacks to "miss Mayberry," at the height of the Ku Klux Klan and racial terrorism? Certainly not. Only whites can "miss Mayberry." Regardless of whether country artists recognize this or not, many of their songs breed a kind of **racist nostalgia**, a yearning among whites for a time when their dominion over nonwhites was surer than it is today.[39]

Racist nostalgia looms large in the American imagination. To find its visual incarnation, we need look no farther than the paintings of Norman Rockwell. An extremely popular and successful artist, Rockwell is best known for his paintings of "typical American life"—some of his favorite subjects being children, families, and patriotism—paintings that in the beginning of the twentieth century adorned *The Saturday Evening Post* and that can now be found on calendars, posters, coffee mugs, and, of course, in museums. A study of Rockwell's life's work reveals that, in his eyes, "typical American life" was white. Not only white, but happy too; American life was bereft of troubles (aside from war, which took place on foreign soil). White people are ice skating in one painting; white people are raking leaves in another. In others, white people are praying or drinking tea or being paid a visit by Santa Claus or being protected by white soldiers. Race was not completely off Rockwell's radar (he composed at least two paintings that dealt with racial segregation), but by and large this thoroughly American artist—perhaps

The white aesthetic presents itself as an un-raced representation of the social world. It desires to speak, not just for white people, but for *all* people.

the twentieth-century artist of America—represented his country as a white utopia where neither people of color nor trouble were to be found.

Norman Rockwell might not have sought to represent whiteness in his paintings any more than did the members of Rascal Flats in "Mayberry." But that is precisely the point. The **white aesthetic** presents itself as an un-raced representation of the social world. It desires to speak, not just for white people (for such a limitation would betray the racial nature of the aesthetic), but for *all* people—even for nature. In other words, by treating "white" as the unexamined artistic default category, the white aesthetic tries to lay claim to "the universal." However, as Pierre Bourdieu has pointed out, "A number of universalistic manifestos or universal prescriptions are no more than the product of (unconscious) universalizing of the particular case. . . . To grant 'humanity' to all, but in a purely formal way, is to exclude from it, under an appearance of humanism, all those who are deprived of the means of realizing it."[40] Norman Rockwell hoped to capture American life in his paintings, but he ended up capturing only a snapshot of white, middle-class America—and a euphemized and sanitized snapshot at that.

The Racist Aesthetic

If the white aesthetic seeks to normalize whiteness, the **racist aesthetic** seeks to depict people of color in negative ways. If the white aesthetic ignores people of color, the racist aesthetic represents them—but never in their full humanity. Rather, it distorts and stereotypes; it infantilizes and demonizes. And its ubiquity today—it is difficult to flip through a magazine or to watch an hour of television programming without seeing the racist aesthetic—demonstrates that nonwhites, regardless of their (relatively modern) presence in the aesthetic field, have yet to gain full control over the representations of themselves.

Take, for example, architecture. Saracenic or Moorish design, adapted by Americans and other Western architects from the styles of medieval Muslim builders from northern Africa and southern Spain, strikes many Americans as alien or "Eastern." Characterized by its onion-shaped domes (think of the Taj Mahal), sharp and vaulted roofs, and minarets, Saracenic architecture primarily is used in America to invoke a feeling of mystery and foreignness. Reserved for buildings that break with normal life—religious structures (for example, synagogues and Mormon temples), museums, and theaters—this architectural style conflates an Eastern design (or, rather, what Americans perceive to be an Eastern design) with spirituality and fantasy. It would be one thing if Saracenic architecture were used to serve many ends—a Saracenic-inspired strip mall, for instance—but since it is used almost exclusively in buildings that host exotic experiences, one cannot help but conclude that Americans interpret Saracenic architecture itself as exotic, along with the people (those of Arab descent) with which it is associated.[41]

Or consider the fact that many comedians promote a racist aesthetic. Amidst America's fascination with the war on terror, Jeff Dunham, the popular and talented ventriloquist, created a puppet character named Achmed the Dead Terrorist. Achmed is a skeleton, all that remains of a suicide bomber, with a turban wrapped around his skull. He talks with a heavy Middle-Eastern accent and berates the audience with the phrase, "Silence! I kill you!" Through Achmed—a "harmless" toy—Dunham is able to caricature Arabs and Islam. He stereotypes Mexican Americans as well—exaggerating their "ethnic-ness"—with his puppet José Jalapeño, a sombrero-topped jalapeño pepper with a long black mustache. African Americans don't escape his ridicule either. They are represented by Sweet Daddy D, a black pimp in flashy clothing. Through Dunham's puppets,

Arabs, Mexican Americans, and African Americans are represented only through their most stereotypical, pejorative—and emphatically *nonwhite*—properties.

Much of Carlos Mencia's material is blatantly racist. Born Ned Arnel Mencía in Honduras to a Mexican mother and Honduran father, Mencia has "Mexican-ized" himself—adopting the name Carlos and rarely mentioning his Honduran roots—and thinks this gives him license to make fun of "beaners" and "wet-backs" on his Comedy Central show. (Note that the racist aesthetic is not reserved for white artists. Nonwhite artists, too, can and often do perpetrate it.) Most recently, Mencia has appeared in a series of Bud Light commercials as a life coach to new immigrants. In an ad that aired during Super Bowl XXXX, Mencia tells a group of immigrant men, "American chicks love the foreign accent" before sending them off to hit on women. What follows is a string of failed interactions that portrays the immigrant men as low and ignorant: an immigrant from Nepal tells a woman she "has the legs of a Sherpa"; one from Africa pres-ents a woman with a chicken, saying, "She has your eyes."

Mencia's brand of humor thrives off its shock value. In this way, it resembles the work of "shock jocks" of talk radio shows, which are full of racial slurs and over-the-top offensive language. Some shock radio shows, such as Chicago's Mancow's Morning Madhouse or New York's El Vacilón de la Mañana, each day draw tens of thousands of listeners. This immense audience tunes in to hear their favorite personalities ridicule Muslims, Jews, women, gays, immigrants, and peo-ple of color. Shock jock Don Imus made headlines in 2007 for calling the black women on the Rutgers women's basketball team "nappy-headed hos." As this sex-ist and racist comment was circulated over the Internet and on news channels, the public voiced their outrage. Imus apologized and was fired by CBS Radio. Eight months later, however, he returned to the airwaves and seemed to have little trou-ble securing business advertisers and high-powered guests. Indeed, John McCain, the Arizona Senator and Republican presidential nominee in 2008, joined Imus during his first day back on the air.[42] Shock jocks often justify their offensive humor by claiming, in the words of New York-base radio host Nick Di Paolo, that they "take shots at everybody." This is certainly untrue, for whites—as a racial group—rarely are the butt of jokes, unlike Native Americans, African Americans, and Chinese, Mexican, and Arab immigrants. But even if such a comment were accurate, it would not excuse the racist content of shock humor, for a dig targeting a group that has been beaten down, day after day, by racial domination does not pack the same punch as one pitched at a privileged group.

If you are a regular television viewer or movie buff, you probably already are aware of the racist aesthetic's prevalence in popular culture. Nonwhite actors often are cast in stereotypical roles. Native American actors, for example, usually appear on screen only as Indians doing "Indian things," as opposed to modern-day executives, athletes, or members of a suburban family. And when Hollywood does attempt to depict Indian life, it often grossly misrepresents tribal ceremonies, showing Indians performing dog-eating or wrist-cutting rituals, or using ceremonies of one tribe to (mis)represent another.[43] Arab-American actors have it equally bad, as they often are depicted as enraged Muslim terrorists. Iranian-American actor Max Jorbrani explains that his career started out with auditions "for terrorist role after terrorist role." He refused to play the game and has turned down many (well-paying) roles that depict Arabs as uncomplicated, violent savages, including the terrorist mastermind of Fox's show *24*, which boasts of 15 million viewers. When viewers see a white villain, Jorbrani explains, they think "Wow, that American's crazy," but on seeing an Iranian-American villain, they think, "Man, those Iranians are crazy."[44]

Countless other examples abound. One thinks of the gratuitous use of the word "nigger" in Quentin Tarantino films, especially in *Pulp Fiction*.[45] One thinks, too, of the endless association of goodness with whiteness and of evil with blackness in the *Lord of the Rings* trilogy. Gandalf, the "white wizard," rides a white horse (Shadofax) and helps the heroes defend the white folks of Rohan and the "White City" of Minan Tirith against the ruthless Uruks, "tall, black, and muscular [creatures] with long, coarse hair that resembles dreadlocks."[46] And Anime, the collection of animated video games, playing cards, television shows, and movies that originated in Japan and now has blossomed into a global enterprise, does not avoid the racist aesthetic. The Nintendo-owned *Pokémon* series features a character named Jynx that is modeled after minstrel caricatures of African Americans. With its blackface and exaggerated lips and breasts, Jynx's main weapon of attack is its sexuality—its sensual dance and "lovely kiss"— which links blackness to hyper-eroticism. Similarly, *Dragon Ball Z* features Mr. Popo, a blackfaced genie whose head is wrapped in a bejeweled turban. Mr. Popo has been described as a "loyal servant" willing to please, resembling, top-to-bottom, the slaves of minstrel shows.[47] That hundreds of thousands of children around the globe are introduced to the racist aesthetic through characters like Jynx and Mr. Popo is disconcerting, to say the least.

The racist aesthetic misrepresents not only people of color but also the very nature of racial domination. It does so in at least three ways. First, it whitewashes history to blunt the sharp edge of past wrongs and replaces nonwhite heroes with white ones. In the film *Mississippi Burning*, for example, two white FBI agents investigate the slayings of Goodman, Schwerner, and Chaney, the three Civil Rights workers who were killed in 1964. The white agents crack the case single-handedly, and justice is served. Thus, the film turns the Civil Rights Movement's "historical enemies—the racist FBI which harassed and sabotaged the movement—into the film's heroes, while turning the historical heroes—the thousands of African Americans who marched and braved beatings and imprisonment and sometimes death—into the supporting cast, passive victim-observers waiting for official White rescue."[48] Indeed, as several film critics have observed, the white male savior of seemingly helpless nonwhite communities is a common trope in movies, one that perhaps began with the 1962 classic, *To Kill a Mockingbird*. Think, for example, of *Black Hawk Down, Three Kings,* or *The Matrix,* to list but a few.[49]

The second way the racist aesthetic distorts racial domination is by pretending it does not exist. But rather than excluding altogether nonwhites and their troubles (like a Norman Rockwell painting), the racist aesthetic includes nonwhites but excludes racial domination. Society is depicted as a kind of racial utopia: racial domination has been vanquished; racial inequalities are non-existent; the history of racial oppression is long forgotten. This is why racial domination never seems a problem between the two lead characters of the *Lethal Weapon* series: Murtaugh, the straight-laced, married black middle-class cop played by Danny Glover, and Riggs, the psychotic, alcoholic divorced white cop played by Mel Gibson. "In [interracial] buddy films such as *Lethal Weapon*," writes anthropologist John Jackson, Jr., "black middle-classness (that is, moral, behavioral, ethical conservatism) and white male marginality combine to depict race without engaging the entrenched discourses of racial difference found in the real world beyond the reel world."[50]

But perhaps the most invidious way the racist aesthetic warps the true nature of racial domination is by depicting it as a purely psychological issue. It reduces racial domination to interpersonal racism—racist attitudes and prejudice—while ignoring institutional racism. When Dr. Phil, the popular television psychologist, dedicated two back-to-back shows to the events of Jena 6, he overlooked the long history of violent racial domination in the South as well as modern-day racial domination in the legal field and, instead, (predictably) preferred pinning the blame on the parents. "Where is the parenting here, on both sides?" he asked.

Or consider the movie *Crash*, which won the Oscar for Best Picture in 2005. *Crash* features a multiethnic cast and grapples with racial and class-based tensions in Los Angeles. Tempers flare between a racist white police officer and black citizens, a wealthy white woman and her Hispanic maid, an Iranian storeowner and a tattooed Hispanic family man, and so the movie goes. Viewers are berated with one jarringly racist exchange and insult after another and, in the end, walk away with the impression that virtually everybody is a racist and that racism is violent and visible and quite conscious. *Crash* should be commended for attempting to confront racial domination, but it should be criticized for doing so in such an elementary and misleading fashion, presenting racism as just a collection of mean attitudes and opinions possessed by whites and nonwhites alike. The movie makes little mention of historical and institutional racism, apart from which interpersonal racism ceases to exist. Even more troubling is the film's tendency to represent racism as something that affects all people equally; having reviewed a mass of sociological evidence in the previous chapters, we know better. With *Crash* we see that some of the most well-intentioned films can do more harm than good when it comes to offering an accurate and complex picture of racial domination.[51]

The Antiracist Aesthetic

Just as art can be used on behalf of racial domination, it can be marshaled on behalf of racial justice. Indeed, art always has functioned as a primary "weapon of the weak," a mode of defense against racial tyranny. Native Americans joke that Custer was well dressed for the Battle of Little Big Horn; when Sioux scouts found his body, he was dressed in an Arrow shirt.[52] Noting that the artistic resistance of dominated groups sometimes takes the form of rejoicing at the misfortunes of their oppressors, anthropologist James Scott recalls that the sinking of the *Titanic* struck many blacks as "a stroke of poetic justice." Some even wrote and sang songs celebrating the event:

> All the millionaires looked at Shine [a black stoker] say,
>
> "Now Shine, oh Shine, save poor me."
>
> Say, "We'll make you wealthier than one Shine can be."
>
> Shine say, "You hate my color and you hate my race."
>
> Say, "Jump overboard and give those sharks a chase."
>
> And everybody on board realized they had to die.
>
> But Shine could swim, and Shine could float,
>
> And Shine could throw his ass like a motorboat.[53]

Subversive art is propelled by the **antiracist aesthetic**, an artistic approach that seeks somehow to throw a wrench in the grinding gears of racial domination. This can be accomplished in several ways.

Instead of ignoring America's brutal past, or twisting history to cast racist whites in a positive light, antiracist art forces its audience to confront American racial history honestly and courageously. This is the impulse behind Kara Walker's powerful artwork. An African-American woman, and one of the youngest recipients of the MacArthur "Genius" Award, Walker specializes in room-sized installations featuring silhouetted depictions of Africans Americans and whites during slavery. Her pieces often feature unsettling images, such as white-on-black violence, the rape of enslaved African girls by older white men, black suicide, and infanticide. The silhouetted shapes command the eye and force you to study them in such a way that you find yourself asking, "Is that really what I see?" and then, "Did that—that monstrosity—really happen?" Walker's work is a direct assault on racist nostalgia and leaves its viewers angered and ashamed, even nauseous.[54] In a similar way, Japanese-American artist Michi Itami confronts the history of Japanese internment camps. In his computer-generated photo collage, "The Irony of Being American," Itami overlays three pictures of his father—one in traditional Japanese dress, one in a business suit, and one in his Army uniform—against a picture of Manzanar, the internment camp where he and his family were held captive.[55]

Subversive art also can provide a direct response to the racist aesthetic, correcting distorted representations of nonwhites and racial domination. Some Native-American artists, for example, have responded sardonically to the pervasive tendency to depict Native Americans as relics of the past. Jimmie Durham's "On Loan from the Museum of the American Indian" displays his personal belongings as museum relics to mock scientists' and artists' all too frequent tendency to portray American Indians only as anthropological subjects to be gazed upon and studied. A photograph of Durham's mother and father is placed against black paper and labeled, "The Indian's Parents (frontal view)." Even more confrontational is James Luna's "The Artifact Piece." This installation features the artist himself, a member of the Luiseño Nation, lying face-up on a bed of sand in a museum case. The displayed Luna is marked with a name tag and other labels that draw attention to his scars, including ones received from bouts of "excessive drinking."[56] These two humorous pieces parody the racist aesthetic to ridicule it: American Indians present their belongings—or, in Luna's case, their selves—as ancient relics stuck in the past in order to demonstrate the absurdity of such a view.

The white aesthetic has not gone unscrutinized by antiracist art. Recently, several artists from across the aesthetic field have attempted to call attention to whiteness through their work.[57] One thinks, for instance, of Roger Shimomura's striking paintings and prints, which address distorted stereotypes of Asian Americans and racist encounters he has experienced personally. In his 2002 acrylic, "Passé," Shimomura depicts a group of well-dressed white women and men discussing an artist's portfolio. The painting is accompanied by the following explanation: "In 2002, Roger was asked to submit a proposal for [an] arts project on a university campus in the state of Washington. The submitted drawing proposed a mural which would explore the complex question as to whether America would be better off continuing to be thought of as a 'melting pot,' or whether it might be more relevant today for America to be more like a 'tossed salad.' A month later Roger was told that he was not awarded the commission due in part to an art historian on the panel who said that the subject was 'soooo passé.'"

One thinks, too, of Nikki Lee. A young, Korean-born artist based in New York, Lee specializes in embedding herself in American subcultures, adopting their dress, postures, and behaviors and then having herself photographed. For her "Yuppie Project," Lee immersed herself in the fast-paced, white-dominated world of Wall Street professionals and emerged with photographs that render whiteness visible. Lee captured the relationship between white privilege and affluence by underscoring the yuppies' expensive clothing, their country-club camaraderie, and their racial exclusivity.[58] In her photographs, whiteness is represented not as the norm but as a curious, tangible something to be objectified and placed in specific social and historical contexts.

The world of poetry has always been—and remains—a hotbed of the antiracist aesthetic. From the pens of poets such as Audre Lorde, Sonia Sanchez, and Sekou Sundiata have come the sternest abominations of all forms of oppression. And spoken-word poets, those who perform their work on stage, recently have emerged as some of the most outspoken critics of racial domination. (Indeed, the spoken-word scene is one of the most multicultural, democratic, and critically minded spaces in contemporary America.) Thus, in his humorous "Super Negro," a young black poet who goes by the name of Al B. Back likens his blackness (and the discrimination he faces because of it) to superpowers:

> I can make you pick me for any sport,
>
> Before you found out that I'm just a poet with seven sisters. . . .
>
> I am so mature, that my face can rearrange in days,
>
> Change in ways that cops everyday need to stop me, and see my ID. . . .
>
> Chickens in fear always bow when they see me.
>
> Surveillance cameras always make it their point to see me.

"In America," a poem penned by Palestinian-American poet Suheir Hammad, links contemporary American society to its colonial past:

> right now you are standing
>
> on stolen land no matter
>
> where you are reading this poem
>
> i promise below you is stolen
>
> land was lakota was navajo
>
> was creek was
>
> and was and is and is and
>
> this fact does not change
>
> because you do not think
>
> about it or you thought
>
> the last Indian died before you were
>
> born or you were born 1/15 apache

Both these poets use the tricks of their trade—Al B. Back marshals blues-tinged comedy and irony; Hammad uses fast-moving style and geographic imagery—to denounce racial domination. In doing so, they hope to unsettle and mature our current modes of comprehension, to remedy the imbalance that results, as Saul Williams says in his poem, "Coded Language," when "Your current frequencies of understanding outweigh/That which has been given for you to understand."

Although television programs and movies have slowly but steadily integrated an antiracist aesthetic into their repertoires—think, for example, of the stereotypes that are turned on their heads in *Grey's Anatomy*—comedians are perhaps popular culture's most creative critics of racial domination. While a good many comedians end up supporting racial domination, many others have used humor to break down stereotypes and to ridicule racism. The "Axis of Evil" comedy troupe, made up of performers of Middle Eastern descent, calls attention to the ways Arab Americans suffer at the hands of racial domination; Margaret Cho's edgy humor takes homophobia and sexism and anti-immigrant sentiment to task; and Dave Chappelle's sketch comedy and stand-up routines scrutinize race relations. Through his character Clayton Bigsby—a blind black man who believes himself to be white and who is an outspoken white supremacist—Chappelle finds a clever and hilarious way to belittle bigotry.

And, of course, the antiracist aesthetic courses through the lyrics of some forms of music. It seeps through the songs of Woody Guthrie, a white American and folk legend from Great Depression times. A staunch defender of worker and immigrant rights, when Guthrie learned of an airplane crash that killed Mexican migrants being deported from California back to Mexico, migrants who were referred to only as "deportees" in the news coverage, he grew incensed and, in response, wrote "deportee," an indictment of the exploitation of immigrants.

The folk tradition of Guthrie has been given new relevance by singers such as Ani di Franco. In songs such as "Subdivision," a critique of white flight, one finds a powerful antiracist message. Juan Díes of the group Sones de Mexico also has followed in Guthrie's footsteps. While translating Guthrie's "This Land Is Your Land" into Spanish, so Mexican migrant workers might hear its protest-pregnant lyrics, Díes added a verse of his own: "In the world there are people who are poor/In the world there are people who are rich/And then there are the others, the travelers/Who are seeking an opportunity." The *corrido,* a Mexican folk ballad that tells a story, has for years been used to chronicle Mexican history. Today, many Mexican immigrants have embraced *corridos* and have begun to write tunes that document their current struggles. Responding to America's repressive anti-immigrant policies, for example, Jose Garcia reaches for his accordion and sings:

> Now they are putting up barriers in front of us so we don't return;
> But that is not going to block us from crossing the United States,
> We leap them like deer; we go under them like moles.[59]

The Promise and Pitfalls of Hip-Hop

Until now we have said little about hip-hop, that cultural movement that combines music, break-dancing, graffiti, deejaying, fashion, and poetry into one distinctive style. Hip-hop is one of the most influential art forms today. (To take but one example, after Busta Rhymes released "Pass the Courvoisier," sales for the French cognac shot through the roof, increasing by 5% in the first quarter of 2002 and by over 10% months later.[60]) It is also one of the most controversial. Indeed, hip-hop is chock full of racial and sexual messages that deserve to be dissected with care through intersectional analysis. The descendent of jazz, black rhetoric, African drumming, quick-tongued poetry and humor, rap—which stands for "rhythm and poetry"—originated in the black ghetto. This unrelentingly urban art form exploded a few brief months after Harlem's Sugarhill Gang released "Rapper's Delight" in 1979 and, since then, has bloomed into a global enterprise worth billions. Today, hip-hop music stands as *the* defining musical movement of this generation. In every consecutive year since 1999, rap has been the second best-selling music category (behind rock).[61] Cornel West calls rap music "the musical expression of the paradoxical cry of desperation and celebration of the black underclass and poor working class."[62] For Trisha Rose, author of the celebrated book, *Black Noise: Rap Music and Black Culture in Contemporary America*, rap represents "the central cultural vehicle for open social reflection on poverty, fear of adulthood, the desire for absent fathers, frustrations about black male sexism, female sexual desires, daily rituals of life as an unemployed teen hustler, safe sex, raw anger, violence, and childhood memories."[63] How, then, might we analyze hop-hop's association with racial domination given the three aesthetic forms described above?

Although rap began as a beat-thumping voice of protest, many have claimed it has ceased to be a positive force. It has become commonplace for rappers to pepper their songs with violent and unblushing homophobic and misogynistic lyrics. And their videos, many of which accurately can be classified as soft-core pornography (especially the "uncensored versions" that appear on YouTube[TM]), often reduce women to mere sexual objects who exist solely to satisfy men's sensual desires. Consider Nelly's "Tip Drill," named after an ugly person used for sex or money. The song's music video shows Nelly and his entourage arriving at a mansion filled with nude and nearly nude black women who proceed to rub their bodies over the fully clothed men and shake their butts in front of the camera. The men slap the women's butts and throw money at their vaginas, an act that reduces the women to prostitutes.

In his overt degradation of women, Nelly is typical. We could easily have selected sexist songs by Ludacris, 50 Cent, or Eminem. It is no wonder, then, that sociologists have found African Americans who listen to rap to be more likely to harbor homophobic and misogynistic attitudes than those who do not.[64]

Add to this the violent lyrics of many popular rap artists, which some politicians have used to justify police crack-downs in black neighborhoods, as well as rap's hypermaterialism, its emphasis on "getting paid" and living luxuriously, manifest in ostentatious displays of gold and diamonds, fancy cars, and expensive liquor in rap videos (consider, for example, Ghostface Killer's "We Celebrate"), and one can begin to understand why some prominent African Americans, such as the Reverends Delman Coates and Calvin Butts, have called for an all-out boycott of rap music.[65] At best, this brand of hip-hop—namely, gangsta rap—fails to function as a cultural movement that advances the cause of social justice; at worst, it helps to support racial domination and masculine (not to mention heterosexual) domination by depicting black men as ultraviolent killers and black women as at-your-service sexual objects.[66]

And yet, and yet: Hip-hop is perhaps the most outspokenly defiant and powerful voice for racial justice emanating from the aesthetic field. Nelly and 50 Cent are not representative of hip-hop's rich diversity. Indeed, progressive-minded rappers, such as Queen Latifa and Lupe Fiasco, sing out against racial and class-based domination and criticize the exploitation of women. Referencing the dilapidated state of American ghettos, the Seattle-based Blue Scholars rap in "Back Home":

> And they say "progress," but the fact is
> Dr. Martin Luther King's legacy is lookin'
> Like the streets we named after 'em:
> Permanently under construction
> The people hustlin'
> Despite the pain and sufferin'.

Some of the harshest critics of hip-hop's sexism, materialism, and violence are hip-hop artists. Go listen to Lauryn Hill's "Superstar" or Saul William's "Black Stacy." They demonstrate clearly that hip-hop has a "socially conscious" dimension. Like all art forms, it is not one-dimensional; it encompasses both racist and antiracist aesthetics. Indeed, rappers are far from one-dimensional. One thinks immediately of Tupac Shakur, who alternated between uncritical acceptance of gangsta motifs and highly critical-minded social commentary. Or of Eminem, who, in one verse, makes light of violence against women, while, in another, he scathingly indicts racial domination, pointing out, as he does in "The Way I Am," that shootings in white suburban schools shock America while black-on-black inner-city violence is hardly considered newsworthy.

Often, people debating hip-hop speak past one another. Someone will criticize hip-hop's sweat-dripped sexism or blood-stained violence, while someone else will call attention to its more "socially conscious" aspects. Hip-hop, like all art forms, is not one-dimensional; it encompasses both racist and antiracist aesthetics. Indeed, rappers themselves are far from one-dimensional. One thinks immediately of Tupac Shakur, who alternated between uncritical acceptance of gangsta motifs and highly critical-minded social commentary. Or of Eminem, who, in one verse, makes light of violence against women, while, in another, scathingly indicts racial domination, pointing out, as he does in "The Way I Am," that shootings in white suburban schools shock America while black-on-black inner-city violence is hardly considered newsworthy: "And look where it's at/middle America/*Now* it's a tragedy./*Now* it's so sad to see./An upper-class city/havin' this happen."[67]

A weapon against racial domination, hip-hop is full of great promise—and great disappointment. The important sociological question, therefore, is this: What social forces act on hip-hop to turn it away or toward its political roots? Corporate pressure is certainly one answer. Major record labels and television stations—many of which have to answer to powerful (and often white) corporate executives—often pressure hip-hop artists to abandon calls for liberation and justice in favor of indulgent consumerism and sexism.[68] As a former hip-hop magazine editor has observed, "MTV has really gotten behind these artists who represent the one small fraction [of hip-hop] that degrades and humiliates Black culture. It's not even about the music or the culture anymore; it's just about the money."[69] Spoken-word artist Taalam Acey makes a similar point in his poem, "Market for Ni$$as":

> The more he shows his draws,
>
> The more he gets applause,
>
> And if he's willing to play the role of society's savage,
>
> Then society will make him a star . . .
>
> Just focus on being a stereotype,
>
> Like, you wake up every morning just dying to fight,
>
> Just snappin' pictures of stackin' riches
>
> Of clappin' triggers and slappin' bitches.

Not only is the minstrelized black image marketable; so, too, is a watered-down representation of black political protest. Music promoters have found a way to **"merchandise dissent,"** to turn the idea of "revolution" itself into a depoliticized commodity.[70] As one art historian has observed, hip-hop's "transgressive and revolutionary underpinnings have not been abandoned, but rather recoded within the matrix of capitalist consumption. . . . Hip-hop uses economic achievement and materialistic braggadocio as a form of resistance to white racism and its economic stronghold on the black community, as opposed to a politically infused transgression."[71] In other words, in mainstream hip-hop, "revolution" is reduced to getting rich: Stick it to "The Man" by buying a Bentley.

Besides examining how corporate and economic forces influence the course of hip-hop, we also should examine if and how hip-hop is unfairly singled out for criticism because it is a distinctly black art form. After all, sexist and violent lyrics are not unique to hip-hop. Country western singers, for example, have penned violent lyrics at least since Johnny Cash. "Early in the morning, while making the rounds/I took a shot of cocaine, and I shot my woman down," Cash sings in "Cocaine Blues." In "Attitude Adjustment," Hank Williams, Jr., gives his girlfriend an "adjustment on the top of her head." In rock music, Neil Young shoots his baby "Down by the River"; the Beatles threaten a woman with death if she ever cheats in "Run for Your Life"; and the lead singer of Better Than Ezra fantasizes about killing his girlfriend and "savor[ing] the sight" in "Porcelain."[72] It is not simply the content of offensive rap lyrics that results in hip-hop being labeled the country's "most dangerous music." It is how those offensive lyrics bring to the surface America's longstanding fear of black men.[73] And, indeed, because hip-hop is intimately connected to African Americans, "criticizing rap or hip-hip becomes a way to utter sweeping condemnations of Black people and Black culture without ever having to explicitly frame such commentary in racial terms."[74]

The Racialization of Art Worlds

The proceeding section dealt with the artistic representation of race or how art depicts racial groups and racial domination. This section deals with the racialization of the aesthetic field or how racial domination guides and structures artistic production and consumption. Gustave Flaubert, the famous French novelist, once complained, "One does not write what one wants."[75] What did he mean? That artists—who often profess to being liberated individuals beholden to nothing and no one—are constrained by the structures of the aesthetic field. The artist's world is not set off from society but is grafted, head to heel, to the social world and its problems.

The Power of the White Gaze

Despite many significant inroads made by nonwhites into Hollywood, the music industry, art museums, and other cultural institutions, whites continue to wield significant control over the arts. As in sports, nonwhites constitute many of the players and performers but few of those who hold the power: owners, curators, producers, directors, or scriptwriters. Studies have concluded that nonwhites are underrepresented in "each and every aspect" of the entertainment industry. For example, nonwhite directors account for less than 3% of those registered with the Directors' Guild of America. Indeed, with the exception of Taiwan-born Ang Lee, every single recipient of the Academy Award for Best Director has been a white man. And nonwhite filmmakers often have to work with a shoe-string budget, as Hollywood producers, who are more than willing to pour millions into summer action blockbusters, seem hesitant to fund films written and produced by nonwhites.[76]

Or consider the (white) corporate domination of radio. Have you ever driven across the country and wondered why many of the radio stations in California sound like the ones in Nebraska, which sound like the ones in North Carolina? It is a safe bet that the similarity is due to the fact that the same company that owns the radio stations in California owns the ones in Nebraska and North Carolina, too. Clear Channel Communications, one of the nation's largest media conglomerates, owns over 1,000 full-power AM and FM radio stations, not to mention 12 XM Satellite radio channels and over 30 television stations. In other words, roughly 1 in 10 radio stations is a Clear Channel station.[77] Clear Channel's domination of the airwaves leaves little room for more critically minded music or political viewpoints that challenge the racial status quo, which is why the Black Eyed Peas are played over and over but many radio listeners have never heard of Aesop Rock or Erykah Badu.

Whites also are overrepresented in positions of power in art museums, constituting a sizeable portion of museum trustees, curators, and directors. It is beyond dispute that artists of color and artworks that challenge racial domination now make frequent appearances in major art museums. But it is also beyond dispute that such museums are bastions of Eurocentrism. In most museums, white European and American artists are the ones most prominently displayed. Museums that wish to provide visitors with a thoroughly non-Eurocentric art education must get by on decidedly less impressive budgets, which is why we tend to find such museums tucked away in small, usually unremarkable buildings and staffed by a cadre of committed volunteers. They tell a different story, yes, but their voice is far softer than the one that booms from New York's Metropolitan Museum of Art or the Chicago Art Institute.[78]

Consider the following example. In 2007, the art scene was shaken by a major exhibition in New York City of drawings by a little known Mexican-American artist named Martin Ramirez. A penniless migrant worker in California, Ramirez had been picked up from the streets in 1931 by police and institutionalized in a mental hospital, where he was diagnosed as a catatonic schizophrenic. Confined to asylums over the next quarter-century, he produced hundreds of drawings "on available bits of paper glued together with a paste made of bread or potatoes and saliva."[79] "Discovered" thereafter by art critics and curators, he is now compared to Picasso and other masters, even hailed as "simply one of the greatest artists of the twentieth century."[80] And yet his exhibition in 2007 took place not at the

Museum of Modern Art, that great citadel of twentieth-century artistic modernism, but at the (decidedly less prestigious) American Folk Art Museum.

As nonwhites continue to be excluded from the highest seats of artistic power and control, it is small wonder that whiteness continues to infuse our conception of the beautiful. Whiteness guides artists and critics as they decide what should be classified as "art" and what should not. The best-known mid-twentieth century sociologist of music, Theodor Adorno, infamously dismissed (black-dominated) jazz as one of "many varieties of rhythmic-spatial music . . . 'sprouting forth everywhere as though they are rooted in nature,'" even as he lavished praise on (white-dominated) classical music, which he described as "expressive-dynamic."[81] Only Duke Ellington earned his grudging respect—but solely on account of Ellington's "tasteful" appropriation of musical ideas already found in compositions by Claude Debussy and Maurice Ravel. In many cases, creations by nonwhites are revered as "art" only when respected white critics—or white establishments or elite artists—revere them as such. To take but another example, African masks and sculpture have been around for centuries, but it was only after famous European artists such as Picasso and Matisse began including African masks in their paintings that the masks appeared to the white-dominated art world as "art."[82] In this case, white artists borrowed images from the nonwhite (indeed, non-Western) world and refurbished that image through an established artistic medium (for example, modernist painting) to incorporate it into the artistic canon.

In other cases, ordinary artifacts and tools created by nonwhites to meet everyday needs are "discovered" by white art critics. For years, the black women of Gee's Bend, a poverty-stricken patch of Alabama, made quilts out of discarded cloth and rags. The quilts were stunning—colorful and complex, the material cut and sewn by hand—and eventually were discovered by museum curators. In 2002, the Houston's Museum of Fine Arts devoted an impressive exhibition to the quilts of Gee's Bend, an exhibition that gripped the nation's attention. Soon, they were shown in some of the nation's most prominent museums and impressive art books were dedicated to them. The (white) discovery of the Gee's Bend quilts did not make them more beautiful or special (and it is still unclear if it has improved the lives of the quilt-makers themselves), but it did make them "art." Once the quilts were hung in Houston's Museum of Fine Arts, they became, as the museum director put it, "works of art that just happened to be made for utilitarian purposes."[83]

With little effort other examples could be highlighted—from the pottery of Native America to the crafts of the Pacific Islands—demonstrating the control cultural elites exercise over the definition of "art." When "folk art" or "outsider art" (these are art historians' terms) are deemed important by these cultural gatekeepers, important enough to be exhibited in museums, important enough to be studied and purchased at high prices, we are able to catch a glimpse of how whiteness conditions their aesthetic decisions. After all, in a majority of cases, art created outside the normal boundaries of an art world—by people who reside outside the normal boundaries of society—is deemed **"naïve art."** A beautiful handmade quilt made by a poor black woman of Alabama is art; a beautiful handmade quilt made by a middle-class white grandmother is not. Why? Because the beauty of "naïve art" is found in its *exotic*—not normal, not white—characteristics. It is found in its Africanism, its Orientalism, its primitivism, all of which come to us filtered though the white aesthetic.[84] As the dominant and normative artistic judgment that pervades the aesthetic field, the unexamined artistic default category, the white aesthetic normalizes whiteness by exoticizing nonwhiteness.

Just as the white aesthetic can turn an ordinary quilt into a masterpiece, it can reward artists whose work supports it and punish artists whose work it finds threatening. Since the first year of the award (1996), the Grammy Award for the Best Rap Album has been given either to rappers whose lyrics are peppered with misogyny and violence (Eminem has won three times) or to those whose music *mostly* avoids discussing social inequalities and racial domination (Kanye West has won three times as well). In 2001, Halle Berry became the first black woman to win an Academy Award for Best Actress. She took home the Oscar for her performance as Leticia Musgrove in *Monster's Ball*. Leticia is a single mother and a "loose woman," whose husband sits on death row. His execution is overseen by Hank Grotowski, a racist jailer played by Billy Bob Thornton. Leticia, often dazed and drunk, shown slouching, legs askew, in revealing clothing, meets Hank, and the two quickly form a desperate, confused, and physical relationship. In one scene, Leticia, writhing in emotional agony, tells Hank, "Make me feel better." What follows is a graphic sex scene, "one of the rawest, most intense sexual scenes in American cinematic history," according to one critic.[85] Eventually, Leticia moves in with Hank. During their first night together, Hank tells her, "I'm gonna take care of you." She replies, "Good, 'cause I really need to be taken care of." Berry won the Oscar, in other words, for her role as a poor, low-life, promiscuous, black woman who needs a white man—indeed, the man who supervised the execution of her husband—to take care of her. (Here, again, is another example of the white male savior.) The role so degraded black women that some black actresses had turned it down before Berry accepted it. Angela Bassett was one of them. When asked why, Bassett replied, "It's about character, darling. I wasn't going to be a prostitute on film. I couldn't do that because it's such a stereotype about black women and sexuality."[86]

The distribution of awards is but one indicator of how institutions within the aesthetic field award nonwhite artists when they do not challenge the dominant, white representation of the social world. One could also analyze artists' fame and fortune. The distance between nonwhite musical artists who do not challenge the racial status quo and those who do—measured, for example, by the prominence of their music videos on MTV or their songs on the radio, how easily one can find their CDs, how often they are featured in *Rolling Stone*, and their net worth—is considerable.

Indeed, the white aesthetic is so powerful that few artists can escape it. Even those who wish to challenge it are forced to acknowledge it. To quote Cornel West once more, the African-American artist driven by an antiracist aesthetic "still seems too preoccupied with how black folk appear to the white normative gaze, too obsessed with showing white people how sophisticated they are, how worthy [they are] of white validation and recognition. . . . The irony of the view of black art as protest . . . [is that] it reduces black people to mere reactors to white power."[87] If artists represent nonwhites only as the **un-stereotype**, they end up responding to white representations of nonwhiteness.[88] To wrest free of the white gaze, artists must depict nonwhites in their full and complex humanity rather than representing them in the soft glow of romanticism, as only as their stereotype's mirror image: *not* criminals, *not* impoverished, and so on. In painting, Horace Pippin, the self-trained African-American artist, achieves such a goal, "portray[ing] black people as 'fully themselves'—that is, as they are outside of the white normative gaze that requires elaborate masks and intricate posturing for black survival and sanity."[89] In literature, one also thinks of Zora Neale Hurston; in film, of Oscar Micheaux.[90]

In the aesthetic field, works and performances that do not align with the white aesthetic tend to be marginalized, pushed to the side. Artists who refuse to "sell out" to racial domination often do not enjoy the perks of artistic success—wealth, fame, long-running television shows, lavish record deals, prominent museum exhibits—as often as those artists who do. Faced with the tension that long has defined the aesthetic field—that between art and money, authenticity and profitability, truth and clichés—artists must choose to what extent, if at all, they will sell out, most of them fully aware of the consequences of their decision.

Alternative viewpoints are relegated to low-budget media sources found on the edges of the aesthetic field: low-power pirate radio stations, ethnic newspapers and websites, a museum that relies on donations (as opposed to government funding) and makes do in a small building on the "bad side" of town.[91] Never in the history of humankind have shouts of protest against racial domination been completely silenced, and today, in some artistic corners, they are perhaps louder than ever. But sometimes it is hard to be heard above all the noise.

The Racial Structures of the Aesthetic Field

Artistic divisions—those separating, say, different styles of dance, musical tastes, fashion senses, or schools of art—map onto racial divisions. Or, as cultural sociologist William Roy put it, "boundaries between aesthetic genres correspond to social boundaries between groups."[92] In the 1930s, country music was so explicitly connected to whiteness that the KKK hosted fiddle contests. Rhythm and blues, by contrast, was linked to blackness, so much so that rhythm and blues records were first called "race records."[93] With respect to this specific division, not much has changed. Country-western, along with polka and rock-and-roll, continue to be associated with whites, while rhythm and blues, along with hip-hop, gospel, funk, and soul, are associated with blacks. Other musical tastes are racially coded as well: cumbia, salsa, and reggaetón, for example, are connected to Latino culture. Indeed, the distribution of musical instruments is related to the distribution of racial groups: the steel guitar with whites; the pipa with Chinese Americans; the sitar with Indian Americans.

In poetry, traditional written poetry is associated with whites, modern spoken-word poetry with nonwhites. In dance, the world of classical ballet is inhabited almost exclusively by white dancers; Latinos tend to be overrepresented on the floors of salsa clubs; and modern dance often features African Americans and African influences. Cooking certainly should be considered an aesthetic expression, and we see racial divisions here, too: White chefs and consumers are over-represented in the organic food movement—as well as in high cuisine restaurants—while soul food is considered a thoroughly black culinary art form. Whiteness can be spotted in grocery stores, where some items—such as tortillas and salsa, chow mein and soy sauce—are grouped in the "ethnic foods" aisle, while other, equally "ethnic" items—for example, spaghetti sauce and French baguettes—are not labeled as such.

Racial divisions are quite apparent in television programming. For years now, television producers have targeted specific racial or ethnic groups with programs supposedly designed to speak to those groups' unique needs and lifestyles. Because it focuses on a narrow segment of society, this practice has become known as **"narrowcasting"** (as opposed to "broadcasting," which targets a general audience). The result is a kind of artistic segregation, where "black programs" are pitched at black viewers, "Jewish programs" at Jewish viewers, "Hispanic programs" at Hispanic viewers, and so forth. Indeed, in multicultural metropolises, such as Los Angeles and New York, one can find weekly programs aired in Assyrian, Armenian, Persian, and Hebrew. Entire television networks are dedicated to narrowcasting, such as the Jewish TV Network, Black Entertainment Television, and American-owned Spanish-language stations, such as Telemundo and Univision.[94]

Like all racial divisions, those found within the aesthetic field are never fixed, impenetrable, or complete. Nor are such divisions timeless. If one were to conduct a historical analysis of the aesthetic field, one would quickly discover how art forms associated, say, with blacks are taken up by whites and then abandoned by blacks. The banjo used to be known as a "Negro instrument"; now it is associated with whites and bluegrass.[95] The piano used to be reserved for the white-dominated world of classical music; but it was "jazzed up," so to speak, by such black artists as Duke Ellington and Ray Charles. Lindy hop swing dance was popularized in the 1920s by blacks in Harlem. It fell out of style after World War II but roared back on the cultural scene in the 1990s, this time as an art form populated by young white professionals.[96] Or consider folk music, which began as the voice of white nationalism before being refashioned in the 1930s as the sound of a multiracial labor movement. It crumbled under the pressures of consumer culture during the 1950s, only to be resurrected again in the 1960s, but this time as an art form predominantly played and listened to by whites. Writing about the re-whitening of folk music in the 1960s, William Roy observes, "What the middle-class youth found aesthetically pleasing about folk music—its anti-commercial simplicity, its musical purity, its evocation of a dissolving past— appealed primarily to whites who wanted out of the mainstream more than African Americans, who had been excluded."[97]

Historically informed socioanalysis demonstrates, once again, that racial divisions (this time in the aesthetic field) that appear natural and timeless are anything but. Indeed, because aesthetic choices can be used to signal and enforce social differences—to divide "us" from "them" (a process about which we shall have more to say later)—the shifting nature of artistic tastes across racial boundaries often is propelled by identity struggles and power relations. Speaking of the role fashion plays in signaling class divisions, German sociologist Georg Simmel observed, "Just as soon as the lower classes begin to copy their style, thereby crossing the line of demarcation the upper classes have drawn and destroying the uniformity of their coherence, the upper classes turn away from this style and adopt a new one, which in its turn differentiates them from the masses; and thus the game goes merrily on."[98] Simmel's point is not exclusive to fashion or to economic divisions. It can be applied to racial divisions and to all kinds of aesthetic choices. When blacks "invade" a traditionally white art form, many whites abandon that art form for something new. The reverse is also true: Many blacks turn their backs on a traditionally black art form when it is taken up by too many whites.[99] Jazz itself, once seen as the quintessential black art form, has come to have predominantly white audiences in recent decades, as blacks have moved on to hip-hop and other musical forms. And so the game goes merrily on.

Highbrow/Lowbrow Culture

But this game—the racialization and re-racialization of art worlds—comes with consequences. For one, not every art form awards its practitioners the same amount of cultural capital. You might recall that, in the previous chapter, we defined cultural capital as "the sum total of one's knowledge of established and revered cultural activities and practices" and demonstrated how cultural capital can be exchanged for other varieties of capital (for example, economic, political, educational). So-called **highbrow culture**, the collection of art forms associated with an upper-class taste and lifestyle, is rich in cultural capital, while **lowbrow culture** or "popular culture," art forms considered more ordinary and associated with the tastes and lifestyles of "the masses," is more or less bereft of it. Ballet, opera, classical music, sculpture, and abstract painting are considered highbrow art forms, while club dancing, popular music, and stand-up comedy are grouped under lowbrow art. In fashion, it is the difference between tailored items plucked fresh off the Milan runway and clothes purchased at the local mall. In cuisine, it is the difference between foie gras and a cheeseburger or between a 1997 Abreu Cabernet Sauvignon and a Budweiser.[100]

The distinction between highbrow and lowbrow corresponds to the distinction between traditionally white and traditionally nonwhite art forms. Indeed, the origin of this artistic division is rooted in racial and class divisions of the nineteenth century. As historian Lawrence Levine has documented, as English cities grew larger and more diverse (owing to processes of immigration and urbanization), the upper class needed to devise a way to set themselves apart from (and above) the masses. One way they did so was by transforming the performing arts. No longer would Shakespearean plays be performed alongside comedy routines and trained animal acts, and no longer were audience members allowed to partake in rowdy behavior (for instance, booing inept actors). By the end of the nineteenth century, the upper class had claimed certain art forms as their own, had developed certain behaviors to accompany those art forms (for example, sitting quietly, no tobacco spitting), and had elevated these forms above other ones.[101] Soon, cultural organizations linked to upper-class taste, such as the symphony orchestra and the art museum, arose and provided an institutional existence to the highbrow/lowbrow distinction.

When this distinction was imported to the United States, it took on a specifically racialized meaning. The new upper-class ideal that came to define the culture and conduct of highbrow art—"orderly, regulated, learned, prosperous, 'civilized'"[102]—became associated with white audiences, while lowbrow behaviors, such as heckling or calling to a friend from across the room, were associated with nonwhite audiences. Affluent whites (as well as whites who wished to appear affluent) approached highbrow art with reverence and stillness, with coolness and calm; poorer nonwhites, in contrast, tended to approach lowbrow art with much more bravado and vim, with honest appraisals uttered aloud. Such behavioral differences remain today, which helps explain why it is not unusual to hear nonblacks voice discomfort when African-American movie- or theatergoers participate more vocally during the show.[103]

Distribution of Live Music Attendees by Ethnicity and Race (percentage)

	Hispanic	White	American African	Other	Total
Percentage of U.S. Population	11.0	72.9	11.5	4.6	100.0
Jazz	6.3	77.0	13.5	3.1	99.9
Classical	5.2	86.2	4.5	4.1	100.0
Opera	6.1	86.4	3.8	3.6	99.9

NOTES: The SPPA measured the number of adults who attended three types of musical performances—jazz, classical, and opera—in the 12-month period ending August 2002. Some rows do not total 100 because of rounding.
SOURCES: 2000 Census and 2002 Survey of Public Participation in the Arts (SPPA).

Variation in Arts Participation among Asian Americans and Hispanics (percentage)

	Asian Americans		Hispanics	
	Natives	Immigrants	Natives	Immigrants
Attended a live performance	100	82	75	60
Attended a museum	100	60	52	35
Considers self an artist	38	24	42	44
Favorite arts activity with others is dance	33	52	52	43

SOURCE: Cultural Initiatives Silicon Valley, Community Creativity Index. 2002.

Just as it was designed to do in the nineteenth century, today the binary coding scheme separating white/highbrow culture from nonwhite/lowbrow culture is marshaled as a mechanism of inclusion and exclusion. Thus fashion statements rooted in African-American history and culture—Afros, dashikis, even flamboyant and colorful suits rooted in the fashion style of the Southern black church— are deemed "inappropriate" for the professional world. American Airlines and Hyatt are but two companies that at one time forbade their employees from wearing braids, a hairstyle traditionally worn by black women. The Hyatt went so far as to label braids an "extreme and unusual hair style."[104] Hip-hop fashion, in particular, has been so deeply linked to negative behavior that it has been banned by several companies. The NBA dress code, for example, forbids its players from wearing "chains, pendants, or medallions" over their clothes, "headgear of any kind," and "sunglasses while indoors" when engaging in team or league business. And some bars and restaurants explicitly forbid their patrons from donning clothes associated with hip-hop fashion. In February 2008, CNN ran a story about the Brooksider Bar of Kansas City, Missouri, which recently instituted a dress code that banned "baggy or saggy clothing," bandannas and

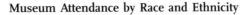

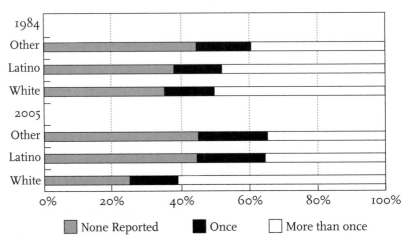

Museum Attendance by Race and Ethnicity

dew rags, stickers and price tags on baseball caps, men's white T-shirts, and necklaces outside one's shirt. The CNN reporter concluded the story with the line: "A neighborhood bar, trying to keep trouble away."[105] "Trouble," apparently, dresses like a black teenager.

Nonwhite audiences face barriers when attempting to access traditionally white highbrow culture. If nonwhites are disproportionately impoverished, as we learned in Chapter 4, then they are also disproportionately denied access to many highbrow art forms and their cultural capital. Opera tickets and violin lessons are expensive. So are locally grown vegetables, which is why the organic food movement (as much an aesthetic movement as a political or nutritional one) appeals mainly to white, middle-class people who can afford to pay $2.15 for a California-grown organic cucumber or $5 for an unprocessed loaf of bread.[106] And besides, to the palates of many poor folks, that fancy bread tastes funny; some prefer Wonder Bread they can buy for 99 cents. They develop, in other words, distaste for the things they cannot afford, as social barriers to highbrow food, culture, and art are transformed into legitimate tastes. If you cannot afford to eat at expensive restaurants, you adapt (perhaps without even knowing it) by twisting that structural barrier into a personal choice. "I hate fancy restaurants," you might profess. "I'd much rather eat at McDonald's." This **taste of necessity**, as Bourdieu calls it, defines the artistic judgments of those who cannot afford to behave otherwise.[107]

This idea of a taste of necessity is all important. Although highbrow art claims to have universal value and significance, the knowledge and tastes required to consume it, that is, meaningfully to experience it, are not universally distributed. Hence, although certain art museums might be relatively accessible in terms of the price of admission, they continue to be frequented not by working-class people, at least proportionately speaking, but by (white) middle- and upper-class audiences. Why? Because only the latter are equipped by the cultivation they have received in their family lives and schooling to understand and appreciate the (primarily Eurocentric) art they encounter there. Others experience only discomfort and say to themselves, "This place isn't for the likes of me." The late-nineteenth-century writer, Émile Zola, dramatized this sentiment in a scene in his novel, *L'Assommoir*. A wedding party of working-class Parisians heads out for a walk and, caught in a rainstorm, ducks into the great art museum, the Louvre. Disheveled and caked with mud, they trudge there uncomprehendingly from gallery to gallery. Zola writes: "More pictures and still more pictures, saints, men and women whose faces meant nothing to anybody, landscapes all black, animals gone all yellow, . . . [all these] were beginning to give them a bad headache."[108] Eventually they leave the museum, in search of another setting where they will feel more at home. Their tastes incline them, that is, toward less highbrow, less intimidating, entertainments. Initially denied access to cultural knowledge that would have allowed them to understand what they saw in the Louvre, they develop dispositions to reject what was initially denied them (by institutions like schools) and, in the end, exclude themselves.

Even nonwhite artists face significant barriers, both explicit and implicit, when seeking to access majority-white art worlds. Talented black dancers, for example, often are denied a position in ballet companies. New York City's two largest ballet corps—American Ballet Theater and New York City Ballet—have never had a black female principal, a lead dancer. Indeed, until recently, only one black woman—Lauren Anderson of Houston Ballet—had been promoted to the rank of principal by a large American ballet company. Many black ballet dancers who have secured a spot feel isolated and singled out against the white backdrop of their fellow dancers. As former black dancer Victoria Johnson confessed, "It's hard to be the only black dancer. You feel separate, and you feel neglected in a certain sense, and it's not that people are trying to make you feel bad, but it's just obviously around you. Everyone else can make a bond by similarity, and you have to make an effort, and making an effort makes you wonder, 'Am I not being true to myself?' It's hard to be strong enough to be in that environment and to not feel wrong."[109]

The racial structures of the aesthetic field, therefore, associate certain art forms with certain racial or ethnic groups and assign to different art forms various degrees of cultural capital. Some of the most sophisticated sociological research on this topic has found that highly educated people (that is, people with a healthy amount of cultural capital) do not reject all forms of lowbrow culture; instead, they tend to reject only those low-status art forms most appreciated by people with the lowest levels of education.[110] When it comes to music, for example, sociologist Bethany Bryson has found that highly educated people tend to profess liking everything but rap, heavy metal, country, and gospel music, musical genres most closely associated with low education.[111] Education, then, promotes cultural tolerance but only to a point. And it is in people's artistic *dislikes* that we are best able to detect how they erect symbolic boundaries between themselves and people they hope to keep at a safe distance. There is a racial element to all of this. Indeed, studies have shown that, compared to people who are fairly tolerant of other racial groups, people who harbor racial prejudice are more likely to reject art forms associated with nonwhite groups, such as Latin music, reggae, gospel, and rap.[112] As we mentioned in our discussion of hip-hop, the rejection of certain (racialized) artistic forms can function as coded language, as a method of putting down certain groups without sounding like a racist.[113] You can express animus against poor whites by claiming to hate NASCAR or monster truck rallies; you can express your anti-Mexican attitudes by observing that Mexican food is disgusting and that Mexican music is simplistic.

In the aesthetic field, then, one confronts a race-based audience segmentation rooted in race-based social divisions.[114] However, taking note of the racial cleavages within the aesthetic field should not blind us to the fact that artistic production is—and has always been—a thoroughly multicultural and multiethnic undertaking. Artistic forms and tastes glide and float across color lines. Aesthetic styles overlap and bleed into one another. Although typically thought of as black music, jazz found inspiration and guidance in the compositions of white military bands. Rock has been categorized as white music, despite the fact that in its early days it drew heavily on rhythm and blues and gospel.[115] Recently, Native-American modernist painters have represented traditional Indian images through techniques borrowed from European artistic movements; and, as we noted above, European artists, such as Picasso, borrowed artistic images from African cultures. Romare Bearden, the great African-American artist, was influenced not only by scenes from his Harlem neighborhood but also by Mexican muralists and French cubists.[116]

Entire musical genres are based on the premise of cross-cultural convergence. Reggaetón, for example, mixes hip-hop, Electonica, reggae, and dance hall influences with bomba, merengue, and other Latin-American musical traditions. And dozens of artists have made a name for themselves specifically by transcending racial divisions within the aesthetic field. Kid Rock's music combines rap, country, and hard rock. DJ Rekha, one of New York City's most popular, overlays the Bhangra music of South Asia with modern hip-hop beats. Los Angeles-based Dengue Fever features a Cambodian-born lead singer, Chhom Nimol, supported by five American-born band members and mixes themes and musical expressions associated with the East with those associated with the West. Cuban-American rapper Pitbull's sound fuses hip-hip with crunk, reggae, and dance hall. And

African-American rapper Kanye West's third album, *Graduation,* is greatly influenced by Japanese pop, so much so that he commissioned Japanese artist Takashi Murakami to design the cover. Less visibly, two of hip-hop's biggest producers, Eric Hermansen and Mikkel Eriksen, are a pair of Norwegians who go by the name Stargate. Together, the duo has written songs for Beyoncé, Shakira, and Lionel Richie.[117] Music, like many American art forms, reflects the country's multicultural mosaic.

Cultural Appropriation

If American art is, in some way or another, a kind of multiracial hybridization—a creolized cultural concoction—can we even speak in terms of "Puerto Rican art" or "Hopi art"? Is there no such thing as Jewish humor, Latin dance, or Irish food? If art forms considered black borrow from those considered white or Asian or French, is there such a thing as a "black aesthetic" or, for that matter, an "Asian-American aesthetic" or a "white aesthetic? The answer is yes. Racialized aesthetics stem from the different ways racial groups have been incorporated into American society. Because Native-American history is different from Asian-American history, and because Native Americans experience different struggles today than Asian Americans do, it should not surprise us that there exists a Native-American aesthetic that differs from an Asian-American aesthetic. One theme that helps define Asian-American poetry, for example, is that of dislocation, the experience of being a perpetual foreigner in America. And the large number of Columbus and Custer jokes that circulate through Indian country are properly understood as constituting Native-American humor.[118]

Claiming that racialized aesthetics exist does imply that they are isolated from one another. In our multicultural society—indeed, our multicultural world, which, since the popularization of the Internet, is ever closer within our grasp—such a claim is untenable. Nor does it suggest that, say, the Asian-American aesthetic is simple and monolithic. Indeed, assuming that certain racial groups must have a unified aesthetic or no aesthetic at all implies that nonwhite groups are homogeneous blobs, void of diversity and internal differences. As one Asian-American art critic has pointed out, "When we speak of Euro-American aesthetics, there is room for diversity and a myriad of cultural influences, many of which came from Asia and other parts of the world. But suddenly when we speak of the possibility of an Asian-American aesthetics, it must either be monolithic or not viable. Our diversity, our myriad of influences, and our history of cultural interactions are problematic only when discussing Asian-American aesthetics, which serves as a direct assault on the one-dimensional and caricaturized terms in which the United States is accustomed to thinking of Asian and Asian-American culture."[119]

Racialized aesthetics, then, reflect their respective groups' shared histories and insights as well as their rich diversity of opinions and tastes. They possess their own flavor but borrow styles from other groups. But when, we must ask, is it appropriate to appropriate another group's culture? Does doing so belittle or celebrate the appropriated group's music, style, or fashion? Does cultural appropriation lead to a more liberated, multicultural democracy or is it another mechanism of racial domination? This section addresses these questions, confronting the thorny issue of cultural appropriation, a topic that has been the subject of great controversy and has caused a good deal of pain.

Making Sense of Cultural Appropriation

Cultural appropriation occurs when members of one ethnic or racial group adopt a cultural product associated with another.[120] Asian fashion has been widely appropriated by non-Asians, as evidenced by the proliferation of Chinese character tattoos and, in the world of women's fashion, Japanese kimonos and Indian saris.[121] Native-American art forms and traditions—or at least *representations* of Native-American art forms and traditions—have been employed by the Boy Scouts of America, New Age gurus, and non-Indian artists. This practice is certainly not unique to America. The white Australian Elizabeth Durack paints aboriginal style works and has even adopted a second identity as Eddie Burrap, an aboriginal man, who, were he actually a real aboriginal person, might have a more legitimate claim to profiting off aboriginal patterns and styles.[122]

One of the most referenced examples of cultural appropriation is the non-black (and especially white) adaptation of African-American culture in general, and hip-hop culture in particular. Hip-hop styles, such as tilted caps, baggy clothes, and fly sayings—styles rooted in the poor black urban experience—have been picked up by nonblacks, many of whom have never set foot in a ghetto. A white person who immerses himself in the hip-hop scene is sometimes pejoratively labeled a "wigga" (a combination of the words "white" and "nigga"), meaning "a young white who wants desperately to be down with hip-hop, who identifies more strongly with black culture than white." (What is most disturbing about this term is not what it says about white hip-hoppers but about black ones. If white hip-hoppers are "wiggas," then are all black hip-hoppers "niggas"?[123]) Since the rapid expansion of hip-hop, many have wondered about its appeal to nonblack youth, especially white middle-class suburban youth. *Why Do White Kids Love Hip-Hop?*, asks Bakari Kitwana in his recent book. He tenders several answers: hip-hop connects with youth's feelings of alienation and their antiestablishment leanings; it allows them to nourish their fascination with black culture; and, on the flip side, it has been very intentional about reaching wider audiences. "As much as white kids chose hip-hop, hip-hop chose white America."[124]

Let us intervene in this debate as sociologists, ever ready to *question* conventional questions. Why do we need to know why young nonblack people love hip-hop? Why is this question posed in the first place? Under what assumptions does it operate? Wondering why whites or Asian Americans connect with hip-hop implies, first, that hip-hop still has not reached the status of "true art," a musical expression that can be enjoyed by everyone. The reason we do not ask why Asian Americans love classical music even though most classical music originally was composed for white upper-class audience, is in part that we treat classical music as pure (read: highbrow) art that transcends racial boundaries. But, clearly, one of the reasons nonblacks jam to Outkast or Wyclef Jean is that their music is fresh and exciting and important. What is more, asking why white kids appreciate hip-hop implies that whites should not love hip-hop and that blacks should. Not only does this stance advance some overarching generalizations about white and black people, it imposes an artificial racial segregation on the aesthetic field.

The point we are driving at is this: it is too simplistic and wholly unsatisfactory to comprehend cultural appropriation as a kind of "ethnic theft" which *always* occurs when insider culture is performed by outsider bodies. It is certainly true that white Americans do not daily bear the weight of racial domination on their shoulders, but it is equally true that such vast diversity exists within nonwhite racial groups that claims like "only blacks can truly understand hip-hop" only help flatten that diversity and should be treated as fallacious. Who has a better chance of understanding the black mother in Alice Walker's short story, "Everyday Use" (a character who tends a small farm and "can kill and clean a hog as mercilessly as a man"), a black man from an affluent suburb or a young Latina from a poor family, who grew up butchering livestock?[125] Who has a better chance of understanding Cherokee culture, the full-blooded Cherokee who lives in Philadelphia and has never set foot on a reservation or an Irish American who grew up on the Cherokee reservation, speaks the language, and partakes in the ceremonies? As one Cherokee leader explains, "I've seen some full-blooded Indians, that I *know* are full-blooded Indians, that are *not* Indians. They don't care about Indian culture, they don't attend Indian functions. . . . I see a blonde-headed person, blue-eyed, that attends ceremonial things and goes to different tribal affairs and things like that. And they try to uphold the Indian tradition. To me, that's a real Indian."[126]

Cultural appropriation, in other words, is not simply about *who* is doing the appropriating but *how* they are doing it. We can distinguish between cultural appropriation that denigrates and that which appreciates; that which supports a racist aesthetic and that which contributes to the antiracist aesthetic. "There is a difference," writes Kitwana, "between 'cultural banditry,' appropriation that comes in the form of an outsider ripping off another culture, and 'acknowledged appropriation,' where the outsider emulates a culture *and* redefines it, while acknowledging its roots."[127]

Racist Appropriation

If some nonwhites are offended by cultural appropriation, it is because for years their art—their very heart and soul, for what is art other than life beautifully rendered?—have been used against them, co-opted by cultural outsiders who twist and distort, malign and fragment their art so as better to exploit, dehumanize, and dominate the very people that art was intended to heal. **Racist appropriation** employs a variety of methods. One is a strategic amnesia. Here, the appropriators not only refuse to credit the racial or ethnic group responsible for the appropriated art form, they also attempt completely to detach that art form from the racial or ethnic group that brought it into the world. One encounters this, for example, in *le jazz,* that peculiar conconction, part classical music and part pseudo-African chic, that was briefly popular in Paris during the 1920s; "there is no need to belabor the point," writes music historian Alex Ross, "that *le jazz* was condescend-ing toward its African-American sources. [Its leading composers] were enjoying a one-night stand with a dark-skinned form, and they had no intention of striking up a conversation with it the following day."[128] A few decades later, white popular singers appropriated rock music from black performers such as Chuck Berry, B. B. King, and Count Basie—and whitewashed it to such an extent that today the genre is associated with whites and often is misunderstood as originating from white performers, which is why Elvis Presley is considered "the King of Rock and Roll" and Eric Clapton is regarded widely as the country's leading blues guitarist.[129] Mos Def in "Rock and Roll" put it this way: "You may dig on the Rolling Stones/ But they ain't come up with that style on they own."

In de-racializing and re-racializing an art form, racist appropriation denies nonwhite groups the ability to profit from their creations. Given the pronounced race-based economic inequalities in America, whites who get rich off an art form co-opted from nonwhites, especially from poor nonwhites, steal not only culture but resources and revenue as well. Additionally, when a successful art form is appropriated from the group in which it originated, that group loses control over the form and, by extension, the ways it is represented. Racist appropriation can be used to exoticize the nonwhite groups and, therefore, to contribute to their status as Other. "Within commodity culture," writes bell hooks, "ethnicity becomes spice, seasoning that can liven up the dull dish that is mainstream white culture. . . . Should youth of any other color not know how to move closer to the Other, or how to get in touch with the 'primitive,' consumer culture promises to show the way. . . . Encounters with Otherness are clearly marked as more exciting, more intense, and more threatening. The lure is the combination of pleasure and danger."[130] Thus, the white appropriation of Native-American culture can entrap

American retailers have reduced the Keffiyeh, a scarf symbolizing Palestinian nationalism, to a trendy accessory divorced from its historical and political significance.

Indianness in representations of the primitive, just as the appropriation of Asian-American culture can bind Asianness to foreignness—thereby contributing to both groups' continued alienation from mainstream America.

When an image slips out of your hand—better: when that image is snatched away by the hand of your oppressor—the very image you created to dismantle racial domination can be used by those who seek to uphold it. Racist appropriation of an art form or cultural style weakens its political power, sometimes to the point of impotence. (Recall, for example, the discursive co-optation, discussed in Chapter 3, practiced by whites who opposed the Civil Rights Movement.) Equally destructive, racist appropriation can be used as a new form of colonialization, where white supremacy is strengthened by the appropriation and purposeful degradation of nonwhite cultures. The result is a kind of modern-day minstrelsy, where nonwhite culture is represented by and for the white gaze.[131] And if the appropriated image comes to overpower the original image—as is usually the case—then the distorted representation of, say, black culture is soon widely regarded as an accurate reflection of black culture. Representation becomes misrecognized as reality.

What disrespectful appropriators often fail to realize (and this gets to the crux of the matter) is this: because nonwhite art is often a cry against oppression and suffering—black spirituals were a sigh of anguish in the face of slave tyranny; hip-hop emerged in an era of mass incarceration as the voice of the abandoned black masses huddled together in America's desolate city centers— those who co-opt that art without acknowledging the suffering that helped inspire it do violence to the artists who created it and the people she or he represents. Imagine that a team of female coworkers decides to participate in a 5-mile jog hosted by the National Breast Cancer Foundation to raise money for breast cancer research. They order pink T-shirts for the event. Failing to realize that pink T-shirts identify them as breast cancer survivors, the coworkers wear the shirts and, during their jog, are over and over mistaken for women who have suffered through breast cancer. When they reach the finish line, onlookers erupt with applause and cheers. But when the onlookers discover that the women are not survivors at all, they feel wronged and angry; this is doubly true of the real survivors in the crowd. Breast cancer survivors are encouraged and respected because of the hell they went through. Why, then, is not the same courtesy extended to people of color, when their artistic expressions of suffering are casually appropriated by those who have never suffered at the hands of racial domination?

For those who have been "down the line," who have been politically misrepresented, economically exploited, socially alienated, and psychologically manipulated, who have been enslaved and murdered and imprisoned because of their skin color, their culture, however they defined it, is a poultice. It sooths; it warms and protects; it is special and reverent. And it burns when their culture is profaned by outsiders who treat it as a kind of "cultural safari" through which to stare at the Other with the impunity one enjoys while staring at a blind person.[132] The essence of racist appropriation is the act of taking "everything but the burden," of enjoying the pleasure without even recognizing the pain.[133]

> Saw whites clap during a sacred dance
>
> Saw young blonde hippie boy with a red stone pipe
>
> > My eyes burned him up
>
> He smiled *This is a Sioux pipe* he said from his sportscar
>
> > *Yes* I hiss *I'm wondering how you got it*
> >
> > *& the name is Lakota not Sioux*
>
> *I'll tell you* he said all friendly and liberal as only
>
> > Those with no pain can be
> >
> > I turned away Can't charm me can't bear to know . . .

Today was a day like TB

you cough & cough trying to get it out

all that comes

is blood & spit

Chrystos, "Today Was a Bad Day Like TB"[134]

Antiracist Appropriation

Do nonwhite groups appropriate white culture? Absolutely. But when appropriation flows in this direction, it does not bring about the same (negative) consequences. That is, when white culture is appropriated by nonwhites, whites as a group do not suffer (materially or symbolically) because of it. Whites have not experienced years of cultural humiliation and debasement or been depicted in a superficial or dehumanizing light. Never in the history of America were whites kidnapped and transported to boarding schools, where they were told that white culture was evil, as were Native Americans; never have a group of powerful nonwhites appeared in "whiteface" and mocked white culture to loud applause, as African Americans were mocked in minstrel shows; and never have grotesque images of whites committing anti-American acts been displayed on posters that hung in American towns, as were those of Japanese Americans during World War II. The white appropriation of nonwhite culture connects with this history of racial domination; the same cannot be said of the nonwhite appropriation of white culture. "The history of the world, my sweet, is who gets eaten and who gets to eat," wrote Stephen Sondheim in the musical, *Sweeney Todd*. With cultural appropriation, the ones who "get eaten" are those who remain at the bottom of America's racial order.[135] Culture appropriation may flow both ways, but in nearly every case raced-based power and privilege are asserted in but one direction.

That said, there are respectful ways to appropriate another group's culture. **Antiracist appropriation** refuses to de-racialize or de-historicize the art form that inspires it but gives credit where credit is due. It does not distort or malign the image in mocking ways; it refuses to use the image in the interest of racial domination. The antiracist artist (or consumer of art) acknowledges the suffering caused by racial domination and, importantly, the role she or he might play in upholding that suffering. And if an artist makes money off an appropriated art form, she or he reinvests some of that money in the nonwhite communities from which the art was borrowed.

"No human culture," writes African-American literary critic Henry Louis Gates, Jr., "is inaccessible to someone who makes the effort to understand, to learn, to inhabit another world."[136] Gates's observation is reaffirmed by the many who have accurately and justly represented another culture in their artwork. Tony Hillerman, a white novelist, set many of his books on the Navajo (or Dineh) reservation and was awarded the Special Friend of the Dineh Award by the Navajo Nation for "authentically portraying the strength and dignity of traditional Navajo culture."[137] Similarly, the Yankton Nation of South Dakota allowed a non-Indian, who had been adopted by a Yankton family and learned to speak their language and participate in tribal culture, to market his artwork as "Indian produced."[138] And, unlike the Beastie Boys and other white artists who have incorporated hip-hop styles and sounds into their music, "Eminem comes across as someone who cares as much (if not more) about maintaining the overall integrity of hip-hop culture as he does about his commercial success."[139]

Cultural appropriation is inevitable. Indeed, when carried out in an antiracist manner, it can help bring about racial justice. As one scholar has put it, "When we have true respect for the Difference of other cultures, then we grant them the potential for challenging our own culture."[140] How, after all, do we expect to come together as a multicultural society, to reach across these imposed racial barriers and build strong coalitions, if we do not understand each other's deep and rich culture, each other's art and music and styles? Asian Americans might gain a deeper understanding of poverty and institutional racism by listening to rap music, just as blacks might come to a fuller awareness of South Asian religion and culture by practicing meditation and yoga. Remember, it's not who is doing the appropriating but how they are doing it.

Unanticipated Consequences

The emotional debates surrounding the dynamics of cultural appropriation have resulted in several unanticipated consequences within the aesthetic field. For one, racial divisions sometimes are reinforced when claims about art forms belonging to specific racial or ethnic groups are marshaled. For example, because certain modern dances have been attributed to African Americans, the latter are often labeled "better dancers." This claim implies that African Americans somehow are "naturally" good dancers, that they come out of the womb that way, a notion that can be used to reify and naturalize racial divisions, just as it can be used to stereotype blacks (for example, if they are good at dancing, they must be bad at school).[141]

Meanwhile, debates about cultural authenticity and appropriation can be especially complex and even disheartening for people who claim multiracial heritage. "If I belong to two worlds," they might wonder, "does this mean I am doomed to be loyal to neither, inauthentic by birthright?" Can a woman, for instance, whose mother is Oneida and whose father is white label her pottery "Oneida art"? Should a man whose mother is Cuban and whose father is Chinese express a kind of ethnic authenticity by learning Spanish or Mandarin? Should the children of African-American and Jewish parents celebrate Hanukkah or Kwanza? Questions such as these can leave biracial and multiracial people feeling confused and frustrated just as, in the opposite direction, they can provoke creative action that blurs racial boundaries and forecasts multicultural possibilities.[142]

What is more, artists who admire and respect other cultures' art but do not want to be labeled a "cultural bandit" may refuse to draw on that art in their own work. This can bring about a kind of aesthetic racial segregation and strengthen the white aesthetic. A white novelist who sets herself the task of writing an epic novel about American society but who is afraid to represent nonwhite groups, for fear of being accused of racist appropriation, might write a book that represents America only as a white nation. The tendency of some racial or ethnic groups to claim a monopoly over their own representations "has had a bad effect on our fiction," according to literary critic Stanley Crouch, "since there are ethnic characters that too many writers do not feel free enough to try and imagine in their work."[143]

Even more ironically, claims about the cultural authenticity of a certain art form—claims reacting against cultural appropriation—can bring about the death of that art form. As "real Indian art" comes to rely more and more on a cultural preservationist ethic, Indian culture becomes smothered by the weight of unchanging tradition. Because traditional storytellers risk being labeled un-Indian if their tales diverge too far from the well-worn path, Indian poetry and literacy, reduced to simple imitation, can become void of creativity. As sociologist Eva Marie Garroutee has stated, "The logic of cultural 'authenticity' may initially support the identity claims of individuals and tribes, only later to destroy them, along with the culture in which they arose."[144] In *Ceremony,* novelist Leslie Marmon Silko, of white, Mexican, and Laguna Pueblo heritage, captures eloquently the tension between tradition and progress as it relates to Native-American practices. "The people nowadays have an idea about the ceremonies," she writes. "They think the ceremonies must be performed exactly as they have always been done. . . . But long ago when the people were given these ceremonies, the changing began, if only in the aging of the yellow gourd rattle or the shrinking of the skin around the eagle's claw, if only in the different voices from generation to generation, singing the chants. . . . The people mistrust this greatly, but only this growth keeps the ceremonies strong. . . . [T]hings which don't shift and grow are dead things."[145]

And from where, we might ask, do our own ideas of "cultural authenticity" come? From no other source than the European colonizer. White explorers charted distant lands in search of "primitive" cultures "uncontaminated" by outside sources; they wanted to set their eyes upon the "authentic" art of these cultures. The notion of cultural authenticity was invented within the context of the colonial enterprise; it was developed to satisfy the white gaze. Accordingly, it carries with it colonialist assumptions, those that divide the world into rigid racial groups and that attribute to those groups certain practices and behaviors.[146] And what about our concept of "cultural ownership," where does that originate? As philosopher Kwame Anthony Appiah has observed, our idea of "cultural ownership" sprouts directly from Western notions of intellectual-property law, which was originally designed to benefit the interests of corporate owners: "Talk of cultural patrimony ends up embracing the sort of hyper-stringent doctrine of property rights . . . that we normally associate with international capital. . . . In the name of authenticity, [we] would extend this peculiarly Western, and modern, conception of ownership to every corner of the earth. The vision is of a cultural landscape consisting of Disney Inc. and the Coca-Cola Company, for sure; but also of Ashanti Inc., Navajo Inc., Maorin Inc., Norway Inc.: All rights reserved."[147]

The Sociology of Art, the Art of Sociology

We have traversed the aesthetic field, discussing sculpture, architecture, painting, dance, performance, television, cinema, photography, fashion, and many varieties of music. In so doing, we have learned that racial domination is found within all art worlds, even if the artists and consumers of those worlds fail to recognize this. Perhaps, too, we have been reminded of the unquestionable, enduring, and prophetic importance of art. The power that media holds over our thinking is breathtaking; and our only hope of preserving a clear and accurate understanding of the world is to interrogate all the representations delivered daily to us at breakneck speed. Passive consumption is not an option, for all art, in some way or another, is political.

Edgar Degas, the famous French impressionist painter, once said, "Painting is easy when you don't know how, but very difficult when you do." The same could be said of sociology. Anyone can look at a painting or a television program or any other piece of art and venture a guess as to how that art form affects the racial order, just as they can (and often do) overlook the art form's racial implications altogether. But it takes a trained eye to conduct a thorough socioanalysis of art, to carry out a triple reading of an artwork, placing it in its overlapping historical and social contexts and deciphering precisely how the art in question affects racial domination (if it supports a white, racist, or antiracist aesthetic) and how racial domination might have affected it. The sociological eye also pays attention to the included and the excluded; it notes the excesses, silences, and omissions when conducting a racial analysis of art. In this chapter, we have provided you with some guidance for effectively objectifying the artistic representations that meet you every day, so that you can better understand the social world and your position within it.

CHAPTER REVIEW

DEMYSTIFYING ART
triple reading

RACE AND ART IN NINETEENTH- AND TWENTIETH-CENTURY AMERICA
human zoos, minstrel shows, blues

RACIAL REPRESENTATION IN ART
racist nostalgia, white aesthetic, racist aesthetic, antiracist aesthetic, merchandise dissent

THE RACIALIZATION OF ART WORLDS
naive art, un-stereotype, narrowcasting, highbrow culture, lowbrow culture, taste of necessity

CULTURAL APPROPRIATION
cultural appropriation, racist appropriation, antiracist appropriation

FROM THEORY TO PRACTICE

1. Carry out a triple reading on some piece of art. This can be a song, painting, movie, or any other cultural creation. Be sure to note the aesthetic, political, and racial properties of the form. Once you have done that, explain how the artwork reflects a white, racist, or antiracist aesthetic.

2. Select one piece of art that, in your mind, reflects the white aesthetic. Defend your selection by explaining how this artwork treats whiteness as the normal, artistic default category. What message does this piece of art convey about the social world? How might this artwork be altered so that it does not reflect the white aesthetic?

3. Participate in some artistic performance you have never experienced. If you are a metal head, attend an opera performance. If you love salsa, attend a modern dance show. Sample a cuisine you have never sampled; attend a spoken-word slam; go to the rodeo. Push your limits and challenge yourself. After attending the performance, write about it, answering the following questions: How did the performance represent race? How might the racial structures of society have affected the performance? How did the performance help you better to understand the kind of art with which you are more familiar? That is, how did it encourage you to be more reflexive about the racialized nature of your aesthetic preferences?

4. Write a fan letter to one of your favorite artists. In it, apply what you have learned in this chapter to her or his art. You might commend this person for advancing an antiracist aesthetic, or you might criticize her or him for nourishing a racist one. You might ask about cultural appropriation or about how he or she makes sense of the racialized nature of audience segmentation. In your letter, be sure to apply at least three concepts and/or ideas featured in this chapter, and be sure to provide illustrations from your artist's body of work.

5. Prepare a piece of art for your next class. You can define art in any way you wish, but you must defend your definition. Your artwork might be a collage, a poem, a song, a video—but it must be your unique creation. Through your art, speak to racial domination. You might consider criticizing other (racist) representations in art. You might address a problem or a historical event you learned about in previous chapters. You might try carrying out an antiracist kind of cultural appropriation. In all cases, be creative and daring. Analyze and explain your artwork using the terms and ideas developed in this chapter.

RECOMMENDED READING

- Martin Berger, *Sight Unseen: Whiteness and American Visual Culture* (Berkeley and Los Angeles: University of California Press, 2005).

- John Dewey, *Art as Experience* (New York: Capricorn Books, 1934).

- bell hooks, *Black Looks: Race and Representation* (Cambridge: South End Press, 1992).

- Ronald Jacobs, *Race, Media, and the Crisis of Civil Society: From Watts to Rodney King* (Cambridge: Cambridge University Press, 2000).

- Michèle Lamont and Marcel Fournier, eds., *Cultivating Differences: Symbolic Boundaries and the Making of Inequality* (Chicago: University of Chicago Press, 1992).

- Ella Shohat and Robert Stam, *Unthinking Ethnocentrism: Multiculturalism and the Media* (New York: Routledge, 1994).

Chapter 9

Associations

A Country of Joiners

"A rich vegetation of associations and organizations for worth-while causes is an American characteristic. Americans are great 'joiners,' and they enjoy 'campaigns' and 'drives' for membership or contributions. Social clubs are plentiful, and even they are taken with a seriousness difficult for a stranger to understand. . . . It is natural for the ordinary American, when he sees something that is wrong, to feel not only that 'there should be a law against it' but also that an organization should be founded to combat it."[1]

So wrote the Swedish social scientist Gunnar Myrdal in 1944. Myrdal would later call associations the "salt of American politics." Organizations, in other words, are the stuff of democracy. For Alexis de Tocqueville, another European who, a century earlier, had much to say about America, associational life helped to cultivate in Americans a spirit of civic virtue and responsibility. "It is difficult to force a man out of himself," Tocqueville wrote, "and get him to take an interest in the affairs of the whole state. [But] the free institutions of the United States and the political rights enjoyed there provide a thousand continual reminders to every citizen that he lives in society. At every moment they bring his mind back to this idea, that it is the duty as well as the interest of men to be useful to their fellows. . . . At first it is of necessity that men attend to the public interest, afterward by choice. What had been calculation becomes instinct. By dint of working for the good of his fellow citizens, he in the end acquires the habit and taste for serving them."[2]

The importance of associations to healthy democracy cannot be overstated. They are the lifeblood of civil society and the very embodiment of community. A government "of the people, for the people, and by the people" requires that its citizens connect with one another—that they work and struggle and deliberate together. American citizenship is predicated on the community bonds its people forge with one another. Those bonds, however, have not always been—and are not always now—the fraternal sort of which Tocqueville spoke so highly. Associations can exclude people from the fruits of full citizenship, just as they can force the democratic state to include them. "In truth," writes political theorist Judith Shklar, "from the nation's beginnings as an independent republic, Americans were torn by 'glaring inconsistencies between their professed principles of citizenship and their deep-seated desire to exclude certain groups permanently from the privileges of membership.' These tensions constitute the real history of its citizens."[3]

This chapter examines how racial domination affects associational life. We have explored the workings of many associations in previous chapters—from political organizations and neighborhood-based groups to educational and artistic guilds—but have not yet fully unpacked the rich complexity of society's associational realm. In this sphere of society, we find social clubs, religious organizations, voluntary associations, and (in the age of the Internet) even virtual associations. Here are Elks Clubs, Masonic Lodges, and Odd Fellows Halls; college feminist societies, fraternities and sororities; community garden groups and Girl Scout troops. Here, too, are neo-Nazis and Klansmen and NAACP members and all sorts of religious followers, including Hasidic Jews, Methodists, Catholics, Sunni Muslims, and Vaishnava Hindus. We begin how we must always begin: with a backward glance that places American organizations in a historical context, examining, specifically, the struggles toward and away from racial integration. We then investigate how voluntary organizations affect and are affected by the racial order and their importance for sustaining a multiethnic democracy. Finally, we increase the magnification and focus on three kinds of organizations that are extremely important to the career of racial domination today: hate groups, Internet-based associations, and religious communities.

The Ordeal of Integration and the Rise of Ethnic Nationalism

After the fall of slavery, Africans Americans and other nonwhite citizens began to rise. Some worked their way out of poverty; others reunited with family members; still others made inroads into political life. America's racial order, which to many eyes appeared rather secure and settled just a few years before the Civil War, was changing at dizzying speeds. "And whites responded to this increasing diversity and the rising black middle class with fear, violent reprisals, and state legislation—their floundering attempts to build a new racial order," observes historian Grace Elizabeth Hale. "Whites created the culture of segregation in large part to counter black success, to make a myth of absolute racial difference,

to stop the rising."[4] With the union intact and slavery abolished, racial segregation arose as one of American society's central organizing principles. It recon-
figured the geography of the nation's neighborhoods, as we learned in Chapter 5,
and it came to dominate all areas of life, transforming America into what one
observer labeled a "Jim Crow jungle."[5] Associational life certainly did not escape
the tide of segregation. As Lillian Smith reflected in her stirring book, *Killers of
the Dream,* "Every little southern town is a fine stage-set for Southern Tradition
to use as it teaches its children the twisting turning dance of segregation. Few
words are needed for there are signs everywhere. *White . . . colored . . . white . . .
colored . . .* over doors of railroad and bus stations, over doors of public toilets,
over doors of theaters, over drinking fountains. . . . There are the signs without
words: big white church on Main Street, little unpainted colored church on the
rim of town; big white school, little ramshackly colored school; big white house,
little unpainted cabins; white graveyard with marble shafts, colored graveyard
with mounds of dirt."[6]

The Segregated Community

After the Civil War, America was wounded and reeling. Its towns, especially
those south of the Mason-Dixon Line, burnt and leveled by battles, needed to
be rebuilt. Its national community, which had lost no less than 2% of its
population—620,000 men, "the same number as those lost in all of America's other wars from the Revolution through Korea combined"[7]—needed to
be resurrected and patched back together. It is perhaps small wonder, then,
that associations proliferated in dramatic fashion during this time. Between
1861 and 1865, men and women formed organizations dedicated to the wartime effort, and those committed to community service continued to spread
long after the fighting stopped. The white chapters of the Independent Order
of Odd Fellows, for example, doubled their number of lodges between 1865
and 1895, while the black chapters experienced an even more impressive
increase. In 1865 black northern chapters of the Odd Fellows had only 5
lodges per 100,000 people; in 1895 they had over 30 lodges per 100,000.[8]
And new associations continued to be formed. Between 1895 and 1899, whites
established roughly 40 new national organizations, and white ethnics, such
as Irish and Polish Americans, established approximately 20 new groups.[9]

Southern whites, in contrast, devastated by the fall of the Confederacy, lagged
behind northern whites and blacks when it came to building associations. "As
losers in the great conflict over demarcation of American nationhood, white
southerners found it harder than the victorious northerners to organize or participate in large-scale civic endeavors in the postwar era."[10] There was, however,
one major exception: the 1865 founding of the Ku Klux Klan. Although the Klan's
racial terrorism was extreme (if widely accepted by white Protestants), many

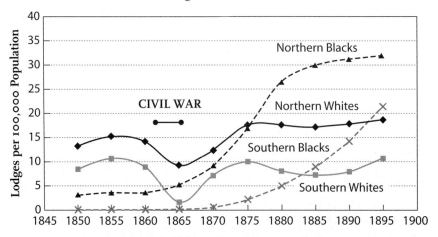

White and Black Odd Fellows Lodges in the North and South before, during, and after the Civil War

other new organizations were formed with the explicit purpose of promoting racial and ethnic conflict. Irish associations were established to wage battle with Italian ones; Protestant groups struggled against Catholic societies. And many social clubs limited their membership to white men. The Elks' membership pamphlet, *What It Means to Be an Elk*, was typical in its declaration that "membership in the Order is limited to white male citizens of the United States . . . who believe in the existence of God."[11] When the Elks spoke of "Charity, Justice, Brotherly Love, and Fidelity," or when the Odd Fellows touted the principles of "Friendship, Love, and Truth," they did not have nonwhites or women in mind. The same was true of most trade unions, churches, business associations, professional societies, and political groups.[12]

As a result, nonwhite organizations sprouted up alongside white ones, as did women's groups alongside those reserved for men. Consider the rise of African-American societies. When whites refused to admit blacks into the Masonic Lodge in 1775, blacks formed their own chapter, inaugurating a pattern that would continue throughout the 1800s and into the twentieth country, when dozens of African-American fraternal societies were established. "As the largest and most extensive sector of popularly rooted social organizations next to churches," write political scientist Theda Skocpol and colleagues in *What a Mighty Power We Can Be*, "African American fraternal lodges and federations likewise nurtured African American solidarity and supported many instances of civil rights advocacy from the nineteenth century, through the post-Civil War and Jim Crow periods, and down to eruption of Civil Rights militancy. . . . In time and places where blacks had few chances to create well-capitalized business

"In time and places where blacks had few chances to create well-capitalized business enterprises, African American fraternal orders expressed and fostered entrepreneurial talents, paid wages to black employees, and allowed blacks to use dues payments to amass considerable institutional capital." —Theda Skocpol

enterprises, African American fraternal orders expressed and fostered entrepreneurial talents, paid wages to black employees, and allowed blacks to use dues payments to amass considerable institutional capital. As of the early 1920s, more than sixty nationally visible 'secret and fraternal organizations' had about 2.2 million members and owned $20 million worth of property."[13]

Toward Integration: Associational Coalition Building

Associational life bent itself to accommodate America's newfound edict of racial segregation. Blacks attended black churches; whites attended white churches; Hispanics attended Hispanic churches, and so on. There were black and Asian-American Boy Scout Troops, segregated military brigades, barber shops, corner stores, and restaurants. There were Mexican Unions in copper industry, black miners unions, and United Hebrew Trades that came up beside the dominant white ones.

But in the wake of racial segregation, a movement toward integration also began to take shape within associational life. Political societies, such as the

Commission on Interracial Coalition, which arose alongside the NAACP, practiced integration in membership and leadership. Veterans associations, such as the Grand Army of the Republic, the Veterans of Foreign Wars, and the American Legion, allowed nonwhite veterans to join integrated chapters in the North.[14] African-American women in the Young Women's Christian Association (YWCA) fought to integrate their organization. In its early years, the YWCA established segregated chapters, subordinated black chapters to white ones, and all but ignored the voices of discontent from its black members. However, beginning in 1920, black women began to organize and challenge the YWCA's stance on racial segregation and, eventually, helped to transform the YWCA from a progressive-minded but segregated organization to one that "put racial justice at the centre of its mission." The YWCA adopted an interracial charter in 1946, a move remembered by Dr. Benjamin Mays, then President of Morehouse College, with these words: "I realize what you have before you, what you are trying to do, and . . . most likely all across the country you will hear people saying, 'The time is not ripe.' . . . In the Christian ethic, the time is always right to do justice. Given your honorable purpose as the Young Women's Christian Association, if the time is not ripe, then it is your job to ripen it!" As the twentieth century pushed forward, the YWCA transformed itself into an anti-racist and fully integrated organization, a transformation symbolized by a new slogan it adopted in 2002: "Eliminating Racism; Empowering Women."[15]

Even some labor unions, traditional mainstays of racial domination and segregation, joined the movement towards integration. As early as 1892, one locale of the United Mine Workers of America not only allowed nonwhites and Eastern European immigrants to join, it also selected "one Hungarian, one [African American], one Polander, one Slav, and one white" to serve as officers.[16] White workers were starting to come around to the idea that their interests and those of nonwhite workers were bound together. As one mid-twentieth-century steelworker put it, "You must forget that the man working beside you is a 'Nigger,' Jew, or 'Pollock.' The man working beside you, be he negro, Jew, or Pollock, is a working man like yourself. . . . You work together—fight together."[17] Indeed, the inclusion of nonwhites into traditionally white unions challenged the dominant image of nonwhites as strikebreakers and discouraged white workers from "[jeopardizing] class solidarity by exhibiting racial antagonism."[18]

After the Civil Rights Movement, many associations erased racially exclusive language from their constitutions and charters, and some actively pursued racial integration. In the 1960s, many Boy Scout troops were desegregated, and in 1970, the Parent-Teacher Association (PTA), which had always practiced segregation, forbade its chapters from limiting membership to white parents only.[19] Slowly but surely, whites embraced integration. In 1977, only 42% of surveyed whites said they would try to change the rules of their club if it excluded blacks. By 1993, 67% of whites said they would. Of course, compared to their white peers, nonwhites always have been stronger proponents of integration. When blacks were asked in 1993 if they would try to change the rules of a social club to which they belonged so that whites were allowed to join, 86% answered yes.[20]

Away from Integration: The Case for Ethnic Nationalism

In the same way as they resisted integrated neighborhoods, many whites opposed the integration of their associations. But just as a small if committed cadre of whites fought *for* racial integration, a small but committed cadre of nonwhites fought *against* it. For these nonwhites, racial integration did not lead to liberation but only to more oppression. Racial segregation and complete independence from whites was the only answer. This ideological movement has come to be known as **ethnic nationalism**; its ambassadors resist cultural and social assimilation and instead champion self-determination, race pride, separatism, and, in some cases, the creation of an independent nation based on racial identity.

As we already know, whites long have advocated for ethnic nationalism, even if they have refused to recognize the racial and ethnic dimensions of their nativism or patriotism: an ethnic nationalism that need not speak its name. One thinks not only of organized white nationalist groups, which we discuss in some detail later on, but also of legal cases that restricted citizenship to whites, the anti-Chinese movement, the white backlash that choked the Civil Rights Movement, and, most recently, anti-Arab sentiment and militia groups that patrol the U.S.-Mexico border.[21] Some nonwhites, too, have championed ethnic nationalism, in one form or another. Here one thinks of nonwhite ethnic nationalist movements, including the American Indian push for sovereignty and Chicano nationalism (or *Chicanismo*). The most influential of these was black nationalism.[22]

The roots of black nationalism stretch clear back to the early days of slavery. Its political philosophy was prevalent in nineteenth-century African-American thought, but it was not until the early twentieth century that black nationalism gained momentum, secured a significant following, and captured the nation's (and the FBI's) attention.[23] The year was 1918. Booker T. Washington had been dead for three years; many African Americans were yearning for a new leader; and a Jamaican immigrant by the name of **Marcus Garvey** was earning a name for himself in Harlem. Garvey was a masterful orator, one who could "throw his voice around three corners without batting an eyelash," as one admirer put it.[24] And the message he advocated with such force and eloquence—one that would jump out of Harlem and spread around the nation and, soon after that, the world—was that of black nationalism.

Garvey was the founding mastermind behind and primary spokesperson for the United Negro Improvement Association (UNIA), which, in its heyday

(1920–1921), most likely had more members than the NAACP. (And, unlike the NAACP, the UNIA placed women in positions of leadership and entirely was led, financed, and staffed by blacks.) For Garvey and the UNIA, the solution to the white domination of blacks could be found only within the collective strength of the black community. Garvey encouraged African Americans to view themselves as Africans first—as people who had had their culture, history, language, identity, and pride stripped from them—and as Americans second. Although other black leaders criticized racist notions of black inferiority and worked to instill in blacks a sense of dignity, it was Garvey who most compellingly and unequivocally argued that blacks all over the world *constituted a powerful nation* with a proud past and a heroic future. Garvey chronicled the glories of African civilization and urged all blacks to band together, embracing their blackness. Garvey did not think blacks were equal to whites; he thought they were better than them.[25] "They tell us that God is white," he bellowed. "That is a lie. They tell us that all of His angels are white, too. To my mind, everything that is devilish is white. They told us that the devil was a black man. There isn't a greater devil in the world than the white man."[26] It was Garvey who popularized the term "white devil." Indeed, his pro-black nationalism often found meaning through antiwhite declarations.

Garvey's **ethnic chauvinism**—or excessive loyalty toward, and belief in the superiority of, a racial or ethnic group, a term applicable in principle to all groups—was not a tangential feature of his black nationalist platform. It was a central one. And it was in the principles of black chauvinism, a direct reversal of white supremacy that resulted in a kind of black supremacy, that Garvey grounded his anti-integrationist stance. Convinced that things would get worse, not better, for blacks, Garvey vied for the complete separation of the races: "This is going to be a 'white man's country,' sooner or later, and the best thing possibly we can do is [to] find a black man's country."[27] Black nationalism was not a movement for equal rights, as was the movement for integration; it was a movement for *black power,* for black-owned businesses and a black-run government with a black military behind it. How, precisely, this vision was to be fulfilled was never fully articulated. Several times, Garvey went so far as to promote a repatriation plan, where all people of African descent would return to Africa to help liberate the continent from white colonialism. "Africa for the Africans, home and abroad," so read the UNIA slogan.[28]

In his anti-integrationist convictions, Garvey had much in common with outspoken white supremacists. Fully aware of this fact, Garvey arranged secret meetings with Edward Clarke, the Imperial Wizard of the KKK. Garvey lost considerable support once news of this unholy alliance spread throughout African-American communities. A "Garvey Must Go" campaign was launched in 1922; a year later, Garvey was convicted of mail fraud; in 1925 he was deported to Jamaica, never to set foot again on American soil. Although black *nationalism* had been around for years, Garvey was the first black *nationalist*—he was the first to build a movement around the idea of a separate, independent black nation.[29]

Without Garvey, the UNIA floundered—and the black nationalist movement with it. Black nationalism would lie dormant until the 1960s, when urban centers erupted in racial uprisings. Some Northern blacks, forced to get by on hard ghetto streets, were growing impatient with Martin Luther King, Jr.'s, message of nonviolence and with the SCLC's failure to achieve in the North the political victories it had enjoyed in the South. It was during his visits to Chicago, New York, and other northern cities that King most fully realized that a minority of blacks disagreed with his philosophy of nonviolence and that some even were ready to employ armed resistance on behalf of the black liberation struggle. A Harlem high school student succinctly captured a growing sentiment in Black America when he told a group of visiting Mississippi high schoolers, "Turning the other cheek is a load of trash. Up here we understand what snake is biting us."[30] A significant minority of African Americans, then, were ready to rally behind another leader, one who would energize a movement that bared more teeth than King's integrationist platform. **Malcolm X** would become that leader.

Malcolm Little was born in 1925 into hard-scrabble poverty. Whereas King grew up in a stable and supportive family, Malcolm's family was riddled with hardship. When Malcolm was 6, his father was killed in a car accident. A few years later, his mother was committed to a mental institution. Malcolm was shuffled between relatives and foster parents and, as a young adult, got caught up in a life of drugs and crime. Convicted of burglary, he was imprisoned between 1946 and 1952. It was in prison that Malcolm remade himself. He began to read voraciously and converted to the Nation of Islam, a small, black separatist religious sect then led by Elijah Muhammad. He abandoned his last name—one that belonged to his ancestors' slave master—and replaced it with the letter X, which stood for his real African name that was "destroyed during slavery." Once released, Malcolm X helped bring about a powerful resurgence of black nationalism.[31]

If Garvey had the United Negro Improvement Association, Malcolm X had the Nation of Islam, which promoted race pride, isolation, and self-discipline. (Unlike the UNIA, however, the Nation of Islam was by and large dominated by men—a pattern that may gradually be changing today, as women assume more positions of leadership within the organization.[32]) Like Garvey, Malcolm X was a beautiful elocutionist; and, also like Garvey, he criticized integration— "We believe that separation is the best way and the only sensible way, not integration," he said in 1963—and advanced a kind of ethnic chauvinism, which tended to downplay or altogether disregard the actions of white antiracists. (Like Garvey, Malcolm X sometimes referred to whites as "snakes" and "devils.") Malcolm X encouraged blacks to cleanse themselves of all thoughts of self-hate and inferiority implanted within them since slavery. As he once observed to a mostly black audience, "I think to teach a man to hate himself is much more criminal than teaching him to hate someone else. And, look at you, who taught you to hate yourself?"

Drawing great inspiration from the uprisings of colonized people in Africa, Asia, and Latin America—uprisings he understood as together constituting a global revolt of nonwhites against their white oppressors—Malcolm X condemned nonviolent protest as weak and ineffective, even cowardly, and argued that violence could play an important role in bringing freedom to African Americans. "Nationalism is the wave of the present and the future," he said. "It is *nationalism* that is bringing freedom to oppressed people around the world. . . . The Africans didn't get it by sitting in. They didn't get it by wading in. They didn't get it by singing, 'We Shall Overcome.' They got it through *nationalism,* and you and I will get it through nationalism." Or, as he put it on another occasion, "You haven't *got* a revolution that doesn't involve bloodshed. And you're afraid to bleed. . . . Long as the white man sends you to Korea, you bled. He sends you to Germany, you bled. He sent you to the South Pacific to fight the Japanese, you bled. You bleed for white people, but when it comes time to seeing your own churches being bombed, and little black girls murdered, you haven't got no blood."[33]

"The purpose of our organization," Malcolm X famously declared, "of Afro-American unity, which has the same aim and objective to fight whoever gets in our way . . . is to bring about the complete independence of people of African descent, . . . to bring about the freedom of these people *by any means necessary.*" Such a phrase—"by any means necessary"—caused a chill to run up the spines of many white Americans. Although Malcolm X's defense of violence was anything but radical—after all, it had been around since the dawn of humanity, and many enslaved African Americans (such as Nat Turner) as well as some white abolitionists (for instance, John Brown), correctly understanding slavery as an all-out war against blacks,[34] had advocated and practiced armed self-defense, while, of course, racist whites long had subscribed to such a position—it did break with the "turn the other cheek" message championed by King and his followers. Accordingly, the FBI kept a close eye on Malcolm X (as they did on King), amassing a thick file that recently was made available to the public.[35] An FBI memorandum from March 4, 1968 reads, "For maximum effectiveness of the Counterintelligence Program, and to prevent wasted effort, long-range goals are being set. [First,] prevent the coalition of militant black nationalist groups. . . . [Second,] prevent the rise of a 'messiah' who could unify, and electrify, the militant black nationalist movement. Malcolm X might have been such a 'messiah.'"[36]

Malcolm X shocked a good number of African Americans, and other non-whites, as well. "He scared the hell out of us, bred as we are to caution, to hypocrisy in the presence of white folks, to the smile that never fades," African-American actor Ossie Davis would remember. "And if all the lies we tell ourselves by way of extenuation were put into print, it would constitute one of the great chapters in the history of man's justifiable cowardice in the face of other men. But Malcolm kept snatching our lies away. He kept shouting the painful truth we whites and blacks did not want to hear from all the housetops. . . . He would make you angry as hell, but he would also make you proud. It was impossible to remain defensive and apologetic about being a Negro in his presence. He wouldn't let you. And you always left his presence with the sneaky suspicion that maybe, after all, you *were* a man!"[37]

Malcolm X would eventually break with the Nation of Islam and some of its separatist leanings. After converting to orthodox Islam, he partook in the Hajj, the sacred pilgrimage to Mecca, and upon seeing Muslims of all races and nationalities come together, after catching a glimpse of the promise of multiracial unity and harmony, he began to rethink his promotion of ethnic chauvinism. And after witnessing some of the gains made by the mainstream of the Civil Rights Movement, he softened his anti-integrationist stance and tempered his proviolence arguments. But we will never know the full impact and development of Malcolm X's modified views toward black nationalism, because he was shot and killed on February 21, 1965, just as few months before his 40th birthday.[38]

The vast majority of blacks during Malcolm X's time believed more in the promise of and movement toward interrogation than in black nationalism and racial separatism. In 1966, 88% of blacks polled approved of Martin Luther King, Jr., and 55% approved of SCLC; by contrast, only 12% approved of Elijah Muhammad, and a paltry 9% backed the Nation of Islam.[39] Nevertheless, a good many blacks resonated with and respected black nationalism, even if they rejected the movement's more militant elements. In the words of James Farmer, "Deep in the heart of every black adult lives some of Malcolm and some of King, side by side."[40]

On the one hand, black nationalism failed. A separate black nation never came to be, and racial integration has become the desired goal. On the other hand, the movement succeeded in striking a tremendous blow to the symbolic violence inflicted by racial domination upon the psyches of black people. As Norman Kelly has put it, "Integration has been a material success but an ideological and spiritual failure; black nationalism, on the other hand, has been an ideological success but a material failure."[41] Despite all its shortcomings, the great triumph of black nationalism was this: it lifted high the heads of millions of African Americans (and perhaps those of a good deal of other nonwhites as well) that for decades had been bowed low under the weight of white supremacy.

Civil Society in a Multiracial Democracy

"Citizens cannot leave politics just to politicians," reasoned German novelist Günter Grass.[42] By participating in associational life—or in civil society, which, you might recall from Chapter 3, is that area of life where we find public debate, community organizing, and citizen-led political mobilization—citizens can help to chart the course of their society. From its inception, America has developed a diverse and active civil society, bursting forth with a rich variety of associations. "Americans of all ages, all stations of life, and all types of dispositions are forever forming associations," wrote Tocqueville. "At the head of any new undertaking, where in France you would find the government or in England some territorial magnate, in the United States, you are sure to find an association."[43] Tocqueville was on to something when he drew our attention to the very American practice of forming and developing associations. As Gabriel Almond and Sidney Verba demonstrated over one hundred years later in their influential book, *The Civic Culture,* compared to citizens in other Western countries, a significantly higher percentage of Americans belong to associations.[44] And America's healthy civil society, a number of social scientists have concluded, has been primarily responsible for bringing about the nation's stable and developed democracy. What, then, is the state of today's all-important civil society? How does racial domination thwart the development of genuine community and multicultural democracy? And what can we do about it?

Racial Variation in Civic Participation

To begin our discussion, we might ask: Do whites participate in civil society at similar rates as nonwhites? The answer, according to a well-developed social-scientific literature, is no. Whites tend to participate at higher rates, whereas people of color are less likely to join voluntary associations and to participate in community activities. As one pair of researchers plainly state, "On average, Whites participate in the most organizations, followed by Blacks, Latinos, and Asians."[45] Nonwhites also exhibit lower degrees of social trust, a fundamental prerequisite of community building. One study found that, while 45% of whites believe that "most people can be trusted," only 27% of Hispanics and Asians and 17% of blacks feel likewise.[46] Racial domination stonewalls interracial solidarity and trust. Speaking of the racial divisions in her community, one resident of the Mississippi Delta observed, "Everything here is segregated. There is no social interaction between the races, and *no trust.* Whites say you can't trust blacks, and blacks say the same thing about whites."[47] Such racial discrepancies

Voter Turnout for Presidential Elections by Race, Citizens Ages 18–29

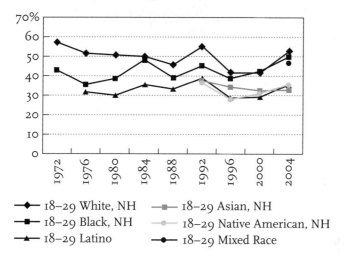

— ◆ — 18–29 White, NH   — ■ — 18–29 Asian, NH
— ■ — 18–29 Black, NH   — ● — 18–29 Native American, NH
— ▲ — 18–29 Latino   — ● — 18–29 Mixed Race

in civil participation are disturbing because they suggest that nonwhites' interests may be underrepresented in the public debate and that civil society may be developing in an uneven and dysfunctional fashion.[48]

Why might whites be out-joining nonwhites? For one, some nonwhites, especially those living and working in some of America's poorest neighborhoods, have withdrawn their support from a nation that first withdrew its support from them. Families living on impoverished Native American reservations in Nebraska or South Dakota, those in run-down barrios along the Southern border or on segregated and bombed-out ghetto streets in Cleveland, Detroit, or Pittsburg— areas created, we have learned, by state and federal policies designed to uphold racial domination—understandably may find it hard to devote their time and energy to a system that historically has ignored their cries and, more, has fostered the conditions that have produced those cries. Most major political movements have not paid these communities much mind. Indeed, the presidential campaign of Barack Obama, which sought uniquely to organize and mobilize nonwhite voters, including those in low-income neighborhoods, is perhaps the exception that proves the rule.

Another factor that helps explain why whites out-participate nonwhites is racialized economic inequality. In fact, studies have shown that this is the primary force behind most of racial variation in associational life. Participating in associational life takes time (attending meetings, organizing events) and money (paying dues, making financial contributions to campaigns), which is why the affluent are overrepresented in civil society. Forty percent of people with annual

Civic Involvement by High- and Low-Income Groups

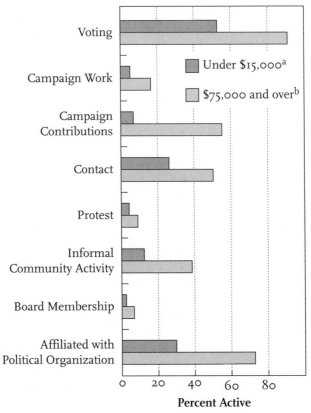

a. N = 483 weighted cases.

b. N = 224 weighted cases.

incomes of $75,000 or higher, but only 15% of people with annual incomes under $15,000, are involved in some informal community activity. Seventy-five percent of people with annual incomes of $75,000 or higher are affiliated with a political organization; the same is true of only 25% of people with annual incomes under $15,000. And although a full 96% of affluent people (those with incomes exceeding $125,000) are affiliated with some organization, only 63% of their poor neighbors (those with incomes below $15,000) report likewise. Only with respect to religious attendance and church membership do the poor participate at similar rates as middle- and upper-class citizens.[49] By and large, residents of poor inner-city neighborhoods are especially cut off from associational life. As we pointed out in Chapter 6, ghetto dwellers often are isolated not only from the social mainstream but also from one another.[50] Indeed, one study has concluded that blacks who regularly come in contact with whites are more active in political organizations than blacks with infrequent contact with whites—further evidence of the alienation and isolation that has come to define some of the country's poorest urban communities.[51]

Because the poor do not participate in community organizations as much as the affluent, and because nonwhites are disproportionately wracked by poverty, we should expect racial variation in associational life to dissipate to a significant degree once economic differences are accounted for. This expectation is precisely what researchers have found. Once economic differences are taken into account, Latinos are just as likely, and blacks even more likely, to participate in voluntary associations as whites.[52] In fact, several analysts have observed that many African Americans are "super joiners." To quote Gunnar Myrdal once again, "Despite the fact that they are predominately lower class, Negroes are more inclined to join associations than are whites; in this respect . . . Negroes are 'exaggerated' Americans."[53]

Unlike blacks and Latinos, however, Asians participate in associational life at significantly lower rates than whites do, regardless of economic differences. There are other factors, then, beside economic differences driving racial variation in civic participation. According to recent sociological research, those factors seem to be associated with the immigrant experience. One's English proficiency and one's time of arrival in the United States can affect one's level of civic participation. Once these factors are accounted for, the gap between Asian and white participation rates narrows, and Latinos seem even more involved than whites in associational life.[54] Indeed, social scientists have found high levels of community building in immigrant enclaves.[55] Sociologist Min Zhou has documented a rise of voluntary associations in New York's Chinatown, associations designed to help new immigrants adjust to American society. These organizations, such as the Chinese Consolidated Benevolent Association and the Chinese-American Planning Council—not to mention the many Buddhist temples and Christian churches sprinkled throughout the enclave—oversee English language classes, career training, and cultural events. They have played a vital role in strengthening community and helping immigrants integrate into American life.[56]

If poor immigrant enclaves are brimming with community associations—Zhou counted over 100 voluntary associations in Chinatown alone—and if one even can find a vibrant associational life in ghetto neighborhoods, then perhaps the very definition of "association" that undergirds the observation that whites associate in civil society at higher rates is too narrow. Better: perhaps the definition is biased toward traditionally white middle-class forms of association. "All too frequently," observes sociologist Robert Wuthnow, "[our idea of civil society] appears to be couched in terms that reflect the traditionally dominant position of the white middle class rather than the growing realities of a racially and ethnically diverse society."[57]

Do your friendship networks mostly consist of people who share your skin color?

Homophily in Associational Life

Today, over half of African Americans who participated in a national survey claimed to have a white friend in whom they could confide and to whom they could speak their minds.[58]

With whom do you choose to associate? Do your friendship networks, social clubs, and favorite spots to hang out mostly consist of people who share your skin color? Researchers studying social networks long have documented the phenomenon of **homophily**. Literally meaning "love of the same," homophily refers to the practice of associating with people like you. "Birds of a feather flock together," as the old adage goes. Homophily applies to age, religion, education, and occupation, but, as one group of sociologists concluded after reviewing over one hundred studies that document homophilous associations, "homophily in race and ethnicity creates the *strongest divides* in our personal environments."[59] You are more likely to associate regularly with people of different class standings, educational levels, and religions than with people of different racial or ethnic groups.

By and large, today's associations remain racially segregated; but today's associational segregation is maintained not so much through active and open discrimination as through a softer kind of exclusion. Whites who belong to a majority-white Rotary Club, for example, might keep their club white, not by turning down nonwhite applications but by actively recruiting women and men from their social circles (for example, their families, work, or religious institutions) who, because of the homophily principle, most likely also are white. They are not pushing "enemies" away so much as pulling friends in.[60] Sociologists have referred to this kind of dynamic as "boundary work."

Boundary work refers to the multiple ways people create, uphold, and traverse social boundaries that separate familiar from unfamiliar, welcome from unwelcome, "us" from "them." The key idea gleaned from the social science of boundary work—one that dates back to the work of anthropologist Fredrik Barth—is that racial and ethnic groups can understand one another as possessing distinct cultures and lifestyles only if they actively distinguish themselves from other groups. To be Persian American is, at base, to be *not*-Arab American, *not*-black, *not*-white, and so forth. To conduct a sociology of boundary work is to assume a fundamentally *relational* view of the social world, of the sort we ourselves have championed in this book. Racial dynamics, as we already know, are driven by overlapping relations between people, institutions, or ideas (for example, whiteness does not exist without blackness). Boundary work is the collection of practices by which people maintain or challenge racial relations of exclusivity and inclusivity.[61] And one of the primary sites of boundary work is the associational field.

More often than not, formal associations, such as churches and social clubs, only deepen—rather than defy—racial divisions. One thinks of the English-Only Movement, which we briefly encountered in Chapter 5, a collection of white-led political organizations that seek to outlaw the use of any language other than English in public settings and on government documents and to make English the official language of towns, states, and—their biggest goal—the nation. The English-Only Movement has gained steam in recent years, riding the tide of a growing anti-immigrant sentiment, and in twenty-eight states English is the official language—an unwelcoming symbolic gesture targeting immigrant communities in general and Spanish speakers in particular, as linguist boundaries map onto racial ones.[62] At the same time, other organizations have criticized the English-Only Movement. The Linguistic Society of America, for example, decries English Only measures "on the grounds that they are based on misconceptions about the role of a common language in establishing political unity, and that they are inconsistent with basic American traditions of linguistic tolerance."[63]

Other examples of formal associations contributing to racial boundary work abound. Think of the clear-cut racial segregation that marks your college or university's sororities and fraternities. Or consider the boundary work carried out by America's Christian churches. "We must face the fact that the church is still the most segregated major institution in America," said a Baptist pastor by the name of Martin Luther King, Jr. "At 11:00 on Sunday morning, when we stand and sing that Christ has no east or west, we stand at the most segregated hour in this nation." If there are two kinds of social capital—a homophilous kind that *binds* you to "your people" and a heterophilous kind that *bridges* racial cleavages—we must conclude that most formal associations dole out the binding kind.

The same is true of more informal associations, those that do not hand out membership cards or charge dues but, nevertheless, are as important to civil society as their more formal counterparts. Here one thinks of boundary work executed by bars and nightclubs (for example, their dress codes, dance styles, musical tastes, drink specials), and the social (and racial) significance of the phrase, "This is my kind of place."[64] One thinks, too, of how different ethnic ceremonies, from Quinceañeras and Bar Mitzvahs to Puerto Rican Pride Parades and Polish Day festivities, reinforce boundaries. And, of course, if we conceive of social boundaries with an intersectional imagination, we realize the many ways in which formal and informal associations reinforce class, gender, sexual, and religious boundaries that further divide racial and ethnic communities. Elite social clubs of the black upper class—such as the Jack and Jill Foundation, a private, invitation-only club that caters to children of wealthy black families—help to distinguish affluent African Americans from poor blacks.[65] And certain religious institutions, such as the Mormon Church or Amish communities, provide their majority-white congregants with practices and beliefs that separate men from women.

Sporting associations—communities of players and fans—are an important part of most the nation's associational life as well. But even the multiracial world of sports is racialized to a significant degree. Athletic divisions map onto racial divisions. Some sports, like rugby, NASCAR, rodeo, and sailing virtually are monopolized by whites. Others, like cricket, bull fighting, and professional soccer are connected to various immigrant communities. And in professional- and collegiate-level sports, not only are nonwhites underrepresented in positions of power and leadership—on the field (quarterbacks, pitchers, coaches) and off (owners, commissioners, general managers)—but also nonwhite (and especially black) athletes sometimes are ridiculed by fans and sportscasters for "having attitude" and for blaspheming the values of the game with their "flashy style."[66] Fans, too, can use coded language to signal racial boundaries through sport affiliations. In Chicago, the Cubs are associated with the city's (white and affluent) northern neighborhoods, while the White Sox are associated with its (nonwhite and poorer) southern districts. In the Bay Area, the 49ers are connected to white and affluent San Francisco, while the Raiders are linked to black and not-so-affluent Oakland.

Our associations, then, remain homophilous and highly segregated. Whether or not the next generation will change this remains to be seen. There are some encouraging signs afoot. The value of multiculturalism is prized by this generation

All or Most Members of Associations That Are the Same Race

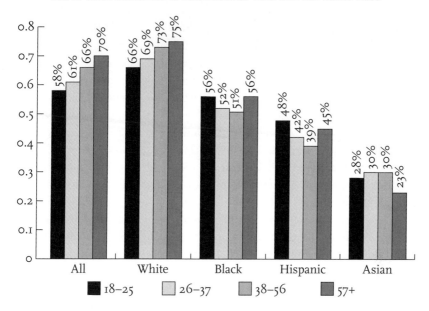

much more than by the last. In the political field, one can find racially integrated organizations fighting for a living wage, health care, or sustainable agriculture; in integrated neighborhoods, community-based associations gather together people of different racial or ethnic heritage to cultivate community and respond to criminal activity; and on college campuses multicultural student coalitions often have a visible presence. Integrated associations, like integrated neighborhoods, are not the norm—not even close—but they may be proliferating. As America grows more racially diverse by the year, and as the creeds of multiculturalism and antiracism continue to be adopted by more and more of its citizens, might that which separates Navajo from Hopi, Cuban from Puerto Rican, Chinese American from white American, African American from Arab American, born citizen from immigrant—the problem of the color line—lessen and blur as the promise of a multicultural democracy is more fully realized? Time will tell, but know this: racial integration of the associational field will not come through a Supreme Court decision or a federally mandated policy; it will come only if people like you take up its charge, influencing the organizations to which you belong and the company you keep.

Racial Domination and the Decline of Social Capital

What, we now ask, is the status of our civil society more generally? Dysfunctional and anemic, answers political scientist Robert Putnam in his modern classic,

Bowling Alone: The Collapse and Revival of American Community. According to Putnam, the current generation (*your* generation, if you are a "traditional" college student who came straight to college from high school) is less interconnected and less engaged in community affairs than the one that came before. And *that* generation (your parents' generation, if you are a traditional college student) was less interconnected than the previous one. In other words, since the end of the Civil Rights Movement, social capital has declined in America. Since the 1960s, "Americans have become perhaps 10%–15% less likely to voice our views publicly by running for office or writing Congress or the local newspaper, 15%–20% less interested in politics and public affairs, roughly 25% less likely to vote, roughly 35% less likely to attend public meetings, both partisan and nonpartisan, and roughly 40% less engaged in party politics and indeed in political and civic organizations of all sorts."[67]

Church congregations, bridge clubs, socialist societies, community-outreach coalitions, and organizations of all hues have thinned and, in some cases, dissolved altogether. In Putnam's view, one informed by an impressive array of evidence, we are becoming more disconnected from and distrustful of one another. Civil society is in trouble. Given the importance of civil society for a healthy democracy—associations are the primary and most effective vehicle through which social change happens; members of organizations are more active in politics and exhibit more competence in the political process than nonmembers; and efficient judiciaries, financial development, high-quality governments, and social welfare all are associated with high levels of social capital and trust[68]—**Putnam's thesis of social decapitalization** should concern us all.

Of course, Putnam's thesis has not gone unchallenged. Some have suggested that it may be biased toward white middle-class forms of association. Others have argued that the thesis may mistake a dramatic reorganization of associations for a decline in social capital. If this is the case, then perhaps bowling leagues have lost members not because Americans are becoming more isolated but because they are choosing to associate in newfangled ways. Odd Fellows halls have been eclipsed by Facebook and My Space. But even Putnam's harshest critics admit that civic engagement, associational life, and political participation—at least in some areas of the country—are not as vibrant today as one would like.[69] If this is the case, what social forces are responsible for the weakening of civil society? Social scientists have pointed to many, including the rise of television, the mass movement of (white) women into the labor force, and the lengthening of the work week. Of particular interest to our purposes, analysts have demonstrated at least two ways in which racial domination contributes to social decapitalization.

First, the suburbanization of America, a process pushed along by white fear and flight, has contributed to the erosion of social capital. Putnam himself

Social Capital and Civic Engagement by Generation (education controlled)

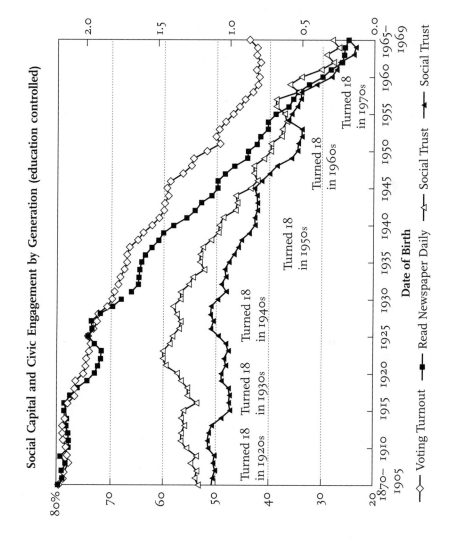

Turned 18 in 1920s Turned 18 in 1930s Turned 18 in 1940s Turned 18 in 1950s Turned 18 in 1960s Turned 18 in 1970s

Date of Birth

1870–1905 1910 1915 1920 1925 1930 1935 1940 1945 1950 1955 1960 1965–1969

—◇— Voting Turnout —■— Read Newspaper Daily —△— Social Trust —▲— Social Trust

recognized this: "Not only are canvassing politicians and Girl Scouts selling cook-ies excluded from exclusive communities, but the affluent residents themselves also appear to have a surprisingly low rate of civic engagement and neighborliness even within their boundaries. . . . Far from seeking small-town connectedness, suburbanites [keep] to themselves, asking little of their neighbors and expecting little in return."[70] The suburbanite values privacy and self-sufficiency, confirming the historian of city planning Lewis Mumford's observation that "the romantic suburb was a collective attempt to live a private life."[71] Here, tools that could be used by a good number of people, such as snow blowers and lawnmowers, are regarded as private property and are locked up in two-car garages; and homeown-ers' associations, with their strict rules and penalties, have emerged as the pri-mary, if not exclusive, community organization in suburban neighborhoods. What is more, the suburbanite simply might not think he has time to participate in associational life on account of his daily commute. Suburbanization helped to create the commute by expanding the distance separating work from home. Today, the average American spends 25 minutes each day commuting to work. That's more than 100 hours a year, time that could be spent organizing and associating with fellow citizens.[72]

As America has become more racially segregated and suburbanized, it has become more racially diverse as well, and this brings us to the second way in which racial domination corrodes American community. Study after study has concluded that social capital and trust for fellow Americans is lower in racially diverse communities.[73] Membership in associations lags in metropolitan areas with greater amounts of racial and ethnic integration and economic inequality. Likewise, nonwhites who live in majority-white suburbs are less involved in community organizing than those who live in majority-nonwhite areas. The pro-liferation of associations and the degree of social trust is highest in states with racially homogeneous populations (such as Minnesota and Maine) and lowest in states with racially heterogeneous populations (Mississippi and New Mexico). These findings make sense given the homophilous nature of social networks. If whites are more likely to associate with other whites, blacks with blacks, Latinos with Latinos, and so forth, then we would expect to observe an increase in social capital in areas that facilitate the formation of segregated associations. In the words of political scientist Rodney Hero, because "social capital is inevitably easier to foster within homogeneous communities[,] . . . there is a deep tension between diversity and connectedness."[74]

Not only are Americans less willing to associate and to trust people of other racial and ethnic groups, they also are less likely to support public programs (such as education and welfare) that they think will disproportionately benefit members of other racial and ethnic groups. This is especially true of whites. In Florida, for example, the average taxpayer is a white senior citizen, but the average public school student is a Latino child. In this state, white taxpayers voice considerably less support for public school expenditures than those in states where most taxpayers and public school students are white. Economists have amassed a good deal of evidence for the **"Florida Effect"** in other states as well, finding that support for public services (from trash pickup and sewer systems to road maintenance and education) is negatively correlated with racial and ethnic diversity.[75] It seems that people, especially white citizens, are more willing to put their tax dollars behind public programs that they think overwhelmingly will benefit members of their own racial group.

Racial domination, then, rips apart civil society in two opposite directions. On the one hand, it had led (and continues to lead) to the creation of segregated suburbs, which foster a kind of lifestyle that can be fundamentally at odds with community building. On the other hand, it divides white from Asian, Asian from black, black from Latino, and so forth, to such a degree that, unless the current generation strives to bridge racial boundaries in sustained and intentional ways, social capital will decline even further as our nation grows more racially diverse.

Identity Politics and the Fragmentation of Civil Society

If civil society's landscape is segregated along racial lines, does this imply that civil society has become fragmented to such a degree that it is very difficult to reach across racial boundaries and debate, deliberate, and commune together? Is America's national culture in jeopardy? Are Americans no longer guided by a core constellation of shared values? These are the questions that bother some analysts, who bemoan the ascendancy of special interests and identity politics. Arising in the wake of the Civil Rights Movement, **identity politics** refers to political action intended to address the unique interests and hardships of groups (such as nonwhites, women, and gays) who historically have faced oppression and who continue to be excluded from mainstream society. Associations such as the NAACP, ethnic newspapers, National Council of La Raza, National Organization for Women, and the Gay and Lesbian Alliance against Defamation are but a handful of organizations (out of hundreds) that are designed to protect and enhance the rights of certain marginalized groups.

Of course, dominant groups—whites, men, heterosexuals—participate in identity politics as well, though oftentimes, as we have already learned, their privileged position in society allows them to promote a political agenda that does not on the surface appear to be a kind of identity politics. Whites do not, in the majority of cases, speak of advocating for "white rights" or of "serving the white community" in the same way that some nonwhite groups advocate for, say, "immigrant rights" or "serving the South Asian community." However, the silence of some white politicians in the face of racial injustice—the fact that they avoid altogether discussing racial inequalities or championing anti-racist programs—most certainly is a form of identity politics, one that supports white majority.

Many have criticized the emergence of identity politics (and its accompanying associations) for splintering civil society.[76] They worry that the growing number of Americans who live in racially homogeneous communities may be "willing to protect [only] their own lifestyles but are unlikely to express interest in broader issues of national importance," resulting in a civil society that resembles a collection of warring camps where "diverse groups have so little in common that they are unable to come to agreement at all."[77] The increasing fragmentation of identity politics, some argue, may cause some Americans to become disillusioned and cynical and to withdraw from civil society altogether. Are such worries justified?

Social-scientific evidence suggests they are not. Americans' political attitudes and interests are not becoming more polarized; in fact, on moral, social, economic, and political issues there is impressive congruence. While so-called **"culture wars"** may wage among political elites and media pundits, at the ground level everyday Americans of all racial identities agree on many important issues.[78] We have our differences, to be sure, but we have much more in common than many people believe. Most of us, regardless of our racial identity, gender, or class upbringing, believe that all people should be provided equal opportunity to succeed, that everyone should be treated equally under the law, and that freedom is a fundamental human right. Most even believe that "the perfect home is a detached single-family house in which each child has a separate bedroom."[79] Indeed, the fact that many Americans agree that civil society is wracked by culture wars is itself evidence *against the actual existence of* culture wars and proof of shared political beliefs![80]

Americans of all stripes see eye-to-eye on many core issues, and yet, today, there are more organizations associated with specific racial or ethnic groups than even before. Even if associations are dwindling, one has little trouble locating political, social, and professional groups that cater to specific racial and ethnic communities. In the last fifty years, for example, Chinese associations in the United States have increased by over 300%, and now nearly a quarter of the world's Chinese associations are located in America.[81] And on college campuses, one finds Native-American coalitions, African-American sororities, Thai-American student organizations, Hillel (the nationwide Jewish student organization), Korean Christian Fellowships, the Muslim Student Association, and the *Movimiento Estudiantil Chicano de Aztlán* (MEChA), to list but a few. The prevalence of such organizations has provoked some to ask, "In this day and age, one that places great value on the concept of multiculturalism, are race- and ethnicity-based organizations still necessary?"

First things first: because whiteness steers the associational field, as it does all fields of life, we cannot address this question without taking a step back to determine how organizations that do not refer to themselves as white organizations nonetheless exist as such. The Christian Coalition of America claims to represent all conservative Christians, even though its membership rolls are made up of primarily middle-class whites. Civil War reenactors, who wear historic uniforms and stage mock battles (thereby participating in one of the fastest growing hobbies in America)—and who, overwhelmingly, want to "fight" for the Confederacy—do not limit their membership to whites only, although it would be hard to imagine many nonwhites participating in their events.[82] And one only need glace at those big group pictures of fraternity and sorority houses to see how "normal" Greek organizations mostly comprise white students from affluent families.

With this in mind, we might return to our question and answer, first, that whites, too, have many associations that cater to their specific needs and desires, even if the word "white" does not appear in their names. But although many (though certainly not all) white groups intentionally or unintentionally ignore or endorse racial domination, many (although certainly not all) nonwhite associations confront and challenge racial domination. Nonwhite professional associations, such as the Society of Black Lawyers, the Association of Asian Probation Staff, the Native American Journalist Association, and the Cuban-American Certified Public Accountants, provide support, mentoring, and training to nonwhites working in organizations structured by institutional racism. They also organize a network of professionals who can challenge racial domination within their organizations.[83] Nonwhite campus organizations provide nonwhite students, especially those attending majority-white institutions, a safe and comfortable space. They also facilitate student-led collective action that confronts the ways colleges and universities reproduce racial domination.[84] And the ethnic press—made up of newspapers, magazines, websites, and blogs that take as their primary audience certain racial or ethnic groups—holds the mainstream (primarily white) news media accountable; increases the visibility of nonwhites in civil society; and addresses issues of particular importance to nonwhite communities often ignored in the popular press (for example, migrant workers' rights; Native-Americans' health care; inner-city poverty). It also specializes in alternative news stories that, in the words of political theorist Nancy Fraser, "formulate oppositional interpretations of [specific groups'] identities, interests, and needs."[85]

Nonwhite associations also can provide nonwhites with temporary solace from a society that privileges and prioritizes whiteness. This is why many middle-class nonwhite families choose to worship and socialize with friends and family members belonging to their own racial or ethnic group, even if they spend most of their workweek with whites.[86] Consider, for example, black barbershops and beauty parlors—staples of urban black communities. Not only are most mainstream (white) hair salons incapable of cutting and styling black hair (especially black women's hair), but black barbershops and beauty parlors also provide their African-American clientele with a thoroughly black space, a protected space, set apart from the surrounding society, threatening and hurtful and dominated by whites. Historically, barbershops and beauty parlors have functioned as key gathering places in black neighborhoods. As Rev. Wyatt Walker, one of Martin Luther King, Jr.'s, top advisors, once put it, barbershops and beauty parlors were "the second-best means of communication" in the black community, second only to the church.[87] According to historian Christiana Greene, during the Civil Rights Era, black barbershops and beauty parlors "fostered an 'invisible' network of grassroots supporters for black demands. . . . [They functioned as] bases for black protest. Beauticians frequently served as confidantes, sharing the personal stories and problems of their patrons. Such intimacies laid the groundwork for political mobilization."[88]

If nonwhite associations provide a refuge from racial domination, and if they can be mobilized to energize and advance an antiracist politics, then nonwhite associations will be necessary so long as our society is fraught with racial domination. Some nonwhite associations, it is true, only exacerbate racial tensions and sour relationships between, say, immigrants and native-born Americans, blacks and Hispanics (the so-called "Black/Brown Divide"), or even antiracist whites and antiracist people of color, thereby decelerating the racial justice movement.[89] And, sometimes, such associations encourage their members to obsess over racial and ethnic differences at the expense of ignoring racial domination and economic injustice. As a result, their focus is diverted away from life-and-death issues—for example, racialized poverty on American Indian reservations; institutional racism within the criminal justice system; the exploitation of Mexican migrant workers—and toward "celebrating diversity."[90] That said, research suggests that white associations, which refuse to refer to themselves as such, are even more responsible for maintaining racial divisions within associational life. Compared to their white counterparts, nonwhites are more likely to favor integration. If this is true, then critics of identity politics, who often blame nonwhite associations for the culture wars they believe to be fractionalizing the civil sphere, have misplaced their animus.

What Is "Political Correctness"?

One final issue deserves mention before we bring our discussion of civil society to a close. Some commentators have suggested that American civil society is now guided by an ethic of "political correctness," which discourages free thought and honest debate, because people are afraid to offend their fellow citizens or, worst of all, to be labeled as "racists." In its most recent incarnation, **political correctness** usually refers to discourse that, while designed to minimize offense to marginalized groups, ends up censoring certain speech or attitudes deemed off-limits. Political correctness, so the logic goes, forbids you to say what is truly on your mind. Former President George H. W. Bush spoke of a left-wing movement of political correctness, a movement to "declare certain topics off-limits, certain expressions off-limits, even certain gestures off-limits."[91] Speaking at American University in 2000, conservative spokesperson Bill Lind had this to say about political correctness: "For the first time in our history, Americans have to be fearful of what they say, of what they write, and of what they think. They have to be afraid of using the wrong word, a word denounced as offensive or insensitive, or racist, sexist, or homophobic."[92]

Who, exactly, does Mr. Lind have in mind when he references Americans who, *for the first time in history,* have to watch what they say? He cannot have African Americans in mind. They have had to choose their words carefully since slavery and Reconstruction, when blacks were tortured and lynched for saying the wrong thing. He cannot be thinking of Native Americans either, because Indian children were beaten at boarding schools if they spoke their native tongue, and Indian adults were killed during the Indian Wars if they practiced certain ceremonies, such as the Ghost Dance, that threatened white colonialism. Perhaps, then, Mr. Lind is speaking only of white Americans. But whites who spoke out against racial domination also had to pay a high price. Bill Moore, the postal worker we met in Chapter 3, gave his life to the Civil Rights Movement; John Brown, a white abolitionist who advocated arming enslaved Africans, was hanged for treason.[93]

To whom, then, is Mr. Lind referring? Who are those Americans who "for the first time in our history have to be fearful of what they say"? They are those who advocate for a kind of white identity politics; it is their voices that have come under attack. The Civil Rights Movement has transformed American discourse in such a way that, for the first time in American history, a significant number of Americans, white and nonwhite, consider racial domination evil.[94] As one sociologist has observed, "By 1970, a new normative climate in the area of race relations had emerged in the United States. . . . Whites, South as well as North, who discriminated became 'racist' rather than regular guys."[95] In post-Civil Rights America, civil society has widened to include a cacophony of voices and opinions. It is not marred by a silencing code of political correctness but by an impressive diversity of opinions. (This certainly includes the loud contingent complaining about "political correctness." Indeed, one need only compare the immense popularity of the term "political correctness" with the relative unpopularity of "racism" to gain a sense of whose voice actually is being drowned out.) This is the mark of a healthy and flourishing associational field.

Hate Groups

Because racist hate groups present a threat to a multiracial democratic society, a chapter on racial domination in associational life cannot help but confront the culture and dynamics of associations such as skinheads, neo-Nazis, Christian Identity chapters, and the KKK. Closely tied with avowedly racist hate groups are **white nationalist organizations,** which believe whites to be genetically superior to African Americans and Hispanics and vie for a separate, exclusively white country. With names such as Euro-American Student Union, Institute for Historical Review, the Conservative Citizens Council, and the New Century Foundation, white nationalist groups might not appear to be hate groups at first blush, but they thrive on racist and anti-Semitic beliefs. Although it has been almost 90 years since the heyday of hate groups—the KKK and its offshoots had more than 5 million members in the 1920s—some scholars have pointed to a recent resurgence in hate groups and hate crimes. According to the Southern Poverty Law Center, there were 884 active hate groups in 2006, up from 708 in 2002. In the last 30 years, KKK membership alone has quadrupled, and today, there may be as many as 50,000 people involved in hate groups.[96] (By comparison the NAACP alone boasts of more than 300,000 members—more than six times the estimated number of women and men involved in hate groups.)

Organized Racism

More than an exaggerated form of everyday racism, the kind of extraordinary or **organized racism** cultivated by hate groups is more intensified and commanding. It is ordered by a unifying racist philosophy that demonizes specific "enemies" and advances certain goals aimed at promoting the white race.[97] Hate groups, writes one analyst, are "filled with evil conspiracies and righteous crusades."[98] In the minds of hate group members, Jews and nonwhites are responsible for most of the world's problems. "The difference between everyday [racism found in routine life] and extraordinary racism [found in hate groups]," writes Kathleen Blee, a leading sociologist of hate groups, "is the difference between being prejudiced against Jews and believing that there is a Jewish conspiracy that determines the fate of individual Aryans, or between thinking that African Americans are inferior to whites and seeing African Americans as an imminent threat to the white race."[99]

History, to hate groups, is a sham, a conspiracy. Many, for example, believe the Holocaust was a hoax, Martin Luther King, Jr., was a fraud, and the accomplishments of white culture have been blotted out in the mainstream historical record.[100] Mirroring the strategies of the white backlash that helped extinguish the Civil Rights Movement, hate groups regularly co-opt the discourse of nonwhite organizations. Parodying the NAACP, some white racists have founded chapters of the National Associations for the Advancement of White People (NAAWP), while the white nationalist movement borrows much of its rhetoric from black nationalism. Indeed, as we have already shown, white hate groups and black nationalists often share many goals and have a strange history of collaboration.

The practices of hate groups are many and diverse. On one end of the spectrum are white nationalists who hope to energize a social movement aimed at establishing a white nation. White nationalism is primarily a symbolic movement based on discourse channeled through leaders, magazines, music, and even comic books. "We believe that we as white people, as European-Americans, have the right to pursue our destiny without interference from other races," states Don Black, founder of the racist website stormfront.org.[101] On the other end of the spectrum are hate groups steeped in a culture of violence. Vandalism, arson, assault, murder, even mass murder and terrorism are the lifeblood of these groups. Violence rests at the core of the white supremacist movement. It is a panacea for its problems and, in the movement's apocalyptic vision of an imminent race war, to which many active racists look forward, violence will bring about the triumph of the white race.[102] For example, Hal Turner, a neo-Nazi radio host, proclaimed in 2006: "All of you who think there's a peaceful solution to these invaders are wrong. We're going to have to start killing these people. I advocate using extreme violence against illegal aliens."[103]

As the debate over immigration has intensified and as people's fear of being "invaded" by Mexican migrants has expanded and deepened, hate groups have responded by lashing out at immigrants and Hispanics (regardless of their immigrant status). Hate crimes directed at Hispanics increased by 35% between 2003 and 2006, and they doubled in California, the state with the largest Hispanic population.[104] There was Pedro Corzo, a Cuban-American who worked as a regional manager for Del Monte Produce in Dateland, Arizona. In January 2004, he was shot and killed by two young white men from Missouri. The killers, 16-year-old Joshua Aston and his 24-year-old cousin, Justin Harrison, shaved their heads and set out on a trek through southern Arizona with the specific intent of murdering Mexicans. There was José Gonzales, a U.S. citizen who in September 2007 returned to his home in Avon Park, Florida, to find his car and garage destroyed by fire and "Fuck Puerto Rico" spray-painted on the garage walls. Gonzales, a car mechanic, lost thousands of dollars worth of tools in the fire. And there was David Richardson, a 16-year-old Latino teenager who in April 2006 was attacked by two skinheads after allegedly trying to kiss a white teenaged woman at a party. The two assailants, yelling racial epithets and "White Power!," broke Richardson's jaw, knocked him unconscious, burned him with cigarettes, attempted to carve a swastika into his chest, poured bleach on him, and, finally, violently sodomized him with a patio umbrella pole. It took thirty surgeries before Richardson, who was confined to a wheelchair and forced to use a colostomy bag, was able to return to school. The attack left him so emotionally and psychologically scarred that a year later he committed suicide by jumping from a cruise ship into the Gulf of Mexico.[105]

These attacks harm not only the direct victims of racial violence but also their families, friends, and, indeed, fellow members of their racial or ethnic groups. Just as lynching spread a spirit of fear throughout the black community during Reconstruction, today the repercussions of hate crimes are felt across nonwhite and immigrant communities. When an Arab American is beaten specifically because he is an Arab American, it puts all Arab Americans on notice; it lets them know there are organized people out there who want to hurt them. White Americans—at least those who are heterosexual, white, and male—rarely experience the weight and pain of this realization.[106]

Who Joins Hate Groups?

Despite popular representations of hate group members as poor, uneducated whites from rural America, white supremacist groups draw from all regions of society. When Blee conducted her in-depth study of women involved in the white supremacist movement—women are prominent in the movement and often are targeted for recruitment by hate groups—she discovered that most were neither poor nor uneducated but possessed college degrees, came from middle-class stable homes, and held steady jobs, working as nurses, engineers, teachers, therapists, and librarians.[107] Others have verified Blee's observation, finding that hate groups have pitched their message to a broad audience and have been somewhat successful, even incorporating highly educated and affluent people into their ranks.[108] Hate groups are most prominent in states with relatively large nonwhite populations, such as Georgia, California, and Pennsylvania. More specifically, studies have shown that the environment in which hate groups best flourish is one with high concentrations of nonwhites and high rates of segregation, where the majority of whites are cordoned off from nonwhite communities.[109]

Hate groups thrive off the erroneous idea that racial relations are a kind of zero-sum game, where nonwhite advancement always results in white loss. Matthew Hale, the former head of a white supremacist group called the World Church of the Creator (now the Creativity Movement)—and a convicted felon currently serving a forty-year sentence for conspiracy to commit murder—has expressed it this way: "The more that the other races obtain, the more white people feel that it's being obtained at their own expense."[110] In holding to such a view, hate groups invert the reality of racial domination, as if, despite all evidence to the contrary, whites were the real victims, today's persecuted minority.[111] Such a misunderstanding can push people to join hate groups.

Whites also are pulled into the hate movement by various recruitment techniques. Leaflets, speakers, 'zines, music, children's books, and face-to-face conversations all are employed by hate groups in pursuit of new members. The Internet quickly has become one of hate groups' favorite recruiting tools. Hate groups were among the earliest users of forms of electronic communication that would eventually evolve into the Internet. White supremacist leaders were utilizing computer bulletin boards as early at 1985, long before the rise of the World Wide Web. Since then, their presence on the Internet has grown by leaps and bounds. In 1995, there were only a handful of websites dedicated to white supremacy; today, there are hundreds. Estimates of the number of hate group websites range from 600 to over 2,000.[112] Cheap and efficient, the Internet is the ideal medium through which hate groups can channel their message around the globe. Because it allows people to camouflage their true identity behind screen names, hate group members are able to post seething racist diatribes without compromising their relationships with unsuspecting neighbors or coworkers. And because cyberspace virtually is unregulated, functioning as a kind of free speech haven where anything goes, where information is unfiltered and rarely is screened for accuracy, white supremacists are able to disseminate their distortions with impunity.[113]

Some hate groups' websites have pages dedicated to children and teens, who are presented with games, music, and "history" lessons. The kids' page on stormfront.org, for example, reads: "My name is Derek. I am 11 years old and I am the webmaster of kids.stormfront.org. I used to be in public school, it is a shame how many white minds are wasted in that system. I am now in home school. I no longer get beat up by *gangs* of nonwhites and I spend most of my day learning, instead of tutoring the slowest kinds in my class."[114] More commonly, however, hate groups' websites attempt to attract young, college-aged women and men. According to one study, nearly half of all extremist websites contain multimedia presentations (music, videos, downloads of speeches) that appeal to the younger generation.[115] One hate group even tries to entice young web browsers with a video game called "Ethnic Cleansing." "The Race War has begun," the game's promotion reads. "Your skin is your uniform in this battle for the survival of your kind. The White Race depends on you to secure its existence. Your peoples [sic] enemies surround you in a sea of decay and filth that they have brought to your once clean and White nation. Not one of their numbers shall be spared."[116]

More underhandedly, hate groups have created dozens of websites that, at first glance, do not appear to be hosted by hate groups. Rather, they present themselves as "natural information sites" where one can learn about American history and society. While researching a term paper on, say, the Holocaust, affirmative action, or slavery, you might pull up a white supremacist website without even knowing it, one that offers an "alternative interpretation" of certain events. (Indeed, if one types "ethnic cleansing" into the Google search engine, the racist video game is listed among the top fifteen sites returned.) Stormfront.org sponsors a page dedicated to Martin Luther King, Jr., that mirrors the site hosted by the King Center. Stormfront's site is slick, professional, and bereft of white supremacist symbols. Indeed, the website is housed at the innocent address: www.martinlutherking.org. It purports to offer a "true historical examination" of King's legacy (one that makes him out to be a communist, a drunk, and a rapist) and even displays downloads of "flyers to pass out at your school." After following a few links, you are transported to more "hard core" white supremacist websites. This is, in fact, a common feature of hate groups' websites. The user might stumble on an innocent-looking webpage, which, for example, presents a rather mainstream argument against affirmative action, but after clicking on a few links, might find herself in the more extremist nether regions of cyberspace.[117]

"The Internet," observes hate group expert Mark Potok, "is allowing the White Supremacy movement to reach into places it has never reached before—middle and upper middle-class, college bound teens. The movement is terribly interested in developing the leadership cadre of tomorrow."[118] He would later remark, "The movement is interested not so much in developing street thugs who beat up people in bars, but [in] college-bound teens who live in middle-class and upper-class homes."[119] In other words, if you are a white college student reading this book, the white supremacist hate movement is interested in you. Therefore, be ever on guard and vigilant with respect to what you read and what you hear. Be mindful of the sources of your information, and be weary of white supremacist propaganda masquerading as truth. If you listen hard enough, you quickly will discover that such propaganda is found not only in the back alleys of the Internet or in underground pamphlets distributed by extremist hate groups but also in more conventional settings as well.

That said, the power of the white supremacist and white nationalist movements should not be overstated. Despite their inflated Internet presence, their true numbers are relatively small (for many hate groups, the leader's house doubles as "headquarters"), and their leaders are relatively powerless (before going to jail, Mathew Hale, whom we met above, lived in the basement of his parents' house).[120] The white supremacist movement is built on a foundation of lies. And try as it might, repackaging its rhetoric or revamping its image, a movement of lies is bound to tumble, like a house of cards, under the weight of the truth. The march toward multicultural democracy and racial justice is far too strong for the white supremacist movement to bear.

Cyber Communities

The power and influence of the Internet is indisputable. In its relatively short existence, the World Wide Web already has emerged as one of our primary, if not *the* primary, sources of information. Open-source websites such as Wikipedia blur the lines between teacher and student, allowing browsers to play the role of expert; and journalism as we know it is undergoing a massive overhaul thanks to the rise of the Internet. Many have pointed to the Internet's potential to energize and strengthen democracy. Indeed, the technologists who helped develop it had precisely this in mind. The Internet, they forecasted, would foster free expression, allowing anyone to speak her or his mind to audiences around the globe. It would strengthen civil society, enabling people to transcend geographic boundaries and work together. And it would democratize knowledge, bringing all that is known within the click of a mouse. Many of these predictions have become reality, as the Internet seems to be a powerful democratic tool. How do we know? "From the most closed regimes like Iraq and Cuba to the more open ones like China and Iran, authoritarian governments have sought in numerous ways to shut out the Internet or to limit its effects on their populations. What better proof could there be that the Net nourishes democracy?"[121]

The Internet's developers had high hopes as well for its ability to build community and bring people together. Indeed, many early admirers believed the Net would operate as a kind of utopian space where social divisions, such as race, gender, and age, would not exist.[122] We now know that this vision did not come to pass: social cleavages are very much alive and well on the Internet. How does racial domination affect virtual associations, and how have people marshaled the Internet to combat it?

The Digital Divide

Before we can discuss how racial domination affects virtual associations, we must examine who, on account of their not having regular access to the Internet, is excluded from these associations in the first place. Studies have shown that nonwhite citizens disproportionately are less likely to own computers and to have regular access to the Internet than their white peers. Compared to Mexican Americans, whites are twice as likely to own a computer and two-thirds as likely to have Internet access. They outpace African Americans as well—blacks are 50% less likely to have Internet access than whites. Regular Internet use is sparse in some immigrant communities (non-English speakers have very low rates of computer ownership and home Internet access), as it is in many poor rural areas, such as American Indian reservations, impoverished white communities, and rural black towns scattered throughout the Mississippi Delta. As of 2003, less than 40% of Hispanic households and roughly 45% of black households nationwide had Internet access, compared to 65% of white households. Income and educational differences explain some, but not all, of these racial disparities—disparities that most likely will not be eradicated in the near future.[123]

Although most Americans can access the Internet at school in the local library—and, compared to whites and Asian Americans, low-income blacks and Hispanics are twice as likely to access the Internet through these means—if they cannot access it at home, their time online significantly is limited.[124] One can use a school or library computer only for a short amount of time (and typically while someone waits impatiently for her or his turn). That which separates those with regular and unfettered home access to the Internet from those without it—the split between people with twenty-four-hour access to valuable information, educational software, social networking websites, local and national news, and medical advice from people without it—has been termed the **digital divide**.[125] If you are an average college student, then you have regular access to the Internet and probably log on every day. Think how different your life would be without it! You would be locked out of libraries upon libraries of vital information—legal advice, nutritional guides, medical information, political activity, traffic reports, job listings—not to mention the entire middle-class professional world, which nowadays does much of its business online. You would be cut off from friends and family members, too, who more and more have come to rely on e-mail and social networking sites to stay in touch.

Sociologist Daniel Bell called knowledge and information the "major structural features of post-industrial society."[126] Those without equal access to this knowledge and information will be left behind by a society in which knowledge is power. They will become "roadkill on the information superhighway," as one scholar, with a penchant for unfortunate if effective metaphors, has put it.[127] The digital divide—that between the technical class and the "digital underclass"—is therefore a serious problem indeed.[128] "The computer is not a toy; it is a site of wealth, power and influence, now and in the future. . . . [For this reason, people of color and those with few resources] cannot afford to be excluded from this new medium. To do so will [put them at] risk [of] becoming the information poor. It will be not to count; to be locked out of full participation in society in the same way that illiterate people have been disenfranchised in a print world."[129]

Virtual Racism

Those privileged enough to have regular Internet access are admitted into a parallel universe teeming with virtual associations and cyber communities. There are large associations, such as eBay and YouTube™ communities, as well as more specialized ones, including chat rooms and electronic bulletin boards.

MUDs (Multi-User Domains) and MOOs (MUD Object Oriented), primarily text-based interactive sites that allow people to talk and play games with one another, paved the way for MMORPGs (Massively Multiplayer Online Role-Playing Games) that bring thousands of players together from across the globe. One such role-playing game, *World of Warfare,* is so popular that Dell sells a computer system designed specifically for it; China, worried its citizens were growing addicted to the game, imposed mandatory limits on the amount of time one can spend playing.[130] Other MMORPGs, such as the popular *Second Life,* allow players to live in a virtual world, complete with virtual property one can buy and sell, as well as virtual jobs, parties, sex, and, of course, virtual characters known as avatars, "your persona in the virtual word."[131]

But these online habitats do not transcend real-life social problems. Several studies have documented the prevalence of racism in cyber communities, even (and especially) in well-traveled, mainstream websites.[132] Consider YouTube[TM]. Some of the website's "power users," those with large fan bases and a high number of subscribers, post videos that degrade people of color. For example, sxephil, whose channel at the time of this writing is the tenth most subscribed on YouTube[TM], often peppers his video with off-the-cuff racist remarks. In "Racism Can Be Fun," he looks into the camera and says, "I'm like a black guy. I also like chicken, playing basketball, banging white chicks, and collecting welfare." But racism on YouTube[TM] is perpetrated much more regularly by users who respond to videos than by those who post them. It is rare to find a well-viewed video that grapples somewhat critically with the topic of racial domination without also seeing a number of blatantly racist comments directed at the person who posted the video or, as is usually the case, at a racial or ethnic group in general. When YouTube[TM] featured several videos in honor of Black History Month in 2008, among which was a video of a speech by Malcolm X and one of a poem entitled "A Black Woman's Smile," several members of the YouTube[TM] community responded with hate. Speaking of Damon Wayans, YouTube[TM]'s guest editor, Gnomewarrior86 wrote, "How did this monkey learn how to speak?" and Wwk99xp3du commented, "I am sick of all these filthy niggers dirtying up our country. Go back to Africa you dirty niggers." Hiding cowardly behind their screen names, protected by complete anonymity, users such as these are able to pollute one of the Internet's most popular websites with hate speech they most likely would not dare use offline.

If you confront someone who believes that racism is dead, simply suggest they spend thirty minutes perusing YouTube[TM]. Chat rooms, too, can be sites where racist transactions take place. According to one study, you have a 60% chance of being exposed to racist hate speech in an unmonitored chat room frequented by teenagers and a 20% chance of encountering it in a monitored one (a chat room with an adult host who can "evict" users if they violate room

Virtual associations can encourage a form of racial tourism, whereby players, through various avatars, temporarily slip into another skin.

rules). The study also found that white teens are just as likely to fall victim to hate speech as their nonwhite peers.[133]

Because one often does not know your racial identity online, many Internet users have come to regard whiteness as the virtual norm. Chat room participants sometimes make assumptions about one's racial identity, especially if one "presents white" by the way they type. As a Korean-America woman who participates in LambdaMOO, a popular chat room with thousands of users, complained, "I never outright . . . said I was Asian, because I felt that IRL [in real life] people already have stereotypes and felt that it would be at least as bad here. . . . But then it bugs me that people just assume you're white if you don't say otherwise."[134]

This woman underscores a fascinating virtual dilemma: that of whether or not to reveal one's racial identity. Although light-skinned people of color have passed (with varying degrees of success) as whites for centuries, the Internet allows all people, regardless of their phenotype, to trade their offline racial identity for a different online one. Online, an Arab-American man can pass as a white woman, just as a white woman can pass as a Native-American teenager. Virtual associations, then, encourage a form of **racial tourism** where players can, through various avatars, temporarily slip into another skin just like vacationers can temporarily travel to a foreign country. On the one hand, racial tourism can denaturalize racial categories and might provide people with a kind of racial freedom that offline life does not permit. On the other hand, too often racial tourism reinforces racial domination through the employment of stereotypes. For example, many white men who pass as Asians do so by relying on exotic caricatures, accentuating the foreignness of their avatars by, for instance, confining them to the popular Asian stereotypes of samurais or geishas. One white American man on LambdaMOO passed as the avatar Geisha Girl, a "petite Japanese girl in her 20s . . . [who] has devoted her entire life to perfecting the tea ceremony and mastering the art of lovemaking . . . [and who] has spent her entire life in the pursuit of erotic experiences."[135] This man represents (indeed, embodies) Japanese femininity through stereotypes of hypereroticism and domestic servitude. Noting the (ironic) social disconnect between virtual race relations and real race relations, communications professor Lisa Nakamura writes in *Cybertypes*, "Peopling the virtual landscape with samurai, homeboys, and sexy Latina women confirms a vision of ethnicity from which many in the offline world are struggling to distance themselves."[136]

Virtual Empowerment

Although a good number of cyber communities are rife with racism, many others promote the empowerment of racially dominated groups and facilitate multiracial coalition building. Antiracist movements have relied on the Internet to circulate information around the world and to increase their visibility in civil society.[137] A committed group of black women, for example, have attempted to improve the health and life quality of underserved populations by using the Internet to close the gap between medical professionals, technical experts, and patients, creating sites such as sisternetonline.org. Native American Nations have built websites devoted to their history, culture, and governance. And antiracist organizations have constructed websites such as whiteantiracist.org and the impressive tolerance.org to join in the struggle against white supremacy.[138]

The Internet also has been marshaled to reconnect members of **diasporic communities**, communities of people or ethnic groups that have been fractured, displaced, and scattered around the world on account of warfare, colonialism, or the slave trade. Thus Vietnamese and Hmong Americans who immigrated to the United States during the Vietnam Wars might use the Internet to reconnect with friends and family members on the other side of the Pacific. Jews whose parents fled Europe during the Holocaust might reach out to fellow Jews in Israel or Russia in an attempt to patch the Jewish community back together. One scholar has examined how Filipino Americans negotiate and create their ethnic identity through the Internet by entering into (virtual) community with women and men in the Philippines. She observed how "members of the diaspora established what Filipino identity means with people back home and how people at home forged an identity with members of the diaspora."[139]

In a similar vein, Native Hawaiians have relied on the Internet to preserve their native culture and language. Twenty years ago, those who spoke the Hawaiian language numbered only in the hundreds, and most speakers were elderly. To avoid the extinction of their language, some Hawaiians started a language revitalization movement, an extension of the larger Hawaiian cultural identity movement that came to the fore in the 1970s and that revived indigenous traditions such as hula, oral chanting, and canoeing. As early as 1994, Hawaiian teachers built an electronic bulletin board, named *Leoki* (Hawaiian for "powerful voice"), devoted to the Hawaiian language. *Leoki* has spread throughout the archipelago and beyond, allowing users to converse in Hawaiian through e-mail, live chats, and virtual conferences.[140] The Internet, then, helped resuscitate the Hawaiian language—and unique perspectives and worldviews connected to that language—and it could help save other endangered languages as well, thousands of which are projected to fade away within the next century.[141]

The promise of forging multiracial, multinational communities on the Internet is immense. In effect, the Internet has shrunk the world to the size of your computer screen, and this is its most important contribution to civil society. Even websites like YouTube™, where racist comments abound, may help move us one step closer to a multicultural democracy simply by bringing people together who otherwise would never have met. The Internet enables people of different racial identities and nationalities to interact and enter into conversation with one another. Whether or not those conversations will divide or unite, repair or tear down, heal or wound is up to you. As the old Hawaiian saying goes, *"I ka ʻōlelo no ke ola, i ka ʻōlelo ke make."* "In the language there is life; in the language there is death."[142]

Religious Associations

If America is a nation of joiners, it is also a nation of believers. According to one nationwide survey, only 3% of Americans do not believe in God. Another study finds that American atheists constitute only 1% of the population. By contrast, atheists make up the majority in other Western countries, constituting over 80% of the population in Sweden and Denmark, for example. America overwhelmingly is a Christian nation, with somewhere between 160 and 260 million of its citizens—up to 85% of the country—following the Christian faith. As little as 20% and as much as 40% of Americans attend a Christian church service on any given Sunday. With 6 million Jews, America's Jewish population is the largest in the world, exceeding even Israel's. There are somewhere between 2 and 6 million Muslims in the United States, along with 3–4 million Buddhists and 1 million Hindus. Together, Muslims, Buddhists, and Hindus make up 4% of the population.[143]

Tolerance of Religious and Racial Groups, Survey Responses

This Group Does Not at All Agree with My Vision of American Society	
Atheist	39.6%
Muslim	26.3%
Homosexual	22.6%
Conservative Christian	13.5%
Recent Immigrant	12.5%
Hispanic	7.6%
Jew	7.4%
Asian American	7.0%
African American	4.6%
White American	2.2%
I Would Disapprove if My Child Wanted to Marry a Member of This Group	
Atheist	47.6%
Muslim	33.5%
African American	27.2%
Asian American	18.5%
Hispanic	18.5%
Jew	11.8%
Conservative Christian	6.9%
White	2.3%

SOURCE: American Mosaic Project Survey, 2003.

Religious Illiteracy and Intolerance

Given that America is one of the most religious nations in the Western world, it is surprising how confused many Americans are when it comes to religion. The majority of Americans cannot name five of the Ten Commandments, one of the Gospels, or the first five books of the Torah.[144] Although Americans have focused much of their political thought and attention on Islam and the Middle East since September 11, 2001, ignorance of Islam is rampant. Case in point: when U.S. Representative Silvestre Reyes, head of the House Intelligence Committee—which oversees the sixteen government agencies, including the CIA and FBI, that make up the U.S. Intelligence Community—was asked if the Al Qaeda terrorist group was associated with Sunni or Shiite Muslims, he failed to answer correctly.[145] In the words of religious studies professor Stephen Prothero, although America is "one of the most religious places on earth," it is also "a nation of religious illiterates."[146]

Where there is ignorance, intolerance and violence are never far behind. Anti-Muslim prejudice and attacks increased in the aftermath of September 11.[147] According to recent polls, whereas 94% of Americans would vote for a black presidential candidate, and 84% would vote for a woman, only 34% would vote for a Muslim. In the words of one commentator, "Calling someone a Muslim is still a slur."[148] Mosques have been vandalized and ridiculed. When Craig Baker, a white man living in Katy, Texas, discovered that his town's Islamic Association planned to erect a mosque next to his property, he projected his outrage by hosting pig races and grilling sausage every Friday evening, the holiest day of the week on the Muslim calendar. One hundred people showed up at the first pig race, despite heavy rain. Although Baker's bigoted display was rooted in a misunderstanding of Islam—Muslims do not despise pigs, they simply refrain from eating them—he managed to get his message across.[149]

Although anti-Semitism has declined significantly in recent years, Jews continue to face discrimination and assaults. Spokesmen for the Nation of Islam, such as Louis Farrakhan and Abdul Muhammad, have made anti-Semitic speeches, including one delivered by Muhammad in which he claimed that "the so-called Jew . . . is sucking our blood in the black community."[150] Such remarks exacerbate the already strained relationships between African Americans and Jews.[151] One can also point to instances of institutional anti-Semitism, such as when the city council of Fort Collins, Colorado—home of Colorado State University—refused to allow a local rabbi to display a 9-foot-tall menorah near the city square, even though the town prominently displayed a Christmas tree and other Christmas decorations during the winter holiday season.[152]

Religious intolerance, then, is yet another force that tears at the fabric of civil society, dividing Christian from Muslim, Muslim from Jew, and so forth. It is a vector we must consider in our intersectional analyses, for failing to account for the many complex ways in which religious conviction drives social action is to fundamentally misinterpret the social world.

Racialization of the Religious Sphere

Does the religious sphere mirror society's racial segregation, or does it buck the tide? By and large, religious associations do not overcome racial divides; in fact, the opposite is true. Religious life is racialized to a high degree. Certain religions, denominations within religions, and places of worship within denominations correspond to certain racial and ethnic groups. Let's start with Christianity. If a church is considered multiracial if no more than 80% of its members belong to a single racial group, then less than 8% of all American churches are multiracial. In nine out of ten churches, 90% of congregants belong to a single racial group. According to a recent study, 43% of Christian churches do not have *a single member* from another racial group, and many others have only a very small percentage. Sunday morning remains, as it did fifty years ago, one of society's most *racially segregated hours.*[153]

Racial-Ethnic Diversity within Religious Communities

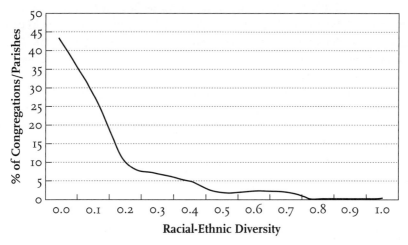

Note: The measurement of racial-ethnic diversity employs the entropy index, where 0 = perfect homogeneity and 1.0 = perfect heterogeneity (mean = .137; standard deviation = .193).

The racial segregation of Christian congregations has led to the development of traditionally white, black, Hispanic, Asian-American, and Native-American churches, each with their own unique rituals, practices, and styles of worship. Many white congregations, such as Southern Baptist, Presbyterian, and Lutheran churches, follow either a traditional style of worship, where old hymns are sung, or a more modern variant, complete with a "contemporary Christian" band. Services tend to be quite professional and regimented, "by the book," and congregants tend to listen quietly and attentively. The black church, however, has since slavery been defined by an energetic, emotional, and "spirit led" style of worship. The Southern revival, the black choir, the fiery preacher, who between proclamations wipes the sweat off his brow, and the "call and response" style of service, peppered with audience members' shouts of "Amen" and "Preach it!" all are emblematic practices found within the black church.[154]

For years, the black church has functioned as the nexus of African-American life, and today it continues to serve that role in many communities. This is one reason why African Americans are perhaps the nation's most religious group.[155] Indeed, a number of scholars have observed that many residents of poor black neighborhoods are "overchurched," meaning that "African Americans [possess] far more churches than they [can] keep up or that [can] be useful in ameliorating the social and economic conditions of the Black population."[156] In many black ghettos across the country, one can find literally dozens of small congregations— storefront churches, home churches, churches that congregate outside—each one fitting itself to different populations within the black community and together reflecting the "kaleidoscopic expression of Black subcultures."[157] Such observations lend some credibility to the depressing cliché that all one finds in rundown neighborhoods are liquor stores and churches. *The Boston Globe* described one of Boston's toughest neighborhoods as follows: "The Four Corners area . . . [comprises] o supermarkets; o bakeries; o hardware stores; o accounting offices; 11 religious organizations; [and] 14 vacant storefronts."[158]

Latinos, for their part, are overwhelmingly Catholic. Seventy percent of Latinos identify as such, and another 23% classify themselves as Protestant. And within Latino Christianity, one finds divisions along ethnic lines—distinct Puerto Rican, Cuban, and Mexican parishes—as well as along generational divides: first-generation immigrants are more likely to be Catholic, while third-generation Latinos are overrepresented in Protestant denominations.[159] The Latino presence in the Catholic Church is so commanding that it is common to hear commentators speak of the "Hispanicization of American Catholicism." Today, Latinos make up roughly 40% of America's Catholic population and have been credited with reviving the Catholicism, which, since the 1960s, has experienced a steady decline in priests, Catholic high schools, Mass attendance, and seminarians. To connect with immigrant congregants, Masses around the country are delivered in Spanish. The priests at Los Angeles's St. Thomas parish went so far as to incorporate mariachi bands (in full regalia) into their services.[160]

Ethnic churches associated with Asian and Arab Americans also are a common feature of America's Christian landscape. Most Arab Americans are Christian, not Muslim, as is often assumed. According to one study, 35% of Arab Americans are Catholic, 18% are Eastern Orthodox (one of the world's largest Christian denominations), and 10% are Protestant. Another 13% have no religious affiliation, and 24% are Muslim. Maronite Christians from Lebanon, Coptic Christians from Egypt, and Chaldeans from Iraq have established ethnic churches.[161] Most Asian Americans are Christian as well, with 26% identifying as Protestant and 20% as Catholic. With 94% identifying as religious and 71% attending church service at least once a month, Filipino Americans are the most religious Asian ethnic group. Korean Americans rank a close second, with 87% identifying as religious and 77% attending church regularly. But, again, many of these Asian-American believers belong not to multiracial congregations but to Filipino or Korean churches, or even to more encompassing Asian-American churches, formed around a pan-Asian congregation instead of a particular ethnic group.[162]

Native Americans, too, have developed their own variant of Christianity. From the 1880s to the 1940s, the United States government prohibited Native Americans from practicing their traditional religions. During this time, missionaries spread Christianity throughout Indian Country. Some tribes, such as Oklahoma's

"Five Civilized Tribes"—the Cherokee, Creek, Choctaw, Seminole, and Chickasaw—converted to Christianity early on. (Anglo-European colonists gave them this name because the tribes adopted many of their customs.) Many members of these tribes integrated into their newfound Christian faith rituals and practices that dated back to pre-Columbus times. The result was the Native American Church, a pan-Indian religious organization that blends mainstream Christianity with indigenous beliefs and traditions.[163] (One scholar has estimated it is roughly 80% Christian and 20% traditional.[164]) Not only does it encourage medicine men to conduct traditional healings, it also (and more controversially) employs peyote in some of its ceremonies. A spineless cactus indigenous to the Southwest, peyote is eaten or drunk during all-night religious ceremonies. Although some non-Indians have labeled peyote a narcotic, many Native Americans see it as a kind of medicine or sacrament.[165]

The last fifty years have witnessed a resurgence of Native-American traditional practices, not just those sewn into Christian belief systems but also those that constitute their own religion. Navajo medicine men work beside non-Indian doctors, who practice modern medicine; Apache Crown Dancers hold a special place in their tribe's religious life; New York's Iroquois Nation conducts religious ceremonies by making use of masks and wampum belts; and after the government lifted its prohibition on the Sun Dance, some Northern plains tribes have reinstituted the ceremony, which requires participants to abstain from food and to suffer through considerable pain as their chest or back is pierced. Perhaps more than any other tribe, "the Pueblos stand out as the most consistent and persistent of the nation's Indian groups in continuing their old ways."[166] During especially important ceremonies, Pueblos often place barricades on the roads leading into their reservation towns so that outsiders cannot enter. Although there is great variety in Indian Country when it comes to traditional religions, one can identify several shared themes and practices that together constitute a unique Indian spirituality and cosmology, including an intimate connection to nature and sacred lands, dancing, and powwows.[167]

Turning now to Buddhism, we see that 61% of America's practicing Buddhists are Asian American, and 34% are white. As in other religions, different Buddhist sects correspond to different ethnic groups. Thus Laotian, Cambodian, Thai, and Sri Lankan Buddhists tend to practice Theravada Buddhism, whereas those with family trees planted in China, Vietnam, or Japan usually practice Mahayana Buddhism. Many Asian immigrants have conformed their Buddhism to the American workweek. Whereas Buddhist temples are an everyday meeting place in many immigrants' home countries, they primarily are frequented only on the weekends in America.[168]

As for Islam, Americans of South Asian descent, who identify ethnically as Pakistani, Indian, Bangladeshi, or Afghan, account for 33% of America's Muslim

Although the majority of mosques have one dominant ethnic group, they are more racially diverse than other religious organizations.

population. African Americans account for 30%, and Arab Americans account for 25%. (Indeed, South Asia is home to more Muslims than the Middle East with Indonesia housing more Muslims than any other country.) Most Muslims in America—two-thirds, in fact—were born outside the U.S. The remaining one-third are mostly African Americans. Although the majority of mosques have one dominant ethnic group, they are more racially diverse than other religious organizations. Ninety percent of all American mosques have at least some Arab Americans and some Americans of South Asian heritage. The Nation of Islam, however, remains exclusively black.[169]

American Judaism is the whitest of all the nation's major religions. As historian Eric Goldstein makes clear in *The Price of Whiteness: Jews, Race, and American Identity*, the relationship between Jewish ethnicity and whiteness always has been uncertain and filled with tension. Throughout the nineteenth and twentieth centuries, Jews worked both to insert themselves into the white mainstream and to preserve their distinct cultural identity. As a result, they always have teetered on the outer boundaries of whiteness, a position they occupy to this day.[170] Although Latinos and African Americans have converted to Judaism in small numbers, most Jews (92%) are of European descent.[171] Although religion and ethnicity often are wound tightly together, in Judaism and Jewish ethnicity the overlap is nearly complete. Although one can be ethnically Jewish and religiously atheist (or Christian or Buddhist), Jewish ethnicity (its food, clothing, holidays, language) is rooted in Jewish religion. Jewishness encompasses religious, cultural, ethnic, and national elements, though these elements, of course, are not found in every person who identifies as a Jew.

Explaining Racial Homophily in Religious Life

After surveying religious associations in America, we are met with the conclusion that they are marked by high levels of racial and ethnic segregation. As sociologists Michael Emerson and Karen Chai Lim have noted, "Despite the racial integration that has been occurring in other institutions, the vast majority of the more than 300,000 religious congregations—*the largest and most active voluntary associations*—involve members who are of the same race."[172] But why? Why is American religious life defined by such clear-cut racial and ethnic schisms?

One reason is that religious associations behave as other associations in civil society do, following the homophily principle. Since religious groups spring from (most likely racially homophilous) social networks and connections based in (most likely racially segregated) neighborhoods, it is small wonder that most reflect preexisting racial divides.[173] Another reason for racial segregation in religious life is that certain religious cultures and habits unintentionally widen racial divisions. Although the white evangelical Christian community has taken impressive steps since the 1980s with respect to racial reconciliation, a good number of white churches have failed seriously to address racial domination. Why? Because most white evangelicals understand racism only on the interpersonal, not the institutional, level.[174] "Despite devoting considerable time and energy to solving the problem of racial division," write the authors of *Divided by Faith*, "white evangelicalism likely does more to perpetuate the racialized society than to reduce it. . . . [This is because] for white evangelicals, the 'race problem' is not racial inequality, and it is not systematic, institutionalized injustice. Rather, white evangelicals view the race problem as (1) prejudiced individuals, resulting in poor relationships and sin, (2) others trying to make it a group or systematic issue when it is not, or (3) a fabrication of the self-interested."[175]

However, nonwhite Christians—as well as white members of multiracial churches—generally have a more accurate understanding of racial domination, one that accounts for its institutional properties. And they are more likely to advance antiracist solutions pitched at structural inequality. As a result, when white and nonwhite Christians talk about racism, many times they are working with very different understandings of the term and, by extension, what a proper Christian response to racial divisions should entail. Indeed, in a recent survey only 4% of white Protestants named racism a key issue that should concern Christians, compared to one-third of black Protestants, a quarter of whom listed racism as *the* most important problem Christians should address.[176]

In other words, many white evangelicals, especially those attending majority-white churches, exhibit in spite of themselves a kind of **interracial incompetence** that seriously impedes their ability to confront racial domination in all its complexity. This incompetence also impedes their ability to attract nonwhites to their services, further contributing to racial divisions within religious life. Many nonwhite places of worship do their part to contribute to these divisions as well. Most Native Americans view their traditional religions as theirs and theirs alone and discourage non-Indians from participating. Many black churches prioritize the black experience, thereby excluding non-blacks. And some ethnic churches perpetuate a kind of ethnic chauvinism that encourages its congregants to distance themselves from less successful immigrants, from "those kind" of Arabs, "those kind" of Mexicans.[177]

Religion and Racial and Ethnic Identity

As the preceding examples demonstrate, religious associations are connected to, and used to promote and preserve, certain racial and ethnic identities. Places of worship that cater to new immigrants, for example, allow them to form friendship ties with fellow immigrants who speak their language and to enjoy similar kinds of food. They also play a large part in preserving immigrant culture. Korean churches conduct their services in Korean, observe Korean holidays, and offer Korean language classes for children. Just as Irish and Italian culture, language, and music were preserved through Catholic parishes during the beginning of the twentieth century, Mexican, Cuban, and Puerto Rican culture thrive in many Catholic parishes. In many neighborhoods, the Greek Orthodox parish, Hindu temple, or Lebanese church is the only major institution that strives to preserve certain ethnic cultures and languages.[178]

For racially dominated groups, the church, mosque, temple, or synagogue often functions as a refuge. Religious associations provide valuable social services. They provide new immigrants with information on naturalization, health care, education, and jobs, which in part is why immigrants tend to become more religious in the United States than they were in their home country.[179] What is more, religious associations provide those denied honor by the surrounding society with social status and prestige. One can be a "big person" on Sunday, even if she or he is a "little person" the rest of the week. An unemployed Native American may be looked on as a respected spiritual leader on the reservation; a black man who works as an underappreciated and overlooked middle manager may be an admired deacon in the National Baptist Convention.[180]

Religious associations also can be powerful agents of social change and political mobilization. Recall that Native American spirituality helped America's indigenous people resist white colonialism, just as it informed the American Indian Movement that rose up in the late 1960s. And the importance of the black church to the Civil Rights Movement cannot be overstated: its congregants served as activists; its preachers as some of the movement's most important voices; its buildings as central meeting spots.[181] Today, some places of worship help energize and strengthen the racial justice movement; others thwart it. Conservative white churches that make up the "religious right" long have served as the base of the Republican Party and have worked to impede racial progress.[182] However, many mainline and liberal white churches have adopted an antiracist stance and have developed programs to confront racial injustice.

Religious associations have played a significant role in defending immigrant rights. For example, Jews, Baptists, Catholics, Quakers, Unitarian Universalists, and other religious groups came together in the early 1980s to form the **Sanctuary Movement.** This interfaith coalition was devoted to providing sanctuary (that is, religious-based asylum) to families suffering from political turmoil and violence that had erupted in some Central American countries. Sanctuary was offered in direct defiance of U.S. immigration law, which resulted in some activists being arrested. Today, the sanctuary movement is spearheaded by the Catholic Church and works to protect undocumented immigrants from deportation.[183] Latino churchgoers think their churches should be actively involved in protecting immigrants. In fact, 74% believe their church should provide help to undocumented immigrants even when doing so is illegal.[184] "I think the church will always side with the rights of people to live where it's best for them to live," remarks Monsignor John Moretta, pastor of Los Angeles's Church of the Resurrection. "We took that position when the Irish came and when the Italians came, and now we are doing the same with the Latinos."[185]

We should emphasize, by way of conclusion, that not all of America's religious organizations are monoracial: some congregations are quite multiracial and exist as a powerful force for integration. How, then, do these religious associations swim against the (homophilous) tide? Sociologists have tendered several answers, but the most important one has to do with organizational priorities. Synagogues, churches, mosques, and temples that make concerted and serious efforts to diversify their congregations often are successful. One thinks of the American Catholic Church, which circulated a letter in 1984 urging its priests to "broaden the embrace" to new immigrant communities. Today, the Catholic Church is one of the most racially integrated religious organizations, with the average parish made up of at least three racial and ethnic groups. One thinks, too, of the new evangelical movement, a mainline Christian movement that stresses social justice and interracial solidarity. Many new evangelical congregations are multiracial, including 35% of megachurches (those with a weekly attendance that exceeds 2,000 people).[186]

Religious associations can affect today's racial order in a variety of ways. Analysts have shown that whites who attend multiracial religious services harbor less prejudice toward nonwhites than those who attend all-white or majority-white services.[187] Others have demonstrated that Conservative Protestant congregations actually contribute to residential racial segregation, whereas Mainline Protestant churches, as well as most Jewish and Muslim congregations, contribute to neighborhood integration.[188] Still others have asserted that religious associations can strengthen civil society by joining people together, fighting against injustice and exploitation, encouraging altruism and community service, helping the poor, and meeting people's emotional needs.[189] Religious associations are a powerful force in today's racial order, just as they have been ever since the founding of the country.

American Promise

In Alexis de Tocqueville's view, the strength and vitality of America's voluntary associations constituted the foremost safeguard of its freedom. Today, from our reflexive and critical perspective, we can see that, although robust and vibrant in many ways, the American associational field continues to be marred by profound racial divisions. The ideals of public-spiritedness, citizenship, and community that so inspired Tocqueville, not to mention later observers of the American scene such as Gunnar Myrdal, will never be realized so long as our civil society is rent with racial separations and discord. We have accordingly stressed throughout this chapter the need to bring out the full democratic potential in our associational life, to bridge racial divides in civil society and to establish a more genuine solidarity in our community organizations, social clubs, and religious congregations. Think how much more powerful civil society would be if we evicted racial domination from its midst, how much louder and clearer our democratic voices would grow. Much work remains to be done. In our associational field reside some of the deepest obstacles to the realization of a racially just society. But there, too, can be found some of its greatest promise.

CHAPTER REVIEW

THE ORDEAL OF INTEGRATION AND THE RISE OF ETHNIC NATIONALISM
ethnic nationalism, Marcus Garvey, ethnic chauvinism, Malcolm X

CIVIL SOCIETY IN A MULTIRACIAL DEMOCRACY
homophily, boundary work, Putnam's thesis of social decapitalization, Florida Effect, identity politics, culture wars, political correctness

HATE GROUPS
white nationalist organizations, organized racism

CYBER COMMUNITIES
digital divide, racial tourism, diasporic communities

RELIGIOUS ASSOCIATIONS
interracial incompetence, Sanctuary Movement

FROM THEORY TO PRACTICE

1. With whom do you choose to associate? Pick an association (religious institution, knitting circle, intramural team,) to which you belong and analyze it in
terms of its racial and ethnic composition. Who is present and absent? Why?
Address these questions by drawing on the information in this chapter.

2. Pay a visit to an event or meeting organized by an association to which
you have never been, preferably one comprising members of a racial or ethnic
group other than your own. The association could be formal (think: church,
political organization) or informal (think: social club, garden guild). Afterward, write about your experience, using the following questions to guide you:
How did you feel during your visit and why? How did the association's event
do boundary work? In your mind, does the association include or exclude
people like you? Finally, what larger historical and social forces (ones you have
learned about throughout this book) help to illuminate what goes on in that
association?

3. Strike up a conversation with someone—stranger or friend—specifically
asking her or his opinion on identity politics or "political correctness." (You may
or may not choose to tell this person you are doing this for a class assignment.)
Afterward, analyze her opinions with a sociological imagination, paying special
attention to how her beliefs rely on certain assumptions about racial domination.
How does she conceive of identity politics or "political correctness"? On what
assumptions about the nature of social reality does her opinions rest? To what
extent do you agree or disagree with her positions?

4. Visit a webpage that functions as a kind of cyber community—that is, any
webpage that allows users to interact and post comments—and conduct a racial
analysis. How is racial domination challenged or upheld by members of that
cyber community? How do members assert, distort, or conceal their racial identity? What might this community tell us about the workings of racial domination
on the Internet?

5. Conduct a reflexive analysis of your own religious beliefs, whether you are a devout Muslim, born-again Christian, searching agnostic, or made-up-your-mind atheist. How do your religious beliefs affect your participation in civil society? How do they influence how you think about racial domination? If you belong to a religious association, how might it impede or promote racial justice?

RECOMMENDED READING

- Kathleen Blee, *Inside Organized Racism: Women in the Hate Movement* (Berkeley and Los Angeles: University of California Press, 2002).

- Michael Emerson and Christian Smith, *Divided by Faith: Evangelical Religion and the Problem of Race in America* (New York: Oxford University Press, 2000).

- Robert Putnam, *Bowling Alone: The Collapse and Revival of American Community* (New York: Touchstone Books, 2000).

- Mario Small, *Villa Victoria: The Transformation of Social Capital in a Boston Barrio* (Chicago: University of Chicago Press, 2004).

- Neil Smelser and Jeffrey Alexander, eds., *Diversity and Its Discontents: Cultural Conflict and Common Ground in Contemporary American Society* (Princeton: Princeton University Press, 1999).

Chapter 10

Intimate Life

Mastering Oneself

You've heard all the sayings, old and tired. "The apple does not fall far from the tree." "Like father like son." "In the end, we all become our mothers." The implication of these clichés, and the dozens more like them, is that, no matter how hard we try, in the end we end up more or less a replica of our parents. But family is not destiny. There is no denying that our families very much shape us into the people we are, and many of us might want to be like our mothers or fathers, or our brothers and sisters, just as an equal number of us might want—need—to be nothing like them. But all of us have a choice. The apple, if it wishes, can fall quite a way from the tree.

We have a choice, too, in the development of our selfhood and identity. We need not be held captive by the whims and worries of our unevaluated selves, the nether region recesses of our psyches. Nor ought we to allow ourselves to be a toy of social forces, tossed about by historical and political powers like so many anchorless rafts at sea.[1] To a significant degree, we can gain control over these things by understanding them intimately. The ancient Greeks had a saying: "Know thyself." By this, they meant that we must submit to self-evaluation, exploring our innermost thoughts and desires as well as the people closest to us, if we ever hope to understand the world around us—let alone gain some control over our lives.

The point is that rigorous reflexivity provides some limited but real power over the forces that would control our imaginations and actions. At the very least, it allows us rationally to assess and perhaps to alter how those forces affect our thinking and behavior. "The true freedom that sociology offers," wrote Bourdieu, "is to give us a small chance of knowing what game we play and of minimizing the ways in which we are manipulated by the forces of the field in which we evolved, as well as by the embodied social forces that operate from within us."[2]

To this end, we here analyze sociologically those aspects of our daily lives that so often avoid socioanalysis: our families and ourselves. We begin with a survey of the history of the family, reaching all the way back to colonial and slavery times and tracking the emergence of interracial and same-sex couples as well as the common tendency to blame all our social problems on the "pathological" (nonwhite) family. We then survey the sociology of race and the family, providing explanations for racial variation in marriage and divorce rates, examining the dynamics of interracial marriage, and focusing on the hardships associated with single motherhood. In the last section, we take up such topics as the racialized nature of the self and the miscommunications that occur within interracial relationships; racial identity formation; and the idea of "racial authenticity" or "keeping it real."

The Family since Colonialism and Slavery

Today, a good many of us—but certainly not all—are encouraged to marry the person we love. And most of us believe that people over the age of 18 should make their own decisions and that the family should not be dominated by the husband. Such ideas are quite new in the American context. In colonial times, the family—certainly the white family—functioned quite differently. Marriages, governed more by economic practicalities than by romance, required parental permission. Because a daughter was thought to belong to her father, in the same way that a gun or a horse belonged to him, she was "given away" at the marriage ceremony in exchange for the groom's promise of financial support, a ritual that continues to this day.[3]

This model of **"family government"** was a recipe for masculine domination. Before World War II, most white women were excluded from the formal labor market. Those few who did work outside the home were paid paltry wages. Indeed, most were not even paid, as many employers refused to pay women directly, choosing instead to pay their husbands. Forced to rely on men to survive, many women were forced into unhappy marriages (just as many gays and lesbians were forced into unhappy heterosexual unions) and were controlled by their husbands, who alone held the purse strings. If a woman wanted to make do on her own, her only options were to inherit a large sum of money from her dead husband or to move to another town, chop off her hair, dress in pants, and try to pass as a man. This gendered system designated public life (work, politics) as male and private life (child rearing, housework) as female. And even today it is often thought that a heterosexual and monoracial marriage, made up of a breadwinning husband and a stay-at-home mom, is a kind of natural and timeless creation. We must remember that this model of the "ideal family" took a considerable amount of social engineering to perfect. It is neither natural nor timeless but originated in America's Puritan past.[4]

The Black Family under Slavery

Since colonial times, racial domination has wreaked havoc on many nonwhite families. Native-American boarding schools separated parents from their children, sometimes, tragically, forever. Citizenship laws that forbade Asian women, and later all Asian immigrants, from entering the country inhibited significantly the development of Asian-American families and communities. And Mexican Repatriation Programs ripped husband from wife, brother from sister, daughter from mother. But no other nonwhite group suffered from a systematic attack on the institution of the family as much as blacks did under slavery. One of the most ruinous impacts of slavery was its assault on the black family and, in particular, on black masculinity and fatherhood.

If the white family was held up as a powerful and sacred union before the nineteenth century, the black family was not even considered a family under the harsh rule of slavery. If slavery allowed white masters to assume absolute control over their enslaved Africans, and if fatherhood in those times required, at minimum, a man to protect and to provide for his wife and children, then we must conclude that slavery all but completely abolished the role of husband and father for most enslaved black men. A slave could not provide for his wife and children (let alone for himself); he could not prevent his wife from being ripped from his arms and shipped to another plantation, where she might be "used for breeding"; he could not stop his master from beating his son or raping his daughter.[5] The historian Willie Lee Rose recalls the case of Jacob, a young slave, who was beaten unrelentingly by his master. When Jacob sought comfort and advice from his father, the latter replied, "Go back to your work and be a good boy, for I cannot do anything for you."[6]

Black motherhood, too, was denied under slavery. Some slave women were forced to sleep, not near their husbands or children, but "on the floor at the foot of a mistress's bed (increasing the chances they would sooner or later be bribed, seduced, or forced into sexual relations with the master)."[7] A slave woman did not have control over her sexuality or her reproductive capabilities: her womb belonged to her white master. So, too, did her breasts, for in many cases lactating mothers had to feed their masters' wives' white babies before nursing their own children. Long before the lactating period was over, slave women were forced back to the fields, their infants placed in "nurseries where their care was in the hands of slaves either too infirm, too old, or too young to work elsewhere."[8] As a result, children were malnourished and many did not survive. Those who did were beaten, sexually molested, put to work, and forced to watch their parents endure the same treatment. Many were shipped to other plantations and never again saw their mothers or fathers.[9] "Because of the omnipresent threat of forced separation by sale, gift, or bequest, the [slave] family was not 'stable,'" writes Jacqueline Jones, with considerable understatement.[10]

White domination of the black body and black family was so total and horrid during these times that some historians convincingly have argued that on many plantations what existed was not a slave "family," in the conventional sense of the term, but rather a "reproductive unit," controlled by the master who desired as many offspring as possible. Slavery made it impossible for slaves to love their spouses and children unreservedly and without hesitation. Toni Morrison captures this sad truth in her novel *Beloved*. As Sethe and Paul D, both former slaves, sit and talk, Sethe recalls her escape from bondage: "It was a kind of selfishness I never knew nothing about before. It felt good. Good and right. I was big, Paul D, and deep and wide and when I stretched out my arms all my children could get in between. I was *that* wide. Look like I loved em more after I got here. Or maybe I couldn't love em proper in Kentucky because they wasn't mine to love." The narrator tells us Paul D's thoughts: "So you protected yourself and loved small. Picked the tiniest stars out of the sky to own; lay down with head twisted in order to see the loved one over the rim of the trench before you slept. Stole shy glances at her between the trees at chain-up. Grass blades, salamanders, spiders, woodpeckers, beetles, a kingdom of ants. Anything bigger wouldn't do. A woman, a child, a brother—a big love like that would split you wide open in Alfred, Georgia. He knew exactly what she meant: to get to a place where you could love anything you chose—not to need permission for desire— well now, *that* was freedom."[11]

Although most slave women, historians agree, remained in monogamous sexual relationships when they could, as did a minority of slave men fortunate enough to assume the (limited) role of father and husband on smaller plantations, a good number of slave men, forced to work for extended periods away from their wives, had multiple sexual partners.[12] (In this way, their sexual relationships mirrored those of many white men.) Sociologist Orlando Patterson has found that slave men "developed a reproductive strategy with two distinctive features." His reflections on this matter deserve to be quoted at length: "First, a man's having as many children as possible would have made most sense, in order to ensure that he would leave progeny who would survive to adulthood. . . . In the absence of any other meaningful ways of expressing manhood, becoming a progenitor would have acquired special value. . . . Under the severe environmental exigencies of slavery, it would have been supremely rational male behavior. The fact that some masters persistently, and nearly all masters at some time, actively encouraged young unattached male slaves to act as human studs would simply have encouraged this reproductive strategy. This tendency would also have been encouraged by the second distinctive feature of male slaves' reproductive behavior, namely, that control over resources did not enter into the decision to have a child. . . . Bringing a child into the world became a virtual obligation of manhood and of ethnic survival that did not entail any consideration of the means whereby one would support it." Patterson concludes by observing that blacks "are still living with the devastating consequences of this male attitude toward reproduction."[13]

The sexual and familial strategies blacks devised to survive two hundred fifty years of forced slavery, while somewhat practical under such an oppressive environment, would prove disastrous after emancipation. Some black men continued their reproductive strategy of populating the earth with as many offspring as possible. By 1900, the average African-American family in the rural South had eight children. With so many mouths to feed, and with so few opportunities for economic advancement, many black families had a difficult time lifting themselves out of poverty. Facing this desperate situation, they accepted the neoslavery terms of sharecropping.[14]

Middle-class black families, in contrast, adopted the white model of family government, the dominant model at the time. Instead of being the non-father and the non-husband, roles thrust on them during slavery, many black men now assumed a paternalistic and patriarchal role as head of the household. Black women were to be controlled and protected, lauded as homemakers and caretakers; they were to be treated, that is, like white women. Patriarchy, then, came to define many black families, just as it had defined white families since colonial times. But, unlike white women, black women, who for centuries had not been treated like "dainty ladies," refused to accept their new-found place in the shadows of their husbands. Ironically, under the vicious system of slavery black women had tasted a kind of gender equality—they often worked alongside black men, picking cotton, harvesting rice, swinging axes—and many were not about to allow one kind of freedom (emancipation) to usher in another kind of oppression (patriarchy). This situation bred a tense spirit of distrust and contempt between black men and women and birthed the stereotype of the "black matriarch," a stereotype about which we will have much to say later.[15]

White control of the black family would continue throughout the twentieth century, most heinously in the form of forced sterilizations sometimes applied to unknowing black women (as well as to Native-American women). "For several decades," writes Dorothy Roberts in *Killing the Black Body: Race, Reproduction, and the Meaning of Liberty,* "peaking in the 1970s, government-sponsored family-planning programs not only encouraged Black women to use birth control but coerced them into being sterilized. While slave masters forced Black women to bear children for profit, more recent policies have sought to reduce Black women's fertility. . . . During the 1970s sterilization became the most rapidly growing form of birth control in the United States, rising from 200,000 cases in 1970 to over 700,000 in 1980. It was a common belief among Blacks in the South that Black women were routinely sterilized without their informed consent and for no valid medical reason. Teaching hospitals performed unnecessary hysterectomies on poor Black women as practice for their medical residents. This sort of abuse was so widespread in the South that these operations came to be known as 'Mississippi appendectomies.'"[16]

The Emergence of Interracial and Same-Sex Unions

Before the Civil War, some white communities were tolerant of interracial marriages between free blacks and whites. Historians estimate that interracial sex was common during the colonial period, when black and white servants worked side-by-side and entered into relationships with one another. But as blacks descended into chattel slavery, white landowners sought to separate white indentured servants from permanent black slaves (lest they join together in open rebellion) by outlawing interracial unions. This gave rise to **antimiscegenation laws** that criminalized interracial marriage and sex.[17] These laws applied not only to black-white unions but to nearly all romantic and sexual intercourse that traversed the color line and that might lead to "race mixing." On the West Coast, for example, relationships between whites and Asians were of particular concern to defenders of the racial status quo.[18]

Of course, in practice antimiscegenation laws applied only to *consenting adults* who longed to be together; white slave masters who had their way with enslaved black women—and children—ignored antimiscegenation statutes. When African-American novelist and critic James Baldwin responded to a question that obsessed white America during the 1960s—"Would you want *your* daughter to marry one?"—he did so with the kind of penetrating deftness that came to define his career. Addressing a white man, he said, "You're not worried about me marrying *your* daughter—you're worried about me marrying your *wife's* daughter. I've been marrying *your* daughter since the days of slavery."[19]

Interracial relationships continued to decline after the fall of slavery. Biracial children posed no threat to slavery because the "one drop rule" classified all people with African-American blood as black and, therefore, subject to bondage. But they did pose a threat to the order of racial segregation that arose postemancipation, an order that attempted to create a bipolar racial system that rigidly separated whites from blacks. During Jim Crow segregation, more antimiscegenation statutes were passed into law, and the lynch mob arose to "protect white women's purity" (and to uphold white patriarchy, as we learned in Chapter 6). The fact that black men often were lynched on fabricated rape charges or simply for whistling at white women, as was the case for young Emmett Till, and the fact that many lynchings involved castration, should unequivocally indicate that the fear of black male sexuality and miscegenation fueled the reign of white

Stylistic Depiction of Interracial Sexual Contact across United States History

| Colonial Slavery Period | Antebelium Period | Reconstruction and Jim Crow | Civil Rights and After |

Time

terrorism that lasted clear into the twentieth century. As Jim Crow segregation reached its peak near the beginning of the twentieth century, interracial marriages fell to their lowest point in U.S. history.[20]

But throughout the twentieth century the family would be remade. Two events, in particular, helped erode parental influence over children as well as masculine dominance over women and thereby reorganized America's gender regime. The first was the Great Depression, which sent thousands of men to the unemployment line and diminished their role as breadwinner. Women and children had to join men in helping make ends meet, forcing men to relinquish total control over family finances. The second event was World War II. With a significant portion of the male workforce fighting oversees, women *en masse* had to pick up the slack. White women, who for centuries had been relegated to the home, marched to the factories to work in assembly lines and contribute to the war effort. Nonwhite women, much more familiar with working outside the home than their white counterparts, worked in the factories as well, often performing the dirtiest and most dangerous tasks. They also filled the void left by the absence of white women in the home, soon becoming overrepresented in the domestic service sector. Significantly, the flood of women into the labor force during the war challenged the demeaning idea that women were unable to do "men's work."[21]

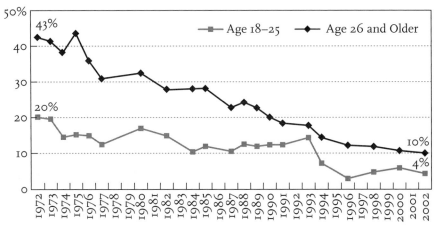

Percentage of Americans Favoring a Ban on Interracial Marriage

America's military men were helping to reinvent the family as well. Thousands of miles away from the demands of their families, gay soldiers were able to express their sexuality in ways that before had been denied them. As one historian has argued, "Once they left the constraints of family life and watchful neighbors, many recruits were surprised to find that military service gave them opportunities to begin a 'coming-out' process. . . . The massive mobilization for World War II relaxed the social constraints of peacetime that had kept gay men and women unaware of themselves and each other."[22]

Not only this, but some heterosexual soldiers of color engaged in relationships with white European women, relationships that would have been strictly forbidden by anti-miscegenation policies in the United States.[23] When the war ended, America had entered a new age in the career of the family. As the century marched into the sixties, the sexual revolution unfolded; the Gay Rights Movement gained steam; the Women's Movement found new energy and launched "a full-scale attack on the exploitative and stultifying effects of women's confinement and dependency as homemaker"; and the Civil Rights Movement gained power and helped alter the course of the nation.[24]

In 1967, the Supreme Court ruled antimiscegenation laws unconstitutional in *Loving v. Virginia,* marking a significant civil rights victory. Accordingly, Americans began to marry across racial divides in record numbers. Interracial marriage increased tenfold between 1960 and 1990.[25] In 1960, there were only 55,000 black-white married couples (living mostly in the north, where interracial marriage was permitted). Today, there are over 331,000 black-white marriages. Similarly, between 1960 and 2000, Asian-white marriages increased from 49,000 to 579,000. There were less than 280,000 Hispanic-white married couples in 1970; today there are well over 1.5 million. Compared to whites and other nonwhite groups, American Indians have the highest rates of intermarriage. In 1990, the majority of American Indians (roughly 60%) were married to non-Indians.[26]

Today the United States is home to over 4.35 million interracially married couples. Men and women involved in interracial marriages have demonstrated that love does not respect racial divides. And as the familial landscape has shifted, so too have Americans' attitudes about marriage. In 1958, 96% of whites disapproved of interracial marriage; by 1997, that percentage had dropped to 33%.[27] Despite such impressive changes, however, nontraditional families remain beyond the pale of complete American acceptance and inclusion. A significant number of white people (one out of three, in fact) still disapprove of interracial marriage, and twenty-six states have added to their constitutions amendments banning gay marriage. Interracial and gay families continue to suffer, if not from legal restrictions, then certainly from family-based control mechanisms, as when parents disown their children for marrying, say, an Arab American.

Backlash: The "Pathological Family" as the Root of All Social Ills

In the midst of all the changes that came on the backs of the Civil Rights and Women's Movements, a backlash emerged, one that continues to dominate our thinking even today. It was a discursive backlash that involved repackaging the problem of racial inequality such that the dysfunctional family, not systemic racial domination, would come to be understood as the root cause of social problems. The change began shortly after the Civil Rights Act of 1964, when President Lyndon Johnson began hinting at the "family problem" in his speeches on civil rights. In doing so, he "shifted the discourse away from the radical vision of 'equal rights' that emanated from the black protest movement of the 1960s back to the standard liberal cant of the 1950s, which held that the black child is stunted by 'circumstances present in the family within which he grows up.' The conceptual groundwork was being laid for a drastic policy reversal: the focus would no longer be on white racism, but rather on the deficiencies of blacks themselves."[28]

This policy reversal, not to mention a massive shift in Americans' ideas about racial domination, came about in 1965 when one of President Johnson's top speech writers, a sociologist named Daniel Patrick Moynihan, published an influential study entitled *The Negro Family: The Case for National Action*. This study, known today simply as the **Moynihan Report**, argued that most of the problems facing African Americans were caused by a "tightening tangle of pathology" within the black family. For Moynihan, female-headed households were detrimental to children's (especially boys') well-being. Without a father, so went the argument, children lacked strong role models, economic resources, discipline, guidance, and structure.[29] "At the center of the tangle of pathology is the weakness of the family structure," wrote Moynihan. "Once or twice removed, it will be found to be the principal source of most of the aberrant, inadequate, or anti-social behavior that did not establish, but now serves to perpetuate, the cycle of poverty and deprivation."[30] In a nutshell, Moynihan, with little empirical evidence but all the right credentials (including a professorship at Harvard), claimed that black female-headed households were to blame for racial inequalities. This thesis became known as the **"pathology of matriarchy."**

Civil rights leaders shot back. Stokley Carmichael, leader of the Student Non-violent Coordinating Committee (SNCC), wrote in 1966: "To set the record straight, the reason we are in the bag we are in isn't because of my mama, it's because of what they did to my mama."[31] But Moynihan's influence was too great, reaching clear into the White House. His report shifted national attention away from programs that attempted to compensate victimized groups for years of suffering and placed it squarely on the "pathological black family."[32] Because Moynihan argued that racial inequality is caused "less by basic defects in the social system than by defects in particular individuals and groups which prevent their adjusting to the system," the solution required changing the deviant and dysfunctional black family, not the racist system—an idea eventually extended to include other nonwhite families as well as those that make up poor white communities.[33] As social problems were turned into individual problems, system-level solutions were passed over in favor of self-help prescriptions.

Moynihan's report long has been discredited by sociologists, who convincingly have demonstrated that it is shortsighted and simply wrong to blame the family for a whole host of society's problems. Moynihan's ideas, however, continue to penetrate discussions about racial domination. A favorite question offered by politicians, talk show hosts, and media spokespeople in search of an explanation for some social problem is, "Where were the parents?" Of course, it would be foolish to discount altogether the importance of the family. But it is equally foolish to explain all social problems by pointing to problems within the family. By now, you should know that individual-level explanations, as well as individual-level solutions, are insufficient, that they fail to account for the country's long legacy of white supremacy, institutional racism, and ongoing discrimination. Moynihan-inspired thinking assumes that the family exists in a kind of social vacuum, insulated from social forces and histories. But, as the preceding discussion has demonstrated, the family is a social creation, conditioned by large-scale social forces, including and especially racial domination.

Race and the Family Today

The family—so much could be said. Some of us attach words such as love, support, and safety to our family; others of us attach such words as pain, isolation, and violence. The family can be a refuge from the burdens of society, just as it can be a space where certain forms of domination thrive. Feminists long have drawn our attention to the hundreds of ways women are disadvantaged within the traditional family arrangement that places men at the helm. The **sexual division of labor** not only infiltrates the economic field, such that certain jobs (maids, nurses, receptionists) are classified as female while others (surgeons, firefighters, engineers) "belong" to males; it also structures family life so that women are assigned the lion's share of the housework and child care. For women who work outside the home, unpaid housework—work often not recognized as such—can amount to a "second shift." After the first shift ends at your job, your second shift begins at home, where you cook dinner, clean house, and take care of the children.[34]

If mainstream feminists have criticized masculine domination, women-of-color feminists have confronted the overlapping modes of oppression that affect them: in particular, the intersection between masculine domination and racial domination. Women-of-color feminists have chided mainstream civil rights leaders for at times silencing women's voices and ignoring their needs, just as they have criticized the mainstream feminist movement for its whiteness, for assuming that the needs of white and nonwhite women are identical. The stereotypes that latch onto white women are different from those that latch onto Arab-American, Asian-American, Hispanic, Native-American, and African-American women. And women of color face unique problems created by the overlapping systems of racial and masculine domination. For example, conditioned by family members and friends to put their needs below those of "the race," many women of color keep quiet about sexism in their communities out of fear of being labeled "race traitors" for speaking out against the actions of nonwhite men.[35]

We would do well to remember these points as we evaluate critically the ways in which racial domination affects family life. We begin with a discussion of racial differences in marriage rates and then turn to the topic of interracial relationships and mixed marriages. Next, in a discussion of divorce we examine how racial domination breaks some families. Last, we explore the racialized aspects of out-of-wedlock births and single motherhood, focusing, in particular, on the hardships of raising a child alone.

Explaining Racial Differences in Marriage Rates

The United States has one of the highest marriage rates in the world, ranking fifteenth overall.[36] For many Americans, marriage brings stability, companionship, and social status, as well as economic perks that come from tax breaks and (for many) two incomes. But racial groups do not marry at similar rates. Some groups have strikingly low rates of marriage; and although marriage has declined for all Americans over the last forty years, some racial groups have experienced more significant declines than others. In 1975, over 60% of white women

Marital Status by Race (percentages)

	White, NH*	Asian American	Hispanic	Black
Married, SP[†]	55	57	47	31
Married, SA[‡]	1	3	4	2
Widowed	7	4	3	6
Divorced	10	5	7	11
Separated	2	1	4	5
Never Married	25	30	35	45
Total	100	100	100	100

NOTES: *Nonhispanic
[†]Spouse Present
[‡]Spouse Absent
SOURCE: U.S. Census Bureau, CPS 2006 (people 15+).

between the ages of 20 and 24 were married; by 1998, that percentage had fallen to 32%. Similarly, almost 50% of black women that same age were married in 1975, but only 15% were in 1998. Today, black women are least likely to marry, compared to other groups. Some analysts estimate that only 1 in 3 will marry in their lifetime. At the opposite end of the spectrum are Hispanic women, who have the highest marriage rates. According to the most recent research, 46% of Mexican-American women between the ages of 20 and 24 are married, relative to 36% of Cubans, 32% of whites, and 16% of blacks.[37] How do we make sense of these drastic differences? Why do Mexican Americans marry at relatively high rates while such a large proportion of African Americans never marry?

Do our answers lie in the fact that certain groups are more likely to cohabitate, that is, to live together as committed romantic partners but not as husband and wife? Cohabitation between heterosexual couples has risen steadily in recent years, so much so, in fact, that today the majority of marriages begin as cohabiting relationships. However, there are virtually no racial differences in cohabitation rates. The proportion of Asian Americans, Native Americans, Hispanics, whites, and blacks who cohabitate is almost identical.[38] Our answers lie elsewhere.

Some scholars have explained the high rates of marriage among Hispanics by pointing to the special importance they place on family relationships. As we noted in Chapter 7, familism is an important component of Hispanic culture, one that may help explain why Mexican Americans are 14% more likely than whites and 30% more likely than blacks to marry. Young Hispanic women, studies have shown, emphasize the importance of getting married and having children and are less focused on achieving academic or career success, compared to Asian Americans, blacks, and whites.[39] As one pair of scholars succinctly put it, "Mexican girls are socialized to become wives and mothers, and less empha-sis is placed on work or school roles."[40]

Additionally, the racialized labor market is structured in such a way as to advantage Hispanics and disadvantage African Americans with respect to mar-riage. Although roughly the same proportion of Hispanics and blacks live below the poverty line, Hispanic men (including recent immigrants) are employed at much higher rates than black men (for reasons discussed in Chapter 4). Because a man with stable employment is a much better "catch" than one without a job, Hispanic men are advantaged when it comes to marriage relative to black men.[41] Indeed, a number of scholars have documented how the disappearance of stable employment opportunities from the inner city has resulted in the growth of a population of black men who are not "marriage material." For William Julius Wilson, job flight has created "a long-term decline in the proportion of black men, and particularly young black men, who are in a position to support a family."[42]

The black male marriage pool has been diminished even further by America's prison boom. The racial disparities in imprisonment, we have already learned, are enormous. Black men are eight times more likely to be in prison than white men. In 2007, 1 in 15 black men were behind bars, as were 1 in 9 black men of marrying age (between 20 and 34)![43] In poor black communities that are intensely policed, black women outnumber black men by sizable margins. In one such neighborhood in Washington, D.C., for example, there are only 62 men for every 100 women. And, once they are released, many men with criminal records do not reenter the marriage pool since many women, concerned about their reputa-tions, do not want to marry someone who has spent time in the slammer.[44]

Latino familism, racialized labor market disadvantage, and the blackening of America's prison boom all help explain racial variation in marriage rates. But there is one more important explanation, one that has caused black women a good deal of pain. Some—but certainly not all—black men prefer to date and later to marry nonblack, and especially white, women. Darker-skinned black women feel especially passed over. "You have to be a black black woman to really understand," one college student observed. "Like when the African-American students' group has a dance, all the men rush to dance with the light-skinned women. All of us black black women are left standing around, like leftovers."[45]

The vast majority of white men, for their part, partner with white women, who for centuries have enjoyed being favored by dominant images of feminine beauty. And the sordid, slavery-stained history between white men and black women may further impede these kinds of relationships. As sociologist Patricia Hill Collins has said, "Traditionally, freedom for Black women has meant freedom *from* White men, not the freedom to choose White men as lovers and friends. Black women who have willingly chosen White male friends and lovers have been severely chastised in African-American communities for selling out the 'race.' Or they are accused of being like prostitutes, demeaning themselves by willfully using White men for their own financial or social gain."[46] Black men, by contrast, do not suffer this level of reproach for going out with nonblack women. "It's all about control and power," writes one analyst. "A Black man is seen as the one who controls the relationship and so his 'race' isn't being downtrodden and trampled. But if a black woman does the same thing, she is being submissive."[47]

In the heterosexual dating and marriage game, many black women are left behind. They are passed over by nonblack and black men alike, both groups buying into an ideal of feminine attractiveness molded by the hands of white supremacy. This has resulted in friction and resentment between light-skinned and dark-skinned black women as well as between black and white women, particularly when white women remain completely oblivious to these dynamics.[48] And it has made many black women feel utterly rejected. "We feel abandoned," admits Gloria Wade-Gayles, African-American woman scholar and critic. "We feel abandoned because we have been abandoned in so many ways, by so many people, and for so many centuries. We are the group of women furthest removed from the concept of beauty and femininity which invades every spot on the planet, and, as a result, we are taught not to like ourselves. . . . The truth is we experience a pain unique to us as a group when black men marry white women and even when they don't. It is a pain our mothers knew and their mothers before them."[49]

Interracial Marriage

Many consider interracial marriage a barometer for racial progress and social integration. Although interracial marriage has increased over the years, as we pointed out earlier, it still accounts for only a small fraction of all U.S. marriages, a mere 6%. And there are considerable differences in interracial marriage across racial boundaries. Whites are the least likely group to intermarry (only 5% do), whereas Native Americans are the most likely, with nearly 60% of all Native Americans married to non-Indians. After Native Americans come Asian Americans, then Hispanics, then African Americans. Indeed, a Hispanic person between the ages of 20 and 34 is nearly twice as likely to enter into an interracial marriage as a black person that same age. Additionally, there are noticeable gender differences for interracial marriage rates, especially for blacks and Asian Americans. Black men, for reasons discussed above, are almost three times as likely as black women to be in interracial marriages. For Asian Americans, the gender dynamic is reversed: nearly 39% of Asian-American women, but only 26% of men, have non-Asian spouses.[50] Some have explained this imbalance by invoking the opposite ways in which Asian-American women and men are stereotyped with respect to their sexuality: namely, the tendency of

Percentage of Intermarriages among Married Individuals, Ages 20–34,
1990 and 2000

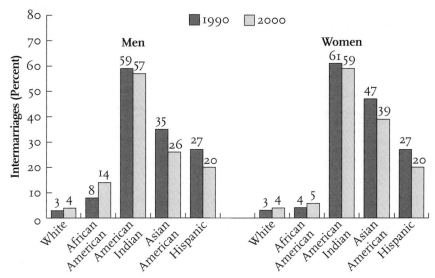

Race/Ethnicity of Married Individuals Ages 20–34

some to consider Asian-American women exotic and hyper-erotic and Asian-American men effete and sexless.[51]

There are countless reasons why people traverse racial borders to marry, including the simplest and most powerful explanation of all: they found someone to love. But some interracial relationships are driven more by a negative dynamic than a positive one. That is, some people form an aversion to dating and marrying within their race. We have already seen how this applies to some black men. Some women and men raised in immigrant families with a domineering father or mother, too, might seek a partner outside their racial or ethnic group so as not to revisit the problems of their parents' marriage. For example, heterosexual Asian-American women often look for non-Asian partners, because they believe many Asian men are sexist. Similarly, some Asian-American men refuse to date Asian women because they want to break away from the traditional "Asian family" mold. And each may find the other unattractive. When a pair of researchers interviewed Asian-American women and men in interracial marriages, they found that "women reported they found Asian-American men physically unattractive, conservative, and boring. . . . Male interviewees complained that Asian-American women were workaholics and too serious about relationships. They claimed that [these] women weren't vivacious and were too laden with Asian baggage."[52]

Still others may be attracted to members of certain ethnic or racial groups who are presented by the dominant culture as exotic objects of sexual desire. Those who accept the commonplace assumptions about the sexuality of black men ("Once you go black, you never go back"), Hispanics ("Latin lovers"), or Asian women ("I have a thing for Asian girls") might seek out interracial relationships to satisfy their ethnic fetishes. Although each interracial marriage is a small assault on racial segregation in intimate life, when the marriage is propelled by **racial aversion** (a variant of symbolic violence applied to prospective lovers of the same race) or **racial fetishism** (a variant of racial tourism with an erotic twist), one wonders if it leads us to take one step forward but two steps back.

"I'm all for interracial marriage, but what about the children?" This question comes up time and again in discussions of mixed-raced unions. In fact, most Americans who disapprove of interracial marriage cite "concerns for children produced by those unions" as one of the primary justifications for their disapproval.[53] Do biracial children have it harder than children from intraracial couples? Not necessarily. As Ronne Hartfield writes in *Another Way Home,* the popular notion of "confused and troubled" biracial children overlooks "stories about the ordinary lives of the vast number of people of color who have occupied the zone of mixed race with ease and sanity for several generations, ordinary nontragic people who, within the category of mulattoness, are productive citizens whose lives, individually and within their communities, are emotionally healthy and socially instructive."[54] It is certainly true that some biracial individuals wrestle with racial identity issues as they transition into adulthood, but psychological research leads us to conclude that their struggles are not worse or more complicated than those faced by other nonwhites whose parents share a racial identity.[55] Plus, if young biracial adults do have a hard time coming to terms with their racial makeup, what needs to change, interracial marriage patterns or the system of racial domination that is the root source of their anguish?

Some biracial and multiracial women and men have grown justifiably tired of people assuming they are "mixed up in the head," because they are half this and part that. (Many are equally annoyed with the often repeated inquiry, "What's your racial background?"[56]) One biracial student named Kimberly uses humor to shine light on the assumptions that buttress this train of thought: "People come up to me and they'll say, 'Do you get confused between being black and white?' I say, 'Well, yeah, you know some mornings I wake up with this craving for fried chicken, and other mornings I just can't get the beat.'" Kimberly goes on to explain her retort, saying, "I want them to see how narrow-minded they're being. What do you think? One day I like fried chicken, and the next I don't? It's not like that."[57] In other words, the idea that biracial and multiracial people are doomed to a life of ethnic confusion assumes it is more "natural" to belong

Multiracial Population Map

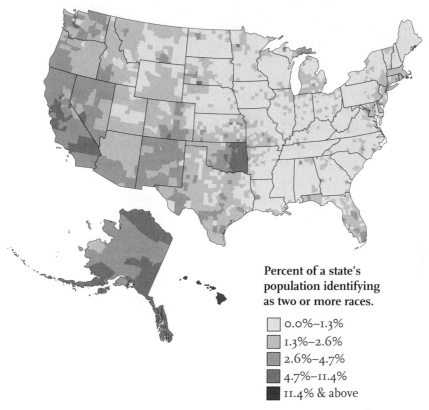

Percent of a state's population identifying as two or more races.

☐ 0.0%–1.3%
☐ 1.3%–2.6%
☐ 2.6%–4.7%
☐ 4.7%–11.4%
■ 11.4% & above

SOURCE: U.S. Census

to only one race and that one's actions and lifestyles are dictated completely by one's racial identity.[58] Neither of these assumptions holds water.

What is more, people like Kimberly, those who claim multiracial heritage, are growing in number. As we mentioned in Chapter 2, 1 in 20 people under the age of 18 claim multiracial heritage.[59] Such projections have led to another popular question in conversations about interracial marriage: "If we are all multiracial, is racial domination on its way out?" Unfortunately, things are not so simple, and there is little evidence that racial domination somehow can be bred out of our society.

First, there is nothing new about interracial unions and multiracial people. Recall that interracial sex and multiracial offspring were common during colonial times and slavery. No one would argue that those were eras of racial harmony. Second, racial domination, as we learned back in Chapter 1, can shape-shift and adjust to demographic changes. It can make—and has made—room in its wide enterprise for degrading multiracial people. Consider the long list of mean epithets reserved for them: from half-breed, zebra, banana, and coconut to sell-out, race traitor, wannabe, and jungle fever.

And, third, interracial marriage is far from universally accepted in the United States and accounts for only a small percentage of all marriages. In 1994, a white high school principal in Wedowee, Alabama, announced during a school assembly that he would not allow interracial couples to attend a school dance. When a multiracial student questioned him about this, the principal called her a "mistake." In 2000, Bob Jones University, a fundamentalist institution, banned interracial dating on campus; it later retracted the policy amid national outrage.[60] And some parents, white and nonwhite alike, actively discourage their children from interracial dating, many times cloaking their own prejudices or ethnic chauvinism in a concern over mixed-race children or "other people's" racism. This helps explain why adolescents are more likely to introduce to their parents a romantic partner who shares their racial identity than one who does not.[61] Someone in an interracial relationship can feel rejected both by people who share their racial identity and by those who share their partner's. A Korean American dating a Puerto Rican might, on the one hand, be ridiculed by her parents and her extended family, who all were hoping she'd meet a "nice Korean boy," and, on the other hand, feel awkward and out of place around her boyfriend's Puerto Rican friends and family, who might harbor anti-Asian sentiments.

Doing the (Racial) Work

Given this hostile climate, it is not surprising that psychologists have documented an association between interracial relationships and high levels of distress, finding, in particular, that Native Americans, white women married to nonwhite men, and Hispanics with nonwhite (but non-Hispanic) spouses have elevated levels of stress and anxiety.[62] What, then, is needed to make an interracial relationship last? If you desire a fulfilling interracial relationship, then, simply, you must be willing to *do the work*. Interracial relationships require each person to engage in a fair amount of **cultural labor.** If you want to grow more intimate with your Jewish partner, you should learn about Jewish history and culture. If you are dating a Mexican American whose family speaks Spanish at home, then, in the interest of growing closer to your partner and her or his family, you should take Spanish lessons. If you desire to grow closer to a second-generation Arab American, you should make the effort to learn more about where his relatives migrated from—their country's history, culture, and mores—but do so respectfully and with humility. If you are getting serious with a white person, you should strive to get in touch with her or his white identity. Cultural labor requires broadening your cultural competence, stepping out of your comfort zone, and trying as much as possible to adopt another perspective on the world.

Some whites never experience being victimized by interpersonal and institutional racism until they begin dating a nonwhite person. Sociologist Heather Dalmage, a white woman married to a black man, explains her experiences: "As an interracially married woman, my experiences are vastly different from other white women. Things like being seated in the back of restaurants, being denied loans, being steered out of white neighborhoods when we search for housing, being pulled over for no reason, and facing hostility from racist whites are experiences most whites never contend with. Because of my experiences, I no longer take white privilege for granted, and in some cases I am no longer seen as a white by other whites."[63] Dalmage has been treated to a first-rate education in racial domination through her marriage. And in order fully to understand her husband—let alone the world in which she herself lives—she has had to do the (racial) work, to divest her white privilege and to come to expect unfair treatment.

We cannot overemphasize the importance of cultural labor. It is a principle that applies to any meaningful relationship that traverses racial boundaries—not only romances and marriages but also friendships and professional associations. It applies as well to parents raising biracial or adopted children whose racial identities differ from their own. A white woman who adopts a black baby, for example, must learn how to braid and style black hair; she must learn to provide her child with tools to defend herself from racial domination; she must know what to do when the child comes home crying after being called "dirty"; she must be vigilant about her whiteness so her child does not unknowingly internalize a white supremacist perspective.[64] This mother, in short, must do some serious cultural labor, learning and relearning. But then again, in our multiracial society, one that grows more diverse by the day, aren't we all required to do the (racial) work? Isn't it rather unacceptable—not to mention thoroughly unpatriotic—to walk through life unaffected by other people's histories and hardships, their joys and jokes and experiences? "We are learning," as Jane Addams once said, "that a standard of social ethics is not attained by travelling a sequestered byway, but by mixing on the thronged and common road where all must turn out for one another, and at least see the size of one another's burden."[65] We heartily agree. And we wager that many of you, having read this far and having learned a considerable amount about racial domination—that is, having already done a great deal of cultural labor—would agree as well.

Divorce

If the U.S. has a fairly high marriage rate, it has an enormously high divorce rate, ranking second only to Aruba in the number of divorces per 1,000 people.[66] Divorce rates have risen since the 1970s, but like marriage rates, they fluctuate widely across race. Immigrant families, for one, experience relatively high levels of divorce. Characterized by change and adjustment, immigrant families are a blending of the old and the new, an amalgamation of influences rooted both in the sending country and the receiving nation. Oftentimes, these families' very definition of what constitutes a "family" must bend to U.S. law and custom. For example, social service agencies narrow Hmong immigrants' notions of a family from extended kin networks of aunts, uncles, cousins, and grandparents to the nuclear family model.[67] And many immigrant parents are surprised and angered by the fact that in America they are not allowed to discipline their children "with the rod," a fact that immigrant children learn quickly. In her research on West African immigrants, sociologist Mary Waters found that these parents "believe that physical punishment is the best way to deal with a child who has misbehaved. They are shocked that this is unacceptable in the United States and consistently told us that it was one of the most disturbing aspects of living [here]."[68]

The biggest threat to the immigrant family is the process of immigration itself. In the majority of cases, immigrant families migrate in bits and spurts. Sometimes one parent migrates first, under an occupational visa, sending for her children and spouse later. Other times, children go ahead of their parents to live with relatives or friends, or to attend a boarding school, their parents following when they are able. One recent study found that 85% of immigrant youth are separated from one or both of their parents during the immigration process.[69] A family that begins to immigrate to the United States may not be reunited for years.[70] And when families do reconnect, ties between spouses may have frayed in transit. They may become weaker still, when parents, forced to find jobs in the immigrant labor market, begin working long hours for meager pay. The immigrant process—demanding, fracturing, all-consuming—unravels a good number of families.

African-American families also are at high risk of divorce. Indeed, African-American marriages are twice as likely to end in divorce as those of whites and native-born Mexican Americans.[71] Why? Again, a significant part of the answer lies in the fact that African Americans disproportionately are incarcerated and impoverished. Incarceration greatly increases the risk of divorce, as does inner-city poverty.[72] As the sociological ethnographer Elliot Liebow explained in *Tally's Corner*, speaking of unemployed black men, "By itself, the plain fact of supporting one's wife and children defines the principal obligation of a husband [for these men]. . . . Few married men, however, do in fact support their families over sustained periods of time. Money is chronically in short supply and chronically a source of dissension in the home. . . . Thus, marriage is an occasion of failure. To stay married is to live with your failure, to be confronted by it day in and day out. It is to live in a world whose standards of manliness are forever beyond one's reach, where one is continuously tested and challenged and continuously found wanting."[73]

If financial hardship and imprisonment can wreak havoc on a marriage, so too can high levels of spousal dissimilarity. Opposites might attract, but many do not stay married. Social scientists have argued that couples with high levels of incompatibility with respect to socioeconomic differences, conflicting views on gender roles, different degrees of educational attainment, and a large age gap are at higher risk of divorce. And studies have shown that black couples exhibit greater spousal dissimilarity than nonblack couples in these key areas.[74] One reason for this is the small African-American marriage pool we discussed earlier: the fewer the choices of potential mates, the greater the chances of incompatibility. Another reason is the historically conditioned incongruence between the ways in which black men and women understand gender roles, an incongruence whose genesis is located in the destruction of the black family under slavery. This has led some black marriages to be defined by a tradition of "love and trouble," wherein relationships are sites of much affection but also of antagonism.[75]

Added to poverty, incarceration, and spousal dissimilarity is yet another explanation for the high black divorce rate: the psychological strain of racial domination. An analogy: A soldier is ordered to leave his family to be deployed in a war zone. Once there, he sees terrible things, does terrible things, and has terrible things done to him. He then returns home to his family, changed. War transformed that marriage from a stable union to a tragically unstable one. Divorce, once considered something that happens to other people, seems imminent. Now consider a black couple. Over the years they collect war stories of their own: job discrimination, police harassment, working but never getting ahead, sending their children to rundown schools, everyday cuts because of their skin color—a slight here, a denied opportunity there. Things add up, as numerous studies that have documented the psychological costs of racism attest.[76] These psychological costs can harm a marriage. Veterans of racial domination, like veterans of war, are at great risk of divorce.

Out-of-Wedlock Births

Relative to other major industrialized countries, the United States ranks near the middle when it comes to the proportion of babies born outside of wedlock. Countries such as Iceland, Sweden, Norway, Britain and France have higher percentages of out-of-wedlock births, while countries like Canada, Ireland, Portugal, Greece, and Japan have lower rates.[77] Since 1995, one in three babies has been born to an unmarried mother in the U.S. (In 1950, the rate was one in twenty.[78]) Out of wedlock births steadily have increased over the last few decades. In 1970, only 12% of all children lived with one parent; in 2000, 25% of children did.[79]

At least since the presidency of Ronald Reagan, single mothers have been stereotyped as immoral, inner-city black delinquents who have more children in order to collect bigger welfare checks. (Absent fathers, however, are mentioned less frequently, a silence that assumes single mothers somehow acted alone in the creation of their babies.) But the truth is that single mothers are "a remarkably diverse group who have arrived at single parenthood through divergent, and

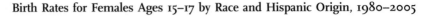

Birth Rates for Females Ages 15–17 by Race and Hispanic Origin, 1980–2005

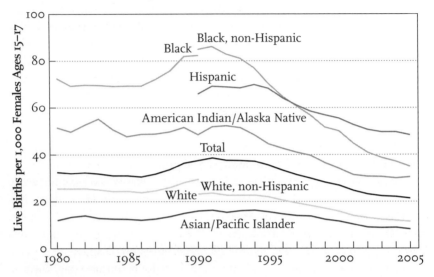

NOTE: Data for 2005 are preliminary. Rates for 1980–1989 are calculated for all Whites and all Blacks. Rates for 1980–1989 are not shown for Hispanics; White, non-Hispanics; or Black, non-Hispanics because information on the Hispanic origin of the mother was not reported on the birth certificates of most states.

often class-segregated paths, and who share middle-class values and struggle to embody them, often at significant cost to themselves."[80]

According to one study, most single mothers are in their early 20s (11% are under 18); most are poor and have very little education (over 30% lack a high school diploma); and, in most cases, the mother and father are in a committed relationship at the time of the birth, although many separate afterward.[81] Racial differences in out-of-wedlock births are considerable and well documented. With nearly 70% of births occurring outside marriage, African Americans have the highest rate of out-of-wedlock birth—and by a wide margin. Fifty-nine percent of Puerto Rican births occur outside of marriage, as do 41% of Mexican-American births and 25% of white births. The majority of white mothers are married (13% are single and 12% are cohabitating); for black mothers, the pattern is reversed: most are single. African Americans also have the highest rate of teenage pregnancy, followed by Mexican Americans, Puerto Ricans, American Indians, whites, and Asian Americans. Hispanic and Native-American teenagers are twice as likely—and black teenagers 2.5 times as likely—to have babies, compared to white teenagers.[82]

What is going on? Once again, two of America's most powerful racial institutions—the economy and the prison—have something to do with these discrepancies. For all racial groups, "the prevalence of fatherhood among prisoners is almost identical to that on the outside." The consequence is that groups that are imprisoned at higher rates, Latinos and especially blacks, also will have larger numbers of children with incarcerated fathers. Nationwide, 3% of children are in this position. A little over 1% of white children have incarcerated dads; for Latino children, the percentage is 3.5%. But *one in eleven* black children—over a million children—have a father behind bars.[83] By extracting the father from the home and community, imprisonment plays a large role in creating single-mother households.

With respect to the economic explanation, a longstanding finding in demography is that poor people have higher fertility rates. The reason is that, as one climbs the economic ladder, childcare costs increase: there are nannies, piano lessons, designer baby clothes, and private schools for which to pay. If fertility rates increase the lower you are on the economic ladder, then, as a rule, black and Hispanics, who are disproportionately poor, will have more children than whites. And several scholars have argued that people who systematically are denied social status in other areas of society, such as the business or academic worlds, may find it in the home. If you were raised on a poverty-stricken reservation or in the ghetto, your chances of becoming a high-powered lawyer or business mogul are slim; but almost anyone can become a parent, one of society's most cherished roles.[84]

As we have repeated throughout this chapter, however, racialized economic inequalities cannot fully explain why nonwhite women, and especially black women, are so much more likely to have children outside marriage than are Asian Americans or whites. "Most of the world's peoples are poor, far poorer than Afro-Americans, but do not experience the marital and familial problems that Afro-Americans do," writes Patterson. "Millions of chronically unemployed men live on the verge of starvation, in urban squalor all over Asia and Latin America without abandoning their wives and children. In America itself, the three-quarters of a century of urban semighetto poverty experienced by the post-famine Irish, and the present condition of the Latino minority . . . have not resulted in men's massive abandonment of their wives and children."[85] Other answers to our question lurk, ones having to do with racial differences in attitudes on sex and childbearing.

One has to do with the sexual strategies of some poor black men, namely, the practice of impregnating multiple women over their lifetimes. Seventeen percent of fathers have multiple children with different women, and black men account for a disproportionate amount of them. One-third of black fathers have had children by two or more women, relative to 16% of Latino and 5% of white fathers.[86] If a man has children by more than one woman, then at least one of those women is raising the child alone or with a stepparent. Indeed, research has suggested that some men who have children by different women spend very little time with any of their children.[87] This reproduction strategy of poor black men, one originally developed as an adaptation to dehumanizing slavery, is a mechanism of symbolic violence through which racial (and economic) domination reproduces itself within poor black communities.[88]

The special value some groups place on motherhood is another explanation for racial differences in out-of-wedlock birth rates. "In the ghetto," observes American sociologist Kenneth Clark, "the meaning of the illegitimate child is not ultimate disgrace. There is not a demand for abortion or for surrender of the child that one finds in more privileged communities. In the middle class, the disgrace of illegitimacy is tied to person and family aspirations. In lower-class families, however, the girl loses only some of her already limited options by having an illegitimate child; she is not going to make a 'better marriage' or improve her economic and social status either way. On the contrary, a child is symbolic of the fact that she is a woman, and she may gain from having something of her own. Nor is the boy who fathers an illegitimate child going to lose, for where is he going? The path to any higher status seems closed to him in any case."[89]

Sociologists Kathryn Edin and Maria Kefalas interviewed over 160 young, urban, and poor single mothers to understand why so many remain unmarried after having children and why they decide to have children even when caring for them may require living hand to mouth. They found that single mothers do not devalue or scorn marriage. On the contrary, they revere it, so much so, in fact, that they refuse to trade vows until they are certain the marriage will last. "The poor women we talked to," Edin and Kefalas write in *Promises I Can Keep: Why Poor Women Put Motherhood before Marriage,* "insist [that marriage] means lifelong commitment. In a surprising reversal of the middle-class norm, they believe it is better to have children outside of marriage than to marry unwisely only to get divorced later."[90] If these single mothers value a stable marriage but in the end conclude it is too risky—because their child's father, who once wooed them with the line, "I want to have a baby with you," now cannot find a job, goes to prison, abuses drugs, or blows his monthly paycheck on stereo equipment—they view parenthood as a "promise they can keep." These women "seldom view out-of-wedlock birth as a mark of personal failure, but instead see it as an act of valor."[91] They understand childbearing as a central part of their womanhood and their worth. Edin and Kefalas sum up their main argument: "While the poor women we interviewed saw marriage as a luxury, something they aspired to but feared they might never achieve, they judged children to be a necessity, an absolutely essential part of a young woman's life, the chief source of identity and meaning."[92]

This is why so few pregnant women in poor neighborhoods consider adoption or abortion as viable options. Unlike their more affluent peers, many are encouraged by their parents to have and raise the child. On learning that her 15-year-old daughter was pregnant, one of the poor black women captured in Carol Stack's important book, *All Our Kin,* encouraged her daughter to keep the baby. "I had you," she said, "and you should have your child. I didn't get rid of you. I loved you and I took care of you until you got to the age to have this one. Have your baby no matter what, there's nothing wrong with having a baby. Be proud of it like I was proud of you."[93] Indeed, social scientists have found that blacks are less supportive of abortion than whites and that white teens are more likely to have abortions than black teens.[94]

The Consequences of Single Motherhood

The major consequences of single motherhood are many. Out-of-wedlock pregnancy decreases teenage women's chances of graduating from high school as well as their likelihood of marrying in the future. And children raised by single mothers, despite their mothers' best efforts, are disadvantaged in a number of ways. They are less likely to be healthy, more likely to have children in their teens, and, when they get older, more likely to have trouble finding steady employment. Children from single-parent households also are more likely to acquire behavioral and psychological problems, to do worse in school, and not to go to college than their peers raised by both biological parents.[95]

Many—but certainly not all—of these negative consequences stem, not from the one-parent family structure per se, but from the economic disadvantage that accompanies marital disruption and single motherhood. In 2003, only 64% of custodial mothers possessed a child support order and, of those, only 45% received the full amount they were due.[96] It is estimated that over 90% of poor noncustodial fathers pay no formal child support. Fathers who contribute little to nothing, low earnings, poor employment status, a lack of affordable childcare, meager public assistance programs, and low levels of wealth result in single-mother families ranking below all other major demographic groups on the economic ladder.[97] Children of single mothers are five times more likely to live below the poverty line than those raised by married parents. Sociologists have referred to the swelling ranks of single mothers among the poor—the fact that increasing numbers live "one sick child away from destitution"[98]—as the **feminization of poverty.**[99]

Many women who are "flat broke with children" rely on welfare to get by. One study of single mothers found that half rely on welfare to make ends meet, whereas the other half struggles in the low-wage labor market. Many poor single mothers find themselves between a rock and a hard place, having "to choose between a welfare system that [pays] far too little to provide for their basic needs and a labor market that [offers] them little more than they could have gotten by staying home."[100] Because most single parents lack the wherewithal to pay

Percentage of Related Children Ages 0–17 Living in Poverty by Family Structure, 1980–2005

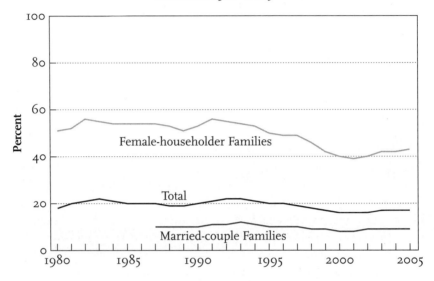

NOTE: Estimates refer to children ages 0–17 who are related to the householder. In 2005, the average poverty threshold for a family of four was $19,971.

for educational expenses (such as private tutoring, textbooks, computers, college tuition, and so forth), their children play with a handicap in school and, by extension, in the labor market. Recognizing the severity of single mothers' financial situations, researchers have shown that the negative effect on children's life chances of living with a single mother declines significantly when income is held constant.[101]

The policy implications of this research are clear. If we truly want to help some of the poorest people in America—low-income single mothers—we should not push for policies that encourage these women to get married (or, in the negative formula, that *punish them* for not being married), as do "marriage incentives" proposed by many politicians.[102] Rather, we should attempt to lift them out of destitution with robust antipoverty initiatives, ones that raise the minimum wage, provide childcare and housing subsidies, and universalize health care. We might also consider more effectively enforcing childcare payments, so that mothers do not have to shoulder the costs of raising children themselves.[103] One thing is certain: as the United States continues to roll back its welfare programs, and as more and more single women are forced into the unskilled, underpaid sections of the labor force, the feminization of poverty will get only worse. And the lives of single mothers and their children will get only harder.[104]

"[Many poor single mothers must] choose between a welfare system that [pays] far too little to provide for their basic needs and a labor market that [offers] them little more than they could have gotten by staying home." —Kathryn Edin and Laura Lein

The Self and Identity Formation

Finally, we arrive at a discussion of the self. With this section on the most intimate of all sociological subjects—your identity and psychology, your emotions and innermost thoughts—we bring Part Two of this book to a close. We start with a discussion of common misunderstandings that occur during interracial communication, misunderstandings that push us further apart. We examine racial identity development and intersectionality, moving from an examination of the interaction order to an analysis of identity formation and contestation. We conclude by interrogating the idea of "racial authenticity," of being true to one's ethnic or racial heritage, including in that discussion the choice of some whites to reject whiteness for an alternative ethnic identity.

Interaction Troubles

The **interaction order** is the face-to-face domain of social life, the mezzanine level between large-scale structure and individual psychology. In this domain we find transactions between two or more persons and all those performances— breathing, standing, laughing, lying, blowing one's nose—that constitute the daily work of impression management. Here the object of study is verbal and nonverbal communication—what one "gives" and "gives off." As Erving Goffman, sociologist par excellence of the interaction order, put it, "The ultimate behavioral materials are the glances, gestures, positionings, and verbal statements that people continuously feed into the situation, whether intended or not."[105] For Goffman, the self is best described as an arrangement of social performances, the face you present to different audiences at different times.[106]

Goffman drew many parallels between society and the stage (which is why his brand of social science has been termed the dramaturgical approach). In life, there is a front stage and a back stage. The front stage is where the performance is given, where we try to impress a certain impression on others. The back stage, in contrast, is where we kick off our shoes and relax a bit, where we feel we do not have to put on a show. The bustling restaurant kitchen, where the five-course meal is prepared among yelling chiefs, banging knives, and clanging dishes, is the back stage; the quiet dining room, where waiters interact solemnly with well-dressed guests, is the front. Your own classroom, where you have adopted a certain kind of performance to impress your professor or peers, is the front stage; your dorm room, where you tell your best friend what you "really think"—or, for that matter, the hallway right outside the classroom door—is the back stage.

When it comes to the drama of race, the distinction between front stage and back stage tends to be much more distinct and clear for people of color than whites. To put it another way, in most of life the front and back stage are almost one for whites when it comes to their racial practices. Because whiteness is the dominant and "normal" racial category in all of society's fields of life, whites need not be reflexive about their whiteness to get ahead in the world. They need not "check their whiteness at the door" to move up the corporate ladder or to excel in school. The same cannot be said for people of color. Most of the time, whites do not need to know terribly much about nonwhites to navigate society; but nonwhites must know about whites to do so. "Of them," wrote Du Bois, "I am singularly clairvoyant."[107] Accordingly, many nonwhites, operating with a double vision, a double consciousness, have developed **racial survival strategies** to navigate white America. One strategy is "testing," the act of "feeling out" members of other racial or ethnic groups to evaluate their level of racial tolerance and understanding. Because of America's legacy of racial domination, some nonwhites are distrustful of whites—and have their guard up around whites until they are confident they are trustworthy or "down with the cause." That is, they might "wear a mask" (another survival strategy) around those who have not yet earned their confidence. Granted, we all wear masks around those not in our inner circle (and even around those who are), but for nonwhites, masking takes on an explicitly racialized character. An ambitious middle-class African American working in a majority white law firm, for example, may attempt to put as much distance between her and her blackness as possible. Of African Americans who join whites at the table of economic or political privilege, Patricia Williams once observed, "You need two chairs at the table, one for you, one for your blackness."[108]

Because many nonwhites think explicitly about their behaviors in these terms and because many whites do not—they do not say to themselves several times a day, "I'm white, and they're not, so I'd better do it this way"—misunderstandings are bound to happen. Consider the way we greet one another. Sociologists who study the minutiae of everyday life have demonstrated that whites and blacks engage in different greeting styles. When a white person goes to meet another, they usually look to categorize the person according to their social roles. Accordingly, they might ask: Where are you from? What do you do? What is your major? How old are you? These questions allow them to assess their interlocutor and response accordingly: "Okay, I'm talking to someone older than me; someone with a good job; someone who lives in a nice neighborhood. I'd better answer her question this way." Whites would rather be asked about information than offer it unsolicited. African Americans, in contrast, prefer greetings that talk about the "here and now." They like to discuss public settings that any person can clearly see and talk about. And instead of petitioning for information directly, they go fishing for it. They hint that information is desired—a practice known as "signifying"—by asking roundabout questions. For example, instead of asking, "How old are you?" an African-American interlocutor might ask, "Did you just graduate from high school?"[109]

Whites find their own style of greeting natural and friendly, while some blacks see it as intrusive and prodding. They feel interrogated. In a similar way, blacks find their own greeting styles respectful and considerate of another's privacy, while some whites find it off-putting and avoidant. It leaves them cold. These innocent communication blimps can easily provoke larger racial assumptions. A misfire in greeting strategies may lead whites to find blacks rude, ignorant, or prejudiced toward white people; and it may lead blacks to find whites nosy, invasive, and motivated by racial reasons ("Why do they want to know so much about me?") These assumptions can slip into generalizations: "Black people are rude." "White people are pushy."[110]

Another common misunderstanding takes place on the job. Blacks are more likely to refuse a work assignment than whites. When neither worker wants the extra assignments, blacks are more likely to say "no" to the boss's face, while whites are more likely to say "yes" before going home and complaining about their boss to their roommates or spouses. Blacks may find whites' tendency to hide their true feelings from their supervisors dishonest—and might come to view whites as immoral and fake. Likewise, whites may interpret the way blacks turn down assignments as intimidating and offensive—and might come to view blacks as lazy and hard to handle. Sociologist Anne Rawls notes: "While it may seem obvious from a White perspective that Black employees need to change their behavior in order to succeed, a reevaluation may be in order. An occasional 'no' might relieve some stress of White employees. . . . [After all,] research has shown that stress on the job is one of the biggest health problems in America."[111]

Some whites find nonwhites, and especially blacks and Hispanics, loud and confrontational. "They're always yelling at one another!" But many blacks and Hispanics have been taught that arguments should be handled "on the spot" and ideally settled before the conversation ends. Sometimes this requires a good deal of energy and movement, interrupting and shouting. If someone backs away from a discussion the moment it heats up, nonwhites often find such behavior disingenuous and pretentious. "If you care about a person," they think, "you don't walk away the moment it gets confrontational. You stay and work it out." Whites, however, sometimes get nervous during a heated discussion, especially if it involves a nonwhite person; they often dread saying something offensive and being labeled a racist. They often view backing away as the diplomatic and polite thing to do. "If you care about a person," they think, "you give them their space and let them cool down. Perhaps they will drop it altogether."[112] Again, the tiniest things can lead to communication misfires and negative declarations about the racialized Other.

Rawls sums up the problem: although whites and nonwhites "appear to occupy the same world geographically, they rarely occupy the same interactional space. Furthermore, even today when they do more often jointly occupy interactional space, because their communities have developed in separation and their Interaction Order practices conflict, the display of moral behavior by members of one group may well look like deviant behavior to members of the other."[113] This can affect even the most critically minded and racially aware person. In his book *Race*, American journalist Studs Terkel recalls a conversation he had with a civil rights lawyer. The lawyer remembered a time when his white wife was driving through a black neighborhood: "The people at all the corners [were] all gesticulating at her. She was very frightened, quickly turned up the window and drove determinedly. She discovered, after several blocks, she was going the wrong way on a one-way street and they were trying to help her. Her assumption was that they were blacks and they were trying to get at her. Mind you, she's a very enlightened woman."[114]

Just because we all are English speakers does not mean we are talking the same language. Racial domination thwarts our efforts at communication, our ability to connect with and truly to understand one another. It has built itself into the interaction order; and it has dug itself deep in our minds and bodies. It directs our conscious and subconscious thinking; it holds sway over our emotions, our feelings of rage and bitterness, disgust and fascination, fear and safety, elation and comfort.[115] It is there in our habits, too, casting us about like so many marionettes on a string.[116]

Are we then damned to go about life as in parallel worlds? Is cross-racial communication superficial at best, impossible at worst? No—*unequivocally no*. Such thinking is poison. Then what is the way out of these interaction troubles? You know the answer: We must do the (racial) work. Interracial and intercultural communication requires vigilant reflexivity. We need to strive as much as possible to "take the view of the other" without necessarily sacrificing our own ideas and pay mind to the social and racial contexts that influence the communication. Instead of attributing some misunderstanding that occurs in a conversation across racial lines to some imaginary characteristics of the other group, we need to strive to extend others the benefit of the doubt. Most people who trip over their words when it comes to race or who say something offensive are well-meaning, and they are more likely to listen and learn from you if you address them with kindness and patience, rather than with anger or pretension. Above all, interracial communication demands a display of humility and respect, which encourages us to enter the conversation, not with something to prove as much as with a desire to learn and understand.

Racial Identity Formation

For many of us, growing up requires developing an identity. This means asking ourselves, "How should I live?" "To whom should I give my loyalty?" "Who am I?" Coming to terms with our racial and ethnic identity, of course, is an important part of this process. For whites, this process often begins much later than it does for people of color, the vast majority of whom are socialized at a young age to understand themselves in racial terms. When whites do begin to think about their racial identity, many find the process unsettling and confusing. A good many would rather think of themselves as individuals, somehow detached from the larger society, than as group members. Others simply refuse to open their eyes to all the evidence of historical and present-day racial injustice—and ardently deny their racial privilege. Psychologists have identified this stage, one marked by a naiveté about racial domination (itself a courtesy of white privilege), as the first and most basic step in white identity formation. Unfortunately, some white people never develop beyond this stage.[117]

But many others do. They begin to understand what race means to them; they begin to come to terms with their whiteness, some through personal encounters (living with an American-Indian roommate in college), others through classes like the one for which you are reading this book. Curious, they begin to pay more attention, to learn about racial domination. This process leads many to become aware of their racial privilege, which provokes feelings of guilt and shame. They feel as the great French philosopher Jean-Paul Sartre must have felt when he wrote, "Our whiteness seems to us to be a strange and livid varnish that keeps our skin from breathing—white tights, worn out at the elbows and knees, under which we would find real human flesh the color of black wine if we could remove them. We think we are essential to the world—suns of its harvests, moons of its tides; we are no more than its fauna, beasts."[118]

Newly awakened, many whites made aware of racial domination desire to fight it but don't know how. Like new religious converts, they can be zealous but unwieldy, passionate but not strategic. They tend to make their "unen-lightened" friends and family members uncomfortable; the latter learn not to mention anything having to do with race in their presence. After their passion subsides, some whites begin to regress, placing the blame not on themselves, or even on racial domination, but on people of color. They trade their guilt for anger, their confessions for accusations, their introspection for finger pointing. "My friends are right," they think. "If there are racial inequalities today, nonwhite people must be at fault. After all, slavery did happen long ago, and I certainly had nothing to do with it. All this talk about racial dom-ination is nonsense."[119]

However, those who have any respect for the truth cannot hold fast to this belief for very long. And, at this stage in the development of their racial identity, whites begin to cultivate a healthy and honest relationship with their whiteness. They begin to come to terms with the ways they are privileged simply because they are white; and they start, in a reflexive mode, to "unlearn their whiteness." They begin to interrogate attitudes they long have held about racial domination and people of color, and they begin spending more time in multiracial settings and with antiracist whites. They realize how they unin-tentionally feed racial domination and learn, too, how they can join in the struggle against racial justice. Here, they gain a healthy white identity. They begin to shed their guilt—after all, being white is nothing to be ashamed of—and to develop a "positive White identity, based in reality, not on assumed superiority."[120]

People do not move through these stages in white identity development—which proceeds from racial naiveté and confusion, through guilt and anger, to resolution and honesty—in a straight line. They do not progress through so many steps toward racial enlightenment. Rather, people move forward and back-ward through these stages during different points in their lives. And, we must point out, the vast majority of white people, those who never are introduced to the realities of racial domination, never move past the first two stages.

Nonwhites, too, go through stages of racial identity development. Many begin with their own brand of naiveté, more or less unaware of racial domination.

This innocence, however, tends to be short-lived, as many nonwhites encounter racism at a very young age. Consider this interaction told to a researcher by white parents who had adopted nonwhite children. While shopping at a mall, the family bumped into a white friend, who proceeded to ask the children what they wanted to be when they grew up. "She asked the oldest daughter, who is Asian, if she was planning to be an accountant, the youngest brother, a sturdy boy of black and Asian heritage, if he wanted to become a golfer like Tiger Woods, and the third child, a Latina girl, if she would like to grow up and become a gardener."[121]

Coming to the realization that you are nonwhite in a society marked by a long history of white racial domination is a painful one. Many nonwhites react by immersing themselves in communities of people that share their racial identity, people who have experienced similar slights and cuts and, therefore, may understand their struggles. During this time, nonwhites might be gripped by anger and frustration at the unfairness of racial domination; they might grow bitter toward people who do not share their racial identity, whites and other nonwhites alike. They might also begin learning about nonwhite history and culture. Latinos, for example, might read about César Chávez and the farm workers movement; African Americans might read up on black nationalism and black power; American Indians might begin paying more respect to their tribal language and customs.[122]

For many nonwhites during this stage, their racial or ethnic identity becomes their master identity; it is what most defines their sense of self. This is why the routine occurrence of being misrecognized as belonging to another racial or ethnic group can be so painful to many nonwhites. One recent study found that American Indians are misidentified more than members of other groups and concluded that those who are often misidentified "are more likely to report psychological distress than correctly classified American Indians. . . . [They] are significantly more likely to report considering suicide, attempting suicide, and believing they will die before the age of 35 than those who are correctly classified."[123]

Just as whites pursuing a mature and healthy racial identity must recognize their privilege in order to take steps to understand themselves as more than "victimizers," nonwhites must work to rethink their blackness or Indianness or Mexicanness or Asianness or Arabness in "ways that take them beyond the role of victim."[124] They come to realize that their whole being cannot be defined by their racial identity alone; that they house multitudes. They develop a critical race consciousness that allows them to channel their animus against white supremacy in constructive ways, criticizing the systems that perpetuate racial domination. They learn to rest confidently and calmly in their nonwhite skin and resist basing their racial identity on ethnic chauvinism (white supremacy's mirror image), which only widens racial divides. Many form interracial coalitions and friendships; others join antiracist organizations.[125]

A central component of developing a nonwhite identity in a country whose past and present are scarred by white supremacy is the formation of a **double consciousness**. What Du Bois wrote about African Americans can be applied to other nonwhite groups as well: "The Negro is a sort of seventh son, born with a veil, and gifted with second-sight in this American world,—a world which yields him no true self-consciousness, but only lets him see himself through the revelation of the other world. It is a peculiar sensation, this double-consciousness, this sense of always looking at one's self through the eyes of others, of measuring one's soul by the tape of a world that looks on in amused contempt and pity. One ever feels his two-ness,—an American, a Negro: two souls, two thoughts, two unreconciled strivings; two warring ideals in one dark body, whose dogged strength alone keeps it from being torn asunder."[126]

Double consciousness, then, is a way of thinking about yourself through two pairs of eyes: one pair belonging to White America, the other belonging to your racial or ethnic group. If you are an African American, it means viewing yourself as you believe whites view you and as you believe blacks view you. Most white Americans never develop this kind of fractured identity because they do not have to look upon themselves with the eyes of dominated groups. This is how one sociologist explained Du Bois's famous idea: "The White American takes the role of the White other toward the self without any fundamental contradiction and thus essentially without being aware of doing so. White Americans do not take the role of Black Americans toward themselves. African Americans, on the other hand, because of the essential inequality and incompatibility between the two communities, are forced to take the role of White others toward themselves and are as a consequence uncomfortably aware of looking at themselves through the veil. . . . The African American, according to Du Bois, is always torn in two directions, held accountable to two communities."[127]

Intersectional Identity

As we have mentioned throughout this book, your racial identity coincides with other aspects of your self to produce a full, complex, intersectional identity. You are not "just Asian." You are also young, a student, Buddhist, man, brother, urbanite, English major, and so forth. Other aspects of your identity regulate your racial identity and vice versa. Consider the commingling of your racial identity and class background. One often hears people associate authentic blackness or Latino heritage with poverty, as if (to quote Fanon) "one is white above a certain financial level."[128] Ice Cube, for example, links "real blackness" to the ghetto in his song, "True to the Game," which chastises a black suburbanite for "trying to be white or a Jew," and threatens to revoke his "ghetto pass" (that is, strip him of his blackness) if he doesn't return to the 'hood and "stop being an Uncle Tom."[129] Accordingly, some middle- and upper-class students of color, on rediscovering their cultural heritage during college, strive to downplay their class status and emphasize their race or ethnicity by, for example, learning Portuguese, growing an afro, studying the Koran, or joining a Native-American coalition.[130]

Geography is also an important component of one's identity. Suburban whiteness contrasts sharply with rural whiteness, which in turn is quite different from urban whiteness. Whiteness fluctuates and shape-shifts as one moves across the country. The whiteness practiced in a southern Louisiana town is very different than the whiteness found in San Francisco's gay-friendly Castro district. A white millionaire who made it big working as a CEO in Albuquerque most likely has a different understanding of her racial identity than one who made his money working as a pig farmer in Minnesota. Indeed, northern whites often fail to recognize their racism as racism precisely because they (still) understand racism to be a fundamentally southern phenomenon: the stuff of backwoods, backwards rural "white trash." This dynamic predates the Civil War, when northern whites chastised southern whites for slavery but refused to welcome blacks into their own neighborhoods, schools, and churches.[131]

Your immigrant status, too, is an influential component of your racial or ethnic identity. A fourth-generation Mexican American most likely will have a different understanding of what it means to be Mexican than one who arrived in America just last year.[132] And within many ethnic communities, struggles take place between recent immigrants and native-born Americans. Some Asian Americans, for example, who all their lives have been treated as foreigners ("No, where are you *really* from?" "Gee, you speak good English!"), harbor anti-Asian immigrant sentiments. As sociologist Mia Tuan writes in *Forever Foreigners or Honorary Whites? The Asian Ethnic Experience Today,* some Asian Americans believe Asian immigrants fuel "the stereotypes that have contributed to their conditional status as 'honorary' but not 'legitimate' Americans." She continues, "After years of carefully cultivating good relations with their non-Asian neighbors, [Asian Americans find] themselves subject to the same hostilities as immigrants. In response, many [become] the harshest critics of the immigrants whom they [see] as spoiling what they had worked so hard to establish—a positive image."[133] Asian immigrants, for their part, respond by criticizing Asian Americans for being big on the "American" and little on the "Asian" because, for example, they cannot speak Chinese or know little about Japanese traditions.

The intersection of race and gender is an especially powerful aspect of one's identity, one we have addressed throughout this book. Racial identity colors one's gender identity, and one's gender identity guides people's understandings of what it means to belong to a certain racial or ethnic group. Thus scholars have identified different racialized variants of masculinity, from the "cool pose" of many young black men and the machismo of some Latino men to the rural white masculinity of some "country boys."[134] Likewise, feminine identity is affected by one's racial or ethnic identity. In some communities, a "real" Chinese woman or a "real" Mexican woman takes care of the house and looks after the children. If these women do not fulfill these roles, they feel as if they are not living up to their ethnic obligations, a feeling enforced by some of their friends and family members. The racialization of Asian femininity is the dynamic behind skin-tone discrimination among some Asian Americans. That is, some Asian-American women associate feminine beauty with whiteness and, accordingly, attempt to stay as white as possible. As a young Cambodian woman reflected, "My dad said one day, 'Don't wear shorts too much. You don't want to have dark legs, because no one will want to marry you.' . . . I get a lot of comments from older adults . . . like, 'Careful you're getting so dark. You better stay out of the sun.'" Another put it even more succinctly: "Shun the sun! That's my sister's cry. Shun the sun!"[135]

"The borderlands dividing racial, ethnic, and national identities and communities constitute ethnosexual frontiers, erotic intersections that are heavily patrolled, policed, and protected, yet regularly are penetrated by individuals forging sexual links with ethnic 'others.'"[136] So writes sociologist Joane Nagel. When we examine the intersection between race and sexuality, we are struck by the observation that racial identity is often defined through certain sexual practices and performances. Immigrant families from India, for example, often construct young women's Indian sexuality explicitly by contrasting it with that of young white women. White women are depicted as feeble and promiscuous; Indian women are considered chaste, traditional, and strong.[137] And, as we already have seen, sexual fantasies—of the sexually predatory black man, the erotic Asian woman, the sexless Asian man, the pure white woman—can result in gross misrepresentations of certain racial groups and can fuel racial resentment and hatred.[138]

Studies have found that homophobia—heterosexist domination of lesbian and gay people, manifest at the institutional and interpersonal levels—is higher among African Americans and Hispanics than whites.[139] The result is that gay and lesbians of color suffer from a kind of **double rejection:** they are ostracized by the larger white society on account of their skin color and rejected from their racial or ethnic community on account of their sexuality.[140] Queering whitens. For many African-American men, authentic black masculinity is undeniably straight. Thus Eldridge Cleaver, author of *Soul on Ice,* was able to articulate forcefully the suffering caused by racial domination but was unable to grasp the unique pain experienced by gay blacks. He went so far as to call James Baldwin's homosexuality "somehow un-black"—and labeled interracial homosexual (as well

Your racial identity coincides with other aspects of your self to produce a full, complex, intersectional identity.

as heterosexual) romantic unions a "racial death wish."[141] Black lesbians, too, often are viewed as "race traitors" and come out (of the closet) to their friends and family members only at great personal cost.[142]

Why do some heterosexual blacks understand homosexuality to be a fundamentally un-black or white phenomenon? Why is the black gay man or lesbian not simply shunned but bleached? Part of the answer lies in the fact that racial logics have sexual components, as we have been demonstrating. But another part is to be found in the historical record. "Among the myths Europeans have created about Africa," writes one historian, "the myth that homosexuality is absent or incidental is the oldest and most enduring. For Europeans, black Africans—of all the native peoples of the world—most epitomized 'primitive man.' Since primitive man is supposed to be close to nature, ruled by instinct, and culturally unsophisticated, he had to be heterosexual, his sexual energies and outlets demoted exclusively to their 'natural' purpose: biological reproduction. If black Africans were the most primitive people in all humanity . . . then they had to be the most heterosexual."[143] Thus, the idea that homosexuality is a white sexual practice is rooted in the colonialist enterprise and the transatlantic slave trade. The (black) notion that associates homosexuality with whiteness and the (white) notion that links hyper (heterosexual) eroticism and promiscuity with blackness are two branches sprung from the same trunk.[144]

The prevalence of homophobia in some nonwhite communities leads to a larger issue: the tendency to focus on the disadvantaged components of your identity while paying little attention to the privileged ones. Many men of color talk about how they are victims of racial domination but rarely reflect on how they perpetuate sexism or homophobia. Many white lesbians fail to interrogate their white privilege because their attention is monopolized by the ways they are disadvantaged by homophobia. Middle-class women of color may be keen on the intersection of race and gender but ignore their own class privileges. Because privilege is often weightless to those who profit from it, you are most likely to select as the most important elements of your identity those which give you the most grief, downplaying your privileged memberships. Just as white people often fail to recognize their white privilege, nonwhite people can fail to recognize their heterosexual, gender, or class advantages. The result is that discussions of racism often have a male bias and discussions of sexism often have a white bias—the key point of the classic anthology *All the Women Are White, All the Blacks Are Men, But Some of Us Are Brave*.[145]

Racial Authenticity

For over one hundred years now, sociologists have shown that your behavior is dictated in large part by your identity. If you identify as a Mormon, for example, you are likely to engage in a set of practices (for example, avoiding caffeine, abstaining from using foul language, going on dates with other Mormons) that align with that identity. The same is true of race.

Race is both marked and made. It is *marked* through America's racial taxonomy, which seeks to divide the nation into distinct categories. In this case, race imposes itself on you. It is *made* through hundreds and thousands of practices: gestures, sayings, tastes, ways of walking, religious convictions, opinions, and so forth. In this case, you perform race. Race as performance is "predicated on actions, on the things one does in the world, on how one behaves." As anthropologist John Jackson, Jr., notes, "You are not black because you are (in essence) black; you are black . . . because of how you act—and not just in terms of one field of behavior (say, intellectual achievement in school) but because of how you juggle and combine many differently racialized and class(ed) actions (walking, talking, laughing, watching a movie, standing, emoting, partying) in an everyday matrix of performative possibilities."[146] Because racial domination attaches to skin color, a dark-skinned person can never completely escape its clutches simply by acting "not black." But that person may choose one saying over another, one kind of clothing over another, one mode of interaction over another, because she believes such an action makes her more or less black. This is why we claim that race is both ascribed and achieved, both marked and made.[147]

Just as men often perform masculinity by professing their love of football and their contempt of ballet, we perform race and ethnicity through certain conscious and unconscious decisions. This includes speaking one's native tongue or melding English with other languages—as in the English and Spanish fusion heard in the Southwest or in the Yiddish-sprinkled English (once) spoken in New York's Lower East Side. Some racial groups do race by staking out a virtual monopoly on certain words, ascriptions, and sayings—not to mention certain linguistic styles and bodily postures—which is why someone who does not identify as black is advised not to call a black man a "brotha" and absolutely is forbidden to call him a "nigga," even if these terms are sometimes employed with frequency and fraternity between African-American friends. We perform ethnicity and race by celebrating certain holidays (for example, Kwanza, Juneteenth, St. Patrick's Day, Rosh Hashanah, Burns Night, Chinese New Year) and by cultivating certain fashions (for instance, wearing dashikis, head-wraps, Crucifix necklaces, burkas, kimonos, Norwegian sweaters, kilts).[148] Those who assume that whiteness is not performed in the same way as blackness or Arabness continue to treat whiteness as the invisible norm and are only fooling themselves. Through fashion choices (think of Abercrombie and Fitch, J. Crew, or Land's End), linguistic styles (think of Dave Chappell's impression of a white accent), and a constellation of many other racial behaviors, tastes, and practices, whiteness is executed.[149] Humor writer Christian Lander has compiled a list of *Stuff White People Like* that includes vintage goods, snowboarding, religions their parents don't belong to, organic food, indie music, irony, hating corporations, bumper stickers, and Frisbee sports.[150]

Such performances rely on a collection of recognizable cultural practices and beliefs that separate insiders from outsiders.[151] "We" are different from "them" because we listen to different music, eat different food, dress differently, and laugh at different jokes. A group's identity pivots on the notion of **racial authenticity.** Racial authenticity seeks to define the essence of Mexicanness or Arabness or whiteness by including or excluding certain behaviors from the repertoire that constitutes a group's aesthetic identity. Statements about how a "real Chinese woman" or a "real Puerto Rican man" or a "real Hmong child" should behave are statements about racial authenticity.

For many groups, racial authenticity often is bought with a pound of flesh; it is deeply tied to histories of suffering. Consider the connection between Jewish

What does it mean to be authentically Jewish? Scottish? Mexican? Chinese? Haitian?

identity and the abstinence from pork. As anthropologist Mary Douglas observed, the pig is no more polluted in The Book of Leviticus than are other animals (for example, the camel, the rock badger), but the pig has come to be singled out among Jews as the filthiest of animals. Why? Because of the special historic role it has played in the humiliation and oppression of Jewish people. Greek conquerors blasphemed the God of Israel by immolating swine on Hebrew altars; and Jewish people were forced to eat pork to symbolize their submission. If they refused, and many did, they often were put to death in the most barbarous fashion. It was the Greek rulers, specifically Antiochus, who "forced into prominence the rule concerning pork as the critical symbol of group allegiance. . . . After such historic acts of heroism [on the part of those who refused to eat the flesh of swine], no wonder the avoidance of pork became a specially powerful symbol of allegiance for the Jewish people."[152] Douglas draws our attention to the intimate connection between the role of suffering in the history of a cultural practice (dietary restrictions) and the accumulation and preservation of a particular pedigree of ethnic identity (Jewish authenticity). The memory of persecution structures many other racial and ethnic practices as well, from an African-American couple jumping over a broom on their wedding day (the act that solidified a union in slave times) to a Jewish groom smashing the glass in his wedding ceremony to symbolize the destruction of the Temple and thus to satisfy the Psalmist's call to "consider Jerusalem as your highest joy."

Within the African-American community, there exists a cultural stock exchange of sorts, where what is being bartered and traded is black authenticity or "black sincerity," as one scholar prefers.[153] We have already alluded to the ways in which socioeconomic and sexual differences mark distinctions among blacks. Nationalism plays an important role here as well, one that allocates different amounts of black authenticity to persons of different national origins. While many blacks during the nineteenth century and even the Civil Rights Era welcomed into their ranks first- and second-generation African and Caribbean immigrants (one thinks of such black leaders as Marcus Garvey and Louis Farrakhan), today the entry fee into the field of blackness is descent, not simply from slaves, but from *American* slaves. One sociologist refers to this as the "new black nativism," which, he claims, is directly responsible for "the growing tendency to define blackness in negative terms, [as] not white in upbringing, kinship, or manner."[154]

Or consider debates about who is a "real Indian." Faced with a deluge of claims to Indian identity that began in the 1960s and only increased with the advent of affirmative action programs, American Indians, more than any other group, have had to develop strict definitions of Indian authenticity to guard against "ethnic fraud." To many, true "Indianness" requires one to be frozen in time, to walk in lockstep with one's ancestors. An African American might lose some of her blackness if she secures a high-paying job in a majority-white corporation or plays in a string quartet, but the penalty is much more severe for an American Indian, who must remain culturally untouched by modernity to be considered a "real Indian" or, more harshly, an Indian at all.[155] In James Clifford's terse words: "Life as an American [means] death as an Indian."[156]

This imperative is enforced by American Indians and non-Indians alike. Some Native Americans act as "ethnic police," making sure no outsiders get in. Disturbed by "Cherokee Grandmother Syndrome," they worry about whites and other non-Indians who "discover" their indigenous heritage (or simply lay false claim to it) to access Native-American spirituality and culture and to qualify for tribal benefits and affirmative action programs. As a result, some Native Americans have established rules or benchmarks separating "real Indians" from "imposters."[157] And to gain a sense of how non-Indians also police Indian authenticity, one need only look to court cases in which tribes hoping to "prove their tribal identity" to white judges and juries were labeled phonies on the grounds that they had traded their horses for cars, were fond of eating at fast-food restaurants, and had taken to relying too much on modern conveniences like washers and dryers and televisions. Indeed, tribes seeking federal recognition from the Office of Federal Acknowledgement (formerly the Branch of Acknowledgement and Research) must not only show they have been a tribe since 1900; they also must marshal evidence produced by non-Indian actors, such as anthropologists, historians, and journalists. The result, many have observed, is that "tribes whose memberships exhibit the most cultural and physical

Do you, in your dress, speech, or presentation of self, do things to make yourself look more (or less) Native American, Asian, Latino, white, or black?

attributes of the mythical, aboriginal 'Indian' will have the greatest likelihood of being acknowledged with federal recognition."[158]

In the final analysis, struggles over racial authenticity essentially are about who is let into the "family." And any dynamic designed with the specific intent of governing behavior and including and excluding people from a community is bound to provide deep satisfaction and meaning to those "let in" as well as a painful sense of rejection for those "kept out." When American Jews attempt to get married in Israel, only to be told by the rabbinic courts that they have to "prove their Jewishness," they often leave defeated and outraged.[159] When a Chinese-American woman is shunned by her family for not marrying a Chinese man, or when a third-generation Mexican American is teased by fellow Mexicans for not knowing Spanish, or when an Arab-American Christian is labeled "less Arab" by his Muslim relatives, it burns and often repels people from their racial or ethnic communities. Speaking of the struggles over Indian authenticity, one sociologist has observed, "So strict and unforgiving a linkage of culture and identity often leaves Indian people with a pervasive legacy of insecurity and pain. Admitting to such sentiments, moreover, may only create more 'evidence' of one's insufficient Indianness for others to attack. . . . The judgment that 'he is not one of us' is a severe enough price that many people of Indian heritage with the potential to make significant contributions to Indian communities may choose not to participate in their traditional cultures at all, rather than risk the effort and be rejected for demonstrated lack of competence. There is probably no surer recipe for extinguishing a culture than this."[160]

Rejecting Whiteness

Whites often feel left out of conversations about racial authenticity and pride. While slogans such as "Black Power" or "Chicano Pride" strike one as empowering and appropriate, "White Power" or "White Pride" are used only by racist groups like the Skinheads. A Native-American student might come to class with a button on her backpack declaring, "Indian and Proud!" But her white peers would not dare come to class with a "White and Proud!" button. Of course, when nonwhites assert a kind of racial or ethnic pride, they are driven by a fundamentally *reactionary* impulse. They are responding to white supremacy. No one would need to demand "Black power" if in reality power were evenly and justly distributed across racial groups. No one would put an "Indian Pride" bumper sticker on their truck if pride were not systematically stripped from Indians in the form of degrading social conditions (consider reservation poverty) and humiliating popular images (consider Indian mascots). Demanding "White Power" or "White Pride," by contrast, is a reaction to a reaction, a protest against a movement seeking racial justice and, therefore, would be a defense of racial domination.

As a result, some whites simply do not know what to do with their whiteness. Many wish they could stake their identity in it, just as many of their nonwhite peers lay free claim to their nonwhiteness, but they know doing so is impossible. In a way, they envy nonwhites—or at least their ability to be proud of their racial identity—and may grow resentful or ashamed. Yet, most learn to live comfortably with their whiteness and go about their lives performing whiteness. A significant minority, however, actively reject their white identity. "To be outside whiteness is to be outside the cold and instrumental realm of modernity," writes one scholar attempting to capture a popular sentiment.[161] To some, whiteness is lifeless and dull; it's sexless and oppressive and painfully normal. Nonwhiteness, by contrast, appears liberated and cool, sexy and interesting. It is, in the minds of many, more fully human. As an American teacher once told Frantz Fanon, "The presence of Negroes beside the whites is in a way an insurance policy on humanness. When the whites feel that they have become too mechanized, they turn to the men of color and ask them for a little human sustenance."[162]

Some whites take brief vacations from their whiteness, as in the case of those who travel to Mexico to participate in mock border-crossing expeditions, a growing tourist industry that promises participants the thrill and danger of what hundreds of real Mexican migrants experience every year. Others, as we alluded to earlier, discover that they have some nonwhite blood coursing through their veins, a heritage denied by their parents and grandparents in more overtly racist times, and strive to "reclaim" their nonwhite heritage. ("What the son wishes to forget," writes one historian, "the grandson wishes to remember."[163]) They undo their whiteness by changing their religious practices, dietary habits, and views on the family—or at least they change *how they understand* these things (once as "normal life," now as the "Cherokee way of life").[164]

And some whites—especially adolescents—attempt to break with their whiteness completely, taking on another racial or ethnic identity. In an ethnography of white students in a majority black school in Texas, Edward Morris discovered that whites often shed their whiteness for blackness. They wore their hair in corn-rows, sagged their jeans, tilted their caps, wore gold chains, and spoke "black English." Some white students were so skilled at passing as nonwhites that, at the beginning of his study, Morris had a hard time distinguishing the white students from their light-skinned nonwhite peers. In this school, nonwhite students used the term "white" to insult and tease those who were overly polite and nerdy. For this reason, many whites attempted to distance themselves as much as possible from their whiteness; this was doubly true of the boys, who tended to link whiteness with soft femininity. Still, this did not mean that white students lost their white privilege. Morris points out that black teachers viewed whites as good and responsible students; these teachers also were reluctant to discipline white students, though they did not hesitate to punish the latter's black and Hispanic peers.[165]

Amy Wilkins discovered similar patterns in her study of a multiracial school in Massachusetts, where some white girls turned themselves into "Puerto Rican wannabes." "The typical Puerto Rican wannabe," observes Wilkins, "rejects white middle-class cultural style, adopting an urban presentation of self associated with people of color. She wears hip-hop clothes and Puerto Rican hairstyles, drinks malt liquor and smokes Newports. She adopts an attitude, acting tough and engaging in verbal and psychical fights. And perhaps most important, she dates and has sex with Black and Puerto Rican men."[166] The Puerto Rican wannabe is criticized by whites and nonwhites alike. Whites construct the wannabes as "good (white) girls gone bad"; nonwhites view them as racially inauthentic and worry they are appropriating, not "real" Puerto Rican culture, but a distorted stereotype of that culture: a collection of negative images and risky behavior. "By participating in behaviors associated with the urban poor and calling them Puerto Rican, the wannabes perpetuate negative stereotypes about people of color. Moreover, wannabes are seen as sacrificing white privilege in favor of Puerto Rican coolness. This trade is degrading because it implies that Puerto Ricans and Blacks devalue ambition and mainstream socioeconomic success, disparaging the efforts of those Puerto Ricans and Blacks who seek upward mobility."[167]

What does it mean when young white women wear dark lip-liner, speak Spanish, and try to become Latina? What do we make of the white teenager who calls himself "white chocolate" and "acts black"? Or, for that matter, how do we make sense of Cambodian-American students who call themselves "the blacks of the Asians," address each other as "niggas," and attempt to align themselves with black students and against Latinos and whites?[168] How does this form of racial passing, one that involves a member of a relatively more privileged group adopting the style of members of a dominated group, affect racial domination? It is, in truth, hard to say. On the one hand, whites who reject their whiteness for another kind of racial performance may end up degrading the racial or ethnic group whose styles they attempt to borrow, especially if their ideas of the "blackness" or "Puerto Ricanness," for example, are nothing more than a shallow collection of stereotypes.[169] This certainly does not apply to all whites who turn their backs on whiteness, but it certainly applies to the Puerto Rican wannabes in Wilkins's study. On the other hand, racial transgression also destabilizes racial categories and unveils their social and performative essence. In this way, it has the effect of rendering racial divisions, often viewed as hard and fast—even natural—porous and bendable.

This is an important point. Racial domination orders the world into neat categories; it seeks to divide and pit those divided against one another. But, in truth, none of us are 100% anything. We are grafted onto one another and penetrated by each other's ideas, culture, and actions. The Swiss psychologist Carl Jung realized this upon visiting the United States during the height of Jim Crow. "The naïve European," he wrote, "thinks of America as a white nation. It is not wholly white, if you please; it is partly colored, [which explains] the slightly Negroid mannerisms of the American. . . . Since the Negro lives within your cities and even within your houses, he also lives within your skin, subconsciously."[170] James Baldwin made the same point some years later, saying, "Each of us, helplessly and forever, contains the other—male in female, female in male, white in black and black in white."[171]

The Problem with "Identity"

The question of one's "true identity" occupies many young minds—and many old ones as well. In fact, the hunt for one's identity might be the quintessential college experience: hence the often repeated refrain, "I found myself in college." Identity-based thinking and politics have their place and have been employed in the service of social justice, but some thinkers have begun to wonder just how useful the concept of "identity" truly is.[172] In our view, there are at least two problematic side effects of America's obsession with identity. First, talk of identity is talk about our differences, which necessarily causes further social divisions. And second, talk of identity necessarily turns our gaze inward, which may cause us to lose sight of other people's hardships. By way of conclusion, let's address each of these side effects in turn.

When we focus on identity, we focus on our differences. This encourages a person to view the world, not as a reflexive thinker who has evaluated the social-scientific evidence, but as someone with a distinct identity. Thus, people often begin their sentences with phrases like: "As a black women," or "Speaking as a gay man," or "For me, a recent immigrant, the truth is. . . ." These kinds of identity-based statements are necessary if we are discussing different experiences, but they sometimes are used to justify questionable claims about how the world works. Consider, for example, the "insider doctrine" of which American sociologist Robert Merton spoke, a doctrine holding that only members of certain groups have access, or at least privileged access, to certain knowledge about the groups to which they belong. According to this doctrine, wrote Merton, "the Outsider, no matter how careful and talented, is excluded in principle from gaining access to the social and cultural truth. In short, [the doctrine] holds that the Outsider has a structurally imposed incapacity to comprehend alien groups, statuses, cultures, and societies."[173] One's position in the racial order conditions one's perceptions—this is the whole idea behind Du Bois's theory of "double consciousness"—but an insider's vantage point *in and of itself* does not lead to scientific discoveries unavailable to the outsider. After all, one would be hard pressed to find a thinker who applied the insider doctrine to members of dominant groups, that is, who actually argued that only capitalists can advance knowledgeable claims about capitalists, men about men, or whites about whites.

"No human culture," writes Henry Louis Gates, Jr., "is inaccessible to someone who makes the effort to understand, to learn to inhabit another world."[174] Scientific insight comes by way of rigorous reflexivity and research; it is not the inevitable result of one's position in society. The notion that all whites, strictly because of their whiteness, are blind to certain dimensions of racial domination, while all nonwhites, strictly because of their nonwhiteness, are keen to these dimensions, is too simplistic a proposition. And this line of thinking may result in whites, even when they are right, repeatedly ceding expertise to nonwhites when it comes to race (as if people of color were the real experts) or in nonwhite thinkers absolving themselves of reflexive practices.

We often hear the refrain, "Respect differences." This is a fine refrain, one that should be heeded. But wouldn't a better one be, "Fight injustice"? After all, there are some differences—those that cause injustice—that should not be respected. We should not respect violence against women, even if it is justified through "cultural or religious differences." We might have to *understand* those differences to help fight violence against women, but it is not necessary to "respect" them if respect here means to leave them be. We should not respect poverty in the same way we respect Islam or Christianity; we should strive to alleviate poverty. As Walter Benn Michaels has said, "For thirty years, while the gap between the rich and the poor has grown larger, we've been urged to respect people's identities—as if the problem of poverty would be solved if we just appreciated the poor. . . . If we can stop thinking of the poor as people who have too little money and start thinking of them instead as people who have too little respect, then it's our attitude toward the poor, not their poverty, that becomes the problem to be solved, and we can focus our efforts of reform not on getting rid of classes but on getting rid of what we like to call classism. . . . The point is not that we should be nicer to the homeless; it's that no one should be homeless."[175]

Are we saying the poor do not deserve our respect? Of course not. What we are saying is this: to truly respect the poor, we should disrespect the hell out of poverty. When we shift our focus from dismantling economic injustice and exploitation to class-based identities, anti-poverty activism can dissolve into shallow talk about such identities.

The same point applies to racial domination, and this leads us to the second side effect of conversations that pivot on the concept of identity—namely, their tendency to be narcissistic. Identity is all about you. It's about your unique place in society and your membership in certain groups. Again, it is important to think through such issues, but it is equally important to be sure not to confine your thinking about racial domination to notions about your racial identity. The trouble starts when you begin to evaluate all racial statements by how much they offend you, a maneuver that places you at the center of the universe. Pretty soon, people learn how to talk about race without causing people to be offended, either by using a polite kind of empty talk with all the right words or by not saying anything at all. Honest dialogue—the kind that offends, sometimes—is swapped out for "diversity talk." And if you are at the center of the universe, then your hardships are the most important, and this kind of thinking leads to useless debates over "who has it worse," as well as to whites' resentment of antiracist policies they believe do not benefit them. There is more to life than you. Should we focus on differences or discrimination? Identity or injustice? "Races" or racial domination?

CHAPTER REVIEW

THE FAMILY SINCE COLONIALISM AND SLAVERY

family government, antimiscegenation laws, *Loving v. Virginia*, Moynihan Report, pathology of matriarchy

RACE AND THE FAMILY TODAY

sexual division of labor, racial aversion, racial fetishism, cultural labor, feminization of poverty

THE SELF AND IDENTITY FORMATION

interaction order, racial survival strategies, double consciousness, double rejection, racial authenticity

FROM THEORY TO PRACTICE

1. In the media frenzy that erupts after a school shooting, many pundits explain the shooter's actions by guessing he was raised in a "dysfunctional family." But as sociologist Katherine Newman demonstrates in her book *Rampage: The Social Roots of School Shootings,* the answer is much more complex than the conventional "blame it on the family" approach. Similarly, analyze a social problem linked to racial domination—such as racial inequality, chronic poverty, behavioral conditions, or even divorce—that many people attribute to a broken family. Explain how the "blame it on the family" approach is a necessary but not sufficient argument. Provide other explanations for the problem at hand and show how those explanations go beyond those that point only to the family.

2. Pick one interracial or cross-cultural relationship in your life and list some steps you could take to do the cultural labor necessary to deepen and enrich that relationship. Next, pick at least one item generated from your list and do the (racial) work! You might, for example, go to a Mosque with a Muslim coworker or to your roommate's majority-white church. You might read a memoir about growing up in a border town, or in South Side Chicago, or in an ethnic enclave. And so on. Finally, write about your experiences, reflecting on this idea of doing the cultural labor.

3. Analyze yourself with respect to racial identity formation. What stage of racial identity formation best describes where you are right now? Does one of the stages described in this chapter under the heading "racial identity formation" best express your current state of mind? Also, analyze how you may have changed to arrive at the stage you are at now. Finally, describe where you would like to go in the future.

4. Conducting an intersectional identity analysis, pinpoint one aspect of your identity which is "privileged." How might you benefit from your religious affiliation, sexuality, class background, and so forth? How does this privileged aspect of your identity coincide with your racial identity? Finally, in a reflexive fashion, explain at least one way your privileged identity might cause others to suffer and offer one way you might allay that suffering.

RECOMMENDED READING

- Patricia Hill Collins, *Black Feminist Thought: Knowledge, Consciousness, and the Politics of Empowerment*, Second Edition (New York: Routledge, 2000).

- Kimberle Crenshaw, "Mapping the Margins: Intersectionality, Identity Politics, and Violence against Women of Color," *Stanford Law Review* 43 (1991): 1241–1299.

- Kathryn Edin and Maria Kefalas, *Promises I Can Keep: Why Poor Women Put Motherhood before Marriage* (Berkeley and Los Angeles: University of California Press, 2005).

- Jennifer Lee and Frank Bean, "America's Changing Color Lines: Immigration, Race/Ethnicity, and Multiracial Identification," *Annual Review of Sociology* 30 (2004): 221–242.

- Ann Rawls, "'Race' as an Interaction Order Phenomenon: W. E. B. DuBois's 'Double Consciousness' Thesis Revisited," *Sociological Theory* (2002) 18: 241–274.

- Michael Rosenfeld, *The Age of Independence: Interracial Unions, Same-Sex Unions, and the Changing American Family* (Cambridge: Harvard University Press, 2007).

PART THREE

RECONSTRUCTION

SINCE KNOWLEDGE IS INSEPARABLE FROM LIFE—THAT IS, FROM PRACTICAL affairs and the struggle to change them for the better—this final section of the book is inseparable from those that came before. That is, it continues an arc that began with our efforts to think in reflexive and historical ways about race, the topic of Part One, and that proceeded with an examination of the relational settings, or fields of life, in which racial domination takes place, the topic of Part Two. In this concluding Part Three, we explore how you can join others in the fight against racial domination.

By "reconstruction" we speak not of the thirteen years that followed the Civil War—and we are well aware of the baggage this word carries in much of the South—but of the act of employing the knowledge you have acquired about racial domination in concerted efforts to overturn it. This requires, first, reconstructing how we think about race in our own lives, and second, using our sharpened analysis to reconstruct how race is discussed—and lived—in society at large. This work can be carried on through different methods and in different settings, from your family's dinner table to the corridors of power in Washington, D.C. In other words, reconstruction of our racial order is a comprehensive endeavor, one encompassing both small-scale interactions and large-scale social and cultural structures.

Reconstruction is an idea borrowed from the well-established philosophical tradition of American pragmatism. It builds on the pragmatist insight that knowledge is not simply a bundle of facts but a tool—a weapon—to be deployed in addressing urgent problems of the day. Knowledge proves its mettle not in the cataloguing of data or the fabrication of abstract theories but in effectiveness in dealing with practical affairs and problematic life-circumstances. The pragmatists called for knowledge relevant to the task of reorganizing or, in their terminology, *reconstructing* experience: making our lives together more just, democratic, and enriching (in the fullest sense of that word).

To engage in effective practical action aimed at overturning racial domination, however, you must also have some sense—and the more explicit that sense, the better—of what a society without racial domination might look like. You must have, in other words, not only an idea of the means with which to struggle on behalf of a reconstructed racial order but also an idea of the ends for which you are struggling. And that, too, is one of our concerns in this final part of the work. As we engage in reflection on what the means *and* the ends of racial reconstruction might entail, we invite you to think about your own vision for society and what can—and must—be done to realize that vision. What are the ends informing your own actions in our racialized world? And by what means are you seeking—and should others seek—to make those ends a lived reality?

Chapter 11

Toward Racial Justice

A Life, Engaged

No, you weren't there. You weren't there when European tradesmen kidnapped families from Africa and dragged them across the ocean, tossing the dead and sick overboard, to be separated and shackled, branded and beaten and worked from dawn till dust. It wasn't your idea to destroy American Indians' way of life, to steal their land, to outlaw their religion, to enforce a system of colonization that brought them to extinction's cliff-edge. "Manifest Destiny" was not your cry; you did not load your guns and push the people of Mexico back until Texas and California were ours. You had nothing to do with America's racist citizenship requirements, which tore so many Asian families apart and led to the brutal exploitation of Asian workers. It wasn't your idea. Blood is not on your hands.

It is true: none of us is personally or directly responsible for the wrongs inflicted by—or to—our ancestors. But all of us are responsible for repairing the damage, for cleaning up the mess. Why? Because responsibility is more—so much more—than simply our duty to answer for deeds we ourselves commit. We can distinguish between **personal** and **civic responsibility**.[1] Personal responsibility is connected to things directly asked of you and wrongs you have committed. If you are a student, it is your personal responsibility to attend lectures and complete assignments; if you steal your roommate's iPod, it is your personal responsibility to return it and make things right.

Civic responsibility, in contrast, is connected to your ability—your power—to change your community and beyond. Whereas personal responsibility has to do with your connection to the *problem,* civic responsibility is about your connection to the *solution.* If a heavy storm causes a levee to break and flood waters to come rushing toward your town, you are not personally responsible for the flood, of course, but you are civically responsible for protecting your town and its citizens. It is not the levee but the sandbag that has your name on it.

The idea of civic responsibility implies we have an obligation to people other than ourselves and our close friends and family. It means we have an obligation to justice; that we are responsible for the dispossessed. This fact remains even if we had nothing to do with bringing about their dispossession. But, honestly, how many of us—white and nonwhite alike—can claim to have nothing to do with the suffering of others?

You are not personally responsible for racial domination, you say? You weren't there at the beginning, that's true enough. But, as we learned in the opening pages of this book, accumulation and disaccumulation, privilege and disadvantage, are inseparable. Where were your shoes, shirt, and underwear made? Didn't part of the money you paid at Foot Locker or Target find its way into the pockets of exploiters running sweatshops in Chinatown or on the Mexican border? Do you water your lawn with water drained from the Hopi Reservation? Do you clean your apartment with chemicals developed in the poor black communities of the Mississippi Delta? Where does your trash go? Is it dumped near the Skull Valley Reservation? Do you secure a feeling of safety by backing "tough on crime" politicians, who build more prisons and lengthen mandatory sentences, causing poor blacks and Latinos to bear the brunt of their scourge? Do you wallow only in your own oppression, refusing to reach out to—or even to notice—other people under the hard heel of domination? Do you believe that your pain is greatest, a conviction that only fortifies racial domination by eroding the possibility of interracial and interethnic coalitions and causing rifts between blacks and Latinos, Chinese and Koreans, poor whites and poor American Indians? Perhaps, when it comes to racial domination, personal and civic responsibility are not so easily divorced. Perhaps our hands are not as clean as we once thought.

"But I have done nothing!" you protest. Exactly: You have done nothing. And doing nothing in the face of oppression is equivalent to doing something, a very large something, to help the oppressors. Today, racial domination persists, not only because politicians and businessmen exploit racial divisions for their own gain but also because millions of us, busy with our own lives, hunker down in the shade, indifferent to the suffering of others. We might hope for the best, but we refuse to "stand in the bright sun and cast a long shadow." As Elie Wiesel once said, "The opposite of love is not hate; it's indifference. The opposite of beauty is not ugliness; it's indifference. The opposite of faith is not heresy; it's indifference. And the opposite of life is not death, but indifference between life and death."[2] You can drop bombs on civilian targets without being the one who pushes the button. You can incarcerate thousands of black men without sitting on the jury. You can contribute to the suffering of America's immigrants without ever doing the deporting yourself. If you fill your belly while someone sitting next to you goes hungry, do you not contribute to their hunger? How is it any different when the distance between you and the starved is increased? Indifference is never neutrality; it is loyalty to the powerful.[3] To quote Lorraine Hansberry, the great African-American playwright, "The acceptance of our present condition is the only form of extremism that discredits us before our children."[4]

Indifference sometimes is the product of ignorance. Some people simply do not know the nature and depth of the problem. But we no longer can claim ignorance. Having read this book and participated in this course, you know much more about racial domination than the average American. In fact, you know more about racial domination than the average sociologist! You know its origin and history and how it penetrates all of society's fields of life, from the political and economic realms to the worlds of associations and intimate relationships. You have learned how to study racial domination as a social analyst, treating it as a complex social construction that deserves to be understood as thoroughly as possible. No claims of living in an era "beyond racism," you have learned from the evidence, are truthful. Hopefully, you have developed the ability critically to analyze and objectify racial domination in your own life and in your communities.

So, what do we do with all this knowledge? What is to be done? And what, exactly, is it that we want? What would a racially just society look like, and how can we each do our part to bring it forth? Indifference is not an option; neither are colorblindness and other fantasies of racial naiveté. Where, then, do we go from here? This chapter leads the way. We begin with a discussion of ends, some goals toward which we ought to strive, followed by a discussion of the means, strategies for achieving those goals. To put it another way, this chapter addresses two questions: What is it we wish to achieve; and how do we achieve it?

What Are the Goals?

Many whites believe that racial equality already has been achieved, while many nonwhites hold that little has changed since the Civil Rights Movement and that things may be getting worse.[5] One side declares, "Racial harmony has arrived." The other side replies, "Racial harmony will never come." But the truth, as Confucius liked to say, lies somewhere in the middle. Two things are undeniable: that racial progress in America has been nothing short of astounding and that racial domination in America has yet to be dismantled. As one sociologist has put it, "It can be said, unconditionally, that the changes that have taken place in the United States over the past fifty years are unparalleled in the history of minority-majority relations. . . . There does not exist a single case in modern or early history that comes anywhere near the record of America in changing majority

Percentage of Americans Favoring Segregated Neighborhoods

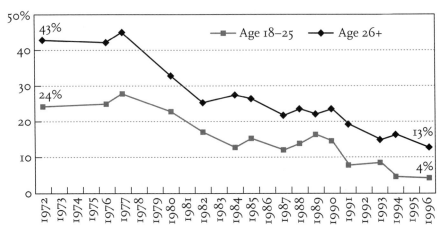

attitudes, in guaranteeing legal and political rights, and in expanding socioeconomic opportunities for its disadvantaged minorities."[6] If we refuse to recognize this fact, we foster an angry spirit of cynicism and nihilism, a spirit of hopelessness that causes whites and nonwhites to throw up their hands and conclude, "If racial equality is hopeless, then why should we do anything to fight it?"

Change *has* come to America. Indeed, some ethnic conflicts viewed as intractable and eternal a mere one hundred years ago hardly exist today. One thinks, for example, of the conflict between Protestants and Catholics, or between Irish and Italians. The historical record demonstrates that what one generation found unrealistic and impossible—idealistic—the succeeding generation made into reality.[7] "What is considered impossible today may be possible tomorrow," observe the authors of *White-Washing Race*. "It is well to remember that in the 1950s few Americans believed that a revolution in civil rights was just around the corner. Jim Crow seemed to be deeply entrenched, racial prejudice too formidable a presence in the minds of white Americans. Yet many people of all races vigorously opposed segregation anyway, not because they knew they would prevail but because they believed that doing so was morally necessary. And in the end they did prevail."[8]

"That's the true genius of America: that America can change. Our union can be perfected. What we've already achieved gives us hope for what we can and must achieve tomorrow." So said Barack Obama on the night he was elected the 44th President of the United States. The election of President Obama was a historic event of global, not just national, significance, for in many other democracies—from France and Israel to Italy and Nigeria—the election of a racial minority to the country's highest political office would be virtually impossible.

One commentator reporting from Gaza summed up the moment this way: "From far away, this is how it looks: There is a country out there where tens of millions of white Christians, voting freely, select as their leader a black man of modest origin, the son of a Muslim. There is a place on Earth—call it America— where such a thing happens."[9] America can change, and it often transforms itself more quickly and drastically on many counts—including race relations— than other developed nations.

We cannot deny the progress of the past, just as we cannot turn a blind eye to the problems of the present—or the pregnant promise of the future. This book has documented thoroughly the troubles of today, but what does the future hold? What do we *want* it to hold? Social science is able to provide a much-needed picture of alternative realities. It can, in a phrase, present us with **real utopias.** Creative and radical alternatives for society "grounded in the real potentials of humanity" as well as in social-scientific and historical research, real utopias are intellectually rigorous, carefully designed blueprints for a better tomorrow.[10] They are the end products of social change; they are realistic renderings of a society more just, equal, and moral than the one we currently inhabit. Real utopias are hopeful but not naïve; realistic but not cynical. They are what Karl Marx had in mind when he spoke of real or "human emancipation" of the working class; what America's founding fathers envisioned when they longed for "a more perfect union"; of what Martin Luther King, Jr., dreamed when he referred to "the promised land."

To work toward racial justice, we must know precisely what we are working toward. Accordingly, in what follows, we sketch three goals, three real utopias, connected to the dismantling of racial domination. This discussion is not a venture in prediction, the stuff of social forecasting; rather, it is an exercise of the imagination. Nor do we paint a complete picture of what a racially just society might look like, a project too rich and expansive for our purposes here. We simply sketch what we believe are three ends essential to the ascension of racial justice, inviting you to fill in the details and, with us, to imagine further possibilities.

A Society Where Racial Domination Is Addressed Intelligently

We use the term *intelligence* deliberately, for what is called for is precisely an application of intelligence in the philosophic sense of that term. To philosophers, intelligence has to do with one's ability to exercise good judgment in a world full of uncertainty. As John Dewey wrote in *The Quest for Certainty,* a person "is intelligent . . . in virtue of his capacity to estimate the possibilities of a situation and to act in accordance with his estimate."[11] For Dewey, our ability to solve the problems we confront was directly connected to our ability accurately to assess those problems and to develop different courses of action.

American sociologist Charles Cooley, a contemporary of Dewey, added that "the test of intelligence is the power to act successfully in new situations. We judge a man to be intelligent when we see that in going through the world he is not guided merely by routine or second-hand ideas, but that when he meets a fresh difficulty he thinks out a fresh line of action appropriate to it, which is justified by its success. . . . It is, then, essentially a kind of foresight, a mental reaction that anticipates the operation of the forces at work and is prepared in advance to adjust itself to them."[12]

Racial domination, like all forms of domination, relies on a tangled collection of distortions, illogic, and lies sometimes misrecognized as truth. Logic, rational decision making, and good sense—the execution of a **racial intelligence**—can shine a bright and revealing light on the obfuscation linked to racial domination; it can lay bare the true nature of the beast. Racial intelligence can promote a political climate where people desire—need—to know the best and latest information on the pressing problems of the day; and it can lead to successful resolution of those problems. We imagine an opening of the American mind, where ideas and science are treated seriously and with respect and where people realize the power of clear thinking. As Kurt Lewin remarked over fifty years ago, "Nothing is more practical than a good theory."[13]

As we already have pointed out, freedom and knowledge, liberation and rational awareness, are welded together. One cannot exist without the other. "Freedom," wrote C. Wright Mills, "is not merely the chance to do as one pleases; neither is it merely the opportunity to choose between set alternatives. Freedom is, first of all, the chance to formulate the available choices, to argue over them—and then, the opportunity to choose. That is why freedom cannot exist without an enlarged role of human reason in human affairs. . . . The social task of reason [, therefore,] is to formulate choices, to enlarge the scope of human decisions in the making of history."[14] Freedom, in a word, goes hand in hand with intelligence, the ability to spread wide your horizon of possibilities and to make sound judgments in respect of them.

In a society such as ours, so filled with misleading language and technologies of mystification, acting intelligently—that is, actively seeking truth rather than passively accepting this or that party line—is itself a powerful political act. Mills knew this well. Not only did he seek, as a public sociologist, to foster critical thinking in the American citizenry as a whole, but he also noted, with respect to more specialized research, that "the very enterprise of social science, as it determines fact, takes on political meaning. In a world of widely communicated nonsense, any statement of fact is of political and moral significance. All social scientists, by the fact of their existence, are involved in the struggle between enlightenment and obscurantism. In such a world as ours, to practice social science is, first of all, to practice the politics of truth."[15]

"The politics of truth?" mocks the cynic. "What is truth?" The question, first of all, is anything but modern, let alone *post*modern, as many would have it. It is, in fact, rather old—and stale. In the biblical account, for example, Pontius Pilate posed the question to Jesus more than 2,000 years ago, before washing his hands, indifferent, and crucifying him. That was no coincidence. For wherever the question, "What is truth?" or, more brashly, the declaration, "There is no truth!" is uttered, indifference, the washing of one's hands of the problem, is nearby. If there is no right or wrong *answer,* so the logic goes, then there is no right or wrong *action.* Is there no better recipe for indifference? The notion that all truth is relative and forever beyond our reach is thoroughly misguided and ought to be discarded. Besides, those who apply such reasoning to the social world would not dare do so to the natural one. The world remains round whether or not you think it so, just as insulin helps diabetics live longer regardless of whether or not you believe this to be true.

Reducing hard-earned facts to "mere words" or "relative truths" is a travesty and an affront to struggles on behalf of racial justice. There *is* a difference between opinion and truth. The latter is those opinions that have been subjected to what Dewey called "the test of consequences," assertions that have been examined and tested and determined collectively and systematically to have warrant.[16] Not all opinions are equal; some are quite wrong and ought to be labeled as such. A black working-class man might perceive that Mexican immigrants are "stealing his job," but that, according to the best available evidence, would be wrong. The evidence also leads us to conclude, contrary to popular belief, that white men have *not* been harmed by affirmative action and that the prison boom has *not* led to a decrease in violent crime. If we believe otherwise, we ought to be corrected. In a democracy, our ideas matter; so we had better get them straightened out, submitting our opinions to the best available evidence, which is usually the way it is done in social science.

A society of racial intelligence would look quite different from the one we have today, in the domains both of everyday life and of high-level policy-making. In everyday life, citizens would, as a matter of disposition, approach problems and conflicts not in terms of their received prejudices and opinions but in a more open-ended, experimentalist spirit, setting alternative proposed solutions to the pragmatic test and seeing what works and what doesn't in furthering a more just and harmonious experience.

In high-level policy-making, there would be what German philosopher Jürgen Habermas has termed a **"scientization of politics and public opinion,"** that is, a situation in which "scientific experts advise the decision makers and [in which] politicians consult scientists in accordance with practical needs."[17] Habermas understood that a relationship of mutual respect between intellectuals and politicians would push us toward a more rational society. Communication between the two parties, he observed, "is like a net of rational discussion stretching between practice and science."[18] In such a world, our politicians would have the best data at their disposal and, crucially, would *want* to be better informed. Political rhetoric would not be chock full of coded language, buzzwords, and manipulations; the days of the political spokesperson adept at dodging questions and masking truth would come to an end. The politics of distortion and extremism would be replaced by a politics educated by history and social science in the same way that modern medicine is educated by chemistry and biology or that modern architecture is educated by physics and engineering.

What is more, instead of making it difficult "for Americans to know what they are up to," politicians would encourage transparency and openness. As political scientists Jacob Hacker and Paul Pierson have written, "Citizens can discipline extraordinarily powerful public figures, just as ordinary consumers in a competitive marketplace can discipline extraordinarily large private corporations. But for competition—whether political or economic—to work, it must be fair. Basic information must be available and accessible, and 'consumers' must have real and effective opportunities to reject 'products' on the basis of that information."[19] We are envisioning a society in which all citizens—from teachers and engineers to domestic workers and truck drivers—would be informed and educated. They would participate in a politics of reason, where their opinions would be tempered by intelligence and the cool-headed evaluation of the best available information. And they would possess a "radical doubt," a skepticism sharpened by the scientific enterprise that would help them better to distinguish truth from falsehood.[20]

This is not a real utopia where the philosopher replaces the king. This is no ivy-league elitist (or scholastic) fantasy. It is, simply, a picture of a world in which people allow, finally, intelligence and rationality—not self-interest or ignorance, not blind opinions or tradition or ideology—to govern their conduct. This goal, this end, is a revolution of ideas, and it constitutes the first and most fundamental step toward crushing racial domination.

A Society That Embraces Racial Justice

Because racial domination has been such a central feature of American society since its inception, it might be difficult to imagine an America where racial justice finally has come to replace injustice. Some people have given up trying.[21] But there is no surer way to guarantee racial domination's continued reign than to conceive of it as intractable and eternal. Imagining alternatives to how we should live is itself a small act of resistance, one that refuses to settle for the world we have inherited and that firmly rejects the defeatist claim, "This is how it is, and how it has always been, so get used to it." Having read this far, you are well versed in the nature of racial injustice in America; but what might a racially just society look like? It would take another book—several others, really—to answer this question thoroughly. But, in what follows, we imagine some real utopias for each of the fields of life reviewed in the previous chapters, in an exercise intended to pry open our imaginations and to stretch the limits of what we believe to be possible.

In the political field, racial justice would come with the advent of a more powerful multicultural democracy, one that lives up to its name (literally, "the rule of the people").[22] Because there is no genuine democracy in societies that muzzle dissenting voices, the new American democracy would value and welcome criticism and would promote (not erode) people's political freedom. Patriotism would be measured by the extent to which we critically evaluate our society and strive to change things for the better—not the extent to which we nod "yes" to everything party officials say. Current systems of "taxation without representation" would come to an end, as poor communities of color, as well as ex-felons, would enjoy political representation that matches that of wealthy white suburbanites. Why, after all, should we settle for a country controlled by a small group of elite citizens instead of a nation where the voice of a single mother scraping by in Gary, Indiana matters just as much as that of the CEO of New York City's most powerful hedge fund company? How can we accept a society in which "the fullness of freedom [is reserved] for those whose income, leisure, and security need no enhancing, and a mere pittance of liberty [is reserved] for the people, who may in vain attempt to make use of their democratic rights to gain shelter from the [powerful]?"[23] In a racially just society, democracy would triumph over oligarchy, and substantive representation would best superficial representation. Appointed officials would be intimately connected to the needs and problems of all citizens, including those living in disadvantaged nonwhite communities. This might require abandoning America's two-party system—the only one of its kind in the democratic world—for a political system where one does not have to choose between Democrats and Republicans. It would most certainly require the revitalization of a powerful and multicultural Civil Rights Movement.[24]

Racial justice in the economic field would mean, first, the complete and total eradication of racialized poverty. "Impossible," whispers the cynic. But why? In a racially just society, the gap between the rich and the poor would narrow, as would income and wealth disparities across race. The simultaneous extraction of immigrant labor and retraction of immigrant rights would cease. America would develop fair policies that treat its poor immigrants as much more than simply an expendable and cheap labor force. Concerns about people trying to survive, no matter their race or nationality, would replace those about borders sketched by the colonizer's hand. And America would help countries such as

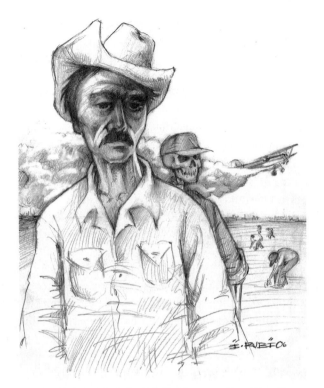

In a racially just society, the simultaneous extraction of immigrant labor and retraction of immigrant rights would cease, and America would develop fair policies that treat its poor immigrants as much more than simply an expendable and cheap labor force.

Mexico revitalize their economy and reduce their poverty, instead of treating those countries as staging grounds where companies can relocate their factories and pay workers a substandard wage. Finally, the skimpy American welfare state—in large part responsible for the millions of citizens living hand-to-mouth today[25]—would expand by generous proportions, such that "the primary obligation of the state" would be to "use its powers and allocate its resources to eradicate poverty and hunger and to assure security of livelihood, security against the major hazards and vicissitudes of life, and the security of decent homes."[26] The welfare state would rise up to exert control over the free market, making sure to protect vulnerable citizens from its erratic whims. In a neoliberal society, the people are controlled by the market; in a racially just democracy, the market would be controlled by the people. The new American welfare state would guarantee people a livable wage; affordable housing; free health care for all; and secure retirement plans. There is good reason to believe that racialized poverty could be considerably reduced if poor communities of color were offered a New Deal comparable to the one offered whites before and after World War II.[27]

A residential field guided by racial justice would not be scarred by drastic segregation but would promote racial integration and multicultural community. More important, it would eliminate the problems associated with racial segregation, such as chronic poverty, educational inequality, and imbalanced political representation. The American state would initiate massive investment in the nation's poorest communities and would nourish and promote self-development and sustainable economic growth on American Indian reservations. Those living in more affluent areas would use their affluence to help others in need, instead of building higher fences. Housing discrimination would be shut down. And we would develop cleaner and more energy-efficient ways to live, so as not to burden poor, nonwhite communities with our trash and pollution.

One of the most racially unjust institutions today is the American criminal justice system. While nonwhites have made gains in the economic and educational fields in the past twenty years, they have lost ground in the legal realm, as evidenced by the gross racial discrepancies in our prison population. In a racially just society, those discrepancies would disappear, as would all forms of racial profiling as well as the pervasive spirit of racialized fear that links blackness to criminality and Arabness to terrorism. If "tough on crime" policies have not made us safer, as the evidence suggests, then we would abandon those policies in favor of more effective and cost-efficient ones. We must think beyond the prison walls, developing alternatives to incarceration that not only decrease racial inequality in punishment but also, unlike our current program of mass incarceration, actually work to decrease crime. A racially just society would mount a proactive assault on the root causes of criminal behavior, instead of relying singularly on reactive programs of harsh punishment. The result would be a safer America—where cities no longer have "streets you shouldn't drive down" or "bad areas of town"—as well as an expansion of freedom in poor nonwhite communities previously subjected to drastic policing measures.

With respect to education, making higher education more affordable— perhaps even free—would open up opportunities for thousands of people, including many people of color, who currently are excluded from the privileges many others enjoy. If freedom is intertwined with intelligence, and intelligence is well cultivated through higher education, then why should college be limited only to those who can afford it plus a relatively small number of underprivileged students who scrape and claw for scholarships? What is more, a racially just society would invest in its poor schools, so that the education a child receives in a wealthy suburb of Los Angeles would not be vastly superior to the one a child receives in Compton. And a racially just society would critically reconstruct its curriculum, replacing Eurocentric accounts of history, art, politics, and philosophy with a more accurate, well-rounded, and multi-cultural program of studies.

In the same vein, the racist aesthetic would be swept out of the aesthetic field by an artistic revolution led by nonwhite and white artists alike, who would renounce caricatured and stereotypical depictions of people of color, as well as distorted and uncomplicated renderings of racism. In their own work, artists would represent people of color in their full humanity, escaping the white gaze and pushing forward our critiques of racial domination much farther than they have been pushed before. Art of this nature, art upholding an antiracist aesthetic, would be richly rewarded.

In a racially just society, our associations would be guided not by the principle of homophily but by an ethic of multiculturalism. Through our associations, we would breach racial and ethnic boundaries instead of reifying them. Hate groups would be a thing of the past; and the Internet would become a conduit through which radical multicultural democracy flourishes and expands its reach. Religious associations would flourish as institutions of justice and equality and would work to foster a spirit of civic responsibility and mutual connectedness. More broadly, a racially just society would entail the galvanization of civil society, where citizens would be involved and deeply invested in community affairs, voting and participating more fully in the political process and working together to fight racial injustice and strengthen nonwhite communities that, for decades, have been overlooked by political elites.

Finally, in the intimate field, a racially just society would disallow stigmas from being attached to interracial marriages. All consenting adults would be free to marry whomsoever they chose, unbound by family and community prejudices or by unjust laws. Aggressive programs would be developed to help single mothers and to abolish the feminization of poverty. The majority of citizens would enthusiastically embrace the concept of "doing the (racial) work." Citizens would cultivate their intercultural competence and their desire to understand the world through multiple perspectives, admitting that, on some occasions, their vision of the world may be neither universal nor correct. As a result, everyday interactions between blacks and Jews, Jews and Muslims, Latinos and whites, whites and American Indians, American Indians and Asians, and so forth, would be defined not by anxiety, anger, or fear but by mutual respect and kindness. Whites would deny their white privilege and use the advantages granted them by racial domination to work on behalf of racial justice. Rejecting feelings of superiority as well as white guilt, both of which stifle positive action, they would embrace a healthy white identity. Nonwhites would abandon any form of ethnic chauvinism and would *decolonize their minds,* evicting from their thinking all traces of internalized white supremacy. No longer would a nonwhite mother fret over her morning cup of coffee about the day her daughter learns that her society deems her less important than her peers with paler skin.

All these ends, these real utopian possibilities, are distant, to be sure, but they are not beyond our collective reach. Like the first flowers of spring after a long hard winter, changes promoting racial justice already are sprouting up all across the nation. The stigma of interracial marriage has been weakened; some American Indian Nations successfully have pulled themselves out of destitution; the Alternatives to Incarceration Movement has developed many practical forms of punishment that have nothing to do with a prison cell; chronic poverty has declined by sizeable margins over the last century. We still have a long row to hoe, but the work has already begun—and we have started to reap some fruits of the harvest.

Since the collapse of the Civil Rights Movement, most of our foot soldiers simply have not known where next to march.[28] During Jim Crow, racial domination was obvious and legal; there was a clear enemy (segregation) and a clear goal (desegregation). But today, racial domination can be more elusive and complicated; it can be ghostlike and difficult to confront. There is a good deal of truth to this, but, as we have seen throughout this book, today racial domination influences all of society's fields of life; its consequences are devastating and, in many cases, its presence undeniable. There are tangible problems in need of tangible solutions. A revitalized Civil Rights Movement—uncompromisingly egalitarian, intersectional, and multicultural—is needed. In the preceding paragraphs, we have offered some direction to that movement, ends it can pursue and, in some cases, is pursuing today. But we have not begun to scratch the surface with respect to envisioning racial justice in America. Much more can be said—and we invite you to say it. You might agree with some of our ideas and disagree with others. But one point is undeniable: we must never become numb to the now; we must never allow ourselves to be lulled into mistaking the present for the permanent; we cannot permit our minds to be closed to the real possibilities tomorrow offers. We can—and must—do better.

A Society That Values and Practices Multiculturalism

Multiculturalism—defined by Habermas as "the equal co-existence of different cultural forms of life within one and the same political community"[29]—is one specific way in which people (especially those belonging to marginalized groups) can be incorporated into society. In his book, *The Civil Sphere*, Jeffrey Alexander juxtaposes multiculturalism to two other modes of incorporation: assimilation and hyphenation.[30]

Assimilation.   **Assimilation** is the age-old American ideal of the melting pot, in which out-groups lose their distinctive identities over time and gradually become absorbed in a preexisting, overarching American identity. The melting pot metaphor was first used in print by a French visitor to America named J. Hector St. John de Crevecoeur, who wrote: "What then is the American, this new man?" He is the one who, "leaving behind him all his ancient prejudices and manners, receives new ones from the new mode of life he has embraced, the government he obeys, and the new rank he holds. He becomes an American by being received in the broad lap of our great Alma Mater. Here individuals of all nations are melted into a new race of men, whose labors and posterity will one day cause great changes in the world."[31] Crevecoeur's words were penned in 1782, during the early years of the American Republic. It was not until the early twentieth century, however, that the metaphor of the melting pot became widely known in the United States. Recall that this was a time of accelerated immigration to the United States, when many new immigrants came from Southern, Central, and Eastern Europe. In 1908, a Jewish playwright named Israel Zangwill wrote a play called *The Melting Pot,* in which a character, an immigrant, made this noteworthy declaration: "Understand that America is God's Crucible, the great Melting-Pot where all the races of Europe are melting and reforming! A fig for your feuds and vendettas! Germans and Frenchmen, Irishmen and Englishmen, Jews and Russians—into the Crucible with you all! God is making the American."[32]

With the premiere of Zengwill's play, the term "melting pot" passed into the American vernacular and became an integral part of Americans' self-image. It continues to be used today. Almost from the beginning, however, there was ambiguity as to what the term meant. Was the "melting together" that was to take place a mutually transformative process, such that new arrivals on American shores would alter the cultural lives of those who had come before, just as the old-timers would transform the identities and mores of the newcomers? Or was the process to work in one direction only, with newer immigrants shedding their previous identities while the "native stock," and its dominant culture, remained unchanged?

The realities of American social life dictated that the latter would become the predominant interpretation. Assimilation would mean that "members of out-groups [would be], in principle, allowed to become members of the society on the condition that they [kept] their stigmatized qualities hidden behind the wall of private life."[33] "You may enter," said the assimilationist, "but only if you leave your old ways behind. You have nothing to teach us; our ways are better than yours. If you'd like to join us, you have to check your culture at the door." One influential spokesperson for assimilationism was Edward A. Ross, one of the key figures of early twentieth-century American social thought. In his view, the "native stock" of white, Anglo-Saxon, British-origin Americans would become, as his critic, Horace Kallen would put it, "the measure and the standard of American that the newcomer [was] to attain . . . by virtue of being heir of the oldest *rooted* economic settlement and spiritual tradition of the white man in America."[34]

Another spokesperson was Robert Park, noted leader of the Chicago School of urban sociology and, in his youth, a publicist and ghostwriter for Booker T. Washington. "In the relations of races," Park asserted, "there is a cycle of events which tends everywhere to repeat itself."[35] This cycle consisted in four sequential stages: contact, conflict, accommodation, and assimilation. At first, when large racial groups came into contact, contestation and competition occurred. Then, after some time, a certain asymmetrical, hierarchical arrangement came to prevail—one of accommodation—in which one race was dominant and the other(s) dominated. However, in the end, assimilation resulted: "Every nation, upon examination, turns out to have been a more or less successful melting pot."[36] Park's view of the "race relations cycle" was less Anglo-centric and more upbeat than that of Ross. (In this respect, it recalled Zangwill's optimistic vision.) For years, sociologists would learn to think of race and ethnicity in its terms.

It is an interesting question—one we leave you to ponder—whether the assimilationist ideal persists in altered form even today, with the "measure and standard," of course, no longer being restricted to Americans of British stock. Do some Americans still believe in something like a "conformity to 'American-ness'" (as in Ross)? Do they still hold to some evolutionist idea of assimilation coming at the end of a trajectory or cycle of race relations (as in Park)? Do they still believe in some variant or other of the old vision of America as a melting pot? Do they still require outsiders who seek inclusion in American life to separate themselves from their outsider qualities, that is, to be purified by climbing into the skin of the insider and publicly accepting her or his traditions, language, religion, and worldview as their own?

Hyphenation. Whatever the answer, assimilation, as a principle and ideal, does not stand alone as a framework for incorporation. Alexander also mentions **hyphenation.** As he explains it, hyphenation, in contrast to assimilation, *does* tolerate outsiders' qualities and so is less rigid than assimilation. However, it also resembles assimilation in that, while tolerating outsiders' qualities, it continues to stigmatize them. What is incorporated under the model of hyphenation is the different person but not her or his different qualities. The latter are still excluded. Hyphenation thus encourages a kind of hybridization (the amalgamation of half-alien/half-citizen) and thereby functions as a midway point between assimilation and multiculturalism.[37]

In scholarly debates, hyphenation sometimes has gone under the banner of "cultural pluralism." The idea harkens back to yet another important thinker of the early twentieth century, Horace Kallen, who wrote about it in an essay published in 1915, "Democracy versus the Melting-Pot." Criticizing Ross's brand of assimilationism, Kallen proposed by contrast a model of "multiplicity in . . . unity, an orchestration of mankind." How many times have you heard it said of America that it is not like a melting pot but a salad bowl? For Kallen, it was like a musical ensemble (different imagery, same idea). "As in an orchestra," he wrote, "every type of instrument has its specific timbre and tonality, founded in its substance and form; as every type has its appropriate theme and melody in the whole symphony, so in society each ethnic group is the natural instrument, its spirit and culture are its theme and melody, and the harmony and disso-nances and discords of them all make the symphony of civilization, with this difference: a musical symphony is written before it is played; in the symphony of civilization the playing is the writing, so that there is nothing so fixed and inevitable about its progressions as in music, so that within the limits set by nature they may vary at will, and the range and variety of the harmonies may become wider and richer and more beautiful." Kallen concluded this passage—and the essay itself—with one additional sentence: "But the question is, do the dominant classes in America want such a society?"[38]

There were two difficulties with Kallen's ideal of the hyphenated, culturally pluralistic society. First, this ideal depicts his ethnic groups—the different instru-ments of his orchestra—as, for their own part, inert and unchanging entities, fixed in their essential traits and characteristics and basically unvarying over time. It also takes these ethnic groups as internally homogeneous and undif-ferentiated and, therefore, is vulnerable to the charge of reification. And second, Kallen's ideal centers itself (as had Ross's ideal of assimilationism) on a process involving only European immigrants. It has nothing whatsoever to say about the massive obstacles hindering the incorporation of nonwhites, problems (in our own terminology) of racial domination. Kallen restricted his concerns, in fact, to what he termed the "Atlantic migration," leaving out of that phrase any reference at all to the Atlantic passage of millions of enslaved Africans.

Although individual members of racialized groups sometimes are labeled (or label themselves) in hyphenated terms, as in the label "Asian-American," the hyphenation model never has succeeded entirely in overcoming the two difficulties faced by Kallen's work, namely, the problems of reification and of race. Nor has it broken entirely free of the assimilationism against which it originally defined itself. For, as Alexander explains it, "Hyphenation is often perceived as a temporary situation, as something that will disappear as mem-bers of insider and outsider groups are absorbed into a more universal, if still culturally distinctive national community. Hyphenated incorporation is a pro-cess, a means rather than an end."[39] These difficulties inherent in the hyphen-ation framework "can be overcome," Alexander continues, "only by moving beyond hyphenation to a multicultural mode that is different not only in degree but in kind."[40]

Multiculturalism. **Multiculturalism,** by contrast to the two previous ways of thinking about incorporation, breaks sharply with assimilationist logic. It welcomes both the outsider *and* her or his qualities. "Multiculturalism dramatically expands the range of imagined life experiences for core-group members. In doing so, it opens up the possibility not just for acceptance and toleration but for understanding and recognition. Insofar as such understandings are achieved, rigid distinctions between core and out-group members break down, and notions of the particular and the universal become much more thoroughly intertwined."[41] In its purest form, multiculturalism abolishes ethnic hierarchies and racial domination. All people, whites and nonwhites, immigrants and native-born citizens, are not simply tolerated; they are valued and, as much as possible, are understood—their differences and similarities acknowledged, accepted, and welcomed.

Let us take a moment to ponder multiculturalism, not only as a partly and selectively realized reality (which it is) but also as a real utopia. Much has been written about it, in a vast and exciting literature that spans philosophy, political theory, cultural studies, as well as sociology. Here we can offer only a few brief ideas. To begin with, in multicultural theory, the ideal America is not one in which all citizens dissolve into a single national identity, an America that would only reproduce the worldviews and lifestyles of the dominant groups. On the contrary, it is a world of multicultural incorporation that rests on two key principles: first, that, drawn shoulder to shoulder in common humanity with others, we have a civic responsibility to all people; and, second, that we must respect each others' differences.[42] Anthony Appiah (who prefers the term "cosmopolitanism"), puts it this way: "There are two strands that intertwine in the notion of cosmopolitanism. One is the idea that we have obligations to others, obligations that stretch beyond those to whom we are related by ties of kith and kin, or even the more formal ties of shared citizenship. The other is that we take seriously the value not just of human life but of particular human lives, which means taking an interest in the practices and beliefs that lend them significance. People are different, the cosmopolitan knows, and there is much to learn from those differences. Because there are so many human possibilities worth exploring, we neither expect nor desire that every person or every society should converge on a single mode of life."[43]

Multiculturalism promotes the "norm of equal inclusion," which, in a racially just world, would become a core component of modern democracies.[44] In such a world, there are no "second-class citizens," and groups currently rendered invisible by political elites finally receive their due recognition. To Canadian philosopher Charles Taylor, failing to recognize fully and to value nonwhites and other dominated groups "shows not just a lack of due respect. It can inflict a grievous wound, saddling its victims with a crippling self-hatred. Due recognition is not just a courtesy we owe people. It is a vital human need."[45] If one of the primary techniques of those championing racial and colonial domination is to convince those they seek to dominate that whiteness and the "white way of life" are superior to all other races and lifestyles, then the aim of the multicultural project is to banish all such ideas of white supremacy and cultural superiority.[46]

Despite our differences—and, indeed, those differences often are far outweighed by our similarities—we all are bound within a common humanity.[47] Abraham Lincoln recognized this as far back as the nineteenth century, arguing that immigrants have a right to claim full American citizenship "as though they were blood of the blood and flesh of the flesh of the men who wrote the Declaration of Independence. So they are."[48] And, long before that, in the second century C.E. to be precise, a playwright by the name of Terence, an enslaved African in Rome, captured this idea with the line: *Homo sum: humani nil a me alienum puto.* "I am human: nothing human is alien to me."[49]

Recognizing this, the multiculturalist cannot deny his or her civic responsibility to dominated groups, and it is here that we witness the convergence of antiracist movements and the multicultural ideal.[50] Multiculturalism demands that we stand with the suffering. It nourishes within us a spirit of solidarity extended not only to our friends or countrymen but to every person inhabiting the planet.[51] Multiculturalism, therefore, is not simply about recognizing other people's identities and cultural scripts; it is also about recognizing their problems—how they are unfairly treated in a democracy that promises them full and equal inclusion—and responding with intelligent and just remedies.[52] For the multiculturalist, racial justice is the value; racial diversity and equality are the results.

"But," the cynic interjects, "wouldn't multiculturalism erode our national culture, undermining American unity and pulling us apart?" Obsessing over our differences, it is true, weakens our democratic potential and breeds animosity. But any multiculturalism worthy of its name does not encourage us to obsess over our differences but inspires us to acknowledge and respect those differences as potential sources of wisdom and good while working *together* to bring more justice into the world. Multiculturalism seeks to draw us nearer, not to push us apart. It does not threaten civic community but nourishes its potential by dismantling racial domination.[53] It does not weaken democracy but strengthens it. Most critics of multiculturalism believe its alternative to be a colorblind society, where we shed our differences and unite under the banner of "American." This train of thought is nothing more than the old idea of assimilation in new garb. It assumes that the stew simmering in the great American melting pot suits everybody's tastes. It also assumes that assimilation melts everyone equally into a new something, even if, in reality, that "new something" is the dominant group projecting itself as the universal American. Whites do not melt; nonwhites do. This means that the alternative to multiculturalism is not national unity but white supremacy.

Multiculturalism seeks to nourish democracy, to strengthen American civil society, making it freer and fuller, wider and warmer, more inclusive and more just. Besides, to deny the goal of multiculturalism is to deny the very essence of America. America always has been multicultural, although it is only in recent years that it has pursued multiculturalism as an ideal. The United States, said Senator Carl Schurz in 1859, was "a great colony of *free humanity* which has not old England but the *world* for its mother country."[54] It took an enormous labor to convince us otherwise; it took a movement of great exertion and coercion, mystification and trickery to present America as a white nation. In America, multiculturalism is the norm; it is racial domination that is its perverse, unnatural substitute—which is why Appiah makes perfect sense when he says, "Cosmopolitanism isn't hard work; repudiating it is."[55]

"Your country?" Du Bois asks the white reader. "How came it yours? Before the Pilgrims landed we were here. . . . Actively we have woven ourselves with the very warp and woof of this nation,—we fought their battles, shared their sorrow, mingled our blood with theirs, and generation after generation have pleaded with a headstrong, careless people to despise not Justice, Mercy, and Truth, lest the nation be smitten with a curse. Our song, our toil, our cheer, and warning have been given to this nation in blood-brotherhood. Are not these gifts worth the giving? Is not this work and striving? . . . Even so," he concludes, "is the hope that sang in the songs of my fathers well sung."[56] That hope, that lonely lit candle surrounded by moonless night, passed from calloused hand to calloused hand throughout American history, is the hope of freedom, of complete inclusion and recognition, of justice and equality. It is, in a word, the hope of multiculturalism—the beloved community.[57]

How Do We Bring about Change?

Like a great locomotive, the movement toward racial equality and justice began slowly, laboriously, and with great effort. But it gained speed with every turn of the wheel and every grate on the track and, soon, it shook the rust off its gears and fired up the engine, and got to rolling. It lumbered forward with great momentum and power and quite literally changed the world. But, since the late 1960s, the movement seems to have lost steam, even in a time when the tenets of antiracism have grown more widely accepted.

Today we find ourselves in a unique historical moment. On the one hand, there has never been a time in American history when so many people reject racism. A mere generation ago, racial segregation was the law of the land and was embraced by millions; today, nothing could seem more anti-American. On the other hand, while racial domination continues to cause a great deal of suffering and makes a mockery of our democracy, many movements for racial justice have faded away. Never has the value of racial equality been so strong while the movement for racial justice is so weak. In *The World Is a Ghetto*, sociologist Howard Winant sums up this most perplexing irony: "Not only in the United States but around the world, a centuries-old pattern of white supremacy has been more fiercely contested and more thoroughly challenged, *in living lifetimes*, than has ever occurred before. As a result, for the first time in modern history, there is widespread support for what had until recently been a 'dream,' Dr. King's dream, let us say, of racial equality. Yet white supremacy is hardly dead. . . . [And] *all around the world the momentum of the struggle against racism is stalemated*."[58]

So, should we throw up our hands in despair? Never. Listen, you are not alone; you are not the only one who cares; you do not have to start from scratch, nor do you have to abandon your own ambitions and personal goals to join in the struggle for racial justice. Our enemy is big, yes, but it is not invincible. "The anvil outlasts the hammer," so goes the old Vietnamese saying. And just because the Civil Rights Movement appears stalemated does not mean that it is dead. Right now, there are thousands upon thousands of people working in the name of multiculturalism and racial liberation. They are running for local office, teaching on reservation schools, giving water to dehydrated border crossers, arguing civil rights lawsuits, and organizing on college campuses and in inner-city neighborhoods and small towns. Of course, on the opposite side of the continuum, there are also thousands upon thousands of people working on behalf of racial domination. Not just members of hate groups, but business owners who discriminate against black applicants, real estate agents who only show Puerto Rican families homes in poor areas of town, movie producers who encourage distorted depictions of Native Americans, and politicians who turn a blind eye to the pressing problems of racial domination. And in the middle are the hordes of the indifferent.

Where do you stand? "I cannot change things," you say. No, it's the other way around: You *cannot but help* change things. By virtue of existing, we change things. We affect people in our classes, dormitories, jobs, families, and social clubs, even if we cannot fully realize exactly how. Even doing nothing, as Elie Wiesel reminds us, influences the trajectory of the world. It is not a question of *if* we will change things but *how* we will—for the better or for the worse.

Real Change and Pseudo Change

Many of us want to leave this world better than we found it. Indeed, a recent survey concluded that a full 43% of college freshman listed "helping promote racial understanding" as one of their *life goals*, and 75% listed "helping others who are in difficulty."[59] These numbers are encouraging and demonstrate that the majority of young students, perhaps not unlike many of you, truly want to make a difference. For them, the next step is to figure out exactly what to do. What kind of change is most effective?

It is necessary, first, to point out that just as some people think they cannot do anything to help but are brimming over with potential, others feel they are doing quite a lot when, in truth, they are doing very little. Widely accepted solutions to racial domination are not always the most effective; in fact, they may be widely accepted precisely because they are ineffective.[60] Consider, for example, the diversity management programs found in many workplaces across America. Diversity management is a fairly new concept, one with roots in affirmative action legislation. During the early 1970s, employers woke up to the fact that they could be subjected to costly lawsuits if they discriminated against women and people of color. To decrease their risk of litigation, they established affirmative action and antidiscrimination offices. But in the 1980s, affirmative action policies were weakened by President Reagan and the Supreme Court, which forced affirmative action specialists—whose livelihoods depended on antidiscrimination efforts—to repackage their services. They did so by filing back the teeth of affirmative action, doing away with more positive and proactive steps to enlarge the representation of women and people of color in the workplace. Then they spun these new (softer) antidiscrimination programs in a different way, rationalizing them not on ethnical grounds—as a judicious response to centuries of racial and masculine domination—but because they made good business sense. A diverse workforce, it was reasoned, would increase a company's effectiveness and competitiveness and would expand its reach to new consumer pools. Many companies were convinced and implemented mandatory "diversity training." Affirmative action thus became diversity management.[61]

Is diversity management enough to dismantle racial domination? Many researchers say no. First, diversity training seems to do nothing to bust through glass ceilings. Studies have shown that such programs leave unaltered the racial and gender mix of companies' supervisory positions.[62] Second, diversity has come to mean many things—diversity of political leanings, religious beliefs, sexual orientation, age, and so on. As the meaning of diversity expands to incorporate more aspects of our lives, the term comes to signal human variation—not historical and structural modes of domination. "Is diversity management really just talking about respecting all individual differences?" asks one observer. "If so, this is problematic and cannot in its present form lead to inclusive organizations. There is a real danger in seeing differences as benign variation among people. It overlooks the role of conflict, power, dominance, and the history of how organizations are fundamentally structured by race, gender, and class."[63] Another concern is that diversity management might reify race in fallacious ways, inflating cultural differences or describing racial differences where none exist. For instance, one antidiscrimination training manual described Latino workers as "family oriented" (versus work oriented) and suggested that blacks "react quickly to changing situations."[64] Overarching statements such as these encourage stereotypical thinking. Finally, one may ask, how could a training session that lasts less than a day—the length of half of such training sessions[65]—have any impact on a force that is centuries old?

The point is not that diversity management programs are useless. Some research suggests that they can encourage tolerance in the workplace, and companies that have taken more serious measures, placing a permanent person or staff of people in charge of antidiscrimination programs, for instance, have created a more integrated workforce.[66] The point is that, when they are critically analyzed, these programs are poor substitutes for more aggressive antiracist initiatives. They are but one step in the right direction, and a small step at that.[67]

When setting out to make a difference, we continually have to ask ourselves, is this prescription for change curing the disease? Is there a stronger medicine out there; or are we taking aspirin when we really need chemotherapy? Is what I'm doing really helping; is it enough? Just because you sport a button with a swastika crossed out does not mean you actually are doing something to fight Neo-Nazism; a poster of Che Guevara hanging in your dorm room does not mean you are part of any revolution; an "Eracism" T-shirt doesn't erase racism. Wearing political buttons and T-shirts and putting up radical posters and bumper stickers is fine and good so long as you realize that buttons, T-shirts, posters, and bumper stickers do not do much by themselves. Real political change is more than a fashion statement.[68] Criticizing so-called conscious hip-hoppers for using "revolution as a catch phrase," Minneapolis-based emcee El Guante raps, "Radio is filled with monotonous crap/But our kids need a lot more than positive rap/So fuck the 'revolution,' join a union/Or run for school board, we need more than music."

What looks like change might be anything but, for there is a difference between **real change** and **pseudo change**, between effective efforts and ineffective ones. We should be careful not to mistake silk roses for the real thing, confusing revolutions on paper with revolutions on the ground or "revolutions in the order of words or texts for revolutions in the order of things, verbal sparring at conferences for 'interventions' in the affairs of the *polis*," that is, the public realm of citizenship and political affairs.[69] For there are initiatives that, on the surface, appear to be fighting racial domination but that, in reality, yield paltry results; and there are some organizations that are more concerned with *appearing* to promote racial justice (that is, with maintaining their own legitimacy) than with actually promoting it. This is the case for companies that hold mandatory diversity trainings but that, when it comes to handing out promotions, pass over qualified nonwhite workers; it is the case, too, for universities that create an

"Office of Diversity Affairs" with two employed staff members while abolishing a similar office that employed six.

Another reason to throw up our hands? No, but a word of caution about picking our battles and choosing our weaponry: Going to war takes wisdom and strategy, reason and foresight—*then* courage. The same is true of our assaults on racial domination. What is needed is not just an impassioned response to racial injustice but an *intelligent* response as well. "We are not in danger of being excessively generous; indeed, most of us are in no danger of meeting . . . our basic obligation. But what's wanted . . . is the exercise of reason, not just explosions of feelings."[70] Where, then, do we start? In what follows we explore four levels or sites of change having to do with (1) ourselves, (2) our inner circle, (3) our institutions, and (4) our nation. These are not stages one proceeds through so much as overlapping areas of struggle. All are important; all are integral elements in the struggle for positive change in racial life. One cannot simply "choose" among them. The intelligent reconstruction of our racial order requires them all, in combination and in creative synthesis.

Changing Ourselves

Leo Tolstoy, perhaps Russia's greatest novelist, once wrote, "Everyone thinks of changing the world, but no one thinks of changing himself." But this is precisely where we must begin. How, after all, could someone claim to be an environmentalist while refusing to conserve water or to recycle? How could someone claim to be a feminist while mistreating the women in his own life? How could any of us claim to be fighting for racial justice without yet critically examining our own prejudices? If we want to help dismantle racial domination, we must first address it within ourselves.

Now, the goal here is not to purify ourselves of all traces of interpersonal racism before getting involved with antiracist movements. If it were, nothing would ever get done, for, if we are honest with ourselves, most of us have prejudices that cling, barnacle-like, to our thoughts and feelings. Asked when she began her lifelong work with poor orphaned children of Calcutta, Mother Teresa replied, "On the day I discovered I had Hitler inside me."[71] Mother Teresa's prejudices and innermost wicked thoughts did not prevent her from doing good work; on the contrary, they propelled her to the frontlines of social action. Our response should be the same. The goal is not perfection but critical self-engagement, not complete purification (an impossibility) but rigorous reflexivity.

Interracial and intercultural competence, moreover, is not a state at which we arrive or something we achieve. It is not a destination but a *process* or, as historian William Cronon puts it, "a way of living in the face of our own ignorance, a way of groping toward wisdom in full recognition of our own folly, a way of educating ourselves without any illusion that our educations will ever be complete."[72] There is no conversion moment, no glorious awakening, where once and for all we come out of the darkness and into the light. There is only a life lived striving and working, succeeding and failing, moving from light to dark and back again. The apt metaphor here is one of training, where day after day we discipline our thoughts and actions so they are not dictated without our consent by forces of domination. This is no simple task, and we can take comfort in St. Augustine's frustrated vent: "Whence is this monstrosity? And why is it? . . . The mind commands the body, and is obeyed instantly; the mind commands itself and is resisted?"[73]

This self-training requires, foremost, identifying our prejudices and attempting to scrutinize and, as much as possible, to evict them. We must pay serious attention to our thoughts and actions, evaluating how we treat people differently because of their racial identity or how we feel about this or that "kind" of person. Knowing ourselves means taking a good hard look in the mirror and being as honest as a reflection about what we see. Many of us are truthful with ourselves far too rarely, and, often we can practice a kind of **disingenuous reflexivity** that errs in two opposite directions. On the one hand, we can search within ourselves and happily report that we are free of all prejudices. "I treat everyone the same," we might declare. "I do not have a racist bone in my body." On the other hand, we can claim, after a thorough inward-looking meditation, that we are wretches, full of only prejudice: "I am so completely racist; I am helpless." One kind of dishonest exaggeration looks inside and finds an angel, seemingly immune to racial domination; the other finds a demon that welcomes racial domination without resistance. But the truth is that we are all made up of a complicated blend of good and evil, courage and cowardice, ignorance and intelligence. The body relies on both the heart and the bowels. Every one of us can locate within ourselves impulses of racism and impulses of racial enlightenment. Honest reflexivity confronts the self in its full complexity, and it does not shy away from the nasty parts but seeks them out in order to set them straight. "We only become what we are by radically negating deep down what others have done to us."[74]

Sociologists and psychologists have developed sophisticated ways to measure unconscious racism. What they have found is that "most persons have deeply held negative associations with minority groups that can lead to subtle discrimination without conscious awareness."[75] After *Seinfeld* star Michael Richards exploded during a stand-up routine at a Los Angeles comedy club, calling audience members "niggers" and saying, "Fifty years ago we'd have you upside down with a fucking fork up your ass" (an obvious allusion to lynching), he took a breath and told the audience, "It shocks you, it shocks you" to discover "what's buried beneath." Plunging through our deepest recesses and reflecting on our unconscious habits and uncritical actions can be shocking. What is the first thought that springs to mind when a large black man steps inside the elevator?

When you see a young Hispanic woman pushing a baby stroller? When you spot an Arab-American man in the airport security line? When you notice a white woman dressed in professional clothes, briefcase in tow? When an Asian-American man raises his hand in class? When a Native-American woman has a drink with you at a party? The first step to changing ourselves is to take notice of these thoughts and to subject them to critical evaluation instead of letting them slip, un-policed, in and out of our consciousness. If we fail to identify and uproot the weeds, we will soon find our minds cluttered with them.

Your thoughts are yours; you must take responsibility for them. But having a racist thought does not make you a bad person or a "racist." It makes you a person who has been influenced by a society up to its neck in racial domination. You might feel ashamed when a racist thought trespasses your mind, but if shame is your only reaction, you have little chance of controlling your prejudices. As Aldous Huxley pointed out, "Rolling in the muck is not the best way of getting clean."[76] To restrain our unconscious racism, we must objectify it and subject it to a historically informed analysis and critique. "The starting point of critical elaboration," said Italian social theorist Antonio Gramsci, "is the consciousness of what one really is, and is 'knowing thyself' as a product of the historical process to date which has deposited in you an infinity of traces, without leaving an inventory."[77] The starting point for the development of a racially sensitive reflexivity, in other words, is the application of a sociological imagination to the self.

This endeavor, a sort of socioanalysis that complements and perhaps even goes further than psychoanalysis, is a reflexive enterprise, in which we objectify all those forces that control our imaginations and actions in order rationally to assess and control how they affect our thinking and behavior. We must never stop asking ourselves: Is my idea correct? From where does my information come? How do I know that this is the truth? How is it that I know the world works in this way? How might my upbringing and racial identity influence my thinking on this matter?

Racial intelligence also requires that we become good listeners, that we "pay attention—to others and to the world around [us]"; that we take note of human achievements in art, music, craftsmanship, poetry, politics, sports, literature, and journalism. It requires that we read and that we learn how to communicate our ideas more clearly to others. If we hope to become people of intelligence, driven by a love of learning and a deep commitment to the truth, we must discipline our minds and reject half-baked, sloppy thinking. We must also invest in others' passions and ideas and "understand the power of other people's dreams and nightmares as well as [our] own." We must acknowledge that "freedom of the individual is possible only in a free community, and vice versa," and therefore understand that our livelihood is inexorably connected to livelihoods of others.[78]

And we must surround ourselves with people who are different from ourselves, who disagree with us, and who can push and challenge our thinking. In a multicultural vein, we should never fear differences or "strangeness." Rather, we should seek them out, knowing full well that our "little shard of mirror cannot reflect the whole."[79]

Perhaps above all, we must develop empathy for the suffering. We must connect our hearts to the groans of the oppressed. You might be the smartest mind of your generation, able to analyze racial domination with precision and brilliance, but if your stomach does not turn when you hear about a hate crime that happened on your campus or when your friend cracks a racist joke or when you pick up the newspaper and read about America's growing anti-immigrant sentiment, then your intelligence is in vain.[80] "If I have the gift of prophecy and can fathom all mysteries and all knowledge," writes the Apostle Paul, "and if I have a faith that can move mountains, but have not love, I am nothing."[81] One does not have to be a Christian to appreciate the wisdom in his observation.

The philosopher Hannah Arendt put it this way: We "do not become just by knowing what is just but by loving justice."[82] Changing ourselves into agents of change, therefore, means changing our minds by cultivating knowledge *and* changing our hearts by cultivating empathy. One kind of change drives the other. The more you learn about racial injustice, the more your heart will break for its victims; likewise, the stronger your passion for justice grows, the more you will want to learn about racial domination and seek out the best prescriptions for change.[83]

A good deal of this work, this self-work, is carried out in solitude. By ourselves, we read and think in the library; we ponder our own thoughts while walking down the street; we imagine a better world while riding on the bus. But this can only take us so far, for reflexivity is a fundamentally *collective* enterprise. We cannot fully change ourselves by ourselves. For our shortcomings to be brought most fully to light, we need to participate in collective dialogues that cut across racial boundaries. The importance of honest discussions that grapple with the complexities of racial domination—and especially of conversations that take place between women and men of different racial identities—cannot be overstated.

Whenever two Americans with different racial identities meet, a whole history of murder and slavery, colonialism and dehumanization, lies between them.[84] Seeing another person *as* black, American Indian, or white is nothing short of seeing hundreds of years of history, ugly and shamefaced, unravel before us. Interracial dialogue means confronting this thing that lies between us. It is not an exercise of pulling off the scab; it is one of addressing the festering wound that never has been adequately treated. As you might already have discovered in this class, talking about race can be painful. Fear and anger, stubbornness and selfishness can choke rational dialogue and get in the way of progress. What is needed is cool-headedness, humility, and respect; in certain instances, what is needed most might be honest contrition; in others, forgiveness.[85]

Weariness and apathy, too, are significant barriers to engaging in these—often exhausting, often maddening—conversations. "I am tired of talking about race," you might say. "Let's just put it all behind us." Most of the time, white students are the ones who voice this complaint, a complaint that itself is a product of white privilege.[86] Nonwhites, whose livelihood depends on overcoming racial domination, do not have much of a choice in the matter; their weariness comes, not from conversations about racial domination, but from the thing itself. Non-Jewish students in Germany, a recent report found, are rather tired of talking about the Holocaust.[87] Should we then silence all talk of the most horrid event in modern history? Of course not—nor should we hush up about racial domination. The legacies of the Holocaust and racial domination do not fade into oblivion if we keep quiet about them—in fact, the opposite is true. To quote Günther Grass, "The job of a citizen is to keep his mouth open."

You want to change the world? The first step is to change yourself or, as Gandhi put it, to "become the change you want to see in the world." It goes without saying that all of us, whites and nonwhites alike, need to carry out this self-work, confronting the many ways that racial domination is alive in our innermost beings, our unconscious habits, dispositions, and postures. Whites need to come face to face with their racial privilege. They need to interrogate how their thinking is informed by a white supremacy that refuses to call itself as such; they need to reject notions of rugged individuality, which encourages them to ignore the power of history and society.[88] Nonwhites, too, need to peel the claws of racial domination off their minds, turning away from all whispers of self-hate, embracing a positive image of their self in a society that day after day projects negative ones. They need to come to the full realization that racial inequalities are the product of racial domination, not of the deficiencies of nonwhites.[89] They must struggle against symbolic violence, investigating how they play a role in reproducing the terms of their own domination. And all of us must strive to understand the world through multiple perspectives.

Changing Our Inner Circle

Racial domination has to be eradicated not only from our ideas and practices but also from the ideas and practices of those nearest us—the persons in our intimate circle. You can have great influence over how your family members and friends think about the world. Perhaps your mother harbors anti-Arab sentiment; perhaps one of your best friends is anti-Semitic. How can you address their racism? Every situation is different and requires a good deal of thought, strategy, and patience on your part. But if there is a single guiding principle for addressing racism in the lives of people closest to you, it is this: *hold them accountable* for their words and deeds—and ask them to do the same to you.

A father sees a group of Mexican-American men and observes, "All these Mexicans. They are taking our jobs away!" Knowing he is misinformed, his son responds, with genuine interest, "Why do you think that?" The father replies, "It's just obvious, isn't it? I mean, you know Bob Kapatrick down the street, he lost his job last year." The son answers, "That really is sad about Mr. Kapatrick, but are you sure he lost his job because of Mexicans? I mean, couldn't there be other factors involved? I read in the paper that a lot of workers from that factory were laid off, including Mexican workers. You know, I used to think that Mexican immigrants took jobs away from Americans, but I've been convinced otherwise. I started reading up on it, and the best evidence out there shows that Mexican immigrants don't take jobs away from native-born citizens. They mainly compete for jobs with other immigrants. What do you think?"

When people with racist beliefs are faced with an alternative interpretation about how the world works, a more intelligent interpretation informed by social science, they have a very difficult time justifying their beliefs. In time, they may come to change their minds and embrace a more informed (and antiracist) understanding of society. But people often grow defensive and uncomfortable when asked to justify their ideas. Accordingly, there are at least **four useful techniques for holding people accountable** for their prejudices. First, take their prejudices seriously. Do not yell at them; do not call them "stupid" or "ignorant"; try not to get too angry. If you blow up on people every time they say something racist, you will not teach them to think differently; you'll only teach them not to say such things around *you*. When confronted with a racist statement—or, more softly, a benign yet misinformed statement about racial domination—realize that the person who uttered the statement matters very much, that their *ideas* matter very much, and that their beliefs most likely are tied to their personal experience. If you want them to listen to you, then you must listen—sincerely—to them.

Second, ask people questions. In the preceding conversation, the son responded to his father's racist remark with a question and inserted questions throughout the conversation. If he had responded with a statement such as "You're wrong!" or "How can you believe such garbage!" or "You're so racist!" he might have blown the teaching opportunity. Questions—posed authentically, not sarcastically or presumptuously—are disarming and inviting. They're also quite natural. If someone says, "I think the Los Angeles Lakers are the best basketball team in the country," the natural response is to ask, "Why?" Similarly, if someone says, "I don't think American Indians want to climb out of poverty," it is equally natural to ask, "Why?" Questions, at bottom, are pursuers of the truth. As such, they are powerful weapons against racist beliefs.[90]

Third, do your homework. How can you hope to change someone's mind if you can't offer them a better interpretation than the one they currently hold? The son was able to offer his father a different way of understanding how Mexican immigrants affect the labor pool because he had read up on the issue. Racial domination's archnemesis is a critically informed citizen. This does not mean you have to memorize statistics (although it's good to store a few in your arsenal) or be able to recite the precise date that marked the beginning of the prison boom. But it does require you to have a firm enough grasp of the relevant research, like the research recorded in this book, that you can clearly articulate educated positions on certain matters. If your knowledge is a bit shaky, don't be afraid to tell your family members or friends that you'll hit the books and get back to them—and be sure you do.

Finally, the worst thing you can do upon being confronted with a racist belief—other than remaining silent—is to turn the conversation into a debate you intend to "win." It is extremely difficult to learn when you are competing. After all, in a debate you are not trying to understand; you are trying to beat your opponent. And it is an extremely rare thing for someone to walk away from a debate having learned anything. In most cases, both winners and losers leave the debate thinking one thing: that the other person is an idiot. You should be firm in your convictions, determined with your questions, and confident in your knowledge, but the goal should be a rational discussion, not a debate in the sense of a verbal sparring match. If you set out to intimidate someone or make them feel stupid, you usually will produce in them the desired effect, losing credibility and perhaps even calcifying their racist or wrongheaded beliefs. If you truly want to change someone's mind, then you have to be willing to be vulnerable and (if appropriate) honest about your own prejudices (we're not perfect, after all). One last thing: think about the timing of your conversation. Sometimes a racist utterance is best addressed on the spot; other times, it is better to confront the person at a later time.

Be prepared for resistance, and gird yourself for the long haul. It will take much more than a single conversation adequately to address your friends' and family members' interpersonal racism. This—it bears repeating—is a process, not a conversion. Understand, too, that, despite your best efforts, you will not always be successful. Some people will go to their graves with their racism. After trying and trying, sometimes the only thing left to do is to move on, expending your energies elsewhere, like fighting for racial justice at the institutional level.

Changing Our Institutions

Racial domination, we know, must be confronted at the interpersonal and institutional levels. There are two kinds of change-oriented institutional action: individual and collective. **Individual action** requires conducting ourselves in a certain manner within the institutions to which we belong so as to promote racial justice. For example, all of us, no matter what our chosen profession, can promote racial justice within our workplaces. After graduation, will you become a police officer? You can decry the pervasive practice of racial profiling, never employing this unfair technique and criticizing other police officers who do. A journalist? You can promote an antiracist form of reporting, cutting through the mystifications of racial domination to clutch hold of the truth. A nurse? You can strive to provide the same level of care to all patients, regardless of their racial identity or socioeconomic status—and you can pull strings for those who need help but lack health insurance, encouraging other nurses to do the same. A teacher? You can petition the school board to promote a multicultural curriculum; speak out against the racist practice of tracking; and teach your students about white privilege. A nutritionist? You can organize fee classes in impoverished neighborhoods, giving lessons on how to live well and eat right. An artist? Work with an antiracist aesthetic and encourage fellow artists not to depict people of color in overly simplistic modes. A lawyer? You can fight for civil rights and speak out against injustices within the criminal justice system. A business owner? You can make sure your firm hires and promotes well-qualified people of color and that it is defined by a healthy and warm racial climate. We easily could go on, but the point is clear: We can be advocates for racial justice in any and all lines of work.

If you work for change within your institutions, you will face obstacles and hardships. There might come a time when racial justice requires you to sacrifice something important to you. It is one thing to write your boss an e-mail, asking him why a white employee was promoted over a more qualified nonwhite one. But what if you were the one promoted? Or perhaps you are a person of color who has climbed the ladder to a position of power within a company but whose very presence in that position allows the company to get away with all kinds of discriminatory practices. Will you let your voice be heard, even if it threatens the position you worked so hard to attain? A few years down the road, when you are looking for a home, will you move into a segregated gated community or invest in a multiracial neighborhood, perhaps in a less affluent part of town with less attractive property values?

Today and in the future, if you fight for racial justice, you might be faced with some tough decisions. They are tough precisely because they require you to endure discomfort or hardship at the expense of doing the right thing. But, as Socrates said long ago, "it is better to suffer wrong than to do wrong."[91] What is needed is courage and integrity. Change never comes without sacrifice. Those who fought in the Civil Rights Movement endured prison and beatings. They were humiliated and spat on. They were fired from their jobs. Their children were threatened and shoved and punched and bullied to tears. They

"Discrimination is morally wrong, politically dangerous, industrially wasteful, and socially silly. It is the duty of whites to stop it, and to do so primarily for their own sakes." —W. E. B. Du Bois

endured depression and weariness; insomnia and terror. Some endured their homes being firebombed; some gave their lives to the movement. What will you endure?

Can we expect whites to endure much, to set aside all claims to white privilege, and actively to work against a system of racial domination from which they benefit? The answer is yes. Since the earliest days of the antiracist movement in America, whites have spoken out against racial injustice and have been persecuted, even killed, as a result.[92] In 1899, after emphasizing the responsibility of nonwhites in the liberation struggle, Du Bois wrote these words: "Discrimination is morally wrong, politically dangerous, industrially wasteful, and socially silly. It is the duty of whites to stop it, and to do so primarily for their own sakes."[93] Why would Du Bois argue that whites should help put an end to racial domination not simply because it is the moral thing to do but "for their own sakes"?

The answer, of course, is that, despite the advantages whites enjoy on account of their skin privilege, whites, too, are afflicted by racial domination. For one, by creating racial antagonisms within the working class, racial domination has reinforced nonwhite *and* white poverty. Moreover, racial domination is costly, and white taxpayers shoulder the bill when they pay for prisons, police officers, and superficial fixes for old and entrenched social problems.[94] Racial domination, studies have shown, takes a psychological toll on whites, who must live in fear of the racialized Other and with a good deal of guilt, depression, and shame.[95] White people also suffer a kind of spiritual cost under the forces of racial domination. For their skin privileges, whites pay with a piece of their humanity. Racism is like a blade without a handle—it cuts both ways. "The price of the liberation of the white people," Baldwin would write, "is the liberation of the blacks [and, we add, all people of color]—the total liberation, in the cities, in the towns, before the law, and in the mind."[96]

Collective action pitched at changing institutions complements individual-level action. Both approaches are important, but collective action is far more effective. If you want to effect real and lasting change within your institutions, then organize others to join you in pushing change forward. In his 1910 novel *Howards End,* British writer E. M. Forster encourages us to *"Only connect!"*[97] This injunction should guide our efforts today. We should connect one person with another, this group with that one, so that, together, we can engage the world through powerful coalitions.

How do we go about doing this? There are two simple guidelines for coalition-building: *join* and *reach*. As for joining, in most cases you do not have to start from scratch. You can seek out organizations already at work and lend a hand. Join a union or an antiracist organization on campus or an interfaith alliance. And once you have joined, reach. Coalition-building means bringing others alongside you in your pursuit of racial justice. Look for unlikely alliances; think of unusual connections. Seek out people in all areas of the institution to join your cause, from the mail room to the corner office. Above all, reach across racial divides. Turn your back on false divisions separating "Latino issues" from "African-American issues" or "class issues" from "race issues" and instead pursue an agenda that unites these causes. Multiracial coalition building is bound to fail unless organizations widen their vision and critically assess how their proposed solutions to institutional problems produce differential effects across race.[98]

Consider an issue at the top of today's feminist agenda: violence against women. If an organization working to protect women from abuse persuades the state to increase the severity of domestic violence laws, it may unintentionally make things worse for victimized black women. The reason is that, because they are fully aware of the rampant mistreatment of young black men within the criminal justice system, black women increasingly are reluctant to turn their abusers over to the police. In fact, studies have shown that, in black communities, the frequency of domestic violence calls decreases as the severity of domestic violence laws increases. The important point, one stressed over and over again by women of color, is that today's feminist movement must be utterly multiracial if it hopes to address the problems of all women. Tokenism simply will not do. Women of color must be placed in positions of leadership; their voices must be heard throughout the organization; and the movement must address their problems with the same commitment and intelligence as it does those of white women.[99]

Workers' rights won by union mobilization demonstrate the importance of interracial alliances. Asian-American and Mexican-American farm workers, along with documented and undocumented immigrants, joined together to fight for more rights and helped energize a movement that would eventually result in the thoroughly multiracial United Farm Workers of America. Chicago's white and black packinghouse workers, whom the business elite long had pitted against one another to drive down the price of labor, overcame ethnic and racial antagonisms to form the powerful United Packinghouse Workers of America union. In 1946, the interracial union went on strike to increase workers' wage—and won. And, as we learned in Chapter 4, Hawaii's racially diverse working-class movement united Native-Hawaiian, Portuguese, Chinese, Japanese, and Filipino workers to win better pay and the institutionalization of antidiscrimination guidelines.[100] In the tradition of the interracial labor movement, we can band together to bring about significant change in our society. "Working in multiracial coalitions of equal members," writes Frank Wu, "united by shared principles, we can create communities that are diverse and just. Together, we can reinvent the civil rights movement."[101]

As we have learned throughout this book, institutional racism is found throughout society. So where do we start? We start where we are, changing the institutions to which we currently belong: our social associations, religious organizations, political parties, and workplaces. And what about the institution to which you now belong: your college or university? How might you promote racial justice on campus? You might review your college's affirmative action policies, evaluating their aggressiveness and effectiveness. You might take a look at the recruitment, retention, and graduation rates for students of color, grading your school on these all-important measures. You might push for more campus resources for students of color and all students from disadvantaged backgrounds, including tutoring services, scholarships, organized activities that raise awareness about white privilege, and university-funded organizations whose sole job is to fight racial domination on campus. You might criticize Eurocentrism in the classroom, encouraging your professors to promote a multicultural curriculum. You might help your university to promote "service-learning activities" that connect students to their surrounding community. You might study other colleges and universities with impressive records of racial justice and high graduation rates for students of color, such as the University of Michigan or Stanford University, to understand how your campus can follow their lead.[102] You might join antiracist groups on campus and participate in their activities. Institutions of higher learning are one of the most effective weapons in the fight against racial domination, and, as students at such an institution, you are in a prime position to bring about change at the educational level.

Changing Our Nation

In the early 1990s, a group of UCLA students fought tooth and nail for a "more inclusive" educational environment, demanding more nonwhite professors and a multicultural curriculum. At the same time, however, the state of California was slashing public education spending by significant margins, forcing UCLA to hike up tuition, thin its resources, and cut positions—all of which made it harder for poor students and students of color to enroll in the university. The important lesson is that, if we are interested in bringing about bold and powerful change, we should commit our energies not only to changing our institutions but also to influencing state and national politics.[103] Institutional change and political change often are inseparable. How, after all, could UCLA hire more faculty of color or institutionalize more multicultural programs if the state did not give the school enough money to do so? Long-lasting, transformative social change will come only if we work to reform political structures as well as state and federal policies.

Racial inequalities have persisted to this day in large part because, for far too long, the American state has refused to develop effective policies aimed at abolishing these disparities. The state has invested, and invested handsomely, in mass incarceration and the development of a police state, but it has invested meagerly in drug treatment or job creation programs. It has invested in tax breaks for large businesses and the nation's elite but invested meagerly in the welfare state, working-class pensions, daycare for single mothers, or universal healthcare. It has invested mightily in warfare and weapons technology but invested meagerly in public education, head start programs, and teachers' salaries.[104] A national antiracist movement would work to reverse these trends and push for intelligent "reforms that would ease the circumstances of people at the bottom of American society."[105]

Recently, intellectuals and activists have worked together to develop innovative policies aimed at eradicating racial and economic injustice in America. Here are some of their ideas. Undocumented immigrants, who work in some of America's most exploitative positions and pay American taxes, deserve more rights, such as the right to social services, public education, healthcare, and legal protection from unfair deportation. Access to the voting booth needs to be further expanded to all Americans, including ex-felons who have done

their time. This could be accomplished by eradicating felon disenfranchisement laws, keeping the polls open twenty-four hours to help working people
who cannot get time off, establishing simple ways for people to vote early,
paying for security guards to staff voting booths so as to curb voter intimidation, and expanding voting legislation so it does not privilege our more privileged citizens.[106]

In the economic field, American wealth could be redistributed so that it is
not concentrated in the hands of a small but enormously influential elite. This
could be accomplished by eliminating tax loopholes that benefit large companies
and the wealthy, enforcing a tax on wealth (such as an estate tax), and reinvest-
ing the money in the nation's poorest neighborhoods and school.[107] Additionally,
the American welfare state—perhaps the skinniest in the developed world—
could be fattened up. We need better unemployment insurance, pensions, subsidies for childcare, and a higher minimum wage; we need universal healthcare,
access to competent doctors and the best medicine available; and our children
need access to well-paid teachers, well-funded schools, and a good public education, no matter where they live. While citizens in industrialized countries much
poorer than ours enjoy such public entitlements, millions of Americans fight to
keep afloat without them.[108]

More toothy legislation could be drafted to put an end to housing discrimination, which robs nonwhite families of the freedom to live where they wish
as well as of a primary source of personal wealth. Real estate firms could be
monitored more closely and sanctioned more severely if they are found guilty
of discrimination. More effort could be committed to the development of
affordable, high-quality housing. And the federal government could develop a
deep-pocketed organization whose sole purpose is the elimination of every
single American ghetto, not in the spirit of "urban renewal" (where poor families are simply shuffled about the city), but with the ultimate goal of forever
wiping out inner-city poverty, isolation, joblessness, and crime. Why does every
major American city have a ghetto? You know the sociological answer to this
question (one having to do with the Great Migration, racial segregation, and
the flight of whites and jobs from city centers), but the political or moral
answer cannot be anything other than "because America has not made the
effort to abolish them."[109]

With respect to the criminal justice system, "tough on crime" policies could
be replaced by "smart on crime" policies that confront the problem of lawbreaking at the root level. Harsh and disproportionate sentences for nonviolent
offenses could be repealed; alternatives to incarceration could be implemented;
and the death penalty—costly and ineffective, racist and brutal—could be abolished. Programs to reduce racial profiling and maltreatment of nonwhites
could be created and enforced. In fact, some scholars wisely have suggested

that we could "make federal and state funding for local police agencies contingent on the development and implementation of strong plans to combat the practices that tend to disproportionately funnel minorities into the criminal justice process."[110]

These are but a small sample of the dozens of reforms carefully outlined and articulated by policy analysts looking to marshal the enormous power of the state in the fight against racial injustice. And, indeed, there are reforms that have yet to be dreamed up by people like you seeking intelligent solutions to some of the country's oldest—but not intractable—problems.

How do we reform policy and social structure? How do we change our nation? Through ongoing, energetic, and collective political action. We can start by lobbying our elected officials, asking them to embrace antiracist reforms. Write them letters; circulate and sign petitions; participate in Internet-based political movements; put your energies behind a candidate willing to fight racism and volunteer for her or his campaign. And never fail to vote.[111] These political activities are the bread-and-butter of democratic participation and the *least* we should do as politically engaged citizens.

As history attests, however, bold reform and transformative social change are brought about, not only through such measures, but also—and primarily— through methods of public protest, including strikes, sustained boycotts, public demonstrations, civil disobedience, racial uprisings, and full-scale revolutions. Democracy entered the world through a revolution, and it is a revolution that we celebrate on the Fourth of July. Slavery was abolished because abolitionists employed revolutionary methods while agitating for slaves' freedom—and because, as Du Bois pointed out, black slaves themselves rose up in rebellion; women gained the right to vote because members of the suffrage movement took to the streets; union strikes during the beginning of the twentieth century helped boost thousands of workers from poverty into the middle class; the Vietnam War drew to a close because the powerful anti-war movement of the 1960s demanded it happen; and segregation folded because antiracist social movements forced its hand.[112] In 1984, Ceéar Chávez reflected on a lifetime spent organizing farm workers with the words, "The UFW [United Farm Workers of America] was the beginning! We attacked that historical source of shame and infamy that our people in this country lived with. We attacked that injustice, not by complaining; not by seeking hand-outs; not by becoming soldiers in the War on Poverty. We organized! Farm workers acknowledged we had allowed ourselves to become victims in a democratic society—a society where majority rule and collective bargaining are supposed to be more than academic theories or political rhetoric. And by addressing this historical problem, we created confidence and pride and hope in an entire people's ability to create the future."[113]

To participate in collective political action—to employ the time-honored methods of public protest—is to engage as fully and completely as possible in civil society and to refuse to "become victims in a democratic society." Of course, some social movements are more effective than others. Why do some movements succeed while others fail? Sociologists have devoted considerable effort to answering this question. In what follows, we organize their findings around **seven components of successful political protest**, stated here as injunctions.

First, *realize you have power*. As sociologist Frances Fox Piven writes, "The rich and the highly placed, including those who control armies and police, usually do prevail in any contest with those who have none of those things—but not always. Sometimes people without things or status or wealth do succeed in forcing institutional changes that reflect, if often only dimly, the needs and aspirations of people lower in the social order."[114] Whence does this power of the masses come? From the fact that society is fundamentally a collection of relations of mutual dependence. Workers rely on capitalists for a paycheck, but capitalists rely on workers' labor; consumers rely on corporations for their goods, but corporations depend on consumers' buying their products; citizens are subject to politicians' decisions, but they also hold great sway over politicians with the power of the vote; and we all depend on one another to uphold the laws and customs of civil society. When we acknowledge these relations of power—and determine how to force the hand of the powerful by exploiting these relations—we have discovered the foundation of political protest. The catch, of course, is that, unlike elite power, which can rest in the hands of a single person, the power of the masses depends on the mobilization of large numbers of people. If one person refuses to buy California grapes, because they were picked by poor Mexican migrant workers laboring under exploitative conditions, their action is virtually undetectable. But if thousands of people join together in boycotting the grapes, the difference can be considerable. Ordinary people, Piven reminds us, are those we have to thank for all the "equalizing reforms that humanized our society, from the founding of the republic, to the emancipation of the slaves, to the rise of the New Deal and Great Society order, to the civil rights acts of the 1960s."[115]

Second, *build coalitions*. The practice of coalition-building discussed under the rubric of institutional change applies as well to social movements fighting for political or structural change. Successful movements accurately identify their targets, their adversaries, as well as their allies: many times, neither group is what one first expects. They also find ways of incorporating multiple institutions—religious organizations, social associations, student groups, unions—into their organizing efforts so that different institutions can work in concert with one another. To do so, they identify points of congruence with other social movements so as to widen their base and appeal.[116] For example,

A Majority of Youth Ages 15–25 Believe That They
Can Make Little Difference in Solving the
Problems of Their Communities

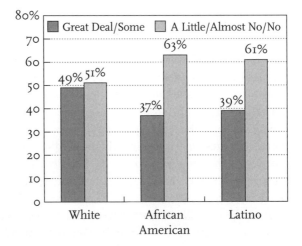

a movement for the eradication of racialized poverty could connect with the environmentalist movement because the adoption of environmentally conscious policies and practices can reduce environmental racism and address the root causes of ethnic conflict (such the decades-long drought that lies at the bottom of the genocidal violence in Darfur) and, therefore, greatly benefit poor communities in America and around the world. As Ban Ki-moon, Secretary-General of the United Nations, advises, "Many of the challenges we face, from poverty to armed conflict, are linked to the effects of global warming. Finding a solution to climate change can bring benefits in other areas. A greener planet will be a more peaceful and prosperous one, too."[117]

Third, *remember that the insurgency matters more than the insurgent organization.* Protest organizations are extremely important and can get quite a lot accomplished, but formal organizations can sometimes end up discouraging instead of promoting social unrest. The main thesis of Frances Fox Piven and Richard Cloward's important book, *Poor People's Movements,* is that "during those brief moments when lower-class groups exert some force against the state, those who call themselves leaders do not usually escalate the momentum of the people's protests. They fail to do so because they are preoccupied with trying to build and sustain embryonic formal organizations in the sure conviction that these organizations will enlarge and become powerful." These efforts deflate the momentum of the movement, as people are pulled "away from the streets and into the meeting rooms." More devastating still, in moments of great potential, windows of revolutionary opportunity, movement leaders obsessed with building their organization rather than with empowering the insurgency often find themselves, hat in hand, at the door of economic or political elites—the very people whose power they are attempting to challenge—asking for resources to sustain their newfound organization. Elites often are happy to comply, as they know it is insurgency, not insurgent organizations, they have to fear.[118] The successful social movement, then, has its priorities in line. It realizes that the power is in the mob not the meeting—that what is powerful is organizing not the organization—and it does not squander rare opportunities to breath fresh life into the discontented masses.

Fourth, *exploit weaknesses in the dominant system.* Racial domination is old and powerful, it is true; but it is not a total system, immune to challenges. The smartest social movements finger its structures, find the weak spots, and tear them open. They identify simple strategies that can have large and far-reaching effects. When a group of Argentineans blocked a bridge that connected Uruguay to Argentina in 2007, protesting the construction of a paper mill that would pollute the Uruguay River and hurt tourism, the protest "not only threatened the plant, but also the Uruguayan economy, exposed fissures in the Mercosur trade alliance, activated international NGOs, and prompted Spain's King Juan Carlos to offer himself as a mediator."[119] All that from a simple bridge blockade. What would happen if members of the Skull Valley Band of Goshutes and community members sympathetic to their plight blocked roads leading into the reservation, turning away trucks full of toxic waste? What would happen if Chinese women organized a walk-out strike to protest horrid working conditions in the underground garment economy? What would happen if millions of Americans refused to buy products from corporations connected to America's private prison industry? Even individual acts of agitation can throw off the system of racial domination. Each of us, in our own fashion, can "throw [our] grain of sand into the well-oiled machinery of resigned complicities."[120] One scholar, for example, makes a convincing case that, should we find ourselves on a jury where a non-white person has been charged with a *nonviolent* offense (such as drug possession or minor theft), we should, regardless of the evidence, hang the jury so as to reverse the course of racial domination within the criminal justice system, if only in that single case.[121]

Fifth, *do not be afraid to break some rules.* Some laws are just; others are not. Successful social movements do not allow unjust laws to stand in their way. This is the central idea undergirding civil disobedience, that tactic of protest on which the Civil Rights Movement relied so heavily—and with great success. Many activities staged by the Movement (for example, Rosa Parks refusing to give up her seat; lunch-counter sit-ins) were effective precisely because they were illegal. The rule-breakers' violations of those laws effectively exposed the latter's injustice and irrationality. For Todd Gitlin, "On the surface, the sit-in protests a bad situation by nonviolently breaking the law. You get arrested—if it comes to that—but you take the moral high ground." But, he continues, sit-ins had a much deeper and more powerful significance. "The sit-in was not an outsider's demand, a request delivered to politicians in hope that they would do the right thing. . . . It was an affirmation, a prefiguration, an act of fertility—a creative act designed to engender a new situation. . . . We who sit in withdraw our willingness. *We don't deplore segregation, we abolish it.* When we cross the color line and sit down in a white-only bus seat or at a lunch counter, we inaugurate a new way of life. When the authorities act or suppress this little utopia that we've launched, they convict themselves in the court of public opinion. We suffer, but—be patient—*they fail.*"[122] Where there are picket signs, there are handcuffs. Throughout the history of America, people have found it impossible to act justly while obeying an unjust law. For a new society to burst forth, the unjust rules holding it back had to be snapped. Henry David Thoreau put it this way: "If it is of such a nature that it requires you to be the agent of injustice to another, then I say, break the law. Let your life be a counter-friction to stop the machine."[123]

Sixth, *plan for the long haul.* The successful social movement develops strategies to support its members throughout the organizing campaign, especially if those people are participating in political action that causes them some hardship. "When workers strike, they need to feed their families and pay the rent; consumer boycotters need to get by for a time without the goods or services they are refusing to purchase."[124] Movements that can address effectively such needs can sustain prolonged political action. The Civil Rights Movement accomplished this by mobilizing resources within the black community, tapping into the network of black churches. For every one person on the frontlines, there was a virtual army of "support staff" cooking food, collecting money, and providing shelter for the organizers.[125] In many cases, activists need to figure out, not only how to mobilize together, but also how to live together, how to survive the insurgency without acquiescing to systems of domination. This is especially important in this day and age, when one finds many avowed antiracist people but very few organized antiracist activists—and where resistance to fundamental racial change remains strong.[126]

Finally, *have fun.* A peculiar injunction? Perhaps, but organizing against racial domination is difficult work. People grow weary and burn out. Or they fall in love with their outrage, overlooking the perhaps small but nonetheless significant victories.[127] They grow bitter and pessimistic and perhaps would not recognize the triumph of justice even if it came. In a successful social movement, people laugh together. They share stories and jokes; they horse around and pull pranks; they respect one another and look forward to working together. They are forward-thinking and optimistic, holding fast to the truism that we have come a long ways and can go much farther. They believe in the promise of democracy. In such a social movement, power is evenly distributed throughout the organization, and control is not monopolized by a cadre of "elite activists" (and neither is the brunt of the labor). Working toward racial justice may require sacrifice; it undoubtedly will result in frustration, anger, and feelings of defeat. But, ask any activist, it will also give you a deep sense of purpose and joy. When you work for something bigger than yourself, something more important than your checking account or your personal ambitions, life grows flush with meaning and importance. Do you long for a life overrunning with significance? That is a life engaged in the fight for justice. You want proof? Steal a glimpse of the calm, soft satisfaction in the eyes of an old civil rights foot soldier.

We Who Believe in Freedom

"It does not require a majority to prevail but rather an irate, tireless minority keen to set brushfires in people's minds." Samuel Adams, one of America's founding fathers, offered these famous lines, words that ring true up to this very hour. It is necessary to remind ourselves time and again that during the Civil Rights Movement, the majority of nonwhite and white Americans stood on the sidelines while a core cadre of committed activists pushed the country forward. The same is true of most major historical events. Analysts have referred to it as the 80/20 phenomenon: the common observation that roughly 80% of social change is brought about by 20% of the population. Sociologist Mario Small has gone even further, suggesting that a community association that involves less than 1% of the total neighborhood population can bring about significant social change in that neighborhood.[128]

Adams was right. When a few impassioned citizens gather together around a single cause, the potential to move the world is in their hands. "Idealist and naïve," dismiss the cynic, coldly and confidently pointing to the countless times people have tried and failed. Yes, there have been failures aplenty—power never cedes ground easily—but we owe many of the freedoms we enjoy today to idealistic souls who joined hands and marched forward as the cynics snickered off to the side.

Collective action is most effective when people break down the racial cleavages that slice civil society into a hundred different groups. The Civil Rights Movement is a prime example of this, and the movement was never more powerful than when blacks were able to incorporate other nonwhites and whites into their liberation struggle.[129] "The present problem of problems," Du Bois once remarked, "is nothing more than democracy beating itself helplessly against the

"It does not require a majority to prevail but rather an irate, tireless minority keen to set brushfires in people's minds."
—Samuel Adams

color bar,—purling, seeping, seething, foaming to burst through . . . [but] held back by those who dream of future kingdoms of greed built on black and brown and yellow slavery."[130] Democracy has poked through the veil bit by bit, letting some light through with each advance, but its full potential has yet to be unleashed on America.

This book has explained how and why racial domination persists; this chapter has explained what you can do about it. The next word is yours. We have said all we can. There is only silence without you. But in you and with you there is hope. What choice do we have but to reconstruct a new society, beautiful and right and, at last, wholly ours?

CHAPTER REVIEW

FROM THEORY TO PRACTICE

1. Select a field of life and imagine it purified of racial domination. Your guiding question: If racial domination were completely banished from this realm of social life, what would that look like? Do not allow your imagination to be tethered to the ground. Be bold. Record your reflections.

2. Imagine a multicultural society. What would that look like? How would your daily life be different in a multicultural society? Record your reflections.

3. List some ways you can work (or perhaps are working) for racial justice in your daily life. List at least one way you can change (1) yourself, (2) the people in your inner circle, (3) an institution to which you belong, and (4) your nation. As you do so, think about what kinds of resistance you might face and what you can do to overcome that resistance.

4. List your career goal. What are some steps you can take in that capacity to dismantle racial domination? How can you work for racial justice specifically as an accountant or social worker or politician or whatever you want to be?

RECOMMENDED READING

- Jeffrey Alexander, *The Civil Sphere* (New York: Oxford University Press, 2006).

- Kwame Anthony Appiah, *Cosmopolitanism: Ethnics in a World of Strangers* (New York: Norton, 2006).

- Paulo Freire, *The Politics of Education: Culture, Power, and Liberation* (Westport: Greenwood, 1985).

- Amy Gutmann, ed., *Multiculturalism: Examining the Politics of Recognition* (Princeton: Princeton University Press, 1994).

- Frances Fox Piven, *Challenging Authority: How Ordinary People Change America* (Lanham: Rowman and Littlefield, 2006).

- James Scott, *Domination and the Arts of Resistance: Hidden Transcripts* (New Haven: Yale University Press, 1990).

Notes

Preface

1. William Faulkner, *Requiem for a Nun* (New York: Vintage 1975 [1951]), Act I, Scene III.

2. Friedrich Nietzsche, "Mixed Opinions and Maxims," in Walter Kaufman, ed., *The Basic Writings of Nietzsche* (New York: Random House, 2000 [1879]), 155.

Chapter 1: Race in the Twenty-first Century

1. Michael Brown, Martin Carnoy, Elliott Currie, Troy Duster, David Oppenheimer, Marjorie Shultz, and David Wellman, *White-Washing Race: The Myth of a Color Blind Society* (Berkeley and Los Angeles: University of California Press, 2003); Joe R. Feagin, Hernan Vera, and Pinar Batur, *White Racism: The Basics*, Second Edition (New York: Routledge, 2001); Eduardo Bonilla-Silva, *Racism without Racists: Color-Blind Racism and the Persistence of Racial Inequality in the United States* (Lanham: Rowman and Littlefield, 2003); Neil Gotanda, "A Critique of 'Our Constitution is Color-Blind,'" in Richard Delgato and Jean Stefancic, eds., *Critical Race Theory: The Cutting Edge*, Second Edition (Philadelphia: Temple University Press, 2000), 35–38.

2. Federal Bureau of Investigation, "Hate Crime Statistics, 1995–2004" (Washington, D.C.: Department of Justice, 1995–2004).

3. United States Bureau of the Census, "Historical Poverty Tables: Table 2, Poverty Status of People by Family Relationship, Race, and Hispanic Origin: 1959–2005" (Washington, D.C.: Government Printing Office, 2006); Bureau of Labor Statistics, "Employment Situation Summary: August 2006" (Washington, D.C.: Department of Labor, 2006); Richard Morin, "Misperceptions Cloud Whites' view of Blacks," *Washington Post*, July 11, 2001, A1; Brown et al., *White-Washing Race*, 35; Feagin et al., *White Racism*, 16; Stephen Cornell and Joseph P. Kalt, eds., "What Can Tribes Do? Strategies and Institutions in American Indian Economic Development" (Los Angeles: American Indian Studies Center, 1992).

4. Virginia Dominguez, "Seeing and Not Seeing: Complicity in Surprise" (New York: Social Science Research Counsel, 2005); Susan Cutter, "The Geography of Social Vulnerability: Race,

Class, and Catastrophe" (New York: Social Science Research Counsel, 2005); Nils Gilman, "What Katrina Teaches about the Meaning of Racism" (New York: Social Science Research Counsel, 2005).

5. Bruce Western, *Punishment and Inequality in America* (New York: Russell Sage Foundation, 2006); Bruce Western and Becky Pettit, "Black-White Wage Inequality, Employment Rates, and Incarceration," *American Journal of Sociology* 111 (2005): 553–578; Michael Tonry, *Malign Neglect: Race, Crime, and Punishment in America* (New York: Oxford University Press, 1995); Alfred Blumstein, "Racial Disproportional of U.S. Prisons Revisited," *University of Colorado Law Review* 64 (1993): 743–760; Thomas Bonczar and Allen Beck, *Lifetime Likelihood of Going to State and Federal Prison* (Washington, D. C.: Bureau of Justice Statistics, 1997); Gail, Chaddock, "U.S. Notches World's Highest Incarceration Rate," *Christian Science Monitor,* August 18, 2003.

6. Émile Durkheim, *The Evolution of Educational Thought* (London: Routledge & Kegan Paul, 1977 [1938]), 11.

7. Melvin Oliver and Thomas Shapiro, *Black Wealth/White Wealth* (New York: Routledge, 1997); Dalton Conley, *Being Black, Living in the Red* (Berkeley and Los Angeles: University of California Press, 1999).

8. *White-Washing Race,* 22

9. Joseph Graves, Jr., *The Race Myth: Why We Pretend Race Exists in America* (New York: Dutton, 2004), 10.

10. Charles Darwin, *The Descent of Man and Selection in Relation to Sex* (Chicago and New York: Rand, McNally & Company, 1871); M. F. Ashley Montagu, *Man's Most Dangerous Myth: The Fallacy of Race* (New York: Columbia University Press, 1942).

11. Graves, *Race Myth,* 16–17.

12. Ian Haney-López, *White by Law: The Legal Construction of Race* (New York: New York University Press, 1996); James Davis, *Who Is Black? One Nation's Definition* (University Park, PA: Pennsylvania State University Press, 1991).

13. Oliver Cromwell Cox, *Caste, Class, and Race: A Study in Social Dynamics* (New York: Doubleday, 1948), 423. Also see Sukhadeo Thorat, ed., *Caste, Race, and Discrimination: Discourses in International Context* (Jaipur: Rawat Publications, 2004); Pauline Kolenda, *Caste, Marriage, and Inequality: Essays on North and South India* (Jaipur: Rawat Publications, 2003); Susan Bayly, *Caste, Society and Politics in India from the Eighteenth Century to the Modern Age* (New York: Cambridge University Press, 2001); André Béteille, *Caste, Class, and Power: Changing Patterns of Stratification in a Tanjore Village,* Second Edition (New York: Oxford University Press, 1996 [1965]).

14. Graves, *Race Myth,* 8.

15. Michael Banton, "Analytical and Folk Concepts of Race and Ethnicity," *Ethnic and Racial Studies* (1979) 2: 127–138, 130.

16. Troy Duster, "Race and Reification in Science," *Science* (2005) 307: 1050–1051.

17. John Hoberman, *Darwin's Athletes: How Sport Has Damaged Black America and Preserved the Myth of Race* (Boston: Houghton Mifflin, 1997).

18. Joseph Graves, Jr., *Emperor's New Clothes: Biological Theories of Race at the Millennium* (New Brunswick: Rutgers University Press, 2001).

19. Jim Holt, "Nobody Does It Better," *The New York Times,* April 16, 2000.

20. Graves, *Race Myth.*

21. Michael Messner, "Masculinities and Athletic Careers," *Gender and Society* 3 (1989): 71–88; Harry Edwards, "The Myth of the Racially Superior Athlete," *The Black Scholar,* November 3, 1971.

22. Richard Herrnstein and Charles Murray, *The Bell Curve: Intelligence and Class Structure in American Life* (New York: The Free Press, 1994).

23. Russell Jacoby and Naomi Glauberman, eds., *The Bell Curve Debate: History, Documents, Opinions* (New York: Times Books, 1995); Steven Fraser, ed., *The Bell Curve Wars: Race, Intelligence, and the Future of America* (New York: Basic Books, 1995); Stephen Jay Gould, *The Mismeasure of Man* (New York: Norton, 1996); Claude Fisher, Michael Hout, Martín Sánchez Jankowski, Samuel Lucas, Ann Swidler, and Kim Voss, *Inequality by Design: Cracking the Bell Curve Myth* (Princeton: Princeton University Press, 1996).

24. Gould, *Mismeasure of Man,* 28.

25. Paul Pierson, *Dismantling the Welfare State? Reagan, Thatcher, and the Politics of Retrenchment* (Cambridge: Cambridge University Press, 1994); Paul Pierson, "Three Worlds of Welfare State Research," *Comparative Political Studies* 33 (2000): 791–821; Margaret Somers and Fred Block, "From Poverty to Perversity: Ideas, Markets, and Institutions over 200 Years of Welfare Debate," *American Sociological Review* 70 (2005): 260–287; Gould, *Mismeasure of Man.*

26. Gould, *Mismeasure of Man,* 60–61.

27. James Baldwin, *The Fire Next Time* (New York: Vintage 1993 [1962]), 104.

28. Pierre Bourdieu, *Language and Symbolic P*ower (Cambridge: Harvard University Press, 2003).

29. See, e. g., Kimberly DeCosta, *Making Multiracials: State, Family, and Market in the Redrawing of the Color Line* (Stanford: Stanford University Press, 2007); Thomas Guglielmo, *White on Arrival: Italians, Race, Color, and Power in Chicago, 1890–1945* (New York: Oxford University Press, 2004); John Jackson, Jr., *Harlemworld: Doing Race and Class in Contemporary Black America* (Chicago: University of Chicago Press, 2001); Robin Sheriff, *Dreaming Equality: Color, Race, and Racism in Urban Brazil* (New Brunswick: Rutgers University Press, 2001); John Hartigan, Jr., *Racial Situations: Class Predicaments of Whiteness in Detroit* (Princeton: Princeton University Press, 1999).

30. Rogers Brubaker, and Frederick Cooper, "Beyond 'Identity,'" *Theory and Society* 29 (2000): 1–47; Mara Loveman, "Is 'Race' Essential?" *American Sociological Review* 64 (1999): 891–898.

31. Kim Williams, *Mark One or More: Civil Rights in Multiracial America* (Ann Arbor: University of Michigan Press, 2006).

32. Mary Waters, *Ethnic Options: Choosing Identities in America* (Berkeley and Los Angeles: University of California Press, 1990); Mary Waters, *Black Identities: West Indian Immigrant Dreams and American Realities* (New York and Cambridge: Russell Sage Foundation, Harvard University Press, 1999).

33. Jack White, "I'm Just Who I Am," *Time,* May 5, 1997, 36.

34. Davis, *Who Is Black?*

35. Allister Sparks, *The Mind of South Africa: The Story of the Rise and Fall of Apartheid* (Johannesburg: Jonathan Ball, 2006); Edward Telles, *Race in Another America: The Significance of Skin Color in Brazil* (Princeton: Princeton University Press, 2004); Thomas Stephens, *Dictionary of Latin American Racial and Ethnic Terminology* (Gainesville: University of Florida Press, 1989); Frank Dikötter, *The Discourse of Race in Modern China* (Stanford: Stanford University Press, 1992); S. N. Eisenstadt, *Japanese Civilization: A Comparative View* (Chicago: University of Chicago Press, 1998); Mary Searle-Chatterjee and Ursula Sharma, *Contextualising Caste: Post-Dumontian Approaches* (Oxford: Blackwell, 1994).

36. Michel Foucault, *The History of Sexuality, Volumes 1–3* (New York: Vintage, 1999 [1984–1976]).

37. David Roediger, *Working toward Whiteness: How America's Immigrants Became White* (New York: Basic Books, 2005); David Roediger, *The Wages of Whiteness: Race and the Making of the American Working Class* (London: Verso, 1991).

38. Stuart Hall, "Race Articulation and Societies Structured in Dominance," in UNESCO, ed., *Sociological Theories: Race and Colonialism* (Paris: UNESCO, 1980, 305–345), 308. Also see Thomas Holt, *The Problem of Race in the Twenty-First Century* (Cambridge: Harvard University Press, 2000); Eduardo Bonilla-Silva, "Rethinking Racism: Toward a Structural Interpretation," *American Sociological Review,* 62 (1997): 465–480.

39. Pierre Bourdieu, *Practical Reason* (Stanford: Stanford University Press, 1998 [1994]), 36.

40. Cf. Ian Haney López, *White by Law: The Legal Construction of Race,* Revised and Updated Tenth Anniversary Edition (New York: New York University Press, 2006 [1996]); Troy Duster, "The 'Morphing' Properties of Whiteness," in Birgit Brander Rasmussen, Eric Klinenberg, Irene Nexica, and Matt Wray, eds., *The Making and Unmaking of Whiteness* (Durham: Duke University Press, 2001), 113–137.

41. DeCosta, *Making Multiracials.*

42. Baldwin, *Fire Next Time,* 104.

43. Cf. Max Weber, "Class, Status, Party," in H. H. Gerth and C. Wright Mills, eds., *From Max Weber: Essays in Sociology* (New York: Oxford University Press), 180–195.

44. Rogers Burbaker, Mara Loveman, and Peter Stamatov, "Ethnicity as Cognition," *Theory and Society* 33 (2004): 31–64; Loveman, "Is 'Race' Essential?"

45. Waters, *Ethnic Options.*

46. Dalton Conley, "Universal Freckle, or How I Learned to Be White," in Birgit Brander Rasmussen, Eric Klinenberg, Irene Nexica, and Matt Wray, eds., *The Making and Unmaking of Whiteness* (Durham: Duke University Press, 2001, 25–42), 37.

47. Charles Hirschman, Richard Alba, and Reynolds Farley, "The Meaning and Measurement of Race in the U.S. Census: Glimpses into the Future," *Demography* 37 (2000): 381–393.

48. Waters, *Black Identities,* 45.

49. Mae Ngai, *Impossible Subjects: Illegal Aliens and the Making of Modern America* (Princeton: Princeton University Press, 2003), 7.

50. Ibid., 7–8.

51. López, *White by Law*, 1.

52. Glenn Loury, *The Anatomy of Racial Inequality* (Cambridge: Harvard University Press, 2001); Christian Joppke, *Immigration and the Nation-State: The United States, Germany, and Great Britain* (Oxford: Oxford University Press, 1999); Rogers Smith, *Civic Ideals: Conflicting Visions of Citizenship in U.S. History* (New Haven: Yale University Press, 1997); Judith Shklar, *American Citizenship: The Quest for Inclusion* (Cambridge: Harvard University Press, 1991).

53. Irene Bloemraad, *Becoming a Citizen: Incorporating Immigrants and Refugees in the United States and Canada* (Berkeley and Los Angeles: University of California Press, 2006).

54. Karen Arenson, "Bias Episodes Rattle a University's Diverse Student Body," *The New York Times*, October 21, 2006.

55. Federal Bureau of Investigation, "Hate Crime Statistics, 1995–2004."

56. Southern Poverty Law Center Intelligence Project, "Active U.S. Hate Groups in 2005" (Montgomery: SPLC, 2005).

57. Philomena Essed, *Everyday Racism* (Claremont: Hunter House, 1991 [1984]).

58. Richard Alba, Rubén Rumbaut, and Karen Marotz, "A Distorted Nation: Perceptions of Racial/Ethnic Group Sizes and Attitudes toward Immigrants and Other Minorities," *Social Forces* 84 (2005): 901–919; Richard Nadeau, Richard G. Niemi, and Jeffrey Levine, "Innumeracy about Minority Populations," *The Public Opinion Quarterly* 57 (1993): 332–347.

59. Shannon Harper and Barbara Reskin, "Affirmative Action at School and on the Job," *Annual Review of Sociology* 31 (2005): 357–379; David Sears, James Sidanius, and Lawrence Bobo (eds.), *Racialized Politics: The Debate about Racism in America* (Chicago: University of Chicago Press, 2000).

60. Loïc Wacquant, "For an Analytic of Racial Domination," *Political Power and Social Theory* 11 (1997): 221–234.

61. Herbert Blumer, "Race Prejudice as a Sense of Group Position," *The Pacific Sociological Review* 1 (1958): 3–7; Bonilla-Silva, "Rethinking Racism."

62. Brown et al., *White-Washing Race*, 43.

63. Kathryn M. Neckerman, *Schools Betrayed: Roots of Failure in Inner-City Education* (Chicago: University of Chicago Press, 2007); Jennie Oaks, *Keeping Track: How Schools Structure Inequality*, Second Edition (New Haven: Yale University Press, 2005).

64. Douglas Harris, *Lost Learning, Forgotten Promises: A National Analysis of School Racial Segregation, Student Achievement, and "Controlled Choice" Plans* (Washington, D.C.: Center for American Progress, 2006); Gary Orfield et al., "The Growth of Segregation in American Schools: Changing Patterns of Separation and Poverty since 1968" (Washington, D.C.: National School Boards Association, 1993); Susan Easton, "The New Segregation: Forty Years after Brown, Cities and Suburbs Face a Rising Tide of Racial Isolation," *Harvard Education Letter* 10, January 1994.

65. Jeffrey Alexander, *The Civil Sphere* (New York: Oxford University Press, 2006); Orlando Patterson, *The Ordeal of Integration: Progress and Resentment in America's "Racial" Crisis* (New York: Basic Civitas Books, 1998).

66. Holt, *Problem of Race in the Twenty-First Century,* 6.

67. Howard Winant, *The World Is a Ghetto: Race and Democracy since World War II* (New York: Basic Books, 2001); Patterson, *Ordeal of Integration;* Ngai, *Impossible Subjects.*

68. Marc Bloch, *The Historian's Craft* (New York: Vintage, 1953), 41, emphasis added.

69. Lawrence Bobo, "Racial Attitudes and Relations at the Close of the Twentieth Century," in Neil Smelser, William Julius Wilson, and Faith Mitchell, eds., *America Becoming: Racial Trends and Their Consequences* (Washington, D.C.: National Academy Press, 2000), 262–299; Howard Schuman, Charlotte Steeh, Lawrence Bobo, and Maria Krysan, *Racial Attitudes in America: Trends and Interpretations,* Revised Edition (Cambridge: Harvard University Press, 1997); Tomás Almaguer, *Racial Fault Lines: The Historical Origins of White Supremacy in California* (Berkeley and Los Angeles: University of California Press, 1994).

70. Holt, *Problem of Race in the Twenty-First Century,* 20.

71. Lillian Smith, *Killers of the Dream,* Revised Edition (New York: Norton, 1961), 96.

72. Feagin et al., *White Racism,* 3.

73. E.g., Tonry, *Malign Neglect.*

74. Joe Feagin, "The Continuing Significance of Race: Antiblack Discrimination in Public Places," *American Sociological Review* 56 (1991): 101–116.

75. Charles Lawrence, III, "The Id, the Ego, and Equal Protection: Reckoning with Unconscious Racism," *Stanford Law Review* 39 (1987): 317–388, 322, emphasis added.

76. Beverly Daniel Tatum, *"Why Are All the Black Kids Sitting Together in the Cafeteria?" and Other Conversations about Race* (New York: Basic Books, 1997), 6.

77. Pierre Bourdieu and Loïc Wacquant, *An Invitation to Reflexive Sociology* (Chicago: University of Chicago Press, 1992), 167.

78. See also Pierre Bourdieu, *Masculine Domination* (Stanford: Stanford University Press, 2001 [1998]).

79. Smith, *Killers of the Dream,* 96.

80. Jean-Paul Sartre, *Anti-Semite and Jew* (New York: Grove, 1960 [1946]), 95.

81. Bourdieu, *Masculine Domination,* 37.

82. Angela Harris, "Race and Essentialism in Feminist Legal Theory," in Richard Delgado and Jean Stefancic, eds., *Critical Race Theory: The Cutting Edge,* Second Edition (Philadelphia: Temple University Press, 2000), 261–274.

83. Kimberlé Crenshaw, "Mapping the Margins: Intersectionality, Identity Politics, and Violence against Women of Color," *Stanford Law Review* 42 (1990): 1241–1299; Chandra Mohanty, *Feminism without Borders: Decolonizing Theory, Practicing Solidarity* (Durham: Duke University Press, 2003); Angela Davis, *Women, Race, and Class* (New York: Vintage, 1983); Patricia Hill Collins, *Black Feminist Thought: Knowledge, Consciousness, and the Politics of Empowerment,* Second Edition (New York: Routledge, 2000).

84. Feagin, "Continuing Significance of Race."

85. Sylvia Walby, "Complexity Theory, Systems Theory, and Multiple Intersecting Social Inequalities," *Philosophy of the Social Sciences* 37 (2007): 449–470; Nira Yuval-Davis, "Intersectionality and Feminist Politics," *European Journal of Women's Studies* 13 (2006): 193–209; Leslie

McCall, "The Complexity of Intersectionality," *Signs: Journal of Women in Culture and Society* 30 (2005): 1771–1800.

86. Kimberlé Crenshaw, "Demarginalizing the Intersection of Race and Sex: A Black Feminist Critique of Antidiscrimination Doctrine, Feminist Theory and Antiracist Politics," *University of Chicago Legal Forum* (1989): 139–167.

87. Cf. Collins, *Black Feminist Thought.*

88. Myra Marx Ferree, "Inequality, Intersectionality and the Politics of Discourse: Framing Feminist Alliances," in Emanuela Lombardo, Petra Meier, and Mieke Verloo, eds., *The Discursive Politics of Gender Equality: Stretching, Bending, and Policy-Making* (New York: Routledge, forthcoming); McCall, "Complexity of Intersectionality."

89. Cf. Mustafa Emirbayer, "Manifesto for Relational Sociology," *American Journal of Sociology* 103 (1997): 281–317; Pierre Bourdieu, *The Rules of Art: Genesis and Structure of the Literary Field* (Stanford, CA: Stanford University Press, 1996 [1992]).

90. Feagin et al., *White Racism,* ix.

91. Conley, "Universal Freckle, or How I Learned to Be White."

92. Amanda Lewis, "'What Group?' Studying Whites and Whiteness in the Era of 'Color-Blindness,'" *Sociological Theory* 22 (2004): 623–646; Amanda Lewis, *Race in the Schoolyard: Negotiating the Color Line in Classrooms and Communities* (New Brunswick: Rutgers University Press, 2003); Ruth Frankenberg, *White Women, Race Matters: The Social Construction of Whiteness* (Minneapolis: University of Minnesota Press, 1993); Stephanie Wildman, *Privilege Revealed: How Invisible Preference Undermines America* (New York: New York University Press, 1996).

93. Toni Morrison, *Playing in the Dark: Whiteness and the Literary Imagination* (New York: Vintage, 1992), 52.

94. Frankenberg, *White Women, Race Matters,* 228–229. Also see Ruth Frankenberg, "The Mirage of an Unmarked Whiteness," in Birgit Brander Rasmussen, Eric Klinenberg, Irene Nexica, and Matt Wray, eds., *The Making and Unmaking of Whiteness* (Durham: Duke University Press, 2001), 72–96.

95. Douglas Massey and Nancy Denton, *American Apartheid: Segregation and the Making of the Underclass* (Cambridge: Harvard University Press, 1993); Devah Pager, "The Mark of a Criminal Record," *American Journal of Sociology* 108 (2003): 937–975; Tonry, *Malign Neglect;* Western, *Punishment and Inequality in America;* Oliver and Shapiro, *Black Wealth/White Wealth;* Conley, *Being Black, Living in the Red.*

96. George Lipsitz, *Possessive Investment in Whiteness: How White People Profit from Identity Politics* (Philadelphia: Temple University Press, 1998), 8–10.

97. Brown et al., *White-Washing Race,* 22.

98. Cited in Kenneth Kinnamon and Michel Fabre, *Conversations with Richard Wright* (Jackson: University Press of Mississippi, 1993), 99.

99. Gotanda, "A Critique of 'Our Constitution Is Color-Blind,'" 36.

100. K. Anthony Appiah and Amy Gutmann, *Color Conscious: The Political Morality of Race* (Princeton: Princeton University Press, 1996), 109.

101. Gotanda, "A Critique of 'Our Constitution Is Color-Blind,'" 35.

102. Lipsitz, *Possessive Investment in Whiteness*, viii.

103. Cited in W. E. B. Du Bois, *Black Reconstruction in America, 1860–1880* (Cleveland: Meridian, 1965 [1935]), pp. 592–594.

104. Lipsitz, *Possessive Investment in Whiteness*, viii–ix.

105. C. Wright Mills, *The Sociological Imagination* (New York: Oxford University Press, 1959).

106. Bourdieu and Wacquant, *Invitation to Reflexive Sociology*, 44.

107. W. E. B. Du Bois, "The Name Negro," in Eric Sundquist, ed., *The Oxford W. E. B. Du Bois Reader* (New York: Oxford, 1996 [1928]), 70–72.

Chapter 2: The Invention of Race

1. Ivan Hannaford, *Race: The History of an Idea in the West* (Baltimore: The Johns Hopkins Press, 1996); Audrey Smedley, *Race in North America: Origin and Evolution of a Worldview*, Second Edition (Boulder: Westview, 1999).

2. Pierre Bourdieu, *Masculine Domination* (Stanford: Stanford University Press, 2001 [1998]); Thomas Holt, *The Problem of Race in the 21st Century* (Cambridge: Harvard University Press, 2000).

3. Stuart Hall, "The West and the Rest: Discourse and Power," in Stuart Hall, David Held, Don Hubert, and Kenneth Thompson, eds., *Modernity: An Introduction to Modern Societies* (Malden: Blackwell, 1996), 185–227.

4. Richard Liggio, "English Origins of Early American Racism," *Radical History Review* 3 (1976): 1–36, 8.

5. Smedley, *Race in North America*.

6. Americo Castro, *The Spaniards* (Berkeley and Los Angeles: University of California Press, 1971); Smedley, *Race in North America*, 65.

7. Henry Kamen, *The Spanish Inquisition* (New Haven: Yale University Press, 1997); Norman Roth, *Conversos, Inquisition, and the Expulsion of the Jews from Spain* (Madison: University of Wisconsin Press, 1995); Smedley, *Race in North America;* Thomas Holt, *Problem of Race in the 21st Century*.

8. Benedict Anderson, *Imagined Communities* (London: Verso, 1983).

9. David Theo Goldberg, *The Racial State* (Malden: Blackwell, 2002).

10. Quoted in Hall, "The West and the Rest," 207.

11. Edward Said, *Orientalism*, 25th Anniversary Edition (New York: Vintage, 1994 [1978]); Hall, "The West and the Rest"; Smedley, *Race in North America*.

12. Juan Gonzalez, *Harvest of Empire: A History of Latinos in America* (New York: Viking, 2000), 6.

13. John Kicza, "First Contacts," in Philip Deloria and Neal Salisbury, eds., *A Companion to American Indian History* (Malden: Blackwell, 2002), 27–45.

14. Russell Thornton, "Health, Disease, and Demography," in Philip Deloria and Neal Salisbury, eds., *A Companion to American Indian History* (Malden: Blackwell, 2002), 68–84; William Denevan, ed., *The Native Population of the Americas in 1492*, Second Edition (Madison: University of Wisconsin Press, 1992); Russell Thornton, *American Indian Holocaust and*

Survival: A Population History since 1492 (Norman: University of Oklahoma Press, 1987); Woodrow Borah and Sherburne Cook, *Essays in Population History*, Three Volumes (Berkeley and Los Angeles: University of California Press, 1971–1979).

15. Melvin Page, ed., *Colonialism: An International Social, Cultural, and Political Encyclopedia* (Santa Barbara: ABC-CLIO, 2003).

16. Hall, "The West and the Rest," 204.

17. Gonzalez, *Harvest of Empire*, 4.

18. Bernal Díaz del Castillo, *The Conquest of New Spain* (New York: Penguin, 1963 [1569]), 216, 235.

19. Tzvetan Todorov, *The Conquest of America: The Question of the Other* (New York: Harper and Row, 1984); Castillo, *Conquest of New Spain*.

20. Michael Meyer and William Sherman, *The Course of Mexican History* (New York: Oxford University Press, 1995); Patricia Seed, *To Love, Honor, and Obey in Colonial Mexico: Conflicts over Marriage Choice, 1574–1821* (Stanford: Stanford University Press, 1988).

21. Martha Menchaca, *Recovering History, Constructing Race: The Indian, Black, and White Roots of Mexican Americans* (Austin: University of Texas Press, 2001); Meyer and Sherman, *The Course of Mexican History*.

22. Menchaca, *Recovering History, Constructing Race*; Castillo, *The Conquest of New Spain*.

23. Bartolomé de Las Casas, *A Short Account of the Destruction of the Indies* (New York: Penguin, 1992 [1542]), 32.

24. David Brion Davis, *Inhuman Bondage: The Rise and Fall of Slavery in the New World* (New York: Oxford University Press, 2006), 98.

25. Gonzalez, *Harvest of Empire*, 14.

26. Smedley, *Race in North America*.

27. Jack Weatherford, *Indian Givers: How the Indians of the Americas Transformed the World* (New York: Fawcett Columbine, 1988); Bruce Johnson, *Forgotten Founders: How the American Indian Helped Shape Democracy* (Boston: The Harvard Common Press, 1987); Henry Steele Commager, *The Empire of Reason: How Europe Imagined and America Realized the Enlightenment* (New York: Doubleday, 1977).

28. Hall, "The West and the Rest."

29. Thornton, "Health, Disease, and Demography."

30. Stephen Cornell, *The Return of the Native: American Indian Political Resurgence* (New York: Oxford University Press, 1988), 52. Also see Francis Jennings, *The Invasion of America: Indians, Colonialism, and the Cant of Conquest* (New York: Norton, 1976); Alfred Crosby, Jr., *The Columbian Exchange: Biological and Cultural Consequences of 1492* (Westport: Greenwood Press, 1972).

31. David Cook, *Born to Die: Disease and New World Conquest, 1492–1650* (Cambridge: Cambridge University Press, 1998), 13.

32. Clark Larsen, "In the Wake of Columbus: Native Population Biology in the Postcontact Americas," *Yearbook of Physical Anthropology* 37 (1994): 109–154; Cary Meister, "Demographic Consequences of Euro-American Contact on Selected American Indian Populations and Their Relationship to the Demographic Transition," *Ethnohistory* 23 (1976): 161–172.

33. Hugh Dempsey, "Smallpox: Scourge of the Plains," in Anthony Rasporich and Max Foran, eds., *Harm's Way: Disasters in Western Canada* (Calgary: University of Calgary Press, 2004, 15–40), 35. Also see Barbara Alice Mann, *George Washington's War on Native America* (Westport: Praeger, 2005).

34. Thornton, *American Indian Holocaust and Survival*, 42–43.

35. Jennings, *The Invasion of America*, 30.

36. Bernard Bailyn, *The Peopling of British North America* (New York: Vintage, 1988); Philip Foner, *Labor and the American Revolution* (Westport: Greenwood, 1976).

37. Smedley, *Race in North America*, 100–101.

38. Theodore Allen, *The Invention of the White Race*, Volumes I and II (London: Verso, 1994 and 1997); David Galenson, *White Servitude in Colonial America: An Economic Analysis* (Cambridge: Cambridge University Press, 1981); Sharon Salinger, *To Serve Well and Faithfully: Labor and Indentured Servants in Pennsylvania* (New York: Heritage, 1987).

39. David Roediger, *The Wages of Whiteness: Race and the Making of the American Working Class* (London: Verso, 1991).

40. Ibid.

41. Quoted in David Brion Davis, *The Problem of Slavery in Western Culture* (Ithaca: Cornell University Press, 1961), 3–4.

42. Orlando Patterson, *Slavery and Social Death: A Comparative Study* (Cambridge: Harvard University Press, 1982), 340.

43. Allen, *Invention of the White Race*.

44. Cornell, *Return of the Native*, 28–32; Smedley, *Race in North America*, 104–105.

45. Smedley, *Race in North America*, 105–106.

46. Ibid., 109.

47. David Eltis, *The Rise of African Slavery in the Americas* (Cambridge: Cambridge University Press, 2000); William Pierson, *From Africa to America: African American History from the Colonial Era to the New Republic, 1526–1790* (New York: Twayne, 1996).

48. Anne Bailey, *African Voices of the Atlantic Slave Trade: Beyond the Silence and the Shame* (Boston: Beacon, 2005); Igor Kopytoff, ed., *The African Frontier: The Reproduction of Traditional African Societies* (Bloomington: Indiana University Press, 1987); David Eltis, *Economic Growth and the Ending of the Transatlantic Slave Trade* (New York: Oxford University Press, 1987); Walter Rodney, *How Europe Underdeveloped Africa* (Washington: Howard University Press, 1972).

49. Hugh Thomas, *The Slave Trade: The Story of the Atlantic Slave Trade: 1440–1870* (New York: Touchstone, 1997), 415.

50. Quoted in Thomas, *Slave Trade*, 412. Also see John Newton, "A Reformed Slave Trader's Regrets, c. 1745–1754," in David Northrup, ed., *The Atlantic Slave Trade* (Lexington: D.C. Heath, 1994), 80–89.

51. Malcolm Cowley and Daniel Mannix, *Black Cargoes: A History of the Atlantic Slave Trade, 1518–1862* (New York: Harold Matson, 1962); Kenneth Kiple and Brian Higgins, "Mortality Caused by Dehydration during the Middle Passage," in Joseph Inikori and Stanley

Engerman, eds., *The Atlantic Slave Trade: Effects on Economies, Societies, and Peoples in Africa, The Americas, and Europe* (Durham: Duke University Press, 1992), 321–338; Thomas, *Slave Trade*, 416–422.

52. Thomas, *Slave Trade*, 424.

53. Geroge Nørregård, *Danish Settlements in West Africa, 1658–1850* (Boston: Boston University Press, 1966), 89. See also Maggie Montesinos Sale, *The Slumbering Volcano: American Slave Ship Revolts and the Production of Rebellious Masculinity* (Durham: Duke University Press, 1997); Eric Taylor, "If We Must Die: A History of Shipboard Insurrections during the Slave Trade" (Los Angeles: University of California, Unpublished Dissertation, 2000).

54. Winthrop Jordan, *White over Black: American Attitudes toward the Negro, 1550–1812* (Chapel Hill: University of North Carolina Press, 1968), 366–367; Thomas, *Slave Trade*, 424.

55. David Richardson, "The Costs of Survival: The Transport of Slaves in the Middle Passage and the Profitability of the 18th-Century British Slave Trade," *Explorations in Economic History* 24 (1987): 178–196.

56. Philip Curtin, *The Atlantic Slave Trade: A Census* (Madison: University of Wisconsin Press, 1969); Paul Lovejoy, "The Volume of the Atlantic Slave Trade: A Synthesis," *Journal of African History* 23 (1982): 473–501; David Henige, "Measuring the Immeasurable: The Atlantic Slave Trade, West Africa Population and the Pyrrhonian Critic," *Journal of African History*, 27 (1986): 295–313; Joseph Inikori and Stanley Engerman, *The Atlantic Slave Trade* (Durham: Duke University Press, 1992).

57. Joseph Miller, *The Way of Death: Merchant Capitalism and the Angolan Slave Trade* (Madison: University of Wisconsin Press, 1988). Also see James Rawley, *The Transatlantic Slave Trade: A History*, Revised Edition (Lincoln: University of Nebraska Press, 2005); John Thornton, *Africa and Africans in Making of the Atlantic World, 1400–1800* (Cambridge: Cambridge University Press, 1998); Rodney, *How Europe Underdeveloped Africa*.

58. Eltis, *Rise of African Slavery in the Americas*, 11.

59. Robert Fogel, *Without Consent or Contract: The Rise and Fall of American Slavery* (New York: Norton, 1989), 29.

60. Deborah Gray White, *Let My People Go: African Americans 1804–1860* (New York: Oxford University Press, 1996); Ronald Bailey, "The Slave(ry) Trade and the Development of Capitalism in the United States: The Textile Industry in New England," in Joseph Inikori and Stanley Engerman, eds., *The Atlantic Slave Trade: Effects on Economies, Societies, and Peoples in Africa, The Americas, and Europe* (Durham: Duke University Press, 1992), 205–246; Fogel, *Without Consent or Contract*.

61. Fogel, *Without Consent or Contract*, 28–29.

62. W. E. B. Du Bois, *Black Reconstruction in America* (Cleveland: Meridian, 1935), 29.

63. Ibid., 700–701.

64. Pem Davidson Buck, *Worked to the Bone: Race, Class, Power, and Privilege in Kentucky* (New York: Monthly Review Press, 2001), 24.

65. William Goodell, *The American Slave Code in Theory and Practice: Its Distinctive Features Shown by Its Statutes, Judicial Decisions, and Illustrative Facts* (Ann Arbor: Scholarly Publishing

Office, University of Michigan Library, 2006); Gary Nash, *Red, White, and Black: The Peoples of Early America,* Third Edition (Englewood Cliffs: Prentice Hall, 1992). John Blassingame, *The Slave Community: Plantation Life in the Antebellum South* (New York: Oxford University Press, 1979).

66. David Brion Davis and Steven Mintz, *The Boisterous Sea of Liberty: A Documentary History of America from Discovery through the Civil War* (New York: Oxford University Press, 1998), 58.

67. Davis, *Who Is Black?;* Haney-López, *White by Law.*

68. Patterson, *Slavery and Social Death,* 51–96; Jordan, *White Over Black,* 103–110, 366–367.

69. Jordan, *White Over Black,* 106.

70. Elizabeth Keckley, *Behind the Scenes; or, Thirty Years a Slave and Four Years in the White House,* in Henry Louis Gates, Jr., and Nellie McKay, eds., *The Norton Anthology of African American Literature,* Second Edition (New York: Norton, 2004, 365–384), 373.

71. Orlando Patterson, *Rituals of Blood: Consequences of Slavery in Two American Centuries* (New York: Basic Books, 1988); Eugene Genovese, *Roll, Jordan, Roll: The World the Slaves Made* (New York: Vintage, 1972).

72. Harriet Jacobs, *Incidents in the Life of a Slave Girl* (1861), in Henry Louis Gates, Jr., and Nellie McKay, eds., *The Norton Anthology of African American Literature,* Second Edition (New York: Norton, 2004, 279–314), 294.

73. Patricia Hill Collins, *Black Sexual Politics: African Americans, Gender, and the New Racism* (New York: Routledge, 2004); David Barry Gaspar and Darlene Clark Hine, eds., *More Than Chattel: Black Women and Slavery in the Americas* (Bloomington: Indiana University Press, 1996); Deborah Gray White, *Ar'n't I a Woman? Female Slaves in the Plantation South* (New York: Norton, 1985); Jacqueline Jones, *Labor of Love, Labor of Sorrow: Black Women, Work, and the Family from Slavery to the Present* (New York: Basic Books, 1985).

74. Dorothy Roberts, *Killing the Black Body: Race, Reproduction, and the Meaning of Liberty* (New York: Pantheon, 1997), 24.

75. Jacobs, *Incidents in the Life of a Slave Girl,* 287–288.

76. Angela Davis, *Women, Race, and Class* (New York: Vintage, 1983); Roberts, *Killing the Black Body.*

77. White, *Ar'n't I a Woman?,* 188.

78. Collins, *Black Sexual Politics;* Patterson, *Rituals of Blood.*

79. Stanley Elkins, *Slavery: A Problem in American Institutional and Intellectual Life* (Chicago: University of Chicago Press, 1959), 82.

80. Patterson, *Slavery and Social Death,* 46.

81. James Scott, *Domination and the Arts of Resistance: Hidden Transcripts* (New Haven: Yale University Press, 1990).

82. Scott, *Domination and the Arts of Resistance;* Patterson, *Slavery and Social Death.*

83. Walter Rucker, *The River Flows On: Black Resistance, Culture, and Identity Formation in Early America* (Baton Rouge: Louisiana State University Press, 2006); Eugene Genovese,

From Rebellion to Revolution: Afro-American Slave Revolts in the Making of the New World (New York: Vintage, 1979); Herbert Aptheker, *American Negro Slave Revolts* (New York: International, 1974 [1943]).

84. Aptheker, *American Negro Slave Revolts*, 4.

85. Herbert Aptheker, *Anti-Racism in U.S. History: The First Two Hundred Years* (New York: Greenwood Press, 1994); W. E. B. Du Bois, *Darkwater: Voices from within the Veil* (New York: Dover 1999 [1920]).

86. David Reynolds, *John Brown, Abolitionist: The Man Who Killed Slavery, Sparked the Civil War, and Seeded Civil Rights* (New York: Vintage, 2006); Stanley Harrold, *The Abolitionists and the South, 1831–1861* (Lexington: University Press of Kentucky, 1995); Larry Ceplair, ed., *The Public Years of Sarah and Angelina Grimké: Selected Writings, 1835–1839* (New York: Columbia University Press, 1989); Merton Dillon, *The Abolitionists: The Growth of a Dissenting Minority* (DeKalb: Northern Illinois University Press, 1974); Russell Nye, *William Lloyd Garrison and the Humanitarian Reformers* (New York: Little Brown, 1969); Aptheker, *Anti-Racism in U.S. History*.

87. Frederick Douglas, "What to the Slave Is the Fourth of July? An Address Delivered in Rochester, New York, on 5 July 1852" in Henry Louis Gates, Jr., and Nellie McKay, eds., *The Norton Anthology of African American Literature*, Second Edition (New York: Norton, 2004, 462–473), 468, 470.

88. Du Bois, *Darkwater*, 102.

89. Quoted in Nell Irvin Painter, *Sojourner Truth: A Life, A Symbol* (New York: Norton, 1996), 167.

90. Leslie Schwalm, *A Hard Fight for We: Women's Transition from Slavery to Freedom in South Carolina* (Urbana: University of Illinois Press, 1997); Eric Foner, *Reconstruction: America's Unfinished Revolution, 1863–1877* (New York: Perennial, 1988).

91. Du Bois, *Black Reconstruction in America*, 611.

92. Michael Vorenberg, *Final Freedom: The Civil War, the Abolition of Slavery, and the Thirteenth Amendment* (New York: Cambridge University Press, 2001); Gao Chunchang, *African Americans in the Reconstruction Era* (New York: Garland, 2000); Eric Anderson and Alfred Moss, Jr., eds., *The Facts of Reconstruction* (Baton Rouge: Louisiana State University Press, 1991).

93. Stewart Tolnay and E. M. Beck, "Black Flight: Lethal Violence and the Great Migration, 1900–1930," *Social Science History* 12 (1991): 347–370; W. J. Cash, *The Mind of the South* (New York: Knopf, 1941); Patterson, *Rituals of Blood*.

94. "Strange Fruit" was composed in 1937 by Abel Meeropol, a.k.a. Lewis Allan. Holiday first performed it two years later. See David Margolick, *Strange Fruit: The Biography of a Song* (New York: Harper Perennial, 2001).

95. Jane Dailey, Glenda Elizabeth Gilmore, and Bryant Simon, eds., *Jumpin' Jim Crow: Southern Politics from Civil War to Civil Rights* (Princeton: Princeton University Press, 2000); Glenda Elizabeth Gilmore, *Gender and Jim Crow: Women and the Politics of White Supremacy in North Carolina, 1896–1920* (Chapel Hill: University of North Carolina Press, 1996).

96. Ira Berlin, *Man Thousands Gone: The First Two Centuries of Slavery in North America* (Cambridge: Harvard University Press, 1998); David Brion Davis, *Slavery and Human Progress* (New York: Oxford University Press, 1984); Eric Williams, *Capitalism and Slavery* (Chapel Hill: University of North Carolina Press, 1944).

97. Gonzalez, *Harvest of Empire.*

98. Enrique Krauze, *Mexico: Biography of Power—A History of Modern Mexico, 1810–1996* (New York: Harper Collins, 1997); Lesley Byrd Simpson, *Many Mexicos,* Fourth Edition (Berkeley and Los Angeles: University of California Press, 1996); David Weber, *The Mexican Frontier, 1821–1846: The American Southwest under Mexico* (Albuquerque: University of New Mexico Press, 1982).

99. Gonzalez, *Harvest of Empire.*

100. Quoted in Arnoldo De León, *They Called Them Greasers: Anglo Attitudes toward Mexicans in Texas, 1821–1900* (Austin: University of Texas Press, 1983), 2–3.

101. Quoted in Juan Gonzalez, *Harvest of Empire,* 44.

102. Menchaca, *Recovering History, Constructing Race;* Weber, *Mexican Frontier.*

103. Weber, *Mexican Frontier,* 274–275; Gonzalez, *Harvest of Empire,* 44.

104. Menchaca, *Recovering History, Constructing Race,* 215–217; Jocelyn Bowden, *Spanish and Mexican Land Grants in the Chihuahua Acquisition* (El Paso: Texas Western Press, 1971).

105. Gonzalez, *Harvest of Empire,* 30.

106. Gloria Anzaldúa, *Borderlands, La Frontera: The New Mestiza,* Second Edition (San Francisco: Aunt Lute Books, 1987).

107. Menchaca, *Recovering History, Constructing Race.*

108. Cornell, *Return of the Native,* 40–45.

109. George Tindall, *America: A Narrative History,* Second Edition (New York: Norton, 1988), 423.

110. Robert Remini, *Andrew Jackson and His Indian Wars* (New York: Viking, 2001); William Anderson, ed., *Cherokee Removal: Before and After* (Athens: University of Georgia Press, 1991); John Ehle, *Trail of Tears: The Rise and Fall of the Cherokee Nation* (New York: Doubleday, 1988); Samuel Carter, *Cherokee Sunset: A Nation Betrayed* (New York: Doubleday, 1976).

111. Quoted in Ronald Takaki, *A Different Mirror: A History of Multicultural America* (Boston: Little Brown, 1993), 97.

112. Cornell, *Return of the Native,* 59.

113. Vine Deloria, Jr., *Custer Died for Your Sins: An Indian Manifesto* (Norman: University of Oklahoma Press, 1988); Takaki, *Different Mirror.*

114. Deloria, *Custer Died for Your Sins,* 35–36.

115. Cornell, *Return of the Native,* 38–40, 54–55.

116. Willard Hughes Rollings, "Indians and Christianity," in Philip Deloria and Neal Salisbury, eds., *A Companion to American Indian History* (Malden: Blackwell, 2002), 121–138; William Coleman, *Voices of Wounded Knee* (Lincoln: University of Nebraska Press, 2000); Dee Brown, *Bury My Heart at Wounded Knee: An Indian History of the American West* (New York: Owl Books, 1971).

117. Lawrence McCaffrey, *Textures of Irish Immigration* (New York: Syracuse University Press, 1992); Naomi Cohen, *Encounter with Emancipation: The German Jews in the United States, 1830–1914* (Philadelphia: Jewish Publication Society, 1984); Lawrence McCaffrey, *The Irish Diaspora in America* (Bloomington: Indiana University Press, 1976); John Higham, *Standers in the Land: Patterns of American Nativism, 1860–1925* (New York: Antheneum, 1985 [1955]).

118. Walt Whitman, "Preface to Leaves of Grass" (1855) in Nina Baym, ed., *The Norton Anthology of American Literature, Volume I,* Fifth Edition (New York: Norton, 1998, 2080–2096), 2080.

119. Lucie Cheng and Edna Bonacich, eds., *Labor Immigration under Capitalism: Asian Workers in the United States before World War II* (Berkeley and Los Angeles: University of California Press, 1984).

120. Said, *Orientalism,* 49.

121. Susie Lan Cassel, ed., *The Chinese in America: A History from Gold Mountain to the New Millennium* (Walnut Creek: AltaMira, 2002); Gary Okihiro, *The Columbia Guide to Asian American History* (New York: Columbia University Press, 2001); Ronald Takaki, *Strangers from a Different Shore: A History of Asian Americans* (London: Little Brown, 1989); Ronald Takaki, *Plantation Life and Labor in Hawaii* (Honolulu: University of Hawaii Press, 1983).

122. Henry Yu, *Thinking Orientals: Migration, Contact, and Exoticism in Modern America* (New York: Oxford University Press, 2001); Cassel, *Chinese in America;* Okihiro, *Columbia Guide to Asian American History;* Cheng and Bonacich, *Labor Immigration under Capitalism;* Takaki, *Strangers from a Different Shore.*

123. *Dutch Flat Chronicles,* August 30, 1877.

124. Mia Tuan, *Forever Foreigners or Honorary Whites? The Asian Ethnic Experience Today* (New Brunswick: Rutgers University Press, 2003); Emma Gee, ed., *Counterpoint: Perspectives on Asian America* (Los Angeles: Asian American Studies Center, University of California, 1976); Stuart Creighton Miller, *The Unwelcome Immigrant: The American Image of the Chinese, 1785–1882* (Berkeley and Los Angeles: University of California Press, 1969); Okihiro, *Columbia Guide to Asian American History;* Takaki, *Strangers from a Different Shore.*

125. Paul Ong and John Liu, "U.S. Immigration Policies and Asian Migration," in Min Zhou and James Gatewood, eds., *Contemporary Asian America: A Multidisciplinary Reader* (New York: New York University Press, 2000), 155–174; Yu, *Thinking Orientals;* Okihiro, *Columbia Guide to Asian American History.*

126. Haney-López, *White by Law.*

127. Ellwood Cubberley, *Changing Conceptions of Education* (New York: Houghton Mifflin, 1909), 14–15.

128. Ibid.

129. David Roediger, *Working toward Whiteness: How America's Immigrations Became White, the Strange Journey from Willis Island to the Suburbs* (New York: Basic Books, 2005).

130. Eric Arnesen, "Whiteness and the Historians' Imagination," *International Labor and Working-Class History* 60 (2001): 3–32; Roediger, *Wages of Whiteness,* 140; Guglielmo, *White on Arrival.*

131. Higham, *Strangers in the Land,* 158–193.

132. Neil Foley, *The White Scourge: Mexicans, Blacks, and Poor Whites in Texas Cotton Culture* (Berkeley and Los Angeles: University of California Press, 1997), 7.

133. Noel Ignatiev, *How the Irish Became White* (London: Routledge, 1996); Roediger, *Working toward Whiteness;* Jacobson, *Whiteness of a Different Color.*

134. Matthew Jacobson, *Whiteness of a Different Color: European Immigrants and the Alchemy of Race* (Cambridge: Harvard University Press, 1999); Arnesen, "Whiteness and the Historians' Imagination," 16.

135. Donald Young, *American Minority Peoples: A Study in Racial and Cultural Conflicts in the United States* (New York: Harpers and Brothers, 1932), 421.

136. Roediger, *Working toward Whiteness,* 22–23.

137. Ignatiev, *How the Irish Became White;* Roediger, *Working toward Whiteness.*

138. Ignatiev, *How the Irish Became White.*

139. Toni Morrison, "On the Backs of Blacks," *Time,* December 2, 1993.

140. Grace Elizabeth Hale, *Making Whiteness: The Culture of Segregation in the South, 1890–1940* (New York: Viking, 1998).

141. Roediger, *Working toward Whiteness.*

142. James Baldwin, *The Price of the Ticket, Collected Nonfiction, 1949–1985* (New York: St. Martin's Press, 1985), p. xx.

143. Du Bois, *Darkwater,* 17.

144. Cornell West, "A Genealogy of Modern Racism," in Philomena Essed and David Theo Goldberg, eds., *Race Critical Theories: Test and Context* (Malden: Blackwell, 2002), 99–112.

145. David Theo Goldberg, *The Racial State* (Malden: Blackwell, 2002), 41–43.

146. Quoted in West, "Genealogy of Modern Racism," 106.

147. Thomas Gossett, *Race: The History of An Idea in America* (New York: Schocken, 1965), 32–34.

148. Quoted in Smedley, *Race in North America,* 161.

149. West, "Genealogy of Modern Racism," 101.

150. Smedley, *Race in North America,* 164–165.

151. Cited in Gould, *Mismeasure of Man,* 154.

152. Richard Lynn, *Eugenics, A Reassessment* (Westport: Praeger, 2001); Philip Reilly, *The Surgical Solution: A History of Involuntary Sterilization in the United States* (Baltimore: The Johns Hopkins Press, 1991).

153. Quoted in M. F. Ashley Montagu, *Man's Most Dangerous Myth: The Fallacy of Race,* Third Edition (New York: Harpers, 1952 [1942]), 153.

154. Daniel Kevles, *In the Name of Eugenics: Genetics and the Uses of Human Heredity* (New York: Knopf, 1985); Reilly, *Surgical Solution.*

155. Montagu, *Man's Most Dangerous Myth,* 164, 168.

156. Holt, *Problem of Race in the Twenty-First Century,* 33.

157. West, "Genealogy of Modern Racism," 108.

158. U.S. Census Bureau, "State and Country Quick Facts," 2005.

159. Richard Alba, Rubén Rumbaut, and Karen Marotz, "A Distorted Nation: Perceptions of Racial/Ethnic Group Sizes and Attitudes toward Immigrants and Other Minorities," *Social Forces* 84 (2005): 901–919; Richard Nadeau, Richard G. Niemi, Jeffrey Levine, "Innumeracy about Minority Populations," *The Public Opinion Quarterly* 57 (1993): 332–347.

160. U.S. Census Bureau, "State and Country Quick Facts," 2005.

161. Nadeau et al., "Innumeracy about Minority Populations."

162. Alba et al., "A Distorted Nation."

163. Blumer, "Race Prejudice as a Sense of Group Position," 3–4.

164. Lincoln Quillian, "Prejudice as a Response to Perceived Group Threat: Population Composition and Anti-Immigrant and Racial Prejudice in Europe," *American Sociological Review* 60 (1995): 586–611; Lawrence Bobo, "'Whites' Opposition to Busing: Symbolic Racism or Realistic Group Conflict?," *Journal of Personality and Social Psychology* 45 (1983): 1196–1210.

165. National Research Council, *The New Americans: Economic, Demographic, and Fiscal Effects of Immigration* (Washington, D.C.: National Academy Press, 1997); U.S. Census Bureau, "State and Country Quick Facts," 2005.

166. U.S. Census Bureau, *Current Population Survey* (Washington, D.C.: U.S. Government Printing Office, 2002).

167. James Smith and Barry Edmonston, *The New Americans: Economic, Demographic, and Fiscal Effects of Immigration* (Washington, D.C.: National Academic Press, 1997).

168. Gustavo Arellano, "¡Ask a Mexican!, Special Half-Breed Edición," *OC Weekly,* September 20, 2007.

169. Jennifer Lee and Frank Bean, "America's Changing Color Lines: Immigration, Race/Ethnicity, and Multiracial Identification," *Annual Review of Sociology* 30 (2004): 221–242.

170. Davis, *Who Is Black?*

171. Mara Loveman and Jeronimo Muniz, "How Puerto Rico Became White: Boundary Dynamics and Inter-Census Racial Reclassification," *American Sociological Review* 72 (2007): 915–939; Brent Staples, "On Race and the Census: Struggles with Categories That No Longer Apply," *The New York Times,* February 5, 2007.

172. Orlando Patterson, *The Ordeal of Integration: Progress and Resentment in America's "Racial" Crisis* (New York: Basic Civitas Books, 1998).

173. Durkheim, *Evolution of Educational Thought.*

Chapter 3: Politics

1. Kay Mills, *This Little Light of Mine: The Life of Fannie Lou Hamer* (New York: Plume, 1994), 119–121.

2. Omi and Winant, *Racial Formation in the United States,* 79.

3. Charles Payne, *I've Got the Light of Freedom: The Organizing Tradition and the Mississippi Freedom Struggle* (Berkeley and Los Angeles: University of California Press, 1995), 42.

4. Doug McAdam, *Freedom Summer* (New York: Oxford University Press, 1988); Payne, *I've Got the Light of Freedom.*

5. Payne, *I've Got the Light of Freedom,* 7–11.

6. Ibid.

7. Andrew Manis, *A Fire You Can't Put Out: The Civil Rights Life of Birmingham's Reverend Fred Shuttlesworth* (Tuscaloosa: University of Alabama Press, 1999).

8. Martin Luther King, Jr., "Letter from Birmingham Jail," in *Why We Can't Wait* (New York: Signet, 2000, 64–84), 68.

9. Aldon Morris, *The Origins of the Civil Rights Movement: Black Communities Organizing for Change* (New York: Free Press, 1984).

10. Ibid., 30.

11. Ibid.

12. Ibid.

13. Stewart Burns, *Daybreak of Freedom: The Montgomery Bus Boycott* (Chapel Hill: North Carolina University Press, 1997).

14. Lynne Olson, *Freedom's Daughters: The Unsung Heroines of the Civil Rights Movement from 1830 to 1970* (New York: Scribner, 2002); Jo Ann Robinson, *Montgomery Bus Boycott and the Women Who Started It: The Memoir of Jo Ann Gibson Robinson* (Knoxville: University of Tennessee Press, 1987).

15. Adam Fairclough, *Better Day Coming: Blacks and Equality, 1890–2000* (New York: Penguin, 2001); Taylor Branch, *Parting the Waters: America in the King Years, 1954–1963* (New York: Simon and Schuster, 1989); David Garrow, *Bearing the Cross: Martin Luther King, Jr., and the Southern Christian Leadership Conference* (New York: HarperCollins paperback, 2004 [1986]).

16. Payne, *I've Got the Light of Freedom*, 93.

17. Morris, *Origins of the Civil Rights Movement*; Payne, *I've Got the Light of Freedom*.

18. King, "Letter from Birmingham Jail," 40.

19. Morris, *Origins of the Civil Rights Movement*; Payne, *I've Got the Light of Freedom*.

20. Robert Moses, Mieko Kamii, Susan McAllister Swap, and Jeffrey Howard, "The Algebra Project: Organizing in the Spirit of Ella," *Harvard Educational Review* 59 (1989): 423–443.

21. Chandler Davidson and Bernard Grofman, eds., *The Quiet Revolution in the South: The Impact of the Voting Rights Act, 1965–1999* (Princeton: Princeton University Press, 1994); Payne, *I've Got the Light of Freedom*, 112.

22. McAdam, *Freedom Summer*.

23. David Garrow, "Commentary," in Charles Eagles, ed., *The Civil Rights Movement in America* (Oxford: University of Mississippi Press, 1986), 59–60.

24. McAdam, *Freedom Summer*, 96.

25. Ibid., 97.

26. King, "Letter from Birmingham Jail," 83.

27. Martin Luther King, Jr., "Address at the Conclusion of the Selma to Montgomery March," in Clayborn Carson and Kris Shepard, eds., *A Call to Conscience: The Landmark Speeches of Martin Luther King, Jr.* (New York: Warner Books, 2001, 111–132), 131.

28. Frank Parker, David Colby, and Minion Morrison, "Mississippi," in Chandler Davidson and Bernard Grofman, eds., *The Quiet Revolution in the South: The Impact of the Voting Rights Act, 1965–1999* (Princeton: Princeton University Press, 1994), 137–154.

29. Morris, *Origins of the Civil Rights Movement*, 287–288.

30. Troy Johnson, Duane Champagne, and Joane Nagel, "American Indian Activism and Transformation: Lessons from Alcatraz," in Troy Johnson, Joane Nagel, and Duane Champagne, eds., *American Indian Activism: From Alcatraz to the Longest Walk* (Urbana: University of Illinois Press, 1997), 9–44.

31. Joane Nagel, *American Indian Ethnic Renewal: Red Power and the Resurgence of Identity and Culture* (New York: Oxford University Press, 1996); Johnson et al., "American Indian Activism and Transformation."

32. Peter Matthiessen, *Sal Si Puedes (Escape If You Can): César Chávez and the New American Revolution* (Berkeley and Los Angeles: University of California Press, 2000); Susan Ferriss and Ricardo Sandoval, *The Fight in the Fields: César Chávez and the Farmworkers Movement* (New York: Harvest, 1997).

33. César Chávez, "Eulogy for Rufino Contreras," in Richard Jay Jensen and John Hammerback, eds., *The Words of César Chávez* (College Station: Texas A&M University Press, 2002), 181–182.

34. Ibid.

35. Michael Suleiman, "Introduction: The Arab Immigrant Experience," Michael Suleiman, ed., *Arabs in America: Building a Future* (Philadelphia: Temple University Press, 1999), 1–21.

36. Edna Bonacich, "A Theory of Middleman Minorities," *American Sociological Review* 38 (1973): 583–594; Michael Suleiman, "Introduction"; Edward Said, *Orientalism*, 287.

37. Michael Suleiman, *Arabs in the Mind of America* (Brattleboro: Amana Books, 1988); Michael Suleiman, "Introduction."

38. William Wei, *The Asian American Movement: A Social History* (Philadelphia: Temple University Press, 1993); Yen Le Espiritu, *Asian American Panethnicty: Bridging Institutions and Identities* (Philadelphia: Temple University Press, 1993), 32–52.

39. Steve Louie and Glenn Omatsu, eds., *Asian Americans: the Movement and the Moment* (Los Angeles: UCLA Asian American Studies Center Press, 2001); Wei, *Asian American Movement*.

40. Payne, *I've Got the Light of Freedom*, 5.

41. Nancy MacLean, *Freedom Is Not Enough: The Opening of the American Workplace* (Cambridge: Harvard University Press, 2006).

42. Dan Carter, *From George Wallace to Newt Gingrich: Race in the Conservative Counterrevolution, 1963–1994* (Baton Rouge: Louisiana State University Press, 1996), 6.

43. Steven Rosenstone, Roy Behr, and Edward Lazarus, *Third Parties in America: Citizen Response to Major Political Failure* (Princeton: Princeton University Press, 1984), 111.

44. Feagin and Vera, *White Racism*, 113. See also "Haldeman Diary Shows Nixon Was Wary of Blacks and Jews," *The New York Times*, May 18, 1994.

45. Carter, *From George Wallace to Newt Gingrich*, 43.

46. Juan Williams, "Reagan, the South, and Civil Rights," *National Public Radio*, June 10, 2004.

47. Cited in Stephen Steinberg, "The Liberal Retreat from Race during the Post-Civil Rights Era," in Wahneema Lubiano, ed., *The House That Race Built: Black Americans, U.S. Terrain* (New York: Pantheon, 1997), 20–21.

48. Ibid.

49. Daniel Patrick Moynihan, "The Negro Family: The Case for National Action," in Lee Rainwater and William Yancey, eds., *The Moynihan Report and the Politics of Controversy* (Cambridge: MIT Press, 1967), 76.

50. Stephen Steinberg, *Turning Back: The Retreat from Racial Justice in American Thought and Policy* (Boston: Beacon, 1995).

51. MacLean, *Freedom Is Not Enough.*

52. King, *Why We Can't Wait*, 125.

53. Steinberg, "The Liberal Retreat from Race during the Post-Civil Rights Era," 23.

54. James Baldwin, Nathan Glazer, Sidney Hook, and Gunnar Myrdal, "Liberalism and the Negro: A Round-Table Discussion," *Commentary* 37 (1964): 25–42, 31.

55. Nicholas Valentino and David Sears, "Old Times There Are Not Forgotten: Race and Partisan Realignment in the Contemporary South," *American Journal of Political Science* 49 (2005): 672–688; Paul Abramson, John Aldrich, and David Rohde, *Change and Continuity in the 2000 and 2002 Elections* (Washington, D.C.: CQ Press, 2003); Jeremy Mayer, *Running on Race: Racial Politics in Presidential Campaigns, 1960–2000* (New York: Random House, 2002).

56. Andrew Hacker, *Two Nations: Black and White, Separate, Hostile, Unequal* (New York: Scribner, 2003), 231.

57. Paul Abramson et al., *Change and Continuity;* Yvette Alex-Assensoh and Lawrence Hanks, eds., *Black and Multiracial Politics in America* (New York: New York University Press, 2000).

58. Louis DeSipio and Rodolfo de la Garza, "Forever Seen as New: Latino Participation in American Elections," in Marcelo Suárez-Orozco and Mariela Páez, eds., *Latinos: Remaking America* (Berkeley and Los Angeles: University of California Press, 2002), 398–409. Rodolfo de la Garza and Louis DeSipio, *Ethnic Ironies: Latino Politics in the 1992 Elections* (Boulder: Westview, 1996).

59. Megan Thee, "Multiple Signs of a Changing Electorate," *The New York Times,* November 6, 2008.

60. Julia Preston, "In Big Shift, Latino Vote Was Heavily for Obama," *The New York Times,* November 7, 2008.

61. Preston, "In Big Shift."

62. Jackie Calmes and Megan Thee, "Polls Find Obama Built Broader Base Than Past Nominees," *The New York Times,* November 5, 2008.

63. U.S. Senate, "Ethnic Diversity in the Senate" (Washington, D.C.: U.S. Senate, 2007); David Canon, *Race, Redistricting, and Representation: The Unintended Consequences of Majority Black Districts* (Chicago: University of Chicago Press, 1999); Hanes Walton, Jr., and Robert Smith, *American Politics and the African American Quest for Universal Freedom,* Third Edition (New York: Addison Wesley Longman, 2000).

64. Memo to Justice Jackson regarding *Terry v. Adams,* 345 U.S. 461 (1953), cited in Charles Ogletree, *All Deliberate Speed: Reflections of the First Half Century of Brown v. Board of Education* (New York: Norton, 2004), 328, n. 15.

65. Robert Carp, Kenneth Manning, and Ronald Stidham, "The Decision-Making Behavior of George W. Bush's Judicial Appointees," *Judicature* 88 (2004): 20–28.

66. Kenny Whitby, *The Color of Representation: Congressional Behavior and Black Constituents* (Ann Arbor: University of Michigan Press, 1997); Kenny Whitby and George Krause, "Race, Issue Heterogeneity and Public Policy: The Republican Revolution in the 104th U.S. Congress and the Representation of African-American Policy Interests," *British Journal of Political Science* 31 (2001): 555–572; Katherine Tate, *Black Faces in the Mirror: African Americans and Their Representatives in the U.S. Congress* (Princeton: Princeton University Press, 2003).

67. Canon, *Race, Redistricting, and Representation.*

68. Michael Dawson, *Black Visions: The Roots of Contemporary African-American Political Ideologies* (Chicago: University of Chicago Press, 2001).

69. Cited in Michael Davis and Hunter Clark, *Thurgood Marshall: Warrior at the Bar, Rebel on the Bench* (New York: Carol Publishing Group, 1992), 375.

70. Carol Swain, *Black Faces, Black Interests: The Representation of African Americans in Congress* (Cambridge: Harvard University Press, 1993).

71. George Billias, *Elbridge Gerry: Founding Father and Republican Statesman* (New York: McGraw-Hill, 1976).

72. David Lublin and Steve Voss, "Racial Redistricting and Realignment in Southern Sate Legislatures," *American Journal of Political Science* 44 (2000): 792–810; David Lublin and Steve Voss, "The Missing Middle: Why Median-Voter Theory Can't Save Democrats from Singing the Boll-Weevil Blues," *Journal of Politics* 65 (2003): 227–237; Kevin Hill, "Does the Creation of Majority Black Districts Aid Republicans? An Analysis of the 1992 Congressional Elections in Eight Southern States," *Journal of Politics* 57 (1995): 384–401.

73. *Shaw v. Reno* (1993).

74. Brown et al., *White-Washing Race,* 198.

75. Alexis de Tocqueville, *Democracy in America* (New York: Perennial Classics 2000 [1835 and 1840]), 251–252.

76. V. O. Key, Jr., *Southern Politics in State and Nation* (Knoxville: University of Tennessee Press, 1984).

77. James Glaser and Martin Gilens, "Interregional Migration and Political Resocialization," *Public Opinion Quarterly* 61 (1997): 72–86; Marylee Taylor, "The Significance of Racial Context," in David Sears, Jim Sidanius, and Lawrence Bobo, eds., *Racialized Politics: The Debate about Racism in America* (Chicago: University of Chicago Press, 2000), 118–136.

78. Carter, *From George Wallace to Newt Gingrich,* 41.

79. Robert Huckfeldt and Carol Weitzel Kohfeld, *Race and the Decline of Class in American Politics* (Urbana: University of Illinois Press, 1989).

80. Donald Kinder and Lynn Sanders, *Divided by Color: Racial Politics and Democratic Ideals* (Chicago: University of Chicago Press, 1996), 17.

81. David Sears, Colette Van Laar, Mary Carrillo, and Rick Kosterman, "Is It Really Racism? The Origins of White Americans' Opposition to Race-Targeted Policies," *Public Opinion Quarterly* 61 (1997): 16–53.

82. Martin Gilens, "'Race Coding' and White Opposition to Welfare," *American Political Science Review* 90 (1996): 593–604.

83. Howard Schuman, Charlotte Steeh, Lawrence Bobo, and Maria Krysan, *Racial Attitudes in America: Trends and Interpretations,* Revised Edition (Cambridge: Harvard University Press, 1997), 126.

84. Steven Tuch and Michael Hughes, "Whites' Racial Policy Attitudes," *Social Science Quarterly* 77 (1996): 723–745; Schuman et al., *Racial Attitudes in America.*

85. Schuman et al., *Racial Attitudes in America,* 157, 169–670.

86. Lee Sigelman and Susan Welch, *Black Americans' Views of Racial Inequality: The Dream Deferred* (Cambridge: Cambridge University Press, 1991); Paul Sniderman and Philip Tetlock, "Reflections on American Racism," *Journal of Social Issues* 42 (1986): 173–187.

87. "Voter Intimidation Efforts In Philadelphia," *National Public Radio,* October 8, 2008; Cindy Chang, "The 2007 Campaign; County G.O.P Asks Candidate to Withdraw over Letter Threat," *The New York Times,* A19, October 20, 2006; People for the American Way Foundation, *The Long Shadow of Jim Crow: Voter Intimidation and Suppression in America Today* (Washington, D.C.: People for the American Way, 2004).

88. Jeff Manza and Christopher Uggen, *Locked Out: Felon Disenfranchisement and American Democracy* (New York: Oxford University Press, 2006).

89. Marc Mauer and Jamie Fellner, *Losing the Vote: The Impact of Felony Disenfranchisement Laws in the United States* (Washington, D.C.: Human Rights Watch, 1998); Manza and Uggen, *Locked Out,* 79–80.

90. Manza and Uggen, *Locked Out.*

91. Carter, *From George Wallace to Newt Gingrich,* 68–72.

92. Ibid., 77.

93. Kathleen Hall Jamieson, *Dirty Politics* (Oxford: Oxford University Press, 1992), 15–17.

94. Tali Mendelberg, *The Race Card: Campaign Strategies, Implicit Messages, and the Norm of Equality* (Princeton: Princeton University Press, 2001); Carter, *From George Wallace to Newt Gingrich.*

95. Herbert Parment, *George Bush: The Life of a Lone Star Yankee* (New York: Scribner, 1997), 336.

96. Jamieson, *Dirty Politics.*

97. Jamieson, *Dirty Politics;* Mendelberg, *Race Card,* 142.

98. Carter, *From George Wallace to Newt Gingrich,* 48.

99. Jonathan Alter and Michael Isikoff, "The Beltway Populist," *Newsweek,* March 4, 1996, 26.

100. Mendelberg, *Race Card,* 6–7.

101. Ibid.

102. Nicholas Valentino, "Crime News and the Priming of Racial Attitudes during Evaluations of the President," *Public Opinion Quarterly* 63 (1999): 293–320.

103. Jeffrey Alexander, *The Civil Sphere* (New York: Oxford University Press, 2006).

104. Bonilla-Silva, *Racism without Racists*, 53–73.

105. James Poniewozik, "Who Can Say What?" *Time*, April 23, 2007, 32–37; Randy Kennedy, "Hey, That's (Not) Funny," *The New York Times*, April 25, 2007.

106. Mari Matsuda, Charles Lawrence III, Richard Delgado, and Kimberlè Crenshaw, *Words That Wound: Critical Race Theory, Assaultive Speech, and the First Amendment* (Boulder: Westview Press, 1993).

107. Poniewozik, "Who Can Say What?"

108. Matsuda et al., *Words That Wound*, 32–34.

109. Ibid., 80.

110. Lisa Lowe, *Immigrant Acts: On Asian American Cultural Politics* (Durham: Duke University Press, 1996); Espiritu, *Asian American Panethnicity.*

111. Mark Toney, "Power Concedes Nothing without Demand: Building Multiracial Organizations with Direct Action," in Fred Pincus and Howard Ehrlich, eds., *Race and Ethnic Conflict: Contending Views on Prejudice, Discrimination, and Ethnoviolence,* Second Edition (Boulder: Westview, 1999) 401–409.

112. Todd Boyd, *The New H.N.I.C.: The Death of Civil Rights and the Reign of Hip-Hop* (New York: New York University Press, 2004).

113. Quoted in Jeff Chang, *Can't Stop Won't Stop: A History of the Hip-Hop Generation* (New York: St. Martin's Press, 2005), 437.

114. Okihiro, *Columbia Guide to Asian American History.*

115. Eileen O'Brien, "Privileged Polemics: White Antiracist Activists," in Fred Pincus and Howard Ehrlich, eds., *Race and Ethnic Conflict: Contending Views on Prejudice, Discrimination, and Ethnoviolence,* Second Edition (Boulder: Westview, 1999), 411–425.

116. Paulo Freire, *The Politics of Education: Culture, Power, and Liberation* (Westport: Greenwood, 1985), 122.

117. http://racetraitor.org/

118. Howard Winant, *The World Is a Ghetto: Race and Democracy since World War II* (New York: Basic Books, 2001), xiv.

119. Kinder and Sanders, *Divided by Color,* 27: 28.

120. K. Anthony Appiah and Amy Gutmann, *Color Conscious: The Political Morality of Race* (Princeton: Princeton University Press, 1996), 109.

121. Lubiano, ed., *The House That Race Built.*

Chapter 4: Economics

1. Nation Master, "Gross National Income by Country," 2007.

2. Donald Barlett and James Steele, *America: What Went Wrong?* (Kansas City: Andrews and McMeel, 1992), ix; Oliver and Shapiro, *Black Wealth/White Wealth,* 6, 29, 69–69; Jackson Dykman, "American by the Numbers," *Time,* October 30, 2006, 41–54.

3. York Bradshaw and Michael Wallace, *Global Inequalities* (Thousand Oaks: Pine Forge, 1996); Harold Kerbo, *Social Stratification and Inequality: Class Conflict in Historical and Comparative Perspective,* Third Edition (New York: McGraw-Hill, 1996).

4. An interview with Isaac Stier. Transcribed by Ann Allen Geoghegan for the Mississippi Slave Narratives from the Work Process Administration Records.

5. Gerald Jaynes and Robin Williams, Jr., eds., *A Common Destiny: Blacks and American Society* (Washington, D.C.: National Academy Press, 1989).

6. Ira Katznelson, *When Affirmative Action Was White: The Untold History of Racial Inequality in Twentieth-Century America* (New York: Norton, 2005).

7. Gwendolyn Mink, *The Lady and the Tramp: Race, Gender, and the Origins of the American Welfare State* (Madison: University of Wisconsin Press, 1990); Michael Brown, *Race, Money, and the American Welfare State* (Ithaca: Cornell University Press, 1999); Robert Lieberman, *Shifting the Color Line: Race and the American Welfare State* (Cambridge: Harvard University Press, 1998); Katznelson, *When Affirmative Action Was White.*

8. Cited in Katznelson, *When Affirmative Action Was White*, 48.

9. Cited in Katznelson, *When Affirmative Action Was White*, 60.

10. Frank Dobbin, "The Origins of Private Social Insurance: Public Policy and Fringe Benefits in America, 1920–1950," *American Journal of Sociology* 97 (1992): 1416–1450; Katznelson, *When Affirmative Action Was White*, 53–79.

11. Eric Goldstein, *The Price of Whiteness: Jews, Race, and American Identity* (Princeton: Princeton University Press, 206); Leonard Dinnerstein, *Anti-Semitism in America* (New York: Oxford University Press, 1994).

12. Katznelson, *When Affirmative Action Was White*, 116.

13. Michael Bennett, *When Dreams Came True: The GI Bill and the Making of Modern America* (McLean: Brassey's Publishing, 1996).

14. David Onkst, "'First a Negro . . . Incidentally a Veteran': Black World War Two Veterans and the G.I. Bill of Rights in the Deep South, 1944–1948," *Journal of Southern History* 31 (1998): 517–543; Kathleen Frydl, "The GI Bill" (Chicago: University of Chicago, Unpublished Dissertation, 2000); Oliver and Shapiro, *Black Wealth/White Wealth.*

15. Katznelson, *When Affirmative Action Was White*, 23.

16. William Julius Wilson, *The Truly Disadvantaged: The Inner City, the Underclass, and Public Policy* (Chicago: University of Chicago Press, 1987); Walter Powell and Kaisa Snellman, "The Knowledge Economy," *Annual Review of Sociology* 30 (2004): 199–220.

17. Richard Hill and Cynthia Negry, "Deindustrializataion and Racial Minorities in the Great Lakes Region, USA," in Stanley Eitzen and Maxine Baca Zinn, eds., *The Reshaping of America: Social Consequences of the Changing Economy* (Englewood Cliffs: Prentice Hall, 1989), 168–178; Sheldon Danziger and Peter Gottschalk, eds., *Uneven Tides: Rising Inequality in America* (New York: Russell Sage Foundation, 1993).

18. Jerome Culp and Bruce Dunson, "Brothers of a Different Color: A Preliminary Look at Employer Treatment of White and Black Youth," in Richard Freeman and Harry Holzer, eds., *The Black Youth Unemployment Crisis* (Chicago: University of Chicago Press, 1986).

19. Paul Pierson, *Dismantling the Welfare State? Reagan, Thatcher, and the Politics of Retrenchment* (Cambridge: Cambridge University Press, 1994); Margaret Somers and Fred Block, "From

Poverty to Perversity: Ideas, Markets, and Institutions over 200 Years of Welfare Debate," *American Sociological Review* 70 (2005): 260–287.

20. Jude Wanniski, *The Way the World Works: How Economies Fail—and Succeed* (New York: Basic, 1978).

21. Frank Levy, *Dollars and Dreams: The Changing American Income Distribution* (New York: Russell Sage Foundation, 1987); Thomas Edsall and Mary Edsall, *Chain Reaction: The Impact of Race, Rights, and Taxes on American Politics* (New York: Norton, 1992); Carter, *From George Wallace to Newt Gingrich*, 60–63.

22. Leslie McCall, *Complex Inequality: Gender, Class, and Race in the New Economy* (New York: Routledge, 2001).

23. Oliver and Shapiro, *Black Wealth/White Wealth*, 2, 30.

24. Herbert Gans, "Race as Class," *Contexts* 4 (2005): 17–21.

25. U.S. Census Bureau, Current Population Survey, *Annual Demographic Survey* (Washington, D.C.: U.S. Government Printing Office, 2007); Leslie McCall, "Sources of Racial Wage Inequality in Metropolitan Labor Markets: Racial, Ethnic, and Gender Differences," *American Sociological Review* 66 (2001): 520–541; Oliver and Shapiro, *Black Wealth/White Wealth*, 24.

26. Edna Bonacich, "A Theory of Ethnic Antagonism: The Split Labor Market," *Annual Review of Sociology* 37 (1972): 547–559; Lawrence Bobo and Vincent Hutchings, "Perceptions of Racial Group Competition: Extending Blumer's Theory of Group Position to a Multiracial Social Context," *American Sociological Review* 61 (1996): 951–972.

27. George Borjas and Marta Tienda, "The Economic Consequences of Immigration," *Science* 235 (1987): 645–652; George Borjas, *Friends or Strangers: The Impact of Immigrants on the U.S. Economy* (New York: Basic, 1990).

28. Kirk Semple, "A Somali Influx Unsettles Latino Meatpackers," *The New York Times*, October 16, 2008.

29. Susan Gonzalez Baker, "Mexican-Origin Women in Southwestern Labor Markets," in Irene Browne, ed., *Latinas and African American Women at Work* (New York: Russell Sage Foundation, 1999), 244–269; McCall, "Sources of Racial Wage Inequality in Metropolitan Labor Markets."

30. Julie Kmec, "Minority Job Concentration and Wages," *Social Problems* 50 (2003): 38–59; Lisa Catanzarite, "Race-Gender Composition and Occupational Pay Degradation," *Social Problems* 50 (2003): 14–37; Irene Browne, Leann Tigges, and Julie Press, "Inequality through Labor Markets, Firms, and Families: The Intersection of Gender and Race-Ethnicity across Three Cities," in Alice O'Connor, Chris Tilly, and Lawrence Bobo, eds., *Urban Inequality: Evidence from Four Cities* (New York: Russell Sage Foundation, 2001), 372–406; Barbara Reskin, Debra McBrier, and Julie Kmec, "The Determinants and Consequences of Workplace Sex and Race Composition," *Annual Review of Sociology* 25 (1999): 335–361; Kimberly Bayard, Judith Hallerstein, David Neumarkm, and Kenneth Troske, "Why Are Racial and Ethnic Wage Gaps Larger for Men Than for Women? Exploring the Role of Segregation Using *New Worker-Establishment Characteristics Database*," in John Haltiwanger, Julia Lane, James Sppletzer, Jules Theeuwes, and Kenneth

Troske, eds., *The Creation and Analysis of Employer-Employee Matched Data* (Amsterdam: Eksevier, 1999), 175–204.

31. William Barnett, James Baron, and Toby Stuart, "Avenues of Attainment: Occupational Demography and Organizational Careers in the California Civil Service," *American Journal of Sociology* 106 (2000): 88–144.

32. CNN, "Racist Party at Campus," May 15, 2007.

33. Oliver and Shapiro, *Black Wealth/White Wealth;* Conley, *Being Black, Living in the Red.*

34. Oliver and Shapiro, *Black Wealth/White Wealth.*

35. Brown et al., *White-Washing Race;* Oliver and Shapiro, *Black Wealth/White Wealth.*

36. Tomas Dye, *Who's Running America?* Seventh Edition (New York: Prentice Hall, 2001); C. Wright Mills, *The Power Elite* (New York: Oxford University Press, 1959).

37. Matthew Hunt, "Race/Ethnicity and Beliefs about Wealth and Poverty," *Social Science Quarterly* 85 (2004): 827–853.

38. Mills, *Power Elite,* 152.

39. Bill Dedman, "The Color of Money," *Atlanta Journal and Constitution,* May, 15–19, 1988; Alicia Munnell, Lynn Browne, James McEneaney, and Geoffrey Tootel, *Mortgage Lending in Boston: Interpreting HMDA Data* (Boston: Federal Reserve Bank of Boston, 1993); Federal Reserve Bulletin, "Expanded HMDA on Residential Lending: One Year Later," *Federal Reserve Bulletin* 78 (1993): 11.

40. Dana Ford, "Minorities Hit Hardest by Housing Crisis," *Reuters,* November 26, 2007.

41. Oliver and Shapiro, *Black Wealth/White Wealth,* 142–150.

42. Patricia Williams, "Of Race and Risk," *The Nation,* December 29, 1997.

43. Oliver and Shapiro, *Black Wealth/White Wealth.*

44. Jim Dwyer, "In a Sea of Foreclosures, an Island of Calm," *The New York Times,* September 26, 2008.

45. Daniel Gross, "Subprime Suspects," *Slate,* October 7, 2008.

46. Karl Polanyi, *The Great Transformation: The Political and Economic Origins of Our Time* (Boston: Beacon, 2001 [1944]), 48. Also see Mark Granovetter, "Economic Action and Social Structure: The Problem of Embeddedness," *American Journal of Sociology* 91 (1985): 481–510.

47. Pierre Bourdieu, *The Social Structures of the Economy* (Cambridge: Polity Press), 197.

48. Mark Robert Rank, *One Nation, Underprivileged: Why American Poverty Affects Us All* (New York: Oxford University Press, 2004), 33–34.

49. U.S. Census Bureau, *Poverty Thresholds for 2006 by Size of Family and Number of Related Children Under 18 Years* (Washington, D.C.: U.S. Government Printing Office, 2006).

50. Susan Mayer and Christopher Jencks, "Poverty and the Distribution of Material Hardship," *The Journal of Human Resources* 24 (1989): 88–114.

51. U.S. Census Bureau, 2005 American Community Survey (Washington, D.C.: U.S. Government Printing Office, 2005); Rank, *One Nation, Underprivileged,* 31.

52. Sharon Lee, "Poverty and the U.S. Asian Population," *Social Science Quarterly* 75 (1994): 541–559.

53. Martin Gilens, *Why Americans Hate Welfare: Race, Media, and the Politics of Antipoverty Policy* (Chicago: University of Chicago Press, 1999).

54. Herbert Gans, *The War against the Poor: The Underclass and Antipoverty Policy* (New York: Basic Books, 1995), 14, 74.

55. John Hartigan, Jr., *Odd Tribes: Toward a Cultural Analysis of White People* (Durham: Duke University Press, 2005), 61.

56. Gunnar Myrdal, *Challenge to Affluence* (New York: Pantheon, 1962), 53. See also Gans, *War against the Poor,* 27–33; Steinberg, *Turning Back,* ch. 6.

57. John Hartigan, Jr., "Unpopular Culture: The Case of 'White Trash,'" *Cultural Studies* 11 (1997): 316–343; Gans, *War against the Poor.*

58. Robin Kelly, *Yo' Mama's Disfunktional: Fighting the Culture Wars in Urban America* (Boston: Beacon Press, 1997), 18.

59. Martin Luther King, Jr., *Where Do We Go from Here: Chaos or Community?* (New York: Harper and Row, 1967), 188.

60. Bradley Schiller, *The Economics of Poverty and Discrimination* (Upper Saddle River: Prentice Hall, 2004); Rank, *One Nation, Underprivileged.*

61. Alejandro Portes and Min Zhou, "The New Second Generation: Segmented Assimilation and Its Variants," *Annals of the American Academy of Political and Social Sciences* 530 (1993): 74–96.

62. David Shipler, *The Working Poor: Invisible in America* (New York: Vintage, 2005); Rank, *One Nation, Underprivileged,* 59.

63. Gilens, *Why Americans Hate Welfare.*

64. Rank, *One Nation, Underprivileged,* 61.

65. Wilson, *Truly Disadvantaged,* 58–59.

66. Mario Luis Small and Monica McDermott, "The Presence of Organizational Resources in Poor Urban Neighborhoods: An Analysis of Average and Contextual Effects," *Social Forces* 84 (2006): 1698–1724.

67. W. E. B. Du Bois, *Souls of Black Folk* (New York: Dover, 1903 [1994]), 5.

68. James Elliot, "Social Isolation and Labor Market Insulation: Network and Neighborhood Effects on Less-Educated Urban Workers," *The Sociological Quarterly* 40 (1999): 199–216; William Julius Wilson, *When Work Disappears.*

69. Paul Jargowsky, *Poverty and Place: Ghettos, Barrios, and the American City* (New York: Russell Sage Foundation, 1997); William Julius Wilson, *The Truly Disadvantaged: The Inner City, the Underclass, and Public Policy* (Chicago: University of Chicago Press, 1987).

70. Mario Luis Small and Katherine Newman, "Urban Poverty after The Truly Disadvantaged: The Rediscovery of the Family, Neighborhood, and Culture," *Annual Review of Sociology* 27 (2001): 23–45; Lincoln Quillian, "Migration Patterns and the Growth of High-Poverty Neighborhoods," *American Journal of Sociology* 105 (1999): 1–37.

71. John Kain, "The Spatial Mismatch Hypothesis: Three Decades Later," *Housing Policy Debate* 3 (1992): 371–460; Wilson, *Truly Disadvantaged,* 40–42; 100–103.

72. St. Clair Drake and Horace Clayton, *Black Metropolis: A Study of Negro Life in a Northern City,* Revised and Enlarged Edition (New York: Harbinger, 1962 [1945]), 206.

73. Cited in Oliver and Shapiro, *Black Wealth/White Wealth*, 18.

74. Jargowsky, *Poverty and Place;* Wilson, *Truly Disadvantaged*, 56–57.

75. William Julius Wilson, *When Work Disappears: The World of the New Urban Poor* (New York: Knopf, 1996), 54.

76. Mary Pattillo-McCoy, *Black Picket Fences: Privilege and Peril among the Black Middle Class* (Chicago: University of Chicago Press, 1999), 208.

77. Jessie Carney Smith and Carrell Horton, eds., *Statistical Record of Black America,* Fourth Edition (Detroit: Gale Research Press, 1997); Frank Wilson, "Rising Tide or Ebb Tide? Recent Changes in the Black Middle Class in the U.S., 1980–1990," *Research in Race and Ethnic Relations* 8 (1995): 21–55; Pattillo-McCoy, *Black Picket Fences.*

78. Evelyn Ititani, "Finding Capital Can Be a Tall Order for Black-Owned Firms," *Los Angeles Times,* May 16 2007; Tammerlin Drummond, "The Million-Dollar Dash," *Time,* December 4, 2000.

79. David Grant, Melvin Oliver, and Angela James, "African Americans: Social and Economic Bifurcation," in Roger Waldinger and Mehdi Bozorgmehr, eds., *Ethnic Los Angeles* (New York: Russell Sage Foundation, 1996), 379–409; Pattillo-McCoy, *Black Picket Fences.*

80. Oliver and Shapiro, *White Wealth/Black Wealth*, 96–97.

81. E. Franklin Frazier, *Black Bourgeoisie* (New York: The Free Press, 1957), 146.

82. Cited in E. Franklin Frazier, *Black Bourgeoisie,* 156.

83. Harvard Project on American Indian Economic Development, *The State of the Native Nations: Conditions under U.S. Policies of Self-Determination* (New York: Oxford, 2007); Stephen Cornell and Joseph Kalt, "Where's the Glue? Institutional and Cultural Foundations of American Indian Economic Development," *The Journal of Socioeconomics* 29 (2000): 443–470; Stephen Cornell and Joseph Kalt, "Sovereignty and Nation-Building: The Development Challenge in Indian Country Today," *American Indian Culture and Research Journal* 22 (1998): 187–214.

84. Cornell and Kalt, "Where's the Glue?"; Cornell and Kalt, "Sovereignty and Nation-Building."

85. David Vinje, "Native American Economic Development on Selected Reservations: A Comparative Analysis," *American Journal of Economics and Sociology* 55 (1996): 427–442; Harvard Project on American Indian Economic Development, *State of the Native Nations.*

86. David Wilkens, *American Indian Politics and the American Political System* (Lanham: Rowman and Littlefield, 2002), 41.

87. Miriam Jorgensen and Jonathan Taylor, *What Determines Indian Economic Success? Evidence from Tribal and Individual Indian Enterprises* (Cambridge: Harvard Project on American Indian Economic Development, 2000); Cornell and Kalt, "Where's the Glue?"; Cornell and Kalt, "Sovereignty and Nation-Building."

88. Cornell and Kalt, "Where's the Glue?," 455–456.

89. Cornell and Kalt, "Sovereignty and Nation-Building," 210.

90. Yoshimi Chitose, "Transitions into and out of Poverty: A Comparison Between Immigrant and Native Children," *Journal of Poverty* 9 (2005): 63–88; Jennifer Van Hook, Susan Brown,

and Maxwell Ndigume Kwenda, "A Decomposition of Trends in Poverty among Children of Immigrants," *Demography* 41 (2004): 649–670; Leif Jensen, "The Demographic Diversity of Immigrants and Their Children," in Rubén Rumbaut and Alejandro Portes, eds., *Ethnicities: Children of Immigrants in America* (New York and Berkeley: The Russell Sage Foundation and the University of California Press, 2001), 21–56.

91. Martha Crowley, Daniel Lichter, and Zhenchao Qian, "Beyond Gateway Cities: Economic Restructuring and Poverty among Mexican Immigrant Families and Children," *Family Relations* 55 (2006): 345–360; Eric Tang, "Collateral Damage: Southeast Asian Poverty in the United States," *Social Text* 62 (2000): 55–79; Chitose, "Transitions into and out of Poverty."

92. Alejandro Portes and Min Zhou, "The New Second Generation: Segmented Assimilation and Its Variants among Post-1965 Immigrant Youth," *Annals of the American Academy of Political and Social Science* 530 (1993): 74–98, 82.

93. Roger Waldinger, "Did Manufacturing Matter? The Experience of Yesterday's Second Generation: A Reassessment," *International Migration Review* 41 (2007): 3–39; Alejandro Portes and Rubén Rumbaut, *Immigrant America: A Portrait* (Berkeley and Los Angeles: University of California Press, 2006); Roger Waldinger, "Ethnicity and Opportunity in the Plural City," in Roger Waldinger and Mehdi Bozorgmehr, eds., *Ethnic Los Angeles* (New York: Russell Sage Foundation, 1996); Min Zhou, "Segmented Assimilation: Issues, Controversies, and Recent Research on the New Second Generation," *International Migration Review* 31 (1997): 975–1008; Alejandro Portes and Min Zhou, "The New Second Generation."

94. Alejandro Portes, "Paths of Assimilation in the Second Generation," *Sociological Forum* 21 (2006): 499–504; Richard Alba and Victor Nee, "Rethinking Assimilation Theory for a New Era of Immigration, *International Migration Review* 31 (1997): 826–874; Wilawan Kanjanapan, "The Immigration of Asian Professionals to the United States, 1988–1990," *International Migration Review* 29 (1994): 7–32; Portes and Rubén, *Immigrant America;* Waldinger, "Did Manufacturing Matter?"

95. Zhen Zeng and Yu Xie, "Asian-Americans' Earnings Disadvantage Reexamined: The Role of Place of Education," *American Journal of Sociology* 109 (2004): 1075–1108.

96. Alejandro Portes, William Haller, and Luis Eduardo Guarnizo, "Transnational Entrepreneurs: An Alternative Form of Immigrant Economic Adaptation," *American Sociological Review* 67 (2002): 278–298; Patrician Landolt, Lilian Autler, and Sonia Baires, "From 'Hermano Lejana' to 'Hermano Mayor': The Dialectics of Salvadorian Transnationalism," *Ethnic and Racial Studies* 2 (1997): 290–315; Alejandro Portes and Julia Sensenbrenner, "Embeddedness and Immigration: Notes on the Social Determinants of Economic Action, *American Journal of Sociology* 98 (1993): 1320–1350.

97. Min Zhou and Regina Nordquist, "Work and Its Place in the Lives of Immigrant Women: Garment Workers in New York City's Chinatown," in Min Zhou and James Gatewood, eds., *Contemporary Asian America: A Multidisciplinary Reader* (New York: New York University Press, 2000), 254–277.

98. Alejandro Portes and Min Zhou, "Self-Employment and the Earnings of Immigrants," *American Sociological Review* 61 (1996): 219–230.

99. Alejandro Portes and Leif Jensen, "The Enclave and the Entrants: Patterns of Ethnic Enterprise in Miami before and after Mariel," *American Sociological Review* 54 (1989): 929–949, 945.

100. Alejandro Portes, "Migration, Development, and Segmented Assimilation: A Conceptual Review of the Evidence," *Annals of the American Academy of Arts and Sciences* 610 (2007): 73–97; Mary Waters and Karl Eschbach, "Immigration and Ethnic and Racial Inequality in the United States," *Annual Review of Sociology* 21 (1995): 419–446; Jimy Sanders and Victor Nee, "Limits of Ethnic Solidarity in the Ethnic Enclave," *American Sociological Review* 52 (1987): 745–767; Jimy Sanders and Victor Nee, "Comment on Portes and Jensen: Problems in Resolving the Enclave Economy Debate," *American Sociological Review* 57 (1992): 415–418; Victor Nee and Brett de Barry Nee, *Longtime California: A Documentary Study of an American Chinatown* (New York: Pantheon, 1973); Alejandro Portes and Leif Jensen, "The Enclave and the Entrants."

101. Zhou, "Segmented Assimilation"; Waters and Eschbach, "Immigration and Ethnic and Racial Inequality in the United States"; Waters, *Black Identities*; Portes, "Migration, Development, and Segmented Assimilation."

102. R. Salvador Oropesa and Nancy Landale, "Immigrant Legacies: Ethnicity, Generation and Children's Familial and Economic Lives," *Social Science Quarterly* 78 (1997): 399–416.

103. Waters, *Black Identities*, 332.

104. Ibid., 332.

105. Philip Moss and Chris Tilly, *Stories Employers Tell: Race, Skill, and Hiring in America* (New York: Russell Sage, 2001).

106. Marc Bendick, Jr., Charles Jackson, and Victor Reinoso, "Measuring Employment Discrimination through Controlled Experiments," *Review of Black Political Economy* 23 (1994): 25–48. Moss and Tilly, *Stories Employers Tell*.

107. Joleen Kirschenman and Kathryn Neckerman, "'We'd Love to Hire Them, but . . .': The Meaning of Race for Employers," in Christopher Jencks and Paul Peterson, eds., *The Urban Underclass* (Washington, D.C.: Brookings Institution, 1991), 203–232.

108. Kirschenman and Neckerman, "'We'd Love to Hire Them, but . . .'," 210.

109. Ivy Kenelly, "'That Single Mother Element': How White Employers Typify Black Women," *Gender and Society* 12 (1999): 168–192; Kirschenman and Neckerman, "'We'd Love to Hire Them, but . . .',"

110. Michael Fix and Raymond Struyk, *Clear and Convincing Evidence* (Washington, D.C.: Urban Institute Press, 1993); Bendick et al., "Measuring Employment Discrimination through Controlled Experiments."

111. Marianne Bertrand and Sendhil Mullainathan, "Are Emily and Greg More Employable Than Lakisha and Jamal? A Field Experiment on Labor Market Discrimination," NBER Working Paper No. 9873, 2004.

112. Devah Pager, "The Mark of a Criminal Record," *American Journal of Sociology* 108 (2003): 937–975.

113. Moss and Tilly, *Stories Employers Tell*.

114. Charles Tilly, *Durable Inequality* (Berkeley and Los Angeles: University of California Press, 1998), 10.

115. Thomas Sugrue, *The Origins of the Urban Crisis: Race and Inequality in Postwar Detroit*, Princeton Classic Edition (Princeton: Princeton University Press, 2005), xviii.

116. Pierre Bourdieu, *Distinction: A Social Critique of the Judgment of Taste* (Cambridge: Harvard University Press, 1984 [1979]); Annette Lareau, *Unequal Childhoods: Class, Race, and Family Life* (Berkeley and Los Angeles: University of California Press, 2003).

117. Roberto Fernandez and Isabel Fernandez-Mateo, "Networks, Race, and Hiring," *American Sociological Review* 71 (2006): 42–71; James Elliot, "Class, Race, and Job Matching in Contemporary Urban Labor Markets," *Social Science Quarterly* 81 (2000): 1036–1051; Gary Green, Leann Tigges, and Daniel Diaz, "Racial and Ethnic Differences in Job-Search Strategies in Atlanta, Boston, and Los Angeles," *Social Science Quarterly* 80 (1999): 263–278.

118. Edna Bonacich, "Advanced Capitalism and Black/White Race Relations in the United States: A Split Labor Market Interpretation," *American Sociological Review* 41 (1976): 34–51.

119. Horace Cayton and George Mitchell, *Black Workers and the New Unions* (Westport: Negro Universities Press, 1970), x.

120. Bonacich, "Advanced Capitalism and Black/White Race Relations in the United States," 50.

121. Edna Bonacich, "A Theory of Ethnic Antagonism: The Split Labor Market," *American Sociological Review* 37 (1972): 547–559, 549.

122. Miriam Jordan, "Carpenters' Union Seeks Immigrants to Spur Clout," *Wall Street Journal*, December 15, 2005.

123. Moon-Kie Jung, "Interracialism: The Ideological Transformation of Hawaii's Working Class," *American Sociological Review* 68 (2003): 373–400.

124. Ibid.

125. Cited in Jung, "Interracialism," 384.

126. Cited in Jung, "Interracialism," 390.

127. Blumer, "Race Prejudice as a Sense of Group Position," 3.

128. Bobo and Hutchings, "Perceptions of Racial Group Competition."

129. Jimmy Santiago Baca, "So Mexicans Are Taking Jobs from Americans," in Maria Mazziotti Gillan and Jennifer Gillan, eds., *Unsettling America: An Anthology of Contemporary Multicultural Poetry* (New York: Penguin, 1994), 115–116.

130. George Wilson and Debra Branch McBrier, "Race and Loss of Privilege: African America/White Differences in the Determinants of Job Layoffs from Upper-Tier Occupations," *Sociological Forum* 20 (2005): 301–321.

131. James Elliott and Ryan Smith, "Race, Gender, and Workplace Power," *American Sociological Review* 69 (2004): 365–386; Ryan Smith and James Elliott, "Does Ethnic Niching Influence Access to Authority? An Examination of Race and Gender in Three Metro Areas," *Social Forces* 81 (2002): 255–279; Gail McGuire and Barbara Reskin, "Authority Hierarchies at Work: The Impacts of Race and Sex," *Gender and Society* 7 (1993): 487–506; Edward Irons and Gilbert Moore, *Black Managers: The Case of the Banking Industry* (New York: Praeger, 1985).

132. Ryan Smith, "Race, Gender, and Authority in the Workplace: Theory and Research," *Annual Review of Sociology* 28 (2002): 509–542; Gail McGuire, "Gender, Race, and The

Shadow Structure: A Study of Informal Networks and Inequality in a Work Organization," *Gender and Society* 16 (2002): 303–322; Joel Podolny and James Baron, "Resources and Relationships: Social Networks and Mobility in the Workplace," *American Sociological Review* 62 (1997): 673–693.

133. Ella Edmondson Bell and Stella Nkomo, *Our Separate Ways: Black and White Women and the Struggle for Professional Identity* (Boston: Harvard Business School Press, 2001); Pamela Braboy Jackson, Peggy Thoits, and Howard Taylor, "Composition of the Workplace and Psychological Well-Being: The Effects of Tokenism on America's Black Elite," *Social Forces* 74 (1995): 543–557; Reskin et al., "The Determinants and Consequences of Workplace Sex and Race Composition."

134. McGuire and Reskin, "Authority Hierarchies at Work," 499.

135. Irene Brown, ed., *Latinas and African American Women at Work: Race, Gender and Economic Inequality* (New York: Russell Sage Foundation, 1999); Melvin Thomas, "Race, Class, and Occupation: An Analysis of Black and White Earnings for Professional and Non-Professional Males, 1940–1990," *Research in Race and Ethnic Relations* 8 (1995): 139–156.

136. Janeen Baxter and Erik Olin Wright, "The Glass Ceiling Hypothesis: A Comparative Study of United States, Sweden and Australia," *Gender and Society* 14 (2000): 275–294; Elliott and Smith, "Race, Gender, and Workplace Power."

137. Ryan Smith, "Racial Differences in Access to Hierarchical Authority: An Analysis of Change over Time, 1972–1994," *Sociological Quarterly* 40 (1999): 367–396; George Wilson, "Pathways to Power: Racial Differences in the Determinants of Job Authority," *Social Problems* 44 (1997): 38–54.

138. James Kluegel, "The Causes and Cost of Racial Exclusion from Job Authority," *American Sociological Review* 43 (1978): 285–301; Erik Olin Wright, Janeen Baxter, and Gunn Elisabeth Birkelund, "The Gender Gap in Workplace Authority: A Cross-National Study, *American Sociological Review* 60 (1995): 407–435.

139. Rosabeth Moss Kanter, *Men and Women of the Corporation* (New York: Basic Books, 1977).

140. Elliott and Smith, "Race, Gender, and Workplace Power," 381.

141. Martin Luther King, Jr., "Showdown for Non-Violence," *Look*, April 16, 1968, 24.

142. Jill Quadagno, *The Color of Welfare: How Racism Undermined the War on Poverty* (New York: Oxford University Press, 1994), 14.

143. Daniel Lichter and Rukamalie Jayakody, "Welfare Reform: How Do We Measure Success?" *Annual Review of Sociology* 28 (2002): 117–141; Alice O'Connor, "Poverty Research and Policy for the Post-Welfare Era," *Annual Review of Sociology* 26 (2000): 547–562; Rank, *One Nation, Underprivileged.*

144. Lichter and Jayakody, "Welfare Reform."

145. Kathryn Edin and Laura Lein, *Making Ends Meet: How Single Mothers Survive Welfare and Low-Wage Work* (New York: Russell Sage Foundation, 1997).

146. Stephen Slivinski, *The Corporate Welfare State: How the Federal Government Subsidizes U.S. Businesses* (Washington, D.C.: Cato Institute, 2007); James Steele and Donald Barlett, *The*

Great American Tax Dodge: How Spiraling Fraud and Avoidance Are Killing Fairness, Destroying the Income Tax, and Costing You (New York: Little, Brown, 2000).

147. Roger Noll and Andrew Zimbalist, eds., *Sports, Jobs, and Taxes: The Economic Impact of Sports Teams and Stadiums* (Washington, D.C.: Brookings Institution Press, 1997).

148. Donald Barlett and James Steele, "Corporate Welfare," *Time*, November 9, 1998.

149. Ibid.

150. Rank, *One Nation, Underprivileged*, 102–104.

151. Administration for Children and Families, *Temporary Assistance to Needy Families Fifth Annual Report to Congress* (Washington, D.C.: Administration for Children and Families, 2003); Jo Anne Schneider, "Pathways to Opportunity: The Role of Race, Social Networks, Institutions, and Neighborhood in Career and Educational Paths for People on Welfare," *Human Organization* 59 (2000): 72–85; United States House of Representatives, Committee on Ways and Means, *Green Book* (Washington, D.C.: Government Printing Office, 1998).

152. Kristen Harknett, "Working and Leaving Welfare: Does Race of Ethnicity Matter?" *Social Science Review* 75 (2001): 359–385; Kathryn Edin and Kathleen Mullan Harris, "Getting Off and Staying Off: Racial Differences in the Work Route of Welfare," in Irene Browne, ed., *Latinas and African American Women at Work* (New York: Russell Sage Foundation, 1999), 270–301.

153. Harknett, "Working and Leaving Welfare."

154. Edin and Harris, "Getting Off and Staying Off."

155. Brown, *Race, Money, and the American Welfare State*, 337–340.

156. Jackson, "Facts Favor Affirmative Action."

157. Joya Misra, Stephanie Moller, Marina Karides, "Envisioning Dependency: Changing Media Depictions of Welfare in the 20th Century," *Social Problems* 50 (2003): 482–504.

158. Edin and Lein, *Making Ends Meet*.

159. Sandra Morgen and Jeff Maskovsky, "The Anthropology of Welfare 'Reform': New Perspectives on U.S. Urban Poverty in the Post-Welfare Era," *Annual Review of Anthropology* 32 (2003): 315–338; Madonna Harrington Meyer, *Care Work: Gender, Labor, and the Welfare State* (New York: Routledge, 2000).

160. Wilson, *Truly Disadvantaged*, 9–10.

161. United States House of Representatives, Committee on Ways and Means, *Green Book* (Washington, D.C.: Government Printing Office, 1993); Rank, *One Nation, Underprivileged*, 104–105; Edin and Lein, *Making Ends Meet*.

162. Gans, *War against the Poor*, 70.

163. Congressional Record, *Debate on the Floor of the House of Representatives about the Personal Responsibility Act of 1995* (Washington, D.C.: Government Printing Office, March 24, 1995); Edsall and Edsall, *Chain Reaction*, 148.

164. Cited in Quadagno, *Color of Welfare*, vii.

165. Rosalee and Rakuya Trice, "Poverty as We Know It: Media Portrayals of the Poor," *Public Opinion Quarterly* 64 (2000); 53–64; Lucy Williams, "Race, Rat Bites and Unfit Mothers: How Media Discourse Informs Welfare Legislation Debate," *Fordham Urban Law Journal* 22 (1995): 1159–1196; Gilens, *Why Americans Hate Welfare*.

166. Cybelle Fox, "The Changing Color of Welfare? How Whites' Attitudes toward Latinos Influence Support for Welfare," *American Journal of Sociology* 110 (2004): 580–625; Lawrence Bobo and James Kluegel, "Status, Ideology, and Dimensions of Whites' Racial Beliefs and Attitudes: Progress and Stagnation," in Steven Tuch and Jack Martin, eds., *Racial Attitudes in the 1990s: Continuity and Change* (Westport: Praeger, 1997).

167. Charlotte Steeh and Maria Krysan, "The Polls—Trends: Affirmative Action and the Public, 1970–1995," *Public Opinion Quarterly* 60 (1996): 128–158.

168. Brown et al., *White-Washing Race,* 25.

169. Shannon Harper and Barbara Reskin, "Affirmative Action at School and on the Job," *Annual Review of Sociology* 31 (2005): 357–379; Samuel Leiter and William Leiter, *Affirmative Action in Antidiscrimination Law and Policy: An Overview and Synthesis* (Albany: State University of New York Press, 2002).

170. David Oppenheimer, "Distinguishing Five Models of Affirmative Action," *Berkeley Women's Law Journal* 4 (1989): 42–61; Harper and Reskin, "Affirmative Action at School and on the Job."

171. Barbara Reskin, *The Realities of Affirmative Action* (Washington, D.C.: American Sociological Association, 1998).

172. Cited in Reskin, *Realities of Affirmative Action,* 10–11.

173. John Ryan, James Hawdon, and Allison Branick, "The Political Economy of Diversity: Diversity Programs in Fortune 500 Companies," *Social Science Research Online* 7 (2002): www.socresonline.org.uk/7/1/ryan.html; Harry Holzer and David Neumark, "Are Affirmative Action Hires Less Qualified? Evidence from Employer-Employee Data on New Hires," *Journal of Labor Economics* 17 (1999): 534–569; Lauren Edelman, "Legal Ambiguity and Symbolic Structures: Organizational Mediation of Civil Rights Law," *American Journal of Sociology* 97 (1992): 1531–1576; Reskin, *Realties of Affirmative Action.*

174. James Button and Barbara Rienzo, "The Impact of Affirmative Action: Black Employment in Six Southern Cities," *Social Science Quarterly* 84 (2003): 1–14; Harry Holzer and David Neumark, "What Does Affirmative Action Do?" *Industrial and Labor Relations Review* 53 (2000): 240–271; Charles Moskos and John Sibley Butler, *All That We Can Be: Black Leadership and Racial Integration the Army Way* (New York: Basic Books, 1996); Kevin Merida, "Study Finds Little Evidence of Reverse Discrimination," *The Washington Post,* March 31, 1995; Holzer and Neumark, "Are Affirmative Action Hires Less Qualified?"; Reskin, *Realities of Affirmative Action.*

175. Miriam Komaromy, Kevin Grumbach, Michael Drake, Karen Vranizan, Nicole Lurie, Dennis Keane, and Andrew Bindman, "The Role of Black and Hispanic Physicians in Providing Health Care for Underserved Populations," *New England Journal of Medicine* 334 (1996): 1305–1310; Nolan Penn, Percy Russell, and Harold Simon, "Affirmative Action at Work: A Survey of Graduates of the University of California at San Diego Medical School," *American Journal of Public Health* 76 (1986): 1144–1146.

176. Faye Crosby, Aarti Iyer, and Sirinda Sincharoen, "Understanding Affirmative Action," *Annual Review of Psychology* 57 (2006): 585–611; Faye Crosby, Aarti Iyer, Susan Clayton, and

Roberta Downing, "Affirmative Action: Psychological Data and the Policy Debates," *American Psychologist* 58 (2003): 93–115; Sam Howe Verhovek, "In Poll, Americans Reject Means but Not Ends of Racial Diversity," *The New York Times*, December 14, 1997; Barbara Reskin and Patricia Roos, *Job Queues, Gender Queues* (Philadelphia: Temple University Press, 1990); Jennifer Hochschild, *Facing Up to the American Dream* (Princeton: Princeton University Press, 1995); Thomas Pettigrew and Joanne Martin, "Shaping the Organizational Context for Black American Inclusion," *Journal of Social Issues* 43 (1987): 41–78.

177. Faye Crosby and Sharon Herzberger, "For Affirmative Action," in R. J. Simon, ed., *Affirmative Action: Pros and Cons of Policy and Practice* (Washington, D.C.: American University Press, 1996); Marylee Taylor, "White Backlash to Workplace Affirmative Action: Peril or Myth?" *Social Forces* 73 (1995): 1385–1414.

178. Richard Morin, "Unconventional Wisdom," *The Washington Post*, January 12, 1997; Liz McMillen, "Policies Said to Help Companies Hire Qualified Workers at No Extra Cost," *The Chronicle of Higher Education*, November 17, 1995; Reskin, *Realities of Affirmative Action;* Crosby and Herzberger, "For Affirmative Action."

179. Wilson, *Truly Disadvantaged*, 113–114.

180. Richard Kahlenberg, *The Remedy: Class, Race, and Affirmative Action* (New York: Basic Books, 1996); Jonathan Leonard, "The Impact of Affirmative Action Regulations and Equal Employment Law on Black Employment," *Journal of Economic Perspectives* 4 (1990): 47; 63; Wilson, *Truly Disadvantaged*.

181. David Williams, James Jackson, Tony Brown, Myriam Torres, Tyrone Forman, and Kendrick Brown, "Traditional and Contemporary Prejudice and Urban Whites' Support for Affirmative Action and Government Help," *Social Problems* 46 (1999): 503–527; Verhovek, "In Poll, Americans Reject Means but Not Ends of Racial Diversity"; Steeh and Krysan, "The Polls."

182. Cited in Reskin, *Realities of Affirmative Action*, 72.

183. Eleanor Holmes Norton, "Affirmative Action in the Workplace," in G. Curry, ed., *The Affirmative Action Debate* (Reading: Addison-Wesley, 1996); Derrick Jackson, "Facts Favor Affirmative Action," *The Boston Globe*, October 30, 1996; Morin, "Unconventional Wisdom"; Reskin, *Realities of Affirmative Action*, 73.

184. Cited in *St. Louis Dispatch*, "Affirmative Action Programs Also Help White Men, Report Says," August 23, 1998.

185. Katznelson, *When Affirmative Action Was White*, 153.

186. Reskin, *Realities of Affirmative Action*, 63, 93.

187. Richard Morin, "Misperceptions Cloud Whites' View of Blacks," *The Washington Post*, July 11, 2001, A1.

Chapter 5: Housing

1. Takaki, *Strangers from a Different Shore*.

2. Thomas Archdeacon, *Becoming American: An Ethnic History* (New York: Free Press, 1983); Rowland Berthoff, *British Immigrants in Industrial America, 1750–1950* (Cambridge: Harvard University Press, 1953).

3. Georg Simmel, "The Stranger," in Donald Levine, ed., *Georg Simmel: On Individuality and Social Forms* (Chicago: University of Chicago Press, 1971 [1908]), 143–149.

4. Stanley Lieberson, *A Piece of the Pie: Blacks and White Immigrants Since 1880* (Berkeley and Los Angeles: University of California Press, 1980); Massey and Denton, *American Apartheid*, 22–23, 46–48.

5. Harvey Zorbaugh, *The Gold Coast and the Slum: A Sociological Study of Chicago's Near North Side* (Chicago: University of Chicago Press, 1929).

6. Robert E. Park, "Human Migration and the Marginal Man," *American Journal of Sociology* 33 (1928): 881–893.

7. Oliver Zunz, *The Changing Face of Inequality* (Chicago: University of Chicago Press, 2000).

8. Eileen Diaz McConnell, "Latinos in the Rural Midwest: The Twentieth-Century Historical Context Leading to Contemporary Challenges," in Ann Millard and Jorge Chapa, eds., *Apple Pie and Enchiladas: Latino Newcomers in the Rural Midwest* (Austin: University of Texas Press, 2004), 26–40; Francisco Balderrama and Raymond Rodríguez, *Decade of Betrayal: Mexican Repatriation in the 1930s* (Albuquerque: University of New Mexico Press, 1995); Zaragosa Vargas, *Proletarians of the North: A History of Mexican Industrial Workers in Detroit and the Midwest, 1917–1933* (Berkeley and Los Angeles: University of California Press, 1993).

9. Peter Hecht, "Mass Eviction to Mexico in 1930s Spurs Apology," *Sacramento Bee*, December 28, 2005.

10. Donald Fixico, "Federal and State Policies and American Indians" in Philip Deloria and Neal Salisbury, eds., *A Companion to American Indian History* (Malden: Blackwell, 2002), 379–96; Donald Fixico, *Termination and Relocation: Federal Indian Policy, 1945–1960* (Albuquerque: University of New Mexico Press, 1986).

11. Kenneth Philip, *Termination Revisited: American Indians on the Trail to Self-Determination, 1933–1953* (Lincoln: University of Nebraska Press, 1999); Fixico, *Termination and Relocation*.

12. Langston Hughes, "The South" in Sondra Kathryn Wilson, *The Crisis Reader: Stories, Poetry, and Essays from the N.A.A.C.P.'s Crisis Magazine* (New York: Modern Library, 1999 [1922]), 24–25.

13. Nicholas Lemann, *The Promised Land: The Great Black Migration and How It Changed America* (New York: Knopf, 1991); James Grossman, *Land of Hope: Chicago, Black Southerners, and the Great Migration* (Chicago: University of Chicago Press, 1991); Drake and Clayton, *Black Metropolis*, 58.

14. Loïc Wacquant, "From Slavery to Mass Incarceration: Rethinking the 'Race Question' in the US," *New Left Review* 13 (2002): 41–60; Allan Spear, *Black Chicago: The Making of a Negro Ghetto, 1890–1920* (Chicago: University of Chicago Press, 1969).

15. Cited in Philip Johnson, *Call Me Neighbor, Call Me Friend: The Case History of the Integration of a Neighborhood on Chicago's South Side* (Garden City: Doubleday, 1965), 17.

16. Thomas Sugrue, *The Origins of the Urban Crisis: Race and Inequality in Postwar Detroit*, Princeton Classic Edition (Princeton: Princeton University Press, 2005); Allan Spear, *Black*

Chicago: The Making of a Negro Ghetto, 1890–1920 (Chicago: University of Chicago Press, 1967); Drake and Clayton, *Black Metropolis.*

17. Sugrue, *Origins of the Urban Housing Crisis,* 43.

18. Oliver and Shapiro, *Black Wealth/White Wealth;* Massey and Denton, *American Apartheid.*

19. Lipsitz, *Possessive Investment in Whiteness,* 6.

20. Dominic Capeci, Jr., *Race Relations in Wartime Detroit: The Sojourner Truth Housing Controversy of 1942* (Philadelphia: Temple University Press, 1985); Sugrue, *Origins of the Urban Housing Crisis,* 45.

21. Kenneth Jackson, "Race, Ethnicity, and Real Estate Appraisal: The Home Owners Loan Corporation and the Federal Housing Association," *Journal of Urban History* 6 (1980): 419–452; Sugrue, *Origins of the Urban Housing Crisis;* Oliver and Shapiro, *Black Wealth/White Wealth.*

22. Sugrue, *Origins of the Urban Housing Crisis,* 54.

23. Ibid., 34–36.

24. Robert Mowitz and Deil Wright, *Profile of a Metropolis: A Case Book* (Detroit: Wayne State University Press, 1962), 405, 412.

25. Robert Caro, *The Power Broker: Robert Moses and the Fall of New York* (New York: Vintage, 1975), 12.

26. Michael White, *Urban Renewal and the Residential Structure of the City* (Chicago: Community and Family Studies Center, 1980); Hirsch, *Making the Second Ghetto.*

27. Caro, *The Power Broker,* 7.

28. Jon Teaford, *Rough Road to Resistance: Urban Revitalization in America* (Baltimore: Johns Hopkins University, 1990); George Squires, ed., *Unequal Partnerships: The Political Economy of Urban Development in Postwar America* (New Brunswick: Rutgers University Press, 1989); Sugrue, *Origins of the Urban Housing Crisis,* 47–51.

29. Ibid., 246.

30. Cited in Sugrue, *Origins of the Urban Housing Crisis,* 210.

31. Ibid., 195.

32. Kenneth Jackson, *Crabgrass Frontier: The Suburbanization of the United States* (New York: Oxford University Press, 1987); Massey and Denton, *American Apartheid,* 53.

33. Kevin Kruse *White Flight: Atlanta and the Making of Modern Conservatism* (Princeton: Princeton University Press, 2005).

34. Massey and Denton, *American Apartheid,* 44.

35. Cited in Sugrue, *Origins of the Urban Housing Crisis,* 247.

36. Drake and Cayton, *Black Metropolis;* Spear, *Black Chicago;* Sugrue, *Origins of the Urban Housing Crisis,* 254–55.

37. Arnold Hirsch, *Making the Second Ghetto: Race and Housing in Chicago 1940–1960* (Chicago: University of Chicago Press, 1998); Gilbert Osofsky, *Harlem: The Making of a Ghetto* (New York: Harper and Row, 1968).

38. Stephen Grant Meyer, *As Long as They Don't Move Next Door: Segregation and Racial Conflict in American Neighborhoods* (Oxford: Rowman and Littlefield, 2000), 71.

39. Patrick Jones, "'Not a Color but an Attitude': Fr. James Groppi and Black Power Politics in Milwaukee," in Komozi Woodard, ed., *Groundwork: Local Black Freedom Movements* (New York: New York University Press, 2005).

40. Meyer, *As Long as They Don't Move Next Door.*

41. Cheryl Harris, "Whiteness as Property," *Harvard Law Review* 106 (1993): 1707–1791.

42. Albert Mayer and Thomas Hoult, *Race and Residence in Detroit* (Detroit: Urban Research Laboratory, Institute for Urban Studies, Wayne State University, 1962), 2.

43. Baldwin, *Notes of a Native Son,* 93.

44. Anthony Perez, Kimberly Berg, and Daniel Myers, "Police and Riots," *Journal of Black Studies* 34 (2003): 153–183; Joe Feagin and Harlan Hahn, *Ghetto Revolts: The Politics of Violence in American Cities* (New York: Macmillian, 1973).

45. Urban American and Urban Coalition, *One Year Later: An Assessment of the Nation's Response to the Crisis Described by the National Advisory Commission on Civil Disorders* (New York: Praeger, 1968).

46. Valerie Reitman and Mitchell Landsberg, "Watts Riots, 40 Years Later," *Los Angeles Times,* August 11, 2005.

47. Herbert Haines, "Black Radicalization and the Funding of Civil Rights: 1957–1970," *Social Problems* 32 (1983): 31–43; James Button, *Black Violence: Political Impact of the 1960s Riots* (Princeton: Princeton University Press, 1978); Feagin and Hahn, *Ghetto Revolts.*

48. Kruse, *White Flight;* Sugrue, *Origins of the Urban Crisis.*

49. Cf. Drake and Cayton, *Black Metropolis,* 97.

50. Massey and Denton, *American Apartheid,* 20.

51. Sean F. Reardon, Stephen A. Matthews, David O'Sullivan, Barrett A. Lee, Glenn Firebaugh, Chad R. Farrell, Kendra Bischoff, "The Geographic Scale of Metropolitan Racial Segregation," *Demography* 45 (2008): 489–514; Camille Zubrinsky Charles, "The Dynamics of Racial Residential Segregation," *Annual Review of Sociology* 29 (2003): 167–207; Reynolds Farley and William Frey, "Changes in the Segregation of Whites from Blacks during the 1980s: Small Steps toward a More Integrated Society," *American Sociological Review* 59 (1994): 23–45; Massey and Denton, *American Apartheid.*

52. Massey and Denton, *American Apartheid,* 67.

53. Charles, "The Dynamics of Racial Residential Segregation."

54. John Logan and Richard Alba, "Locational Returns to Human Capital: Minority Access to Suburban Community Resources," *Demography* 30 (1993): 243–268.

55. Massey and Denton, *American Apartheid,* 112–114.

56. Richard Alba and John Logan, "Minority Proximity to Whites in Suburbs: An Individual-Level Analysis of Segregation," *American Journal of Sociology* 98 (1993): 1388–1427.

57. Nancy Denton, "Are African Americans Still Hypersegregated?" in Robert Bullard, J. Eugene Grigsby, III, and Charles Lee, eds., *Residential Apartheid: The American Legacy* (Los Angeles: UCLA Center for African American Studies, 1994), 49–79.

58. Massey and Denton, *American Apartheid,* 77.

59. Richard Alba, John Logan, and Brian Stults, "How Segregated Are Middle-Class African Americans?" *Social Problems* 47 (2000): 543–558; John Logan, Richard Alba, and Shu-Yin Leung,

"Minority Access to White Suburbs: A Multi-Region Comparison," *Social Forces* 74 (1996): 851–882; Massey and Denton, *American Apartheid*, 85–87.

60. Public Policy Forum, "Housing Diversity and Choices: A Metro Milwaukee Opinion Survey," *Public Policy Forum Regional Report* 1 (2004): 1–12.

61. Reynolds Farley, Charlotte Steeh, Maira Krysan, Tara Jackson, and Keith Reeves, "Stereotypes and Segregation: Neighborhoods in the Detroit Area," *American Journal of Sociology,* 100 (1994): 750–780; Reynolds Farley, Howard Schuman, S. Bianchi, Diane Colasanto, and S. Hatchett, "Chocolate City, Vanilla Suburbs: Will the Trend toward Racially Separate Communities Continue?" *Social Science Research,* 7 (1978): 319–344.

62. Farley et al., "Chocolate City, Vanilla Suburbs"; Massey and Denton, *American Apartheid*.

63. David Cutler, Edward Glaeser, and Jacob Vigdor, "The Rise and Decline of the American Ghetto," *Journal of Political Economy* 107 (1999): 455–506; Chicago Commission on Human Relations, *1990 Hate Crime Report* (Chicago: City of Chicago Commission on Human Relations, 1991).

64. Massey and Denton, *American Apartheid*, 15.

65. Matthew Desmond, "Eviction and the Reproduction of Urban Poverty: Fieldnotes," October 2008.

66. Sabiyha Prince, *Constructing Belongingness: Class, Race, and Harlem's Professional Workers* New York: Routledge, 2004); Monique Taylor, *Harlem between Heaven and Hell* (Minneapolis: University of Minnesota Press, 2000).

67. Mary Pattillo, "Black Middle-Class Neighborhoods," *Annual Review of Sociology* 31 (2005): 305–329, 322.

68. Elizabeth Bruch and Robert Mare, "Neighborhood Choice and Neighborhood Change," *American Journal of Sociology* 112 (2006): 667–709.

69. U.S. Department of Housing and Urban Development, *Housing Discrimination Study, 2000* (Washington, D.C.: Department of Housing and Urban Development, 2000); George Galster, "Research on Discrimination in Housing and Mortgage Markets: Assessment and Future Directions," *Housing Policy Debate* 3 (1992): 639–683.

70. Nathan Glazer, "Race and the Suburbs," in Charles Abrams, Otto Koenigsberger, Steven Groák, and Beverly Bernstein, eds., *The Work of Charles Abrams: Housing and Urban Renewal in the USA and the Third World: A Collection of Papers* (Oxford: Pergamon Press, 1981), 175–180.

71. Susan Bertram, *An Audit of Real Estate Sales and Rental Markets of Selected Southern Suburbs* (Homewood: South Suburban Housing Center, 1988).

72. John Yinger, "The Racial Dimension of Urban Housing Markets in the 1980s," in Gary Tobin, ed., *Divided Neighborhoods: Changing Patterns of Racial Segregation* (Newbury Park: Sage, 1987), 43–67.

73. Massey and Denton, *American Apartheid*, 104.

74. U.S. Department of Housing and Urban Development, *Housing Discrimination Study*.

75. John Yinger, *Closed Doors, Opportunities Lost: The Continuing Costs of Housing Discrimination* (New York: Russell Sage Foundation, 1995).

76. Margery Turner, John Edwards, and Maris Mikelsons, *Housing Discrimination Study: Analyzing Racial and Ethnic Steering* (Washington, D.C.: U.S. Department of Housing and Urban Development, 1991).

77. Vincent Roscigno and Griff Tester, "Sex Discrimination in Housing," in Vincent Roscigno, ed., *The Face of Discrimination* (New York: Rowman and Littlefield, 2007), 187–202.

78. National Law Center on Homelessness and Poverty, *Housing Discrimination against Abused Women* (Washington, D.C.: National Law Center on Homelessness and Poverty, Domestic Violence Project, 2008).

79. James H. Carr and Isaac F. Megbolugbe, "The Federal Reserve Bank of Boston Study on Mortgage Lending Revisited," *Journal of Housing Research* 4 (1993): 277–313, 277. See also Gary A. Dymski, "Discrimination in the Credit and Housing Markets: Findings and Challenges," in William Rodgers, III, ed., *Handbook on the Economics of Discrimination* (Northampton: Edward Elgar Publishing, 2006), 215–259.

80. Karen Orren, *Corporate Power and Social Change: The Politics of the Life Insurance Industry* (Baltimore: Johns Hopkins University Press, 1982).

81. Gregory Squires and William Valez, "Neighborhood Racial Composition and Mortgage Lending: City and Suburban Differences," *Journal of Urban Affairs* 9 (1987): 217–232; Massey and Denton, *American Apartheid*, 107.

82. Alba et al., "How Segregated Are Middle-Class African Americans?"; Logan et al., "Minority Access to White Suburbs."

83. Yinger, *Closed Doors, Opportunities Lost*.

84. William Julius Wilson, *When Work Disappears: The World of the New Urban Poor* (New York: Vintage, 1996); Kirschenman and Neckerman, "'We'd Love to Hire Them, but. . . .'"

85. Douglas Massey and Mary Fischer, "Does Rising Income Bring Integration? New Results for Blacks, Hispanics, and Asians," *Social Science Research* 20 (1999): 316–326; Pattillo-McCoy, *Black Picket Fences*.

86. Massey and Denton, *American Apartheid*, 14.

87. Daphne Kenyon, *The Property Tax-School Funding Dilemma* (Cambridge: Lincoln Institute of Land Policy, 2007).

88. Charles, "The Dynamics of Racial Residential Segregation."

89. Sugrue, *The Origins of the Urban Housing Crisis*, 229.

90. Pierre Bourdieu, *The State Nobility* (Stanford: Stanford University Press, 1996 [1989]), 1.

91. James Baldwin, "Fifth Avenue, Uptown," in *The Price of the Ticket: Collected Nonfiction 1948–1985* (New York: St. Martin's Press, 1985 [1960], 205–213), 210.

92. Kenneth Clark, *Dark Ghetto: Dilemmas of Social Power*, Second Edition (Hanover: Wesleyan University Press, 1989 [1965]), 32–33. Also see John Dixon, Colin Tredoux, and Beverley Clack, "On the Micro-Ecology of Racial Division: A Neglected Dimension of Segregation," *South African Journal of Psychology* 35 (2005): 395–411.

93. John Hartigan, *Racial Situations: Class Predicaments of Whiteness in Detroit* (Princeton: Princeton University Press, 1999).

94. Mehdi Bozorgmehr, Claudia Der-Martirosian, and Geroges Sabagh, "Middle Easterners: A New Kind of Immigrant," in Roger Waldinger and Mehdi Bozorgmehr, eds., *Ethnic Los Angeles* (New York: Russell Sage Foundation, 1996), 345–378; Roger Waldinger, "Immigration and Urban Change," *Annual Review of Sociology* 15 (1989): 211–232; Alba and Nee, "Rethinking Assimilation Theory for a New Era of Immigration."

95. Douglas Massey, "Ethnic Residential Segregation: A Theoretical Synthesis and Empirical Review," *Sociology and Social Research* 69 (1985): 315–350.

96. Peter Marcuse, "The Enclave, the Citadel, and the Ghetto: What Has Changed in the Post-Fordist U.S. City," *Urban Affairs Review* 33 (1997): 228–264; Min Zhou, *Chinatown: The Socioeconomic Potential of an Urban Enclave* (Philadelphia: Temple University Press, 1992).

97. John Logan, Wenquan Zhang, Richard Alba, "Immigrant Enclaves and Ethnic Communities in New York and Los Angeles," *American Sociological Review* 67 (2002): 299–322.

98. U.S. Department of Housing and Urban Development, *Housing Discrimination Study*.

99. Logan et al., "Immigrant Enclaves and Ethnic Communities in New York and Los Angeles," 320.

100. Jennifer Lee, *Civility in the City: Blacks, Jews, and Koreans in Urban America* (Cambridge: Harvard University Press, 2002); Roger Waldinger, *Still a Promised City? African Americans and New Immigrants in Postindustrial New York* (Cambridge: Harvard University Press, 1996).

101. Lee, *Civility in the City*.

102. Rick Hampson, "Studies: Gentrification a Boost for Everyone," *USA Today*, April 19, 2005.

103. Richard Taub, Garth Taylor, and Jan Dunham, *Paths of Neighborhood Change* (Chicago: University of Chicago Press, 1984).

104. Massey and Denton, *American Apartheid*, 19.

105. Loïc Wacquant, *Urban Outcasts: A Comparative Sociology of Advanced Marginality* (Cambridge: Polity Press, 2007).

106. Louis With, "The Ghetto," in Albert Reiss, ed., *Louis Wirth: On Cities and Social Life* (Chicago: University of Chicago Press, 1964 [1927]), 84–98.

107. Mark Cordon, "Public Housing, Crime and the Urban Labor Market: A Study of Black Youths in Chicago," working paper, Malcolm Wiener Center for Social Policy, Harvard University, 1991, 4. See also Sugrue, *Origins of the Urban Housing Crisis*, 81, 86–87.

108. Caro, *Power Broker*, 20.

109. U.S. Department of Housing and Urban Development, "HUD's Public Housing Program," 2007.

110. Sudhir Venkatesh, *American Project: The Rise and Fall of a Modern Ghetto* (Cambridge: Harvard University Press, 2000).

111. Cited in Beverly Wright and Robert Bullard, "Black New Orleans: Before and after Hurricane Katrina," in Robert Doyle Bullard, ed., *The Black Metropolis in the Twenty-First Century: Race, Power, and Politics of Place* (Lanham: Rowman & Littlefield, 2007, 173–198), 189.

112. Associated Press, "In New Orleans, A Brutal Urban Renewal," October 12, 2005.

113. Loïc Wacquant, "Territorial Stigmatization in the Age of Advanced Marginality," *Thesis Eleven* 91 (2007): 66–77, 67.

114. Venkatesh, *American Project*, 5.

115. U.S. National Advisory Commission on Civil Disorders, *The Kerner Report* (New York: Pantheon Books, 1988), 2.

116. Edward Blakely and Gail Snyder, *Fortress America: Gated Communities in the United States* (Washington, D.C.: Brookings Institute, 1997).

117. Kevin Romig, "The Upper Sonoran Lifestyle: Gated Communities in Scottsdale, Arizona," *City and Community* 4 (2005): 67–86; Kristen Hill Maher, "Workers and Strangers: The Household Service Economy and the Landscape of Suburban Fear," *Urban Affairs Review* 38 (2003): 751–786.

118. David Bauder, "Group Points Out O'Reilly Race Comments," *Washington Post*, September 25, 2007.

119. Allan Berube and William Frey, "A Decade of Mixed Blessings: Urban and Suburban Poverty in Census 2000," in Allan Berube, Bruce Katz, and Robert Lang, eds., *Redefining Urban and Suburban America: Evidence from the 2000 Census* (Washington, D.C.: Brookings Institute, 2005), 111–136.

120. Pattillo-McCoy, *Black Picket Fences;* Charles, "The Dynamics of Racial Residential Segregation."

121. Allen Liska, John Logan, and Paul Bellair, "Race and Violent Crime in the Suburbs," *American Sociological Review* 63 (1998): 27–38; Pattillo, "Black Middle-Class Neighborhoods"; Pattillo-McCoy, *Black Picket Fences.*

122. Karyn Lacy, "Black Spaces, Black Places: Strategic Assimilation and Identity Construction in Middle-Class Suburbia," *Ethnic and Racial Studies* 27 (2004): 908–930.

123. France Winddance Twine, "Brown-Skinned White Girls: Class, Culture, and the Construction of White Identity in Suburban Communities," in Ruth Frankenberg, ed., *Displacing Whiteness: Essays in Social and Cultural Criticism* (Durham: Duke University Press, 1997, 214–224), 233.

124. Richard Alba and Victor Nee, *Remaking the American Mainstream: Assimilation and Contemporary Immigration* (Cambridge: Harvard University Press, 2003); Richard Alba, John Logan, Brian Stults, Gilbert Marzan, and Wenquan Zhang, "Immigrant Groups and Suburbs: A Reexamination of Suburbanization and Spatial Assimilation," *American Sociological Review* 64 (1999): 446–460; John Horton, *The Politics of Diversity: Immigration, Resistance, and Change in Monterey Park, California* (Philadelphia: Temple University Press, 1992).

125. Susie Ling, "History of Asians in the San Gabriel Valley," IMDiversity.com, downloaded October 20, 2008. See also John Horton and Jose Calderon, *The Politics of Diversity: Immigration, Resistance, and Change in Monterey Park, California* (Philadelphia: Temple University Press, 1995).

126. United States Census Bureau, "Estimates of U.S. Urban Population," 2003.

127. C. Matthew Snipp, "Understanding Race and Ethnicity in Rural America," *Rural Sociology* 61 (1989): 125–142, 127.

128. Maggie Rivas-Rodriguez, *Mexican Americans & World War II* (College Station: University of Texas Press, 2005); Jeffrey Harris Cohen, *The Culture of Migration in Southern Mexico* (College Station: University of Texas Press, 2004).

129. American Immigration Law Foundation, *Mexican Immigrant Workers and the U.S. Economy: An Increasingly Vital Role* (Washington, D.C.: Immigration Policy Focus, 2002).

130. Doris Slesinger and Max Pfeffer, "Migrant Farm Workers," in Cynthia Duncan, *Rural Poverty in America* (Westport: Auburn House, 1992), 125–154; Snipp, "Understanding Race and Ethnicity in Rural America."

131. Martha Crowley, Daniel Lichter, and Zhenchao Qian, "Beyond Gateway Cities: Economic Restructuring and Poverty among Mexican Immigrant Families and Children," *Family Relations* 55 (2006): 345–360; Joan Anderson, "The U.S. Mexico Border: A Half Century of Change," *The Social Science Journal* 40 (2003): 535–554.

132. Julie Murphy Erfani, "Whose Security? Dilemmas of U.S. Border Security in the Arizona-Sonora Borderlands." Paper presented at the European and North American Border Security Policies in Comparative Perspective Conference, Victoria, British Columbia, 2006; Brian Bennett, "Do-It-Yourself Border Patrol," *Time*, May 28, 2005.

133. Jeffrey Ressner, "How Immigration Is Rousing the Zealots," *Time*, May 29, 2006.

134. Snipp, "Understanding Race and Ethnicity in Rural America."

135. Russell Thornton, *The Cherokees: A Population History* (Lincoln: University of Nebraska Press, 1990), 174–15.

136. Eva Marie Garroutte, *Real Indians: Identity and the Survival of Native America* (Berkeley and Los Angeles: University of California Press, 2003), 67.

137. Robert Bullard, *Dumping on Dixie: Race, Class, and Environmental* Quality (Boulder: Westview Press, 2000), 98.

138. Robert Bullard, *Environment and Morality: Confronting Environmental Racism in the United States* (Geneva: United Nations Research Institute for Social Development, 2004); Winona LaDuke, *All Our Relations: Native Struggles for Land Rights and Life* (Boston: South End Press, 1999).

139. Margot Roosevelt, "Utah's Toxic Opportunity," *Time*, March 8, 2006.

140. Bullard, *Environment and Morality*; Harvard Project on American Indian Economic Development, *State of the Native Nations*.

141. Deborah Robinson, *Environmental Racism: Old Wine in a New Bottle* (Geneva: World Council of Churches, 2000); Dallas Morning News, "Study: Public Housing Is Too Often Located Near Toxic Sites," October 3, 2000.

142. Bullard, *Environment and Morality*, iii.

143. United States Department of Health and Human Services, Agency for Toxic Substances and Disease Registry, *Health Consultation (Exposure Investigation): Calcasieu Estuary (aka Moss-ville)* (Lake Charles, Calcasieu Parish, Louisiana: CERLIS No. LA002368173, November 19, 1999); Robinson, *Environmental Racism*.

144. Environmental Sustainability Committee, *Nationwide Waste Statistics* (Houghton: Environmental Sustainability Committee, 2007).

145. Wacquant, "Territorial Stigmatization in the Age of Advanced Marginality."

146. Cash, *Mind of the South*, vii.

147. Hartigan, *White Tribes*.

148. Andrea Voyer, "Living Difference and Talking Diversity: Interactions, Identifications, and Institutions," unpublished working paper, University of Wisconsin—Madison, Department of Sociology; Jerry Harkavy, "Somalis Find New Lives, Adjustments to Lewiston," *Lewiston Sun Journal*, 2007.

149. Southern Poverty Law Center, "Maine Town's Diversity Rally Outdraws Hate-Group Gathering," March 2004.

150. Alex Kotlowitz, "Our Town," *The New York Times Magazine*, August 5, 2007.

151. Ibid., 37.

152. Ibid., 33.

153. Mary Waters and Tomás Jiménez, "Assessing Immigrant Assimilation: New Empirical and Theoretical Challenges," *Annual Review of Sociology* 31 (2005): 105–125; Richard Alba, John Logan, Any Lutz, and Brian Stults, "Only English by the Third Generation? Loss and Preservation of the Mother Tongue among the Grandchildren of Contemporary Immigrants," *Demography* 39 (2002): 467–484.

154. Kotlowitz, "Our Town."

155. Voyer, "Living Difference and Talking Diversity."

156. Abdelmalek Sayad, *The Suffering of the Immigrant* (Cambridge: Polity Press, 2004), 220.

157. Tony Horwitz, "Immigration—and the Curse of the Black Legend," *The New York Times*, July 9, 2006.

158. Sayad, *Suffering of the Immigrant*, 218–220.

159. Carlos Fuentes, *The Buried Mirror: Reflections on Spain and the New World* (New York: Houghton Mifflin, 1999).

160. Sayad, *Suffering of the Immigrant*, 216.

161. Ingrid Ellen, *Sharing America's Neighborhoods: The Prospects for Stable Racial Integration* (Cambridge: Harvard University Press, 2000); Charles, "Dynamics of Racial Residential Segregation," 2000.

162. Feagin, Vera, and Batur, *White Racism*, 7.

163. Baldwin, "Fifth Avenue, Uptown," 213.

164. Mireya Navarro, "The Mexican Will See You Now," *The New York Times*, June 24, 2007.

Chapter 6: Crime and Punishment

1. John Dewey, *How We Think* (Mineola: Dover, 1997 [1910]), 13.

2. Sister Helen Prejean, *The Death of Innocents: An Eyewitness Account of Wrongful Executions* (New York: Knopf, 2006).

3. Said, *Orientalism*, xxiii.

4. Deborah Cray White, *Too Heavy a Load: Black Women in Defense of Themselves, 1894–1994* (New York: Norton, 1999), 25.

5. Quoted in Fairclough, *Better Day Coming*, 25.

6. Cash, *Mind of the South*, 119.

7. Patricia Schechter, *Ida B. Wells-Barnett and American Reform, 1880–1930* (Chapel Hill: University of North Carolina Press, 2001), 85–87; Mary Frances Berry, *The Pig Farmer's Daughter and Other Tales of American Justice: Episodes of Racism and Sexism in the Courts from 1865 to the Present* (New York: Vintage, 1999).

8. Glenda Gilmore, *Gender and Jim Crow: Women and the Politics of White Supremacy in North Carolina, 1896–1920* (Chapel Hill: University of North Carolina Press, 1996).

9. Amy Dru Stanley, *From Bondage to Contract: Wage Labor, Marriage, and the Market in the Age of Slave Emancipation* (Cambridge: Cambridge University Press, 1998), 108–110.

10. Wacquant, "From Slavery to Mass Incarceration," 53.

11. David Oshinsky, *Worse Than Slavery: Parchman Farm and the Ordeal of Jim Crow Justice* (New York: Free Press, 1996), 45. Also see David Garland, *Punishment and Modern Society: A Study in Social Theory* (Chicago: University of Chicago Press, 1990), 104–105; Martha Myers, *Race, Labor, and Punishment in the New South* (Columbus: Ohio State University Press, 1998).

12. David Garland, "Introduction: The Meaning of Mass Imprisonment," in David Garland, ed., *Mass Imprisonment: Social Causes and Consequences* (London: Sage, 2001).

13. Bruce Western, *Punishment and Inequality in America* (New York: Russell Sage Foundation, 2006).

14. Eric Schlosser, "The Prison-Industrial Complex," *The Atlantic Monthly*, December 1998.

15. The Pew Center on States, *One in 100: Behind Bars in America 2008* (Washington, D.C.: Pew Charitable Trust, 2008); Adam Liptak, "1 in 100 U.S. Adults behind Bars, New Study Says," *The New York Times*, February 28, 2008.

16. The Economist, *Pocket World in Figures, 2007 Edition* (London: The Economist Newspaper, 2007); Katherine Beckett and Theodore Sasson, *The Politics of Injustice: Crime and Punishment in America*, Second Edition (Thousand Oaks: Sage, 2004); Western, *Punishment and Inequality in America*.

17. Elain Leeder, ed., *Women, Prison, and Therapy* (New York: Routledge, 2007); Ann Jacobs and Sarah From, *Hard Hit: The Growth in the Imprisonment of Women, 1977–2004* (New York: Women's Prison Association, 2006); Prisoner Action Coalition, *Women in California Prisons* (Berkeley: Prisoner Action Coalition, 2000).

18. Western, *Punishment and Inequality in America*, 16.

19. Ibid., 15–25.

20. Ibid., 27.

21. Western, *Punishment and Inequality in America*, 48; Beckett and Theodore Sasson, *The Politics of Injustice*, 14, 18.

22. Western, *Punishment and Inequality in America*, 41.

23. Alfred Blumstein and Allen Beck, "Population Growth in U.S. Prisons, 1980–1996," in Michael Tonry, ed., *Prisons: Crime and Justice—A Review of the Research* (Chicago: University of Chicago Press: 1999), 17–61.

24. Michael Tonry, *Malign Neglect: Race, Crime, and Punishment in America* (New York: Oxford University Press, 1995); Western, *Punishment and Inequality in America*, 42–43, 47.

25. Joan Petersilia, *When Prisoners Come Home: Parole and Prisoner Reentry* (New York: Oxford University Press, 2003); Sasha Abramsky, *Hard Time Blues: How Politics Built a Prison Nation* (New York: Dunne Books, 2002); Western, *Punishment and Inequality in America*, 62–64.

26. Beckett and Sasson, *Politics of Injustice*, 49.

27. Joseph Davey, *The Politics of Prison Expansion: Winning Elections by Waging War on Crime* (Westport: Praeger, 1998); Western, *Punishment and Inequality in America*, 60–61.

28. Quoted in Nancy Marion, *A History of Federal Crime Control Initiatives, 1960–1993* (Westport: Praeger, 1994), 70.

29. Lord Windelsham, *Politics, Punishment and Populism* (New York: Oxford University Press, 1998); Beckett and Sasson, *Politics of Injustice*, 52–65.

30. Angela Y. Davis, *Abolition Democracy: Beyond Prisons, Torture, and Empire* (New York: Seven Stories Press, 2005); Angela Y. Davis, *Are Prisons Obsolete?* (New York: Seven Stories Press, 2003); Nils Christie, *Crime Control as Industry: Towards Gulags, Western Style* (New York: Routledge, 2000).

31. Schlosser, "Prison-Industrial Complex."

32. Rose M. Brewer, "The Racialization of Crime and Punishment: Criminal Justice, Color-Blind Racism, and the Political Economy of the Prison Industrial Complex," *American Behavioral Scientist* 51 (2008): 625–644; Julia Sudbury, *Global Lockdown: Gender, Race and the Rise of the Prison Industrial Complex around the World* (New York: Routledge, 2005).

33. Schlosser, "Prison-Industrial Complex."

34. Tonry, *Malign Neglect*, 94.

35. Beckett and Sasson, *Politics of Injustice*, 48.

36. Urban American and Urban Coalition, *One Year Later: An Assessment of the Nation's Response to the Crisis Described by the National Advisory Commission on Civil Disorders* (New York: Praeger, 1968).

37. Leo Caroll and Pamela Irving Jackson, "Minority Composition, Inequality and the Growth of Municipal Police Forces," *Sociological Focus* 15 (1982): 327–346; Susan Welch, "The Impact of Urban Riots on Urban Expenditures," *American Journal of Political Science* 19 (1975): 741–760

38. Pamela Oliver, "Repression and Crime Control: Why Social Movement Scholars Should Pay Attention to Mass Incarceration as a Form of Repression," *Mobilization* 13 (2008): 1–24.

39. Western, *Punishment and Inequality in America*.

40. Michel Foucault, *Discipline and Punish: The Birth of the Prison* (New York: Vintage, 1999 [1975]), 24.

41. Steven Barkan and Steven Cohn, "Why Whites Favor Spending More Money to Fight Crime," *Social Problems* 52 (2005): 300–314; Barry Glassner, *Culture of Fear: Why Americans Are Afraid of the Wrong Things* (New York: Basic Books, 1999).

42. Eric Lambert, "Worlds Apart: The Views on Crime and Punishment among White and Minority College Students," *Criminal Justice Studies* 18 (2005): 99–121.

43. Ted Chiricos, Michael Hogan, and Marc Gertz, "Racial Composition of Neighborhood and Fear of Crime," *Criminology* 35 (1997): 107–129; Wesley Skogan, "Crime and the Racial Fears of White Americans," *The Annals of the American Academy of Political and Social Science* (1995) 539: 59–71; Ralph Taylor and Jeanette Covington, "Community Structural Change and Fear of Crime," *Social Problems* 40 (1993): 374–397.

44. Lincoln Quillian and Devah Pager, "Black Neighbors, Higher Crime? The Role of Racial Stereotypes in Evaluations of Neighborhood Crime," *American Journal of Sociology* 107 (2001): 717–767.

45. Ted Chiricos, Ranee McEntire, and Marc Gertz, "Perceived Racial and Ethnic Composition of Neighborhood and Perceived Risk of Crime," *Social Problems* 48 (2001): 322–340. See also Gertrude Moeller, "Fear of Criminal Victimization: The Effect of Neighborhood Racial Composition," *Sociological Inquiry* 59 (1989): 208–221.

46. Glassner, *Culture of Fear,* xxi.

47. Helen Benedict, *Virgin or Vamp: How the Press Covers Sex Crimes* (New York: Oxford University Press, 1992).

48. Glassner, *Culture of Fear,* xxiii.

49. Jeffrey Kluger, "How Americans Are Living Dangerously," *Time,* November 26, 2006.

50. Mary Douglas and Aaron Wildavsky, *Risk and Culture: An Essay on the Selection of Technical and Environmental Danger* (Berkeley and Los Angeles: University of California Press, 1982).

51. Tom Smith, *What Americans Say about Jews* (New York: American Jewish Committee, 1991); Sniderman and Piazza, *Scar of Race.*

52. Loïc Wacquant, "Race as Civic Felony," *International Social Science Journal* 181 (2005): 127–142; Émile Durkheim, *The Division of Labor in Society* (New York: Free Press, 1997 [1893]).

53. Richard Wright, *Native Son* (New York: HarperCollins, 1998 [1939]), 400.

54. Lambert, "Worlds Apart," 110.

55. Joe Soss, Laura Langbein, and Alan Metelko, "Why Do White Americans Support the Death Penalty?" *The Journal of Politics* 65 (2003): 397–421; Devon Johnson, "Punitive Attitudes on Crime: Economic Insecurity, Race Prejudice, or Both?" *Sociological Focus* 12 (2001): 33–54; Mark Peffley and Jon Hurwirz, "Whites' Stereotypes of Blacks: Sources and Politics Consequences," in Jon Hurwirz and Mark Peffley, eds., *Perception and Prejudice: Race and Politics in the United States* (New Haven: Yale University Press, 1998), 58–99; Barkan and Cohn, "Why Whites Favor Spending More Money to Fight Crime."

56. Lynette Holloway, "Bankrupt, Goetz Still Owes Victim," *The New York Times,* August 2, 1996.

57. Armour, "Race *Ipsa Loquitur.*"

58. Ibid.

59. Ibid., 192.

60. Christine Hauser and Anahad O'Connor, "Virginia Tech Shooting Leaves 33 Dead," *The New York Times*, April 16, 2007.

61. Patrick Buchanan, "The Dark Side of Diversity," www.townhall.com, May 1, 2007.

62. Eyal Press, "Do Immigrants Make Us Safer?" *The New York Times Magazine*, December 3, 2006.

63. "A War on Janitors," *The New York Times*, October 20, 2008.

64. Susan Bibler Coutin, "Contesting Criminality: Illegal Immigration and the Spatialization of Legality," *Theoretical Criminology* 9 (2005): 5–33; Mae Ngai, *Impossible Subjects: Illegal Aliens and the Making of Modern America* (Princeton: Princeton University Press, 2003); Michael Welch, *Detained: Immigration Laws and the Expanding INS Jail Complex* (Philadelphia: Temple University Press, 2002).

65. Anrew Karmen, *New York Murder Mystery: The True Story behind the Crime Crash of the 1990s* (New York: New York University Press, 2006); Amie Nielsen, Matthew Lee, and Ramiro Martinez, Jr., "Integrating Race, Place and Motive in Social Disorganization Theory: Lessons from a Comparison of Black and Latino Homicide Types in Two Immigrant Destination Cities," *Criminology* 43 (2005): 837–872; Ramiro Martinez, Jr., *Latino Homicide: Immigration, Violence, and Community* (New York: Routledge, 2002); Matthew Lee, Ramiro Martinez, Jr., and Richard Rosenfeld, "Does Immigration Increase Homicide? Negative Evidence from Three Border Cities," *The Sociological Quarterly* 42 (2001): 559–580.

66. Robert Sampson, Jeffrey Morenoff, and Stephen Raudenbush, "Social Anatomy of Racial and Ethnic Disparities in Violence," *American Journal of Public Health* 95 (2005): 224–232; Lesley Williams Reid, Harald Weiss, Robert Adelman, and Charles Jaret, "The Immigration-Crime Relationship: Evidence across U.S. Metropolitan Areas," *Social Science Research* 34 (2005): 757–780.

67. Robert Sampson, "Open Doors Don't Invite Criminals," *The New York Times*, March 11, 2006.

68. Robert Sampson, Doug McAdam, Heather MacIndoe, and Simon Weffer, "Civil Society Reconsidered: The Durable Nature and Community Structure of Collective Civic Action," *American Journal of Sociology* 111 (2005): 673–714; Robert Sampson and Steve Raudenbush, "Systematic Social Observation of Public Spaces: A New Look at Disorder in Urban Neighborhoods," *American Journal of Sociology* 105 (1999): 603–651; Robert Sampson et al., "Social Anatomy of Racial and Ethnic Disparities in Violence."

69. Jane Jacobs, *The Death and Life of Great American Cities* (New York: Random House, 1961), 32.

70. Rubén Rumbaut, Roberto Gonzales, Golnaz Komaie, and Charlie Morgan, *Debunking the Myth of Immigrant Criminality: Imprisonment among First- and Second-Generation Young Men* (Washington, D.C.: Migration Policy Institute, 2006); Portes and Rumbaut, *Immigrant America*.

71. Drake Bennett, "If There's a Link between Urban Crime and Immigration, Sociologists Say, It's Probably Not What You Think," *The Boston Globe*, January 1, 2006.

72. Elliott Barkan, "Return of the Nativists? California Public Opinion and Immigration in the 1980s and 1990s," *Social Science History* 27 (2002): 229–283; Yueh-Ting Lee, Victor Ottati, and Imtiaz Hussain, "Attitudes toward 'Illegal' Immigration into the United States: California Proposition 187," *Hispanic Journal of Behavioral Sciences* 23 (2001): 430–443.

73. Irene Jung Fiala, "Anything New? The Racial Profiling of Terrorists," *Criminal Justice Studies* 16 (2003): 53–58.

74. Jeffrey Alexander, "From the Depths of Despair: Performance, Counterperformance, and 'September 11,'" *Sociological Theory* 22 (2004): 88–105.

75. Diane Lauderdale, "Birth Outcomes for Arabic-Named Women in California before and after September 11," *Demography* 43 (2006): 185–201; Costas Panagopoulos, "Arab and Muslim Americans and Islam in the Aftermath of 9/11," *Public Opinion Quarterly* 70 (2006): 608–624; American-Arab Anti-Discrimination Committee Research Institute, *Report on Hate Crimes and Discrimination against Arab Americans: September 11, 2001 to October 11, 2002* (Boston: American-Arab Anti-Discrimination Committee Research Institute, 2003).

76. Panagopoulos, "Arab and Muslim Americans and Islam in the Aftermath of 9/11."

77. Nadine Naber, "Ambiguous Insiders: An Investigation of Arab American Invisibility," *Ethnic and Racial Studies* 23 (2000): 37–61.

78. Jack Shaheen, *Real Bad Arabs: How Hollywood Vilifies a People* (Northampton: Olive Branch Press, 2001), 1.

79. Debra Merskin, "The Construction of Arabs as Enemies: Post-September 11 Discourse of George W. Bush," *Mass Communication and Society* 7 (2004): 157–175; Leti Volpp, "The Citizen and the Terrorist," in Mary Dudziak, ed., *September 11 in History: A Watershed Moment?* (Durham: Duke University Press, 2003), 147–162.

80. Alexander, "From the Depths of Despair," 94.

81. Detroit Free Press, *100 Questions and Answers about Arab Americans: A Journalist's Guide* (Detroit: Free Press, 2007); Naber, "Ambiguous Insiders."

82. Leti Volpp, "Disappearing Acts: On Gendered Violence, Pathological Cultures, and Civil Society" *PMLA* 121 (2006): 1632–1638.

83. American-Arab Anti-Discrimination Committee Research Institute, *Report on Hate Crimes and Discrimination against Arab Americans.*

84. Neil MacFarquhar, "Borders Spells Trouble for Arab American," *The New York Times,* April 29, 2007.

85. Fiala, "Anything New?"; Panagopoulos, "Arab and Muslim Americans and Islam in the Aftermath of 9/11."

86. Bill Dedman, "Fighting Terror—Words of Caution on Airport Security: Memo Warns Against Use of Profiling as a Defense," *The Boston Globe,* October 12, 2001.

87. Cited in Glassner, *Culture of Fear,* xiii.

88. Lauderdale, "Birth Outcomes for Arabic-Named Women in California before and after September 11."

89. Strobe Talbot and Nayan Chanda, *The Age of Terror: America and the World After September 11* (New York: Basic Books, 2002).

90. Anne McClintock, *Imperial Leather: Race, Gender, and Sexuality in the Colonial Conquest* (New York: Routledge, 1995), 12; Said, *Orientalism*, xxi.

91. Quoted in Lanita Jacobs-Huey, "'The Arab Is the New Nigger': African American Comics Confront the Irony and Tragedy of September 11," *Transforming Anthropology* 12 (2006): 60–64, 60–61.

92. Sudhir Venkatesh, *Off the Books: The Underground Economy of the Urban Poor* (Cambridge: Harvard University Press, 2006), 12.

93. United Nations Office on Drugs and Crime, *World Drug Report 2007* (New York: United Nations, 2007); "Class A Capitalists," *London Guardian*, April 21, 2002.

94. Substance Abuse and Mental Health Services Administration, *National Survey on Drug Use and Health* (Washington, D.C.: U.S. Department of Health and Human Services, 2006).

95. Andrew Papachristos and David Kirk, "Neighborhood Effects on Street Gang Behavior," in James F. Short, Jr. and Lorine A. Hughes, eds., Studying Youth Gangs (Lanham: AltaMira Press, 2006), 63–84; Robert Bursik and Harold Grasmick, *Neighborhoods and Crime: The Dimensions of Effective Community Control* (New York: Lexington Books, 1993).

96. Theo Emery, "In Nashville, a Street Gang Emerges in a Kurdish Enclave," *The New York Times*, July 15, 2007; Brenda Coughlin and Sudhir Venkatesh, "The Urban Street Gang after 1970," *Annual Review of Sociology* 29 (2003): 41–64; Eric Schneider, *Vampires, Dragons, and Egyptian Kings: Youth Gangs in Postwar New York* (Princeton: Princeton University Press, 1999); Irving Spergel, *The Youth Gang Problem: A Community Approach* (New York: Oxford University Press, 1995).

97. C. Ronald Huff, *Gangs in America*, Second Edition (Thousand Oaks: Sage, 1996); Martín Sánchez Jankowski, *Islands in the Street: Gangs and American Urban Society* (Berkeley and Los Angeles: University of California Press, 1991); Padilla, *The Gang as an American Enterprise*; Coughlin and Venkatesh, "The Urban Street Gang after 1970."

98. Steven Levitt and Sudhir Venkatesh, "An Economic Analysis of a Drug-Selling Gang's Finances," *The Quarterly Journal of Economics* 115 (2000): 755–789.

99. Avelardo Valdez, "Drug Markets in Minority Communities: Consequences for Mexican American Youth Gangs," in Ruth Peterson, Lauren Krivo, and John Hagan, eds., *The Many Colors of Crime: Inequalities of Race, Ethnicity, and Crime in America* (New York: New York University Press, 2006), 221–236.

100. Philippe Bourgois, *In Search of Respect: Selling Crack in El Barrio* (New York: Cambridge University Press, 1995), 4.

101. Katherine Newman, *No Shame in My Game: The Working Poor in the Inner City* (New York: Vintage and Russell Sage Foundation, 1999).

102. Venkatesh, *Off the Books*, 4, 7.

103. Edwin Sutherland, *White Collar Crime, the Uncut Version* (New Haven: Yale University Press, 1983 [1949]), 7.

104. Kent Kerley and Heith Copes, "The Effects of Criminal Justice Contact on Employment Stability for White-Collar and Street-Level Offenders," *International Journal of Offender Therapy and Comparative Criminology* 48 (2004): 65–84.

105. U.S. Department of Justice, *National Criminal Justice Reference Services* (Washington, D.C.: U.S. Department of Justice, 2007); Federal Bureau of Investigation, *Financial Crimes Report to the Public* (Washington, D.C.: U.S. Department of Justice, 2005).

106. Randall Gordon, Thomas Bindrim, Michael McNicholas, and Teresa Walden, "Perceptions of Blue-Collar and White-Collar Crime: The Effect of Defendant Race on Simulated Juror Decisions," *Journal of Social Psychology* 128 (1987): 191–197.

107. Jeffrey Reiman, *The Rich Get Richer and the Poor Get Prison: Ideology, Class, and Criminal Justice,* Sixth Edition (Boston: Allyn and Bacon, 2001).

108. David Harvey, *A Brief History of Neoliberalism* (New York: Oxford University Press, 2005).

109. Quoted in Reiman, *The Rich Get Richer and the Poor Get Prison,* 58.

110. Sonia Frias and Ronald Angel, "The Risk of Partner Violence among Low-Income Hispanic Subgroups," *Journal of Marriage and Family* 67 (2005): 552–564; Richard Gelles, "Estimating the Incidents of Violence against Women," *Violence against Women* 6 (2000): 784–804; Marchel'le Renise Barber, "Why Some Men Batter Women: Domestic Violence is America's Most Common Crime—And Why Some Women Take It," *Ebony,* October 1990.

111. National Coalition against Domestic Violence, *Sexual Assault* (Washington, D.C.: NCADV Public Policy Office, 2007); U.S. Department of Justice, *National Crime Victimization Survey* (Washington, D.C.: Bureau of Justice Statistics, 2006); Barbara Nagel, Hisaka Matsuo, Kevin McIntyre, and Nancy Morrison, "Attitudes toward Victims of Rape: Effects of Gender, Race, Religion, and Social Class," *Journal of Interpersonal Violence* 20 (2005): 725–737.

112. Callie Rennison and Mike Planty, "Nonlethal Intimate Partner Violence: Examining Race, Gender, and Income Patterns," *Violence and Victims* 18 (2003): 433–443.

113. Diane Purvin, "At the Crossroads and in the Crosshairs: Social Welfare Policy and Low-Income Women's Vulnerability to Domestic Violence," *Social Problems* 54 (2007): 188–210; National Coalition against Domestic Violence, *Immigrant Victims of Domestic Violence* (Washington, D.C.: NCADV Public Policy Office, 2007); U.S. Department of Justice, Bureau of Justice Statistics, *Intimate Partner Violence in the U.S.* (Washington, D.C., Department of Justice, 2007); Carolyn West, "Black Women and Intimate Partner Violence: New Directions for Research," *Journal of Interpersonal Violence* 19 (2004): 1487–1493; Carolyn West, *Violence in the Lives of Black Women Battered, Black, and Blue* (New York: Haworth, 2002); Richard Tolman and Jody Raphael, "A Review of Research on Welfare and Domestic Violence," *Journal of Social Issues* 56 (2000): 655–682; Frias and Ronald Angel, "The Risk of Partner Violence among Low-Income Hispanic Subgroups."

114. Margaret Abraham, *Speaking the Unspeakable: Marital Violence among South Asian Immigrants in the United States* (New Brunswick: Rutgers University Press, 2000).

115. Kimberle Crenshaw, "Mapping the Margins: Intersectionality, Identity Politics, and Violence against Women of Color," *Stanford Law Review* 43 (1991): 1241–1299; National Coalition against Domestic Violence, *Immigrant Victims of Domestic Violence;* Margaret Abraham, *Speaking the Unspeakable.*

116. Crenshaw, "Mapping the Margins," 1249, 1264.

117. Gary Lafree, *Rape and Criminal Justice: The Social Construction of Assault* (Boulder: Wadsworth, 1980); Crenshaw, "Mapping the Margins," 1269.

118. Jonathan Markovitz, "Anatomy of a Spectacle: Race, Gender, and Memory in the Kobe Bryant Rape Case," *Sociology of Sport Journal* 23 (2006): 396–418; Crenshaw, "Mapping the Margins," 1268.

119. Janet Lauritsen, *How Families and Communities Influence Youth Victimization* (Washington, D.C.: U.S. Department of Justice, Office of Juvenile Justice and Delinquency Prevention, 2003).

120. Cited in Crenshaw, "Mapping the Margins," 1255.

121. Nellie McKay, "Remembering Anita Hill and Clarence Thomas: What Really Happened When One Black Woman Spoke Out," in Toni Morrison, ed., *Race-ing Justice, En-gendering Power* (New York: Pantheon, 1992, 269–89), 277–278.

122. Katheryn Russell-Brown, *Protecting Our Own: Race, Crime, and African Americans* (Oxford: Rowman and Littlefield, 2006).

123. Crenshaw, "Mapping the Margins," 1273.

124. Cornell West, *Race Matters,* Second Edition (New York: Vintage, 2001), 37

125. Johnetta Betsche Cole and Beverley Guy-Sheftell, *Gender Talk: The Struggle for Women's Equality in African American Communities* (New York: Ballantine, 2003); see also Tessa Lowinske Desmond, "'Something within Me That Banishes Pain': Black Women's Literature as a Space for Healing," unpublished Master's Thesis, University of Wisconsin—Madison, 2005; Patricia Hill Collins, *Black Feminist Thought,* 146–148.

126. Toya Like and Jody Miller, "Race, Inequality, and Gender Violence: A Contextual Examination," in Ruth Peterson, Lauren Krivo, and John Hagan, eds., *The Many Colors of Crime: Inequalities of Race, Ethnicity, and Crime in America* (New York: New York University Press, 2006), 157–176.

127. Federal Bureau of Investigation, *Unified Crime Report* (Washington, D.C.: U.S. Department of Justice, 2007); Alfred Blumstein and Joel Wallman, "The Crime Drop and Beyond," *Annual Review of Law and Social Science* 2 (2006): 125–146; Kathleen Kingsbury, "The Next Crime Wave," *Time,* December 11, 2006; United Nations, *Seventh United Nations Survey of Crime Trends and Operations of Criminal Justice Systems, 1998–2000* (New York: United Nations Office on Drugs and Crime, 2001); Beckett and Sasson, *The Politics of Injustice,* Ch. 3.

128. Robert Sampson and Lyndia Bean, "Cultural Mechanisms and Killing Fields: A Revised Theory of Community-Level Racial Inequality," in Ruth Peterson, Lauren Krivo, and John Hagan, eds., *The Many Colors of Crime: Inequalities of Race, Ethnicity, and Crime in America* (New York: New York University Press, 2006), 8–36; Blumstein and Wallman, "The Crime Drop and Beyond."

129. Glassner, *Culture of Fear,* 111.

130. Karen Sternheimer, "Do Video Games Kill?" *Contexts* 6 (2007): 13–17; David Courtright, *Violent Land* (Cambridge: Harvard University Press, 1996); Patrick Cooke, "TV Causes Violence?" *The New York Times,* August 14, 1993.

131. Glassner, *Culture of Fear,* xix.

132. Josh Sugarman and Michael Rand, *More Gun Dealers Than Gas Stations: A Study of Federally Licensed Firearms Dealers in America* (Washington, D.C.: Violence Policy Center, 1992); Blumstein and Joel Wallman, "The Crime Drop and Beyond," 132–133.

133. Franklin Zimring and Gordon Hawkins, *Crime Is Not the Problem: Lethal Violence in America* (New York: Oxford University Press, 1997); Beckett and Sasson, *Politics of Injustice,* 28–29.

134. Robert Sampson and William Julius Wilson, "Toward a Theory of Race, Crime, and Urban Inequality," in John Hagan and Ruth Peterson, eds., *Crime and Inequality* (Stanford: Stanford University Press, 1995), 37–54.

135. María Vélez, "Toward an Understanding of the Lower Rates of Homicide in Latino versus Black Neighborhoods," in Ruth Peterson, Lauren Krivo, and John Hagan, eds., *The Many Colors of Crime: Inequalities of Race, Ethnicity, and Crime in America* (New York: New York University Press, 2006), 91–107.

136. Ruth Person and Lauren Krivo, "Macrostructural Analyses of Race, Ethnicity, and Violent Crime: Recent Lessons and New Directions for Research," *Annual Review of Sociology* 31 (2005): 331–356; Ruth Person and Lauren Krivo, "Racial Segregation and Black Urban Homicide," *Social Forces* 71 (1993): 1001–1026.

137. Scott South and Steven Messner, "Crime and Demography: Multiple Linkages, Reciprocal Relations," *Annual Review of Sociology* 26 (2000): 83–106; Sampson and Bean, "Cultural Mechanisms and Killing Fields."

138. Sampson and Bean, "Cultural Mechanisms and Killing Fields," 12–13.

139. Bruce Rankin and James Quane, "Neighborhood Poverty and the Social Isolation of Inner-City African American Families," *Social Forces* 79 (2000): 139–164; Frank Furstenberg, "How Families Manage Risk and Opportunity in Dangerous Neighborhoods," in William Julius Wilson, ed., *Sociology and the Public Agenda* (Thousand Oaks: Sage, 1993), 231–254. Carol Stack, *All Our Kin: Strategies for Survival in a Black Community* (New York: Basic Books, 1974).

140. Elijah Anderson, *Code of the Streets* (New York: Norton, 1999).

141. Eric Stewart, Christopher Schreck, and Ronald Simons, "'I Ain't Gonna Let No One Disrespect Me': Does the Code of the Street Reduce or Increase Violent Victimization among African American Adolescents?" *Journal of Research in Crime and Delinquency* 43 (2006): 427–458.

142. Orlando Patterson, "A Poverty of the Mind," *The New York Times,* March 26, 2006.

143. Robert Sampson and John Laub, "Urban Poverty and the Family Context of Delinquency," *Child Delinquency* 65 (1994): 538–545.

144. Oliver, "Repression and Crime Control."

145. Stewart D'Alessio and Lisa Stolzenberg, "Race and the Probability of Arrest," *Social Forces* 81 (2003): 1381–1397.

146. Brian Stults and Eric Baumer, "Racial Context and Police Force Size: Evaluating the Empirical Validity of the Minority Threat Hypothesis," *American Journal of Sociology* 113 (2007): 507–546; Stephanie Kent and David Jacobs, "Minority Threat and Police Strength from 1980 to 2000: A Fixed-Effects Analysis of Nonlinear and Interactive Effects in Large U.S. Cities," *Criminology* 43 (2005): 731–760.

147. Brown et al., *White-Washing Race,* 149.

148. David Harris, "'Driving While Black' and All Other Traffic Offenses: The Supreme Court and Pretextual Traffic Stops," *Journal of Criminal Law and Criminology* 87 (1999): 544–582; Timothy Flanagan and Michael Vaughn, "Public Opinion about Police Abuse and Force," in William Geller and Hans Toch, eds., *Police Violence* (New Haven: Yale University Press, 1996), 113–128.

149. Patrick Langan, Lawrence Greenfield, Steven Smith, Matthew Durose, and David Levine, *Contacts between Police and the Public: Findings from the 1999 National Survey* (Washington, D.C.: U.S. Department of Justice, 2001); State of New Jersey, Office of the Attorney General, *Selected Highlights of the Interim Report of the State Police Review Team Regarding Allegations of Racial Profiling* (Trenton: Office of the Attorney General, 1999).

150. Quoted in Russell-Brown, *Protecting Our Own,* 67.

151. Langan et al., *Contacts between Police and the Public,* 7.

152. Russ Buettner and Ray Rivera, "For Owners of Strip Club in Police Shooting, a Decade of Raids and Suits," *The New York Times,* December 3, 2006; CNN, "Mayor: Police Barrage at Groom 'Unacceptable,'" November 27, 2006.

153. Glassner, *Culture of Fear,* 114.

154. Quoted in Reiman, *The Rich Get Richer and the Poor Get Prison,* 109.

155. Reiman, *The Rich Get Richer and the Poor Get Prison,* 127. See also Wendy Leo Moore, *Reproducing Racism: White Space, Elite Law Schools, and Racial Inequality* (Oxford: Rowman & Littlefield 2007).

156. Richard Lacayo, "You Don't Always Get Perry Mason," *Time,* June 1, 1992.

157. Julie Rawe, "Congress's Bad Habit," *Time,* November 19, 2007.

158. Adam Liptak, "Whittling Away, but Leaving a Gap," *The New York Times,* December 17, 2007.

159. Clarence Page, "Injustice is Bigger than Jena 6," *Chicago Tribune,* September 24, 2007; Darrell Steffensmier, Jeffrey Ulmer, and John Kramer, "The Interaction of Race, Gender, and Age in Criminal Sentencing: The Punishment Cost of Being Young, Black, and Male," *Criminology* 36 (1998): 763–798; James Nelson, *Disparities in Processing Felony Arrests in New York State, 1990–1992* (Albany: New York State Division of Criminal Justice Services, 1995); Brown et al., *White-Washing Race,* 142–143.

160. Donald F. Tibbs and Tryon P. Woods, "The Jena 6 and Black Punishment: Law and Raw Life in the Domain of Non-Existence," *Seattle Journal for Social Justice,* forthcoming.

161. Richard Jones, "In Louisiana, a Tree, a Fight and a Question of Justice," *The New York Times,* September 19, 2007; Richard Jones, "Louisiana Protest Echoes the Civil Rights Era," *The New York Times,* September 21, 2007; Page, "Injustice Is Bigger Than Jena 6."

162. Mary Frances Berry, *Black Resistance/White Law: A History of Constitutional Racism in America* (New York: Penguin, 1995); Tibbs and Woods, "The Jena 6 and Black Punishment."

163. Richard Dieter, *The Death Penalty in Black and White: Who Lives, Who Dies, Who Decides* (Washington, D.C.: Death Penalty Information Center, 1998); David Baldus, Charles Pulaski, and George Woodworth, "Comparative Review of Death Sentences," *Journal of Criminal Law and Criminology* 4 (1983): 661–753.

164. Innocence Project, *Fact Sheet* (New York: Innocence Project, 2008); Death Penalty Information Center, *Innocence and the Death Penalty* (Washington, D.C.: Death Penalty Information Center, 2008).

165. Susan Howell, Huey Perry, Matthew Vile, "Black Cities/White Cities: Evaluating the Police," *Political Behavior* 26 (2004): 45–68; United States Department of Justice, *Sourcebook of Criminal Justice Statistics 1999* (Washington, D.C.: Bureau of Justice Statistics, 2000).

166. Ross Matsueda, Kevin Drakulich, and Charis Kubrin, "Race and Neighborhood Codes of the Street," in Ruth D. Peterson, Lauren J. Krivo, and John Hagan, eds., *The Many Colors of Crime: Inequalities of Race, Ethnicity, and Crime in America* (New York: New York University Press, 2006), 199–220; Charis Kubrin and Ronald Weitzer, "Retaliatory Homicide: Concentrated Disadvantage and Neighborhood Culture," *Social Problems* 50 (2003): 157–180; Anderson, *Code of the Street;* Sampson and Bean, "Cultural Mechanisms and Killing Fields."

167. Jeffrey Kluger, "The Paradox of Supermax," *Time,* February 5, 2007.

168. Pager, "Mark of a Criminal Record."

169. Bruce Western and Becky Pettit, "Incarceration and Racial Inequality in Men's Employment," *Industrial and Labor Relations Review* 54 (2000): 3–16; Harry Holzer, *What Employers Want: Job Prospects for Less Educated Workers* (New York: Russell Sage Foundation, 1996); Wacquant, "From Slavery to Mass Incarceration;" Pager, "Mark of a Criminal Record;" Western, *Punishment and Inequality in America,* 111–115.

170. Western, *Punishment and Inequality in America,* 108–120.

171. Katherine Edin, Timothy Nelson, Rechelle Paranal, "Fatherhood and Incarceration as Potential Turning Points in the Criminal Careers of Unskilled Men," in Mary Patillo, David Weiman, and Bruce Western, eds., *Imprisoning America: The Social Effects of Mass Incarceration* (New York: Russell Sage Foundation, 2004); Sara McLanahan and Gary Sandefur, *Growing Up with a Single Parent: What Hurts, What Helps* (Cambridge: Harvard University Press, 1994); Western, *Punishment and Inequality in America,* Ch. 6.

172. Beckett and Sasson, *The Politics of Injustice,* 60; Glassner, *Culture of Fear,* xvii.

173. Wacquant, "From Slavery to Mass Incarceration," 57.

174. Western, *Punishment and Inequality in America,* 185.

175. Bureau of Justice Statistics, *Census of State Adult Correctional Facilities, 1979* (Washington, D.C.: Bureau of the Census, 1997); Western, *Punishment and Inequality in America,* 174–185.

176. Anne Morrison Piehl and John DiIulio, "Does Prison Pay? Revisited," *Brookings Review* 13 (1995): 21–25; Western, *Punishment and Inequality in America,* 177.

177. David Anderson, "The Deterrence Hypothesis and Picking Pockets at the Pickpocket's Hanging," *American Law and Economics Review* 4 (2002): 295–313; Bureau of Justice Statistics, *Drug and Crime Facts, 1994* (Washington, D.C.: Department of Justice, 1995); Western, *Punishment and Inequality in America,* Ch. 7.

178. Kingsbury, "The Next Crime Wave," 74.

179. Brown et al., *White-Washing Race,* 152.

180. Gaston Bachelard, *The Psychoanalysis of Fire* (Boston: Beacon Press, 1964), 1.

181. Loïc Wacquant, "The Advent of the Penal State Is Not Destiny," *Social Justice* 28 (2001): 81–87.

182. Lisa Spanierman, V. Paul Poteat, Amanda Beer, and Patrick Ian Armstrong, "Psychological Costs of Racism to Whites: Exploring Patterns through Cluster Analysis," *Journal of Counseling Psychology* 53 (2006): 434–441.

Chapter 7: Education

1. Alexis de Tocqueville, *Democracy in America* (News York: HarperCollins, 2000 [1835/1840]), 12, emphasis ours; Sara Rimer and Alan Finder, "Harvard Steps Up Financial Aid," *The New York Times,* December 10, 2007.

2. Mills, *Sociological Imagination,* 166.

3. Cf. Pierre Bourdieu, *The Field of Cultural Production* (New York: Columbia University Press, 1993), 84.

4. K. Tsiania Lomawaima, "American Indian Education: *By* Indians versus *For* Indians," in Philip Deloria and Neal Salisbury, eds., *A Companion to American Indian History* (Malden: Blackwell, 2002), 422–440.

5. Zitkala-Sa, *The School Days of an Indian Girl* (New York: Atlantic Monthly, 1900), 187.

6. Interview with Virgil "Smoker" Marchand, conducted by Jennifer Mason-Ferguson, February 28, 1997. Courtesy of Eastern Washington University, Art Department.

7. Brenda Child, *Boarding School Seasons: American Indian Families, 1900–1940* (Lincoln: University of Nebraska Press, 1996); K. Tsiania Lomawaima, *They Call It Prairie Light: The Story of Chilocco Indian School* (Lincoln: University of Nebraska Press, 1994).

8. Lewis Meriam, *The Problem of Indian Administration* (Baltimore: Johns Hopkins University Press for the Institute for Government Research, 1928), 11.

9. Bill Curry, "Hunt Begins for Long-Missing Students," *Globe and Mail,* October 27, 2008.

10. Lomawaima, "American Indian Education," 422–423.

11. Ibid.

12. Fairclough, *Better Day Coming,* 48; Myrdal, *American Dilemma,* 894.

13. Myrdal, *American Dilemma,* 894.

14. Fairclough, *Better Day Coming,* 48.

15. Ibid., 41–42.

16. James Anderson, *The Education of Blacks in the South, 1986–1935* (Chapel Hill: University of North Carolina Press, 1988); Basil Matthews, *Booker T. Washington: Educator and Inter-Racial Interpreter* (London: SCM Press, 1949); Fairclough, *Better Day Coming,* Ch. 3.

17. Lawrence Friedman, "Life 'In the Lion's Mouth': Another Look at Booker T. Washington," *Journal of Negro History* 59 (1974): 337–351; Louis Harlen, *Separate and Unequal: Public School Campaigns and Racism in the Southern Seaboard States, 1901–1915* (New York: Atheneum, 1968); Fairclough, *Better Day Coming,* 46.

18. Fairclough, *Better Day Coming,* 54.

19. Du Bois, *Souls of Black Folk*, 67.

20. Ibid., 31, 34–35.

21. Ibid., 106.

22. Cited in Myrdal, *American Dilemma*, 884. Also see Hortense Powdermaker, *After Freedom: A Cultural Study in the Deep South* (Madison: University of Wisconsin Press, 1993 [1939]).

23. Cited in Myrdal, *American Dilemma*, 881.

24. James Patterson, *Brown v. Board of Education: A Civil Rights Milestone and Its Troubled Legacy* (New York: Oxford University Press, 2001).

25. Frederick Aguirre, "*Mendez v. Westminster School District:* How It Affected *Brown v. Board of Education*," *Journal of Hispanic Higher Education* 4 (2005): 321–332; Criag Allan Kaplowitz, *LULAC, Mexican Americans, and National Policy* (College Station: Texas A&M University Press, 2005).

26. Cited in Fairclough, *Better Day Coming*, 220.

27. Fairclough, *Better Day Coming*, 222–223.

28. King, *Why We Can't Wait*, 4.

29. Elizabeth Jacoway, *Turn Away Thy Son: Little Rock, The Crisis That Shook the Nation* (New York, Free Press, 2007); Tony Allan Freyer, *Little Rock on Trial: Cooper v. Aaron and School Desegregation* (Lawrence: University Press of Kansas, 2007).

30. Melba Patillo Beals, *Warriors Don't Cry: A Searing Memoir of the Battle to Integration Little Rock's Central High* (New York: Simon and Schuster, 1995).

31. J. Harvie Wilkinson, III, *From Brown to Bakke: The Supreme Court and School Integration, 1954–1978* (New York: Oxford University Press, 1981), 81.

32. Fairclough, *Better Day Coming*, 324.

33. Thomas Adams Upchurch, *Race Relations in the United States, 1960–1980* (Westport: Greenwood Publishing Group, 2007); Wilkinson, *From Brown to Bakke*.

34. Du Bois, *Black Reconstruction*, 714, 725, 722.

35. Fairclough, *Better Day Coming*, 175.

36. Takaki, *Different Mirror*.

37. Ibid., 12.

38. Joseph Agassi, *Science and History: A Reassessment of the Historiography of Science* (New York: Springer, 2008); Richard Hughes, "A Hint of Whiteness: History Textbooks and Social Construction of Race in the Wake of the Sixties," *The Social Studies* 98 (2007): 210–208; Tony Sanchez, "The Depiction of Native Americans in Recent (1991–2004) Secondary American History Textbooks: How Far Have We Come?" *Equity & Excellence in Education* 40 (2007): 311–320; Manning Marable, *Living Black History: How Reimagining the African-American Past Can Remake America's Racial Future* (New York: Basic Civitas Books, 2006).

39. Du Bois, *Black Reconstruction*, 722.

40. Arthur Levine and Jeanette Cureton, "The Quiet Revolution: Eleven Facts about Multiculturalism and Curriculum," *Change* 24 (1992): 24–29.

41. Rebecca Aanerud, "Fictions of Whiteness: Speaking the Names of Whiteness in U.S. Literature," in Ruth Frankenberg, ed., *Displacing Whiteness: Essays in Social and Cultural Criticism*

(Durham: Duke University Press, 1999), 35–59. Frances Maher and Mary Kay Thompson Tetreault, "Learning in the Dark: How Assumptions of Whiteness Shape Classroom Knowledge," *Harvard Educational Review* 67 (1997): 321–349.

42. Morrison, *Playing in the Dark,* 85

43. Ibid., 52, 5.

44. Deloria, *Custer Died for Your Sins,* 92–93.

45. Mohanty, *Feminism without Borders,* 193.

46. Tukufu Zuberi and Eduardo Bonilla-Silva, eds., *White Logic, White Methods: Race and Social Science* (Lanham: Rowman & Littlefield, 2008).

47. Mohanty, *Feminism without Borders,* 200.

48. Vincent, Tinto, *Leaving College: Rethinking the Causes and Cures of Student Attrition,* Second Edition (Chicago: University of Chicago Press, 1993).

49. Joe R. Feagin, Hernan Vera, Nikitah Imani, *The Agony of Education: Black Students at White Colleges and Universities* (New York: Routledge, 1996).

50. Ashby Plant and Patricia Devine, "The Antecedents and Implications of Interracial Anxiety," *Personality and Social Psychology Bulletin* 29 (2003): 790–801; Yolanda Suarez-Balcazat et al., "Experiences of Differential Treatment among College Students of Color," *Journal of Higher Education* 74 (2003): 428–444.

51. Nahal Toosi, "UW Minority Students Alone in a Sea of White," *Milwaukee Journal Sentinel,* May 24, 2007; Glassner, *Culture of Fear,* 121.

52. David Berg, "Bringing One's Self to Work: A Jew Reflects," *The Journal of Applied Behavioral Science* 38 (2002): 397–415.

53. Cf. Mohanty, *Feminism without Borders,* 203.

54. bell hooks, "Representing Whiteness in the Black Imagination" in Ruth Frankenberg, ed., *Displacing Whiteness: Essays in Social and Cultural Criticism* (Durham: Duke University Press, 1999, 165–179), 167.

55. Monica Biernat and Melvin Manis, "Shifting Standards and Stereotype-Based Judgments," *Journal of Personality and Social Psychology* 66 (1991): 5–20.

56. Rhea Steinpreis, Katie Anders, and Dawn Ritzke, "The Impact of Gender on the Review of the Curricula Vitae of Job Applicants and Tenure Candidates: A National Empirical Study," *Sex Roles* 41(1999): 509–528.

57. Cited in Glassner, *Culture of Fear,* 121.

58. CNN, "Racist Party at Campus."

59. Jennifer Mueller, Danielle Dirks, and Leslie Houts Picca, "Unmasking Racism: Halloween Costuming and Engagement of the Racial Order," *Qualitative Sociology* 30 (2007): 315–335; Toosi, "UW Minority Students Alone in a Sea of White."

60. U.S. Department of Justice, *Hate Crimes on Campus: The Problem and Efforts to Confront It* (Washington, D.C.: Office of Justice Programs, 2001).

61. Ibid.

62. Ella Baker, "Voices," in Dara Byrne, ed., *The Unfinished Agenda of the Selma-Montgomery Voting Rights March* (New York: Wiley, 2005), 108.

63. Jorge Chapa and Belinda De La Rosa, "Latino Population Growth, Socioeconomic and Demographic Characteristics, and Implications for Educational Attainment," *Education and Urban Society* 36 (2004): 130–149; National Center for Education Statistics, *Status and Trends in the Education of Hispanics* (Washington, D.C.: United States Department of Education, 2003); Michael White and Gayle Kaufmann, "Language Use, Social Capital, and School Completion among Immigrant and Native Born Ethnic Groups," *Social Science Quarterly* 78 (1997): 385–398.

64. Stephanie Bohon, Monica Kirkpatrick Johnson, and Bridget Gorman, "College Aspirations and Expectations among Latino Adolescents in the United States," *Social Problems* 53 (2006): 207–225; Sylvia Hurtado, Karen Kurotsuchi Inkelas, Charles Briggs, and Byung-Shik Rhee, "Differences in College Access and Choice among Racial/Ethnic Groups: Identifying Continuing Barriers," *Research in Higher Education* 38 (1997): 43–75; National Center for Education Statistics, *Status and Trends in the Education of Hispanics;* Chapa and De La Rosa, "Latino Population Growth, Socioeconomic and Demographic Characteristics, and Implications for Educational Attainment."

65. David Karen, "Changes in Access to Higher Education in the United States: 1980–1992," *Sociology of Education* 75 (2002): 191–210; Samuel Peng, *Attainment Status of Asian Americans in Higher Education* (Washington, D.C.: U.S. Department of Education, Center for Education Statistics, 1988).

66. U.S. Census Bureau, *Statistical Abstract of the United States* (Washington, D.C.: U.S. Government Printing Office, 2002); Alexander Astin, *Minorities in American Higher Education* (San Francisco: Jossey-Bass, 1982).

67. Matthew Desmond and Ruth N. López Turley, "Staying Home for College: An Explanation for the Hispanic-White Education Gap," *Social Problems,* forthcoming; Marta Tienda and Faith Mitchell, *Hispanics and the Future of America* (Washington, D.C.: National Academy Press, 2006); Belinda Williams, "What Else Do We Need to Know and Do?" in Belinda Williams, ed., *Closing the Achievement Gap* (Alexandria, VA: Association for Supervision and Curriculum Development, 2003), 13–24.

68. Dana Wood, Rachel Kaplan, and Vonnie McLoyd, "Gender Differences in the Educational Expectations of Urban, Low-Income African American Youth: The Role of Parents and the School," *Journal of Youth and Adolescence* 36 (2007): 417–427; Stephanie Bohon, Monica Kirkpatrick Johnson, and Bridget Gorman, "College Aspirations and Expectations among Latino Adolescents in the United States," *Social Problems* 53 (2006): 207–225; Robert Crosnoe, "The Diverse Experiences of Hispanic Students in the American Educational System," *Sociological Forum* 20 (2005): 561–588; Linda Datcher Loury, "Siblings and Gender Differences in African-American College Attendance," *Economics of Education Review* 23 (2004): 213–229; National Center for Education Statistics, *Status and Trends in the Education of Hispanics* (Washington, D.C.: United States Department of Education, 2003); George Vernez and Lee Mizell, *Goal: To Double the Rate of Hispanics Earning a Bachelor's Degree* (Washington, D.C.: RAND Corporation, Center for Research on Immigration Policy, 2002).

69. Desmond and Turley, "Staying Home for College."

70. Ronald Ferguson, "What Doesn't Meet the Eye: Understanding and Addressing Racial Achievement Gaps in High Achieving Suburban School Systems," (Washington, D.C.: North Central Regional Educational Laboratory Working Paper #ED 474 390, 2002).

71. Simon Cheng and Brian Powell, "Under and Beyond Constraints: Resource Allocation to Young Children from Biracial Families," *American Journal of Sociology* 112 (2007): 1004–1094; Lala-Carr Steelman and Brian Powell, "Sponsoring the Next Generation: Parental Willingness to Pay for Higher Education," *American Journal of Sociology* 96 (1991): 1505–1529.

72. Robert Bradley and Robert Corwyn, "Socioeconomic Status and Child Development," *Annual Review of Psychology* 53 (2002): 341–369; Dalton Conley, *Being Black, Living in the Red* (Berkeley and Los Angeles: University of California Press, 1999); Jeanne Brooks-Gunn and Greg Duncan, "The Effects of Poverty on Children," *The Future of Children* 7 (1997): 57–71; Kao and Thompson, "Racial and Ethnic Stratification in Educational Achievement and Attainment."

73. Michele Lamont and Annette Lareau, "Cultural Capital: Allusions, Gaps, and Glissandos in Recent Theoretical Developments," *Sociological Theory* 6 (1988): 153–168; Pierre Bourdieu, *Distinction: A Social Critique of the Judgment of Taste* (Cambridge: Harvard University Press, 1984 [1979]).

74. Matthijs Kalmijn and Gerbert Kraaykamp, "Race, Cultural Capital, and Schooling: An Analysis of Trends in the United States," *Sociology of Education* 69 (1996): 22–34; Paul DiMaggio, "Cultural Capital and School Success: The Impact on Status Culture Participation on the Grades of U.S. High School Students," *American Sociological Review* 47 (1982): 189–201.

75. Pierre Bourdieu and Jean-Claude Passeron, *The Inheritors: French Students and Their Relation to Culture* (Chicago: University of Chicago Press, 1979 [1964]), 17.

76. Bourdieu, *Distinction*, 6.

77. Betty Hart and Todd Risley, *Meaningful Differences in the Everyday Experience of Young American Children* (Baltimore: Brookes Publishing, 1995). See also Jeanne Brooks-Gunn and Lisa Markman, "The Contribution of Parenting to Ethnic and Racial Gaps in School Readiness," *The Future of Children* 15 (2005): 139–168.

78. Lareau, *Unequal Childhoods*.

79. Paul Tough, "What It Takes to Make a Student," *The New York Times Magazine*, November 26, 2006, 49.

80. Eric Margolis, Michael Soldatenko, Sandra Acker, and Marina Gair, "Peekaboo: Hiding and Outing the Curriculum," in Eric Margolis, ed., *The Hidden Curriculum in Higher Education* (New York: Routledge, 2001, 1–19), 4–5. See also Philip Jackson, *Life in Classrooms* (New York: Holt, Rinehart, and Winston, 1968).

81. Buffy Smith, *Demystifying the Higher Education System: Rethinking Academic Cultural Capital, Social Capital, and the Academic Mentoring Process* (Madison: University of Wisconsin, unpublished Ph.D. dissertation, 2004).

82. Vincent Roscigno and James Ainsworth-Darnell, "Race, Cultural Capital, and Educational Resources: Persistent Inequalities and Achievement Returns," *Sociology of Education* 72 (1999): 158–179; Kalmijn and Kraaykamp, "Race, Cultural Capital, and Schooling," DiMaggio, "Cultural Capital and School Success."

83. Paul DiMaggio and Francie Ostrower, "Participation in the Arts by Black and White Americans," *Social Forces* 68 (1990): 753–778.

84. Bourdieu and Wacquant, *Invitation to Reflexive Sociology*, 119.

85. Angel Steidel and Josefina Contreras, "A New Familism Scale for Use with Latino Populations," *Hispanic Journal of Behavioral Sciences* 25 (2003): 312–330; Angela Valenzuela and Sanford Dornbusch, "Familism and Social Capital in the Academic Achievement of Mexican Origin and Anglo Adolescents," *Social Science Quarterly* 75 (1994): 18–36.

86. Andrew Fuligni, Vivian Tseng, and May Lam, "Attitudes toward Family Obligations among American Adolescents with Asian, Latin American, and European Backgrounds," *Child Development* 70 (1999): 1030–1044; Min Zhou and Carl Bankston, *Growing Up American: How Vietnamese Children Adapt to Life in the United States* (New York: Russell Sage Foundation, 1998); Carola Suarez-Orozco and Marcelo Suarez-Orozco, *Transformations: Immigration, Family Life, and Achievement Motivation among Latino Adolescents* (Stanford: Stanford University Press, 1995).

87. Shana Pribesh and Douglas Downey, "Why Are Residential and School Moves Associated with Poor School Performance?" *Demography* 36 (1999): 521–534; Zhenchao Quian and Sampson Lee Blair, "Racial/Ethnic Differences in Educational Aspirations of High School Seniors," *Sociological Perspectives* 42 (1999): 605–625; Renee Smith-Maddox, "The Social Networks and Resources of African American Eighth Graders: Evidence from the National Education Longitudinal Study of 1988," *Adolescence* 34 (1999): 169–183; Wenfan Yan, "Successful African American Students: The Role of Parental Involvement," *Journal of Negro Education* 68 (1999): 5–22.

88. Natalia Sarkisian, Mariana Gerena, and Naomi Gerstel, "Extended Family Ties among Mexicans, Puerto Ricans, and Whites: Superintegration or Disintegration?" *Family Relations* 55 (2006): 331–344; Daphna Oyserman, Heather Coon, and Markus Kemmelmeier, "Rethinking Individualism and Collectivism: Evaluation of Theoretical Assumptions and Meta-Analyses," *Psychological Bulletin* 128 (2002): 3–72; Yolanda Flores Niemann, Andrea Romero, and Consuelo Arbona, "Effects of Cultural Orientation on the Perception of Conflict between Relationship and Educational Goals for Mexican American College Students," *Hispanic Journal of Behavioral Sciences* 22 (2000): 46–63; Lynn Okagaki and Peter Frensch, "Parenting and Children's School Achievement: A Multiethnic Perspective," *American Educational Research Journal* 35 (1998): 125–144; Algea Harrison, Melvin Wilson, Charles Pine, Samuel Chan, and Raymond Buriel, "Family Ecologies of Ethnic Minority Children." *Child Development* 61 (1990): 347–362; Fabio Sabogal, Gerardo Marin, Regina Otero-Sabogal, Barbara Banoss Marin, and Eliseo Perez-Stable, "Hispanic Familism and Acculturation: What Changes and What Doesn't?" *Hispanic Journal of Behavioral Sciences* 9 (1987): 397–412; Valenzuela and Dornbusch, "Familism and Social Capital in the Academic Achievement of Mexican Origin and Anglo Adolescents."

89. Robert Ream, "Counterfeit Social Capital and Mexican American Underachievement," *Educational Evaluation and Policy Analysis* 25 (2003): 237–262; James Valadez, "The Influence of Social Capital on Mathematics Course Selection by Latino High School Students," *Hispanic Journal of Behavioral Sciences* 24 (2002): 319–339; Ricardo Stanton-Salazar and Sanford Dornbusch, "Social Capital and the Reproduction of Inequality: Information Networks among Mexican-Origin High-School-Students," *Sociology of Education* 68 (1995): 116–135.

90. Jeanne Brooks-Gunn and Lisa Markman, "The Contribution of Parenting to Ethnic and Racial Gaps in School Readiness," *The Future of Children* 15 (2005): 139–168.

91. Alejandro Portes, "Social Capital: Its Origins and Applications in Modern Sociology," *Annual Review of Sociology* 24 (1998): 1–24; Alejandro Portes and Patricia Landolt, "The Downside of Social Capital," *The American Prospect* 26 (1996): 18–21; Lynn Okagaki and Robert Sternberg, "Parental Beliefs and Children's School Performance," *Child Development* 64 (1993): 36–56; Rubén Rumbaut, "Ties That Bind: Immigration and Immigrant Families in the United States," in Alan Booth, Ann Crouter, and Nancy Landale, eds., *Immigrants and the Family: Research and Policy on U.S. Immigrants* (Mahwah: Erlbaum, 1977), 3–45; Niemann et al., "Effects of Cultural Orientation on the Perception of Conflict between Relationship and Educational Goals for Mexican American College Students."

92. Clifford Geertz, *The Interpretation of Cultures* (New York: Basic Books, 1973), 216–217.

93. Steinberg, *Ethnic Myth*, 129.

94. Frank Wu, *Yellow: Race in America Beyond Black and White* (New York: Basic Books, 2002), 64–65.

95. John Ogbu and Herbert Simons, "Voluntary and Involuntary Minorities: A Cultural-Ecological Theory of School Performance with Some Implications for Education," *Anthropology and Education Quarterly* 29 (1998): 155–188.

96. Richard Zweigenhaft and G. William Domhoff, *Diversity in the Power Elite: Have Women and Minorities Reached the Top?* (New Haven: Yale University Press, 1998); Morrison Wong and Charles Hirschman, "The New Asian Immigrants," in William McCready, ed., *Culture, Ethnicity, and Identity* (New York: Academic Press, 1983), 395–397; Julian Stanley, "Family Background of Young Asian Americans Who Reason Extremely Well Mathematically," *Journal of the Illinois Council of the Gifted* 1 (1988): 11.

97. U.S. Bureau of the Census, *Educational Attainment in the United States: 2003* (Washington, D.C.: Government Printing Office, 2003); Wu, *Yellow*, 51.

98. Jean Yonemura Wing, "Beyond Black and White: The Model Minority Myth and the Invisibility of Asian American Students," *The Urban Review* 39 (2007): 455–487; Yoonsun Choi, "Academic Achievement and Problem Behaviors among Asian Pacific Islander American Adolescents," *Journal of Youth and Adolescence* 36 (2007): 403–415.

99. Uri Treisman, "Studying Students Studying Calculus: A Look at the Lives of Minority Mathematics Students in College," *College Mathematics Journal* 23 (1992): 362–372.

100. Kimberly Goyette and Yu Xie, "Educational Expectations of Asian American Youths: Determinants and Ethnic Differences," *Sociology of Education* 72 (1999): 22–36; Yongmin Sun, "The Academic Success of East-Asian American-Students: An Investment Model," *Social Science Research* 27 (1998): 432–456; Elliot Mordkowitz and Herbert Ginsburg, "Early Academic Socialization of Successful Asian-American College Students," paper presented at the Annual Meeting of the American Educational Research Association, San Francisco, CA, April 16–20, 1986; Esther Lee Yao, "A Comparison of Family Characteristics of Asian-American and Anglo-American High Achievers," *International Journal of Comparative Sociology* 26 (1985): 198–208.

101. Simon Cheng and Brian Starks, "Racial Difference in the Effects of Significant Others on Students' Educational Expectations," *Sociology of Education* 75 (2002): 306–327; Jennifer Hochschild, *Facing Up to the American Dream: Race, Class, and the Soul of the Nation* (Princeton: Princeton University Press, 1995).

102. Cited in Wu, *Yellow,* 60–61.

103. William Peterson, "Success Story, Japanese American Style," *The New York Times,* January 9, 1966.

104. Wu, *Yellow,* 41. See also Keith Osajima, "Asian Americans as the Model Minority; An Analysis of the Popular Press Image in the 1960s and 1980s," in Min Zhou and James Gatewood, eds., *Contemporary Asian America: A Multidisciplinary Reader* (New York: New York University Press, 2000), 449–458.

105. Wu, *Yellow,* 68.

106. Eliza Noh, "Asian American Women and Suicide: Problems of Responsibility and Healing," *Women and Therapy* 30 (2007): 87–107; Eliza Noh, *Suicide among Asian American Women: Influences of Racism and Sexism on Suicide Subjectification* (Berkeley and Los Angeles: University of California Press, 2002).

107. The phrase "buried above ground" comes from English Poet William Cowper, who penned the line after one of his many suicide attempts. See Kay Redfield Jamison, *Nigh Falls Fast: Understanding Suicide* (New York: Vintage, 1999).

108. All quoted in Wu, *Yellow,* 48.

109. Edna Bonacich, "A Theory of Middleman Minorities," *American Sociological Review* 38 (1973): 583–594; Hubert Blalock, Jr., *Toward a Theory of Minority Group Relations* (New York: John Wiley, 1967).

110. Michael Lind, *The Next American Nation: The New Nationalism and the Fourth American Revolution* (New York: Free Press, 1995), 210.

111. John Ogbu, "Collective Identity and the Burden of 'Acting White': Black History, Community, and Education," *The Urban Review* 36 (2004): 1–35.

112. Scott, *Domination and the Arts of Resistance,* epigraph.

113. Ogbu, "Collective Identity and the Burden of 'Acting White' in Black History, Community, and Education," 28–29.

114. Marvin Lynn, "Race, Culture, and the Education of African Americans," *Educational Theory* 56 (2006): 107–119; John Ogbu, *Black American Students in an Affluent Suburb: A Study of Academic Disengagement* (Mahwah: Lawrence Erlbaum, 2003); Claude Steele, "Race and the Schooling of Black Americans," *The Atlantic Monthly,* April 1993; Laura Inez Luster, "Schooling, Survival, and Struggles: Black Women and the GED" (Stanford: Stanford University, unpublished Ph.D. Dissertation, 1992); William Labov, *Language in the Inner City: Studies in the Black English Vernacular* (Philadelphia: University of Pennsylvania Press, 1972).

115. Ferguson, "What Doesn't Meet the Eye."

116. Audre Lorde, *Sister Outsider: Essays and Speeches* (Berkeley: The Crossing Press, 1984), 110–113.

117. Orlando Patterson, *The Ordeal of Integration: Progress and Resentment in America's "Racial" Crisis* (New York: Basic Civitas Books, 1998).

118. Payne, *I've Got the Light of Freedom*; Morris, *Origins of the Civil Rights Movement*; Fairclough, *Better Day Coming*.

119. Karolyn Tyson, "Weighing In: Elementary-Age Students and the Debate on Attitudes towards School among Black Students," *Social Forces* 80 (2002): 1157–1189; James Ainsworth-Darnell and Douglas Downey, "Assessing the Oppositional Culture Explanation for Racial/Ethnic Differences in School Performance," *American Sociological Review* 63 (1998): 536–553.

120. Angel Harris, "Optimism in the Face of Despair: Black-White Differences in Beliefs about School as a Means for Upward Social Mobility," *Social Science Quarterly* 89 (2008): 629–651; Angel Harris, "I (Don't) Hate School: Revisiting 'Oppositional Culture' Theory of Blacks' Resistance to Schooling," *Social Forces* 85 (2006): 797–834; Monica Johnson, Robert Crosnow, and Glen Elder, Jr., "Students' Attachment and Academic Engagement: The Role of Race and Ethnicity," *Sociology of Education* 74 (2001): 318–334; Karolyn Tyson, William Darity, and Domini Castellino, "Breeding Animosity: The Significance of School Placement Pattters in the Development of a 'Burden of Acting White,'" Duke University, Terry Sanford Institute for Public Policy, unpublished manuscript, 2004.

121. Prudence Carter, *Keepin' It Real: School Success beyond Black and White* (New York: Oxford University Press, 2005), 53.

122. Patricia J. Williams, *The Alchemy of Race and Rights: Diary of a Law Professor* (Cambridge: Harvard University Press, 2001); Moore, *Reproducing Racism*.

123. Carter, *Keepin' It Real,* 65–66.

124. James Baldwin, *Notes of a Native Son* (Boston: Beacon Press, 1955), 15.

125. Pierre Bourdieu, *Masculine Domination* (Stanford: Stanford University Press, 2001 [1998]), 39.

126. Claude Steele and Joshua Aronson, "Stereotype Threat and the Intellectual Test Performance of African Americans," *Journal of Personality and Social Psychology* 69 (1995): 797–811, 797.

127. Steele and Aronson, "Stereotype Threat and the Intellectual Test Performance of African Americans," 808.

128. Ibid.

129. Jim Blascovich, Steven Spencer, Diane Quinn, and Claude Steele, "African Americans' High Blood Pressure: The Role of Stereotype Threat," *Psychological Science* 12 (2001): 225–229.

130. Catherine Good, Joshua Aronson, and Jayne Ann Harder, "Problems in the Pipeline: Stereotype Threat and Women's Achievement in High-Level Math Courses," *Journal of Applied and Developmental Psychology* 28 (2008): 17–28; Toni Schmader and Michael Johns, "Converging Evidence That Stereotype Threat Reduces Working Memory Capacity," *Journal of Personality and Social Psychology* 85 (2003): 440–452; Jean-Claude Croizet and Theresa Claire, "Extending the

Concept of Stereotype Threat to Social Class: The Intellectual Underperformance of Students from Low Socioeconomic Backgrounds," *Personality and Social Psychology Bulletin* 24 (1998): 588–594.

131. Joshua Aronson, Michael Lustina, Catherine Good, and Kelli Keough, "When White Men Can't Do Math: Necessary and Sufficient Factors in Stereotype Threat," *Journal of Experimental Social Psychology* 35 (1999): 29–46.

132. Jonathan Kozol, *Savage Inequalities: Children in American's Schools* (New York: HarperCollins, 1991).

133. Ibid., 112.

134. Kathryn Neckerman, *Schools Betrayed: Roots of Failure in Inner-City Education* (Chicago: University of Chicago Press, 2007); Jeannie Oaks, *Keeping Track: How Schools Structure Inequality,* Second Edition (New Haven: Yale University Press, 2005).

135. Douglas Harris, *Lost Learning, Forgotten Promises: A National Analysis of School Racial Segregation, Student Achievement, and "Controlled Choice" Plans* (Washington, D.C.: Center for American Progress, 2006); Susan Easton, "The New Segregation: Forty Years after Brown, Cities and Suburbs Face a Rising Tide of Racial Isolation." *Harvard Education Letter* 10, January 1994; Gary Orfield, *The Growth of Segregation in American Schools: Changing Patterns of Separation and Poverty since 1968* (Washington: National School Boards Association, 1993).

136. Sheryll Cashin, *The Failure of Integration: How Race and Class Are Undermining the American Dream* (New York: Public Affairs, 2004); Richard Valencia, "Inequalities and the Schooling of Minority Students in Texas: Historical and Contemporary Conditions," *Hispanic Journal of Behavioral Sciences* 22 (2000): 445–459; Gary Orfield and John Yun, "Resegregation in American Schools," working paper, The Civil Rights Project, Harvard University, 1999.

137. Hamilton Lankford, Susanna Loeb, and James Wyckoff, "Teacher Sorting and the Plight of Urban Schools: A Descriptive Analysis," *Educational Evaluation and Policy Analysis* 24 (2000): 37–62; Walk Haney, "The Myth of the Texas Miracle in Education," *Educational Policy Analysis Archives* 8, 2000, available at: http://epaa.asu.edu/epaa/v8n41; Tough, "What It Takes to Make a Student"; Valencia, "Inequalities and the Schooling of Minority Students in Texas."

138. Sam Roberts, "New Demographic Racial Gap Emerges," *The New York Times,* May 17, 2007; Tough, "What It Takes to Make a Student."

139. Cashin, *The Failure of Integration,* 205–206.

140. Bowen Paulle, *Anxiety and Intimidation in the Bronx and the Bijlmer: An Ethnographic Comparison of Two Schools* (Amsterdam: Dutch University Press, 2005).

141. Kozol, *Savage Inequalities,* 18.

142. Douglas Harris, *Lost Learning, Forgotten Promises: A National Analysis of School Racial Segregation, Student Achievement, and "Controlled Choice" Plans* (Washington, D.C.: Center for American Progress, 2006); Carolyn Herrington and Douglas Harris, "Accountability, Standards, and the Growing Achievement Gap: Lessons from the Past Half-Century," *American Journal of Education* 112 (2006): 209–238.

143. Quoted in Cashin, *The Failure of Integration,* 220.

144. Samuel Lucas and Mark Berends, "Race and Track Location in U.S. Public Schools," *Research in Social Stratification and Mobility* 25 (2007): 169–187; Jeannie Oaks, *Keeping Track: How Schools Structure Inequality,* Second Edition (New Haven: Yale University Press, 2005); Samuel Lucas, "Effectively Maintained Inequality: Education Transitions, Track Mobility, and Social Background Effects," *American Journal of Sociology* 106 (2001): 1642–1690; Roslyn Arlin Mickelson, "Subverting Swann: First- and Second-Generation Segregation in Charlotte-Mecklenberg Schools," *American Educational Research Journal* 38 (2001): 215–252.

145. Annette Lareau and Erin McNamara Horvat, "Moments of Social Inclusion and Exclusion: Race, Class, and Cultural Capital in Family-School Relationships," *Sociology of Education* 72 (1999): 37–53; William Lacy and Ernest Middleton, "Are Educators Racially Prejudiced? A Cross-Occupational Comparison of Attitudes," *Sociological Focus* 14 (1981): 87–95.

146. Lucas and Mark Berends, "Race and Track Location in U.S. Public Schools," 172, emphasis ours.

147. Adam Gamoran, "The Stratification of High School Learning Opportunities," *Sociology of Education* 60 (1987): 135–155.

148. Cf. Wu, *Yellow,* 132–133.

149. Eric Grodsky, "Compensatory Sponsorship in Higher Education," *American Journal of Sociology* 112 (2007): 1662–1712; William Bowen and Derek Bok, *The Shape of the River: Long Term Consequences of Considering Race in College and University Admissions* (Princeton: Princeton University Press, 1998).

150. Scott Plous, "Ten Myths about Affirmative Action," in Scott Plous, ed., *Understanding Prejudice and Discrimination* (New York: McGraw-Hill, 2003), 206–212; Bowen and Bok, *The Shape of the River.*

151. Brown et al., *White-Washing Race,* 122.

152. Peter Schmidt, *Color and Money: How Rich White Kids Are Winning the War over College Affirmative Action* (New York: Palgrave MacMillian, 2007); Peter Schmidt, "At the Elite Colleges—Dim White Kids," *Boston Globe,* September 28, 2007; Joe Klein, "There's More Than One Way to Diversify," *Time,* December 18, 2006.

153. Bowen and Bok, *The Shape of the River;* Brown et al., *White-Washing Race.*

154. Wilson, *Truly Disadvantaged,* 147.

155. Jonathan Glater and Alan Finder, "Schools Diversity Based on Income Segregates Some," *The New York Times,* July 15, 2007; Klien, "There's More Than One Way to Diversify."

156. Jerome Karabel, *The Chosen: The Hidden History of Admission and Exclusion at Harvard, Yale, and Princeton* (Boston: Houghton Mifflin Company, 2005).

157. Sigal Alon and Marta Tienda, "Diversity, Opportunity, and the Shifting Meritocracy in Higher Education," *American Sociological Review* 72 (2007): 487–511.

158. Klein, "There's More Than One Way to Diversify."

159. Shelby Steele, *The Content of Our Character: A New Vision of Race in America* (New York: St. Martin's Press, 1990); Plous, "Ten Myths about Affirmative Action."

160. Patricia Gurin et al., "Diversity and Higher Education: Theory and Impact on Educational Outcomes," *Harvard Educational Review* 72 (2002): 330–366; Ernest Pascarella et al., "Influences on Students' Openness to Diversity and Challenge in the First Year of College," *Journal of Higher Education* 67 (1996): 174–196; Alexander Astin, "Diversity and Multiculturalism on the Campus: How Are Students Affected?" *Change* 25 (1993): 44–50.

Chapter 8: Aesthetics

1. W. E. B. Du Bois, "Criteria for Negro Art," in Eric Sundquist, ed., *The Oxford W. E. B. Du Bois Reader* (New York: Oxford University Press, 1996 [1927], 324–328), 324.

2. *USA Today,* "Average Home Has More TVs Than People," *USA Today,* September 21, 2006.

3. Robyn Autry, "The Cultural Politics of Truth, Memory, and Reconciliation at Museums in the United States and South Africa," unpublished manuscript, University of Wisconsin—Madison, Department of Sociology, February 2008; Stephen Weil, *Making Museums Matter* (Washington: Smithsonian Institution Press, 2001); American Association of Museums, *Trust and Education: Americans' Perception of Museums: Key Findings of the Lake, Snell Perry February 2001 Survey* (Washington, D.C.: American Association of Museums, 2001).

4. Herman Gray, *Watching Race: Television and the Struggle for "Blackness"* (Minneapolis: University of Minnesota Press, 1995).

5. John Dewey, *Art as Experience* (New York: Capricorn Books, 1934), 12.

6. Cf. Pierre Bourdieu, *The Political Ontology of Martin Heidegger* (Stanford: Stanford University Press, 1991 [1988]).

7. Martin Berger, *Sight Unseen: Whiteness and American Visual Culture* (Berkeley and Los Angeles: University of California Press, 2005), 100.

8. Charmaine Nelson, "Edmonia Lewis's *Death of Cleopatra:* White Marble, Black Skin and the Regulation of Race in American Neoclassical Sculpture," in Deborah Cherry and Janice Helland, eds., *Local/Global: Women Artists in the Nineteenth Century* (Burlington: Ashgate, 2006), 223–243.

9. Nicolas Bancel, Pascal Blanchard, and Sandrine Lemaire, "Ces zoos humains de la République coloniale," *Le Monde diplomatique,* Août 2000; Paul Greenhalgh. *Ephemeral Vistas: The Expositions Universelles, Great Exhibitions and World's Fairs, 1851–1939* (Manchester: Manchester University Press, 1988); Berger, *Sight Unseen,* 108–109.

10. Mitch Keller, "Scandal at the Zoo," *The New York Times,* August 6, 2006; Rachel Adams, *Sideshow U.S.A.: Freaks and the American Cultural Imagination* (Chicago: University of Chicago Press, 2001).

11. Karen Sotiropoulos, *Staging Race: Black Performers in Turn of the Century America* (Cambridge: Harvard University Press, 2006); Dale Cockerll, *Demons of Disorder: Early Blackface Minstrels and Their World* (New York: Cambridge University Press, 1997); Eric Lott, *Love and Theft: Blackface Minstrelsy and the American Working Class* (New York: Oxford University Press, 1993).

12. Julia Kristeva, *The Powers of Horror: An Essay on Abjection* (New York: Columbia University Press, 1982 [1980]).

13. Vijay Prashad, *The Karma of Brown Folk* (Minneapolis: University of Minnesota Press, 2000), 28–30.

14. Nelson, "Edmonia Lewis's *Death of Cleopatra.*"

15. Du Bois, *Souls of Black Folk,* 156.

16. James Baldwin, *The Fire Next Time* (New York: Vintage 1993 [1962]), 41–42.

17. Craig Werner, *A Change Is Gonna Come: Music, Race, and the Soul of America* (New York: Plume, 1998).

18. Cornel West, "On Afro-American Music: From Bebop to Rap," in Cornel West, ed., *The Cornel West Reader* (New York: Basic Books, 1999, 474–484), 475.

19. Cited in bell hooks, *Black Looks: Race and Representation* (Cambridge: South End Press, 1992), 30.

20. Werner, *Change is Gonna Come,* 89.

21. Cited in Berger, *Sight Unseen,* 108–109.

22. Black Hawk Hancock, "Learning How to Make Life Swing," *Qualitative Sociology* 20 (2007): 113–133, 113.

23. Vicki Mayer, *Producing Dreams, Consuming Youth: Mexican Americans and Mass Media* (New Brunswick: Rutgers University Press, 2003).

24. Phillip Brian Harper, "Extra-Special Effects: Televisual Representation and the Claims of 'the Black Experience,'" in Sasha Torres, ed., *Living Color: Race and Television in the United States* (Durham: Duke University Press, 1999), 62–81; Zora Neale Hurston, "What White Publishers Won't Print," in Winston Napier, ed., *African American Literary Theory: A Reader* (New York: New York University Press, 2000 [1947]), 54–57.

25. Vincent Brook, *Something Ain't Kosher Here: The Rise of the "Jewish" Sitcom* (New Brunswick: Rutgers University Press, 2003).

26. Mel Watkins, "Richard Pryor, Iconoclastic Comedian, Dies at 65," *The New York Times,* December 11, 2005.

27. Gray, *Watching Race,* 81.

28. hooks, *Black Looks,* 126. See Howard Becker, *Art Worlds* (Berkeley and Los Angeles: University of California Press, 1982).

29. Berger, *Sight Unseen,* 1.

30. Guy Trebay, "Ignoring Diversity, Runways Fade to White," *The New York Times,* October 14, 2007.

31. American Psychological Association, "Segregation Ruled Unequal, and Therefore Unconstitutional," *Psychology Matters,* July 2007; Ann duCille, "Dyes and Dolls: Multicultural Barbie and the Merchandising of Difference," in Jacqueline Bobo, Cynthia Hudley, Claudine Michel, eds., *The Black Studies Reader* (New York: Routledge, 2004), 265–280; Kenneth Clark, and Mamie Clark, "Emotional Factors in Racial Identification and Preference in Negro Children," *Journal of Negro Education* 19 (1950): 341–350; Kenneth Clark, and Mamie Clark, "Skin Color as a Factor in Racial Identification of Negro Preschool Children," *The Journal of Social Psychology* 11 (1940): 159–169.

32. Carrie Stetler, "Ethnic Plastic Surgery Grows Popular as Attitudes Change," *Seattle Times*, July 22, 2006. See also Bonnie Berry, *Beauty Bias: Discrimination and Social Power* (Westport, Greenwood Press, 2007); Kathy Davis, *Dubious Equalities and Embodied Differences: Cultural Studies on Cosmetic Surgery* (Lanham: Rowman & Littlefield, 2003).

33. Andrew Lam, "Plastic Surgery as Racial Surgery," *New America Media,* March 29, 2007.

34. Dwight McBride, *Why I Hate Abercrombie and Fitch: Essays on Race and Sexuality* (New York: New York University Press, 2005), 85–86.

35. Quoted in McBride, *Why I Hate Abercrombie and Fitch,* 86.

36. Ibid.

37. Dana Mastro and Susannah Stern, "Representations of Race in Television Commercials: A Content Analysis of Prime-Time Advertising," *Journal of Broadcasting and Electronic Media* 47 (2003): 638–647.

38. Max Blumenthal, "Toby Keith's Pro-Lynching Publicity Tour Hits Colbert, CBS and More," *Huffington Post,* July 29, 2008.

39. Cf. Renato Rosaldo's term "imperial nostalgia." See his *Culture and Truth: The Remaking of Social Analysis* (Boston: Beacon Press, 1988).

40. Bourdieu, *Pascalian Meditations,* 65.

41. Berger, *Sight Unseen,* 81–84.

42. Jacques Steinberg, "Imus Is Back, Chastened but Still Proudly Obnoxious," *The New York Times,* December 4, 2007; Jacques Steinberg, "Shock Radio Shrugs at Imus's Fall and Roughs Up the Usual Victims," *The New York Times,* May 6, 2007.

43. Ella Shohat and Robert Stam, *Unthinking Ethnocentrism: Multiculturalism and the Media* (New York: Routledge, 1994), 194.

44. Amar Bakshi, "How the World Sees America," *Post Global,* August 30, 2007.

45. John Jackson, Jr., *Harlemworld: Doing Race and Class in Contemporary Black America* (Chicago: University of Chicago Press, 2001), ch. 6.

46. Sue Kim, "Beyond Black and White: Race and Postmodernism in *The Lord of the Rings* Films," *Modern Fiction Studies* 50 (2004): 875–907.

47. David Pilgrim, "New Racist Forms: Jim Crow in the 21st Century," paper written for Jim Crow Museum of Racist Memorabilia, Ferris State University, 2001; Carole Boston Weatherford, "Japan's Bigoted Exports to Kids," *The Christian Science Monitor,* May 4, 2000.

48. Shohat and Stam, *Unthinking Ethnocentrism,* 178–179.

49. Wendy Leo Moore and Jennifer Pierce, "Still Killing Mockingbirds: Narratives of Race and Innocence in Hollywood's Depiction of the White Messiah Lawyer," *Qualitative Sociology* 3 (2007): 171–187; Hernán Vera and Andrew M. Gordon, *Screen Saviors: Hollywood Fictions of Whiteness* (Lanham: Rowman & Littlefield Publishers, 2003).

50. Jackson, *Harlemworld,* 197. See also Robyn Wiegman, *American Antimonies: Theorizing Race and Gender* (Durham: Duke University Press, 1995).

51. Melba Joyce Boyd, "Collateral Damages Sustain in the Film *Crash,*" *Souls* 9 (2007): 253–265.

52. Deloria, *Custer Died for Your Sins*, 149.

53. Scott, *Domination and the Arts of Resistance*, 42.

54. Gwendolyn Dubois Shaw, *Speaking the Unspeakable: The Art of Kara Walker* (Durham: Duke University Press, 2004).

55. Michi Itami, "The Irony of Being American," in Phoebe Farris-Dufrene, ed., *Voices of Color: Art and Society in the Americas* (Atlantic Highlands: Humanities Press, 1997) 20–28.

56. Jean Fisher, "In Search of the 'Inauthentic': Disturbing Signs in Contemporary Native-American Art," in Kymberly Pinder, ed., *Race-ing Art History: Critical Readings in Race and Art History* (New York: Routledge, 2002), 331–340.

57. See Maurice Berger, *White: Whiteness and Race in Contemporary Art* (Baltimore: University of Maryland Center for Art and Visual Culture, 2004).

58. Maurice Berger, "Picturing Whiteness: Nikki S. Lee's Yuppie Project—Photography," *Art Journal* 60 (2001): 54–57.

59. Randal Archibald, "Far From Home, Mexicans Sing Age-Old Ballads of a New Life," *The New York Times*, July 6, 2007; Taki Telonidis, "Immigrant Songs Offer New Twist on Old Sounds," *National Public Radio*, September 16, 2007.

60. Lynette Holloway, "Hip-Hop Sales Pop: Pass the Courvoisier And Count the Cash," *The New York Times*, September 2, 2002.

61. Recoding Industry Association of America, "2003 Consumer Profile."

62. West, "On Afro-American Music," 482.

63. Trisha Rose, *Black Noise: Rap Music and Black Culture in Contemporary America* (Hanover: Wesleyan University Press, 1994), 18.

64. Michael C. Dawson, "'Dis Beat Disrupts': Rap, Ideology, and Black Political Attitudes," in Michèle Lamont, ed., *The Cultural Territories of Race: Black and White Boundaries* (Chicago: University of Chicago Press, 1999) 318–342.

65. Rose, *Black Noise*.

66. Paul Gilroy, *Against Race: Imagining Political Culture beyond the Color Line* (Cambridge: Harvard University Press, 2000); Adolph Reed, Jr., "The Allure of Malcolm X," in Joe Wood, ed., *Malcolm X: In Our Own Image* (New York: St. Martins, 1992), 203–232.

67. Gilbert Rodman, "Race . . . and Other Four-Letter Words: Eminem and the Cultural Politics of Authenticity," *Popular Communication* 4 (2006): 95–121.

68. Dawson, "'Dis Beat Disrupts.'"

69. Quoted in Bakari Kitwana, *Why White Kids Love Hip-Hop: Wankstas, Wiggers, Wannabes, and the New Reality of Race in America* (New York: Basic Civitas Books, 2005), 67–68.

70. Harper, "Extra-Special Effects."

71. Derek Conrad Murray, "Hip-Hop vs. High Art: Notes on Race as Spectacle," *Art Journal* 63 (2004): 4–19, 10.

72. Edward Armstrong, "The Rhetoric of Violence in Rap and Country Music," *Sociological Inquiry* 63 (1993): 64–83; Glassner, *Culture of Fear*, 121–127.

73. Kimberlè Crenshaw, "Beyond Racism and Misogyny: Black Feminism and 2 Live Crew," in Mari Matsuda, Charles Lawrence III, Richard Delgado, and Kimberlè Crenshaw, eds., *Words*

That Wound: Critical Race Theory, Assaultive Speech, and the First Amendment (Boulder: Westview Press, 1993), III–136; Amy Binder, "Constructing Racial Rhetoric," *American Sociological Review* 58 (1993): 753–767.

74. Rodman, "Race . . . and Other Four-Letter Words," 105.

75. Cited in Pierre Bourdieu, *Rules of Art: Genesis and Structure of the Literary Field* (Stanford: Stanford University Press, 1995 [1992]), I.

76. Norman Denzin, *Reading Race: Hollywood and the Cinema of Racial Violence* (Thousand Oaks: Sage, 2002); Shohat and Stam, *Unthinking Ethnocentrism,* 184–187.

77. Ben Bagdikian, *The New Media Monopoly,* Revised Edition (Boston: Beacon, 2004); Todd Wirth, "Nationwide Format Oligopolies," *Journal of Radio and Audio Media* 8 (2001): 249–270.

78. Institute of Museum and Library Services, *African American History and Culture in Museums: Strategic Crossroads and New Opportunities* (Washington, D.C.: Institute of Museum and Library Services, 2004); Lewis Mumford, *The Culture of Cities* (Fort Washington: Harvest Books, 1970).

79. Roberta Smith, "Outside In," *The New York Times,* January 26, 2007.

80. Ibid.

81. Robert W. Witkin, "Why Did Adorno 'Hate' Jazz?" *Sociological Theory* 18 (2000): 145–170.

82. Patricia Leighten, "The White Pearl and *L'Art nègre:* Picasso, Primitivism, and Anticolonialism," in Kymberly Pinder, ed., *Race-ing Art History: Critical Readings in Race and Art History* (New York: Routledge, 2002), 233–260; Anna Chave, "New Encounters with *Les Demoiselles d'Avignon:* Gender, Race, and the Origins of Cubism," in Kymberly Pinder, ed., *Race-ing Art History: Critical Readings in Race and Art History* (New York: Routledge, 2002), 261–287.

83. Peter Marzio, "Foreword" to John Beardsley, William Arnett, Paul Arnett, and Jane Livingston, *The Quilts of Gee's Bend* (Atlanta: Tinwood Books, 2002).

84. Said, *Orientalism.*

85. David Pilgrim, "Jezebel Stereotypes," paper written for Jim Crow Museum of Racist Memorabilia, Ferris State University, 2002.

86. Allison Samuels, "Angela's Fire," *Newsweek,* July 1, 2002, 55.

87. Cornel West, "Horace Pippin's Challenge to Art Criticism," in Cornel West, ed., *The Cornel West Reader* (New York: Basic Books, 1999, 447–455), 454–455.

88. hooks, *Black Looks,* Ch. 8.

89. West, "Horace Pippin's Challenge to Art Criticism," 452.

90. Robert Stepto, *From Behind the Veil: A Study of Afro-American Narrative,* Second Edition (Urbana: University of Illinois Press, 1991); hooks, *Black Looks,* Ch. 8.

91. Peter Brinson, "Liberation Frequency: The Free Radio Movement and Alternative Strategies of Media Relations," *The Sociological Quarterly* 47 (2006): 543–568; Ronald Jacobs, *Race, Media, and the Crisis of Civil Society: From Watts to Rodney King* (Cambridge: Cambridge University Press, 2000); Ronald Jacobs, "Race, Media, and Civil Society," *International Sociology* 14 (1999): 355–372.

92. William Roy, "Aesthetic Identity, Race, and American Folk Music," *Qualitative Sociology* 25 (2002): 459–469, 460.

93. Richard Peterson, *Creating Country Music: Fabricating Authenticity* (Chicago: University of Chicago Press, 1997); Paul Oliver, *Songsters and Saints: Vocal Traditions on Race Records* (Cambridge: Cambridge University Press, 1984).

94. Hamid Naficy, "Narrowcasting in Diaspora: Middle Eastern Television in Los Angeles," in Sasha Torres, ed., *Living Color: Race and Television in the United States* (Durham: Duke University Press, 1999), 82–96.

95. Lott, *Love and Theft*.

96. Hancock, "Learning How to Make Life Swing."

97. Roy, "Aesthetic Identity, Race, and American Folk Music," 467.

98. Georg Simmel, "Fashion," in Donald Levine, ed., *Georg Simmel: On Individuality and Social Forms* (Chicago: University of Chicago Press, 1971 [1908]), 299.

99. Annette Lynch and Mitchell Strauss, *Changing Fashion: A Critical Introduction to Trend Analysis and Meaning* (Oxford: Berg Publishers, 2007).

100. Diana Crane, "High Culture versus Popular Culture Revisited: A Reconceptualization of Recorded Cultures," in Michèle Lamont and Marcel Fournier, eds., *Cultivating Differences: Symbolic Boundaries and the Making of Inequality* (Chicago: University of Chicago Press, 1992), 58–74; Bourdieu, *Distinction*.

101. Lawrence Levine, *Highbrow, Lowbrow: The Emergence of Cultural Hierarchy in America* (Cambridge: Harvard University Press, 1988). See also Paul DiMaggio, "Cultural Entrepreneurship in Nineteenth-Century Boston, Pt. 1," *Media, Culture and Society* 4 (1982): 33–50.

102. Jason Kasson, *Rudeness and Civility: Manners in Nineteenth-Century Urban America* (New York: Hill and Wang, 1990).

103. Berger, *Sight Unseen*, 104.

104. *Glamour*, "Your Race, Your Looks," February 2008; E. R. Shipp, "Braided Hair Style at Issue in Protests Over Dress Codes," *The New York Times*, September 23, 1987.

105. CNN, "Bar Institutes Dress Code," February 11, 2008.

106. Rachel Slocum, "Whiteness, Space, and Alternative Food Practice," *Geoform* 38 (2007): 520–533.

107. Bourdieu, *Distinction*, Ch. 7.

108. Emile Zola, *L'Assommoir*, Trans. Leonard Tancock (London: Penguin [1970 (1876)]), 90, 91.

109. Gia Kourlas, "Where Are All the Black Swans?" *The New York Times*, May 6, 2007.

110. Omar Lizardo and Sara Skiles, "Cultural Consumption in the Fine and Popular Arts Realms," *Sociology Compass* (2008): 1–18; Omar Lizardo, "How Cultural Tastes Shape Personal Networks," *American Sociological Review* 71 (2006): 778–807; Richard Peterson and N. Anand, "The Production of Cultural Perspective," *Annual Review of Sociology* 30 (2004): 311–334.

111. Bethany Bryson, "Anything but Heavy Metal: Symbolic Exclusion and Musical Dislikes," *American Sociological Review* 61 (1996): 884–899. See also Shin-Kap Han, "Unraveling the Brow: What and How of Choice in Musical Preference," *Sociological Perspectives* 46 (2003): 435–459.

112. Michèle Lamont and Sada Aksartova, "Ordinary Cosmopolitanisms: Strategies for Bridging Racial Boundaries among Working-Class Men," *Theory, Culture, and Society* 19 (2002): 1–25; Bryson, "Anything but Heavy Metal."

113. Cf. Bonilla-Silva, *Racism without Racists.*

114. Lizardo and Skiles, "Cultural Consumption in the Fine and Popular Arts Realms."

115. Rodman, "Race . . . and Other Four-Letter Words," 107.

116. Lucy Lippard, *Mixed Blessings: New Art in a Multicultural America* (New York: Pantheon Books, 1990); Ralph Ellison, "The Art of Romare Bearden," in Ralph Ellison, *Going to the Territory* (New York: Vintage, 1986), 227–238.

117. Ben Sisario, "Wizards in the Studio, Anonymous on the Street," *The New York Times,* May 6, 2007.

118. Gargi Chatterjee and Augie Tom, "Is There an Asian American Aesthetics?" in Min Zhou and James Gatewood, eds., *Contemporary Asian America: A Multidisciplinary Reader* (New York: New York University Press, 2000), 627–635.; Deloria, *Custer Died for Your Sins,* Ch. 7.

119. Chatterjee and Tom, "Is There an Asian American Aesthetics?," 631.

120. James Young, "Profound Offense and Cultural Appropriation," *The Journal of Aesthetics and Art Criticism* 63 (2005): 135–146.

121. Bill Cunningham, "Look East," *The New York Times,* April 29, 2007.

122. Young, "Profound Offense and Cultural Appropriation," 138.

123. Kitwana, *Why White Kids Love Hip-Hop,* 113.

124. Ibid., 44.

125. Cf. Johnson, *Appropriating Blackness,* 236–238.

126. Quoted in Eva Marie Garroutee, *Real Indians: Identity and Survival of Native America* (Berkeley and Los Angeles: University of California Press, 2003), 76.

127. Kitwana, *Why White Kids Love Hip-Hop,* 124.

128. Alex Ross, *The Rest Is Noise: Listening to the Twentieth Century* (New York: Farrar, Straus and Giroux, 2007), 101.

129. Greg Tate, "Nigs R Us, or How Blackfolk Become Fetish Objects," in Greg Tate, ed., *Everything but the Burden: What White People Are Taking from Black Culture* (New York: Harlem Moon, 2003), 1–14.

130. hooks, *Black Looks,* 26.

131. Ibid.

132. Kevin Powell, *Someday We'll All Be Free* (New York: Soft Skull Press, 2006).

133. Tate, *Everything but the Burden.*

134. Chrystos, "Today Was a Bad Day Like TB," in Maria Mazziotti Gillan and Jennifer Gillan, eds., *Unsettling America: An Anthology of Contemporary Multicultural Poetry* (New York: Penguin, 1994), 61.

135. hooks, *Black Looks*.

136. Henry Louis Gates, Jr., "'Authenticity,' or the Lesson of Little Tree," *The New York Times Book Review*, November 24, 1991, 26.

137. Young, "Profound Offense and Cultural Appropriation," 145.

138. Garroutee, *Real Indians*, 78.

139. Rodman, "Race . . . and Other Four-Letter Words," 110.

140. Dwight Conquergood, "Performing as a Moral Act: Ethnical Dimensions of the Ethnography of Performance," *Literature in Performance* 5 (1985): 1–13, 9.

141. Hancock, "Learning How to Make Life Swing."

142. Kerry Rockquemore, David L. Brunsma, Joe R. Feagin, *Beyond Black: Biracial Identity in America* (Lanham: Rowman & Littlefield, 2007); Loretta Winters and Herman DeBose, *New Faces in a Changing America: Multiracial Identity in the 21st Century* (Thousand Oaks: Sage, 2003).

143. Stanley Crouch, *The Artificial White Man: Essays on Authenticity* (New York: Basic Civitas Books, 2004), 6.

144. Garroutee, *Real Indians*, 78.

145. Leslie Marmon Silko, *Ceremony* (New York: Penguin, 1977), 126.

146. Fisher, "In Search of the 'Inauthentic.'"

147. Kwame Anthony Appiah, *Cosmopolitanism: Ethnics in a World of Strangers* (New York: Norton, 2006), 130.

Chapter 9: Associations

1. Myrdal, *American Dilemma*, 810.

2. Tocqueville, *Democracy in America*, 511, 512–513.

3. Judith Shklar, *American Citizenship: The Quest for Inclusion* (Cambridge: Harvard University Press, 1991), 14–15. See also Rogers Smith, *Civic Ideals: Conflicting Visions of Citizenship in U.S. History* (New Haven: Yale University Press, 1997).

4. Hale, *Making Whiteness*, 21.

5. Myrdal, *American Dilemma*, 632.

6. Lillian Smith, *Killers of the Dream*, 95.

7. Geoffrey Ward, "Death's Army," *The New York Times Book Review*, January 27, 2008.

8. Theda Skocpol, *Diminished Democracy: From Membership to Management in American Civic Life* (Norman: University of Oklahoma Press, 2003), 55.

9. Theda Skocpol, Ariane Liazos, and Marshall Ganz, *What a Mighty Power We Can Be: African American Fraternal Groups and the Struggle for Racial Equality* (Princeton: Princeton University Press, 2006), 31.

10. Skocpol, *Diminished Democracy*, 54. See also Drew Gilpin Faust, *The Republic of Suffering: Death and the American Civil War* (New York: Knopf, 2008).

11. Cited in Skocpol, *Diminished Democracy*, 180.

12. David Roediger, *Working toward Whiteness: How America's Immigrants Became White* (New York: Basic Books, 2005); John Stanfield, "Ethnic Pluralism and Civic Responsibility in Post-Cold

War America," *Journal of Negro Education* 61 (1992): 287–300; Myrdal, *American Dilemma*, 631–639; Skocpol, *Diminished Democracy*, 179–180.

13. Skocpol et al., *What a Mighty Power We Can Be*, 11, 13. See also Anne Firor Scott, "Most Invisible of All: Black Women's Voluntary Associations," *Journal of Southern History* 1 (1990): 3–22.

14. Michael Schudson, *The Good Citizen: A History of American Civic Life* (Cambridge: Harvard University Press, 1998); Debra Minkoff, *Organizing for Equality: The Evolution of Women's and Racial-Ethnic Organizations in America, 1955–1985* (New Brunswick: Rutgers University Press, 1995); Skocpol, *Diminished Democracy*, 140–141; 180–181; Myrdal, *American Dilemma*, 842–847.

15. Helen Laville, "If the Time Is Not Ripe, Then It Is Your Job to Ripen the Time! The Transformation of the YWCA in the USA from Segregated Association to Interracial Organization, 1930–1965," *Women's History Review* 15 (2006): 359–383; Adrienne Lash Jones, "Struggle among Saints: African American Women and the YWCA, 1870–1920," in Nina Mjagkij and Margaret Spratt, eds., *Men and Women Adrift: The YMCA and the YWCA in the City* (New York: New York University Press, 1997), 160–184; Judith Weisenfeld, *African American Women and Christian Activism: New York's Black YWCA, 1905–1945* (Cambridge: Harvard University Press, 1998).

16. Paul Moreno, *Black Americans and Organized Labor: A New History* (Baton Rouge: Louisiana State University Press, 2007); Eric Anderson, "Passion and Politics: Race and the Writing of Working-Class History," *The Journal of the Historical Society* 6 (2006): 323–356; Michelle Brattain, *The Politics of Whiteness: Race, Workers, and Culture in the Modern South* (Princeton: Princeton University Press, 2001); William A. Sundstrom, "The Color Line: Racial Norms and Discrimination in Urban Labor Markets, 1910–1950," *The Journal of Economic History* 54 (1994): 382–396; Roediger, *Working toward Whiteness*, 49; Katznelson, *When Affirmative Action Was White*.

17. Quoted in Roediger, *Working toward Whiteness*, 213.

18. Drake and Cayton, *Black Metropolis*, 326.

19. Skocpol, *Diminished Democracy*, 181.

20. Howard Schuman, Charlotte Steeh, Lawrence Bobo, and Maria Krysan, *Racial Attitudes in America: Trends and Interpretations*, Revised Edition (Cambridge: Harvard University Press, 1997), 142–144; 254–256.

21. Gary Gerstle, *American Crucible: Race and Nation in the Twentieth Century* (Princeton: Princeton University Press, 2002).

22. José-Antonio Orosco, "Neighborhood Democracy and Chicana/o Cultural Citizenship in Armando Réndon's *Chicano Manifesto*," *Ethics, Place and Environment* 10 (2007): 121–139; Komozi Woodard, *A Nation within a Nation: Amiri Baraka (LeRoi Jones) and Black Power Politics* (Chapel Hill: University of North Carolina Press, 1999); Ignacio García, *Chicanismo The Forging of a Militant Ethos among Mexican Americans* (Tucson: University of Arizona Press, 1997); Anthony Smith, *Nationalism in the Twentieth Century* (New York: New York University, 1979).

23. Dexter Gordon, *Black Identity: Rhetoric, Ideology, and Nineteenth-Century Black Nationalism* (Carbondale: Southern Illinois University Press, 2003).

24. Quoted in Fairclough, *Better Day Coming*, 116.

25. Robert Hill, ed., *The Marcus Garvey and UNIA Papers Volume X, Africa for the Africans, 1921–1922* (Berkeley and Los Angeles: University of California Press, 2006); Thandeka Chapman, "Foundations of Multicultural Education: Marcus Garvey and the United Negro Improvement Association," *Journal of Negro Education,* 73 (2004), 424–434; Robert Hill, ed., *The Marcus Garvey and UNIA Papers Volume IX, Africa for the Africans, 1921–1922* (Berkeley and Los Angeles: University of California Press, 1995).

26. Quoted in Fairclough, *Better Day Coming,* 118.

27. Ibid., 124.

28. Hale, *Making Whiteness,* 26–27.

29. Fairclough, *Better Day Coming,* ch. 6. See also Hill, *Marcus Garvey and UNIA Papers Volume X.*

30. Thomas Sugrue, "Crabgrass-Roots Politics: Race, Rights, and Reaction against Liberalism in the Urban North, 1940–1964," *Journal of American History* 82 (1995): 551–578.

31. Malcolm X and Alex Huxley, *The Autobiography of Malcolm X* (New York: Ballantine Books, 1964).

32. Jeff Fleischer, "Nation of Islam Women Look Up and Out," *Women's News,* August 2, 2005.

33. George Breitman, ed., *Malcolm X Speaks: Selected Speeches and Statements* (New York: Grove Press, 1994).

34. David Reynolds, *John Brown, Abolitionist: The Man Who Killed Slavery, Sparked the Civil War, and Seeded Civil Rights* (New York: Vintage, 2006).

35. Clayborne Carson, *Malcolm X: The FBI File* (New York: Carroll and Graf Publishers, 1991). See also Doug McAdam, *Political Process and the Development of Black Insurgency, 1930–1970,* Second Edition (Chicago: University of Chicago Press, 1982).

36. Carson, *Malcolm X,* 17.

37. Ossie Davis, "On Malcolm X," in *The Autobiography of Malcolm X,* 525–526.

38. Clayborne Carson, "1965: A Decisive Turning Point in the Long Struggle for Voting Rights," *Crisis* 112 (2005): 16–20; Clayborne Carson, "The Unfinished Dialogue of Martin Luther King, Jr., and Malcolm X," *Souls* 7 (2005), 12–19; James Tyner, *The Geography of Malcolm X: Black Radicalism and the Remaking of American Space* (New York: Routledge, 2005); Fairclough, *Better Day Coming,* ch. 14.

39. Algernon Austin, *Achieving Blackness: Race, Black Nationalism, and Afrocentrism in the Twentieth Century* (New York: New York University Press, 2006), 174–177.

40. James Farmer, *Lay Bare the Heart: An Autobiography of the Civil Rights Movement* (Fort Worth: Texas Christian University Press, 1985), 224.

41. Norman Kelley, "The Specter of Nationalism," *New Politics* 6 (1996), 13.

42. Cited in Simon Szreter, "The State of Social Capital: Bringing Back in Power, Politics, and History," *Theory and Society* 31 (2002): 573–621.

43. Tocqueville, *Democracy in America,* 513.

44. Gabriel Almond and Sidney Verba, *The Civic Culture: Political Attitudes and Democracy in Five Nations* (Newbury Park: Sage, 1989 [1963]), Ch. 10.

45. Michael Stoll and Janelle Wong, "Immigration and Civic Participation in a Multiracial and Multiethnic Context," *International Migration Review* 41 (2007): 880–908, 898. See also Pei-te Lien, Mary Margaret Conway, and Janelle Wong, eds., *The Politics of Asian Americans: Diversity and Community* (New York: Routledge, 2004); Michael Stoll, "Race, Neighborhood Poverty, and Participation in Voluntary Associations," *Sociological Forum* 16 (2001): 529–557; Pei-te Lien, *The Making of Asian America through Political Participation* (Philadelphia: Temple University Press, 2001).

46. Robert Putnam, "Tuning In, Tuning Out: The Strange Disappearance of Social Capital in America," *Political Science and Politics* 28 (1995): 664–683. See also John Jackson, Jr., *Racial Paranoia: The Unintended Consequences of Political Correctness* (New York: Basic Books, 2008).

47. Quoted in Cynthia Duncan, "Social Capital in America's Poor Rural Communities," in Susan Saegert, J. Phillip Thompson, and Mark Warren, eds., *Social Capital and Poor Communities* (New York: Russell Sage Foundation, 2001, 60–86), 71.

48. Sidney Verba, Kay Lehman Schlozman, and Henry E. Brady, *Voice and Equality: Civic Voluntarism in American Politics* (Cambridge: Harvard University Press, 1995).

49. Kay Lehman Schlozman, Sidney Verba, and Henry E. Brady, "Civic Participation and the Equality Problem," in Theda Skocpol and Morris Fiorina, eds., *Civic Engagement in American Democracy* (Washington and New York: Brookings Institute and Russell Sage Foundation, 1999), 427–460. See also Don Eberly and Ryan Streeter, *The Soul of Civil Society: Voluntary Associations and the Public Value of Moral Habits* (Lanham: Lexington Books, 2002), Ch. 5.

50. Bruce Rankin and James Quane, "Neighborhood Poverty and the Social Isolation of Inner-City African American Families," *Social Forces* 79 (2000): 139–164; Stack, *All Our Kin*.

51. Sean-Shong Hwang, Kevin M. Fitzpatrick, and David Helms, "Class Differences in Racial Attitudes: A Divided Black America?" *Sociological Perspectives* 41 (1998): 367–380.

52. Mario Luis Small, "Racial Differences in Networks: Do Neighborhood Conditions Matter?" *Social Science Quarterly* 88 (2007): 320–343; Natasha Hritzuk and David Park, "The Question of Latino Participation: From an SES to a Social Structural Explanation," *Social Science Quarterly* 81 (2000): 151–177; Ester Fuchs, Roert Shapiro, and Lorraine Minnite, "Social Capital, Political Participation, and the Urban Community," in Susan Saegert, J. Phillip Thompson, and Mark Warren, eds., *Social Capital and Poor Communities* (New York: Russell Sage Foundation, 2001), 290–324; Stoll, "Race, Neighborhood Poverty, and Participation in Voluntary Associations"; Verba, Schlozman, Brady, *Voice and Equality*.

53. Myrdal, American Dilemma, 952. See also Skocpol, Liazos, and Ganz, *What a Mighty Power We Can Be*, 6–8, 61–69.

54. Stoll and Janelle Wong, "Immigration and Civic Participation in a Multiracial and Multiethnic Context," 900.

55. Sampson, McAdam, MacIndoe, and Weffer, "Civil Society Reconsidered"; Sampson and Raudenbush, "Systematic Social Observation of Public Spaces"; Robert Sampson et al., "Social Anatomy of Racial and Ethnic Disparities in Violence"; Waldinger, *Still a Promised City?*

56. Min Zhou, "Social Capital in Chinatown: The Role of Community-Based Organizations and Families in the Adaptation of the Younger Generation," in Min Zhou and James Gatewood,

eds., *Contemporary Asian America: A Multidisciplinary Reader* (New York: New York University Press, 2000), 315–335; Min Zhou, *Chinatown*.

57. Robert Wuthnow, "Democratic Liberalism and the Challenge of Diversity in Late-Twentieth-Century America," in Neil Smelser and Jeffrey Alexander, eds., *Diversity and Its Discontents: Cultural Conflict and Common Ground in Contemporary American Society* (Princeton: Princeton University Press, 1999, 19–36), 32. See also Mario Small, *Villa Victoria: The Transformation of Social Capital in a Boston Barrio* (Chicago: University of Chicago Press, 2004).

58. Miller McPherson, Lynn Smith-Lovin, and Mathew Brashears, "Social Isolation in America: Changes in Core Discussion Networks over Two Decades," *American Sociological Review* 71 (2006): 353–375; Orlando Patterson, *The Ordeal of Integration: Progress and Resentment in America's "Racial" Crisis* (Washington, D.C.: Civitas, 1997); Christopher Ellison and Daniel Powers, "The Contact Hypothesis and Racial Attitudes among Black Americans," *Social Science Quarterly* 75 (1994): 385–400.

59. Miller McPherson, Lynn Smith-Lovin, and James Cook, "Birds of a Feather: Homophily in Social Networks," *Annual Review of Sociology* 27 (2001): 415–444, 415, emphasis ours. See also Jason Kaufman, *For the Common Good? American Civic Life and the Golden Age of Fraternity* (New York: Oxford University Press, 2002); Amy Davis, Linda Renzulli, and Howard Aldrich, "Mixing or Matching? The Influence of Voluntary Associations on the Occupational Diversity and Density of Small Business Owners' Networks," *Work and Occupations* 33 (2006): 42–72.

60. Kaufman, *For the Common Good?*

61. Mark Pachucki, Sabrina Pendergrass, and Michèle Lamont, "Boundary Processes: Recent Theoretical Developments and New Contributions," *Poetics* 35 (2007): 331–351; Michèle Lamont and Virág Molnár, "The Study of Boundaries in the Social Sciences," *Annual Review of Sociology* 28 (2002): 167–195; Michèle Lamont and Marcel Fournier, eds., *Cultivating Differences: Symbolic Boundaries and the Making of Inequality* (Chicago: University of Chicago Press, 1992); Kathryn Manzo, *Creating Boundaries: The Politics of Race and Nation* (Boulder: Lynne Rienner, 1996); Fredrik Barth, *Ethnic Groups and Boundaries* (Boston: Little Brown, 1969).

62. Edward Finegan and John Rickford, eds., *Language in the USA: Themes for the Twenty-First Century* (New York: Cambridge University Press, 2004); Roseann Duenas Gonzalez and Ildiko Melis, eds., *Language Ideologies: Critical Perspectives on the Official English Movement* (Philadelphia: Lawrence Erlbaum Associates, 2001).

63. Linguistic Society of America, "Resolution: English Only," December 28, 1986.

64. Reuben Buford May and Kenneth Sean Chaplin, "Cracking the Code: Race, Class, and Access to Nightclubs in Urban America," *Qualitative Sociology* 31 (2008): 57–72; David Grazian, *On the Make: The Hustle of Urban Nightlife* (Chicago: University of Chicago Press, 2008).

65. Lawrence Otis Graham, *Our Kind of People: Inside America's Black Upper Class* (New York: HarperCollins, 1999).

66. William Rhoden, *Forty Million Dollar Slaves: The Rise, Fall, and Redemption of the Black Athlete* (New York: Crown, 2006).

67. Robert Putnam, *Bowling Alone: The Collapse and Revival of American Community* (New York: Touchstone Books, 2000), 46.

68. Erzo Luttmer, "Group Loyalty and the Taste for Redistribution," *Journal of Political Economy* 109 (2001): 500–528; Stephen Knack and Philip Keefer, "Does Social Capital Have an Economic Payoff? A Cross-Country Investigation," *Quarterly Journal of Economics* 112 (1997): 1251–1288; Rafael La Porta, Florencio Lopez-de-Silanes, Andrei Shleifer, and Robert Vishney, "Trust in Large Organizations," *American Economic Review* 87 (1997): 333–338; Skocpol, *Diminished Democracy*, 8–11; Almond and Verba, *Civic Culture*, 245–265.

69. Jean Cohen, "Does Voluntary Association Make Democracy Work?" in Neil Smelser and Jeffrey Alexander, eds., *Diversity and Its Discontents: Cultural Conflict and Common Ground in Contemporary American Society* (Princeton: Princeton University Press, 1999); 263–292; Szreter, "The State of Social Capital"; McPherson, Smith-Lovin, and Brashears, "Social Isolation in America."

70. Putnam, *Bowling Alone*, 210. See also M. P. Baumgartner, *The Moral Order of a Suburb* (New York: Oxford University Press, 1988); Kenneth Jackson, *Crabgrass Frontier: The Suburbanization of the United States* (New York: Oxford University Press, 1985).

71. Lewis Mumford, *The Culture of Cities* (New York: Harcourt Brace, 1938), 215.

72. Nancy Gibbs, "One Day in America," *Time*, November 13, 2007; National Public Radio, "Study: Americans Commute an Average 25 Minutes," October 12, 2007; U.S. Census Bureau, *Americans Spend More Than 100 Hours Commuting to Work Each Year, Census Bureau Reports* (Washington, D.C.: U.S. Department of Commerce, 2005).

73. James Wong, *Democracy's Promise: Immigrants and American Civic Institutions* (Ann Arbor: University of Michigan Press, 2006); Jennifer Glanville, "Voluntary Associations and Social Network Structure: Why Organizational Location and Type are Important," *Sociological Forum* 19 (2004): 465–491; Dora Costa and Matthew Khan, "Civic Engagement and Community Heterogeneity: An Economist's Perspective," *Perspectives on Politics* 1 (2003): 103–111; Alberto Alesina, Reza Baqir, and William Easterly, "Public Goods and Ethnic Divisions," *Quarterly Journal of Economics* 11 (1999): 1243–1284. Putnam, *Bowling Alone*, 291–294, 362; Stoll and Wong, "Immigration and Civic Participation in a Multiracial and Multiethnic Context."

74. Rodney Hero, "Social Capital and Racial Inequality in America," *Perspectives on Politics* 1 (2003): 113–122, 120.

75. Amy Rehder Harris, William Evans, and Robert Schwab, "Education Spending in an Aging America," *Journal of Public Economics* 81 (2001): 449–472; Claudia Goldin and Lawrence Katz, "Human Capital and Social Capital: The Rise of Secondary Schooling in America, 1910 to 1940," *Journal of Interdisciplinary History* 29 (1999): 683–723; Costa and Khan, "Civic Engagement and Community Heterogeneity"; Luttmer, "Group Loyalty and the Taste for Redistribution."

76. Satya Mohanty, Linda Martin Alcoff, Michael Hames-Garcia, and Paula Moya, eds., *Identity Politics Reconsidered* (New York: Palgrave Macmillan, 2005); Michael Kenny, *The Politics of Identity: Liberal Political Theory and the Dilemmas of Difference* (Cambridge: Polity Press, 2004); Todd Gitlin, *The Twilight of Common Dreams: Why America Is Wracked by Culture Wars* (New York: Owl Books, 1996); Francis Fukuyama, *Trust: The Social Virtues and the Creation of Prosperity* (New York: Free Press, 1995).

77. Wuthnow, "Democratic Liberalism and the Challenge of Diversity in Late-Twentieth-Century America," 22, 24.

78. Delia Balassarri and Peter Bearman, "Dynamics of Political Polarization," *American Sociological Review* 72 (2007): 784–811; Morris Fiorina, with Samuel Abrams, and Jeremy Pope, *Culture Wars? The Myth of Polarized America* (New York: Pearson Longman, 2005); John Evans, "Have Americans' Attitudes Become More Polarized? An Update," *Social Science Quarterly* 84 (2003): 71–90.

79. Claude Fischer, "Uncommon Values, Diversity, and Conflict in City Life," in Neil Smelser and Jeffrey Alexander, eds., *Diversity and Its Discontents: Cultural Conflict and Common Ground in Contemporary American Society* (Princeton: Princeton University Press, 1999), 213.

80. John Hall and Charles Lindholm, *Is America Breaking Apart?* (Princeton: Princeton University Press, 1999), xi.

81. Li Minghuan, *"We Need Two Worlds": Chinese Immigrant Associations in a Western Society* (Amsterdam: Amsterdam University Press, 1999), 222–224.

82. Tony Horwitz, *Confederates in the Attic: Dispatches from the Unfinished Civil War* (New York: Vintage, 1999).

83. Coretta Phillips, "The Re-Emergence of the 'Black Spectre': Minority Professional Associations in the Post-Macpherson Era," *Ethnic and Racial Studies* 30 (2007): 375–396; Coretta Phillips, "Facing Inwards and Outwards? Institutional Racism, Race Equality and the Role of Black and Asian Professional Associations," *Criminal Justice* 5 (2005): 357–377.

84. John Allen, "Kappa Komeback," *On Wisconsin* 108 (2007): 35–43; Tamara Brown, Gregory Parks, and Clarenda Phillips, eds., *African American Fraternities And Sororities: The Legacy and the Vision* (Lexington: University Press of Kentucky, 2005).

85. Nancy Fraser, "Rethinking the Public Sphere: A Contribution to the Critique of Actually Existing Democracy," in Craig Calhoun, ed., *Habermas and the Public Sphere* (Cambridge: MIT Press, 1992, 109–142): 123. See also Houston Baker, Jr., "Critical Memory and the Black Public Sphere," *Public Culture* 7 (1994): 3–33; Steven Gregory, "Race, Identity and Political Activism: The Shifting Contours of the African American Public Sphere," *Public Culture* 7 (1994): 147–164; Jacobs, *Race, Media, and the Crisis of Civil Society.*

86. Karyn Lacy, *Blue-Chip Black: Race, Class, and Status in the New Black Middle Class* (Berkeley and Los Angeles: University of California Press, 2007).

87. Quoted in Christina Greene, *Our Separate Ways: Women and the Black Freedom Movement in Durham, North Carolina* (Chapel Hill: University of North Carolina Press, 2005), 27.

88. Ibid., 27. See also Craig Marberry, *Cuttin' Up: Wit and Wisdom from Black Barber Shops* (New York: Doubleday, 2005).

89. Manning Marable, "Beyond Racial Identity Politics: Towards a Liberation Theory for Multicultural Democracy," in Richard Delgato and Jean Stefancic, eds., *Critical Race Theory: The Cutting Edge,* Second Edition (Philadelphia: Temple University Press, 2000), 448–454.

90. Walter Benn Michaels, *The Trouble with Diversity: How We Learned to Love Identity and Ignore Inequality* (New York: Holt, 2006); Wuthnow, "Democratic Liberalism and the Challenge of Diversity in Late-Twentieth-Century America," 33.

91. Joshua Glenn, "PC Generation, 1964–1973," *The Boston Globe,* January 22, 2008.

92. Bill Lind, "The Origins of Political Correctness," Accuracy in Academia Lecture, 2000, found at www.academia.org.

93. Reynolds, *John Brown, Abolitionist.*

94. Joel Olson, *The Abolition of White Democracy* (Minneapolis: University of Minnesota Press, 2004); Alexander, *Civil Sphere,* Ch. 14.

95. Bart Landry, *New Black Middle Class* (Berkeley and Los Angeles: University of California Press, 1987), 78, 83.

96. Southern Poverty Law Center Intelligence Project, "Hate Groups, Militias on Rise as Extremists Stage Comeback," (Montgomery: SPLC, 2004); Jack Glaser, Jay Dixit, and Donald Green, "Studying Hate Crime with the Internet: What Makes Racists Advocate Racial Violence?" *Journal of Social Issues* 58 (2002): 177–193; Eduardo Bonilla-Silva, *White Supremacy and Racism in the Post-Civil Rights Era* (Boulder: Lynne Rienner Publishers, 2001), 118; Barbara Perry, "'Button-Down Terror': The Metamorphosis of the Hate Movement," *Sociological Focus* 33 (2000): 113–131; Jack Levin and Jack McDevitt, *Hate Crimes: The Rising Tide of Bigotry and Bloodshed* (New York: Plenum Press, 1993); Southern Poverty Law Center Intelligence Project, "Active U.S. Hate Groups in 2005."

97. Rory McVeigh and David Sikkink, "Organized Racism and the Stranger," *Sociological Forum* 20 (2005): 497–522; Josh Adams and Vincent Roscigno, "White Supremacists, Oppositional Culture and the World Wide Web," *Social Forces* 84 (2005): 759–778.

98. Randy Blazak, "White Boys to Terrorist Men: Target Recruitment of Nazi Skinheads," *American Behavioral Scientist* 44 (2001): 982–1000, 994.

99. Kathleen Blee, *Inside Organized Racism: Women in the Hate Movement* (Berkeley and Los Angeles: University of California Press, 2002), 75–76.

100. Blee, *Inside Organized Racism.*

101. Cited in Carol Swain, *The New White Nationalism in America: Its Challenge to Integration* (New York: Cambridge University Press, 2002), 18.

102. Barbara Perry, "Hate Crimes and Identity Politics," *Theoretical Criminology* 6 (2002): 485–491; "'White Men Are This Nation:' Right-Wing Militias and the Restoration of Rural American Masculinity," *Rural Sociology* 65 (2000): 582–604; Blee, *Inside Organized Racism.*

103. Brentin Mock, *Immigration Backlash: Hate Crimes against Latinos Flourish* (Montgomery: Southern Poverty Law Center Intelligence Project, 2007).

104. Gordana Rabrenovic, "When Hate Comes to Town: Community Response to Violence against Immigrations," *American Behavioral Scientist* 51 (2007): 349–360; Mock, "Immigration Backlash."

105. Mock, "Immigration Backlash."

106. Christopher Lyons, "Stigma or Sympathy? Attributions of Fault to Hate Crime Victims and Offenders," *Social Psychology Quarterly* 69 (2006): 39–59; Kathleen Blee, "Racial Violence in the United States," *Ethnic and Racial Studies* 28 (2005): 599–619; Joachim Savelsberg and Ryan King, "Institutionalizing Collective Memories of Hate: Law and Law Enforcement in Germany and the United States," *American Journal of Sociology* 111 (2005): 579–616.

107. Blee, *Inside Organized Racism*, 7, 9, 189–190.

108. Michael Barkun, *Religion and the Racist Right: The Origins of the Christian Identity Movement* (Chapel Hill: University of North Carolina Press, 1994).

109. Rory McVeigh, "Power Devaluation, the Ku Klux Klan, and the Democratic National Convention of 1924," *Sociological Forum* 16 (2001): 1–31; Blazak, "White Boys to Terrorist Men"; McVeigh and David Sikkink, "Organized Racism and the Stranger."

110. Cited in Swain, *New White Nationalism in America*, 336.

111. E. M. Beck, "Guess Who's Coming to Town: White Supremacy, Ethnic Competition, and Social Change," *Sociological Focus* 33 (2000): 175–191; Mitch Berbrier, "The Victim Ideology of White Supremacists and White Separatists in the United States," *Sociological Focus* 44 (2000): 175–191.

112. Phyllis Gerstenfeld, Diana Grant, and Chau-Pu Chiang, "Hate Online: A Content Analysis of Extremist Internet Sites," *Analyses of Social Issues and Public Policy* 3 (2003): 29–44; Brian Levin, "History as a Weapon: How Extremists Deny the Holocaust in North America," *American Behavioral Scientist* 44 (2001): 1001–1031; CNN, "Hate Group Web Sites on the Rise," February 23, 1999.

113. Perry, "'Button-Down Terror'"; Adams and Roscigno, "White Supremacists, Oppositional Culture and the World Wide Web"; Gerstenfeld et al., "Hate Online."

114. Cited in Swain, *New White Nationalism in America*, 326.

115. Gerstenfeld et al., "Hate Online."

116. Ibid., 39.

117. Elissa Lee and Laura Leets, "Persuasive Storytelling by Hate Groups Online: Examining Its Effects on Adolescents," *American Behavioral Scientist* 45 (2002): 927–957; Gerstenfeld et al., "Hate Online."

118. Cited in Swain, *New White Nationalism in America*, 32.

119. CNN, "Hate Group Web Sites on the Rise."

120. Eli Lehrer, "On the Fringe," *Policy Review* 117 (2003): book reviews.

121. Leslie David Simon, Javier Corrales, and Donald Wolfensberger, *Democracy and the Internet: Allies or Adversaries?* (Washington, D.C.: Woodrow Wilson Center Press, 2002), 1.

122. Nicholas Negroponte, *Being Digital* (New York: Knopf, 1995).

123. Michael Marriott, "Digital Divide Closing as Blacks Turn to Internet," *The New York Times*, March 31, 2006; Robert Fairlie, "Explaining Differences in Access to Home Computers and the Internet: A Comparison of Latino Groups to other Ethnic and Racial Groups," *Electronic Commerce Research* 7 (2007): 265–291; Robert Fairlie, "Race and the Digital Divide," *Berkeley Electronic Journal of Economic Analysis and Policy* 3 (2004): available at www.bepress.com/bejeap.

124. Blanca Gordo, "Overcoming Institutional Marginalization," in David Silver and Adrienne Massanari, eds., *Critical Cyber-Culture Studies* (New York: New York University Press, 2006), 140–158.

125. Alondra Nelson, Thuy Linh N. Tu, and Alicia Hines, eds., *TechniColor: Race, Technology, and Everyday Life* (New York: New York University Press, 2001); U.S. Department of

Commerce, *Falling through the Net: Toward Digital Inclusion* (Washington, D.C.: Department of Commerce, 2000); U.S. Department of Commerce, *Falling through the Net II: New Data on the Digital Divide* (Washington, D.C.: Department of Commerce, 1998).

126. Daniel Bell, *The Coming of Post-Industrial Society: A Venture in Social Forecasting* (New York: Basic Books, 1973).

127. Lisa Nakamura, *Cybertypes: Race, Ethnicity, and Identity on the Internet* (New York: Routledge, 2002), xii.

128. Karen Evans, *Maintaining Community in the Information Age: The Importance of Trust, Place and Situated Knowledge* (New York: Palgrave, 2004).

129. Dale Spender, *Nattering on the Net: Women, Power, and Cyberspace* (Melbourne: Spinifex Press, 1995), xvi.

130. BBC, "China Imposes Online Gaming Curbs," August 25, 2005.

131. Urs Gattiker, *The Internet as a Diverse Community: Cultural, Organizational, and Political Issues* (Mahwah: Lawrence Erlbaum, 2001).

132. Emily Noelle Ignacio, "E-scaping Boundaries: Bridging Cyberspace and Diaspora Studies through Nethnography," in David Silver and Adrienne Massanari, eds., *Critical Cyber-Culture Studies* (New York: New York University Press, 2006), 181–193; Beth Kolko, Lisa Nakamura, and Gilbert Rodman, eds., *Race in Cyberspace* (New York: Routledge, 1999); Nakamura, *Cybertypes.*

133. Brendesha Tynes, Lindsay Reynolds, and Patricia Greenfield, "Adolescence, Race, and Ethnicity on the Internet: A Comparison of Discourse in Monitored vs. Unmonitored Chat Rooms," *Journal of Applied Developmental Psychology* 25 (2004): 667–684.

134. Cited in Nakamura, *Cybertypes,* 47.

135. Ibid., 43.

136. Ibid., 56.

137. Michael Dartnell, *Insurgency Online: Web Activism and Global Conflict* (Toronto: University of Toronto Press, 2006); Diana Saco, *Cybering Democracy: Public Space and the Internet* (Minneapolis: University of Minnesota press, 2002); Evans, *Maintaining Community in the Information Age;* Simon et al., *Democracy and the Internet.*

138. Bharat Mehra, "An Action Research (AR) Manifesto for Cyberculture Power to 'Marginalized' Cultures of Difference," in David Silver and Adrienne Massanari, eds., *Critical Cyber-Culture Studies* (New York: New York University Press, 2006), 205–215.

139. Ignacio, "E-scaping Boundaries," 187. See also, Emily Noelle Ignacio, *Building Diaspora: Filipino Community Formation on the Internet* (New Brunswick: Rutgers University Press, 2005).

140. Mark Warschauer, "Language, Identity, and the Internet," in Beth Kolko, Lisa Nakamura, and Gilbert Rodman, eds., *Race in Cyberspace* (New York: Routledge, 1999), 151–170.

141. The Group of Eight: Australia's Leading Universities, *Languages in Crisis: A Rescue Plan for Australia* (Manuka: Group of Eight, 2007); Stephen May, "Uncommon Languages: The Challenges and Possibilities of Minority Language Rights," *Journal of Multilingual and Multicultural Development* 21 (2000): 366–385.

142. Warschauer, "Language, Identity, and the Internet."

143. The Pluralism Project, *Statistics by Tradition* (Cambridge: Harvard University, 2008); Michael Martin, ed., *The Cambridge Companion to Atheism* (New York: Cambridge University Press, 2005); Michael Hout and Claude Fisher, "Americans with 'No Religion': Why Their Numbers Are Growing," *American Sociological Review* 67 (2002): 165–190; United States Bureau of the Census, *Self-Described Religious Identification of Adult Population: 1990–2001* (Washington, D.C.: Government Printing Office, 2002); Ihsan Bagby, Paul Perl, and Bryan Froehle, *The Mosque in America: A National Portrait* (Washington, D.C., Council on American-Islamic Relations, 2001); C. Kirk Hadaway and P. L. Marler, "Did You Really Go to Church This Week? Behind the Poll Data," *The Christian Century*, May 6, 1998; Russell Ash, *The Top 10 of Everything* (New York: DK Publishing, 1997); Martin Bauman, "The Dharma Has Come West: A Survey of Recent Studies and Sources," *Journal of Buddhist Ethics* 4 (1997): available at http://jbe.la.psu.edu.

144. Stephen Prothero, *Religious Literacy: What Every American Needs to Know—And Doesn't* (New York: HarperCollins, 2007).

145. Damien Cave, "For Congress: Telling Sunni and Shiite," *The New York Times*, December 17, 2006. See also Resa Aslan, *No God but God: The Origins, Evolution, and Future of Islam* (New York: Random House, 2006).

146. Prothero, *Religious Literacy*.

147. James Wellman, "Is Religious Violence Inevitable?" *Journal for the Scientific Study of Religion* 43 (2004): 291–306; Robert Wuthnow, "The Challenge of Diversity," *Journal for the Scientific Study of Religion* 43 (2004): 159–170.

148. Nicholas Kristof, "Obama and the Bigots," *The New York Times*, March 9, 2008.

149. CNN, "Mosque Plans Trigger Neighbor's Pig Races," December 31, 2006.

150. Michael Kotzin, "Louis Farrakhan's Anti-Semitism: A Look at the Record," *The Christian Century*, March 2, 1994.

151. Yvonne Chireau and Nathaniel Deutsch, ed., *Black Zion: African American Religious Encounters with Judaism* (New York: Oxford University Press, 2000).

152. Martin Forstenzer, "Offering Support for a Menorah, Unofficially," *The New York Times*, December 12, 2006.

153. George Yancey and Michael Emerson, "Integrated Sundays: An Exploratory Study into the Formation of Multiracial Churches," *Sociological Focus* 36 (2003): 111–126; Michael Emerson and Karen Chai Kim, "Multiracial Congregations: An Analysis of their Development and a Typology," *Journal for the Scientific Study of Religion* 42 (2003): 217–227; Kevin Dougherty, "How Monochromatic Is Church Membership? Racial-Ethnic Diversity in Religious Community," *Sociology of Religion* 64 (2003): 65–85; Michael Emerson and Christian Smith, *Divided by Faith: Evangelical Religion and the Problem of Race in America* (New York: Oxford University Press, 2001).

154. Michael Battle, *The Black Church in America: African American Christian Spirituality* (Malden: Blackwell, 2006).

155. Barry Kosmin and Egon Mayer, *American Religious Identification Survey* (New York: The Graduate Center of the City University of New York, 2001).

156. Omar McRoberts, *Streets of Glory: Church and Community in a Black Urban Neighborhood* (Chicago: University of Chicago Press, 2003), 7.

157. Ibid., 139.

158. *The Boston Globe*, "Turning Around Four Corners," November 8, 1999.

159. David Badillo, *Latinos and the New Immigrant Church* (Baltimore: Johns Hopkins University Press, 2006); Gastón Espinosa, Virgilio Elizondo, and Jesse Miranda, *Hispanic Churches in American Public Life: Summary of Findings* (Notre Dame: Institute for Latino Studies, 2003).

160. David Rieff, "Nuevo Catholics," *The New York Times Magazine*, December 24, 2006.

161. Samia El-Badry, *Arab American Demographics* (Alexandria: Allied Media Corporation, 2008); Arab American Institute, "Arab American Demographics," available at www.aaiusa.org.

162. Russell Jeung, *Faithful Generations: Race and New Asian American Churches* (New Brunswick: Rutgers University Press, 2005); Pei-te Lien and Tony Carnes, "The Religions Demography of Asian American Boundary Crossing," in Tony Carnes and Fenggang Yang, eds., *Asian American Religions: The Making and Remaking of Borders and Boundaries* (New York: New York University Press, 2004), 38–54; Fenggang Yang, Helen Rose Ebaugh, "Transformations in New Immigrant Religions and Their Global Implications," *American Sociological Review* 66 (2001): 269–288.

163. R. Murray Thomas, *Manitou and God: North-American Indian Religions and Christian Culture* (Westport: Praeger, 2007); Vine Deloria, Jr., *For This Land: Writings on Religion in America* (New York: Routledge, 1999),

164. Deloria, *For This Land*, 125.

165. Michael Hittman, "Native American Church/Peyote Movement," in Suzanne Crawford and Dennis Kelley, eds., *American Indian Religious Traditions: An Encyclopedia*, Volume Two (Santa Barbara: ABC-CLIO, 2005), 599–617.

166. Deloria, *For This Land*, 123.

167. Joseph Epes Brown, *Teaching Spirits: Understanding Native American Religious Traditions* (New York: Oxford University Press, 2001); Deloria, *For This Land*.

168. Carl Bankston, III. "Sangha of the South: Laotian Buddhism and Social Adaptation in Rural Louisiana," in Min Zhou and James Gatewood, eds., *Contemporary Asian America: A Multidisciplinary Reader* (New York: New York University Press, 2000), 357–371; Kosmin and Mayer, *American Religious Identification Survey*.

169. Andrea Elliot, "Muslim Immigration Has Bounced Back," *The Seattle Times*, September 10, 2006; Edward Curtis, IV, *Islam in Black America: Identity, Liberation, and Difference in African-American Islamic Thought* (Albany: State University of New York Press, 2002); Bagby et al., *Mosque in America*.

170. Eric Goldstein, *The Price of Whiteness: Jews, Race, and American Identity* (Princeton: Princeton University Press, 2006).

171. Kosmin and Mayer, *American Religious Identification Survey*; Chireau and Deutsch, *Black Zion*.

172. Emerson and Kim, "Multiracial Congregations," 217, emphasis ours.

173. Rodney Stark and Roger Finke, *Acts of Faith: Explaining the Human Side of Religion* (Berkeley and Los Angeles: University of California Press, 2000); Emerson and Kim, "Multiracial Congregations," 219.

174. Penny Edgell and Eric Tranby, "Religious Influences on Understandings of Racial Inequality in the United States," *Social Problems* 54 (2007): 263–288; Victor Hinojosa and Jerry Park, "Religion and the Paradox of Racial Inequality Attitudes," *Journal for the Scientific Study of Religion* 42 (2004): 229–238.

175. Emerson and Smith, *Divided by Faith,* 170, 116–117.

176. Ibid., 86–87.

177. Elaine Howard Ecklund, "'Us' and 'Them': The Role of Religion in Mediating and Challenging the 'Model Minority' and Other Civic Boundaries," *Ethnic and Racial Studies* 28 (2005): 132–150; McRoberts, *Streets of Glory.*

178. Pyong Gap Min, "The Structure and Social Functions of Korean Immigrant Churches in the United States," in Min Zhou and James Gatewood, eds., *Contemporary Asian America: A Multidisciplinary Reader* (New York: New York University Press, 2000), 372–391; Silvano Tomasi, *Religious Experience of Italian Americans* (New York: American Italian Historical Association, 1973).

179. Min, "The Structure and Social Functions of Korean Immigrant Churches in the United States"; Emerson and Kim, "Multiracial Congregations"; Badillo, *Latinos and the New Immigrant Church.*

180. Frances Kostarelos, *Feeling the Spirit: Faith and Hope in an Evangelical Black Storefront Church* (Columbia: University of South Carolina Press, 1995); E. Franklin Frazier, *The Negro Church in America* (New York: Schocken Books, 1963); Min, "The Structure and Social Functions of Korean Immigrant Churches in the United States."

181. Cornel West, *Prophesy Deliverance! An Afro-American Revolutionary Christianity*, Anniversary Edition (Louisville: Westminster John Know Press, 2002 [1982]); Morris, *Origins of the Civil Rights Movement;* Deloria, *For This Land.*

182. Ann Burlein, *Lift High the Cross: Where White Supremacy and the Christian Right Converge* (Durham: Duke University Press, 2002); Barkun, *Religion and the Racist Right.*

183. Pierrette Hondagneu Sotelo, *God's Heart Has No Borders: How Religious Activists Are Working for Immigrant Rights* (Berkeley and Los Angeles: University of California Press, 2008); Pierrette Hondagneu Sotelo, ed., *Religion and Social Justice for Immigrants* (New Brunswick: Rutgers University Press, 2007); Hillary Cunningham, *God and Caesar at the Rio Grande: Sanctuary and the Politics of Religion* (Minneapolis: University of Minnesota Press, 1995); Gregory L. Wiltfang and Doug McAdam, "The Costs and Risks of Social Activism: A Study of Sanctuary Movement Activism," *Social Forces* 69 (1991): 987–1010.

184. Espinosa et al., *Hispanic Churches in American Public Life: Summary of Findings,* 17.

185. Cited in David Rieff, "Nuevo Catholics," 85–86.

186. Gregory Stanczak, "Strategic Ethnicity: The Construction of Multi-Racial/Multi-Ethnic Religious Community," *Ethnic and Racial Studies* 29 (2006): 856–881; Robert Webber, *The Younger Evangelicals* (Grand Rapids: Baker Books, 2002); Scott Thumma, *Megachurches*

Today, 2000 (Hartford: Hartford Institute for Religious Research, 2001); Penny Edgell Becker, "Making Inclusive Communities: Congregations and the 'Problem of Race,'" *Social Problems* 45 (1998): 451–472; Nancy Tatom Ammerman, *Congregation and Community* (New Brunswick: Rutgers University Press, 1997); John McGreevy, *Parish Boundaries: The Catholic Encounter with Race in the Twentieth-Century Urban North* (Chicago: University of Chicago Press, 1996); Jeung, *Faithful Generations,* 151–156; Emerson and Kim, "Multiracial Congregations"; Dougherty, "How Monochromatic Is Church Membership?"

187. George Yancey, "An Examination of the Effects of Residential and Church Integration on Racial Attitudes of Whites," *Sociological Perspectives* 42 (1999): 279–304.

188. Troy Blanchard, "Conservative Protestant Congregations and Racial Residential Segregation: Evaluating the Closed Community Thesis in Metropolitan and Nonmetropolitan Counties," *American Sociological Review* 72 (2007): 416–433.

189. Robert Wuthnow, "Can Religion Revitalize Civil Society? An Institutional Perspective," in Corwin Smidt, ed., *Religion as Social Capital: Producing the Common Good* (Waco: Baylor University Press, 2003), 191–209.

Chapter 10: Intimate Life

1. Bourdieu and Wacquant, *Invitation to Reflexive Sociology,* 183.

2. Ibid., 198.

3. Michael Rosenfeld, *The Age of Independence: Interracial Unions, Same-Sex Unions, and the Changing American Family* (Cambridge: Harvard University Press, 2007); Richard Godbeer, *Sexual Revolution in Early America* (Baltimore: Johns Hopkins University Press, 2002); Michael Drake, ed., *Time, Family and Community: Perspectives on Family and Community History* (Oxford: Blackwell, 1994); Edmund Morgan, *The Puritan Family: Religion and Domestic Relations in Seventeenth-Century New England* (New York: Harper, 1966 [1944]).

4. Judith Stacy, *Brave New Families: Stories of Domestic Upheaval in Late Twentieth Century America* (New York: Basic Books, 1991); Lillian Faderman, *Odd Girls and Twilight Lovers: A History of Lesbian Life in Twentieth-Century America* (New York: Penguin, 1991); Rosenfeld, *The Age of Independence.*

5. Orlando Patterson, "Broken Bloodlines: Gender Relations and the Crisis of Marriages and Families among Afro-Americans," in Orlando Patterson, *Rituals of Blood: Consequences of Slavery in Two American Centuries* (New York: Basic Books, 1998).

6. Willie Lee Rose, *Slavery and Freedom* (New York: Oxford University Press, 1982), 37–48.

7. Jacqueline Jones, *Labor of Love, Labor of Sorrow: Black Women, Work, and the Family from Slavery to the Present* (New York: Basic Books, 1985), 27.

8. William Dunaway, *The African-American Family in Slavery and Emancipation* (New York: Cambridge University Press, 2003); Wilma King, *Stolen Children: Slave Youth in Nineteenth-Century America* (Bloomington: Indiana University Press, 1995), 13.

9. Deborah Gray White, *Ar'n't I a Woman? Female Slaves in the Plantation South* (New York: Norton, 1985).

10. Jones, *Labor of Love, Labor of Sorrow,* 32.

11. Toni Morrison, *Beloved* (New York: Plume, 1988), 162.

12. Göran Therborn, *Between Sex and Power: Family in the World, 1900–2000* (New York: Routledge, 2004); Robert William Fogel, *Without Consent or Contract: The Rise and Fall of American Slavery* (New York: Norton, 1989); Edith Clarke, *My Mother Who Fathered Me* (London: Allen and Unwin, 1957); W. E. B. Du Bois, *The Negro American Family* (Cambridge: MIT Press, 1970 [1908]); Patterson, "Broken Bloodlines."

13. Patterson, "Broken Bloodlines," 42–43.

14. Tamara Hareven, *Families, History, and Social Change: Life-Course and Cross Cultural Perspectives* (Boulder: Westview, 2000); Donna Franklin, *Ensuring Inequality: The Structural Transformation of the African-American Family* (New York: Oxford University Press, 1997); Stewart Tolnay, "Black Family Formation and Tenancy in the Farm South, 1900," *American Journal of Sociology* 90 (1984): 305–325.

15. Frank Furstenberg, "The Making of the Black Family: Race and Class in Qualitative Studies in the Twentieth Century," *Annual Review of Sociology* 33 (2007): 429–448; John Dollard, *Caste and Class in a Southern Town* (Madison: University of Wisconsin Press, 1989); Hortense Powdermaker, *After Freedom: A Cultural Study of the Deep South* (New York: Viking, 1939); Jones, *Labor of Love, Labor of Sorrow;* Patterson, "Broken Bloodlines."

16. Roberts, *Killing the Black Body,* 56, 90.

17. Aaron Gullickson, "Black/White Interracial Marriage Trends, 1850–2000," *Journal of Family History* 31 (2006): 289–312; Martha Hodes, *White Women, Black Men: Illicit Sex in the Nineteenth-Century South* (New Haven: Yale University Press, 1997): Joel Williamson, *New People: Miscegenation and Mulattoes in the United States* (Baton Rouge: Louisiana State University Press, 1995); Gary Mills, "Miscegenation and the Free Negro in Antebellum 'Angle' Alabama: A Reexamination of Southern Race Relations," *The Journal of American History* 68 (1981): 16–34.

18. Dennesh Sohoni, "Creating the Excluded: Anti-Misegination Laws and the Consruction of Asian Identity," paper presented at the American Sociological Association Conference, Montreal, August 2006; Kevin Johnson, ed., *Mixed Race America and the Law: A Reader* (New York: New York University Press, 2003).

19. Cited in Timothy Tyson, *Blood Done Sign My Name* (New York: Three Rivers Press, 2004), 39.

20. Gullickson, "Black/White Interracial Marriage Trends, 1850–2000."

21. Cecilia Conrad, "Racial Trends in Labor Market Access and Wages: Women," in Neil Smelser, William Julius Wilson, and Faith Mitchell, eds., *America Becoming: Racial Trends and Their Consequences, Volume II* (Washington, D.C.: National Academy Press, 2001), 124–151; Rosenfeld, *Age of Independence;* Stacy, *Brave New Families;* Jones, *Labor of Love, Labor of Sorrow.*

22. Allan Bérubé, *Coming Out under Fire: The History of Gay Men and Women in World War Two* (New York: Free Press, 1990), 6.

23. Renee Romano, *Race Mixing: Black-White Marriage in Postwar America* (Cambridge: Harvard University Press, 2003).

24. Stacy, *Brave New Families,* 12.

25. Jennifer Lee and Frank Bean, "America's Changing Color Lines: Immigration, Race/Ethnicity, and Multiracial Identification," *Annual Review of Sociology* 30 (2004): 221–242.

26. Rachel Moran, *Interracial Intimacy: The Regulation of Race and Romance* (Chicago: University of Chicago Press, 2001); Gary Sandefur, Molly Martin, Jennifer Eggerling-Boeck, Susan Mannon, and Ann Meier, "An Overview of Racial and Ethnic Demographic Trends," in Neil Smelser, William Julius Wilson, and Faith Mitchell, eds., *America Becoming: Racial Trends and Their Consequences,* Volume I (Washington, D.C.: National Academy Press, 2001), 40–102; Rosenfeld, *Age of Independence,* 4, 68–71, 80–82.

27. Howard Schuman, Charlotte Steeh, Lawrence Bobo, and Maria Krysan, *Racial Attitudes in America: Trends and Interpretations,* Revised Edition (Cambridge: Harvard University Press, 1997), 106–107, 242–243.

28. Steinberg, "The Liberal Retreat from Race during the Post-Civil Rights Era," 22.

29. Timothy Biblarz and Adrian Raftery, "Family Structure, Educational Attainment, and Socioeconomic Success: Rethinking the 'Pathology of Matriarchy,'" *American Journal of Sociology* 105 (1999): 321–365.

30. Daniel Patrick Moynihan, "The Negro Family: The Case for National Action," in Lee Rainwater and William Yancey, eds., *The Moynihan Report and the Politics of Controversy* (Cambridge: MIT Press, 1967), 76.

31. Cited in Jones, *Labor of Love, Labor of Sorrow,* 313.

32. Steinberg, "The Liberal Retreat from Race during the Post-Civil Rights Era."

33. Christopher Jencks, "The Moynihan Report," in Lee Rainwater and William Yancey, eds., *The Moynihan Report and the Politics of Controversy* (Cambridge: MIT Press, 1967), 443.

34. Arlie Russell Hochschild, *The Second Shift* (New York: Avon Boons, 1990); R. W. Connell, *Gender and Power* (Stanford: Stanford University Press, 1987).

35. Deborah King, "Multiple Jeopardy, Multiple Consciousness: The Context of a Black Feminist Ideology," in Beverly Guy-Sheftall, ed., *Words of Fire: An Anthology of African-American Feminist Thought* (New York: The New Press, 1995), 294–317; bell hooks, *Feminist Theory: From Margin to Center* (Boston: South End Press, 1984); Collins, *Black Feminist Thought;* Jones, *Labor of Love, Labor of Sorrow;* Mohanty, *Feminism without Borders.*

36. Economist, *Pocket World in Figures, 2007 Edition,* 88–89.

37. Nancy Landale and R. S. Oropesa, "Hispanic Families: Stability and Change," *Annual Review of Sociology* 33 (2007): 381–405; Jay Teachman, Lucky Tedrow, and Kyle Crowder, "The Changing Demography of America's Families," *Journal of Marriage and the Family* 62 (2000): 1234–1246.

38. Pamela Smock, "Cohabitation in the United States: An Appraisal of Research Themes, Findings, and Implications," *Annual Review of Sociology* 26 (2000): 1–20; Larry Bumpass and Hsien-Hen Wu, "Trends in Cohabitation and Implications for Children's Family Contexts in the U.S.," *Population Studies* 54 (2000): 29–41; Larry Bumpass and Hsien-Hen Wu, "Cohabitation: How Families of U.S. Children Are Changing," *Focus* (2000): 4–7.

39. Nancy Foner, "The Immigrant Family: Cultural Legacies and Cultural Changes," in Marcelo Suárez-Orozco, Carola Suárez-Orozco, and Desitée Baolian Qin, eds., *The New*

Immigration: An Interdisciplinary Reader (New York: Routledge, 2005), 157–166; Elena Flores, Jeanne Tschann, Barbara VanOss Martin, and Philip Pantoja, "Marital Conflict and Acculturation among Mexican American Husbands and Wives," *Cultural Diversity and Ethnic Minority Psychology* 10 (2004): 39–52; Patricia East, "Racial and Ethnic Differences in Girls' Sexual, Marital, and Birth Expectations," *Journal of Marriage and the Family* 60 (1998): 150–162; Anne Roschelle, *No More Kin: Exploring Race, Class, and Gender in Family Networks* (Thousand Oaks: Sage, 1997).

40. Landale and Oropesa, "Hispanic Families," 396.

41. Brian Duncan, V. Joseph Hotz, and Stephen Trejo, "Hispanics in the U.S. Labor Market," in Marta Tienda and Faith Mitchell, eds., *Hispanics and the Future of America* (Washington, D.C.: National Academies Press, 2006), 228–290; Valerie Kincade Oppenheimer, "The Continuing Importance of Men's Economic Position in Marriage Formation," in Linda Waite, Christine Bachrach, Michelle Hindin, Elizabeth Thomson, and Arland Thornton, eds., *Ties That Bind: Perspectives on Marriage and Cohabitation* (Hawthorne: Aldine de Gruyter, 2000), 283–301; Valerie Kincade Oppenheimer, "A Theory of Marriage Timing," *American Journal of Sociology* 94 (1988): 563–591.

42. Wilson, *Truly Disadvantaged,* 83. See also Scott South and Glenna Spitze, "Determinants of Divorce over the Marital Life Course," *American Sociological Review* 51 (1986): 583–590; Teachman et al., "The Changing Demography of America's Families," 1237–1238.

43. Adam Liptak, "U.S. Imprisons One in 100 Adults, Report Finds," *The New York Times,* February 29, 2008.

44. William Sabol and James Lynch, "Assessing the Longer-Run Consequences of Incarceration: Effects on Families and Employment," in Darnell Hakins, Samuel Myers, Jr., and Randolph Stone, eds., *Crime Control and Social Justice: The Delicate Balance* (Westport: Greenwood Press, 2003); Western, *Punishment and Inequality in America,* 139–145.

45. Maureen Reddy, *Crossing the Color Line: Race, Parenting, and Culture* (New Brunswick: Rutgers University Press, 1994), 81.

46. Collins, *Black Feminist Thought,* 162.

47. Annecka Marshall, "Sensuous Sapphires: A Study of the Social Construction of Black Female Sexuality," in Mary Maynard and June Purvis, eds., *Researching Women's Lives from a Feminist Perspective* (London: Taylor and Francis, 1994, 106–124), 119.

48. Mary McCullough, *Black and White Women as Friends: Building Cross-Race Friendships* (Cresskill: Hampton Press, 1998).

49. Gloria Wade-Gayles, *Rooted against the Wind* (Boston: Beacon Pres, 1996), 110.

50. Zhenchao Qian and Daniel Lichter, "Social Boundaries and Marital Assimilation: Interpreting Trends in Racial and Ethnic Intermarriage," *American Sociological Review* 72 (2007): 68–94; Rosalind Berkowitz King and Jenifer Bratter, "A Path toward Interracial Marriage: Women's First Partners and Husbands across Racial Lines," *The Sociological Quarterly* 48 (2007): 343–369; Christine Batson, Zhenchao Qian, and Daniel Lichter, "Interracial and Intraracial Patterns of Mate Selections among America's Diverse Black Population," *Journal of Marriage and the Family* 68 (2006): 658–672; Tavia Simmons and Martin O'Connell,

Married-Couple and Unmarried-Partner Households, 2000 (Washington, D.C.: Bureau of the Census, 2003); Randall Kennedy, *Interracial Intimacies: Sex, Marriage, Identity, and Adoption* (New York: Pantheon, 2003); Lee and Bean, "America's Changing Color Lines."

51. Yen Le Espiritu, *Asian American Women and Men: Labor, Laws, and Love* (Lanham: Rowman & Littlefield, 2008).

52. Colleen Fong and Judy Yung, "In Search of the Right Spouse: Interracial Marriage among Chinese and Japanese Americas," in Min Zhou and James Gatewood, eds., *Contemporary Asian America: A Multidisciplinary Reader* (New York: New York University Press, 2000), 589–605, 599.

53. Eduardo Bonilla-Silva, Carla Goar, and David Embrick, "When Whites Flock Together: The Social Psychology of White Habitus," *Critical Sociology* 32 (2006): 229–253.

54. Ronne Hartfield, *Another Way Home: The Tangled Roots of Race in One Chicago Family* (Chicago: University of Chicago Press, 2004), xv. See also Barbara Katz Rothman, *Weaving a Family: Untangling Race and Adoption* (Boston: Beacon Press, 2005).

55. Jeana Bracey, Mayra Bámaca, and Adriana Umaña-Taylor, "Examining Ethnic Identity and Self-Esteem among Biracial and Monoracial Adolescents," *Journal of Youth and Adolescence* 33 (2004): 123–132; Grace Koa, "Racial Identity and Academic Performance: An Examination of Biracial Asian and African American Youth," *Journal of Asian American Studies* 2 (1999): 223–249; Maria Root, ed., *The Multicultural Experience: Racial Borders as the New Frontier* (Thousand Oaks: Sage, 1996); Ana Mari Cauce et al., "Between a Rock and a Hard Place: Social Adjustment of Biracial Youth," in Maria Root, ed., *Racially Mixed People in America* (Thousand Oaks: Sage, 1992), 207–222.

56. Elliott Lewis, *Face: My Journeys in Multiracial America* (New York: Carroll and Graf, 2006); SanSan Kwan and Kenneth Speirs, eds., *Mixing It Up: Multiracial Subjects* (Austin: University of Texas Press, 2004).

57. Cited in Heather Dalmage, *Tripping the Color Line: Black-White Multiracial Families in a Racially Divided World* (New Brunswick: Rutgers University Press, 2000), 29.

58. Wendy Roth, "The End of the One-Drop Rule? Labeling of Multiracial Children in Black Intermarriages," *Sociological Forum* 20 (2005): 35–67.

59. Lee and Bean, "America's Changing Color Lines."

60. *The New York Times*, "The Trouble with Wedowee," August 12, 1994; Heather Dalmage, *Tripping the Color Line*, 6–7.

61. Kara Joyner and Grace Kao, "Interracial Relationships and the Transition to Adulthood," *American Sociological Review* 70 (2005): 563–581; Maria Root, *Love's Revolution: Interracial Marriage* (Philadelphia: Temple University Press, 2001); Romano, *Race Mixing*.

62. Jenifer Bratter and Karl Eschbach, "'What about the Couple?' Interracial Marriage and Psychological Distress," *Social Science Research* 35 (2006): 1025–1047.

63. Dalmage, *Tripping the Color Line*, 21.

64. Reddy, *Crossing the Color Line*, 80–85. See also Allen Fisher, "Still 'Not Quite as Good as Having Your Own'? Toward a Sociology of Adoption," *Annual Review of Sociology* 29 (2003): 335–361; Jiannbin Lee Shiao and Mia Tuan, "Korean Adoptees and the Social Context of Ethnic Exploration," *American Journal of Sociology* 113 (2008): 1023–1066.

65. Jane Addams, *Democracy and Social Ethics* (Urbana: University of Illinois Press, 2002 [1902]), 7.

66. Economist, *Pocket World in Figures, 2007 Edition*, 88–89.

67. Sucheng Chan, *Hmong Means Free* (Philadelphia: Temple University Press, 1994). See also Nazli Kibria, "Household Structure and Family Ideologies: The Dynamics of Immigrant Economic Adaptation among Vietnamese Refugees," *Social Problems* 41 (1994): 81–96.

68. Mary Waters, "Immigrant Families at Risk: Factors That Undermine Chances for Success," in Alan Booth, Ann Crouter, and Nancy Landale, eds., *Immigration and the Family: Research and Policy on U.S. Immigrants* (Malwah: Lawrence Erlbaum, 1997, 79–87), 84. See also Nancy Foner, "The Immigrant Family: Cultural Legacies and Cultural Changes," in Marcelo Suárez-Orozco, Carola Suárez-Orozco, and Desitée Baolian Qin, eds., *The New Immigration: An Interdisciplinary Reader* (New York: Routledge, 2005), 157–166.

69. Carola Suárez-Oroz, Irina Todorova, and Josephine Louie, "Making Up for Lost Time: The Experience of Separation and Reunification among Immigrant Families," in Marcelo Suárez-Orozco, Carola Suárez-Orozco, and Desitée Baolian Qin, eds., *The New Immigration: An Interdisciplinary Reader* (New York: Routledge, 2005), 179–196.

70. Waters, "Immigrant Families at Risk," 81.

71. Megan Sweeney and Julie Phillips, "Understanding Racial Differences in Marital Disruption: Recent Trends and Explanations," *Journal of Marriage and the Family* 66 (2004): 639–650; Jason Fields and Lynne Casper, *America's Families and Living Arrangements: March 2000* (Washington, D.C.: Bureau of the Census, 2001); Teachman et al., "The Changing Demography of America's Families."

72. Western, *Punishment and Inequality in America*, Ch. 6.

73. Elliot Liebow, *Tally's Corner: A Study of Negro Streetcorner Men* (Boston: Little, Brown and Company, 1967), 131, 135–136.

74. Andrew Clarkwest, "Spousal Dissimilarity, Race, and Marital Dissolution," *Journal of Marriage and Family* 69 (2007): 639–653.

75. Collins, *Black Feminist Thought*, 151–160.

76. Jennifer Hickes Lundquist, "The Black-White Gap in Marital Dissolution among Young Adults: What Can a Counterfactual Scenario Tell us?" *Social Problems* 53 (2006): 421–441; Douglas Massey, "Segregation and Stratification: A Biosocial Perspective," *The Du Bois Review* 1 (2004): 7–25; Bruce McEwan, "Allostasis and Allostatic Load: Implications for Neuropsychopharmacology," *Neuropsychopharmacology* 22 (2000): 108–124.

77. Kathleen Kiernan, "European Perspectives on Nonmarital Childbearing," in Lawrence Wu and Barbara Wolfe, eds., *Out of Wedlock: Causes and Consequences of Nonmarital Fertility* (New York: Russell Sage Foundation, 2001), 77–108.

78. Kathryn Edin and Maria Kefalas, *Promises I Can Keep: Why Poor Women Put Motherhood before Marriage* (Berkeley and Los Angeles: University of California Press, 2005), 2.

79. Maria Cancian and Daniel Meyer, "Responding to Changing Family Organization," *Focus* 22 (2002): 87–92; Lawrence Wu and Barbara Wolfe, "Introduction," in Lawrence Wu and Barbara Wolfe, eds., *Out of Wedlock: Causes and Consequences of Nonmarital Fertility* (New York:

Russell Sage Foundation, 2001), xiii–xxxii; Lawrence Wu, Larry Bumpass, and Kelly Musick, "Historical and Life Course Trajectories of Nonmarital Childbearing," in Lawrence Wu and Barbara Wolfe, eds., *Out of Wedlock: Causes and Consequences of Nonmarital Fertility* (New York: Russell Sage Foundation, 2001), 3–48.

80. Cameron Lynne Macdonald, "Life without Father: Single Mothers in the New America," *Qualitative Sociology* 31 (2008): 89–94. See also Rosanna Hertz, *Single by Chance, Mothers by Choice: How Women Are Choosing Parenthood without Marriage and Creating the New American Family* (New York: Oxford University Press, 2006); Margaret Nelson, *The Social Economy of Single Motherhood: Raising Children in Rural America* (New York: Routledge, 2005).

81. Irwin Garfinkel and Sara McLanahan, "Unwed Parents: Myths, Realities, and Policymaking," *Focus* 22 (2002): 93–97.

82. Jason Fields, *America's Families and Living Arrangements: 2003* (Washington, D.C.: Bureau of the Census, 2004): Kelleen Kaye, "Differences in Nonmarital Childbearing across States," in Lawrence Wu and Barbara Wolfe, eds., *Out of Wedlock: Causes and Consequences of Nonmarital Fertility* (New York: Russell Sage Foundation, 2001), 49–76; Sandefur et al., "An Overview of Racial and Ethnic Demographic Trends"; Wu et al., "Historical and Life Course Trajectories of Nonmarital Childbearing"; Landale and Oropesa, "Hispanic Families: Stability and Change"; Teachman et al., "The Changing Demography of America's Families."

83. Western, *Punishment and Inequality in American*, 137–138.

84. Reanne Frank and Patrick Heuveline, "A Crossover in Mexican and Mexican-American Fertility Rates: Explanations and Evidence for an Emerging Paradox," *Demographic Research* 12 (2005): 77–104; Warren Robinson, "The Economic Theory of Fertility over Three Decades," *Population Studies* 51 (1997): 63–74.

85. Patterson, "Broken Bloodlines," 25.

86. Karen Benjamin Guzzo and Frank Furstenberg, Jr., "Multipartnered Fertility among American Men," *Demography* 44 (2007): 583–601.

87. Ronald Mincy and Chien-Chung Huang, "The 'M' Word: The Rise and Fall of Interracial Coalitions on Fathers and Welfare Reform," paper presented at the Welfare Reform and Child Well-being Conference, Bowling Green State University, March 1, 2002.

88. Patterson, "Broken Bloodlines"; Collins, *Black Feminist Thought*.

89. Kenneth Clark, *Dark Ghetto: Dilemmas of Social Power* (New York: Harper and Row, 1965), 72.

90. Edin and Kefalas, *Promises I Can Keep*, 9.

91. Ibid., 9.

92. Ibid., 6.

93. Stack, *All Our Kin*, 47.

94. Ted Jelen and Clyde Wilcox, "Causes and Consequences of Public Attitudes toward Abortion: A Review and Research Agenda," *Political Research Quarterly* 56 (2003): 489–500; Robert Joseph Taylor, M. Belinda Tucker, Linda Chatters, and Rukmalie Jayakody, "Recent Demographic Trends in African American Family Structure," in Robert Joseph Taylor, James Jackson, and Linda Chatters, eds., *Family Life in Black America* (Thousand Oaks: Sage, 1997),

14–62; Clyde Wilcox, "Race Differences in Abortion Attitudes: Some Additional Evidence," *The Public Opinion Quarterly* 54 (1990): 248–255; Sandefur et al., "An Overview of Racial and Ethnic Demographic Trends."

95. Michelle Ver Ploeg, "Children from Disrupted Families as Adults: Family Structure, College Attendance and College Completion," *Economics of Education Review* 21 (2002): 171–184; Andrew Cherlin, "New Developments in the Study of Nonmarital Childbearing," in Lawrence Wu and Barbara Wolfe, eds., *Out of Wedlock: Causes and Consequences of Nonmarital Fertility* (New York: Russell Sage Foundation, 2001), 390–402; Sara McLanahan and Gary Sandefur, *Growing Up with a Single Parent: What Hurts, What Helps* (Cambridge: Harvard University Press, 1994).

96. Timothy Grall, *Custodial Mothers and Fathers and Their Child Support: 2003* (Washington, D.C.: Bureau of the Census, 2006); Elaine Sorensen and Chava Zibman, "Getting to Know Poor Fathers Who Do Not Pay Child Support," *Social Service Review* 75 (2001): 420–434.

97. Ruth N. López Turley and Matthew Desmond, "Contributions to College Costs by Married and Divorced Parents," Institute for Research on Poverty, University of Wisconsin—Madison, 2008; Martha Hill, "The Role of Economic Resources and Remarriage in Financial Assistance for Children of Divorce," *Journal of Family Issues* 13 (1992): 158–178; Sara McLanahan and Karen Booth, "Mother-Only Families: Problems, Prospects, and Politics," *Journal of Marriage and the Family* 51 (1989): 557–580.

98. Edin and Lein, *Making Ends Meet*, 2.

99. Karen Christopher, "A 'Pauperization' of Motherhood'? Single Motherhood and Women's Poverty over Time," *Journal of Poverty* 9 (2005): 1–23. Sara McLanahan and Erin Kelley, "The Feminization of Poverty: Past and Present," in Janet Saltzman Chafetz, ed., *Handbook of the Sociology of Gender* (New York: Kluwer Academic Publishing, 1999), 127–146; Cancian and Meyer, "Responding to Changing Family Organization," 87.

100. Edin and Lein, *Making Ends Meet*, 5. See also Joanna Lipper, *Growing Up Fast* (New York: Picador, 2003); Lillian Rubin, *Families on the Fault Line: America's Working Class Speaks about the Family, the Economy, Race, and Ethnicity* (New York: HarperCollins, 1994).

101. Suet-Ling Pong and Dong-Beom Ju, "The Effects of Change in Family Structure and Income on Dropping out of Middle and High School," *Journal of Family Issues* 21 (2000): 147–169; Sara McLanahan, "Family Structure and the Reproduction of Poverty," *American Journal of Sociology* 90 (1985): 873–901; Ver Ploeg, "Children from Disrupted Families as Adult."

102. Sharon Hays, *Flat Broke with Children: Women in the Age of Welfare Reform* (New York: Oxford University Press, 2003).

103. Christopher Jencks, "Foreword," to Edin and Lein, *Making Ends Meet*.

104. Jane Collins and Victoria Mayer, *Both Hands Tied: Welfare and the Low Wage Labor Market* (Chicago: University of Chicago Press, forthcoming); Jason DeParle, *American Dream: Three Women, Ten Kids, and a Nation's Drive to End Welfare* (New York: Penguin Press, 2004).

105. Erving Goffman, *Interaction Ritual* (Garden City: Anchor Books, 1967), 1.

106. Erving Goffman, "The Interaction Order: American Sociological Association, 1982 Presidential Address," *American Sociological Review* 48 (1983): 1–17; Erving Goffman, *The Presentation of Self in Everyday Life* (Garden City: Anchor Books, 1959).

107. W. E. B. Du Bois, "The Souls of White Folk," in W. E. B. Du Bois, *Darkwater: Voices from within the Veil* (Mineola, NY: Dover, 1999 [1920]), 17.

108. Patricia Williams, "The Pantomime of Race," in Patricia Williams, ed., *Seeing a Colorblind Future: The Paradox of* Race (New York: Noonday Press, 1997, 17–30), 27.

109. Douglas Maynard and Don Zimmerman, "Topical Talk Ritual and the Social Organization of Relationships," *Social Psychology Quarterly* 47 (1984): 301–316; Ann Rawls, "'Race' as an Interaction Order Phenomenon: W. E. B. DuBois's 'Double Consciousness' Thesis Revisited," *Sociological Theory* (2002) 18: 241–274.

110. Rawls, "'Race' as an Interaction Order Phenomenon."

111. Ibid., 268.

112. Thomas Kochman, *Black and White: Styles in Conflict* (Chicago: Free Press, 1981); William Labov, *Language in the Inner City* (Philadelphia: University of Pennsylvania Press, 1972); Rawls, "'Race' as an Interaction Order Phenomenon."

113. Rawls, "'Race' as an Interaction Order Phenomenon."

114. In Studs Terkel, *Race: How Blacks and Whites Think and Feel about the American Obsession* (New York: New Press, 1992), 289.

115. Jessica Decuir-Gunby and Meca Williams, "The Impact of Race and Racism on Students' Emotions: A Critical Race Analysis," in Paul Schutz and Reinhard Pekrun, ed., *Emotions in Education* (Burlington: Elsevier, 2007), 205–219; Roxanna Harlow, "Race Doesn't Matter But . . .": The Effect of Race on Professors' Experiences and Emotion Management in the Undergraduate College Classroom," *Social Psychology Quarterly* 66 (2003): 348–363; Kiran Mirchandani, "Challenging Racial Silences in Studies of Emotion Work: Contributions from Antiracist Feminist Theory," *Organization Studies* 24 (2003): 721–742.

116. Shannon Sullivan, *Revealing Whiteness: The Unconscious Habits of Racial Privilege* (Bloomington: Indiana University Press, 2006).

117. Daniel Traber, *Whiteness, Otherness, and the Individualism Paradox from Huck to Punk* (New York: Palgrave, 2007); Shawn Utsey and Carol Gernat, "White Racial Identity Attitudes and the Ego Defense Mechanisms Used by White Counselor Trainees in Racially Provocative Counseling Situations," *Journal of Counseling and Development* 80 (2002): 475–483; Janet Helms, *Black and White Racial Identity: Theory, Research, and Practice* (Westport: Greenwood, 1990); Tatum, *Why Are All the Black Kids Sitting Together in the Cafeteria?*

118. Jean-Paul Sartre, "Black Orpheus," in Jean-Paul Sartre, *"What Is Literature?" and Other Essays* (Cambridge: Harvard University Press, 1988), 291–330.

119. Cynthia Levine-Rasky, ed., *Working through Whiteness: International Perspectives* (Albany: State University of New York Press, 2002); Helms, *Black and White Racial Identity*; Tatum, *Why Are All the Black Kids Sitting Together in the Cafeteria?*

120. Tatum, *Why Are All the Black Kids Sitting Together in the Cafeteria?*, 94. See also Milton Bennett, "Towards a Developmental Model of Intercultural Sensitivity," in R. Michael Paige, ed. *Education for the Intercultural Experience* (Yarmouth: Intercultural Press, 1993); Janet Bennett, "Cultural Marginality: Identity Issues in Intercultural Training," in R. Michael Paige, ed. *Education for the Intercultural Experience* (Yarmouth: Intercultural Press, 1993).

121. Gail Steinberg and Beth Hall, *Inside Transracial Adoption* (Indianapolis: Perspective Press, 2000), 92.

122. Carol Lee, "Interrogating Race and Ethnicity as Constructs in the Examination of Cultural Processes in Developmental Research," *Human Development* 45 (2002): 282–290; Sabine Elizabeth French, Edward Seidman, LaRue Allen, J. Lawrence Aber, "Racial/Ethnic Identity, Congruence with the Social Context, and the Transition to High School," *Journal of Adolescent Research* 15 (2000): 587–602; William Cross, *Shades of Black: Diversity in African American Identity* (Philadelphia: Temple University Press, 1991).

123. Mary Campbell and Lisa Troyer, "The Implications of Racial Misclassification," *American Sociological Review* 72 (2007): 750–765, 758, 760.

124. Tatum, *Why Are All the Black Kids Sitting Together in the Cafeteria?*, 108.

125. Judith Howard, "Social Psychology of Identities," *Annual Review of Sociology* 26 (2000): 367–393; Tatum, *Why Are All the Black Kids Sitting Together in the Cafeteria?*; Cross, *Shades of Black*.

126. Du Bois, *Souls of Black Folk*, 2.

127. Rawls, "'Race' as an Interaction Order Phenomenon," 244.

128. Fanon, *Black Skin, White Masks*, 44.

129. Johnson, *Appropriating Blackness*, 30.

130. Johnson, *Appropriating Blackness*, 239–240.

131. Hartigan, *Odd Tribes*; Hartigan, *Racial Situations*.

132. Jill Denner and Bianca Guzmán, eds., *Latina Girls: Voices of Strength in the United States* (New York: New York University Press, 2006); Ed Morales, *Living in Spanglish: The Search for Latino Identity in America* (New York: St. Marin's Press, 2002).

133. Mia Tuan, *Forever Foreigners or Honorary Whites? The Asian Ethnic Experience Today* (New Brunswick: Rutgers University Press, 2003), 147, 149. See also Ellen Alexander Conley, *The Chosen Shore: Stories of Immigrants* (Berkeley and Los Angeles: University of California Press, 2004); Sayad, *Suffering of the Immigrant*.

134. Bryant Keither Alexander, *Performing Black Masculinity: Race, Culture, and Queer Identity* (Lanham: Altamira, 2006); Matthew Desmond, *On the Fireline: Living and Dying with Wildland Firefighters* (Chicago: University of Chicago Press, 2007); bell hooks, *We Real Cool: Black Men and Masculinity* (New York: Routledge, 2003); Richard Majors, *Cool Pose: The Dilemmas of Black Manhood in America* (New York: Touchstone, 1993).

135. Joanne Rondilla and Paul Spickard, *Is Lighter Better? Skin-Tone Discrimination among Asian Americans* (Lanham: Rowman & Littlefield, 2007), 51.

136. Joane Nagel, "Ethnicity and Sexuality," *Annual Review of Sociology* 26 (2000): 107–133. See also Abdul JanMohamed, "Sexuality on/of the Racial Border: Foucault, Wright, and the Articulation of 'Racialized Sexuality,'" in Donna Stanton, ed., *Discourses of Sexuality: From Aristotle to AIDS* (Ann Arbor: University of Michigan Press, 1992), 117–137.

137. Sharmila Rudrappa, *Ethnic Routes to Becoming American: Indian Immigrants and the Cultures of Citizenship* (New Brunswick: Rutgers University Press, 2004). See also Yen Le Espiritu, "We Don't Sleep around Like White Girls Do": Family, Culture, and Gender in Filipina American Lives," *Signs: Journal of Women and Culture in Society* 26 (2001): 415–440; Monisha

Das Gupta, "What Is Indian about You?" A Gendered, Transnational Approach to Ethnicity," *Gender and Society* 11 (1997): 573–596.

138. Joshua Gamson and Dawne Moon, "The Sociology of Sexualities: Queer and Beyond," *Annual Review of Sociology* 30 (2004): 47–64; Michael Kimmel and Rebecca Plante, eds., *Sexualities: Identities, Behaviors, and Society* (New York: Oxford University Press, 2004); Henry Yu, "Mixing Bodies and Cultures: The Meaning of America's Fascination with Sex between 'Orientals' and 'Whites,'" in Martha Hodes, ed., *Sex, Love, Race: Crossing Boundaries in North American History* (New York: New York University Press, 1999), 423–463.

139. Beniot Denizet-Lewis, "Double Lives on the Down Low," *The New York Times Magazine*, April 3, 2003; Estelle Freedman, "The Prison Lesbian: Race, Class, and the Construction of the Aggressive Female Homosexual, 1915–1965," in Martha Hodes, ed., *Sex, Love, Race: Crossing Boundaries in North American History* (New York: New York University Press, 1999), 423–443; Rafael Díaz, *Latino Gay Men and HIV: Culture, Sexuality, and Risk Behavior* (New York: Routledge, 1997); Rosenfeld, *Age of Independence.*

140. Marla Brettschneider, *The Family Flamboyant: Race Politics, Queer Families, Jewish Lives* (New York: State University of New York, 2006); Earl Ofari Hutchinson, "My Gay Problem, Your Black Problem," in Devon Carbado, ed., *Black Men on Race, Gender, and Sexuality: A Critical Reader* (New York: New York University, 1999), 303–305; David Eng and Alice Hom, eds., *Queer in Asian America* (Philadelphia: Temple University Press, 1998).

141. Eldridge Cleaver, *Soul on Ice* (New York: McGraw-Hill, 1968), 101–102.

142. Niels Teunis and Gilbert Herdt, eds., *Sexual Inequalities and Social Justice* (Berkeley and Los Angeles: University of California Press, 2007); Chong-suk Han, "They Don't Want to Cruise Your Type: Gay Men of Color and the Racial Politics of Exclusion," *Social Identities* 13 (2007): 51–67; Martin Manalansan, IV, "Queer Intersections: Sexality and Gender in Migration Studies," *International Migration Review* 20 (2006): 224–249; Johnson, *Appropriating Blackness.*

143. Quoted in Johnnetta Betsch Cole and Beverly Guy-Sheftall, *Gender Talk: The Struggle for Women's Equality in African American Communities* (New York: Ballantine, 2003), 165.

144. Patricia Hill Collins, *Black Sexual Politics: African Americans, Gender, and the New Racism* (New York: Routledge, 2004).

145. Gloria Hull, Patricia Bell Scott, and Barbara Smith, eds., *All the Women Are White, All the Blacks Are Men, but Some of Us Are Brave* (New York: The Feminist Press, 1982).

146. Jackson, *Harlemworld*, 171, 188.

147. E. Patrick Johnson, *Appropriating Blackness: Performance and the Politics of Authenticity* (Durham: Duke University Press, 2003).

148. See Barbara Summers, *Black and Beautiful: How Women of Color Changed the Fashion Industry* (New York: HarperCollins, 2001); David Thomas and Naomi Campbell, eds., *Soul Style: Black Women Redefining the Color of Fashion* (New York: Universe Publishing, 2000).

149. John Hartigan, *Racial Situations: Class Predicaments of Whiteness in Detroit* (Princeton: Princeton University Press, 1999); Patricia Williams, "The Pantomime of Race," in Patricia Williams, ed., *Seeing a Colorblind Future: The Paradox of* Race (New York: Noonday Press, 1997, 17–30); Jackson, *Harlemworld*, 185.

150. Christian Lander, *Stuff White People Like: The Definitive Guide to the Unique Taste of Millions* (New York: Random House, 2008).

151. Roy, "Aesthetic Identity, Race, and American Folk Music," 461.

152. Mary Douglas, *Natural Symbols: Explorations in Cosmology* (New York: Routledge, 2003 [1970]), 42–43.

153. John Jackson, Jr., *Real Black: Adventures in Racial Sincerity* (Chicago: University of Chicago Press, 2005).

154. Orlando Patterson, "The New Black Nativism," *Time*, February 8, 2007.

155. Jack Forbes, *Black Africans and Native Americans: Color, Race, and Caste in the Evolution of Red-Black Peoples* (Oxford: Blackwell, 1988).

156. James Clifford, "Identity in Mashpee," in James Clifford, ed., *The Predicament of Culture* (Cambridge: Harvard University Press, 1988).

157. Kathleen Fizgerlad, *Beyond White Ethnicity: Developing a Sociological Understanding of Native American Identity Reclamation* (Lanham: Lexington Books, 2007); Joane Nagel, *American Indian Ethnic Renewal: Red Power and the Resurgence of Identity and Culture* (New York: Oxford University Press, 1996).

158. Anne Merline McCulloch and David Wilkins, "Constructing Nations within States: The Quest for Federal Recognition by the Catawaba and Lumbee Tribes," *American Indian Quarterly* 19 (1995): 361–388, 369.

159. Gershom Gorenberg, "How Do You Prove You're a Jew?" *The New York Times Magazine*, March 2, 2008.

160. Garroutee, *Real Indians*, 81.

161. Alastair Bonnett, *White Identities: Historical and International Perspectives* (Essex: Prentice Hall, 2000), 78.

162. Fanon, *Black Skin, White Masks*, 129.

163. Cited in Fizgerlad, *Beyond White Ethnicity*, 2.

164. Fizgerlad, *Beyond White Ethnicity*; Nagel, *American Indian Ethnic Renewal*.

165. Edward Morris, *An Unexpected Minority: White Kids in an Urban School* (New Brunswick: Rutgers University Press, 2006), 112. See also Dalton Conley, *Honky* (Berkeley and Los Angeles: University of California Press, 2000).

166. Amy Wilkins, "Puerto Rican Wannabes: Sexual Spectacle and the Marking of Race, Class, and Gender Boundaries," *Gender and Society* 18 (2004): 103–121, 104. See also Amy Wilkins, *Wannabes, Goths, and Christians: The Boundaries of Sex, Style, and Status* (Chicago: University of Chicago Press, 2008).

167. Wilkins, "Puerto Rican Wannabes," 113.

168. Annegret Staiger, "'Hoes Can Be Hoed Out, Players Can Be Played Out, But Pimp Is for Life'—The Pimp Phenomenon as Strategy of Identity Formation," *Symbolic Interaction* 28 (2005): 407–428.

169. Wilkins, "Puerto Rican Wannabes"; Fizgerlad, *Beyond White Ethnicity*.

170. Cited in Henry Louis Gates, Jr., "The Close Reader; Both Sides Now," *The New York Times*, May 4, 2003.

171. Ibid.

172. Rogers Brubaker and Frederick Cooper, "Beyond 'Identity,'" *Theory and Society* 28 (2000): 1–47.

173. Robert K. Merton, "Insiders and Outsiders: A Chapter in the Sociology of Knowledge," *American Journal of Sociology* 78 (1972): 9–47, 15.

174. Henry Louis Gates, Jr., "'Authenticity,' or the Lesson of Little Tree," *The New York Times Book Review,* November 24, 1991, 26.

175. Michaels, *The Trouble with Diversity,* 7, 19–20, 192.

Chapter 11: Toward Racial Justice

1. Hannah Arendt, *Responsibility and Judgment* (New York: Schocken Books, 2003).

2. Elie Wiesel, quoted in *U.S. News & World Report,* October 27, 1986.

3. Freire, *Pedagogy of the Oppressed.*

4. Robert Nemiroff, *To Be Young Gifted and Black: A Portrait of Lorraine Hansberry in Her Own Words* (New York: Samuel French, 1969), 72.

5. Brown et al., *White-Washing Race,* 224–225.

6. Patterson, *Ordeal of Integration,* 16.

7. W. E. B. Du Bois, *The Philadelphia Negro: A Social Study* (Philadelphia: University of Pennsylvania Press, 1996 [1899]), 386.

8. Brown et al., *White-Washing Race,* 248.

9. Ethan Bronner, "For Many Abroad, an Ideal Renewed," *The New York Times,* November 5, 2008.

10. Erik Olin Wright, "Preface: The Real Utopias Project," in Archon Fung and Erik Olin Wright, eds., *Deepening Democracy: Institutional Innovations in Empowered Participatory Governance* (London: Verso, 2003), vii–viii. See also Pierre Bourdieu, *Firing Back: against the Tyranny of the Market 2* (New York: New Press, 2003), 17–25.

11. John Dewey, *The Quest for Certainty, The Later Works, 1925–1953,* Volume 4 (Carbondale: Southern Illinois University Press, 1988 [1929]), 170.

12. Charles Horton Cooley, *Social Process* (Carbondale: Southern Illinois University Press, 1966 [1918]), 351.

13. Kurt Lewin, *Field Theory in Social Science: Selected Theoretical Papers* (New York: Harper and Row, 1951), 169.

14. Mills, *Sociological Imagination,* 174.

15. Ibid., 178.

16. John Dewey, *Reconstruction in Philosophy,* in *John Dewey: The Middle Works, 1899–1924,* Volume 12 (Carbondale: Southern Illinois University Press, 1988 [1920]), 171, 169.

17. Jürgen Habermas, *Toward a Rational Society: Student Protest, Science, and Politics* (Boston: Beacon, 1970 [1968]), 67.

18. Ibid., 71.

19. Jacob Hacker and Paul Pierson, *Off Center: The Republican Revolution and the Erosion of American Democracy* (New Haven: Yale University Press, 2005), 15–16.

20. Leith Mullings, "Interrogating Racism: Toward an Antiracist Anthropology," *Annual Review of Anthropology* 24 (2005): 667–693; Joe Feagin and Hernán Vera, *Liberation Sociology* (Cambridge: Westview, 2001); Cynthia Willett, *The Soul of Justice: Social Bonds and Racial Hubris* (Ithaca: Cornell University Press, 2001).

21. Cf. Derrick Bell, *And We Are Not Saved: The Elusive Quest for Racial Justice* (New York: Basic Books, 1987).

22. Hacker and Pierson, *Off Center*.

23. Polanyi, *Great Transformation*, 265.

24. Rogers Smith, "Toward a More Perfect Union: Beyond Old Liberalism and Neoliberalism," in Adolph Reed, Jr., *Without Justice for All: The New Liberalism and Our Retreat from Racial Equality* (Boulder: Westview Press, 1999), 327–353.

25. Wacquant, *Urban Outcasts*.

26. David Harvey, *A Brief History of Neoliberalism* (New York: Oxford University Press, 2005), 183.

27. Katznelson, *When Affirmative Action Was White*.

28. Winant, *World Is a Ghetto*.

29. Jürgen Habermas, "Intolerance and Discrimination," *International Journal of Constitutional Law* 1 (2003): 2–12, 4.

30. Alexander, *Civil Sphere*, ch. 17.

31. J. Hector St. John de Crevecoeur, *Letters from an American Farmer* (New York: Penguin, 1981 [1782]), 66.

32. Israel Zangwill, *The Melting Pot* (New York: Arno Press, 1932 [1909]).

33. Alexander, *Civil Sphere*, 8.

34. Horace Kallen, "Democracy versus the Melting Pot: A Study of American Nationality," *The Nation*, February 18, 1915, 192.

35. Robert Ezra Park, "Our Racial Frontier on the Pacific," in *Race and Culture* (New York: Free Press, 1950 [1926]), 150.

36. Robert Ezra Park, "Human Migration and the Marginal Man," in *Race and Culture*, 346.

37. Alexander, *Civil Sphere*, 431–435, 450.

38. Horace Kallen, "Democracy versus the Melting Pot: A Study of American Nationality," *The Nation*, February 25, 1915, 220.

39. Alexander, *Civil Sphere*, 450.

40. Ibid.

41. Ibid, 450–451.

42. Will Kymlicka, *Multicultural Citizenship: A Liberal Theory of Minority Rights* (New York: Oxford University Press, 1995).

43. Appiah, *Cosmopolitanism*, xv.

44. Brian Barry, *Culture and Equality: An Egalitarian Critique of Multiculturalism* (Cambridge: Harvard University Press, 2001); Kymlicka, *Multicultural Citizenship*; Habermas, "Intolerance and Discrimination."

45. Charles Taylor, "The Politics of Recognition," in Amy Gutmann, ed., *Multiculturalism: Examining the Politics of Recognition* (Princeton: Princeton University Press, 1994), 25–74.

46. Frantz Fanon, *The Wretched of the Earth* (New York: Grove 2004 [1963]).

47. Anne Phillips, *Multiculturalism without Culture* (Princeton: Princeton University Press, 2007); Lila Abu-Lughod, "Writing against Culture," in Richard Fox, ed., *Recapturing Anthropology: Working in the Present* (Santa Fe: School of American Research Press, 1991).

48. Quoted in Alexander, *Civil Sphere,* 431.

49. Quoted in Appiah, *Cosmopolitanism,* III.

50. Keith Banting and Will Kymlicka, "Introduction: Multiculturalism and the Welfare State: Setting the Context," in Keith Banting and Will Kymlicka, eds., *Multiculturalism and the Welfare State: Recognition and Redistribution in Contemporary Democracies* (New York: Oxford University Press, 2006), 1–48.

51. Alexander, *Civil Sphere;* Appiah, *Cosmopolitanism.*

52. Cf. Richard Thompson Ford, *Racial Culture: A Critique* (Princeton: Princeton University Press, 2005); Phillips, *Multiculturalism without Culture.*

53. Banting and Kymlicka, "Introduction," II, 17.

54. Lawrence Fuchs, "Thinking about Immigration and Ethnicity in the United States," in Donald Horowitz and Gerard Noiriel, eds., *Immigration in Two Democracies: French and American Experience* (New York: New York University Press, 1992, 39–65), 45.

55. Appiah, *Cosmopolitanism,* xx.

56. Du Bois, *Souls of Black Folk,* 162–163.

57. Floya Anthias and Cathie Lloyd, eds., *Rethinking Antiracisms: From Theory to Practice* (New York: Routledge, 2002); bell hooks, *Killing Rage: Ending Racism* (New York: Henry Holt and Company, 1995); Bourdieu, *Masculine Domination,* 109–112.

58. Winant, *World Is a Ghetto,* 289, xiv. See also Howard Winant, *The New Politics of Race: Globalism, Difference, Justice* (Minneapolis: University of Minnesota Press, 2004).

59. Sylvia Hurtado, et al., *Findings from the 2005 Administration of Your First College Year (YFCY): National Aggregates* (Los Angeles: Higher Education research Institute, UCLA, 2007).

60. Elisabeth Lasch-Quinn, *Race Experts: How Racial Etiquette, Sensitivity Training, and New Age Therapy Hijacked the Civil Rights Revolution* (New York: Norton, 2001).

61. Erin Kelley and Frank Dobbin, "How Affirmative Action Became Diversity Management: Employer Response to Antidiscrimination Law, 1961 to 1996," *American Behavioral Scientist* 41 (1988): 960–984.

62. Alexandra Kalev, Frank Dobbin, and Erin Kelly, "Best Practices or Best Guesses? Diversity Management and the Remediation of Inequality," *American Sociological Review* 71 (2006): 589–917.

63. Cited in John Wrench, "Diversity Management Can Be Bad for You," *Race and Class* 46 (2003): 73–84, 80.

64. Wrench, "Diversity Management Can Be Bad for You," 77.

65. Cited in Kelley and Dobbin, "How Affirmative Action Became Diversity Management."

66. Lisa Takeuchi Cullen, "Employee Diversity Training Doesn't Work," *Time*, April 26, 2007; Jacqueline Hood, Helen Muller, and Patricia Seitz, "Attitudes of Hispanics and Anglos Surrounding a Workforce Diversity Intervention," *Hispanic Journal of Behavioral Sciences* 23 (2001): 444–458.

67. See Joyce Bell and Douglass Hartmann, "Diversity in Everyday Discourse: The Cultural Ambiguities and Consequences of 'Happy Talk,'" *American Sociological Review* 72 (2007): 895–914.

68. See Alastair Bonnett, *Anti-Racism* (London: Routledge, 2000); Sheilah Mann, "What the Survey of American College Freshman Tells Us about Their Interest in Politics and Political Science," *Political Science and Politics* 32 (1999): 263–268.

69. Bourdieu, *Firing Back*, 19–20.

70. Appiah, *Cosmopolitanism*, 170.

71. Quoted in Walter Kalaidjian, *The Edge of Modernism: American Poetry and the Traumatic Past* (Baltimore: Johns Hopkins University Press, 2006), 59.

72. William Cronon, "'Only Connect . . .': The Goals of a Liberal Education," *The American Scholar* 67 (1998): 73–80, 79.

73. Cited in Hanna Arendt, *The Life of the Mind*, Volume Two: *Willing* (New York: Harcourt Brace Jovanovich, 1978), 93.

74. Jean-Paul Sartre, "Preface" to Franz Fanon, *The Wretched of the Earth* (New York: Grove 2004 [1963]), li.

75. Lincoln Quillian, "Does Unconscious Racism Exist?" *Social Psychology Quarterly* 71 (2008): 6–11, 6. Also see Lincoln Quillian, "New Approaches to Understanding Racial Prejudice and Discrimination," *Annual Review of Sociology* 32 (2006): 299–328.

76. Aldous Huxley, *Brave New World* (New York: Perennial, 1998 [1932]), vii.

77. Antonio Gramsci, *Selections from the Prison Notebooks* (New York: International Publishers, 1999 [1971]), 324.

78. Cronon, "'Only Connect.'"

79. Appiah, *Cosmopolitanism*, 8.

80. Feagin, et al., *White Racism*, 229–250.

81. 1 Corinthians 13:2, *NIV*.

82. Arendt, *Life of the Mind*, 104.

83. Anne Pedersen, Iain Walker, and Mike Wise, "'Talk Does Not Cook Rice': Beyond Anti-Racism Rhetoric to Strategies for Social Action," *Australian Psychologist* 40 (2005): 20–30; Walter Stephen and Krystina Finlay, "The Role of Empathy in Improving Intergroup Relations," *Journal of Social Issues* 55 (1999): 729–743.

84. Cf. Sartre, "Preface" to Fanon, *Wretched of the Earth*, lxii.

85. Patterson, *Ordeal of Integration;* Tatum, *Why Are All the Black Kids Sitting Together in the Cafeteria?*

86. Marc Rich and Aaron Castelan Cargile, "Beyond the Breach: Transforming White Identities in the Classroom," *Race Ethnicity and Education* 7 (2004): 351–365.

87. Roger Boyes, "Comic Book Depiction of Holocaust Upsets Jews," *London Times*, June 21, 2005.

88. Judith Katz, *White Awareness: A Handbook for Anti-Racism Training* (Norman: Oklahoma University Press, 1978).

89. Bell, *And We Are Not Saved*, 228–229.

90. Paul Kivel, *Uprooting Racism: How White People Can Work for Racial Justice*, Revised Edition (Gabriola Island: New Society Publishers, 2002 [1997]), 113–114.

91. Arendt, *Responsibility and Judgment*, 151; quoted from Plato's *Gorgias*.

92. See Cooper Thompson, Emmett Schaefer, and Harry Bond, *White Men Challenging Racism: 35 Personal Stories* (Durham: Duke University Press, 2003); Becky Thompson, *A Promise and a Way of Life: White Antiracist Activism* (Minneapolis: University of Minnesota Press, 2001); Aptheker, *Anti-Racism in U.S. History*.

93. Du Bois, *The Philadelphia Negro*, 394.

94. Brown et al., *White-Washing Race*; Feagin et al., *White Racism*.

95. Spanierman et al., "Psychological Costs of Racism to Whites."

96. James Baldwin, *Fire Next Time*, 97.

97. Cf. Cronon, "'Only Connect.'"

98. Anne-Marie Fortier, "Pride Politics and Multiculturalist Citizenship," *Ethnic and Racial Studies* 28 (2005): 559–578.

99. Roberts, *Killing the Black Body*; Collins, *Black Feminist Thought*; Crenshaw, "Mapping the Margins."

100. John Brueggemann and Terry Boswell, "Realizing Solidarity: Sources of Interracial Unionism During the Great Depression," *Work and Occupations* 25 (1998): 436–482; Rich Halpern and Roger Horowitz, *Meatpackers: An Oral History of Black Packinghouse Workers and Their Struggle for Racial and Economic Equality* (New York: Twayne Publishers, 1996); James Barrett, *Work and Community in the Jungle: Chicago's Packinghouse Workers, 1894–1922* (Bloomington: University of Illinois Press, 1987); Jung, "Interracialism."

101. Wu, *Yellow*, 325.

102. Brown et al., *White-Washing Race*, 244.

103. Gitlin, *Twilight of Common Dreams*.

104. Brown et al., *White-Washing Race*, 230.

105. Frances Fox Piven, "Can Power from Below Change the World?" *American Sociological Review* 73 (2008): 1–14, 1.

106. Frances Fox Piven and Richard Cloward, *Why Americans Still Don't Vote: And Why Politicians Want It That Way* (Boston: Beacon Press, 2000); Kivel, *Uprooting Racism*, 179–186.

107. Donald Barlett and James Steele, *America: Who Really Pays the Taxes?* (New York: Simon and Schuster, 1994).

108. Greg Duncan, Aletha Huston, and Thomas Weisner, *Higher Ground: New Hope for the Working Poor and Their Children* (New York: Russell Sage Foundation, 2007); Christopher Jencks, *Rethinking Social Policy: Race, Poverty, and the Underclass* (New York: HarperPerennial, 1992); Hays, *Flat Broke with Children*, 215–240.

109. Wilson, *When Work Disappears*; Wacquant, *Urban Outcasts*.

110. Brown et al., *White-Washing Race,* 242.

111. Piven and Cloward, *Why Americans Still Don't Vote.*

112. Jack Metzgar, *Striking Steel: Solidarity Remembered* (Philadelphia: Temple University Press, 2000); Piven, "Can Power from Below Change the World?"

113. Cesar Chavez, "Address to the Commonwealth Club of California, 1984," in Kenneth Bridges, ed., *Freedom in America* (Upper Saddle River: Pearson, Prentice Hall, 2008 [1979], 424–430), 426.

114. Piven, "Can Power from Below Change the World?," 4.

115. Ibid, 1. See also Frances Fox Piven, *Challenging Authority: How Ordinary People Change America* (Lanham: Rowman and Littlefield, 2006).

116. David Meyer and Nancy Whittier, "Social Movement Spillover," *Social Problems* 4 (1994): 277–298.

117. Ban Ki-moon, "The Right War," *Time,* April 28, 2008.

118. Frances Fox Piven and Richard Cloward, *Poor People's Movements: Why They Succeed, How They Fail* (New York: Pantheon, 1977), xi–xii.

119. Piven, "Can Power from Below Change the World?," 8.

120. Bourdieu, *Firing Back,* 65.

121. Paul Butler, "Racially Based Jury Nullification: Black Power in the Criminal Justice System," in Richard Delgato and Jean Stefancic, eds., *Critical Race Theory: The Cutting Edge,* Second Edition (Philadelphia: Temple University Press, 2000), 194–203.

122. Todd Gitlin, *Letters to a Young Activist* (New York: Basic Books, 2003), 49–50.

123. Henry David Thoreau, "Resistance to Civil Government," 1849.

124. Piven, "Can Power from Below Change the World?," 11.

125. Morris, *Origins of the Civil Rights Movement.*

126. Rodney Hero and Robert Preuhs, "Multiculturalism and Welfare Politics in the USA: A State-Level Comparative Analysis," in Keith Banting and Will Kymlicka, eds., *Multiculturalism and the Welfare State: Recognition and Redistribution in Contemporary Democracies* (New York: Oxford University Press, 2006), 121–151; Winant, *New Politics of Race,* 57–62.

127. Gitlin, *Letters to a Young Activist,* 143.

128. Small, *Villa Victoria,* 177.

129. Alexander, *Civil Sphere.*

130. Du Bois, *Darkwater,* 33.

Credits

Text Credits

CHAPTER 1 P. 18: Melissa Nobles, "History Counts: A Comparative Analysis of Racial/Color Categorization in US and Brazilian Censuses," *American Journal of Public Health* 90 (2000): 1738–1745, pp. 1739, table 1. Reprinted by permission of American Journal of Public Health; p. 19: Melissa Nobles, "History Counts: A Comparative Analysis of Racial/Color Categorization in US and Brazilian Censuses," *American Journal of Public Health* 90 (2000): 1738–1745, pp. 1739, table 2. Reprinted by permission of American Journal of Public Health; p. 35: THE BOONDOCKS © 2000 Aaron McGruder. Dist. By UNIVERSAL PRESS SYNDICATE. Reprinted with permission. All rights reserved. **CHAPTER 2** P. 69: Russell Thornton, *American Indian Holocaust and Survival: A Population History Since 1492* (Norman: University of Oklahoma Press, 1987), p. xvii, Figures P-1 and P-2; p. 80: Maps from *Atlas of American History*, 1993 © by Rand McNally, R.L. 09-S-50. Used by permission; p. 84: Stanley Lieberson, *A Piece of the Pie: Black and White Immigrants Since 1880* (Berkeley: University of California Press, 1980), p. 20. Used by permission of University of California Press; p. 88: Stanley Lieberson, *A Piece of the Pie: Black and White Immigrants Since 1880* (Berkeley: University of California Press, 1980), p. 28. Used by permission of University of California Press; p. 96: Michael Olander, Emily Hoban Kirby, and Krista Schmitt, Fact Sheet: Attitudes of Young People Toward Diversity (CIRCLE: The Center for Information & Research on Civil Learning & Engagement, February 2005), p. 1, graph 1. Reprinted permission; p. 98: Source: *Time*, "America by the Numbers," October 30, 2006. **CHAPTER 3** P. 125: Pew Research Center, "Party Identification Trend, By Demographic Groups," http://people-press.org/commentary/pdf/95.pdf. Reprinted by permission of Pew Research Center for the People + the Press; p. 126: Pew Research Center, "Party Identification Trend, By Demographic Groups," http://people-press.org/commentary/pdf/95.pdf. Reprinted by permission of Pew Research Center for the People + the Press; p. 134: Figure 3.8, "Attitudes toward principle of school integration and toward federal implementation of school integration," page 126 reprinted by permission of the publisher from *Racial Attitudes in America: Trends and Interpretations*, Revised Edition by Howard Schuman, Charlotte Steeh and Lawrence Bobo, Cambridge, Mass.: Harvard University Press, Copyright © 1985, 1997 by the President and

UCLA, CivilRightsProject.ucla.edu; p. 339: Gary Orfield and Chungmei Lee, "Racial Transformation and the Changing Nature of Segregation," *The Civil Rights Project*, Harvard University, January 2006, p. 14; figure 2. Reprinted by permission of Gary Orfield, The Civil Rights Project at UCLA, CivilRightsProject. ucla.edu; p. 342: "Harlem (2) [What happens to a dream defedrred . . . "]" from THE COLLECTED POEMS OF LANGSTON HUGHES by Langston Hughes, edited by Arnold Rampersad with David Roessel, Associate Editor, copyright © 1994 by the Estate of Langston Hughes. Used by permission of Alfred A. Knopf, a division of Random House, Inc.   **CHAPTER 8** P. 355: "Notes on Commercial Theater," from THE COLLECTED POEMS OF LANGSTON HUGHES by Langston Hughes, edited by Arnold Rampersad with David Roessel, Associate Editor, copyright © 1994 by the Estate of Langston Hughes. Used by permission of Alfred A. Knopf, a division of Random House, Inc.; p. 370: Source: "Super Negro" by Al B Back; p. 370: Source: "In America" by Suheir Hammad; p. 371: Source: Jose Garcia, "Now they are putting up barriers . . ."; p. 373: Source: "Back Home" by Blue Scholars; p. 374: "Market for Ni$$as" by Taalam Acey. Reprinted by permission of the author; p. 383: Carole Rosenstein, Diversity and Participation in the Arts: Insights from the Bay Area (New York: Urban Institute, 2005), p. 1, table 1 from www.urbaninstitute.org/UploadedPDF/311252_diversity_in_arts.pdf; p. 383: Carole Rosenstein, Diversity and Participation in the Arts: Insights from the Bay Area (New York: Urban Institute, 2005), p. 2, table 3 from www.urbaninstitute.org/UploadedPDF/311252_diversity_ in_arts.pdf; p. 384: SCS Fact Sheet, Museum Attendance, Population Shifts, and Changing Tastes, May 2005, figure 4 "Museum Attendance by Ethnicity," from http://lewis.sppsr.ucla.edu/special/ socalsurvey/Socal%20FS_Issue7_letter.pdf. Reprinted by permission; p. 393: "Today Was a Bad Day Like TB" by Chrystos. Reprinted by permission of Wales Literary Agency, Inc.   **CHAPTER 9** p. 402: Charles R. Brooks, *The Official History and Manual of the Grand United Order of Odd Fellows in America* (Freeport, NY: Books for Libraries Press, 1971; Reprint of 1902 ed); p. 411: Mark Hugo Lopez and Emily Kirby, Electoral Engagement Among Minority Youth (CIRCLE: The Center for Information & Research on Civil Learning & Engagement, July 2005), p. 2 graph 3 from http://www.civicyouth.org/PopUps/ FactSheets/FS_04_Minority_vote.pdf. Reprinted by permission; p. 412: Kay Lehman Schlozman, Sidney Verba, and Henry E. Brady, "Civic Participation and the Equality Problem," in Theda Skocpol and Morris Fiorina, eds., *Civic Engagement in American Democracy* (Washington and New York: Brookings Institute and Russell Sage Foundation, 1999), 427–60, p. 434, figure 12–1. Copyright © 1999, the Brookings Institution and the Russell Sage Foundation. Used with permission; p. 417: Michael Olander, Emily Hoban Kirby, and Krista Schmitt, Fact Sheet: Attitudes of Young People Toward Diversity (CIRCLE: The Center for Information & Research on ?Civil Learning & Engagement, February 2005), p. 14, graph 20. Reprinted by permission; p. 419: Robert Putnam, "Tuning In, Tuning Out: The Strange Disappearance of Social Capital in America, The 1995 Ithiel de Sola Pool Lecture," *Political Science and Politics* 28 (1995): 664–83, p. 675, figure 5. Reprinted by permission of The Sagalyn Literary Agency for the author; p. 437: Penny Edgell, Joseph Gerteis and Douglas Hartmann, "Atheists as 'Other': Moral Boundaries and Cultural Membership in American Society," *American Sociological Review* 71 (2006): 211–34, p. 218, table 1. Reprinted by permission; p. 439: Kevin D. Dougherty, "How Monochromatic is Church Membership? Racial-Ethnic Diversity in Religious Community," *Sociology of Religion* 64 (2003): 65–85, p. 75, figure 1.   **CHAPTER 10** P. 455: Aaron Gullickson, "Black/White Interracial Marriage Trends, 1850–2000," *Journal of Family History* 31 (2006): 289–312, p. 291, figure 1. Reprinted by permission of Sage Publications, Inc.; p. 456: Michael Olander, Emily Hoban Kirby, and Krista Schmitt, Fact Sheet: Attitudes of Young People Toward Diversity (CIRCLE:

The Center for Information & Research on ?Civil Learning & Engagement, February 2005), p. 8, graph 11. Reprinted by permission; p. 460: US Census, 2006 (table designed by Ruth Lopez Turley, Department of Sociology, University of Wisconsin at Madison) from www.ssc.wisc.edu/~rturley/Soc134/ Minority%20Families.ppt#304,1,MaritalStatus Reprinted by permission of Ruth Turley; p. 463: Zhenchao Qian and Daniel Lichter, "Social Boundaries and Marital Assimilation: Interpreting Trends in Racial and Ethnic Interrrmariage," *American Sociological Review* 72 (2007): 68–94, p. 76, figure 1. Used by permission; p. 466: US Census, Multiracial Population Map from www.censusscope.org/us/ map_multiracial.html. CensusScope.org is produced by the Social Science Data Analysis Network (SSDAN.net). Reprinted by permission.   **CHAPTER 11** P. 504: Michael Olander, Emily Hoban Kirby, and Krista Schmitt, Fact Sheet: Attitudes of Young People Toward Diversity (CIRCLE: The Center for Information & Research on ?Civil Learning & Engagement, February 2005), p. 9, graph 12. Reprinted by permission; p. 538: Mark Hugo Lopez and Emily Kirby, Electoral Engagement Among Minority Youth (CIRCLE: The Center for Information & Research on Civil Learning & Engagement, July 2005), p. 6 graph 10. Reprinted by permission.

Photo Credits

P. 8: Nikki S. Lee "The Hispanic Project (25)", 1998, Fujiflex print; p. 13: © John Blackford/AA Reps; p. 31: Jeff Wall, Mimic, 1982. Transparency in lightbox, 198 × 228.5 cm; 70 Kara Walker "Untitled" 1995 Cut paper; p. 89: Hebrew Union College Library; p. 93: Courtesy: Carrie Mae Weems/Jack Shainman Gallery, New York.; p. 113: © Charles Moore/Black Star; p. 114: Photo by Robert W. Kelley// Time Life Pictures/Getty Images; p. 118: © Rick Tejada-Flores/Alturas Films; p. 160: © Bob Adelman/ Corbis; p. 177: www.schnews.org.uk; p. 179: Ann Johansson/The New York Times/Redux; p. 183: © Michael Jacobson Hardy; p. 207: © The Phillips Collection, Washington, D.C. Any reproduction of this digitized image shall not be made without the written consent of The Phillips Collection, Washington, D.C.; p. 213: Walter P. Reuther Library, Wayne State University; p. 231: © Camilo Jose Vergara; p. 251: © Bettmann/Corbis; p. 252: *Without Sanctuary: Lynching Photography in America*, plates 25 and 26; p. 268: © Copyright 2010 John Annerino; p. 272: © Steve Raymer/Corbis; *283* Camilo Jose Vergara; p. 315: © Eric Haase/Contact Press Images; p. 324: © Gayle Shomer Brezicki; p. 330: Reprinted through the courtesy of the Editors of TIME Magazine © 2009 Time Inc.; p. 352: Grande piscine de Brousse de J.L. Gérôme, inventaire PH-976; Chantilly, musée Condé © Musée Condé; p. 360: © Richard Marshall; p. 363: © Printed by permission of the Norman Rockwell Family Agency. Copyright © 1943 Norman Rockwell Family Entities; p. 391: Rucksackshop.com; p. 403: James VanDerZee, American, 1886–1983, Elks, c. 1930s, Gelatin silver print, 16.8 × 23.7 cm (image); 19.4 × 25.2 cm (support). Restricted gift of Anstiss and Ronald Krueck in memory of her mother, Florence Pierson Hammond, 2000.330, The Art Institute of Chicago. Photography © The Art Institute of Chicago; p. 414: © Robin Bowman; p. 434: Stephane De Sakutin/AFP/Getty Images; p. 442: © Joni Brook; p. 475: copyright 2003 Alex Garcia; p. 485: Jupiter Images; p. 488: Nahum Budin / PhotoStock-Israel; p. 490: © Erica Lord, *Untitled (I Tan To Look More Native)*; p. 598: © Ivan Rubio, *Dying Fields*; p. 622: © Milo Hess; p. 634: Declan Haun, American, 1937–94. Protester Carrying "Justice" Sign, Monroe, North Carolina, August 26, 1961. Gelatin-silver print, 9 1/4" X 7 1/4". Museum purchase, gift of Patricia L. Raymond, M.D., and in memory of Alice R. and Sol B. Frank. Chrysler Museum of Art, Norfolk, VA. 97.20.

Index